Spanish American Literature

A Collection of Essays

Series Editors

David William Foster
Arizona State University

Daniel Altamiranda
Universidad de Buenos Aires

A GARLAND SERIES

Contents of the Series

Theoretical Debates in Spanish American Literature

Edited with introductions by

David William Foster
Arizona State University

Daniel Altamiranda
Universidad de Buenos Aires

GARLAND PUBLISHING, INC.
A MEMBER OF THE TAYLOR & FRANCIS GROUP
New York & London
1997

Library of Congress Cataloging-in-Publication Data

Theoretical debates in Spanish American literature / edited with
   introductions by David William Foster and Daniel Altamiranda.
       p.   cm. — (Spanish American literature ; 1)
   Includes bibliographical references.
       ISBN 0-8153-2677-7 (set : alk. paper). — ISBN 0-8153-2676-9
   (v. 1 : alk. paper)
       1. Spanish American literature—20th century—History and
   criticism. 2. Politics and literature—Latin America.
   3. Imperialism in literature. 4. Literature and society—Latin
   America. 5. Reportage literature, Spanish American—History and
   criticism. 6. Sex role in literature. 7. Postmodernism (Literature)—
   Latin America. 8. Ethnicity in literature.
   I. Foster, David William. II. Altamiranda, Daniel. III. Series.
   PQ7081.A1T44 1997
   860.9'358—dc21   97-40788
                                                         CIP

Printed on acid-free, 250-year-life paper
Manufactured in the United States of America

Contents

Series Introduction

Many and varied are the factors that underlie the growing interest in recent decades in the literary production of Latin American writers, such as, for instance, the international recognition of several Latin American writers such as the Argentine Jorge Luis Borges, the Colombian Gabriel García Márquez, the Mexican Carlos Fuentes, and the Chilean Pablo Neruda, to name only a few of the most renowned figures. Out of these writers, two are Nobel Prize Literature winners: García Márquez and Neruda. Another factor that has fueled this interest is their commercial success and the accompanying cultural diffusion of the so-called Boom of Latin American fiction. And last but not least, is the new and vigorous feminist body of writing, quite unique in Hispanic letters for the richness and variety of its innovations.[1]

Despite the fact that the task of translating some authors into English, such as the Cuban Alejo Carpentier, had begun a little before the crucial decade of the 1960s, it is only beginning in this latter period that there arises an explosion of publishing activity oriented toward making Latin American texts known among English-speaking readers. Furthermore, the creation of Latin American studies programs in numerous North American universities resulted in the institution of a specific field of research that comes to be considered a natural adjunct of Spanish literature. It is evident that all of the interest is not an exclusive result of the internal development of literary history, as though such a thing could occur in the abstract, but rather it presupposes a concrete response to the sociopolitical circumstances of the period: the triumph of the Castro Revolution in 1959, which turned Cuba into a center of enormous political and cultural consequences and whose influence began to be felt early on in the farthest reaches of Latin America.

The factors mentioned above provided the context for the development of extensive research programs whose goals included the elaboration and periodic examination of the literary canon, the analysis of specific texts, authors, periods, and problems. All of this activity has resulted in innumerable dissertations, theses, and books published by academic and trade presses, as well as articles that appeared in journals traditionally devoted to literary history and philology, along with the flourishing of new specialized journals and the organization of national and international congresses on specific themes.

In the face of such an enormous proliferation of commentary and study, it is necessary to offer students undertaking the study of Latin American literature a body of basic texts to assist them in providing an initial orientation in the diverse research areas that have emerged. Consequently, we have chosen to include essays and articles that have appeared in periodical publications, some of which are difficult to obtain by the Anglo-American student. These articles are not limited to philological minutiae or the discussion of highly specific aspects. Rather, they address major texts and problems from an interpretive and critical point of view. Although principally directed toward neophyte students, the present selection will undoubtedly be useful to advanced students and researchers who find themselves in need of a quick source of reference or who wish to consult newer issues and approaches to Spanish American literary studies.

Notes

[1] Although the term "Latin America" will be used throughout as a synonym of "Spanish American," it should be noted that, in its most precise usage, the former includes the other non-Spanish but Romance language-speaking areas to the south of the United States and in the Caribbean. This collection has not sought to include a representation of Portuguese and French-speaking authors on the assumption that it will be used principally in nonresearch institutions where Brazilian and Francophone Caribbean literature is not customarily taught.

Volume Introduction

This volume brings together papers relative to various theoretical questions that have been recent points of debate in the area of Spanish American literary studies. Our attempt has been to offer under the heading of each one of the subthemes a selection of essays and studies that, while they in no way exhaust or provide conclusive commentaries on issues that are still open to debate, provide varying perspectives, to the degree that they model diverse theoretical positions as they constitute contrasting ideological stances and alternative focuses on a particular question. Rather than presenting a monolithic and hegemonic vision of each topic, we have chosen to showcase, at least in part, the multiplicity of stances that have been adopted in each case. Clearly, the aspects that have been selected do not take into account all of the problematics that have merited critical consideration. Thus, the reassessment of the vanguard movements or the matter of magical realism constitutes some of the theoretical themes that we have excluded, and not because we believe them to be issues that have been superseded or been completely settled. In fact, their currency will be detected in subsequent volumes in the context of the production of specific authors.

Rather, we have opted for providing space to selected fundamental issues that bring into play the relationship between Spanish American literary studies and general issues concerning literary, theoretical, and critical studies in general. Therefore, the volume is subdivided into six sections: 1. Colonial and Postcolonial Issues; 2. Documental and Testimonial Writing; 3. Gender Studies; 4. Postmodernism in Latin America; 5. Ethnic Issues; and 6. Politics, History, and Nation.

Colonial and Postcolonial Issues

This section opens with a long work by the Cuban Roberto Fernández Retamar, "Caliban: Notes Towards a Discussion of Culture in Our America" (1971). As Fredric Jameson observes in the prologue to the translation of a selection of Fernández Retamar's writings, this essay occupies in the Latin American intellectual world a place similar to the one held by Edward Said's *Orientalism* within North American thought. In effect, it deals with an early postcolonial position, and it was written in the effervescent climate of the confrontation between intellectuals of the left and the right that took place at the beginning of the 1970s as a consequence of the so-called "Padilla case" in Cuba.[1]

Fernández Retamar undertakes to correct the cultural interpretation established at the outset of the century by the Uruguayan José Enrique Rodó in a celebrated essay, *Ariel* (1900). The Cuban's rereading of the Shakespearian fantasy recasts the scheme of identifications in the following manner:

> Prospero invaded the islands, killed our ancestors, enslaved Caliban, and taught him his language to make himself understood. What else can Caliban do but use that same language—today he has no other—to curse him, to wish that the 'red plague' would face on him?

Thus, Prospero occupies here the place of the colonizer, the European man, and Caliban that of the colonized, whose active resistance can only be expressed, in view of the historical circumstances, via the language of the other. In this allegorical structure, the figure of Ariel corresponds to that of the intellectual who must decide on which side to be.

Although with time the international political context has changed, the virulence of some of its observations has diminished, and personal attacks can only be read today with a sardonic smile of complicity, "Calibán" continues to be a valuable cultural document that attests to an ideological conflict of vast repercussions. While Fernández Retamar's essay constitutes a foundational text for Latin American thought, it also attests to the climate of intolerance (political, homophobic, etc.) that prevailed among intellectuals during the 1960s and 1970s.

Basing himself on a consciously postcolonial attitude that refers not only to the long colonial period of the Spanish in Latin America but also to the most recent period of North American neocolonialism, Fernández Retamar reinterprets a series of archetypical examples drawn from Latin American literature. On the one hand, he contributes toward the construction of an image of the Cuban José Martí as a forerunner of the leaders of the Cuban Revolution. In order to do this, he contrasts his stance toward the Indian (as well as toward the black) with that of another thinker from the nineteenth century, the Argentine Domingo Faustino Sarmiento, and he extends the contrast to include the different position taken by both intellectuals with respect to the development of the United States and its eventual expansionism. While Sarmiento proposed to his fellow citizens the model of the United States as worthy of emulating, Martí insisted on the threat that the North American model represented to the autonomy of the southern republics.

With regard to more recent literature, Fernández Retamar contributes to the demarcation of the image of Jorge Luis Borges as a colonial writer who represents a declining social class whose values can in no way be said to coincide with the need for social revolution that the Cuban writer defends. There can be no doubt that this image, which clearly is not entirely gratuitous, has been sufficiently extended that many Latin American intellectuals of the left considered it for years to be inappropriate to concern themselves with Borges except in terms of some of his heavy-handed political declarations. But Borges is only one of the writers labeled by Fernández Retamar as right-wing intellectuals. His list also includes Carlos Fuentes, Emir Rodríguez Monegal (an Uruguayan scholar working in the United States), and the Cuban novelist Severo Sarduy.

More recently, Walter D. Mignolo has observed that postcolonial theories and, in general, the question of the postcolonial has not provoked the same interest as the issue of postmodernism has, an issue that has been debated extensively in Latin American intellectual circles since the mid-1980s. It is evident that the term postcolonial bears some irritating implications for the thinkers of the region. In order to overcome this factor, Mignolo proposes that we understand 'postcolonial' as "an opportunity to criticize the legacy of modernity" in the realm of the periphery. Mignolo's essay helps to assign a different place to a series of Latin American texts that can be taken to constitute a tradition of postcolonial discursiveness. It would include a constellation of writers not usually brought together by the literary history of high modernism, writers that were considered marginal or even nonliterary. But beyond what one could consider theoretical writing, postcolonialism has awakened an interest in the reconsideration of an array of materials from the period of the Spanish and Portuguese empires in Latin America. This interest has unquestionably been influenced by the fifth centennial celebration of 1492.

Another concept of interest is presented by William Luis in the last essay included in this section. Beginning with an analysis of the textual interventions of the various editors of the Juan Francisco Manzano's *Autobiografía* (Autobiography), the author presents the concept of cultural translation that contributes to an understanding, among other specific phenomena of Latin American literary history, of the particular vision of the chroniclers of the Indies (the traditional Hispanic name for the New World) who played a fundamental role in the demarcation of "Latin American reality." Concomitantly, the first writers to identify with the New World, who were culturally conditioned to express themselves in the language of the dominant culture, were obliged to "translate" concepts and experiences of the pre-Columbian world into the terminology of the discourse of the conqueror. Luis's paper concludes with some observations and examples on how the process of cultural translation works in Neo-Rican[2] writing, which opens the question out toward especially recent phenomena.

Documental and Testimonial Writing

As various critics have suggested, the testimonial as a narrative form has come to constitute the most original contribution of recent Latin American writing. In fact, new forms identified with the testimonial have sparked the interest of researchers both inside and outside the community of Hispanic scholars, and non-Hispanicists of renowned theoretical fame like Fredric Jameson and Gayatri Spivak have taken notice of it. While some have pointed out the enormous impact that the publication of the translation of Truman Capote's *In Cold Blood* (1965) had in the Hispanic world, it does not seem reasonable to attempt to explain the vitality of the testimonial on the basis of this influence only. Rather, there exists a long tradition of writing in the region that makes use of testimonial elements.

In his article on documentary narrative, a concept that includes the testimonial, David William Foster notes the connection of these forms to New Journalism and, as a consequence, the continuity between creative writing and the production of documentary texts, since it can be observed in both expressive modalities the use of similar strategies for the process of textual elaboration.

The most recent critical essays on these narrative forms have followed two divergent although complementary lines. On the one hand, John Beverley, a critic committed to an ideological examination of literature and its institutions, considers Latin American testimonial as a new mode for the manifestation of the social conflicts that plague the continent,[3] and he offers the following definition:

> By testimony I mean a novel or novella-length narrative in book or pamphlet (that is, printed as opposed to acoustic) form, told in the first-person by a narrator who is also the real protagonist or witness of the events he or she recounts, and whose unit of narration is usually a 'life' or a significant life experience (1989, 12–13).

Beverley views the testimonial as characterized by a particular intentionality on the part of the narrator in a unique communicative situation that aspires toward a degree of active participation of the individuals involved in the "literary" exchange. Given its relation to the concrete social situation of its source, the testimonial cannot conceive of itself as a fictional form nor assimilate itself to the novel. In effect, rather than associating itself with this literary form, which is privileged in the contemporary bourgeois world, the testimonial appears to be the expressive medium adopted by marginal groups that count on the support of a wide variety of intellectuals, journalists, and writers.

Elzbieta Sklodowska, in contrast to Beverley, concentrates on the process through which the interpretive community of specialized critics of Spanish American literature has legitimated a block of nonfiction texts that have traditionally fallen outside the canon, so as to constitute a "new" genre. From her point of view, the testimonial contract is based on the capacity of the narrator to forge a pact of verisimilitude that allows for the underscoring of the coexistence of voices in the text—the voice of the person providing the testimonial and the voice of the person undertaking the interpretation of that testimonial. These voices are discernible in terms of the fissures that occur between the universe of the narrator and that of the text's readers.

Gender Studies

This section includes feminist oriented essays, as well as a block of recent work that concerns itself with the constitution and construction of sexual and gender identity and its literary manifestations. In the first place, one must take into account that the methods of analysis and interests that derive from European and American sources do not always correlate optimally with the discussion of Latin American culture, since the cultures of the region codify in different ways the distribution of sexual roles. These differences not only occur between Latin America and the United States and Europe, but also among the various societies that make up Latin America.

In the second place, it is necessary to bear in mind that a preoccupation for the place that woman occupies in society has not been absent from Latin American thought. The case of the Mexican Rosario Castellanos, considered a founder of Mexican feminism, is a case in point, and her collection, *Mujer que sabe latín* (A Woman Who Knows Latin; 1973) brings together essays that many consider correctly to be the first significant analysis of the image of woman in Western culture and in Mexico specifically.

For this section we have chosen to include only two out of the numerous papers available dealing with feminist concerns. The first one is Jean Franco's analysis of the ideological elements structuring the first histories of Latin America literature, based on the idea of nation as the articulation of meaning, which leads to a systematic exclusion of women from the canon. As the representation of a feminist place in criticism on the literature of the region, this essay explores the relations of power, the problem of textual authority, and the poetic voice. Along the same revisionist line, Lucía Guerra Cunningham points out the significant role played in women's literary production by the effort of self-definition. The detection of ambiguities and silences in the novels written by women from romanticism to the present day allows the author to identify textual fissures in which one can read the passage from the concept of identity subordinated to the logic of the patriarchy to a new conceptualization that is more autonomous and individual in nature.

Without the establishment of a feminist program that has questioned the bases of Western culture, an inquiry along similar lines having to do with the construction of identity would not have been possible. This inquiry with respect to specific societies has attained a degree of sophistication in the process of laying bear the heterogeneity of complex factors that overdetermine identity: not only the issue of sexual and racial differences, but also how subjects are constituted via language and cultural representations that surround them. Francine Masiello establishes a productive relationship between these themes and the end of the nineteenth century, and she goes on to deal with melodrama as a trope that links literary discourse with the discourse of journalism during the last part of the nineteenth century. In terms of these temporal coordinates, the interest in identifying the manifestations of an alternative sexuality outside the confines of what is considered normal is presented as a constant that contributes to the definition of the ideological systems of the novel as well as to that of the state, which had embarked at that time of the traumatic process of modernization. Lilian Manzor-Coats, with an interest in the way in which Latino identity is configured, studies how that specific configuration gets represented in Cuban theater produced in the United States. Beginning with a careful reading of several theatrical works, she reconstructs the history of a series of efforts at deconstructing traditional forms of the theater and Cuban culture, with the goal of matching them with the new cultural coordinates in which individuals must pursue their lives. Both essays, therefore, underscore how identity is the result of cultural transformations.

Postmodernism in Latin America

Since the mid-1980s, the ongoing debate surrounding postmodernism[4] has been heatedly joined by Latin American intellectuals whose commentaries and discussions continue to multiply. For some critics, it makes no sense to speak of postmodernity in Latin America, since the processes of modernization were, at best, partial and uneven.

On the one hand, the diverse modernizing impulses to be found in Latin American history have not been consistent, nor have they resulted in substantive modifications of society. On the other, these thinkers believe that postmodernism, understood as something that goes beyond the modern, cannot take place because there was, properly speaking, no full modernity. Nevertheless, if one can include within the orbit of postmodernity the cultural logic of late capitalism—that is, the result of the socioeconomic conditions proper to the postindustrial world, including the asymmetric distribution of relations of economic power among developed and developing countries—one then ought to be able to extend the limits of such a cultural logic beyond highly industrialized societies. In fact, carrying this observation a step further, one concludes that such postmodern societies have come to discover, with the end of the cold war, that the conditions of backwardness and socioeconomic inequality are not a phenomenon that is purely external to them.

In the first essay in this section, George Yúdice provides a general panorama of the problems that modernity produced in certain sectors of Latin American society and how those sectors attempt to avoid their inclusion in the politics of hegemonic representation.

Alfonso de Toro insists on the necessity to define the corpus of narrative literature that could be considered postmodern, and he offers a panorama of the emergence of the question in various areas of contemporary culture, and at the same time underlines how the phenomenon is global in nature. In response to the tendency to classify all narrative production since 1960 as postmodern, de Toro attempts to identify a series of structural features that can be taken to be unquestionably postmodern and that will serve as characterizing elements in the construction of the corpus.

Emil Volek approaches the issue of postmodernism from a different point of view. He discusses the concept of magical realism, with the goal of placing it in the context of postrealist Western literature, both modern and postmodern. According to Volek, magical realism is one of the signs of the current malaise of Western modernity, which serves to convert it into sort of a first attribute of Latin American postmodernity that even antedates the theoretical discussion of the question.

Ethnic Issues

If the so-called discovery of America at the end of the fifteenth century brought into contact the cultures of the New World and Europe, a contact with African cultures followed almost immediately. African cultures were brutally transported as slaves to the new and barely conquered territories. This second contact, whose nature and historical development have always occupied a subordinate place vis-à-vis the political and cultural interest that the former provoked from virtually the very outset of modernity, has begun slowly to be reevaluated by literary and cultural historians. Although this new interest took place in the broad context of the recognition and evaluation of the existence of contrahegemonic discourses in Latin American culture, which includes many diverse minority groups (Jews, Chicanos, Asians of differing ethnic backgrounds, and so on), we have chosen to offer a representation of study that takes into account the manifestations of Afro-American culture.

José Piedra takes as his point of departure for the process of the construction of an Afro-American identity the criteria of linguistic standardization that Spain imposed as the cultural mark of imperialism. Adhering to the observations by the grammarian Antonio de Nebrija, a norm of correction is established for colonial literature such that access to writing can only be achieved via the process of assimilation to the official culture and, more specifically, as the incorporation of Peninsular models. This dynamic is particularly crucial when one examines the limits of the canon and revises the work of writers who belong to racial minority, particularly aborigines and blacks, for whom the demands of social status went so far as to make it necessary to obtain certificates of whiteness, which was the only way in which they could, for example, pursue higher learning. Piedra's thesis maintains that it is necessary to trace the origin in these historical conditions of modern Afro-American writing.

Even though Josaphat Bekunuru Kubayanda concerns himself with a body of problematics similar to that of Piedra, he concentrates on discovering the characteristics of contemporary writers who are the heirs of transplanted African cultures. The critic observes that the Latin American literary tradition of blacks is oriented principally toward questions of group identity, such as genealogy, the identity and existential anguish of subgroups whose access to cultural expression beyond the group to which they belong demands the adoption of the language and culture of the master.

Finally, Richard Jackson analyses the production of various contemporary black authors who take up the theme of slavery. These writers do not limit themselves to dealing with the theme in order to compensate for historical excesses that Africans transplanted to the Americas and their descendants suffered. They attempt, in the final analysis, to bring about a change in a collective conscience that has been heir to a broad system of prejudices associated with human skin color. Thus, this writing presents the general reader with a series of strategies designed to restructure the pattern of symbolic values underlying the racist myths of the West regarding blacks.

The three studies selected for inclusion contribute to the identification of a new and different literary corpus of writing that has been excluded in general from the canon on the basis of considerations such as the socioethnic identity of its authors or the distance between them and values considered to be emblematic of the European and Western tradition. But, beyond this appropriate reconsideration of the literary tradition, these works represent a sample of the thematic and methodological possibilities that open up the study of ethnic questions in the field of literary research, as well as also a warning of homogenizing results, whether the latter are deliberate or not, that have underlain a large part of traditional scholarship.

Politics, History, and Nation

A rapid overview of the studies presented up to now demonstrates the degree of importance that political considerations have played in Spanish American literary studies. Even, in the case of those critics who, for ideological reasons, have as their goal the elimination from their research of any openly political consideration, the relationship between politics and literature, abundantly documented in literary texts, both canonical and noncanonical, constitutes a basic axis for the metacommentary produced in and on Latin America.

The first article of this section, by Enrico Mario Santí, analyzes precisely this relationship in terms of the space created by the Cuban Revolution for a political debate among Latin American writers and intellectuals. After identifying a series of elements that liberal intellectuals share with those on the left—the opposition to dictatorial regimes, a critical posture in the face of North American influence, and the defense of intellectual freedom—Santí attempts to adopt a posture midway between both extremes in order to define the function of the Latin American intellectual, who ought, at least, to model two features: on the one hand, a reformist stance toward society and the state and, on the other, a moral function.

Alejandro Losada's study undertakes to formulate an explanatory model of Latin American literature as the practice of diverse, basically urban, social groups in the historical context of the efforts at modernization in the nineteenth century. Taking as his basis the study of Peruvian Romantic literature, Losada discusses the validity of Eurocentric criteria of periodization transplanted to Latin America. The author insists that a true comprehension of national culture is possible only when one takes into account how certain enlightened groups operated, groups that were dependent on the oligarchic elites, in an effort to represent modernity in the context of a fundamentally traditional social structure.

Marc Zimmerman, one of the instigators of a Marxist-based social criticism in the United States, introduces the problem of migrant groups that, although they have a long history in Latin America, produce in the latter part of the twentieth century a series of new conditions for cultural production. In the first place, Zimmerman concentrates on the place of researchers, critics, and writers in Latin America who were forced to abandon their respective countries as a consequence of authoritarian regimes. But he also analyzes the situation of those groups that migrated to the United States and, as a result, were driven to recontextualize themselves in a profound way in order to initiate processes of acculturation that, unquestionably, have affected and will go on to affect literary practices.

By contrast, Hernán Vidal inaugurates the discussion of the ideological implications that lead to the adoption of the notion of otherness as it comes to manifest itself in recent criticism. Beginning with the concept of national culture as the articulation and neutralization that imposes the hegemonic capacity of a power sector on the different alternatives for projects of socioeconomic development that can emerge in a specific society, as well as taking into consideration the situation of Chile during the 1970s and 1980s under military rule, Vidal discusses the limitations and inadequacy of the notion of otherness and its epistemological implications.

As has already been stated, the mosaic of essays and studies included in this volume do not cover every aspect in which the contemporary debate among specialists in Latin American literature has fragmented. Nevertheless, we believe that it does constitute a sufficiently broad and representative display of the fundamental lines that are at the present moment open for discussion.

Notes

[1] The Padilla case involved the political persecution and incarceration of the 1968 Unión Nacional de Escritores y Artistas' Prize winner, Heberto Padilla. This case constituted a first expression of the Castro's cultural policy, reluctant to tolerate any manifestation of dissidence.

[2] Neo-Ricans are Puerto Ricans principally identified with communities in the U.S., mainly in New York and New Jersey.

[3] "Continent" is used by Latin Americanists to refer to the geographic entity called Latin America.

[4] The English concepts of *modernism/postmodernism* should not be identified with the Spanish *modernismo/postmodernismo* which, in Latin American literary history, designates specific early twentieth-century movements (see volume 3).

Colonial and
Postcolonial Issues

Roberto Fernández Retamar

CALIBAN

NOTES TOWARDS A DISCUSSION OF CULTURE IN OUR AMERICA

A QUESTION

A EUROPEAN JOURNALIST, and moreover a leftist, asked me a few days ago, "Does a Latin American culture exist?" We were discussing, naturally enough, the recent polemic regarding Cuba which ended by confronting, on the one hand, certain bourgeois European intellectuals (or aspirants to that state) with a visible colonialist nostalgia; and on the other, that body of Latin American writers and artists who reject open or veiled forms of cultural and political colonialism. The question seemed to me to reveal one of the roots of the polemic, and could also be expressed another way: "Do you exist?" For to question our culture is to question our very existence, our human reality itself, and thus to be willing to take a stand in favor of our irremediable colonial condition, since it suggests that we would be but a distorted echo of what occurs elsewhere. This elsewhere is of course the metropolis, the colonizing centers, whose "right wings" have exploited us and whose supposed "left wings" have pretended and continue to pretend to guide us with pious solicitude; in both cases, with the assistance of local intermediaries of varying persuasions.

This article appeared for the first time in *Casa de Las Américas* (Havana), 68 (Sept.–Oct., 1971). It is that journal, and that issue specifically, to which the author refers in the text. [editor's note]

While this fate is to some extent suffered by all countries emerging from colonialism—those countries of ours which enterprising metropolitan intellectuals have ineptly and successively termed *barbarians, peoples of colour, underdeveloped countries, third world*—I think the phenomenon achieves a singular crudeness with respect to what Martí called "our *mestizo* America." Although the unquestionable thesis that every man and even every culture is *mestizo* could easily be defended, and although this seems especially valid in the case of colonies, it is nevertheless apparent that in both the ethnic as well as the cultural aspects, capitalist countries long ago achieved a relative homogeneity. Almost before our eyes certain readjustments have been made. The white population of the United States (diverse, but of common European origin) exterminated the aboriginal population and thrust the black population aside, thereby affording itself homogeneity in spite of diversity, and offering a coherent model which its Nazi disciples attempted to apply even to other European conglomerates—an unforgiveable sin that led some members of the bourgeoisie to stigmatize in Hitler what they applauded as a healthy Sunday diversion in Westerns and Tarzan films. Those movies proposed to the world—and even to those of us who are kin to the communities under attack and who rejoiced in the evocation of our own extermination—the monstrous racial criteria which has accompanied the United States from its beginnings to the genocide in Indochina. Less apparent (and in some cases perhaps less cruel) is the process by which other capitalist countries have also achieved relative racial and cultural homogeneity at the expense of *internal* diversity.

Nor can any necessary relationship be established between *mestizaje* [racial intermingling; racial mixture—ed. note] and the colonial world. The latter is highly complex[1] despite basic structural affinities. It has included countries with well-defined millennial cultures, some of which (India, Vietnam) have suffered (or are presently suffering) direct occupation, and others,

---

[1] Cf. Yves Lacoste. *Les pays sous-developpés* (Paris, 1959), pp. 82–4.

such as China, which have suffered indirect occupation. It also comprehends countries with rich cultures, but less political homogeneity, which have been subjected to extremely diverse forms of colonialism (the Arab world). There are other countries, finally, whose fundamental structures were savagely dislocated by the dire activity of the European (the peoples of black Africa), despite which they continue to preserve a certain ethnic and cultural homogeneity. (Indeed, the latter occurred despite the colonialists' criminal and unsuccessful attempts to prohibit it.) In these countries, *mestizaje* naturally exists to a greater or lesser degree, but it is always accidental and always on the fringe of its central line of development.

But within the colonial world, there exists a case unique to *the entire planet:* a vast zone for which *mestizaje* is not an accident, but rather the essence, the central line: ourselves, "our *mestizo* America." Martí, with his excellent knowledge of the language, employed this specific adjective as the distinctive sign of our culture—a culture of descendants, both ethnically and culturally speaking, of aborigines, Africans, and Europeans. In his "Letter from Jamaica" (1815), the Liberator Simón Bolívar had proclaimed: "We are a small human species: we possess a world encircled by vast seas, new in almost all its arts and sciences." In his message to the Congress of Angostura (1819), he added:

Let us bear in mind that our people is neither European nor North American, but a composite of Africa and America, rather than an emanation of Europe; for even Spain fails as a European people because of her African blood, her institutions and her character. It is impossible to assign us with any exactitude to a specific human family. The greater part of the native peoples have been annihilated; the European has mingled with the American and with the African, and the latter has mingled with the Indian and with the European. Born from the womb of a common mother, our fathers, different in origin and blood, are foreigners; all differ visibly in the epidermis, and this dissimilarity leaves marks of the greatest transcendence.

Even in this century, in a book as confused as the author

himself but full of intuitions (*La raza cósmica*, 1925), the Mexican José Vasconselos pointed out that in Latin America a new race was being forged, "made with the treasure of all previous ones, the final race, the cosmic race."[2]

This singular fact lies at the root of countless misunderstandings. Chinese, Vietnamese, Korean, Arab or African cultures may leave the Euro-North American enthusiastic, indifferent, or even depressed. But it would never occur to him to confuse a Chinese with a Norwegian, or a Bantu with an Italian; nor would it occur to him to ask whether they exist. Yet, on the other hand, some Latin Americans are taken at times for apprentices, for rough drafts or dull copies of Europeans, including among these latter whites who constitute what Martí called "European America." In the same way our entire culture is taken as an apprenticeship, a rough draft or a copy of European bourgeois culture ("an emanation of Europe," as Bolívar said). This last error is more frequent than the first, since confusion of a Cuban with an Englishman or a Guatemalan with a German tends to be impeded by a certain ethnic tenacity. Here the *rioplatenses* appear to be less ethnically, although not culturally, differentiated. The confusion lies in the root itself, because as descendants of numerous Indian, African, and European communities, we have only a few languages with which to understand one another: those of the colonizers. While other colonials or ex-colonials, in metropolitan centers, speak among themselves in their own language, we Latin Americans continue to use the languages of our colonizers. These are the *linguas francas* capable of going beyond the frontiers which

---

[2] A Swedish summary of what is known on this subject can be found in Magnus Mörner's study, *La mezcla de razas en la historia de América Latina*, translation, reviewed by the author, by Jorge Piatigorsky, Buenos Aires, 1969. Here it is recognized that "no part of the world has witnessed such a gigantic mixing of races as the one that has been taking place in Latin America and the Caribbean [Why this division?] since 1492," p. 15. Of course, what interests me in these notes is not the irrelevant biological fact of the "races" but the historical fact of the "cultures": *vid.* Claude Lévi-Strauss: *Race et histoire* (1952), (Paris, 1968), *passim.*

neither the aboriginal nor creole languages succeed in crossing. Right now as we are discussing, as I am discussing with those colonizers, how else can I do it except in one of their languages, which is now also *our* language, and with so many of their conceptual tools which are now also *our* conceptual tools? This is precisely the extraordinary outcry which we read in a work by perhaps the most extraordinary writer of fiction who ever existed. In *The Tempest*, William Shakespeare's last play, the deformed Caliban—enslaved, robbed of his island, and taught the language by Prospero—rebukes him thus: "You taught me language, and my profit on't/ Is, I know how to curse. The red plague rid you/ For learning me your language!" (*The Tempest*; Act 1, Scene ii.)

TOWARD THE HISTORY OF CALIBAN

CALIBAN IS Shakespeare's anagram for "cannibal," an expression which he had already used to mean anthropophagus, in the third part of *Henry IV* and *Othello*, and which comes in turn from the word "carib." Before the arrival of the Europeans, whom they resisted heroically, the Carib Indians were the most valiant and war-like inhabitants of the very lands which we occupy today. Their name lives on in the term Caribbean Sea (referred to genially by some as the American Mediterranean; just as if we were to call the Mediterranean the Caribbean of Europe). But the name *carib* in itself—as well as in its deformation, *cannibal*—has been perpetuated in the eyes of Europeans above all as a defamation. It is the term in this sense which Shakespeare takes up and elaborates into a complex symbol. Because of its exceptional importance to us, it will be useful to trace in some detail its history.

In the *Diario de Navegación* (Navigation Log Books) of Columbus there appear the first European accounts of the men who were to occasion the symbol in question. On Sunday, 4 November 1492, less than a month after Columbus arrived on the continent which was to be called America, one reads the following entry: "He learned also that far from the place there were men with one eye and others with dogs' muzzles,

who ate human beings."[3] On 23 November, this entry:
". . . which they said was very large [the island of Haiti] and
that on it lived people who had only one eye and others called
cannibals, of whom they seemed to be very afraid." On 11
December it is noted ". . . that *caniba* refers in fact to the people of El Gran Can," which explains the deformation undergone by the name *carib*—also used by Columbus. In the very
letter of 15 February, 1493, "dated on the caravelle off the
island of Canaria" in which Columbus announces to the world
his "discovery," he writes: "I have found, then, neither monsters nor news of any, save for one island [Quarives], the
second upon entering the Indies, which is populated with people held by everyone on the islands to be very ferocious, and
who eat human flesh."[4]

This *carib/cannibal* image contrasts with another one of the
American man presented in the writings of Columbus: That
of the *Arauaco* of the Greater Antilles—our *Taino* Indian
primarily—whom he describes as peaceful, meek, and even
timorous and cowardly. Both visions of the American aborigine
will circulate vertiginously throughout Europe, each coming
to know its own particular development: the *Taino* will be
transformed into the paradisical inhabitant of a utopic world;
by 1516 Thomas More will publish his *Utopia*, the similarities
of which to the island of Cuba have been indicated, almost to
the point of rapture, by Ezequiel Martínez Estrada.[5] The
Carib, on the other hand, will become a *cannibal*—an anthro-
pophage, a bestial man situated on the margins of civilization,

---

[3] Cited, along with subsequent references to the *Diario*, by Julio C. Salas.
*Etnografía americana. Los indios caribes. Estudio sobre el origen del Mito de
la antropofagia* (Madrid, 1920). The book exposes "the irrationality of
[the] charge that some American tribes devoured human flesh, maintained in
the past by those interested in enslaving [the] Indians and repeated by the
chroniclers and historians, many of whom were supporters of slavery." (p. 211)

[4] *La carta de Colón anunciando el descubrimiento del nuevo mundo. 15 de
febrero—14 de marzo, 1493* (Madrid, 1956), p. 20.

[5] Ezequiel Martínez Estrada, "El Nuevo Mundo, la Isla de Utopía y la Isla
de Cuba," *Casa de las Américas*, 33 (noviembre-diciembre, 1965). This issue
is entitled, *Homenaje a Ezequiel Martínez Estrada*.

who must be opposed to the very death. But there is less of a contradiction than might appear at first glance between the two visions; they constitute, simply, options in the ideological arsenal of a vigorous emerging bourgeoisie. Francisco de Quevedo translated "utopia" as "There is no such place." With respect to these two visions, one might add: "There is no such man." The notion of an edenic creature comprehends, in more contemporary terms, a working hypothesis for the bourgeois left, and as such offers an ideal model of the perfect society free from the constrictions of that feudal world against which the bourgeoisie is in fact struggling. Generally speaking, the utopic vision throws upon these lands projects for political reforms unrealized in the countries of origin. In this sense its line of development is far from extinguished. Indeed, it meets with certain perpetuators—apart from its radical perpetuators who are the consequential revolutionaries—in the numerous advisors who unflaggingly propose to countries emerging from colonialism magic formulas from the metropolis to solve the grave problems colonialism has left us and which, of course, they have not yet resolved in their own countries. It goes without saying that these proponents of "There is no such place" are irritated by the insolent fact that the place *does* exist and, quite naturally, has all the virtues and defects not of a project but of genuine reality.

As for the vision of the *cannibal*, it corresponds—also in more contemporary terms—to the right-wing of that same bourgeoisie. It belongs to the ideological arsenal of politicians of action, those who perform the dirty work in whose fruits the charming dreamers of utopias will equally share. That the Caribs were as Columbus depicted them (and after him, an unending throng of followers) is about as probable as the existence of one-eyed men, men with dog-muzzles or tails, or even the Amazons mentioned by the explorer in his pages where Greco-Latin mythology, the medieval bestiary, and the novel of chivalry all play their part. It is a question of the typically degraded vision offered by the colonizer of the man he is colonizing. That we ourselves may have at one time believed in this version only proves to what extent we are infected with the ideology of the enemy. It is typical that we have applied the term *cannibal* not to the extinct aborigine of our isles, but, above all, to the African black who appeared in those shameful Tarzan films. For it is the colonizer who brings us together, who reveals the profound similarities existing above and beyond our secondary differences. The colonizer's version explains to us that owing to his irremediable bestiality, there was no alternative to the extermination of the Carib. What it does not explain is why, even before the Carib, the peaceful and kindly Arauaco was also exterminated. Simply speaking the two groups suffered equally one of the greatest ethnocides recorded in history. (Needless to say, this line of action is still more alive than the earlier one.) In relation to this fact, it will always be necessary to point out the case of those men who, being on the fringe both of Utopianism (which has nothing to do with the actual America) and of the shameless ideology of plunder, stood in their midst opposed to the conduct of the colonialists, and passionately, lucidly, and valiantly defended the flesh-and-blood aborigine. In the forefront of such men stands the magnificent figure of Father Bartolomé de Las Casas, whom Bolívar called "the apostle of America," and whom Martí extolled unreservedly. Unfortunately, such men were exceptions.

One of the most widely disseminated European Utopian works is Montaigne's essay "De los caníbales" ("On Cannibals") which appeared in 1580. There we find a presentation of those creatures who "keep their natural properties and virtues, which are the true and useful ones, vigorous and alive."[6]

Giovanni Floro's English translation of the *Essays* was published in 1603. Not only was Floro a personal friend of Shakespeare, but the copy of the translation that Shakespeare owned and annotated is still preserved. This piece of information would be of no further importance, but for the fact that it proves beyond a shadow of doubt that the book was one of the direct sources of Shakespeare's last great work, *The Tempest*

---

[6] Miguel de Montaigne: *Ensayos*, trans. C. Román y Salamero, Vol. I (Buenos Aires, 1948), p. 248.

(1612). Even one of the characters of the play, Gonzalo, who incarnates the Renaissance humanist, at one point closely glosses entire lines from Floro's Montaigne, originating precisely in the essay "On Cannibals." This fact makes the form in which Shakespeare presents his character *Caliban/cannibal* even stranger. Because if in Montaigne—in this case, as unquestionable literary source for Shakespeare—"there is nothing barbarian or savage in these nations . . . what happens is that everyone calls what is foreign to his own customs *barbarian*,"[7] in Shakespeare, on the other hand, *Caliban/cannibal* is a savage and deformed slave who cannot be degraded enough. What has happened is simply that in depicting Caliban, Shakespeare, an implacable realist, here takes *the other option* of the emerging bourgeois world. Regarding the utopian vision, it does indeed exist in the work but is unrelated to Caliban; as was said before, it is expressed by the harmonious humanist Gonzalo. Shakespeare thus confirms that both ways of considering the American, far from being in opposition, were perfectly reconcilable. As for the concrete man, present him in the guise of an animal, rob him of his land, enslave him so as to live from his toil, and at the right moment, exterminate him; this latter of course, only as long as there was someone who could be depended on to perform the arduous tasks in his stead. In one revealing passage, Prospero warns his daughter that they could not do without Caliban: "We cannot miss him: he does make our fire,/ Fetch in our wood, and serves in offices/ that profit us" (I, ii). The Utopian vision can and must do without men of flesh and blood. After all, *there is no such place*.

There is no doubt at this point that *The Tempest* alludes to America, that its island is the mythification of one of our islands. Astrana Marín, who mentions the "clearly Indian (American) ambience of the island," recalls some of the actual voyages along this continent that inspired Shakespeare and even furnished him, with slight variations, with the names of not a few of his characters: Miranda, Fernando, Sebastian, Alonso,

---

[7] *Loc. cit.*

Gonzalo, Setebos.[8] More important than this is the knowledge that Caliban is our Carib.

We are not interested in following all the possible readings that have been made of this notable work since its appearance,[9] and shall merely point out some interpretations. The first of these comes from Ernest Renan who published his drama *Caliban: Suite de La Tempête* in 1878.[10] In his work, Caliban is the incarnation of the people presented in their worst light, except that this time his conspiracy against Prospero is successful and he achieves power—which ineptitude and corruption will surely prevent him from retaining. Prospero lurks in the darkness awaiting his revenge, and Ariel disappears. This reading owes less to Shakespeare than to the Paris Commune which had taken place only seven years before. Naturally, Renan was among the writers of the French bourgeoisie who savagely took part against the prodigious "assault of heaven."[11] Beginning with this event, his anti-democratic feeling stiffened even further. "In his *Philosophical Dialogues*," Lidsky tells us, "he believes that the solution would lie in the creation of an *elite* of intelligent beings who alone would govern and possess the secrets of science."[12] Characteristically, Renan's aristocratic and pre-Fascist elitism and his hatred of the common people of his country are united with an even greater hatred for the inhabitants of the colonies. It is instructive to hear him express himself along these lines.

---

[8] William Shakespeare, *Obras completas*. Trans. with an Introductory Study and Notes by Luis Astrana Marín (Madrid, 1961), pp. 107–8.

[9] Thus, e.g., Jan Kott notes that until the nineteenth century "there were several Shakespearean scholars who attempted to read *The Tempest* as a biography in the literal sense, or as an allegorical political drama." Jan Kott, *Apuntes sobre Shakespeare*, Trans. J. Maurizio (Barcelona, 1969), p. 353.

[10] Ernest Renan: *Caliban, Suite de La Tempête. Drame Philosophique* (Paris, 1878).

[11] V. Arthur Adamov. *La Commune de Paris (8 mars-28 mars 1871): Anthologie* (Paris, 1959); and especially Paul Lidsky, *Les écrivains contre la Commune* (Paris, 1970).

[12] Paul Lidsky: *op. cit.*, p. 82.

We aspire [he says] not to equality but to domination. The country of a foreign race must again be a country of serfs, of agricultural laborers or industrial workers. It is not a question of eliminating the inequalities among men but of broadening them and making them law.[13]

And on another occasion:

The regeneration of the inferior or bastard races by the superior races is within the providential human order. With us, the common man is nearly always a *declassé* noble man, his heavy hand is better suited to handling the sword than the menial tool. Rather than work he chooses to fight, that is, he returns to his first state. *Regere imperio populos—* that is our vocation. Pour forth this all-consuming activity onto countries which, like China, are crying aloud for foreign conquest [. . .] Nature has made a race of workers, the Chinese race, with its marvelous manual dexterity and almost no sense of honor; govern them with justice, levying from them, in return for the blessing of such a government, an ample allowance for the conquering race, and they will be satisfied; a race of tillers of the soil, the black [. . .]; a race of masters and soldiers, the European race [. . .] *Let each do that which he is made for, and all will be well.*[14]

It is unnecessary to gloss these lines, which as Césaire rightly says, came from the pen, not of Hitler, but of the French humanist Ernest Renan.

The initial destiny of the Caliban myth on our own American soil is a surprising one. Twenty years after Renan had published his *Caliban,* in other words, in 1898, the United States intervened in the Cuban war of independence against Spain and subjected Cuba to its tutelage, converting her as of 1902 (and until 1959) into her first *neocolony;* while Puerto Rico and the Philippines became colonies of a traditional nature. The fact—which had been anticipated by Martí years before—moved the Latin American *intelligentsia.* Elsewhere I have recalled that "ninety-eight" is not only a Spanish date that gives its

---

[13] Cited by Aimé Césaire in *Discours sur le colonialisme.* 3rd ed. (Paris, 1955), p. 13. This is a remarkable work, and I have incorporated many of its hypotheses (partially trans. in *Casa de las Américas,* 36–37 [mayo-agosto, 1966], an issue dedicated to *Africa en américa*).

[14] *Ibid.,* pp. 14–15.

name to a complex group of writers and thinkers of that country, but it is also, and perhaps most importantly, a Latin American date which should serve to designate a no less complex group of writers and thinkers on this side of the Atlantic, generally known by the vague name of *modernistas*.[15] It is "ninety-eight"—the visible presence of North American imperialism in Latin America—already foretold by Martí, which informs the later work of someone like Darío or Rodó.

In a speech given by Paul Groussac in Buenos Aires on 2 May 1898, we have an early example of how Latin American writers of the time would react to this situation:

Since the Civil War and the brutal invasion of the West [he says], the *Yankee* spirit had rid itself completely of its formless and "Calibanesque" body, and the old world has contemplated with disquiet and terror the newest civilization that intends to supplant our own, declared to be in decay.[16]

The Franco-Argentine writer Groussac feels that "our" civilization (obviously understanding by that term the civilization of the "old world," of which we Latin Americans would, curiously enough be a part) is menaced by the Calibanesque Yankee. It seems highly improbable that the Algerian or Vietnamese writer of the time, trampled underfoot by French colonialism, would have been ready to subscribe to the first part of such a criterion. It is also frankly strange to see the Caliban symbol—in which Renan could with exactitude see, if only to abuse, the people—being applied to the United States. But nevertheless, despite this blurred focus characteristic, on the other hand, of Latin America's unique situation, Groussac's reaction implies a clear rejection of the Yankee danger by Latin American writers. This is not, however, the first time that such a rejection was expressed on our continent. Apart from cases of Hispanic writers such as Bolívar and Martí, among others,

---

[15] *Vid.* R.F.R., "Modernismo, noventiocho, subdesarrollo," read at the 3rd Congress of the International Association of Hispanists, Mexico City, Aug. 1968; collected in *Ensayo de otro mundo*, 2nd ed. (Santiago de Chile, 1969).

[16] Quoted in José Enrique Rodó. *Obras completas.* Introducción, Prólogo y Notas por Emir Rodríguez Monegal (Madrid, 1957), p. 193.

Brazilian literature presents the example of Joaquín de Sousa Andrade or Sousândrade, in whose strange poem, *O Guesa Errante*, stanza X is dedicated to "O inferno Wall Street," ". . . a *Walpurgisnacht* of corrupt stockbrokers, petty politicians, and businessmen."[17] There is besides José Verissimo, who in an 1890 treatise on national education impugned the United States with his "I admire them, but I don't esteem them."

We do not know whether the Uruguayan José Enrique Rodó—whose famous phrase on the United States: "I admire them, but I don't love them," coincides literally with Verissimo's observation—knew the work of the Brazilian thinker, but it is certain that he was familiar with Groussac's speech, essential portions of which were reproduced in *La Razón* of Montevideo on 6 May 1898. Developing and embellishing the idea outlined in it, Rodó published in 1900, at the age of twenty-nine, one of the most famous works of Latin American literature: *Ariel*. North American civilization is implicitly presented there as Caliban (scarcely mentioned in the work), while Ariel would come to incarnate—or should incarnate—the best of what Rodó did not hesitate to call more than once "our civilization" (pp. 223 and 226). In his words, just as in those of Groussac, this civilization was identified not only with "our Latin America" (p. 239), but with the ancient Romania, if not with the Old World as a whole. The identification of Caliban with the United States, proposed by Groussac and popularized by Rodó, was certainly a mistake. Attacking this error from one angle, José Vasconcelos commented that "if the Yankees were only Caliban, they would not represent any great danger."[18] But this is doubtless of little importance next to the relevant fact that the danger in question had clearly been pointed out. As Benedetti rightly observed, "perhaps Rodó erred in naming the danger, but he did not err in his recognition of where it lay."[19]

---

[17] *Vid.* Jean Franco, *The Modern Culture of Latin America: Society and the Artist* (London, 1967), p. 49.

[18] José Vasconcelos: *Indología.* 2nd edition (Barcelona, n.d.), p. XXIII.

[19] Mario Benedetti, *Genio y figura de José Enrique Rodó* (Buenos Aires, 1966), p. 95.

Some time afterward, the French writer Jean Guéhenno—
who while he was surely unaware of the work by the colonial
Rodó, knew of course Renan's work from memory—restated
the latter's Caliban thesis in his *Calibán Parle* (Caliban
Speaks) published in Paris in 1928. This time, however, the
Renan identification of Caliban/the people is accompanied by
a positive evaluation of Caliban. One must be grateful to
Guéhenno's book—and it is about the only thing for which
gratitude is due—for having offered for the first time an ap-
pealing version of the character.[20] But the theme would have
required the hand or the rage of a Paul Nizan to be effectively
realized.[21]

Much sharper are the observations of the Argentine, Aníbal
Ponce, in his 1935 work *Humanismo burgués y humanismo
proletario.* The book—which a student of Che's thinking con-
jectures must have exercised influence on the latter[22]—devotes
the third chapter to "Ariel, or the Agony of an Obstinate Illusion." In commenting on *The Tempest*, Ponce says that "those
four beings embody an entire era: Prospero is the enlightened
despot who loves the Renaissance; Miranda, his progeny;
Caliban, the suffering masses [Ponce will then quote Renan,
but not Guéhenno]; and Ariel, the genius of the air without
any ties to life."[23] Ponce points up the equivocal nature of Caliban's presentation, one which reveals "an enormous injustice

---

[20] The penetrating but negative vision of Jan Kott causes him to be irritated
by this fact. "For Renan," he says, "Caliban personifies the Demos. [. . .]
Caliban is successful in carrying out a crime against Prospero. Guéhenno's
work is an apology of Caliban/the people. Both interpretations are trivial.
Shakespeare's Caliban has more grandeur" (*op. cit.*, p. 398).

[21] Guéhenno's weakness in approaching this theme with any profundity is
apparent from his increasingly contradictory prefaces to successive editions
of the book (Second Edition, 1945, Third Edition, 1962) down to his book
of essays *Calibán et Próspero* (Paris, 1969) where according to one critic,
Guéhenno is converted into "a personage of bourgeois society and beneficiary
of its culture," who judges Prospero "more equitably than in the days of
Calibán Parle." (Pierre Henri Simon in *Le Monde*, 5 July, 1969.)

[22] Michael Lowy: *La Pensée de Che Guevara* (Paris, 1970), p. 19.

[23] Aníbal Ponce: *Humanismo burgués y humanismo proletario* (Havana,
1962), p. 83.

on the part of a master." In Ariel he sees the intellectual, tied to Prospero in "less burdensome and crude a way than Caliban, but also in his service." His analysis of the conception of the intellectual ("A mixture of slave and mercenary") coined by Renaissance humanism, a concept which "taught as nothing else could an indifference to action and an acceptance of the established order," and which even today is for the intellectual in the bourgeois world "the educational ideal of the governing classes," constitutes one of the most penetrating essays written on the theme in our America.

But this examination, although made by a Latin American, still took only the European world into account. For a new reading of *The Tempest*—for a new consideration of the problem—it was necessary to await the emergence of the colonial countries, which begins around the time of the Second World War. That abrupt presence led the busy technicians of the United Nations to invent, between 1944 and 1945, the term *economically underdeveloped area* in order to dress in attractive (and profoundly confusing) verbal garb what had until then been called *colonial areas* or *backward areas*.[24]

Concurrently with this emergence, there appeared in Paris in 1950 O. Mannoni's book *Psychologie de la colonisation*. Significantly, the English edition of this book (New York, 1956) was to be called *Prospero and Caliban: The Psychology of Colonization*. To approach his subject Mannoni has created, no less, what he calls the "Prospero complex," defined as "the sum of those unconscious neurotic tendencies that delineate at the same time the 'picture' of the paternalist colonial and the portrait of 'the racist whose daughter has been the object of an [imaginary] attempted rape at the hands of an inferior being.' "[25] In this book, probably for the first time, Caliban is identified with the colonial. But the odd theory that the latter suffers from a "Prospero-complex" which leads him neurotical-

---

[24] J. L. Zimmerman. *Países pobres, países ricos: La brecha que se ensancha.* Trans. by G. González Aramburo (Mexico City, 1966), p. 7.

[25] O. Mannoni. *Psychologie de la colonisation* (Paris, 1950), p. 71. Quoted by Frantz Fanon in *Peau noire, masques blancs*. Second Edition (Paris [c. 1965]), p. 106.

ly to require, even to anticipate, and naturally to accept the presence of Prospero/colonizer, is roundly rejected by Frantz Fanon in the fourth chapter ("The So-Called Dependence Complex of Colonized Peoples") in his 1952 book *Black Skin, White Masks*.

Although he is (apparently) the first writer in our world to assume our identification with Caliban, the writer from Barbados George Lamming is unable to break the circle traced by Mannoni.

Prospero [says Lamming] has given Caliban languages; and with it an unstated history of consequences, an unknown history of future intentions. This gift of language meant not English, in particular, but speech and concept as a way, a method, a necessary avenue towards areas of the self which could not be reached in any other way. It is this way, entirely Prospero's enterprise, which makes Caliban aware of possibilities. Therefore, all of Caliban's future—for future is the very name of possibilities—must derive from Prospero's experiment, which is also his risk. Provided there is no extraordinary departure which explodes all of Prospero's premises, then Caliban and his future now belong to Prospero . . . Prospero lives in the absolute certainty that Language, which is his gift to Caliban, is the very prison in which Caliban's achievements will be realized and restricted.[26]

In the decade of the sixties, the new reading of *The Tempest* ultimately established its hegemony. In *The Living World of Shakespeare* (1964), the Englishman John Wain will tell us that Caliban

has the pathos of the exploited peoples everywhere, poignantly expressed at the beginning of a three-hundred year wave of European colonization; even the lowest savage wishes to be left alone rather than be "educated" and made to work for someone else, and there is an undeniable justice in his complaint: "for I am all the subject that you have,/ Which once was mine own king." Prospero retorts with the inevitable

---

[26] George Lamming. *The Pleasures of Exile* (London, 1960), p. 109. In commenting on these opinions of Lamming, the German Janheinz Jahn observes their limitations and proposes an identification of Caliban/negritude. *Neo-African Literature*. Trans. O. Coburn and U. Lehrburger (New York, 1968), pp. 239–42.

answer of the colonist: Caliban has gained in knowledge and skill (though we recall that he already knew how to build dams to catch fish, and also to dig pig-nuts from the soil, as if this were the English countryside). Before being employed by Prospero, Caliban had no language: ". . . thou didst not, savage,/ Know thy own meaning, but wouldst gabble like/ A thing most brutish." However, this kindness has been rewarded with ingratitude. Caliban, allowed to live in Prospero's cell, has made an attempt to ravish Miranda. When sternly reminded of this, he impertinently says, with a kind of slavering guffaw, "Oh ho! Oh ho!—would it have been done!/ Thou didst prevent me; I had peopled else/ This isle with Calibans." Our own age [Wain concludes] which is much given to using the horrible word "miscegenation," ought to have no difficulty in understanding this passage.[27]

At the end of that same decade, in 1969, and in a highly significant manner, Caliban would be taken up with pride as our symbol by three Antillian writers—each of whom expresses himself in one of the three great colonial languages of the Caribbean. In that year, independently of one another, the Martinican writer Aimé Césaire published his dramatic work in French, *Une tempête. Adaptation de "La Tempête" de Shakespeare pour un théâtre nègre;* the Bardbadian Edward Brathwaite, his book of poems *Islands* in English, among which there is one dedicated to "Caliban"; and the author of these lines, an essay in Spanish "Cuba hasta Fidel" which discusses our identification with Caliban.[28] In Césaire's work, the characters are the same as those of Shakespeare. Ariel, however, is a mulatto slave, while Caliban is a black slave; in addition, Eshú, "a black god-devil" appears. Prospero's remark when Ariel returns full of scruples, after having unleashed—following Prospero's orders but against his own conscience—the tempest with which the work begins is curious indeed: "Come now!" Prospero says to him, "Your crisis! It's always the same with

---

[27] John Wain. *El mundo vivo de Shakespeare.* Trad. de J. Silés (Madrid, 1967), pp. 258–9.

[28] Aimé Césaire. *Une tempête. Adaptation de "La Tempête" de Shakespeare pour un théâtre nègre* (Paris, 1969); Edward Brathwaite. *Islands* (London, 1969); R.F.R. "Cuba hasta Fidel," *Bohemia* (19 September 1969).

intellectuals!" Brathwaite's poem called "Caliban" is dedicated, significantly, to Cuba: "In Havana that morning . . ." writes Brathwaite, "It was December second, nineteen fifty-six./ It was the first of August eighteen thirty-eight./ It was the twelfth October fourteen ninety-two./ How many bangs how many revolutions?"[29]

OUR SYMBOL

O UR SYMBOL then is not Ariel, as Rodó thought, but rather Caliban. This is something that we, the *mestizo* inhabitants of these same isles where Caliban lived, see with particular clarity: Prospero invaded the islands, killed our ancestors, enslaved Caliban, and taught him his language to make himself understood. What else can Caliban do but use that same language—today he has no other—to curse him, to wish that the "red plague" would fall on him? I know no other metaphor more expressive of our cultural situation, of our reality. From Túpac Amaru, *Tiradentes*, Toussaint-Louverture, Simón Bolívar, Father Hidalgo, José Artigas, Bernardo O'Higgins, Benito Juárez, Antonio Maceo and José Martí, to Emiliano Zapata, Augusto César Sandino, Julio Antonio Mella, Pedro Albizu Campos, Lázaro Cárdenas, Fidel Castro and Ernesto Che Guevara; from the Inca Garcilaso de la Vega, the *Aleijadinho*, the popular music of the Antilles, José Hernández, Eugenio María de Hostos, Manuel Gonzáles Prada, Rubén Darío (yes, when all is said and done), Baldomero Lillo and Horacio Quiroga, to Mexican muralism, Héctor Villalobos, César Vallejo, José Carlos Mariátegui, Ezequiel Martínez Estrada, Carlos Gardel, Pablo Neruda, Alejo Carpentier, Nicolás Guillén, Aimé Césaire, José María Arguedas, Violeta Parra, and Frantz Fanon—what is our history, what is our culture, if not the history and culture of Caliban?

---

[29] The new reading of *The Tempest* has now become a common one throughout the colonial world of today. I want only, therefore, to mention a few examples. On concluding these notes, I find a new one in the essay by James Nggui (of Kenya) "Africa y la descolonización cultural," in *El Correo*, January 1971.

As regards Rodó, if it is indeed true that he erred in his symbols, as has already been said, it is no less true that he was able to point with clarity to the greatest enemy of our culture in his time—and in ours—and that is enormously important. Rodó's limitations (and this is not the moment to elucidate them) are responsible for what he saw unclearly or failed to see at all.[30] But what is worthy of note in his case is what he did indeed see and what continues to retain a certain amount of validity and even virulence.

Despite his failings, omissions, and ingenuousness [Benedetti has also said], Rodó's vision of the Yankee phenomenon, rigorously situated in its historical context, was in its time the first launching pad for other less ingenuous, better informed and more foresighted formulations to come [. . .]. The almost prophetic substance of Rodó's Arielism still retains today a certain amount of validity.[31]

These observations are supported by indisputable realities. We Cubans are well aware that Rodó's vision served for later, less ingenuous and more radical formulations simply by turning to the work of our own Julio Antonio Mella, on whose development the influence of Rodó was decisive. In "Intelectuales y tartufos" ("Intellectuals and Tartuffes," 1924), a vehement work written at the age of twenty-one, Mella violently attacks the false intellectual values of the time—opposing them with such names as Unamuno, José Vasconcelos, Ingenieros and Varona. He writes, "The intellectual is the worker of the mind.

---

[30] "It is improper," Benedetti has said, "to confront Rodó with present-day structures, statements, and ideologies. His time was different from ours [. . .] his true place, his true temporal homeland was the nineteenth century" (*op. cit.*, p. 128).

[31] *Op. cit.*, p. 109. Even greater emphasis on the current validity of Rodó will be found in Arturo Ardao's book *Rodó: su americanismo* (Montevideo, 1970), which includes an excellent anthology of the author of *Ariel*. On the other hand, as early as 1928, José Carlos Mariátegui, after rightly recalling that "only a socialist Latin or Ibero-America can effectively oppose a capitalist, plutocratic, and imperialist North America," adds: "The myth of Rodó has not yet acted—nor has it ever acted—usefully and fruitfully upon our souls." J.C.M.: "Aniversario y balance" (1928) in *Ideología y política* (Lima, 1969), p. 248.

The worker! That is, the only man who in Rodó's judgement is worthy of life . . . he who takes up his pen against iniquity just as others take up the plow to fecundate the earth, or the sword to liberate peoples, or a dagger to execute tyrants."[32]

Mella would again quote Rodó with devotion during that year[33] and in the following he was to help found the Ariel Polytechnic Institute in Havana.[34] It is opportune to recall that in this same year, 1925, Mella was also among the founders of Cuba's first Communist party. Without a doubt, Rodó's *Ariel* served as a "launching pad" for the meteoric revolutionary career of this first organic Marxist-Leninist in Cuba and one of the first on the continent.

As further examples of the relative validity which Rodó's anti-Yankee argument retains even in our day, we can point to enemy attempts to disarm such an argument. A strange case is that of Emir Rodríguez Monegal, for whom *Ariel*, in addition to "material for philosophic or sociological meditation, *also* contains pages of a polemic nature on political problems *of the moment*. And it was precisely this *secondary* but undeniable condition that determined its immediate popularity and dissemination." Rodó's essential position against North American penetration would thus appear to be an afterthought, a *secondary* fact in the work. It is known, however, that Rodó conceived it immediately after American intervention in Cuba in 1898, *as a response to the deed*. Rodríguez Monegal says:

The work thus projected was *Ariel*. In the final version *only two direct allusions* are found to the historical fact which was its primary motive force [. . .] both allusions enable us to appreciate how Rodó has *transcended* the initial historical circumstance to arrive fully at the essential problem: The proclaimed decadence of the Latin race.[35]

---

[32] *Hombres de la Revolucion. Julio Antionio Mella* (La Habana, 1971), p. 12.

[33] *Op. cit.*, p. 15.

[34] *Vid*. Erasmo Dumpierre. *Mella* (La Habana c. 1965), p. 145; and also José Antonio Portunondo: "Mella y los intelectuales" (1963), which is reproduced in *Casa de las Américas*, No. 68, 1971.

[35] Emir Rodríguez Monegal. *Rodó, op. cit.*, p. 192–193. (my emphasis—R.F.R.).

The fact that a servant of imperialism such as Rodríguez Monegal, afflicted with the same "Nordo-mania" which Rodó denounced in 1900, tries so coarsely to emasculate his work, only proves that it does indeed retain a certain virulence in its formulation—something which we would approach today from other perspectives and with other means. An analysis of *Ariel* —and this is absolutely not the occasion to make one—would lead us also to stress how, despite his background and his anti-Jacobinism, Rodó combats in it the anti-democratic spirit of Renan and Nietzsche (in whom he finds "an abominable, reactionary spirit," p. 224), and exalts democracy, moral values, and emulation. But undoubtedly the rest of the work has lost the immediacy that its gallant confrontation with the United States and the defense of our values still retains.

Put into perspective, it is almost certain that these lines would not bear the name they have were it not for Rodó's book, and I prefer to consider them also as an homage to the great Uruguayan, whose centenary is being celebrated this year. That the homage contradicts him on not a few points is not strange. Medardo Vitier has already observed that "if there should be a return to Rodó, I do not believe that it would be to adopt the solution he offered concerning the interests of the life of the spirit, but rather to reconsider the problem."[36]

In proposing Caliban as our symbol, I am aware that it is not entirely ours, that it is also an alien elaboration, although in this case based on our concrete realities. But how can this alien quality be entirely avoided? The most venerated word in Cuba—*mambí*—was disparagingly imposed on us by our enemies at the time of the war for independence, and we still have not totally deciphered its meaning. It seems to have an African root, and in the mouth of the Spanish colonists implied the idea that all *independentistas* were so many black slaves— emancipated by the very war for independence—who of course constituted the bulk of the liberation army. The *independentistas*, white and black, adopted with honor something that colonialism meant as an insult. This is the dialectic of Caliban. To

---

[36] Medardo Vitier. *Del ensayo americano* (Mexico, 1945), p. 117.

offend us they call us *mambí*, they call us *Black*; but we reclaim as a mark of glory the honor of considering ourselves descendants of the *mambí*, descendants of the rebel, runaway, *independentista* Black—*never* descendants of the slave holder. Nevertheless, Prospero, as we well know, taught his language to Caliban and, consequently, gave him a name. But is this his true name? Let us listen to this speech made in 1971:

To be completely precise, we still do not even have a name; we still have no name; we are practically unbaptized—whether as Latin Americans, Ibero-Americans, Indo-Americans. For the imperialists, we are nothing more than despised and despicable peoples. At least that was what we were. Since Girón they have begun to change their thinking. Racial contempt—to be a creole, to be a *mestizo*, to be Black, to be, simply, a Latin American, is for them contemptible.[37]

This, naturally, is Fidel Castro on the tenth anniversary of the victory at Playa Girón.

To assume our condition as Caliban implies rethinking our history from the *other* side, from the viewpoint of the *other* protagonist. The *other* protagonist of *The Tempest* (or as we might have said ourselves, *The Hurricane*) is not of course Ariel, but rather Prospero.[38] There is no real Ariel-Caliban polarity: both are slaves in the hands of Prospero, the foreign magician. But Caliban is the rude and unconquerable master of the island, while Ariel, a creature of the air, although also a child of the isle, is the intellectual—as both Ponce and Césaire have seen.

AGAIN MARTÍ

THIS CONCEPTION of our culture had already been articulately expressed and defended in the last century by the first among us to understand clearly the concrete situation of what he called—using a term I have referred to several times

---

[37] Fidel Castro: Speech of April 19, 1971.
[38] Jan Kott, *op. cit.*, p. 377.

—"our *mestizo* America": José Martí,[39] to whom Rodó planned to dedicate the first Cuban edition of *Ariel* and about whom he intended to write a study similar to those he devoted to Bolívar and Artigas, a study which in the end he unfortunately never realized.[40]

Although he devoted numerous pages to the topic, the occasion on which Martí offered his ideas on this point in a most organic and concise manner was in his 1891 article "Our America." I will limit myself to certain essential quotations. But I should first like to offer some prior observations on the destiny of Martí's work.

During Martí's lifetime, the bulk of his work, scattered throughout a score of continental newspapers, enjoyed widespread fame. We know that Rubén Darío called Martí *Maestro* (as, for other reasons, his political followers would also call him during his lifetime) and considered him the Latin American whom he most admired. We shall soon see, on the other hand, how the harsh judgments on the United States which Martí commonly made in his articles were well known in his time, and were the cause of acerbic criticism by the pro-Yankee Sarmiento. But the particular manner in which Martí's writings circulated—he made use of journalism, oratory, and letters, but *never published a single book*—bears no little responsibility for the relative oblivion into which the work of the Cuban hero fell after his death in 1895. This alone explains the fact that nine years after his death—and twelve from the time Martí stopped writing for the continental press, devoted as he was after 1892 to his political tasks—an author as absolutely ours and as far above suspicion as the twenty-year-old Pedro Henríquez Ureña could write in 1904, in an article on

---

[39] *Vid.* Ezequiel Martínez Estrada, "Por una alta cultural popular y socialista cubana" (1962), in *En Cuba y al servicio de la Revolución cubana* (Havana, 1963); R.F.R., "Martí en su (tercer) mundo" (1964), in *Ensayo de otro mundo, cit.*: Noël Salomon, "José Martí et la prise de conscience latinoamericanine," in *Cuba Sí*, 35–36 (4th trimester, 1970, 1st trimester, 1971); Leonardo Acosta, "La concepción histórica de Martí," *Casa de las Américas*, 67 (julio-agosto, 1971).

[40] José Enrique Rodó, *op. cit.*, pp. 1359 and 1375.

Rodó's *Ariel,* that the latter's opinions on the United States are "much more severe than those formulated by two of the greatest thinkers and most brilliant psycho-sociologists of the Antilles: Hostos and Martí."[41] Insofar as this refers to Martí, the observation is completely erroneous; and given the exemplary honesty of Henríquez Ureña, it led me first to suspect, and later to verify, that it was due simply to the fact that during this period the great Dominican had not read, *had been unable to read* Martí adequately. Martí was hardly *published* at the time. A text such as the fundamental "Our America" is a good example of this fate. Readers of the Mexican newspaper *El Partido Liberal* could have read it on January 30, 1891. It is possible that some other local newspaper republished it,[42] although the most recent edition of Martí's *Complete Works* does not indicate anything in this regard. But it is most likely that those who did not have the good fortune to obtain said newspaper knew nothing about the article—the most important document published in America from the end of the past century until the appearance in 1962 of the Second Declaration of Havana—for almost twenty years, at the end of which time it appeared in book form (Havana, 1910) in the irregular collection in which publication of the complete works of Martí was begun. For this reason, Manuel Pedro González is correct when he asserts that during the first quarter of this century the new generations did not know Martí. "A minimal portion of his work" was again put into circulation starting with the eight volumes published by Alberto Ghiraldo in Madrid in 1925. Thanks to the most recent appearance of several editions of his complete works—actually still incomplete—"he has been rediscovered and reevaluated."[43] González is thinking above all of the dazzling literary qualities of this work ("the literary

---

[41] Pedro Henríquez Ureña. *Obra crítica* (Mexico, 1960), p. 27.

[42] Ivan Schulman (*Martí, Casal y el Modernismo,* Havana, 1969, p. 92) has discovered that it had been *previously* published on January 10, 1891, in *La Revista Ilustrada de Nueva York.*

[43] Manuel Pedro González, "Evolución de la estimativa martiana," *Antología crítica de José Martí.* Compiled with an Introduction and Notes by M.P.G. (Mexico, 1960), p. xxix.

glory" as he says). Could we not add something, then, regarding the works' fundamental ideological aspects? Without forgetting very important prior contributions, there are still some essential points which explain why today, after the triumph of the Cuban Revolution and because of it, Martí is being "rediscovered and reevaluated." It was no mere coincidence that in 1953 Fidel named Martí as the intellectual author of the attack on the Moncada Barracks; nor that Che should use a quotation from Martí—"It is the hour of the furnace, and only light should be seen"—to open his extremely important "Message to the Tricontinental Congress" in 1967. If Benedetti could say that Rodó's time "is different from our own [. . .] his true place, his true temporal homeland is the nineteenth century," we must say, on the other hand, that Martí's true place was the future and, for the moment, this era of ours which simply cannot be understood without a thorough knowledge of his work.

Now, if that knowledge, because of the curious circumstances alluded to, was denied or available only in a limited way to the early generations of this century, who frequently had to base their defense of subsequent radical arguments on a "first launching pad" as well intentioned but at the same time as weak as the nineteenth century work *Ariel*, what can we say of more recent authors to whom editions of Martí are now available, but who nevertheless persist in ignoring him? I am thinking, of course, not of scholars more or less ignorant of our problems, but, on the contrary, of those who maintain a consistently anti-colonialist attitude. The only explanation of this situation is a painful one: we have been so thoroughly steeped in colonialism that we read with real respect only those anti-colonialist authors *disseminated from the metropolis*. In this way we cast aside the greatest lesson of Martí; thus we are barely familiar with Artigas, Recabarren, Mella, and even Mariátegui and Ponce. And I have the sad suspicion that if the extraordinary texts of Che Guevara have enjoyed the greatest dissemination ever accorded a Latin American, the fact that he is read with such avidity by our people is to a certain extent due to the prestige his name has even in the metropolitan capitals where, to be sure, he is frequently the object of the most shameless manipulation. For consistency in our anti-colonialist attitude, we must in effect turn to those of our people who have incarnated and illustrated that attitude in their behavior and thinking.[44] And in this sense, there is no case more useful than that of Martí.

I know of no other Latin American author who has given so immediate and so coherent an answer to another question put to me by my interlocutor, the European journalist whom I mentioned at the beginning of these lines (and whom, if he did not exist, I would have had to invent, although this would have deprived me of his friendship, which I trust will survive this monologue): "What relationship," this guileless wit asked me, "does Borges have with the Incas?" Borges is almost a *reductio ad absurdum* and, in any event, I shall discuss him later. But it is only right and fair to ask what relationship we, the present inhabitants of this America in whose zoological and cultural heritage Europe had played an unquestionable part, have to the primitive inhabitants of this same America —those peoples who constructed or were in the process of constructing admirable cultures, and were exterminated or martyred by Europeans of various nations, about whom neither a white nor black legend can be built—only an infernal truth of blood which, together with deeds such as the enslavement of Africans, constitutes their eternal dishonor. Martí, whose father was from Valencia, and whose mother was from the Canaries, who wrote the most prodigious Spanish of his—and our—age, and who came to have the greatest knowledge of the Euro-North American culture ever possessed by a man of our America, also asked this question. And answered it as follows: "We

---

[44] Nonetheless, this should not be understood to mean that I am suggesting that those authors who have not been born in the colonies should not be read. Such a stupidity is untenable. How could we propose to ignore Homer, Dante, Cervantes, Shakespeare, Whitman, to say nothing of Marx, Engels or Lenin? How can we forget that even in our own day there are *Latin American* thinkers who have not been born here? Lastly, how can we defend intellectual Robinson-Crusoism at all without falling into the greatest absurdity?

are descended from Valencian fathers and Canary Island mothers, and feel the enflamed blood of Tamanaco and Paramaconi coursing through our veins; we see the blood which fell amid the brambles of Mount Calvary as our own, along with that shed by the naked and heroic Caracas as they struggled breast to breast with the gonzalos in their iron-plated armor."[45]

I presume that the reader, if he is not a Venezuelan, will be unfamiliar with the names evoked by Martí. So was I. This lack of familiarity is but another proof of our subjection to the colonialist perspective of history which has been imposed on us, causing names, dates, circumstances, and truths to vanish from our consciousness. Under other circumstances—but closely related to these—did not the bourgeois version of history try to erase the heroes of the Commune of 1871, the martyrs of the first of May 1886 (significantly reclaimed by Martí)? At any rate, Tamanaco, Paramaconi, "the naked and heroic Caracas" were natives of what is today called Venezuela, of *Carib or very closely related origin,* who heroically fought against the Spaniards at the beginning of the conquest. This means that Martí *has written* that he feels *Carib blood, the blood of Caliban* coursing through his veins. This will not be the only time he expresses such an idea, which is central to his thinking. Again making use of such heroes,[46] he was to repeat some time later: "We must stand with Guaicaipuro, Paramaconi [heroes of Venezuela, probably of Carib origin], Anacaona, Hatuey [heroes of the Antilles, of Arauaco origin], and not with the flames that burned them, nor with the ropes that bound them, nor with the steel that beheaded them, nor with the dogs that devoured them."[47] Martí's rejection of the ethnocide that Europe practiced is *total*. No less total is his identification with

---

[45] José Martí, "Autores americanos aborígenes," 1884. *Obras completas,* VIII, 336–7.

[46] To Tamanaco he dedicated a beautiful poem: "Tamanaco of the Plumed Crown," *Obras completas,* XXII, 237.

[47] José Martí, "Fragmentos" (1885–95). *Obras completas,* XXII, 27.

the American peoples that offered heroic resistance to the invader, and in whom Martí saw the natural forerunners of the Latin American *independentistas.* This explains why in the notebook in which this last quotation appears, he continues writing, almost without transition, on Aztec mythology ("no less beautiful than the Greek"), on the ashes of Quetzacoatl, on "Ayachucho on the solitary plateau," on "Bolívar, like the rivers . . ." (pp. 28–29).

Martí, however, dreams not of a restoration now impossible, but of the future integration of our America—an America rising organically through a firm grasp of its true roots, to the heights of authentic modernity. For this reason, the first quotation in which he speaks of feeling valiant Carib blood coursing through his veins continues as follows:

It is good to open canals, to promote schools, to create steamship lines, to keep abreast of one's own time, to be on the side of the vanguard in the beautiful march of humanity. But in order not to falter because of a lack of spirit or the vanity of a false spirit, it is good also to nourish oneself through memory and admiration, through righteous study and loving compassion, on that fervent spirit of the natural surroundings in which one is born—a spirit matured and quickened by those of every race which issue from such surroundings and find their final repose in them. Politics and literature flourish only when they are direct. The American intelligence is an indigenous plumage. Is it not evident that America itself was paralyzed by the same blow that paralyzed the Indian? And until the Indian is caused to walk, America itself will not begin to walk well. ("Autores aborígenes, americanos," *op. cit.*)

Martí's identification with our aboriginal culture was thus accompanied by a complete sense of the concrete tasks imposed upon him by his circumstances. Far from hampering him, that identification nurtured in him the most radical and modern criteria of his time in the colonial countries.

Naturally, Martí's approach to the Indian was also applied to the Black.[48] Unfortunately, while in his day serious enquiries

---

[48] *Vid.,* e.g., "Mi raza," *Obras completas,* II, 298–300, where we read:

An individual has no special right because he belongs to one race or another: to speak of a human being is to speak of all rights [. . .] If one into American aboriginal cultures (which Martí studied passionately) had already been undertaken, only in the twentieth century would there appear similar studies with regard to the African cultures and their considerable contribution to the makeup of our *mestizo* America (Frobenius, Delafosse, Suret-Canale; Ortiz, Ramos, Herskovits, Roumain, Metraux, Bastide, Franco).[49] And Martí died five years before the dawning of our century. In any event, in his treatment of Indian culture and his concrete behavior with regard to the Black, he left a very clear outline of a "battle plan" in this area.

In this way is his Calibanesque vision of the culture of what he called "our America" formed. Martí is, as Fidel was later to be, aware of how difficult it is even to find a name which in designating us defines us conceptually. For this reason, after several attempts, he favored that modest descriptive formula which above and beyond race, language, and secondary circumstances, embraces the communities that live, with their common problems, "from the [Rio] Bravo to the Patagonia," and which are distinct from "European America." I have al-

---

says that in the Black there is no aboriginal fault or virus which incapacitates him from leading his human life to the full, one is speaking the truth [. . .], and if this defense of nature is called racism, the name does not matter; for it is nothing if not natural decency and the voice crying from the breast of the human being for the peace and life of the country. If it be alleged that the condition of slavery does not suggest any inferiority of the enslaved race, since white Gauls with blue eyes and golden hair were sold as slaves with iron rings around their necks in the markets of Rome, that is good racism, because it is pure justice, and helps to remove the prejudices of the ignorant white man. But there righteous racism ends.

And further on: "A human being is more than white, more than mulatto, more than Black. Cuban is more than white, more than mulatto, more than Black." Some of these questions are treated in Juliette Oullion's paper, "La discriminación racial en los Estados Unidos vista por José Martí," *Anuario martiano*, 3 (La Habana, 1971), which I was unable to use since it appeared after these notes were completed.

[49] *Vid. Casa de las Américas,* 36–37 (mayo-agosto, 1966), devoted to *Africa en América.*

31

ready said that although it is found scattered throughout his very numerous writings, this conception of our culture is aptly summarized in the article-manifesto "Our America," and I direct the reader to it: to his insistence upon the idea that one cannot "rule new peoples, with a singular and violent composition, with laws inherited from four centuries of free practice in the United States, or nineteen centuries of monarchy in France. One does not stop the blow in the chest of the plainsman's horse with one of Hamilton's decrees. One does not clear the congealed blood of the Indian race with a sentence of Sieyès"; to his deeply-rooted concept that "the imported book has been conquered in America by the natural man. Natural men have conquered the artificial men of learning. *The authentic mestizo has conquered the exotic Creole*" (my emphasis—R.F.R.); and finally to his fundamental advice:

The European university must yield to the American university. The history of America, from the Incas to the present, must be taught letter perfect, even if that of the Argonauts of Greece is not taught. Our own Greece is preferable to that Greece which is not ours. We have greater need of it. National politicians must replace foreign and exotic politicians. Graft the world onto our republics, but the trunk must be that of our republics. And let the conquered pedant be silent: there is no homeland of which the individual can be more proud than our unhappy American republics.

THE REAL LIFE OF A FALSE DILEMMA

IT is impossible not to see in this text—which, as has been said, summarizes in lightning fashion Martí's judgement on this essential problem—his violent rejection of the imposition of Prospero ("the European university [. . .] the European book [. . .] the Yankee book"), which *"must yield"* to the reality of Caliban ("the Latin American university [. . .] the Latin American enigma"): "The history of America, from the Incas to the present day must be taught letter perfect even if that of the Argonauts of Greece is not taught. Our Greece is preferable to that Greece which is not ours." And later: "Common cause must be made with the oppressed so as to secure the system against the interest and customs of the oppressors."

But our America has also heard, expressed with vehemence by a talented and energetic man who died three years before this work appeared, the thesis which was the exact opposite: the thesis of Prospero.[50] The interlocutors were not called then Prospero and Caliban, but rather *civilization and barbarism,* the title which the Argentine Domingo Faustino Sarmiento gave to the first edition (1845) of his great book on Facundo Quiroga. I do not believe that autobiographical confessions are of much interest here, but since I have already mentioned, by way of self-inflicted punishment, the forgettable pleasures of the westerns and Tarzan films by which we were innoculated, unbeknownst to us, with the ideology which we verbally repudiated in the Nazis (I was twelve years old when the Second World War was at its height), I must also confess that only a few years afterwards, I read this book passionately. In the margins of my old copy, I find my enthusiasms, my rejections of the "tyrant of the Republic of Argentina" who had exclaimed: "Traitors to the American cause!" I also find, a few pages later, the comment: "It is strange how one thinks of Perón." It was many years later, specifically after the triumph of the Cuban Revolution in 1959 (when we began to live and to read the world in another way) that I understood I had not been on the best side in that otherwise remarkable book. It was not possible to be simultaneously in agreement with *Facundo* and with "Our America." What is more, "Our America"—along with a large part of Martí's entire work—is an implicit, and at times, explicit dialogue with the Sarmiento theses. If not, what then does this lapidary sentence of Martí's mean: "*There is no battle between civilization and barbarism,* only between false erudition and nature." Eight years before "Nuestra América" appeared (1891)—within Sarmiento's lifetime

---

[50] I refer to the dialogue within Latin America itself. The despicable opinion that America earned in Europe's eyes can be followed in some detail in Antonello Gerbi's vast, *La disputa del Nuevo Mundo: Historia de una polémica 1750–1900.* Trans. Antonio Alatorre (Mexico, 1960), *passim.*

—Martí had already spoken (in the sentence I have quoted more than once) of the "pretext that civilization, which is the vulgar name under which contemporary European man operates, has the natural right to seize the land of foreigners, which is the name given by those who desire foreign lands to every contemporary human being who does not come from Europe or European America."[51] In both cases, Martí *rejects* the *false* dichotomy that Sarmiento, falling into the trap adroitly set by the colonizer, takes for granted. For this reason, when I said some time ago that "In coming out on the side of 'barbarism' Martí foreshadows Fanon and our Revolution"[52] (a phrase that some hasty people, without noticing the quotation marks, misunderstood—as if Fanon, Fidel, and Che were apostles of barbarism) I wrote "barbarism" in this way, between quotation marks, to indicate that in fact there was no such state. The presumed barbarism of our peoples was invented with crude cynicism by "those who desire foreign lands"; those who, with equal effrontery, give the "popular name" of "civilization" to the "contemporary" human being "who comes from Europe or European America." What was surely more painful for Martí was to see a man of our America—a man whom, despite incurable differences, he admired in his positive aspects[53]—fall into this very grave error. Thinking of figures such as Sarmiento, it was Martínez Estrada, who had *previously* written so many pages extolling Sarmiento, in *1962* wrote in his book *Diferencias y semejanzas entre los países de la América Latina* (Similarities and Differences among Latin American Countries):

---

[51] José Martí, "Una distribución de diplomas en un colegio de los Estados Unidos," 1883. *Obras Completas*, VIII, 442.

[52] R.F.R. *Ensayo de otro mundo, op. cit.*, p. 15.

[53] "Sarmiento, the real founder of the Republic of Argentina," he says of him, for example, in a letter dated 7 April 1887 to Fermín Valdés Domínguez, shortly after a warm literary elogy which the Argentine had publicly made of him. (*Obras completas*, XX, 325.) Nevertheless, it is significant that Martí, always so mindful of Latin American values, *did not publish a single work on Sarmiento*, not even on the occasion of his death in 1888. It is difficult not to relate this silence to Martí's often reiterated criterion that silence was his way of censuring.

We can immediately establish the premise that those who have worked, in some cases patriotically, to shape social life in complete accordance with models of other highly developed countries, whose practices are the result of an organic process over the course of centuries, have betrayed the cause of the true emancipation of Latin America.[54]

I lack the necessary information to discuss here the virtues and defects of this bourgeois antagonist and shall limit myself to pointing out his opposition with Martí, and the coherence between his thought and conduct. As a postulator of *civilization*, which he found incarnated in archetypal form in the United States, he advocated the extermination of the indigenous peoples according to the savage Yankee model; what is more, he adored that growing Republic to the north which had by midcentury still not demonstrated so clearly the flaws that Martí would later discover. In both extremes—and they are precisely that: extremes, margins of their respective thinking—he and Martí differed irreconcilably.

Jaime Alazraki has studied with some care "El indigenismo de Martí y el antindigenismo de Sarmiento."[55] ("The Indigenism of Martí and the Anti-indigenism of Sarmiento.") I refer the reader interested in the subject to this essay. Here I shall

---

[54] Ezequiel Martínez Estrada, "El colonialismo como realidad," *Casa de las Américas*, 33 (noviembre-diciembre, 1965), 85. These pages originally appeared in his book *Diferencias y semejanzas entre los países de la América Latina* (Mexico, 1962) and were written in that country in 1960; that is to say, after the triumph of the Cuban Revolution, which led Martínez Estrada to make considerable restatements of his ideas. See, for example, his "Retrato de Sarmiento," a lecture given at the Biblioteca Nacional de Cuba on December 8, 1961. In it he said, "A rigorous and impartial study of the political behavior of Sarmiento in government effectively verifies the fact that many of the evils characterizing the oligarchic politics of Argentina were introduced by him"; and also: "He was contemptuous of the people, he was contemptuous of the ignorant masses, the ill-clad masses, without understanding that this is the American people." *Revista de la Biblioteca Nacional* (julio-septiembre, 1965), 14 and 16.

[55] Jaime Alazraki: "El indigenismo de Martí y el antindigenismo de Sarmiento," *Cuadernos Americanos* (mayo-junio, 1965). The conclusion of this essay—and almost the same quotations—appear in the work of Antonio Sacoto "El indio en la obra literaria de Sarmiento y Martí," *Cuadernos Americanos* (enero-febrero, 1968).

only draw on some of the quotations from the works of both included in that study. I have already mentioned some of Martí's observations on the Indian. Alazraki recalls others:

No more than peoples in blossom, no more than the bulbs of peoples, were those the valiant conquistador marched upon; with his subtle craftiness of the old-time opportunist, he discharged his powerful fire-arms. It was a historic misfortune and a natural crime. The well-formed stalk should have been left standing, the entire flowering work of Nature could then be seen in all its beauty. The conquistadors stole a page from the Universe!

And further:

Of all that greatness there remains in the museum scarcely a few gold cups, a few stones of polished obsidian shaped like a yoke, and one or two wrought rings. Tenochtitlán does not exist, nor Tulan, the city of the great fair, Texcuco, the city of the palaces, is no more. Indians of today, passing before the ruins, lower their heads and move their lips as if saying something; they do not put on their hats again until the ruins are left behind.

For Sarmiento, the history of America is the "bands of abject races, a great continent abandoned to savages incapable of progress." If we want to know how he interpreted the maxim of his compatriot Alberdi that "to govern is to populate," we must read this: "Many difficulties will be presented by the occupation of so extensive a country; but there will be no advantage comparable to that gained by the extinction of the savage tribes." That is to say, for Sarmiento, to govern is also to *depopulate* the nation of its Indians (and gauchos). And what of the heroes of the resistance against the Spaniards, those magnificent men whose rebellious blood Martí felt coursing through his veins? Sarmiento has also questioned himself about them. This is his response:

For us, Colocolo, Lautaro, and Caupolicán, notwithstanding the noble and civilized garb with which they are adorned by Ercilla, are nothing more than a handful of loathesome Indians. We would have them hanged today were they to reappear in a war of the Araucanos against Chile, a country which has nothing to do with such rabble.

This naturally implies a vision of the Spanish conquest radically different from that upheld by Martí. For Sarmiento, "Spanish—repeated a hundred times in the odious sense of impious, immoral, ravisher and imposter—is synonymous with civilization, with the European tradition brought by them to these countries." And while for Martí, "there is no racial hatred, because there are no races," the author of *Conflicto y armonías de las razas en América* (Conflict and Harmony among the Races in America) bases himself thus on pseudo-scientific theories:

It may be very unjust to exterminate savages, suffocate rising civilizations, conquer peoples who are in possession of a privileged piece of land. But thanks to this injustice, America, instead of remaining abandoned to the savages, incapable of progress, is today occupied by the Caucasian race—the most perfect, the most intelligent, the most beautiful and the most progressive of those which people the earth. Thanks to these injustices, Oceania is filled with civilized peoples, Asia begins to move under the European impulse, Africa sees the times of Carthage and the glorious days of Egypt reborn on her coasts. Thus, the population of the world is subject to revolutions that recognize immutable laws; the strong races exterminate the weak ones and the civilized peoples supplant the savages in the possession of the earth.

There was no need then to cross the Atlantic and seek out Renan to hear such words: a man of this America was saying them. The fact is that if he did not learn them on this side of the ocean, they were at least reinforced for him here—not in our America, but in the other, "European America," of which Sarmiento was the most fanatical devotee in our mestizo lands during the nineteenth century. Although in that century there is no shortage of Latin Americans who adored the Yankees, our discovery of people among us equal to Sarmiento in their devotion to the United States would be due above all to the ranting sepoyism in which our twentieth-century Latin America has been so prodigal. What Sarmiento wanted for Argentina was exactly what the United States had achieved for itself. The last words he wrote (1888) were: "We shall catch up to the United States [...] Let us become the United States." His travels in that country produced in him a genuine bedazzlement, a never-ending historical orgasm. He tried to establish in his homeland the bases for an enterprising bourgeoisie, similar to what he saw there. Its present fate makes any commentary unnecessary.

What Martí saw in the United States is also sufficiently well known that we need not dwell upon the point. Suffice it to recall that he was the first militant anti-imperialist of our continent; that he denounced over a period of fifteen years "the crude, inequitable, and decadent character of the United States, and the continued existence therein of all the violence, discord, immorality, and disorder for which the Hispano-American peoples are censured"[56]; that a few hours before his death on the battlefield, he confided in a letter to his great friend, the Mexican Manuel Mercado: "everything I have done to this day, and everything I shall do is to that end [. . .] to prevent in time the expansion of the United States into the Antilles and to prevent her from falling, with ever greater force, upon our American lands."[57]

Sarmiento did not remain silent before the criticism which Martí—frequently from the very pages of *La Nación*—levelled against his idolized United States. He commented on one occasion on this incredible boldness:

Don José Martí lacks only one requirement to be a journalist [. . .] He has failed to regenerate himself, to educate himself, so to speak, to receive inspiration from the country in which he lives, as one receives food so as to convert it into life-giving blood [. . .] I should like Martí to give us less of Martí, less of the pure-bred Spaniard and less of the South American, and in exchange, a little more of the Yankee—the new type of modern man [. . .] It is amusing to hear a Frenchman of the *Courier des Etats-Unis* laughing at the stupidities and political incompetence of the Yankees, whose institutions Gladstone proclaims the supreme work of the human race. But to criticize with magisterial airs that which a Latin American, a Spaniard sees there, with a confetti of political judgment transmitted to him by the books of other nations—

---

[56] José Martí, "La verdad sobre los Estados Unidos," *Páginas escogidas.* Selección y Prólogo de R.F.R. Tomo I (La Habana, 1971), p. 392.

[57] *Op. cit.*, p. 149.

as if trying to see sunspots through a blurred glass—is to do the reader a very grave injustice and lead him down the path of perdition [. . .] Let them not come to us, then, with their insolent humility of South Americans, semi-Indians and semi-Spaniards, to find evil [. . .].[58]

Sarmiento, who was as vehement in his praise as in his invective, here places Martí among the "semi-Indians." This was in essence true, and for Martí, a point of pride; but we have already seen what it implied in the mouth of Sarmiento . . .

For these reasons, and despite the fact that highly esteemed writers have tried to point out possible similarities, I think it will be understood how difficult it is to accept a parallel between these two men, such as the one elaborated by Emeterio S. Santovenia in two hundred sixty-two sloppy pages: *Genio y acción: Sarmiento y Martí* (La Habana, 1938). A sample will suffice. According to this author: "above and beyond the discrepancies in the achievements and limitations of their respective projections concerning America, there does emerge a coincidence [*sic*] in their evaluation [those of Sarmiento and Martí] of the Anglo-Saxon role in the development of political and social ideas that fertilized the tree of total emancipation in the new world." (p. 73)

This luxuriant undergrowth of thought, syntax and metaphor gives some indication of what our culture was like when we were part of the "free world," of which Sr. Santovenia (as well as being one of Batista's ministers in his moments of leisure) was so eminent a representative.

ON THE FREE WORLD

BUT THE PORTION of the free world which corresponds to Latin America can boast today of much more memorable figures. There is Jorge Luis Borges, for example, whose name seems to be associated with that adjective. The Borges I have in mind is the one who only a short time ago dedicated his

---

[58] Domingo Faustino Sarmiento. *Obras completas.* (Santiago de Chile-Buenos Aires, 1885–1902), Volume XLVI, *Páginas literarias*, p. 166–73.

(presumably good) translation of Whitman's *Leaves of Grass* to United States President, Richard Nixon. It is true that this man wrote in 1926, "I want to speak to the Creoles—to those who feel their existence deeply rooted in our lands, not to those who think the sun and the moon are in Europe. This is a land of born exiles, of men nostalgic for the far-off and the foreign: they are the real *gringos*, regardless of their parentage, and I do not address myself to them."[59] It is also true that Sarmiento is presented in that book as a "North American Indian brave, who loathed and misprized anything Creole."[60] But the fact is *that Borges* is not the one who has gone down in history. This memorious individual decided to forget the little book of his youth, written only a few years after having been a member of "the sect, the blunder called Ultraism." In his eyes that book and the ideas in it were also a blunder. Pathetically faithful to his class,[61] it was a different Borges who would become so well known, attain such great circulation abroad, and experience the public acclaim of innumerable literary prizes— some of which are so obscure that he would seem to have awarded them himself. The Borges in question, to whom we shall dedicate a few lines here, is the one who echoes Sarmiento's grotesque "We belong to the Roman Empire," with this declaration not of 1926, but of 1955: "I believe that our tradition is Europe."[62]

It might seem strange that the ideological filiation of such an energetic and blustering pioneer would come to be manifest today in a man so sedate, a writer such as Borges—the archetypal representative of a bookish culture which on the surface seems far removed from Sarmiento's constant vitality. But this

[59] Jorge Luis Borges. *El tamaño de mi esperanza* (Buenos Aires, 1926), p. 5.
[60] *Op. cit.*, p. 6.
[61] On the ideological evolution of Borges with respect to his class-attitudes, *vid.* Eduardo López-Morales, "Encuentro con un destino sudamericano," *Recopilación de textos sobre los vanguardismos en la America Latina*. Prólogo y materiales seleccionados por Oscar Collazos (La Habana, 1970); and, for a Marxist approach to the author, *vid.* Jaime Mejía Duque, "De nuevo Jorge Luis Borges," *Literatura y realidad* (Medellín, 1969).
[62] Jorge Luis Borges, "El escritor argentino y la tradición," *Sur*, 232 (enero-febrero, 1955), p. 7.

strangeness only demonstrates how accustomed we are to judging the superstructural products of our continent, if not of the whole world, without regard to their concrete structural realities. Except by considering these realities, how would we recognize the insipid disasters who are the bourgeois intellectuals of our time as descending from those vigorous and daring thinkers of the rising bourgeoisie? We need only consider our writers and thinkers in relation to the classes whose world view they expound in order to orient ourselves properly and outline their true filiations. The dialogue we have just witnessed between Sarmiento and Martí was, more than anything else, a class confrontation.

Independently of his (class) origin, Sarmiento is the implacable ideologue of an Argentine bourgeoisie which is attempting to transport bourgeois policies of the metropolitan centers (particularly North America) to its own country. To be successful it must impose itself, like all bourgeoisies, upon the popular classes; it must exploit them physically and condemn them spiritually. The manner in which a bourgeoisie develops at the expense of the popular classes' brutalization is memorably demonstrated, taking England as an example, in some of the most impressive pages of *Das Kapital*. "European America," whose capitalism succeeded in expanding fabulously—unhampered as it was by a feudalistic order—added new circles of hell to England's achievements: the enslavement of the Negro, and the extermination of the indomitable Indian. These were the models to which Sarmiento looked, and which he proposed to follow faithfully. He is perhaps the most consequential and the most active of the bourgeois ideologues on our continent during the nineteenth century.

Martí, on the other hand, is a conscious spokesman of the exploited classes. "Common cause must be made with the oppressed," he told us, "so as to secure the system against the interests and customs of the oppressors." And, since beginning with the conquest Indians and Blacks have been relegated to the base of the social pyramid, making common cause with the oppressed came largely to be the same as making common cause with Indians and Blacks—which is what Martí does. These Indians and those Blacks had been intermingling among themselves, and with some Whites, giving rise to the *mestizaje* which is at the root of our America, where—according to Martí—"the authentic *mestizo* has conquered the exotic creole." Sarmiento is a ferocious racist, because he is an ideologue of the exploiting classes in whose ranks the "exotic creole" is found. Martí is radically anti-racist, because he is a spokesman for the exploited classes within which the three races are fusing. Sarmiento opposes what is essentially American in order to inculcate—with blood and fire, just as the conquistadors had tried to do—alien formulae here. Martí defends the autochthonous, the genuinely American. This does not mean, of course, that he foolishly rejected whatever positive elements might be offered by other realities: "Graft the world onto our republics," he said, "but the trunk must be that of our republics." Sarmiento also sought to graft the world onto our republics, but he would have their trunks uprooted in the process. For that reason, if the continuators of Martí are found in Mella and Vallejo, Fidel and Che, and in the new culture of revolutionary Latin America, the heirs of Sarmiento (in spite of his complexity) are, in the final analysis, those representatives of the Argentine vice-bourgeoisie, who are, moreover, a defeated class. Because the dream of bourgeois development which Sarmiento envisaged was not even a possibility. There was simply no way an eventual Argentine bourgeoisie could develop. Latin America was a late arrival to that fiesta, for as Mariátegui wrote: "The time of free competition in the capitalist economy has come to an end, in all areas and in every aspect. We are now in an era of monopolies, of empires. The Latin American countries are experiencing a belated entry into competitive capitalism. The dominant positions are already well established. The fate of such countries, within the capitalist order, is that of simple colonies."[63]

Incorporated into what is called with a bit of unintentional humor the "Free World," our countries—in spite of our shields, anthems, flags and presidents—would inaugurate a new form of not being independent: neo-colonialism. The

---

[63] José Carlos Mariátegui, "Aniversario y balance," *Ideología y Política* (Lima, 1969), p. 248.

bourgeoisie, for whom Sarmiento had outlined such delightful possibilities, became no more than a vice-bourgeoisie, a modest local shareholder in imperial exploitation—first the English, then the North American.

It is in this light that one sees more clearly the connections between Sarmiento, whose name is associated with grand pedagogical projects, immense spaces, railways, ships; and Borges, the mention of whom evokes mirrors which multiply the same miserable image, unfathomable labyrinths and a sad, dimly-lit library. But apart from this, if the "American-ness" of Sarmiento is always taken for granted (while it is obvious in him, this is not to say he represents the positive pole of that "American-ness"), I have never been able to understand why it is denied to Borges. Borges is a typical colonial writer, the representative among us of a now powerless class for whom the act of writing—and he is well aware of this, for he is a man of diabolical intelligence—is more like the act of reading. He is not a European writer; there is no European writer like Borges. But there are *many* European writers—from Iceland to the German expressionists—whom Borges has *read*, shuffled together, collated. European writers belong to very concrete and provincial traditions—reaching the extreme case of a Péguy, for example, who boasted of never having read anything but French authors. Apart from a few professors of philology, who receive a salary for it, there is only one type of man who really knows in its entirety the literature of Europe: the colonial. Only in the case of mental imbalance can a learned Argentine writer ever boast of having read nothing but Argentine—or even Spanish language—authors. And Borges is not imbalanced. On the contrary, he is an extremely lucid man, one who exemplifies Martí's idea that intelligence is only one—and not necessarily the best—part of a man.

The writing of Borges comes directly from his reading, in a peculiar process of phagocytosis which identifies him clearly as a colonial and the representative of a dying class. For him the creation *par excellence* of culture is a library; or better yet, a museum—a place where the products of culture from abroad are assembled. A museum of horrors, of monsters, of splendors, of folkloric data and artifacts (those of Argentina seen with the eye of a curator)—the work of Borges, written in a Spanish difficult to read without admiration, is one of the American scandals of our time.

Unlike some other important Latin American writers, Borges does not pretend to be a leftist. Quite the opposite. His position in this regard leads him to sign a petition in favor of the Bay of Pigs invaders, to call for the death penalty for Debray, or to dedicate a book to Nixon. Many of his admirers who deplore (or say they deplore) these acts maintain that there is a dichotomy in the man which permits him, on the one hand, to write slightly immortal books and, on the other, to sign political declarations which are more puerile than malicious. That may well be. It is also possible that no such dichotomy exists, and that we ought to accustom ourselves to restoring unity to the author of "The Garden of Forking Paths." By that I do not propose that we should find errors of spelling or syntax in his elegant pages, but rather that we read them for what, in the final analysis, they are: the painful testimony of a class with no way out, diminished to saying in the voice of one man, "The world, unfortunately, is real; I, unfortunately, am Borges."

It is interesting that the writing/reading of Borges is enjoying a particularly favorable reception in capitalist Europe at the moment when Europe is itself becoming a colony in the face of the "American challenge." In a book of that very title, Jean-Jacques Servan-Schreiber explains with unmasked cynicism: "Now then, Europe is not Algiers or Senegal!"[64] In other words, the United States cannot do to Europe what Europe did to Algiers and Senegal! I have bad news for Europe. It seems that in spite of everything they can indeed do it; they have, in fact, been doing it now for some time. And if this occurs in the area of economics—along with complex political derivations—the European cultural superstructure is also manifesting obvious colonial symptoms. One of them may well be the apogee of Borges' writing/reading.

But of course the heritage of Borges, whose kinship with

---

[64] Jean-Jacques Servan-Schreiber. *El desafío americano* (La Habana, 1968), p. 41.

Sarmiento we have already seen, must be sought above all in Latin America, where it will imply a further decline in impetus and quality. Since this is not a survey, but rather a simple essay on Latin American culture, I shall restrict myself to a single example. I am aware that it is a very minor one; but it is none-theless a valid symptom. I shall comment on a small book of criticism by Carlos Fuentes, *La nueva novela hispanoamericana* ("The New Spanish American Novel") (Mexico, 1969).

A spokesman for the same class as Borges, Fuentes also evinced leftist whims in his younger days. The former's *El tamaño de mi esperanza* ("The Extent of My Hope") corre-sponds to the latter's *La muerte de Artemio Cruz* (*The Death of Artemio Cruz*). And to continue judging Fuentes by that book, without question one of our good novels, would be as senseless as continuing to judge Borges by his early book. The difference being that Borges, who is more consistent (and in all ways more estimable; Borges, even though we differ so greatly from him, is a truly important writer), decided to adopt openly his position as a man of the right; while Fuentes operates as such, but attempts to conserve, from time to time, a leftist terminology which does not lack, of course, references to Marx. In *The Death of Artemio Cruz*, a secretary who is fully integrated into the system synthesizes his biography in the following dialogue:

> "You're very young. How old are you?"
> "Twenty-seven."
> "When did you receive your degree?"
> "Three years ago. But . . ."
> "But what?"
> "Theory and practice are different."
> "And that amuses you? What did they teach you?"
> "A lot of Marxism. So much that I even wrote my thesis on sur-plus value."
> "It ought to be good training, Padilla."
> "But practice is very different."
> "Is that what you are, a Marxist?"
> "Well, all my friends were. It's a stage one goes through."[65]

---

[65] Carlos Fuentes. *La muerte de Artemio Cruz* (Mexico, 1962), p. 27.

This dialogue expresses clearly enough the situation of a certain sector of the Mexican intelligentsia which, though it shares Borges' class circumstances and behavior patterns, differs from him, for purely local reasons, in certain superficial aspects. I am thinking, specifically, of the so-called Mexican literary *mafia,* one of whose most conspicuous figures is Carlos Fuentes. This group warmly expressed its sympathy for the Cuban Revolution until, in 1961, the Revolution proclaimed itself and proved to be Marxist-Leninist—that is, a revolution which has in its forefront a worker-peasant alliance. From that day on, the support of the *mafia* grew increasingly diluted, up to the last few months when—taking advantage of the wild vociferation occasioned by a Cuban writer's month in jail—they broke obstreperously with Cuba.

The symmetry here is instructive: in 1961, at the time of the Bay of Pigs, the only gathering of Latin American writers to express in a manifesto its desire that Cuba be defeated by mercenaries in the service of imperialism was a group of Argentines centered around Borges.[66] Ten years later, in 1971, the only national circle of writers on the continent to exploit an obvious pretext for breaking with Cuba and calumniating the conduct of the Revolution was the Mexican *mafia.* It is a simple changing of the guard within an identical attitude.

In that light one can better understand the intentions of Fuentes' short book on the new Spanish American novel. The development of this new novel is one of the prominent features of the literature of these past few years, and its circulation beyond our borders is in large part owing to the world-wide attention our continent has enjoyed since the triumph of the Cuban Revolution in 1959.[67]

Logically, this new novel has occasioned various interpreta-

---

[66] No one has preserved a copy of the manifesto. There does exist, however, a copy of the article in which Ezequiel Martínez Estrada responded to it: "Réplica a una declaración intemperante," *En Cuba y al servicio de la Revolución cubana* (La Habana, 1963).

[67] I have dealt further with this point in my essay, "Intercomunicación latino-americana y nueva literatura" (1969), for a collective volume on contemporary Latin American literature, to be published by UNESCO.

tions, numerous studies. That of Carlos Fuentes, despite its brevity (less than one hundred pages), comprehends a thoroughgoing position-paper on literature and politics, which clearly synthesizes a shrewd rightist viewpoint within our countries.

Fuentes is quick to lay his cards on the table. In the first chapter, exemplarily entitled "Civilization and Barbarism," he adopts for openers, as might be expected, the thesis of Sarmiento: during the nineteenth century "it is possible for only one drama to unfold in this medium: that which Sarmiento established in the subtitle of *Facundo*—Civilization and Barbarism." That drama constitutes the conflict "of the first one hundred years of Latin American society and its novel." (p. 10) The narrative corresponding to this conflict comprehends four factors: "an essentially alien [to whom?] natural order," which was "the real Latin American protagonist"; the dictator on a national or regional scale; the exploited masses; and a fourth factor, "the writer, *who invariably stands on the side of civilization and against barbarism.*" (p. 11-12, my emphasis), a fact which, according to Fuentes, implies "a defense of the exploited," etc.; but Sarmiento revealed what it consisted of in fact. The polarity which characterized the nineteen-hundreds, he continues, does not go unchanged in the following century. "In the twentieth century the intellectual himself is forced to struggle within a society which is, internally and externally, much more complex," a complexity owing to the fact that these countries will be penetrated by imperialism, while some time later there will take place "a revolt and upsurge . . . in the underdeveloped world." Among the international factors which must be taken into account in the twentieth century, Fuentes forgets to consider socialism. But he slips in this opportune formula: "we have the beginning of the transition from epic simplism to dialectical complexity." (p. 13) "Epic simplism" was the nineteenth century struggle in which, according to Fuentes, "the writer [he means writers *like him*] invariably stands on the side of civilization and against barbarism," that is, becomes an unconditional servant of the new oligarchy and a harsh enemy of the American masses. "Dialectical complexity" is the form that collaboration takes in the twentieth century, when the oligarchy in question has revealed itself as a mere intermediary for imperialist interests and "the writer" such as Fuentes must now serve two masters. Even when it is a question of such well-heeled masters, we have known since the Holy Scriptures that this does imply a certain "dialectical complexity," especially when one attempts to make everyone believe he is in fact serving a third master—the people. Notwithstanding its slight omissions, the synthesis offered by the lucid Fuentes of one aspect of imperialist penetration in our countries is interesting. He writes:

In order to intervene effectively in the economic life of each Latin American country, it requires not only an intermediary ruling class, but a whole array of services in public administration, commerce, publicity, business management, extractive and refining industries, banking, transportation, and even entertainment: bread and circuses. General Motors assembles automobiles, takes home profits, and sponsors television programs. (p. 14)

As a final example (even though that of General Motors is always valid) it might have been more useful to mention the C.I.A., which organizes the Bay of Pigs invasion and pays, via transparent intermediaries, for the review *Mundo Nuevo*, one of whose principal ideologues was none other than Carlos Fuentes.

With these political premises established, Fuentes goes on to postulate certain literary premises, before concentrating on the authors he will study (Vargas Llosa, Carpentier, García Márquez, Cortázar, and Goytisolo), and concludes with more observations of a political nature. I am not interested in lingering over his criticism *per se*, but simply in underscoring a few of its ideological lines which are, in any case, apparent: at times, this little book seems a thoroughgoing ideological manifesto.

A critical appreciation of literature requires that we start off with a concept of criticism itself; one ought to have answered the elemental question: What is criticism? The modest opinion of Krystina Pomorska (in *Russian Formalist Theory and its Poetic Ambiance*—Mouton, 1968) would seem acceptable. According to Tzvetan Todorov,

. . . she defends the following thesis: every critical method is a general-ization upon the literary practice of its time. Critical methods in the period of Classicism were elaborated as a function of Classical literary works. The criticism of the Romantics reiterates the principles (the irrational, the psychological, etc.) of Romanticism itself.[68]

Reading Fuentes' criticism on the new Spanish American novel, then, we are aware that his "critical method is a generali-zation upon the literary practice of its time"—the practice of *other* literatures, that is, *not* the Spanish American. All things considered, this fits in perfectly with the alienated and alienat-ing ideology of Fuentes.

After the work of men like Alejo Carpentier, whom some profiteers of the *boom* have tried in vain to disclaim, the un-dertaking assumed by the new Spanish American novel—an undertaking which, as certain critics do not cease to observe, might appear accomplished by now or "surpassed" in the narra-tive of capitalist countries—implies a reinterpretation of our history. Indifferent to this incontestable fact—which in many cases bears an ostensible relationship to the new perspectives the Revolution has afforded our America, and is in no small way responsible for the diffusion of our narrative among those with a desire to know the continent about which there is so much discussion—Fuentes dissipates the flesh and blood of our novels, the criticism of which would require, first of all, gen-eralizations and judgments upon the vision of history presented in them, and, as I have said, calmly applies to them schemes derived from other literatures (those of capitalist countries), now reduced to mere linguistic speculations.

The extraordinary vogue enjoyed by linguistics in recent years has moved more than one person to conclude that "the twentieth century, which is the century of so many things, would seem to be above all the century of linguistics."[69] Even though we would say, that among those "many things" the establishment of socialist governments and decolonization carry much more weight as outstanding features of this century.

---

[68] Tzvetan Todorov, "Formalistes et futurists," *Tel Quel*, 30 (1968), 43.
[69] Carlos-Peregrín Otero. *Introducción a la lingüística transformacional* (Mexico, 1970), p. 1.

I might add as a modest personal example regarding this vogue that as recently as 1955, when I was a student of linguistics under André Martinet, linguistic matters were confined in Paris to university lecture halls. Outside the classroom we talked with our friends about literature, philosophy and politics. Only a few years later, linguistics—whose structuralist dimension, as Lévi-Strauss describes it, had engulfed other social sciences—was in Paris the obligatory theme of all discussions. In those days literature, philosophy and politics all ran afoul *of structuralists.* (I am speaking of some years ago; presently, structuralism seems to be on the decline. However, in our part of the world the insistence on such an ideology will last for some time yet.)

Now I have no doubt that there exist specifically scientific factors to which we can credit this vogue of linguistics. But I also know that there are *ideological* reasons for it over and above the subject-matter itself. With respect to literary studies it is not difficult to determine these ideological reasons, from Russian formalism to French structuralism, the virtues and limitations of which cannot be shown without considering them. And among them is the attempt at ahistorization peculiar to a dying class: a class which initiated its trajectory with daring *utopias* in order to chase away time and endeavors now, in the face of adversity, to congeal that trajectory via impossible *uchronics.* In any case, one must recognize the convergence between these studies and their respective conterminous literatures. However, when Fuentes glosses over the concrete reality of the current Spanish American novel and attempts to impose upon it systems derived from other literatures and other critical methodologies, he adds—with a typically colonial attitude —a second level of ideolization to his critical outlook. In a word, this is summed up in his claim that our present-day narrative—*like that of apparently coetaneous capitalist countries*—is above all a feat of language. Such a contention, among other things, allows him to minimize nicely everything in that narrative having to do with a clear historical concretion. Furthermore, the manner in which he lays the foundations of his linguistic approach demonstrates a pedantry and a provincialism typical of the colonial wishing to demonstrate to those in the metropolis that he too is capable of grappling with fashionable themes *from abroad,* and wishing at the same time to enlighten his fellow countrymen, in whom he is confident of finding an ignorance ,even greater than his own. This is the sort of thing he spews forth:

Change comprehends the categories of process and speech, of diachrony; structure comprehends those of system and language, of synchrony. The point of interaction for all these categories is the word— which joins diachrony and synchrony, speech and language through discourse; along with process and system, through the event, and even event and discourse themselves. (p. 33)

These banalities (which any handy little linguistics manual could have taken care of), nonetheless should arouse in us more than a smile. Fuentes is elaborating as best he can here a consistent vision of our literature, of our culture—a vision which significantly coincides in its essentials with that proposed by writers like Emir Rodríguez Monegal and Severo Sarduy.

It is revealing that for Fuentes the thesis of the preponderant role of language in the new Spanish American novel finds its basis in the prose of Borges, "without which there would simply not exist a modern Spanish American novel," since, according to Fuentes, "the ultimate significance" of that prose is "to bear witness, first off, that Latin America is lacking a language and must therefore establish one." This singular triumph is achieved by Borges, Fuentes continues, "in his creation of a new Latin American language which, by pure contrast, reveals the lie, the acquiescence and the duplicity of what has traditionally passed for 'language' among us." (p. 26)

Naturally, based on such criteria the ahistorization of literature can attain truly delirious expressions. We learn, for example, that Witold Gombrowicz' *Pornography*

could have been related by a native of the Amazon jungles and that neither nationality nor social class, in the final analysis, explain the difference between Gombrowicz and the possible narrator of the same initiation myth in a Brazilian jungle. Rather, it is explained precisely by the possibility of combining discourse in different ways. Only on the basis of the universality of linguistic structures can there be conceded, *a posteriori,* the peripheral data regarding nationality and class. (p. 22)

And, consequently, we are told as well that "it is closer to the truth, in the first instance, to understand the conflict in Spanish American literature *as related to certain characteristics of the literary endeavor*" (p. 24, my emphasis), rather than to history; furthermore:

The *old* obligation to denounce is transformed into a *much more arduous* enterprise: the critical elaboration of everything which has gone unspoken in our long history of lies, silences, rhetoric and academic complicities. *To invent a language is to articulate all that history has concealed.* (p. 30, my emphasis)

Such an interpretation, then, allows Fuentes to have his cake and eat it too. Thus conceived, literature not only withdraws from any combatant role (here degraded by a clever adjective: "the *old* obligation to denounce"), but its withdrawal, far from being a retreat, becomes a *"much more arduous* enterprise," since it is to articulate no less than *"all that history has concealed."* Further on we are told that our true language is in the process of being discovered and created, and that "in the very act of discovery and creation it threatens, *in a revolutionary way,* the whole economic, political and social structure erected upon a vertically false language." (pp. 94-5, my emphasis)

This astute, while at the same time superficial, manner of expounding right-wing concerns in left-wing terminology reminds us—though it is difficult to forget for a single moment —that Fuentes is a member of the Mexican literary *mafia,* the qualities of which he has attempted to extend beyond the borders of his country.

Furthermore, that these arguments constitute the projection onto literary questions of an inherently reactionary political platform is not conjecture. This is said throughout the little book, and is particularly explicit in its final pages. Besides the well-known attacks on socialism, there are observations like this one: "Perhaps the sad, immediate future of Latin America will see fascist populism, a Peronist sort of dictatorship, capable of carrying out various reforms only in exchange for a suppression of revolutionary impulse and civil liberties." (p. 96) The "civilization vs. barbarism" thesis appears not to have changed in the least. But in fact it has—it has been aggravated by the devastating presence of imperialism in our countries. In response to this reality, Fuentes erects a scarecrow: the announcement that there is opening before us

. . . a prospect even more grave. That is, in proportion to the widening of the abyss between the geometrical expansion of the technocratic world and the arithmetic expansion of our own ancillary societies, Latin America is being transformed into a world which is *superfluous* [Fuentes' emphasis] to imperialism. Traditionally we have been exploited countries. *Soon we will not even be that.* [my emphasis] It will no longer be necessary to exploit us, for technology will have succeeded in—to a large extent it can already—manufacturing substitutes for our single-product offerings. (*Ibid.*)

In light of this, and recalling that for Fuentes the revolution has no prospects in Latin America—he insists upon the impossibility of a "second Cuba" (p. 96), and cannot accept the varied, unpredictable forms the process will assume—we should almost be thankful that we are not superfluous to imperialist technology, that it is not manufacturing substitutes (as *it can already*) for our poor products.

I have lingered perhaps longer than necessary on Fuentes because he is one of the most outstanding figures among the new Latin American writers who have set out to elaborate in the cultural sphere a counter-revolutionary platform which, at least on the surface, goes beyond the coarse simplifications of the program, "Appointment with Cuba," broadcast by the Voice of the United States of America. But the writers in question already had an adequate medium: the review, *Mundo Nuevo* ("New World"), financed by the C.I.A.,[70] whose ideological foundations are summed up by Fuentes' short book in a manner which the professorial weightiness of Emir Rodríguez Monegal or the neo-Barthean flutterings of Severo Sarduy—

---

[70] Ambrosio Fornet's analysis of the publication in "*New World* en español," *Casa de las Américas*, 40 (enero-febrero, 1967), has lost none of its validity.

the magazine's other two "critics"—would have found difficult to achieve. That publication, which also gathered together the likes of Guillermo Cabrera Infante and Juan Goytisolo, is to be substituted shortly by another, which will apparently rely upon more or less the same team, along with a few additions. I am speaking of the review *Libre* ("Free"). A fusion of the two titles speaks for itself: *Mundo Libre* ("Free World").

THE FUTURE BEGUN

THE ENDEAVOR to include ourselves in the "Free World" —the hilarious name which capitalist countries today apply to themselves and bestow in passing on their oppressed colonies and neo-colonies—is a modern version of the nineteenth-century attempt by creole exploiting classes to subject us to a supposed "civilization"; and this latter, in its turn, is a repetition of the designs of European conquistadors. In all these cases, with only slight variations, it is plain that Latin America does not exist except, at the very most, as a *resistance* which must be overcome in order to implant *true* culture, that of "the modern peoples who gratify themselves with the epithet of civilized."[71] Pareto's words here recall so well those of Martí, who wrote in 1883 of civilization as "the vulgar name under which contemporary European man operates."

In the face of what the conquistadores, the creole oligarchs and the imperialists and their flunkies have attempted, our culture—taking this term in its broad historical and anthropological sense—has been in a constant process of formation, our authentic culture: the culture created by the *mestizo* populace, those descendants of Indians and Blacks and Europeans who Bolívar and Artigas led so well; the culture of the exploited classes, of the radical petite bourgeoisie of José Martí, of the poor peasantry of Emiliano Zapata, of the working class of Luis Emilio Recabarren and Jesús Menéndez; the culture "of the hungry Indian masses, of the landless peasants, of the ex-

---

[71] Vilfredo Pareto. *Tratado de la sociología general*, Vol. II. Cited by José Carlos Mariátegui. *Ideología y política*, p. 24.

ploited workers" mentioned by the *Second Declaration of Havana* (1962), "of the honest and brilliant intellectuals who abound in our suffering Latin American countries"; the culture of a people which now encompasses "a family numbering two hundred million brothers" and which "has said: Enough!, and has begun to move."

That culture—like every living culture, especially at its dawn—is on the move. It has, of course, its own distinguishing characteristics, even though it was born—like every culture, although in this case in a particularly planetary way—of a synthesis. And it does not limit itself in the least to a mere repetition of the elements which formed it. This is something which the Mexican Alfonso Reyes, while he directed his attention to Europe more often than we would have wished, has underscored well. On speaking with another Latin American regarding our culture as one of synthesis, he says:

Neither he nor I were understood by our European colleagues, who thought we were referring to the resume or elemental compendium of the European conquests. According to such a facile interpretation, the synthesis would be a terminal point. But that is not the case: here the synthesis is the new point of departure, a structure composed of prior and dispersed elements which—like all structures—transcends them and contains in itself new qualities. H_2O is not only a union of hydrogen and oxygen; it is, moreover, water.[72]

This is especially apparent if we consider that the "water" in question is formed not only from European elements, which are those Reyes emphasizes, but also from the indigenous and the African. But even with his limitations, it is still within Reyes' capacity to state at the end of that piece:

I say now before the tribunal of international thinkers within reach of my voice: we recognize the right to universal citizenship which we have won. We have arrived at our majority. Very soon you will become used to reckoning with us.[73]

---

[72] Alfonso Reyes, "Notas sobre la inteligencia americana," *Obras completas.* Tomo XI (Mexico, 1960), p. 88n.

[73] *Op. cit.,* p. 90.

These words were spoken in 1936. Today that "very soon" has already arrived. If we were asked to indicate the date which separates Reyes' hope from our certainty—considering the usual difficulties in that sort of thing—I would say 1959, the date the Cuban Revolution came to power. One could also go along marking some of the dates which are milestones in the advent of that culture. The first, relating to the indigenous peoples' resistance and Black slave revolts against European oppression, are imprecise. The year 1780 is important: it marks the uprising of Túpac Amaru in Peru. In 1803, the independence of Haiti. In 1810, the beginning of revolutionary movements in various Spanish colonies in America—movements extending well into the century. In 1867, the victory of Juárez over Maximilian. In 1895, the beginning of the final stage of Cuba's war against Spain—a war which Martí foresaw as an action against emerging Yankee imperialism. In 1910, the Mexican Revolution. In the twenties and the thirties, Sandino's resistance in Nicaragua and the establishment on the continent of the working class as a vanguard force. In 1938, the nationalization of Mexican petroleum by Cárdenas. In 1944, the coming to power of a democratic regime in Guatemala, which will be radicalized in office. In 1946, the beginning of Juan Domingo Perón's presidency in Argentina, under which the "shirtless ones" will become an influential force. In 1952, the Bolivian revolution. In 1959, the triumph of the Cuban Revolution. In 1961, the Bay of Pigs: the first military defeat of Yankee imperialism in America, and the declaration of our Revolution as Marxist-Leninist. In 1967, the fall of Che Guevara while leading a nascent Latin American army in Bolivia. In 1970, the election of socialist president Salvador Allende in Chile.

These dates, seen superficially, might not appear to have a very direct relationship to our culture. But, in fact, the opposite is true. Our culture is—and can only be—the child of revolution, of our multisecular rejection of all colonialisms. Our culture, like every culture, requires as a primary condition our own existence. I cannot help but cite here, although I have done so before elsewhere, one of the occasions on which Martí spoke to this fact in the most simple and illuminating way. "Letters, which are expression, cannot exist," he wrote in 1881, "so long as there is no essence to express in them. Nor will there exist a Spanish American Literature until Spanish America exists." And further on: "Let us lament now that we are without a great work of art; not because we do not have that work, but because it is a sign that we are still without a great people which would be reflected in it."[74] Latin American culture, then, has become a possibility *in the first place* because of the many who have struggled, the many who still struggle, for the existence of that "great people" which, in 1881, Martí still referred to as Spanish America but which some years later he would prefer to name more accurately, "Our America."

But this is not, of course, the only culture forged here. There is also the culture of anti-America, that of the oppressors, of those who tried (or are trying) to impose on these lands metropolitan schemes, or simply, tamely reproduce in a provincial fashion what might have authenticity in other countries. In the best of cases, to repeat, it is a question of the influence of

those who have worked, in some cases patriotically, to shape social life in accordance with models of other highly-developed countries, whose practices are the result of an organic process over the course of centuries [and thus] have betrayed the cause of the true emancipation of Latin America.[75]

This anti-America culture is still very visible. It is still proclaimed and perpetuated in structures, works, ephemerides. But without a doubt, it is suffering the pangs of death, just like the system upon which it is based. We can and must contribute to a true assessment of the history of the oppressors and that of the oppressed. But of course, the triumph of the latter will be the work, above all, of those for whom history is a function not of erudition, but of deeds. It is they who will achieve the definitive triumph of the true America, reestablishing—this time in a different light—the unity of our immense continent.

---

[74] "Cuaderno de apuntes—5" (1881). *Obras completas*, XXI, p. 164.

[75] Ezequiel Martínez Estrada, "El colonialismo como realidad," cited in note 54.

"Spanish America, Latin America—call it what you wish," wrote Mariátegui,

will not find its unity in the bourgeois order. That order divides us, perforce, into petty nationalisms. It is for Anglo-Saxon North America to consummate and draw to a close capitalist civilization. The future of Latin America is socialist.[76]

Such a future, which has already begun, will end by rendering incomprehensible the idle question regarding our existence.

AND ARIEL NOW?

THE Ariel of Shakespeare's great myth, which we have been following in these notes, is, as has been said, the intellectual from the same island as Caliban.[77] He can choose between serving Prospero—the case with intellectuals of the anti-American persuasion—at which he is apparently unusually adept, but for whom he is nothing more than a timorous slave; or allying himself with Caliban in his struggle for true freedom. It could be said that I am thinking, in Gramscian terms, above all of the "traditional" intellectuals: those whom the proletariat, even during the period of transition, must assimilate in the greatest possible number, while it generates its own "organic" intellectuals.

It is common knowledge, of course, that a more or less im-

---

[76] José Carlos Mariátegui. *Siete ensayos de interpretación de la realidad peruana* (La Habana, 1964), p. xii.

[77] "Intellectual" in the broad sense of the word, as employed by Gramsci in his classic pages on the subject, to which I heartily subscribe. As they are sufficiently known, I do not feel it necessary to comment on them here: *vid.* Antonio Gramsci, *Los intelectuales y la organización de la cultura* (1930), tr. Raul Sciarretta (Buenos Aires, 1960). In the preparatory seminar for the Cultural Congress of Havana, 1967, the word was used by us in this same broad sense and, recently, Fidel has taken up the question again in the first National Congress on Education and Culture. There he rejected the notion that such a denomination be enjoyed by a small group of "witch-doctors" which "has monopolized the title of intellectual," to the exclusion of "teachers, engineers, technicians, researchers. . . ."

portant segment of intellectuals at the service of the exploited classes usually comes from the exploiting classes, with which they have broken radically. This is the classic, to say the least, case of such supreme figures as Marx, Engels and Lenin. The fact had been observed already in the Manifesto of the Communist Party (1848) itself, where Marx and Engels wrote:

In times when the class-struggle nears the decisive hour, the process of dissolution going on within the ruling class, in fact, within the whole range of old society, assumes such a violent, glaring character, that a small section of the ruling class cuts itself adrift and joins the revolutionary class, the class that holds the future in its hands. . . . So now a portion of the bourgeoisie goes over to the proletariat and, in particular, a portion of the bourgeois ideologists, who have raised themselves to the level of comprehending theoretically the historical movements as a whole.[78]

If this is obviously valid with regard to the most highly developed capitalist nations—the ones Marx and Engels had in mind in the *Manifesto*—something more must be added in the case of our countries. Here that "sector of bourgeois ideologists" to which Marx and Engels refer experiences a second form of rupture: except for that sector proceeding organically from the exploited classes, the intelligentsia which considers itself revolutionary[79] must break all ties with its class of origin (frequently the petite-bourgeoisie) and must besides sever the nexus *of dependence* upon the metropolitan culture from which it has learned, nonetheless, a language as well as a conceptual and technical apparatus. That language will be of profit, to use Shakespearean terminology, in cursing Prospero. Such was the case with José María Heredia, who exclaimed in the finest Spanish of the first third of the nineteenth century, "The vilest

---

[78] Carlos Marx y Federico Engels, *Manifesto del Partido comunista*, in *Obras escogidas en dos tomos* (Moscú, s.f.), tomo I, p. 32.

[79] We would do well to recall here that more than forty years ago Mariátegui wrote, "This is a moment in our history when it is not possible, in effect, to be nationalist and revolutionary without also being socialist." José Carlos Mariátegui. *Siete ensayos*. p. 26n.

of traitors might serve him,/ But the tyrant's passion is all in vain./ For the sea's immense and rolling waves/ Span the distance from Cuba to Spain." It was also the case of José Martí. After spending fifteen years in the United States—which would allow him to become completely familiar with modernity, and to detect within that country the emergence of North American imperialism—he wrote: "I have lived in the monster and I know its entrails; and my sling is the sling of David." While I can foresee that my suggestion that Heredia and Martí went about cursing will have an unpleasant ring in the ears of some, I wish to remind them that "vile traitors" and "monster" do have something to do with curses. Both Shakespeare and reality would appear to argue well against them. And Heredia and Martí are only archetypal examples. More recently we have not been lacking either in individuals who attribute the volcanic violence in some of Fidel's recent speeches to deformations—Caliban, let us not forget, is always seen as deformed by the hostile eye—in our Revolution. Response to his address at the first National Congress on Education and Culture is one example of this. That some of those shocked should have praised Fanon (others, perhaps had never heard of him; since they have as much to do with politics, in the words of Rodolfo Walsh, as with astrophysics), and now attribute an attitude which is at the very root of our historical being to a deformation or to foreign influence, might be a sign of any number of things. Among them, total incoherence. It might also be a question of total ignorance, if not disdain, regarding our concrete realities, past and present. This, most assuredly, does not qualify them to have very much to do with our future.

The situation and tasks of the intellectual in the service of the exploited classes differ, of course, depending upon whether it is a question of a country where the revolution has yet to triumph or one where the revolution is already underway. And, as we have recalled above, the term "intellectual" is broad enough to counter any attempts at simplification. The intellectual can be a theoretician and leader like Mariátegui or Mella; a scholar, like Fernando Ortiz; or a writer like César

Vallejo. In all these cases their concrete example is more instructive than any vague generalization. For very recent discussions of this with respect to writers, the reader might consult some of the essays in this issue; in particular, that of Mario Benedetti. ["Las prioridades del escritor" ("The Writer's Priorities"), *Casa de las Américas*, 68 (sept.-oct., 1971).]

The situation, as I said, is different in countries where the Latin American masses have at last achieved power and set in motion a socialist revolution. The encouraging case of Chile is too immediate to allow for any conclusions to be drawn. But the socialist revolution in Cuba is more than twelve years old, and by this time it is possible to point out certain facts. Although, owing to the nature of this essay, I propose to mention here only a few salient characteristics.

This Revolution—in both practice and theory, absolutely faithful to the most exacting popular Latin American tradition —has satisfied in full the aspiration of Mariátegui. "We certainly do not wish for socialism in Latin American to be a carbon copy," he said. "It must be a heroic creation. With our own reality, in our own language, we must give life to Indo-American socialism."[80]

That is why our Revolution cannot be understood without a knowledge of "our own reality," "our own language," and to these I have referred extensively. But the unavoidable pride in having inherited the best of Latin American history, in struggling in the front ranks of a family numbering 200 million brothers and sisters, must not cause us to forget that as a consequence we form part of another even larger vanguard, a planetary vanguard—that of the socialist countries emerging on every continent. This means that our inheritance is also the world-wide inheritance of socialism, and that we commit ourselves to it as the most beautiful, the most lofty, the most combative chapter in the history of humanity. We feel as unequivocally our own socialism's past: from the dreams of the utopian socialists to the impassioned scientific rigor of Marx

---

[80] José Carlos Mariátegui, "Aniversario y balance," p. 249.

("That German of tender spirit and iron hand," as Martí said) and Engels; from the heroic endeavor of the Paris Commune of a century ago to the startling triumph of the October Revolution and the abiding example of Lenin; from the establishment of new socialist governments in Europe as a result of the defeat of fascism in World War II to the success of socialist revolutions in such "underdeveloped" Asian countries as China, Korea and Viet Nam. When we affirm our commitment to such a magnificent inheritance—one which we aspire besides to enrich with our own contributions—we are well aware that this quite naturally entails shining moments as well as difficult ones, achievements as well as errors. How could we not be aware of this when on making *our own* history (an operation which has nothing to do with *reading* the history of others) we find ourselves also subject to achievements and errors, just as all *real* historical movements have been and will continue to be!

This elemental fact is constantly being recalled, not only by our declared enemies but even by some supposed friends, whose only apparent objection to socialism is, at bottom, that it exists —in all its grandeur and with its difficulties in spite of the flawlessness with which this written swan appears in books. And we cannot but ask ourselves why we should go on offering explanations to those supposed friends with regard to the problems we face in *real-life* socialist construction. Especially when their consciences allow them to remain integrated into exploiting societies, or in some cases even to abandon our neo-colonial countries and request, hat in hand, a place in those very societies. No, there is no reason to give any explanation to that sort of people who, were they honest, should be concerned about having so much in common with our enemies. The frivolous way in which some intellectuals who call themselves leftists (and who, nonetheless, don't seem to give a damn about the masses) rush forth shamelessly to repeat word for word the same critiques of the socialist world proposed and promulgated by capitalism only demonstrates that they have not broken with capitalism as radically as they might perhaps think. The natural consequence of this attitude is that under the guise of rejecting error (something upon which any opposing factions can come to an agreement), socialism as a whole, reduced arbitrarily to such errors, is rejected in passing; or there is the deformation and generalization of a concrete historical moment and, extracting it from its context, the attempt to apply it to other historical moments which have *their own characteristics, their own virtues and their own defects.* This is one of the many things that, with respect to Cuba, we have learned in the flesh.

During these years, in search of original and above all *genuine* solutions to our problems, an extensive dialogue on cultural questions has taken place in Cuba. This very magazine has published a number of contributions to the dialogue. I am thinking particularly of the round table in which we participated, with a group of colleagues, in 1969.[81]

And, of course, the leaders of the Revolution themselves have not been remiss in expressing opinions on these matters. Even though, as Fidel has said, "we did not have our Yenan conference"[82] before the triumph of the Revolution, since that time there have taken place discussions, meetings and congresses designed to grapple with these questions. I shall limit myself to recalling a few of the many texts by Fidel and Che. Regarding the former, there is his speech at the National Library of 30 June 1961, published that year and known since then as *Words to the Intellectuals*; his speech of 13 March 1969 in which he dealt with the democratization of the university and to which we referred a number of times in the above-mentioned round table; and finally, his contribution to the recent Congress on Education and Culture which we published, together with the Declaration of that Congress in number 65-66 of this review. Of course, these are not by any means the only occasions on which Fidel has taken up cultural problems, but I think

---

[81] "Diez años de revolución: El intelectual y la sociedad," *Casa de las Américas*, 56 (septiembre-octubre, 1969), also published under the title, *El intelectual y la sociedad* (Mexico, 1969).

[82] Fidel Castro. *Palabras a los intelectuales* (La Habana, 1961), p. 5.

they offer a sufficiently clear picture of the Revolution's criteria in this regard.

Although a decade has passed between the first of these speeches—which I am convinced has scarcely been read by many of its commentators, who limit themselves to quoting the odd sentence or two out of context—and the most recent one, what an *authentic* reading of both demonstrates above all is a consistency over the ten-year period. In 1971, Fidel has this to say about literary and other artistic works:

We, a revolutionary people, value cultural and artistic creations in proportion to what they offer mankind, in proportion to their contribution to the revindication of man, the liberation of man, the happiness of man . . . Our evaluation is political. There can be no esthetic value where the human content is absent. There can be no esthetic value in opposition to man. Esthetic value cannot exist in opposition to justice, in opposition to the welfare or in opposition to the happiness of man. It cannot exist!

In 1961, he had declared:

It is man himself, his fellow man, the redemption of his fellow man that constitutes the objective of the revolutionary. If they ask us revolutionaries what matters most to us, we say the people, and we will always say the people. The people in the truest sense, that is, the majority of the people, those who have had to live in exploitation and in the cruelest neglect. Our basic concern will always be the great majority of the people, that is, the oppressed and exploited classes. The prism through which we see everything is this: whatever is good for them will be good for us; whatever is noble, useful and beautiful for them will be noble, useful and beautiful for us.

And those words of 1961, so often cited out of context, must be returned to that context for a full understanding of their meaning:

Within the Revolution, everything; outside the Revolution, nothing. Outside the Revolution, nothing, because the Revolution also has its rights; and the first right of the Revolution is to be, to exist. No one, to the extent that the Revolution understands the interests of the people, to the extent that the Revolution expresses the interest of the nation as a whole, can maintain any right in opposition to it.

But consistency is not repetition. The correspondence between the two speeches does not mean that the past ten years have gone by in vain. At the beginning of his *Words to the Intellectuals* Fidel had recalled that the economic and social revolution taking place in Cuba was bound inevitably to produce in its turn a revolution in the culture of our country. The decisions proclaimed in the 1969 speech on the democratization of the university along with those of the 1971 speech at the National Congress on Education and Culture correspond, among other things, to the very transformation mentioned already in 1961 as an outcome of the economic and social revolution. During those ten years there has been taking place an uninterrupted radicalization of the Revolution, which implies a growing participation of the masses in the country's destiny. If the agrarian reform of 1959 will be followed by an agrarian revolution, the literacy campaign will inspire a campaign for follow-up courses, and the later announcement of the democratization of the university already supposes that the masses have conquered the domains of so-called high culture. Meanwhile in a parallel way, the process of syndical democratization brings about an inexorable growth in the role played by the working class in the life of the country.

In 1961 this could not yet have been the case. In that year the literacy campaign was only just being carried out. The foundations of a truly new culture were barely being laid. By now, 1971, a great step forward has been taken in the development of that culture; a step already foreseen in 1961, one involving tasks which must inevitably be accomplished by any revolution that calls itself socialist: the extension of education to all of the people, its firm grounding in revolutionary principles, and the construction and safeguarding of a new, socialist culture.

To better understand the goals as well as the specific characteristics of *our* developing cultural transformation, it is useful to compare it to similar processes in other socialist countries. The creation of conditions by which an entire people who have lived in exploitation and illiteracy gains access to the highest levels of knowledge and creativity is one of the most beautiful achievements of a revolution.

Cultural questions also engaged a good part of Ernesto Che Guevara's attention. His study, *El socialismo y el hombre en Cuba* (*Man and Socialism in Cuba*), is sufficiently well known to make comment on it unnecessary here. But the reader should be warned, above all, against following the example of those who take him *à la carte,* selecting for example his censure of a certain conception of socialist realism but not his censure of decadent art under modern capitalism and its continuation in our society—or vice-versa.[83] Or who forget with what astonishing clarity he foresaw certain problems of our artistic life, expressing himself in terms which, on being taken up again by pens less prestigious than his own, would raise objections no one dared make to Che himself.

Because it is less known than *Man and Socialism in Cuba,* I would like to close by citing at some length the end of a speech delivered by Che at the University of Las Villas on 28 December 1959, that is, at the very beginning of our Revolution. The University had made him Professor *honoris causa* in the

---

[83] While a certain narrow conception of socialist realism—which Che rejects in his article along with the phony vanguardism attributed to capitalist art today and its negative influence among us—has not damaged our art in the way he suggested, some harm has been done by an extemporaneous fear of that conception. The process has been described thus: "For ten years Cuban novelists eluded skillfully the dangers of a narrative which would lead to schematism and paralysis. On the other hand, the greater portion of their works evince an air of timidity from which poetry and documentary film, for example, have freed themselves (and from which the writer of short stories will perhaps free himself) [. . .] if the new narrative, given the climate of artistic freedom in which it developed, had passed through an epic phase of ingenuous exaltation of reality, perhaps it might have discovered at least its own *tone,* which would have demanded in turn the discovery of new forms. That way we would be able to discuss today, in a manner of speaking, epic vanguardism in the Cuban narrative [. . .] The danger should have been incurred *proceeding from* a fall, instead of attempting to avoid one, for the fact that one does not *fall* into pamphletism does not guarantee that he will escape mimetism and mediocrity." Ambrosio Fornet, "A propósito de Sacchario," *Casa de las Américas,* 64 (enero-febrero, 1971).

School of Pedagogy, and Che's speech was to express his gratitude for the distinction. He did so, but what he did above all
was to propose to the University, to its professors and students,
a transformation which all of them—and us—had to undergo
in order to be considered truly revolutionary, truly useful:

I would never think of demanding that the distinguished professors or
the students presently associated with the University of Las Villas perform the miracle of admitting to the University the masses of workers
and peasants. The road here is long; it is a process all of you have lived
through, one entailing many years of preparatory study. What I do
ask, based on my own limited experience as a revolutionary and rebel
commandante, is that the present students of the University of Las
Villas understand that study is the patrimony of no one, and that the
place of study where you carry out your work is the patrimony of no
one—it belongs to all the people of Cuba, and it must be extended to
the people or the people will seize it. And I would hope—because I began the whole series of ups and downs in my career as a university
student, as a member of the middle class, as a doctor with middle-class
perspectives and the same youthful aspirations that you must have; and
because I have changed in the course of the struggle, because I am
convinced of the overwhelming necessity of the Revolution and the
infinite justice of the people's cause—I would hope for those reasons
that you, today proprietors of the University will extend it to the people.
I do not say this as a threat, so as to avoid its being taken over by them
tomorrow. I say it simply because it would be one more among so many
beautiful examples in Cuba today: that the proprietors of the Central
University of Las Villas, the students, offer it to the people through
their revolutionary Government. And to the distinguished professors,
my colleagues, I have to say something similar: become Black, mulatto,
a worker, a peasant; go down among the people, respond to the people,
that is, to all the necessities of all of Cuba. When this is accomplished
no one will be the loser; we all will have gained and Cuba can then
continue its march toward the future with a more vigorous step, and
you will not need to include in your cloister this doctor, commandante,
bank president, and today Professor of Pedagogy who now takes leave
of you.[84]

---

[84] Ernesto Che Guevara, "Que la Universidad se pinte de negro, de mulato,
de obrero, de campesino," *Obras, 1957–1967* (La Habana, 1970), tomo II,
p. 37–8.

That is to say, Che proposed that the "European university," as Martí would have said, yield before the "American university." He proposed to Ariel, through his own luminous and sublime example if ever there was one, that he seek from Caliban the honor of a place in his rebellious and glorious ranks.

—HAVANA, 7-20 June 1971.

—Translated by Lynn Garafola,
David Arthur McMurray, Robert Márquez

OCCIDENTALIZACIÓN, IMPERIALISMO, GLOBALIZACIÓN: HERENCIAS COLONIALES Y TEORÍAS POSTCOLONIALES

POR

WALTER D. MIGNOLO
Duke University

1.- El proceso de occidentalización a partir de finales del siglo xv legó a la historia cultural de lo que se conoce hoy como América Latina una preocupación particular: hasta dónde Latinoamérica es parte de Occidente; es el extremo occidente o un espacio donde lo occidental es lo extraño frente a los legados de las culturas Amerindias y Africanas. El sentimiento de pertenecer o no a Occidente, de pertenecer más o menos, varía según las regiones culturales y la trayectoria étnica y social de los grupos humanos y las personas. Las trayectorias son diferentes también en los Andes, Mesoamérica y el Caribe. Durante el siglo xix el proceso de occidentalización generó la Doctrina Monroe y con ella una conciencia "americana" del Hemisferio Occidental, que si bien no fue abrazada por todos, tuvo sin embargo impacto político y entusiastas defensores. A mediados del siglo xx, el debate adquirió un nuevo carácter y una nueva dimensión en la medida en que la pregunta fundamental pasó a explorar el lugar de América en la historia, teniendo en cuenta los sucesivos procesos de expansión imperial (España y Portugal, primero, Francia e Inglaterra después), trazando las diferencias entre la América del Sur y la del Norte, las cuales comenzaron a separarse hacia principios del siglo xx, cuando el impulso imperial de Estados Unidos desplazó la "fraternidad" americana presupuesta en la Doctrina Monroe, enfatizó la política de la ubicación ("location") geo-cultural y, con ella, las variables de raza y género.

Curiosamente, tales preocupaciones provienen de un tipo de pensamiento que se entronca con una particular herencia colonial: la hispano-portuguesa. La herencia colonial inglesa y francesa generan, en cambio, un tipo distinto de relación con Occidente. La diferencia se nota en pensadores de la América Hispana que, desde los años cincuenta hasta la fecha, fueron modificando su posición frente a Occidente en la medida en que fueron escuchando más voces descolonizadoras de Africa y de Asia. En 1959, cuando escribió *América en la historia*, el filósofo mexicano Leopoldo Zea tenía una posición ambivalente, aunque tendiente a la celebración, del proceso de occidentalización del globo y de universalización de la cultura (Zea 1959). Al leer hoy aquellas páginas, la lectura es también ambivalente puesto que, por un lado, se percibe un esfuerzo por pensar críticamente el occidentalismo y, por otro, un apego demasiado cercano a Toynbee. Zea no cuestionó, en ese momento, el hecho de que el lugar de la enunciación de Toynbee coincidía con el ·

del discurso de la occidentalización.[1] En cambio, en su libro más reciente, *Discurso desde la civilización y la barbarie* (1958), su crítica al occidentalismo es más decisiva y va acompañada de la necesidad de "ir más allá" de él. Es interesante comparar lo que Zea tiene que decir sobre Hegel en 1958 y en 1968. En 1988 Zea se hace cargo del discurso sobre Próspero y Calibán y es a partir de esta perspectiva que reinterpreta las lecciones de filosofía de la historia, de Hegel. Mientras que en 1959 Hegel le permitía justificar y celebrar la expansión occidental, en 1988 le sirve para criticarla, como ya lo había hecho George Lamming, también en los cincuenta, en sus ensayos recogidos en *The Pleasure of Exile* (1960).

Enrique Dussel ofrece un caso distinto y complementario al de Leopoldo Zea. En su *Filosofía de la liberación*, 1980, Dussel plantea abierta la cuestión geopolítica actual y la crítica de la colonización. Así, la "filosofía de la liberación" se aproxima a perspectivas de crítica y teoría postcoloniales, si bien el propio Dussel la concibe como una empresa intelectual postmoderna. La creencia de que la filosofía de la liberación es postmoderna, dice Dussel, se basa en el hecho de que la filosofía Europea moderna, antes del *cógito* cartesiano pero sobre todo a partir de él, situó a los seres humanos en relación a sus propias fronteras: los cronistas y letrados castellanos contribuyeron en esta tarea, sigue Dussel, al preguntarse si los amerindios eran seres humanos (esto es, si eran racionales y racionales a la europea), ubicándolos (allocating them), sin que ellos tuvieran oportunidad de ubicar a los castellanos ni de ubicarse ellos con respecto a los castellanos. Mientras que en 1980 Dussel veía la filosofía de la liberación como una toma de posición postmoderna, podríamos decir hoy que la filosofía de la liberación es más cercana a la perspectiva postcolonial que postmoderna. No se trata, por cierto, de una polémica para llevar las aguas al molino de uno o del otro de los "post," pero sí de tener en cuenta que la crítica de Dussel es una crítica a la occidentalización desde la experiencia periférica de la colonización.[2] Por eso, en aquel momento, la cuestión geopolítica era crucial para Dussel y la organización del espacio geo-político se hacía con la convicción de que no es lo mismo nacer en New York que nacer en Chiapas (sic!).

Pero hay más razones para pensar que la filosofía de la liberación contribuye más a la crítica y teoría postcolonial que a la postmoderna. Sé que preguntarse dónde termina lo postmoderno y empieza lo postcolonial, o viceversa, es una pregunta de difícil respuesta. En América Latina la complicación es aún mayor puesto que si bien los debates sobre la

---

[1] Una rearticulación actual de las tesis de Toynbee, en la que se busca reemplazar el modelo geopolítico basado en la distinción entre "primer", "segundo," y "tercer" mundo, se encuentra en el debatido artículo de S. P. Huntington. La hipótesis de Huntington es importante para cualquier reflexión sobre herencias coloniales y teorías postcoloniales: "World politics is entering a new phase, and intellectuals have not hesitated to proliferate visions of what it will be ... It is my hypothesis that the fundamental source of conflict in this new world will not be primarily ideological or primarily economic. The great divisions among humankind and the dominating source of conflict will be cultural. Nations states will remain the most powerful actors in world affairs, but the principal conflicts of global politics will occur between nations and groups of different civilizations. The clash of civilization will dominate global politics" (Huntington 1993, 22).

[2] El asunto aquí, como lo planteó Anthony Apiah hace algunos años, es de decidir si el "post" en "postcolonial" es lo mismo que el "post" en "postmoderno".

postmodernidad llevan ya varios años y variadas publicaciones, la postcolonialidad no despertó el mismo interés.[3] Las teorías postcoloniales fueron y son todavía, una asunto más ligado a Asia y a África que a América Latina. Lo cual no deja de tener interés si se piensa que los primeros siglos del proceso de occidentalización tuvo su escenario en lo que es hoy América Latina, durante la expansión de los imperios hispano y portugués. En cambio, la herencia colonial inglesa y francesa produjo, en las islas del Caribe, un tipo de pensamiento que si bien no se autoidentifica como "postcolonial" tiene todas las carácterísticas de los trabajos que hoy se aceptan como tales.[4] Dussel llama "filosofía colonial" a la filosofía exportada desde Europa hacia África, Asia y América Latina y, con algunas diferencias, en las primeras colonias portuguesas e inglesas. Así, Dussel concibe las sucesivas independencias en las Américas como emancipación no sólo del mercantilismo, sino también de la filosofía colonial. De modo que al llegar al período de la recuperación de la crisis industrial en Europa, hacia 1850, los centros imperiales comenzaron una segunda ola de expansión colonial cuando el mundo Árabe, el África negra, India, el sudeste Asiático y China pasaron a ser los nuevos centros de expansión, ya no mercantil, sino monopólica e imperial. En ello ve Dussel un proceso de recolonización intelectual mediante el cual los "filósofos colonizados," olvidaron su pasado y ya no regresaron al legado de formas de pensamiento anterior a la segunda ola de colonización, económica e intelectual.

La tercera etapa de expansión la sitúa Dussel después de la segunda guerra mundial, cuando se produce la "tercera revolución industrial", ya no mecánica y mercantil, tampoco industrial y monopolista, sino en el esfuerzo hacia la transnacionalización de capitales y en el incremento en las técnicas de comunicación. Esto es, lo que hoy llamaríamos "globalización". En definitiva, lo que buscaba Dussel con la filosofía de la liberación era una "filosofía explícita para la emancipación anticolonial". Veía un proceso en marcha, un grupo de pensadores que se situaban en un espacio diferencial de enunciación (el espacio "hermenéutico adecuado y desde la perspectiva correcta", según Dussel) aunque lamente que tal pensamiento no sea todavía propiamente filosofía. El ejemplo paradigmático de Dussel es el de Frantz Fanon.

Argumentos como el que acabo de resumir sugieren hoy —como ya dije— una perspectiva postcolonial, aunque en el momento en que Dussel escribe tal marco discursivo no estaba todavía disponible. Sin embargo, la búsqueda y la esperanza de Dussel de que una filosofía anticolonial se adapte a las reglas del juego de la filosofía europea moderna (por ejemplo, Fanon es un discurso crítico y de emancipación pero no es filosofía) no es sólo pedirle "peras al olmo" sino que es también mantenerse en el circuito de la filosofía "colonial", en cualquiera de sus tres etapas. Es quizás este respeto a las formas discursivas "correctas", lo que mantiene a Dussel apegado a los valores y criterios de la modernidad.

---

[3] Me solidarizo con quienes se sientan irritados o incómodos con el término "postcolonial" (Klor de Alva, 1992; Shohat 1993, Dirlik 1994). No entiendo por "postcolonial" un momento en el cual se han superado los colonialismos, sino desde una posición crítica frente a sus legados. En este sentido, entiendo "postcolonial" de la misma manera que algunos entienden "postmoderno", como un momento de crítica a los legados de la modernidad. Las teorías "postcoloniales", en consecuencia, serían las repuestas críticas periféricas a la modernidad. Es decir, una perspectiva postcolonial frente a la modernidad y a la postmodernidad, diferentes caras del mismo cubo.

[4] Ortiz (1940); Fernández Retamar (1981); Fanon (1961); Glissant (1981).

Es también por esta razón que Dussel concibe la filosofía de la liberación como un posición postmoderna en vez de postcolonial. Quizás una posición más explícitamente postcolonial sostendría que la emancipación intelectual exige que las reglas y el orden del discurso de la modernidad sea transgredido, que los panfletos anticolonialistas que no son todavía filosofía, parafraseando a Dussel, se conviertan en nuevos géneros que lleven la emancipación intelectual no sólo por los caminos del "contenido" sino también de la desarticulación de las formaciones discursivas (por ejemplo, "la" filosofía), en las que se consolidó el pensamiento moderno. Quizás, finalmente, este tironeo en Dussel se deba a que el espacio lingüístico e intelectual desde donde piensa (por ejemplo, su lugar de enunciación), se entronque con la lengua y las herencias culturales de la primera etapa de la expansión colonial, esto es, del castellano.

En otros terrenos, en cambio, Dussel mantiene posiciones que lo acercan a premisas que reconocemos hoy como postcoloniales. Repito, no trato de valorar a Dussel cuando se acerca a lo uno o a lo otro. Me interesa más, en cambio, registrar críticas a la occidentalización que se sitúan en distintos espacios hermenéuticos o epistemológicos. Así, el sentimiento de pensar en y desde la periferia (Dussel) o en los espacios-entre-medio (por ejemplo, los espacios conflictivos y superpuestos de instituciones y saberes europeos con instituciones y saberes no-europeos),[5] creados a lo largo de la expansión colonial, es lo que a mi juicio legitima la crítica postcolonial frente a (y la distingue de) la crítica postmodernista.

Cito, finalmente, unos párrafos de Dussel en los cuales construye un lugar postcolonial de enunciación al articular su crítica a la modernidad como un fenómeno eurocéntrico:

> Modernity is, for many (for Jurgen Habermas or Charles Taylor, for example), an essentially or exclusively European phenomenon. In these lectures, I will argue that modernity is, in fact, a European phenomenon, but one constituted in a dialectical relation with a non-European alterity that is its ultimate content. Modernity appears when Europe affirms itself as the "center" of the World History that it inaugurates; the "peripher" that surrounds this center is consequently part of its self-definition [...]

> According to my central thesis, 1492 is the date of the "birth" of modernity, although its gestation involves a preceding "intrauterine" process of growth [...] So, if 1492 is the moment of birth of modernity as a concept, the moment of origin of a very particular muth of sacrificial violence, it also marks the origin of a process of concealment or misrecognition of the non-European [...]

> Understanding this, I believe, allows Latin America to also rediscover its "place" in the history of modernity. *We* (itálicas mías, WM), were the *first periphery* of modern Europe; that is, we suffered globally from our moment of origin on a constitutive process of modernization (...) that afterward would be applied in Africa and Asia [...]

> The myth of origin that is hidden in the emancipatory "concept" of modernity, and that continues to underlie philosophical reflection and many other theoretical positions in European and North American thought, has to do above all with the connection of

---

[5] Ver Santiago (1971); Bhabha (1992).

Eurocentrism with the concomitant "fallacy of developmentalism". The fallacy of developmentalism consists in thinking that the path of Europe's modern development must be followed unilateraly by every other culture [...][6]

El argumento de Dussel comienza a reencontrarse con el de Zea, en la medida en que ambos retoman la falacia "progresista" en Kant (en su concepción iluminista de la razón) y en Hegel en su idea geográfica (por ejemplo, del este hacia al oeste) del desarrollo histórico, en sus lecciones de filosofía de la historia. En ambos casos, "1492" es la referencia a un largo proceso de occidentalización, de expansión colonial y, finalmente, de globalización cuyas consecuencias culturales y filosóficas (no sólo económicas), están todavía hoy en debate; un debate en el que la crítica y teoría postcoloniales encuentran su lugar de enunciación y de práctica oposicional.

2.- Un tipo de respuesta (y resistencia) a la occidentalización, que es único en América Latina, es la de Rodolfo Kusch (Argentina 1920-1979). Es también significativo que Dussel no prestara atención a una reflexión tan relevante para sus propios argumentos. En el momento en que escribió *Filosofía de la liberación* (1980), Dussel no prestaba todavía atención a la posibilidad de pensar a partir de las ruinas del pensamiento indígena, un aspecto que incorporó en su última obra, *1492: El encubrimiento del otro. Hacia el origen del mito de la modernidad* (1992), donde intentó un esfuerzo por construir una hermenéutica desde el "otro".[7] Fue esta necesidad, precisamente, la que obsesionó a Rodolfo Kusch durante unos veinte años de tarea intelectual, desde *América profunda* (1963) hasta *Esbozo de una antropología filosófica americana* (1978).

Rodolfo Kusch comienza al prólogo de su libro *El pensamiento indígena y popular en América* (1970), como sigue:

> La búsqueda de un pensamiento indígena no se debe sólo al deseo de exhumarlo científicamente, sino a la necesidad de rescatar un estilo de pensar que, según creo, se da en el fondo de América y mantiene cierta vigencia en las poblaciones criollas (Kusch 1970. 11).

Hoy somos quizás más sospechosos sobre al proyecto de "buscar un pensamiento indígena", simplemente porque no estaríamos seguros de que haya tal cosa. Seríamos más proclives a aceptar la ubicación de las herencias del pensamiento indígena y las huellas de sus transformaciones desde la colonia hasta nuestros días. Pero habría que reflexionar más, sin embargo, no sólo en lo que Kusch trata de rescatar, sino cómo propone hacerlo: el proyecto no se "debe sólo al deseo de *exhumarlo científicamente*, sino a la necesidad de *rescatar un estilo de pensar* que, según creo, se da en el fondo de América y que mantiene cierta vigencia en las poblaciones criollas". "Exhumarlo científicamente" implicaría imponer sobre un "estilo de pensar" otro estilo de pensar que yace en "otra parte". En cambio, "rescatar un estilo de pensar" implica la búsqueda de ciertas raíces, ciertas referencias o ciertos puntos de apoyo que no sean, precisamente, las raíces y los puntos de

---

[6] Dussel (1993a).
[7] Dussel (1993b); Mignolo (1988).

apoyo que dieron lugar a la configuración de estilos de pensar entre los cuales se cuenta la posibilidad de exhumar científicamente otros estilos de pensar. Si seguimos el proyecto de Kusch hasta sus últimas consecuencias, su propuesta es radical puesto que nos invita a fundar formas de pensamiento sobre estilos que habían sido considerados como interesante material etnográfico pero no como formas de pensamiento en su propio derecho. A medida que se desarrolla el argumento vamos comprendiendo que Pachacuti Yamki y Kant son pensadores situados al mismo nivel, aunque ellos operen en distintas condiciones sociales y a partir de distintas premisas cosmológicas.

El proyecto de Kusch pone sobre la mesa de trabajo la posibilidad de una reorientación de los estudios coloniales y de una reubicación de las culturas en el momento de mayor globalización en la historia de la humanidad, globalización que reemplaza o transforma el proceso de occidentalización cuyo comienzo situamos hacia 1500. La alternativa entre "exhumación científica" y "estilo de pensar" es la alternativa entre las transformaciones del discurso colonial que da cuenta de otros estilos de vida y de pensamiento y la emergencia de lo que podríamos llamar (en este contexto), discurso postcolonial: resistencia a la occidentalización y la globalización —por un lado, y producción creativa de estilos de pensar que marquen constantemente la diferencia con el proceso de occidentalización. Esto es, la constante producción de lugares diferenciales de enunciación. De modo que el esfuerzo de Kusch por *rescatar* un estilo de pensar se transforma en su propio proyecto de *continuarlo* como resistencia a la occidentalización y como una forma de crear las condiciones y de "pensar en América" (aunque no necesariamente el proyecto utópico y lógicamente insostenible de fundar un "pensamiento Americano"). Las condiciones de pensamiento en América no son las que produjeron ni el pensamiento de Confucio, ni el de Platón, ni el de Ibn-Khaldun ni el de Kant o el de Heidegger. Pensar en o desde (América, el exilio, la cárcel Pacífico, etc.), son casos particulares donde el *dictum* de Anton Shammas tendría su plena vigencia: "Home is the only thing you don't leave home without".[8] En casos como "América" o "circum-Pacífico" el lugar de enunciación se confunde con la política de la ubicación geocultural. En el caso del exilio, en los intersticios de las zonas geoculturales.

Kusch introduce un concepto fundamental para entender lo que podría ser un "estilo de pensar" que daría lugar a una extensión de él: el concepto de "fagocitación". Cito lo que Kusch escribió en 1963 para definir el concepto:

> Los técnicos de la filosofía de la cultura ya han hallado el concepto de "aculturación"[9] para explicar el contacto de culturas. No lo han aplicado abiertamente a América pero resulta tentador hacerlo, aunque con ello no se obtenga otra cosa que enunciados sin compromiso. Nos serviría para entender que hubo simplemente un paso de la cultura europea hacia América, ya que se trataba de la Europa ciudadana del siglo xv y una América meramente agraria, y todo consistía en que las cosas pasaran de un lado a otro.

---

[8] Shammas (1994).

[9] Ortiz (Ortiz 1940) introdujo el concepto de "transculturación" como correctivo de "aculturación" muchos años antes. El hecho de que Kusch lo ignore puede ser un buen indicador de la falta de comunicación que debilita a los intelectuales "postcoloniales", que mutuamente se ignoran. La centralización en la metrópoli y la falta de comunicación entre los centros coloniales es un conocido caso de la estrategia de "dividir y gobernar".

Pero como ya venimos encarando el problema desde otro ángulo, podemos afirmar que la aculturación se produce sólo en un plano material, como la arquitectura o la vestimenta, en cambio, en otros órdenes pudo haberse producido un proceso inverso, diríamos de *fagocitación* de lo blanco por lo indígena. Quizás hubo siempre una acción simultánea de los dos procesos pero nuestros ideales de progresismo nos impiden ver a este último. La fagocitación se da en un terreno de imponderables, en aquel margen de inferioridad de todo lo nuestro, aunque de elementos aculturados, respecto a lo europeo, ahí donde adquirimos nuestra personalidad nacional, cuando somos netamente argentinos, peruanos, chilenos o bolivianos y también en ese hecho tan evidente de nuestra mala industria o nuestra peor educación pública. Es cuando tomamos conciencia de que algo nos impide ser totalmente occidentales aunque nos lo propongamos (Kusch 1963: 158-159).

La conciencia del mestizaje, de las fronteras y de los espacios entre medio, de ser y no ser, de ser lo uno y lo otro, etc., se ha agudizado con el proceso de globalización. En América Latina, el concepto de "transculturación", introducido por Fernando Ortiz, es una de las más tempranas tomas de conciencia teórica del asunto. Hacia finales de los sesenta, Frantz Fanon (1959) conceptualizó las zonas fronterizas como zonas de expansión colonial y como zonas de violencia, más que de contacto. Más tarde, Silviano Santiago (1971), habló del "entre-discurso" (o quizás el "discurso intermedio") para teorizar situaciones y sentimientos de la historia de las prácticas culturales en América Latina. Gloria Anzaldúa (1987) recontextualizó la noción de "mestizaje" para conceptualizar la experiencia fronteriza al decir que: "*Mestizaje* is the reality of our life and not Chicanismo. *Mestizaje* is the heart of our art. We bleed in *mestizaje*, we eat and sweat and cry in *mestizaje*. But the Chicana/o is inside the *mestiza/o*". Haroldo de Campos (1978) se apropió de la noción de "canibalismo" para dar cuenta del discurso intermediario desde otra perspectiva: la apropiación digestiva de la cultura europea en la historia cultural del Brasil. Es en este contexto donde podemos ubicar la idea de "fagocitosis" de Kusch y, al mismo tiempo, sugerir *que todas estas conceptualizaciones son propuestas teóricas postcoloniales para dar cuenta de diferentes herencias y legados coloniales.*

Así, podemos introducir una distinción significativa entre "discursos coloniales" y "discursos poscoloniales". Los primeros han sido descrito/como discursos producidos por agentes colonizadores (por ejemplo, la filosofía colonial de Dussel), ligados a instituciones políticas, administrativas o educativas de los centros metropolitanos de colonización. Los "discursos poscoloniales", serían discursos producidos tanto como discursos oposicionales a los primeros, como aquéllos que buscan nuevas formas y energías creativas despegadas de las instituciones políticas, administrativas y educativas coloniales. Pero también aquí hay zonas intermedias. En primer lugar, porque los discursos poscoloniales ponen de relieve las fuerzas de oposición después de las independencias nacionales, pero oscurecen formas de resistencia y de oposición antes del proceso de construcción nacional y en el interior mismo de situaciones coloniales. En segundo lugar, porque hay distintos tipos de "discursos poscoloniales". Aquéllos, por un lado, producidos por los líderes de la construcción nacional en la América Hispana, que proponían la independencia de España (por ejemplo, un colonialismo agonizante), a la vez que celebraban los imperialismos emergentes, como el británico y el francés, primero, y el estadounidense, luego. Y —por otro lado— aquéllos que hacia los años veinte (quizás con la única excepción de Martí a finales del siglo diecinueve), proponían nuevas formas de pensamiento poscolonial en la medida en que avisoran claramente las dimensiones de los nuevos imperialismos, todavía nacientes a principios del siglo diecinueve. Es en este segundo tipo de "discursos (y teorías) poscoloniales" en que podemos situar la teorización de las fronteras, de los espacios intermedios y de los legados de la semiosis colonial.

La "fagocitación" (y el pensamiento de los bordes y de los espacios entre medio como legados coloniales) es muy distinta de la síntesis hegeliana. Una interpretación dialéctica, sugiere Kusch, no se podrá pensar a la manera de Hegel:

> Para Hegel, la síntesis es una *Aufhebung* o sea, literalmente, una *elevación* o, como bien lo dice él mismo, "una elevación sobre lo finito". Esto supone buscar un mejoramiento en el sentido europeo y llevaría a justificar eso que dimos en llamar el ser en América. Como todo proceso dialéctico tiene su correlación con la realidad, tomada así en el sentido de buscar la *elevación*, significaría, que nuestra cultura de costa podría imponer su punto de vista mediante la fuerza e imponer plenamente una cultura montada sobre objetos. Pero, lo primero es falso, porque ni policía, ni moral, ni educacion, podrán llevar a cabo una *elevación* en el sentido del *ser*, porque eso sería ir contra la vida; ni tampoco el occidente europeo podrá seguir girando por mucho tiempo en torno a una exégesis exclusiva de los objetos (Kusch 1963: 171).

La síntesis que busca Kusch es la articulación de polaridades clásicas/el pensamiento moderno en América, como el de civilización y barbarie o costa y sierra en Perú. Kusch traduce estas oposiciones a una más fundamental, la del *ser* y la del *estar*: "La división de costa y sierra —que es típicamente peruana— reproduce a las claras este problema esencial de América: el que se refiere al distanciamiento del *ser* y el *estar*, y también el enfrentamiento dialéctico entre ambos" (165). Kusch insiste, basado en su propia vivencia de campo y en las de otros, en el hecho de que para las poblaciones indígenas las formas marginales de occidentalización no siempre son atractivas o envidiables. Hay, es cierto, migraciones de poblaciones indígenas a los centros urbanos, migraciones sin retorno, por decirlo así, y de distintas formas de adaptación. Pero básicamente, sostiene Kusch, es difícil pensar la síntesis hegeliana en una configuración social donde no es claro cuál de los dos componentes de la síntesis debe ser considerado como *elevación*, si la del *ser* o la del *estar*:

> ... en el plano estricto de la cultura (como praxis, agregado mío, WM) y no de civilización (como estado de cosas, agregado mío, WM), sólo cabe hablar en América de un probable predominio del *estar* sobre el *ser*, porque el *estar*, como visión del mundo, se da también en la misma Europa [...]. Por todo ello, no cabe hablar de una *elevación* sino más bien — en tanto se trata de un planteo nuevo para el occidental— de una distensión o, mejor, *fagocitación* del *ser* por el *estar*, antodo todo como un *ser* alguien, fagocitado por un *estar* aquí (Kusch 1963: 171).

En la medida en que Kusch concibe la modernidad como el avance y triunfo del "ser alguien" (y Colón es un buen ejemplo, tanto por la fecha como por la manera de encuadrar su proyecto), sobre el "estar," tal avance no se da sólo "sobre" las culturas nativas de Tawantinsuyu o de Anáhuac, sino también sobre formas de vida de la emergente Europa cristiana, en oposición y sobrevivencia, al avance de la civilización islámica. Es por eso que la fagocitación del *ser* por el *estar* es vista por Kusch como la "solución" americana al problema más amplio de la conjunción occidentalización-modernidad que comienza hacia finales del siglo XV y cuyos resultados actuales los vemos en la creciente globalización. El descubrimiento, conquista y colonización del Nuevo Mundo (como se suele describir todavía el acontecimiento y procesos posteriores), no es de relevancia particular para la historia de América y de España (tal como lo construyó la historiografía y la conciencia nacionalista, tanto en uno como en otro lado del Atlántico), sino fundamentalmente para la historia de la occidentalización del planeta, para la historia de una conciencia planetaria que va irrefutablemente unida a los procesos de colonización.[10]

Kusch explica mejor su noción de "fagocitación" al decir que al ser tomada como un acontecimiento de orden universal, se produce en un nivel que escapa a la conciencia histórica que Simmel, en la referencia de Kusch, colocaba en el umbral de la conciencia histórica y que, en nuestros días, podríamos analogar al "inconsciente político" de Jameson. Pero lo que es importante, en la elaboración de Kusch, es la relevancia que tiene su análisis —detenido— del manuscrito de Santacruz Pachacuti para elaborar su idea de la "fagocitación".

> Vivir consiste, entonces, en mantener el equilibrio entre orden y caos, que son las causas de la transitoriedad de todas las cosas, y ese equilibrio está dado por una débil pantalla mágica que se materializa en una simple y resignada sabiduría o en esquemas de tipo mágico. Nuestra cultura occidental, en cambio, se diferencia en que suprime de todos los opuestos, el lado malo, casi como si pretendiera que todo fuera orden ... Pero en este sentido nos aventaja el indio. Por eso resulta interesante el dato que nos trae Kubler, cuando nos dice que los indios consideraban a Cristo y al diablo como hermanos. Y eso es verdad porque si el indio suprimiera al diablo y lo sacara de su conciencia, ese mundo adquiriría demasiada tensión y perdería su arraigo o, lo que es lo mismo, perdería su control sobre el granizo y el trueno, que son precisamente los antagonistas del dios (1963: 176).

Al proponer la fagocitación como un proceso universal, Kusch está lejos de articular su propuesta en términos binarios, nativos vs. europeos. Y menos aún, formularlo como la esquemática cuestión del "otro", que sitúa el *ser* (el sí mismo, el ser alguien) como punto de referencia y como *locus* de enunciación que postula la otredad. Kusch sitúa el *ser* (ser alguien, el ser que define el "otro" (bárbaro, salvaje, iletrado, etc.) no-europeo) en el contexto de la modernidad, en ese período precisamente cuya gestación coincide con la colonización del Nuevo Mundo y, más aún, con la ubicación de una parte del planeta (igual en edad que todas las otras) como "nueva". Así, Kusch lleva el planteo desde la historicidad de la colonización a un nivel ontológico:

> Y evadiéndonos del plano indígena, diremos, ya en un terreno ontológico, si se quiere, que esa fagocitación ocurre en la misma medida en que la gran historia —o sea del *estar*— distorsiona, hasta engullirla, a la pequeña historia —la del *ser*—. Y es que la

---

[10] Esta tesis está ya en germen en varios momentos del pensamiento Americano y en la historia cultural en América del Sur, al menos desde los años cincuenta, Zea, 1959; O'Gorman, 1958.

fagocitación es una ley primitiva que consiste en que sea natural que haya distensión y que la tensión, como la del *ser*, sea antinatural o circunstancial. (Kusch, 1963: 177).

Kusch caracteriza el *estar* —en la conciencia de Occidente— como pasivo y femenino. La herencia del pensamiento indígena, que Kusch elabora a partir de Pachacuti Yamki, enseña que el *principio* no es un masculino sino lo masculino y lo femenino encarnados en un ente, Viracocha. Kusch interpreta que la preponderancia del *ser*, en el pensamiento moderno occidental, es una imposición de lo masculino sobre lo femenino. A partir de aquí puede entonces criticar, en los pensadores y constructores de la nación (en el siglo xix), la arraigada creencia de que ser civilizados es una cuestión de virilidad. Esta idea, que persiste en el siglo XIX, comienza a gestarse en el siglo XVI cuando el proceso "civilizador" comienza a imponer el *ser* sobre el *estar* y a construir la idea de la masculinidad del ser y la virilidad del proceso civilizador. Kusch argumenta sobre la base de una carta del español Manuel Carrillo Albornoz al argentino Cisneros, en los momentos previos a la independencia argentina, en la cual habla de la "afeminación que causan estos países". Kusch persigue esta idea en los escritos de varios próceres e intelectuales argentinos decimonónicos y concluye de la siguiente manera:

> Es evidente que no estaba errado el español (Albornoz). Detrás del término *afeminamiento* y de las expresiones utilizadas en las cartas mencionadas, se advierte que lo americano ejerce una acción nefasta sobre la mentalidad europea. Más allá del simple soporte geográfico, América pareciera provocar una cierta desazón, y como los próceres estaban empeñados en estabilizar la existencia en términos de *homo faber*, echan al muladar la *afeminación* de una América negra, todo lo otro, lo que no se logra resolver.[11]

La hermenéutica desde el "otro" que formuló Dussel en su último libro[12] en relación al legado de las culturas amerindias, estaba en las indagaciones de Kusch en 1963 y lo formula aún de manera más directa en 1970, en su libro *El pensamiento indígena y popular en América*. En ese trabajo, tomando como punto de referencia el "mapamundi" de Guaman Poma, lee la organización del espacio en ese mapa como alternativa, y no como "concepción previa", a la cartografía europea. No lo lee, tampoco, como expresión de formas precolombinas auténticas de organizar el espacio, sino como lugar donde se manifiesta el conflicto intercultural, donde la fagocitosis tiene su germinación. Esto es, en la apropiación que hace Guaman Poma de la cartografía y de la organización europea del espacio para rearticular (o reconvertir), lo que proviene de otra memoria. No se trata en Kusch de una "hermenéutica desde el otro" sino, mejor, una hermenéutica del espacio-entre-medio como lo formulara Silviano Santiago (Santiago 1971), o del "nepantla" Nahua (Pat Mora), o de la frontera y la nueva mestiza (Anzaldúa 1987); o, en fin, de la "transculturación" concebida por Fernando Ortiz.

3.- No deja de ser extraño que el debate sobre la postmodernidad tenga ya varios años y varias publicaciones en América Latina, pero que la postcolonialidad —en cambio— no

---

[11] Kusch (1970): 135.
[12] Dussel, 1993b.

haya despertado el mismo interés. No es este el lugar para preguntarse por qué sucedieron así las cosas. Con estas notas quiero subrayar distintas maneras de responder, en América Latina, al proceso de occidentalización. Esto es, de responder a las herencias coloniales mediante teorías postcoloniales. Uno podría preguntarse por qué este tipo de teorías tuvo tanto arraigo, en cambio, en la intelectualidad relacionada con Asia, el mundo Árabe o África. Es curioso que las teorías (respuestas) postcoloniales hayan surgido en las regiones culturales que experimentaron la segunda etapa de occidentalización, aquélla llevada adelante fundamentalmente por Inglaterra y Francia. Pero es curiosamente Frantz Fanon, un caribeño que por escribir en francés y por haber vivido en una experiencia y legado colonial distinto al hispano, no tuvo mucho arraigo en Hispanoamérica. Y son otros escritores caribeños, como Cesaire, Lamming, Glissant quienes desde los años cincuenta practican un tipo de crítica y teoría postcolonial. De ellos aprendió mucho Roberto Fernández Retamar cuyo *Calibán* fue leído y se sigue leyendo como un discurso hispanoamericano, aunque un tanto extraño para los legados de las colonias españolas en América.

Todo ello me lleva a enfatizar la necesidad de repensar las herencias coloniales y las teorías postcoloniales junto a una reconfiguración geopolítica y geocultural de las Américas. La división tanto geopolítica como geocultural (particularmente geolingüística), es el resultado de distribuciones y clasificaciones coloniales. Esto es, son herencias coloniales, en el propio sentido de la palabra herencia. La incomunicación (o la poca y dificultosa) comunicación entre Hispanoamérica, Brazil y las islas del Caribe (cuyas lenguas oficiales son tanto el español como el francés y el inglés), es obra tanto de la distribución geocultural colonialista como de los resabios de las herencias coloniales en la organización y distribución del saber. Una de las tareas (quizás de descolonización intelectual) que la teorización postcolonial nos puede ayudar a llevar adelante es la de repensar la superposición de herencias coloniales, en áreas culturales como las Américas y el Caribe, en vez de hacerlo siguiendo una división de fronteras lingüísticas y sus correspondientes cronologías lingüístico-económico-imperiales. En consecuencia, las teorías postcoloniales pueden convertirse en un instrumento útil para la reorganización del saber, la política cultural y la programación curricular, medios particulares de llevar adelante la descolonización intelectual; o, si se quiere, de tomar en serio el hecho de que los "orígenes" no están en Grecia sino en cualquier lugar. Esto es, de tomar en serio la política de la ubicación geocultural como de la ética y política de la enunciación.

Al leer a Edouard Glissant (1981), por ejemplo, en su crítica a las nociones de Literatura y de Historia como instrumentos de colonización (por ejemplo, reorganización hegemónica y supresión de las formas de expresión caribeña), se subraya la importancia de la lengua (colonial o imperial, poco importa en este caso), en el mantenimiento de nociones y prácticas inventadas para cubrir necesidades en otros suelos y cómo éstas se convierten en formas de represión y de control (justificadas en valores culturales), en regiones colonizadas (o reguladas por distintos imperialismos):

> [...] History is written with a capital H. It is a totality that excludes other histories that do not fit into that of the West. *Perhaps therein lies the link between Bossuet (Providence) and Marx (the class struggle): this ethnocentric principle unites the mechanics of the Historical process (the Christian God, the proletariat of industrialized nations) with the*

sould of the West. The hierarchical system instituted by Hegel (ahistory, prehistory, History) corresponds clearly with the literary ideology of his time.

Literature attains a metaexistence, the all-powerfulness of a sacred sign, which will allow people with writing to think it is justified to dominate and rule people with and oral civilization. And the last Western attempt to conceptualize a History, that of Toynbee, will organize the Total System based on a discriminatory sequence (great civilizations, great states, great religions) indispensable in such a project.

It is against this double hegemony of a History with a capital H and a Literature consacrated by the absolute power of the written sign that the people who until now inhabited the hidden side of the earth fought, at the same time they were fighting for food and freedom.[13]

Estas observaciones están ligadas al argumento que construye Glissant sobre la enseñanza de diversas literaturas ("on the teaching of literatures") en francés fuera de Francia. El problema que ve Glissant es uno de locaciones asignadas por la hegemonía de las culturas imperiales y, en este caso, de Francia. De tal modo que la enseñanza presupone una comparación y de la comparación entre literaturas francesas fuera de Francia y la literatura francesa en Francias, las primeras salen perdiendo porque la comparación se hace según las reglas del juego establecidas para la segunda. Algo semejante ocurrió con las literaturas hispánicas fuera de España en el siglo XIX y principios del XX, hasta el momento en que la literatura del "boom" modifica la perspectiva. Modificación que implica cierto riesgo: la producción de una literatura postcolonial que es reconocida por los valores hegemónicos de las culturas colonizadoras. Glissant, en cambio, busca otras soluciones. Esto es, expresiones que "salen" por así decirlo del círculo de la práctica literaria o que ponen a la literatura "fuera de lugar", en el baile, en el canto, en el teatro popular, en los relatos orales, etc. Pero es aquí donde viene la objeción: "These are not literatures (en francés fuera de Francia) that allow a human being to understand himself and to be himself".[14] Michele Cliff puso de relieve el mismo problema al señalar que, en Jamaica, el inglés de la isla se compara, y trata de ser domado, por el inglés imperial ("the King's English").

6.- El proceso de occidentalización es más ancho y más largo, por así decirlo, de lo que ocurrió en los siglos, XVI al XVIII en el Caribe, México y Perú. El Caribe es quizás el ejemplo donde los sucesivos estratos de colonización (de expansión imperial y de occidentalización), se perciben en sus continuidades y rupturas. La América hispana, en general, pasó por el período de la construcción nacional en la difícil encrucijada de desprenderse de la herencia colonial (o imperial) hispánica y tratar de negociar otro tipo de relaciones con los imperialismos sucesivos dominantes, el inglés y el francés primero y el norteamericano después. La cuestión para el futuro de los estudios coloniales es dónde poner el acento: en la división lingüística (por ejemplo, aquellas áreas donde la occidentalización estuvo ligada al español, al portugués, al francés o al inglés); a la división geo-cultural (por ejemplo, los Andes, Mesoamérica, el Caribe), o en los sucesivos momentos de desplazamiento de la conceptualización amerindia de su propio territorio y su reemplazo

---

[13] Glissant, 1981, 75-76.
[14] Glissant, 1981, 171.

por construcciones imaginarias del discurso colonial (o imperial): Indias Occidentales, Nuevo Mundo, América, Hemisferio Occidental, etc.

En todo caso, el lugar de la crítica y teoría postcoloniales sería el de la permanente construcción de lugares diferenciales de enunciación en los marcos discursivos (por ejemplo, discurso colonial) construidos por los sucesivos momentos del proceso de occidentalización: desde la expansión mercantilista hasta la globalización pasando por la revolución industrial y la expansión capitalista. Como prácticas culturales, la crítica y la teoría postcoloniales contribuirían a mantener en constante vigilancia, hasta disolverlos, conceptos que conservan las divisiones imperiales entre Oriente y Occidente, entre primer y tercer mundo, entre salvajes y civilizados, entre centro y periferia. En la medida en que estos conceptos y polaridades tienden a ser negados hoy por ciertos discursos académicos, pero siguen teniendo vigencia en diversos discursos sociales, la cuestión no es la de repetir que la división entre "primer y tercer mundo" es falsa o que "centro y periferia" es un mito, si no la de desmontar las condiciones de posibilidad y las motivaciones de necesidad que produjeron esas construcciones imaginarias y que todavía hoy las mantienen. Las cuestiones fundamentales siguen siendo, todavía:

—si el "orientalismo" es todo discurso que produce una imagen (por ejemplo, una locación imaginaria) del Oriente, ¿hasta qué punto es posible la "relocación imaginaria", por parte de los sujetos que son localizados como orientales, sin caer en nuevas formas de "orientalismo"?

—dado que una pregunta semejante se podría hacer con respecto al "occidentalismo" como construcción imaginaria que se produce en el mismo gesto de construir el "orientalismo", ¿cuáles son las diferencias entre la construcción del "extremo Occidente" o del "hemisferio occidental" y el "orientalismo?"

Mi respuesta tentativa a estas preguntas es, al mismo tiempo, una justificación de la crítica y la teoría postcoloniales: mientras que "orientalismo" y "extremo Occidente" son construcciones imaginarias, "occidentalismo" es, en cambio, la construcción del *lugar de la enunciación* que hace posible la construcción del "Oriente y del extremo Occidente". La crítica y la teoría postcoloniales tienen, entre una tarea posible, ganar lo que fue negado por la occidentalización (entendida "expansión del lugar de enunciación"). Esto es, construir nuevos lugares legítimos de enunciación que hagan posible la re-locación de las construcciones imaginarias (Oriente, extremo Occidente), producida expansión occidental, por el crecimiento monstruoso de la creencia de que el lugar de enunciación es sólo uno, el de Occidente: esto es, el de las humanidades (filosofía, historia literatura, etc.) y de la historia de la ciencia (sociales y naturales), cuya necesidad constante es la de remitirse al pensamiento griego como referencia del origen. Kusch nos enseña a escuchar otras voces, voces de igual consistencia pero "subalternizadas" por el *locus* de enunciación colonial que se construyó, a partir del siglo XVI, distribuyendo y desplazando identidades que, a finales del XX, tratamos de redistribuir y resituar. En suma, el proceso de "allocation of meaning" engendrado y mantenido por el discurso colonial, va acompañado por el proceso de "relocation of meaning" que el primero engendra como la otra cara de la moneda, y por el proceso más reciente en que la crítica y las teorías postcoloniales intentan repensar los dos procesos anteriores (y sus consecuencias actuales), como práctica oposicional.

BIBLIOGRAFÍA

Appiah, Anthony. "Is the Post— in Postmodernism Postcolonial?" *Critical Inquiry* 17/2: 336-357.

Bhabha, Hommi. (in Greemblat).

Dirlik, Arif. "The Postcolonial Aura: Third World Criticism in the Age of Global Capitalism". *Critical Inquiry* 20/2 (1994): 328-356.

Dussel, Enrique. "Eurocentrism and Modernity (Introduction to the Frankfurt Lectures)". *Boundary 2* 20/3 (1993a): 65-76.

Dussel, Enrique. *Philosophy of Liberation* (1980). Translated from Spanish by Aquilina Martinez and Christine Morkovsky. New York: Orbis Book, 1988.

Dussel, Enrique. *1492. El encubrimiento del otro. Hacia el origen del mito de la modernidad.* Madrid: Nueva Utopia, 1993.

Fanon, Frantz. *Los condenados de la tierra* (1961). Traducción de Julieta Campos. México: Fondo de Cultura Económico, 1963.

Fernández Retamar, Roberto. "Calibán: apuntes sobre la cultura en nuestra América". *Para el perfil definitivo del hombre.* La Habana: Editorial Letras Cubanas,1981. 219-290.

Glissant, Edouard. *Caribbean Discourse. Selected Essays* (1981). Translated by Michael Dash. Charlottsville: University of Virginia, 1989.

Huntington, Samuel P. "The Clash of Civilizations?" *Foreign Affairs* 72/3 (1993): 22-49.

Klor de Alva, Jorge. "Colonialism and Post Colonialism as (Latin) American Mirages". *Colonial Latin American Review* I/1-2: 3-25.

Kusch, Rodolfo. *El pensamiento indígena y popular en América.* Buenos Aires: Hachette, 1970.

Lamming, George. *The Pleasure of Exile* (1960). Ann Arbor: Michigan University Press, 1992.

Mignolo, Walter D. "Anahuac y sus otros: la cuestión de la letra en el Nuevo Mundo". *Revista Latinoamericana de Crítica Literaria*, 28 (1988): 29-53.

O'Gorman, Edmundo. *La invención de América.* México: UNAM, 1958.

Ortiz, Fernando. *Contrapunto cubano del tabaco y del azúcar* (1940). Caracas: Biblioteca Ayacucho, 1978.

Santiago, Silviano. "O entre-lugar do discurso latino-americano". *Uma literatura nos tropicos: essaios sobre dependencia cultural.* (1971). São Paulo: Editora Perspectiva, 1978.

Shammas, Anton. "Going Home: The Case of Palestine, Michigan". Lectured delivered at Duke University, February of 1994. Manuscript version.

Shohat, Ella. "Notes on the 'Post-Colonial'". *Social Text* 31/32 (1993): 99-113.

Zea, Leopoldo. *América en la historia.* México: Fondo de Cultura Económica, 1959.

Zea, Leopoldo. *Discurso desde la marginación y la barbarie.* Barcelona: Anthropos, 1988.

Culture as Text:
The Cuban/Caribbean Connection

WILLIAM LUIS *for Sandro Sticca*

The translation of Latin American literature reached a milestone during the literary explosion caused by the novel of the Boom period in the decade of the 60s. The Boom was a period of literary experimentation and creativity in which Latin American authors received international notoriety, as was the case with Borges, who was awarded the Fomentor Prize with Beckett in 1961. The translation of Latin American literature mainly into English and French, but also into Swedish, Hungarian, Italian, German, Norwegian, and Russian gave it international recognition and appeal. In this essay, I am going to look at the issues raised by the conference on "Translating Latin America," April 19–21, as a corolla around Cuba and the Caribbean. I shall take up the crucial role of Cuba in the Boom and post-Boom periods, the role of translation in exporting the nexus of cultures, and the emblematic anomaly of Juan Francisco Manzano, the Cuban slave autobiographer. Manzano's text represents the problematic role of translation and will serve as a transition to the treatment of Spanish in several concrete examples from Garcilaso de la Vega, El Inca, to the Nuyorican poet Tato Laviera.

Political and historical circumstances helped to promote the translation of Latin American works and the novel of the Boom period. Some of the most important events of the Boom pertained to changing events in Cuba. Castro's Revolution occurred a few years before the publication of such master works as Gabriel García Márquez's *Cien años de soledad*, Guillermo Cabrera Infante's *Tres tristes tigres*, Carlos Fuentes *La muerte de Artemio Cruz*, Mario Vargas Llosa's *La casa verde*, and Julio Cortázar's *Rayuela*. At the outset of the Revolution, Cuba received the support of many intellectuals, including the authors who would soon be associated with the Boom. In turn, the Castro government promoted writers who were sympathetic to the Revolution and some of them became international figures. The Revolution and the subsequent Cuban Missile Crisis brought both the Island and the Caribbean and Latin America to the attention of world opinion. Cuba and the Caribbean threatened to become the space which marked the beginning of World War Three.

Castro's initial emphasis on social, educational, and cultural programs and his attempt to spread revolutions throughout Latin America and the Caribbean were challenged by Kennedy's Alliance for Progress, an economic program which intended to address the issues of poverty and economic development, believed to be the stronghold of Communism. Hugh Thomas pointed out that the economic package for Latin America was an idea Castro had proposed in Argentina while attending a meeting of the committee of 21 Latin American countries, in the Organization of American States. At the meeting Castro stated the the United States should provide Latin America with $30 billion over a ten year period. Kennedy publicized the idea of the Alliance in his campaign for the presidency and, during his stay in office, he stated that his program needed $20 billion.[1] Referring to the Alliance, Thomas would later state, "Had it not been for the Cuban issue, doubtless such a scheme would never have received any backing."[2]

The Alliance for Progress promoted the types of programs which were already in place in Cuba. The emphasis on education, literacy, and culture was accompanied by an increased number of publishing houses and books. After the fall of Batista, Cuba experienced in the early 60s a literary explosion of its own. The initiative began with the controversial literary supplement *Lunes de Revolución* (1959–61), edited by Guillermo Cabrera Infante, which gave a voice to young Cuban writers, but also to others from Latin America and Europe. Writers of *Lunes de Revolución* promoted a vernacular literature, recognized the importance of foreign literature, and translated many works from the French, English, and other languages. Soon after, other cultural and literary organizations were founded on the Island. With the backing of the National Council of Culture, groups such as the Unión Nacional de Escritores y Artistas de Cuba (UNEAC) and the Instituto Cubano de Artes e Industrias Cinematográficos (ICAIC) successfully rivaled *Lunes de Revolución* to influence the development of culture with their own journals and publishing houses. The demise of *Lunes* represented a political shift in Castro and his government, away from the supporters of the 26th of July Movement and towards those of the Communist Party. The changes in cultural policy in Cuba culminated with the Padilla Affair of 1971 which created a split among intellectuals and Boom writers, dividing them into two groups: those in support of and those against the Revolution. The Padilla Affair ended the unity among Latin American writers and signaled the start of the post-Boom period.[3]

Events in the United States played an important part in the emergence of the Boom novel and the translation of Latin American literature. During the 60s, many universities throughout the United States established new Latin American Studies programs and strengthened existing ones to follow events in Cuba and other Caribbean and Latin American countries and continued to focus attention on the region. Curiosity about Latin America spread throughout the United States, and literature in translation evolved as a way of understanding the cultures of the neighbors to the South. Literature became an avenue of interpreting the complexity of Latin American thought and culture.

Translations from Spanish into English did exist before the decade of the 60s, but with the novel of the Boom period there is a noticeable increase in the number of works translated. Immediately preceeding the Boom period, in the decade of the 50s, René L.F. Durand and Harriet de Onís took on the challenging task of translating Alejo Carpentier's works. Durand led the way by translating into French *El reino de este mundo* (1949) as *Le Royaume de ce monde* in 1954 and De Onis the same novel into English as *The Kingdom of This World* in 1957. Durand continued his interest in Carpentier and provided readers with a translation of *Los pasos perdidos* (1953) as *Le Partage des eaux* in 1956, and *El acoso* (1956) as *Chasse à l'homme* in 1958, and De Onís translated the same works as *The Lost Steps* in 1956 and *Manhunt* in 1959. In the decade of the sixties, Durand continued to make a career of translating Carpentier's works and Onís's task was taken over by John Sturrock.

An explosion of translations from the Spanish to the English accompanied the works published during the Boom period, as well as the formation of translation centers and programs. A significant number of Latin American works in translation began to make their way into the *New York Times Book Review* and some, like *One Hundred Years of Solitude* and *Hopscotch* even became best sellers.

Without a doubt, Gregory Rabassa is the most important translator of Latin American works and is mainly responsible for introducing them to a North American audience. Rabassa accepted the challenge by translating the best and most difficult writers, such as García Márquez, Vargas Llosa, Lezama Lima, and Cortázar. Rabassa's master translations include García Márquez's *One Hundred Years of Solitude* and Cortázar's *Hopscotch* (1966). Margaret Sayers Peden, whose own translations include Fuentes's *The Hydra Head, Terra Nostra,* and *Distant Relations,* expressed what many readers felt about *Hopscotch* and Rabassa's translation: "This book, this translation must surely be considered one of the breakthrough publications in Latin American literature in the English-speaking world, setting the stage for many works to follow. . . . The translation, as indicated, is similarly a milestone in Spanish American literature."[4]

The textual strategies contained in contemporary Latin American literature allowed for an easy marriage between literature and criticism, insofar as the literature proposed its own theory of criticism. *Rayuela* addressed the question of how we read and offered a more daring way of deciphering the novel. The reader is provided with a Table of Directions and is encouraged to read the novel not in a conventional way, that is, from beginning to end, but to skip sections, to jump back and forth in a prescribed manner until the reading is completed, surprisingly without ever setting eyes on Chapter 55 (In reality, the reading is never completed since chapter 131, the last chapter, refers you to chapter 58, the next to last chapter, which in turn refers you back to chapter 131). In fact, the reader is inspired to make up his own "Tablero de dirección," and each combination of chapters produces a different reading and understanding of the work. *Tres tristes tigres* proposes a theory of translation and reproduces a short story in its different stages of translation. The novel also captures or translates the voices of some of Cuba's best known authors into the pages of the novel. However, for Cabrera Infante, translation is an act of betrayal.

Indeed, literature and criticism have helped to define and redefine translation. One of the most recent works of criticism to do so is Gustavo Pérez Firmat's *The Cuban Condition,* a work which considers Cuban culture to be translational insofar as the presence of foreign models in Cuba is restated within the same culture. Pérez Firmat shows that in Cuba, foreign elements have been absorbed and have become an integral part of Cuban culture. Pérez Firmat considers Cuba's lack of an insular culture to be "translation sensibility" and, for him, "Cuban style *is* a translation style."

Pérez Firmat concentrates on 20th-century Cuban literature and relies on the works of Fernando Ortiz to identify four concepts essential for understanding Cuban culture: transculturation, the impact of the coming together of cultures; *cubanía*, a self awareness and wanting of what is Cuban; *ajiaco*, a stew or hodgepodge of sorts; and *catauro*, literal Cubanisms. Each of these concepts is a Cuban translation of a hegemonic term: "*transculturation* for acculturation, *ajiaco* for melting pot; *catauro* for dictionary; and *cubanía* for *cubanidad*."[5] Pérez Firmat's assertions have broader implications insofar as they provide a framework to explore how other cultures are integrated and translated into a national one. In present-day Cuban culture they suggest a restatement of the presence of Soviet culture for those living on the Island and that of North American culture for the Cuban exile community.

Translation as defined by Cabrera Infante and Pérez Firmat poses interesting problems which are present in their complexity in the 19th century with Juan Francisco Manzano's slave autobiography.[6] Manzano's slave autobiography, which is at the center of the emergence of Cuban narrative, was requested by Cuban critic Domingo Del Monte. An opponent of slavery and the slave trade, Del Monte found literary merit in Manzano's poetry and, although it was prohibited, he helped the slave publish his *Poesías líricas* (1821) and *Flores pasageras* [sic] (1830). More importantly, Del Monte encouraged Manzano to write his autobiography which he completed in 1835, and one year later members of the Del Monte literary salon rewarded the slave by purchasing his freedom. For Manzano, writing resulted in the slave's physical liberation. In his autobiography, Manzano tells us that he learned to read and write on his own and experienced two types of slavery: under his kind masters he was treated as if he were a white child and under the Marquesa de Prado Ameno he was punished as a common slave.

As it was to be expected, Manzano did not have a total command of the Spanish language and wrote his autobiography with numerous grammatical mistakes. However, in order to make it presentable to members of the literary salon, Del Monte asked Anselmo Suárez y Romero to correct Manzano's text and make it readable. By correcting Manzano's grammar, Suárez y Romero in effect translates Manzano's original into standard Spanish. In comparing Manzano's autobiography with Suárez y Romero's version, I have noticed that not only did Suárez y Romero translate Manzano's autobiography, but significantly altered the manuscript, thus, providing the reader with a text other than what the slave had written.[7] If the original revealed the psychic complexity of a slave who experienced both sides of the slavery system, Suárez y Romero eliminated all positive references to Manzano's cruel mistress, including his rhetorical claims that "He loved her as a mother." Among other things, Manzano wanted to make known his talents, justify his escape to Havana, and protect himself against his mistress. Suárez y Romero translated Manzano's life; he rearranged the sequence of events and punishments in order to make Manzano's life even more unbearable than what the slave had lived, thus making Manzano's denunciation against slavery stronger than what the slave had intended. Suárez y Romero's translation of Manzano's original betrays the slave and his autobiography and strips it of the complexity of his life and the rhetorical strategies he employed.

Del Monte encouraged members of his literary salon to oppose slavery and the slave trade. By the time Del Monte asked Suárez y Romero to correct Manzano's autobiography, Richard Madden, the British arbiter in Mixed Court, had already arrived in Cuba and was collecting information for his antislavery portfolio, information he would present to the Antislavery Convention in London. I believe that Madden's presence in Cuba was the principal reason Suárez y Romero rewrote Manzano's life. He, and perhaps with the consent of Del Monte, changed the text to make the strongest case possible against slavery in Cuba, altered the manuscript, and produced not the slave Manzano, but the slave the white patrons wanted him to be.

Madden translated into English not Manzano's autobiography, but Suárez y Romero's translation of it, possibly believing he had received a corrected version of the slave's life. Madden published Manzano's "autobiography," along with some of his own poems, some of Manzano's, and interviews with Del Monte, under the title *Poems by a Slave in the Island of Cuba* in London in 1840.

Needless to say, in his translation Madden made some changes of his own, producing yet another version of the one Suárez y Romero had corrected.[8]

Manzano's autobiography becomes even more interesting when we realize that his original text disappeared for many decades and was not published until 1937 by José Luciano Franco.[9] Not Manzano's original, but Suárez y Romero's translation circulated in the 19th century. The few references to Manzano's autobiography that exist are to Suárez y Romero's text and to Madden's translation. Nevertheless, Manzano's original was finally published by Franco. But Franco's edition should only be viewed as another translation of the original. In his *Suite para Juan Francisco Manzano*, Roberto Friol has shown that Franco did not copy the slave poet's autobiography accurately.[10] A careful comparison between the manuscript housed in the Biblioteca Nacional José Martí and the one published in 1937 reveals significant discrepancies between the two texts.[11] The illegible and crossed out words contained in the original manuscript have been filled in taking into account Franco's knowledge of the period but also his own literary concerns. Not until 1975 did Ivan Schulman provide readers with a modern version of Manzano's autobiography.[12] Currently there are three Spanish translations and one English translation of Manzano's original autobiography, and each one represents a different aspect of Manzano's life.

If we were to take Pérez Firmat's formulations and our own ideas on the Manzano texts to their ultimate conclusions, in still broader terms, translation implies the passage of a sign from one medium or text to another, even if it were to take place in the same language. From this perspective Saussure's binary opposition between speech and language is useful.[13] The "language" spoken in each of the Spanish American countries can be understood as a speech act within the broader Spanish language and the shifts of the *parole* among various nations can be interpreted as translations of sorts. José Donoso has asserted that one of the characteristics of the Boom period is that writers of the different countries found out about each other and began to read one another's works.[14] I would also add that these same writers became aware of the individual use of language spoken in the Spanish American world and the need to translate or understand them. Some critics would argue that readers are wise to use a dictionary of local or national uses to comprehend, for example, *Tres tristes tigres* written in Cuban, Luis Rafael Sánchez's *La guaracha del Macho Camacho* written in Puerto Rican, or José Agustín's *Cuál es la onda* written in Mexican. As an anthropologist, Ortiz was already aware of the nature of the Cuban *parole* when he began to research his *Un catauro de cubanismos*.[15]

A similar argument can be made about understanding the various intra-related cultures contained within a country's dominant one. For example, in his *Biografía de un cimarrón*, Miguel Barnet provides the reader with a translation of Afro-Cuban slave and black culture. And in *Me llamo Rigoberta Menchú*, Elizabeth Burgos does the same with the Quiché culture of Guatemala. Moreover, a case can be made to illustrate that marginal or isolated individuals like Manzano, Esteban Montejo, and Rigoberta Menchú are translating themselves in order to make their stories available to a broader reading audience. That is, they are viewing their slave or Amerindian past not as they lived it, but from the perspective of an outsider. Therefore, they recuperate the past and translate it in order for it to be understood in the present. It should be noted that in so doing, the informant manipulates his own discourse to present the reader with a partial reading of his/her past. As in the case of the editor of Manzano's autobiography, anthropologists Barnet and Burgos, despite appearances, do not provide their readers with the accounts transcribed, but with a translation of them. Due to his/her knowledge of the subject matter and the dominant language, the anthropologist gives the manuscript a certain consistency in the chronology, language, and events, which at times may include a reordering of them, unfamiliar to the informant or absent in the "original" text. When referring to his testimonial novel *La canción de Rachel*, Barnet stated, " 'This is her story, her life as she told it to me and as I later told it back to her.' Many things are implicit in that statement."[16]

The concept of cultural translation appears to be a fundamental component of the New World. For Europeans, the New World existed in their works before Columbus's first voyage. And Columbus and other European conquerers and explorers attempted to record their findings from a cultural and historic referent, that is, as it was understood from a Spanish or European perspective. This was certainly the case with the chroniclers of the New World such as Bartolomé de las Casas, Gonzalo Fernández de Oviedo, Francisco de Herrera y Tordesillas, Lope de Aguirre, and Felipe Guaman Poma de Ayala. It is as if European writers were imposing familiar ideas and concepts on a new reality and were therefore translating what they saw and experienced into a language which they and others like them could understand. In recent times, the works of anthropologists like Levi Strauss, but also Barnet and Burgos, continue a similar task. During the periods of the conquest and colony, Europeans imposed a language and culture on the native inhabitants of America and also on other racial groups brought to work in the New World, such as Africans and Chinese. All were discouraged from using their own languages and when dealing with their white masters or employers, they were forced to translate themselves into terms prescribed by the dominant European culture.

The coming together of a dominant and a non-dominant culture, one imposing itself on the other and the second attempting to liberate itself from the first, is at the origin of the problematic of the "discovery" of the New World and of translation. Garcilaso de la Vega, el Inca, embodies both. He was the first mediator to narrate Latin America and to translate it from within. The son of an Inca noblewoman and of a Spanish conqueror, Garcilaso mediated between two languages and cultural perspectives. In his *Myth and Archive: A Theory of Latin American Narrative*, Roberto González Echevarría shows that legal writing was at the origin of the literatures of Spain and Latin America. Garcilaso, the Inca had an excellent command of Spanish and as his father's scribe, he learned the legal rhetoric used in the 16th century. However, I propose that when writing both his *Comentarios reales* and the *Historia general del Perú*, Garcilaso translated his native knowledge about the pre-Inca empires into Spanish, a language with preconceived cultural and legal referents. As a translator, he captures concepts and structures of one language and culture and reorganizes and transforms them into the dominant discourse of the times.

The figure of the Inca represents translation as a mediated form of understanding that which is foreign or, according to contemporary criticism, as an attempt to capture a trace of a lost origin. The Inca was the illegitimate son of Sebastián Garcilaso de la Vega, who married Doña Luisa Martel de los Ríos. The Inca's father had his mother, Chimpu Ocllo, marry Spaniard Juan del Pedroche. The Inca's illegitimacy is emblematic of a theory of translating Latin American culture as text. The Inca mediated between his parent's languages and cultures when he wrote about the pre-Inca and Inca civilizations and European historiography, that is, he had to translate from the native, mother language and culture to that of his estranged father and his stepfather. As González Echevarría points out, "By the time Garcilaso wrote his masterpiece, the history of America had been told and retold by numerous historians, explorers, and discoverers, so that what the Inca undertook was, of necessity, a revisionist task."[17] From our perspective, Garcilaso, the mediator, offered a more genuine translation of the history of Latin America, one which situated him closer to the original (mother) texts. In the *Comentarios reales* and the *Historia general del Perú*, he mediates between the cultures and corrects previous texts by inscribing his family and himself in Western history. In essence, the Inca was documenting his legitimacy which the courts had refused to recognize. El Inca is twice the heir of the lands of Peru: first as a direct descendant of Inca nobility and second as the son of the conqueror Sebastián Garcilaso de la Vega with entitlement to all privileges and exemptions.

Just as El Inca and Manzano and other marginal people who are forced to employ another language and translate between cultures, in contemporary society, Puerto Rican writers born and living in New York are doing the same with important distinctions. I propose that the Caribbean is a floating metaphor. The interaction of cultures and migration of Caribbean people is not limited to the geographical space known as the Caribbean, but is also present in the United States. Cities such as New York, Miami, and Newark are Caribbean cities of sorts. The coming together of different cultures in the United States has produced a bilingual and bicultural literature best associated with the Nuyorican authors. Writers such as Tato Laviera, Nicolasa Mohr, and Pedro Pietri, to name only three, are concerned with translating their experiences from one cultural framework to another and (at times) back again. These authors and their works have become a filter which separates an experience, event, or emotion and interprets it from two distinct points of view, one pertaining to the North American cultural experience and the other to the Hispanic or Puerto Rican one. They translate themselves and write, think, and speak in two (native) languages. Laviera's *La Carreta Made a U-Turn* (1981) is a rewriting of René Marqués's widely acclaimed play *La carreta* (1953), which narrates the migratory process a family must undergo, from the countryside, to the city, abroad to New York City, and back again to the Island. However, being closer to the New York experience, for Laviera, *la carreta* does not return to Puerto Rico but stays in New York to chronicle life and struggles of those who chose to make the City their home. In his works, Laviera is careful to write in both Spanish and English and to concern himself with issues pertinent to the Island and the mainland and their respective cultures.[18]

Closer to our concerns is Laviera's "Asimilao," which is written in both Spanish and English and addresses the issue of translation. The poem reads as follows:

assimilated? que assimilated,
brother, yo soy asimilao,
asi mi la o si es verdad
tengo un lado asimilao.
You see, they went deep .... Ass
oh .... they went deeper ... SEE
oh, oh, ... they went deeper ... ME
but the sound LAO was too black
for LATED, LAO could not be
tran*slated*, assimilated,
no, asimilao, melao,
it became a black
spanish word but
we do have asimilados
perfumados and by the
last count even they
were becoming asimilao
how can it be analyzed
as american? asi que se
chavaron
trataron
pero no
pudieron
con el AO
de la palabra
principal, deles gracias a los prietos
que cambiaron asimilado al popular asimilao.[19]

The poem raises the issues of bilingualism, biculturalism, self awareness, and pride. The poetic voice is attempting to define a place between the center and the margin, the dominant language and the popular one, high culture and popular culture, the white world and the black one. The poetic voice recognizes that he lives in one world, but is resistant to accepting or translating certain words, expressions, habits, or aspects of his Hispanic culture. Some things cannot be translated nor are they negotiable.

Note that the poem is written in two languages beginning with English, but with Spanish slowly introduced until it gains in intensity towards the end and overpowers the dominant language. Conceptually, the poem progresses from "assimilated," translates it to *asimilado* and ends by producing the popular *asimilao*. There is an implicit shift which takes place from "asi mi la o" to "asi mi lao," insofar as it underscores "my side," or "my point of view."

The duality of the two cultures seen in Laviera's works is also present in *Memorias de Bernardo Vega*, the first work to narrate the history of Puerto Ricans in New York. Vega, who was born in Puerto Rico but spent most of his adult life in New York, traces the origin of Puerto Ricans and Cubans in the United States to the middle of the 19th century. As a product of two cultures, Vega straddles the fence between the lives of Puerto Rican immigrants who arrive in New York and those of mainstream North Americans. At the end of his memoirs, Vega abandons writing to help elect Henry Wallace, the presidential candidate of the "Third Party." Vega is the only one able to represent the Puerto Rican experience in New York to newly arriving immigrants from the Island and to those belonging to the dominant North American culture. He is native to both cultures.

As critics and translators interpret certain experiences in one language or culture to readers in another, with an increasing number of Puerto Rican and other Caribbean or Latin American writers living in the United States and writing in two languages, they will have to confront still another dimension of the problematics of translating culture as text.

SUNY-Binghamton

NOTES

1. Hugh Thomas, *The Cuban Revolution* (New York: Harper and Row, 1977), 433.

2. Ibid., 528.

3. For a review of the literary and cultural background leading up to the Padilla Affair see: Seymour Menton, *Prose Fiction of the Cuban Revolution* (University of Texas Press, 1975), 123–56. Also see: Lourdes Casal, *El caso Padilla* (Miami: Ediciones Universal, 1971). The Padilla Affair ended the good will that existed among intellectuals who supported the Revolution and initiated an end to the Boom period. See my intoduction to *Voices from Under: Black Narrative in Latin America and the Caribbean* (Westport, Ct.: Greenwood Press, 1984). For additional characteristics of the post-Boom, see: Donald Shaw, "Towards and Description of the Post-Boom," *BHS*, 66 (1989): 87–94 and Roberto González Echevarría, *La ruta de Severo Sarduy* (Hanover, N.H.: Ediciones del Norte, 1987).

4. *Handbook of Latin American Studies*, 42 (1980): 683.

5. Gustavo Pérez Firmat, *The Cuban Condition: Translation and Identity in Modern Cuban Literature* (Cambridge: Cambridge University Press, 1989), 31.

6. For a detailed explanation of Juan Francisco Manzano, see my chapter "Textual Multiplications: Juan Francisco Manzano's *Autobiografía* and Cirilo Villaverde's *Cecilia Valdés*," *Literary Bondage: Slavery in Cuban Narrative* (University of Texas Press, 1990), 82–100.

7. I analyze the Suárez y Romero version in my "Autobiografía de esclavo Juan Francisco Manzano: versión de Suárez y Romero," in *La historia en la literatura iberoamericana*, ed. Raquel Chang-Rodríguez and Gabriela de Beer (Hanover, N.H.: Ediciones del Norte, 1989), 259–68.

8. In a comparison between the Spanish and the English, the reader notices, for example, that "famosa asienda" is translated as "beautiful estate," "don Jaime Florid" appears as "don Jaime Florido;" and the "conde de Jibacoa" is both the "count of J." and the "count of G." See: *The Life and Poems of a Cuban Slave*, ed. Edward Mullen (Hamden, Conn.: Archon Books, 1981).

9. *Autobiografía, cartas y versos de Juan Francisco Manzano*, ed. José Luciano Franco (Havana: Municipio de La Habana, 1937).

10. See Roberto Friol, *Suite para Juan Francisco Manzano* (Havana: Editorial Arte y Literatura, 1977).

11. I have been able to confirm this observation after studying the Manzano original at the Biblioteca Nacional José Martí, in December, 1989. I would like to thank Araceli García Carranza for helping me to obtain a microfilm of Manzano's original text.

12. *Autobiografía de un esclavo*, ed. Ivan Schulman (Madrid: Ediciones Guadarrama, 1975).

13. Saussure, *Course in General Linguistics*, ed. Charles Bally and Albert Sechehaye, trans. Wade Baskin (New York: Philosophical Library, 1959), part 1.

14. José Donoso, *Historia personal del "boom"* (Barcelona: Anagrama, 1972).

15. *Un catauro de cubanismos* (Havana: no pub., 1923).

16. "The Documentary Novel," *Cuban Studies/Estudios Cubanos*, 11, no. 1 (1981): 25.

17. *Myth and Archive: A Theory of Latin American Narrative* (Cambridge: Cambridge University Press, 1990), 46.

18. *La Carreta Made a U-Turn* (Houston: Arte Público Press, 1981). The information about Laviera is revealed in an unpublished interview with the poet entitled "From New York to the World: An Interview With Tato Laviera."

19. *AmeRican* (Houston: Arte Público Press, 1985), 54.

Documental and
Testimonial Writing

Latin American Documentary Narrative

Pero es que muchos se olvidan, con disfrazarse de magos a poco costo, que lo maravilloso comienza a serlo de manera inequívoca cuando surge de una inesperada alteración de la realidad (el milagro), de una revelación privilegiada de la realidad, de una iluminación inhabitual o singularmente favorecedora de las inadvertidas riquezas de la realidad, de una ampliación de las escalas y categorías de la realidad, percibidas con particular intensidad en virtud de una exaltación del espíritu que lo conduce a un modo de "estado límite."

¿Pero qué es la historia de América toda sino una crónica de lo real-maravilloso?

But many forget, disguising themselves as cheap magicians, that the marvelous manifests itself unequivocally only when it derives from an unexpected alteration of reality (the miracle), from a privileged revelation of reality, from an unaccustomed or singularly advantageous illumination of the unnoticed richness of reality, from an amplification of the registers and categories of reality, perceived with a special intensity by virtue of an exhaltation of the spirit, which it transports to a sort of "critical state."

But what is the history of America if not a chronicle of the marvelous real?

(Carpentier 131–32, 135; my trans.)

I

ALEJO CARPENTIER'S famous statement concerning the fabulous quality of Latin American reality, on which Gabriel García Márquez later elaborated in his definitive novel of Latin America, *Cien años de soledad* (1976; *One Hundred Years of Solitude*), possesses a double critical importance: it both stresses the interpretation of spurious categories like empirical reality and imaginative fantasy and underscores by implication the continuity between documentary history and narrative fiction.[1] Scholars have routinely characterized contemporary Latin American fiction as predominantly a social testimonial. They may resist applying sociopolitical commentary to the narratives written between 1848 and 1916, that is, between Domingo Faustino Sarmiento's *Facundo (Life in the Argentine Republic in the Days of the Tyrants)*, about the Rosas dictatorship in Argentina, and Mariano Azuela's *Los de abajo* (*The Underdogs*), the most eloquent example of the novel of the Mexican Revolution of 1910. But there is little doubt that first with the novels of social realism and then with contemporary fiction treating the conflicts of Latin American society, fiction has emerged as an especially productive form of documentary.[2] Perhaps the most sustained example is the work of David Viñas, who for almost thirty years has been projecting a revisionist history of Argentine society in his novels (see Rodríguez Monegal).

Many recent novels concern a key phenomenon of Latin American society, the dictator (see Castellanos and Martínez). Augusto Roa Bastos' *Yo el Supremo* (1975; 'I the Supreme') is an outstanding example of these novels. Through the first-person narrative of José Gaspar Rodríguez de Francia (1766–1840), Paraguay's enlightened, utopian despot, the novel represents not only all the contradictions of early independent Latin America but the entire Liberal tradition up to the present day as well. In this sense, Roa Bastos' novel is the quintessential Latin American historical novel: it deals with the arbitrary violence and unremitting oppression of dictatorial regimes, it abounds in historical references and incorporates a wide range of explicit documentary materials, it annuls mere chronological limitations in order to range over the entire span of Paraguayan and Latin American history, and it proceeds with a clear projection of the ideological problems of writing in a society in which vast segments of the population are illiterate and in which discourse is the privilege of a despotic elite ("dictator," of course, derives from *dictare*; and the textual basis of the novels, from Francia's act of dictating his memoirs [see Foster and Miliani]).

Thus, it would be an easy task to enumerate a lengthy list of contemporary Latin American works of fiction that detail the specific facts of a complex Latin American society. Julio

Cortázar's novel on revolutionary exiles, *El libro de Manuel* (1973; *The Book of Manuel*), incorporates explicit documentary material on violence against the third world. José Donoso's *Casa de campo* (1978; 'Country House') allegorizes the right-wing military coup in Chile in 1973. Edmundo Desnoe's *Memorias del subdesarrollo* (1965; *Memories of Underdevelopment*) portrays the tensions of revolutionary change in Cuba. Jorge Asis' *Los reventados* (1974; 'The Exhausted') concerns Perón's "triumphal" return to Argentina in 1973, and a long line of other Argentine novels deals with the Peronista phenomenon (see Avellaneda, Goldar, and Borello). Carlos Fuentes' *La cabeza de la hidra* (1978; *Hydra Head*) uses a spy-novel framework to treat Mexico's emergence as an oil-rich superpower. One could extend the list much further, and one could adduce, moreover, parallel examples from the contemporary Latin American theater, particularly in countries like Argentina, Cuba, Mexico, and Brazil, where there is a tradition of using public spectacle for sociohistorical information (see Lyday and Woodyard and Bissett).

With this wide array of literary materials, it is not surprising to discover a particularly impressive emphasis on documentary or nonfiction narrative. Although critics have written a great deal about the nonfiction novel in recent American literature, the form is fundamentally an outgrowth of the new journalism, and some have questioned whether it belongs in the mainstream of current novelistic practice (see Hellmann, Hollowell, Zavarzadeh, and Weber). By contrast, it would be possible to define documentary fiction to include many of the novels mentioned above, novels signed by some of the foremost figures in contemporary Latin American fiction. Certainly, Cortázar's *El libro de Manuel* is a paradigmatic example, with its intercalation of photographically reproduced newspaper clippings in the fictional text. From the social ethnographies inspired by Oscar Lewis to the many works provoked by institutional violence, documentary narrative is fundamental to Latin American literature (for the relation between violence and art, see Dorfman).

Rather than merely inventory the many forms such a genre has assumed in Latin America, I examine in detail five particularly representative examples. Significantly, none of these examples specifically uses documentary materials, as does Cortázar's novel or Manuel Puig's footnote-laden

El beso de la mujer araña (1976; *The Kiss of Spider Woman*), which treats Eros versus civilization in politically and sexually repressive Argentina. And none involves an independently definable fictional component as, again, we have in Cortázar's novel or in the Lukácsian historical novels of David Viñas. The five titles I study here are based on texts attributed to real people: a former black slave in Cuba, students involved in a massacre in Mexico, the victim of a concentration camp in Chile, survivors of a summary political execution in Argentina, and a Colombian sailor lost at sea. What distinguishes these works is not their fundamentally documentary nature, which routinely prompts libraries to classify them as nonfiction. Rather, all have authors who are important novelists, all display a high degree of novelistic interest, and, most significant, all overtly involve the difficulties of narrating a segment of Latin American reality. As García Márquez notes in the introduction to his documentary narrative *Relato de un náufrago*, which I examine below, the story of his narrator's ten days at sea "was so detailed and fascinating that my only literary problem was to find a reader who would believe it" (8; my trans.). This foregrounded attention to the relation between writing and reality, between narrative and fact, between detached novelist and involved participant links the documentary narrative to the intricacies of fiction in Latin America.

II

Originally published in 1957, *Operación masacre* ('Operation Massacre') by Rodolfo Walsh is easily the most authentic example of documentary narrative in Latin American fiction (see Ford, the only in-depth study of Walsh's documentary writings). Where Julio Cortázar's *El libro de Manuel* uses actual documents to highlight the fictional narrative (see Morello-Frosch), Walsh blends true materials gathered in his investigations and narrative strategies to make a rhetorically effective presentation of an actual event. Published almost ten years before Truman Capote's much-touted "nonfictional novel" *In Cold Blood*, *Operación masacre* anticipates the techniques credited to Capote. Walsh sets out to recreate the senseless massacre of a group of innocent citizens in the area of the capital of Buenos Aires province, La Plata, located about fifty kilometers south of the national capital. (For a fictional treatment of these events, see Szichman.) In June 1956, a year after Juan Perón was deposed, Peronist military officers stationed at the Campamento de Mayo base made an abortive attempt to overthrow the "liberation" military government. Although this government had claimed that it would operate on the principle of "neither victors nor vanquished," it enacted severe reprisals against Peronist sympathizers, and Walsh reports the summary execution of a group of men taken from a private home where they had putatively gathered to listen to a fight on the radio. The police, claiming that these men were part of the plot to overthrow the government and that they had used the home to store arms, transported them to a field and shot them. Approximately a half dozen men either escaped in the dark or survived the executioners' volley of shots, and Walsh pieces the event together based on their stories. Although some of the men were Peronist sympathizers, no evidence linked them to the attempt to overthrow the anti-Peronist government.

Hampered by the problem of identifying and locating the survivors and harassed by a military dictatorship unwilling to admit to such a fatal mistake, Walsh evolved his story over a ten-year period and it appeared in two preliminary versions before the final text was published in 1969. (It is significant that this final version was published by Jorge Alvarez, one of the most dedicated publishers of countercultural materials during the brief period in the late sixties and early seventies when an open diversity of public opinion was permitted in Argentina.)

The prologue to the third and definitive edition of Walsh's narrative provides insights into the problems of investigative reporting in a repressive society, of maintaining an appropriate authorial stance toward one's material, and of distinguishing fact and fiction in a country where reality often outstrips the most creative imaginations. Walsh feels particularly constrained to speak of how he came to discover the first thread that would lead him into the labyrinth of an event with no official reality. Divided into three sections, with vignettelike subdivisions ("Las personas" 'The Persons,' "Los hechos" 'The Facts,' "La evidencia" 'The Evidence'), *Operación* appears as a seamless piece of fiction. One could even read the prologue, with its highly subjective rhetoric concerning the narrator's commitment to his material,

as an integral part of the fictional narrative or as simply one more clever strategy to engage the interest of the reader. In this sense, *Operación* would belong to the *Lord Jim* family of narratives, in which a singular story, recovered by chance, holds interest for its apparent exotic remoteness from the secure comfort of the reader. Nevertheless, Walsh demands implicitly that his reader recognize the contemporary historical references of his narrative: allusions to the Peronist period and its collapse, to the protagonists of the 1955 "revolution of liberation" and to the abortive uprising against them at the Campamento de Mayo, to subsequent political unrest in the country, and to official attempts to thwart investigation.

Thus Walsh's narrative, despite its superficial similarities to much modern fiction, demands to be read as a sociohistorical document in which the techniques of fiction enhance the texture of truth and the density of human experience, as they do in Truman Capote's work several years later. Walsh's experience concerns a terrible and unprovoked act of injustice but not an unexplained one, given the reality of contemporary Argentine politics. What requires explanation, what constitutes the core of mystery, is not that such an event took place but rather who was involved and how that event may be reconstructed in a convincing fashion. The goal of the narrator becomes the act of revelation for the reader in the act of narrative recreation.

In this way, *Operación* is based on a structure of reduplication: reading the narrative creation repeats the narrator's discovery of a clandestine event, an event that according to official reality never took place, a conspiratorial lie—a fiction— propagated to discredit a noble movement of national liberation from Juan Domingo Perón's dictatorship. A strategic risk, therefore, underlies *Operación*: the willingness of the reader to believe the claims of a highly fictionalized narrative about an unverifiable massacre rather than the official version that nothing took place. The unquestionable success of Walsh's book may be based less on the effectiveness of his narrative talents than on the cooperative skepticism of a reading public resigned to the mendacity of official accounts. Nevertheless, Walsh's fictionalized strategies serve as an effective ironic counterpoint to the claim that a massacre never happened or that it involved not innocent victims but counterrevolutionary agents. Walsh's "fiction" overtly challenges the "fiction" of the official explanation of the events of mid-1956. Significantly, one of the final sections of the narrative is entitled "La justicia ciega" 'Blind Justice.'

What are some of the fictional techniques Walsh uses both to enhance his narrative rhetorically and to juxtapose it ironically to the fabric of official lies? The most obvious is the dramatic reenactment of dialogues among the participants. Walsh bases his investigation on individual interviews of the survivors and other persons implicated in the massacre. Yet such dramatic reenactments, which must be fictional, constitute the narrator's understanding of the information given him piecemeal by a number of different sources. The narrator frames these narrative recreations with necessarily hypothetical interpretations of the participants' mental states. The second novelistic strategy, one particularly associated with modern fiction, is the "mosaic narrative." Instead of relating events in a strictly chronological order, the narrative presents first the protagonists (the opening section of *Operación*), followed by the event—summarized with the leisure of a psychological novel moving among the consciousnesses of the participants—and by the concluding section, in which the narrator analyzes the judicial treatment of the case with the goal of undermining the government's self-serving explanations. Thus, the narrator sets the action interest aside in favor of exploring the complex reactions of individuals involved in an irrational historical process that they only vaguely understand although they are its sacrificial victims.

The following type of segment helps the reader assess how Walsh uses documentary information gathered from the participants, psychological speculation, and dramatic recreation:

Ya casi ha terminado de cenar Francisco Garibotti— un bife con huevos fritos comió esa noche—cuando llaman a la puerta.
Es don Carranza.
¿Qué viene a hacer Nicolás Carranza?
—Vino a sacármelo. Para que me lo devolvieran muerto—recordará Florinda Allende con rencor en la voz.

Francisco Garibotti has almost finished eating (steak with fried eggs is what he ate that evening) when someone comes to the door.
It's Don Carranza.
What can Nicolás Carranza want?

"He came to take him away from me. So I would get him back dead," Florinda Allende was to recall with bitterness in her voice.   (29; my trans.)

The unannounced transition from the pluperfect arrival of Nicolás Carranza, to the present rhetorical question posed to the reader, and then to the "future past" reply that Garibotti's wife makes when the investigative reporter asks her the same question is an outstanding example of Walsh's effective narrative strategies. By contrast with the rather flat autobiographical narrative of *Biografía de un cimarrón* (see sec. 6 below), the unhighlighted reporting of *La noche de Tlatelolco* (sec. 3), or the explicit disjunction of fiction and document in *El libro de Manuel*, the narrative texture of *Operación* is particularly novelistic in blending into a single discourse the disparate elements of narrative speculation and authentic quotation.

Yet another novelistic device is a form of narrative withholding characteristic of detective fiction. Walsh effects a suspenseful rhythm in his narrative by withholding information at certain points, by shifting focus from one person to another or from one circumstance to another, and by overtly referring to unknown elements (the final section of the first part is entitled "Las incógnitas" 'Unknown Elements'), to what "we will never know." He gives a general outline of events in the prologue, but by momentarily defying the reader's natural desire for a full explanation at any one point in the exposition, Walsh uses one of the hoariest techniques of the storyteller's art. By playing on the parallel between the reader's desire to know and the participants' inability to explain the tragic circumstances in which they are caught and on the homology between narrator's and reader's discovery of a nefarious event, Walsh constructs perhaps the most sophisticated example of Latin American documentary narrative in the service of sociopolitical awareness. The narrator's cry of frustration in the face of too much reality anticipates that of readers unable to withstand the onslaught of a truth they cannot repeal (10).

III

If the Vietnam War marked an American loss of innocence, the events surrounding the massacre of students by police at Tlatelolco, or the Plaza de las Tres Culturas, on the night of 2 October 1968 had a similar impact on Mexico's self-image. Where the citizen of the United States had to recognize that American military involvement might be base and self-serving rather than noble, the firing on students exercising their constitutional right of assembly brought to the attention of the Mexican public an ugly truth: despite Mexico's tradition of stable government under the strong "guided democracy" of the ruling PRI (Institutional Revolutionary Party), repression of civil liberties and human rights could assume the same proportions in Mexico as it had in Argentina or Paraguay. The massacre followed a series of student protests that spanned the summer months and early fall; it occurred when a large array of foreign correspondents and tourists was in Mexico for the Olympic games; and it proved to the students and their supporters that the government of Gustavo Díaz Ordaz and the ruling oligarchy supporting him would not tolerate serious dissent: these were all elements that contributed to the tremendous psychological impact of the Tlatelolco incident (see Campos Lemus, Mora, and Barros Sierra).

Indeed, Tlatelolco has acquired such a profound meaning in contemporary Mexican culture that it has inspired a book-length essay by Octavio Paz (*Postdata*; trans. as *The Other Mexico: Critique of the Pyramid*) and virtually a subgenre of contemporary Mexican literature (see Leal and Franco). *La noche de Tlatelolco* (1971; published in English as *Massacre in Mexico*) by Elena Poniatowska is the only documentary narrative besides Cortázar's *El libro de Manuel* and Barnet's *Biografía de un cimarrón* translated into English. It is the most documentary of the texts studied in this essay and, consequently, the least "novelistic" in terms of fictional elements or devices.[3] Nevertheless, it is novelistic in the sense that it sustains a complex narrative texture. And, although *Noche* has a place in a bibliography of contemporary Mexican social history, critics read it as an important contribution to the contemporary Latin American novel. To read *Noche* as more novel than document does not detract from its quality as documentary testimonial. Rather—as is true for all recent documentary and historical fiction in Latin America—such a reading testifies to the continuity of fiction and reality in that culture and to the importance of productive "mythic" factuality.[4]

The nearly three hundred pages of *Noche* are divided into two roughly equal sections, "Ganar la calle" 'Take to the Streets' and "La noche de Tlatelolco." The first part refers to the various student demonstrations and skirmishes with police during the summer of 1968 and the second to the confrontation on 2 October, in which the police, apparently obeying orders to end the protest activities, opened fire on the unarmed students. But there is no clear break between the two sections, and the development of the material is chronological in only a general fashion. Poniatowska evidently means to relate the two phases of the 1968 events as more than simply a time sequence of escalating violence. While it is apparent that the protests did not accidentally coincide with Mexico's hosting of the Olympic games, both the author and her interviewees maintain that the movement developed out of natural causes and did not arise from an effort to embarrass the government in its sponsorship of the games (naturally, as the first Latin American country to host the games, Mexico took sponsorship seriously; to a great degree it was meant to signify Mexico's mature international stature). Poniatowska and the students, teachers, intellectuals, and members of the general public whom she interviewed insist that a general pattern of repression of dissent had emerged in Mexico. The Díaz Ordaz government, either cynically or stupidly, seemed determined to exercise the dictatorial control associated with military regimes in Latin America and not with the sort of functioning democracy Mexico claimed to be. Moreover, the fact that events took place in the Plaza de las Tres Culturas has been interpreted as symbolic of Mexico's ties to the blood sacrifice of its Aztec roots.

But Poniatowska only suggests this interpretation; it was left to writers like Octavio Paz and Carlos Fuentes to provide adequate literary elaboration.[5] Instead, Poniatowska treats the material as documentary. She skillfully weaves together fragments, usually a few lines to half a page in length although occasionally longer, based on interviews she conducted with participants and bystanders: many of both groups were still incarcerated over a year after the incident, when she was working on the manuscript. (On the structure of *Noche*, see Christ.) She punctuates these fragments with slogans taken from the banners and signs carried by the students, as well as with material from various other documentary sources, such as newspaper reports and official declarations. Finally, on very few occasions, Poniatowska intervenes to offer her own point of view. Otherwise, with the exception of statements in the interviews addressed to her by name, she limits her authorial presence to the not insignificant ordering of the material that we read.[6]

Although Poniatowska includes material from officials and citizens who attribute seditious and immoral objectives to the students, the overall tone of *Noche* creates the sense of a tragic event that transcended the power of the participants to control it. The massacre at Tlatelolco was neither an isolated "accident" nor the folly of a particular dictatorial ambition but rather the dramatic example of repression inherent in the Mexican system of government. If Rodolfo Walsh's *Operación masacre* depends for its impact on the willingness of the reader to believe that savage torture and illegal executions are integral to Argentine life, Poniatowska's narrative derives its force from the incredulity of the reader, mirrored in the statements of the individuals Poniatowska interviewed, that such events could happen in Mexico, a country that in the twentieth century has claimed to be above the human-rights infringements characteristic of Latin America. When Poniatowska includes material referring to the arbitrary behavior of the police toward students and bystanders, the disappearance of individuals whisked away in broad daylight in unmarked cars, the refusal of authorities to answer inquiries concerning the arrested or the detained, the excessive sentences imposed in violation of accepted legal principles, the torture sessions at police headquarters, and finally, the government's violent explosion against its own citizens at Tlatelolco, she challenges the sacred myths of modern Mexico. Her publisher's difficulty in keeping the book in print when it appeared in 1971 shows that there were readers willing to risk the challenge to their incredulity.

These features lead us to consider the narrative aspects of *Noche* and its place, as documentary, among contemporary Latin American novels. A conventional novel like Carlos Fuentes' *La cabeza de la hidra* (1978) treats a fictional circumstance as though it were real—*Cabeza*, the first Mexican espionage novel by a major writer, deals with American, Jewish, and Arab intrigue over Mexico's huge petroleum industry. Poniatowska's documentary, by contrast, deals with a real event so monumental and terrible that it seems

unbelievable to participants, witnesses, and, in the final instance, the readers of her text (indeed, there must be otherwise intelligent Mexicans who doubt that the massacre at Tlatelolco took place). Thus, the author's goal is not to present an "academic" analysis of a particular moment in recent Mexican history but to recreate the sense and the feel of an event in order to highlight its inescapable reality.

From a novelist's point of view, Poniatowska eschews the procedure of serializing a number of individual and discrete interviews—the strategy popularized by Oscar Lewis in his oral anthropological research—in favor of the mosaic patterning so characteristic of contemporary fiction. That is to say, although she interviewed a number of individuals, she does not present the words of any one of the principal interviewees as a block. Rather, the text of *Noche* moves back and forth among a basic cast of speakers, and one would need to gather quotes spread over the full extent of *Noche* to recover the testimony given by a specific person. The declarations of each individual (and it is reasonable to suppose that Poniatowska interviewed some persons in one session, others in several) are fragmented in order to provide clusters of comments on significant topics: police brutality, the causes of the movement, the role of students, the reactions of bystanders, the attitudes of teachers and administrators toward the protest movement, and so on. One section, for example, deals with participants' emotional reactions to memories of Tlatelolco (152–53).

It could be argued that such a textual strategy is paradigmatically documentary and antithetical to fictional narrative. After all, historical novels, while they may seek to recreate an era or an event, focus on the internal coherence and identity of specific individuals; even documentary narratives like Capote's *In Cold Blood* strive for a sense of the feelings and motivations of concrete individuals. By contrast, Poniatowska's use of her interview material makes it difficult to derive a sense of any single participant, with the exception of two or three whose words recur with special emphasis. Nevertheless, *Noche*, in repudiating the need to portray individual "psychologies," is in the mainstream of contemporary fiction, especially of the Latin American novel. Juan Rulfo's *Pedro Páramo* (1955), Cortázar's *Rayuela* (1963; *Hopscotch*), Fuentes' *La región más transparente* (1958; *Where the Air Is Clear*), Puig's *La traición de Rita Hayworth* (1968; *Betrayed by Rita Hayworth*), and Severo Sarduy's *De donde son las cantantes* (1967; *From Cuba with a Song*) are novels based on narrative and "psychological" fragmentation, in which discrete individuals and events must be pieced together (see Fuentes, *Nueva novela* 16–23, and Jitrik). Vargas Llosa's *La casa verde* (1966; *The Green House*) illustrates this procedure well, for its characters have different names as they participate in different but homologous situations. Thus, *Noche* is an excellent example of the nonpsychological novel, with parallels in the fiction of John Barth, Donald Barthelme, and others. One cannot speak of *Noche* as more "authentic" or "real" because of its overt use of interview materials and the fragmentation that impedes the sense of "round characters," to use E. M. Forster's famous term. Rather, the ironic framing—the foregone conclusion as the point of departure for the chain of events represented—the authorial intervention in organizing the material gathered, the eloquent juxtaposition of oral texts with various other sources, the interplay between personal commentaries and impersonal, antiphonic choruses like the banners and posters are conscious artistic decisions that lend *Noche* its special narrative and novelistic texture.

IV

It would perhaps be an error to associate documentary narrative with unusually dramatic events in the sociopolitical life of a society: institutional violence is such an ordinary part of Latin America that one must conclude that its appearance in Latin American literature has been predominantly documentary rather than fictional since the time of independence and the first sense of lost ideals and myths. Nevertheless, observers have perceived events like the Tlatelolco massacre or the military coup in Chile in 1973 as quantum jumps in the contest between democratic ideals and official repression. It is therefore not surprising that the inevitable fictional treatments are complemented by documentary narratives responding to the urgency of "reality" with the symbolic power of literature. We have seen how Poniatowska's narrative of the Tlatelolco massacre is predicated on the strategy of disbelief. In opposition to the cliché that fiction asks us to believe in the reality of an imaginary narrative space, Poniatowska takes a historically definable

context and demands that we believe that the otherwise incredible can occur. Juan Rulfo asks us to believe that in the fictional realm of *Pedro Páramo* the dead continue the discourse of life; in *La noche de Tlatelolco*, Poniatowska asks us to believe that official repression has reached such a point in Mexico that the incredible may take place: innocent citizens, exercising the constitutional right of assembly and free expression, may be massacred by a cynical government.

The military takeover in Chile spurred a truly impressive body of literature: virtually every Chilean writer of note has attempted to render an adequate portrayal of the Allende phenomenon. The Union Popular government triggered not only one of the most vicious military coups in recent Latin American history but also a tragic collective loss of innocence, a realization of just how fragile the much-touted Chilean liberal and democratic tradition was. (See the collection edited by Skármeta and his introduction; see also the journal *Literatura Chilena en el Exilio* and "Coloquio sobre literatura chilena.") Narrative treatments range from the allegorical *Casa de campo* (1978) by Chile's major novelist, José Donoso, to the barely controlled denunciations like Fernando Alegría's *Paso de los gansos* (1975; 'Goose Step') and Antonio Skármeta's *Soñé que la nieve ardía* (1975; 'I Dreamed the Snow Was Burning'). In a documentary vein, Enrique Lafourcade's *Salvador Allende* (1973) and Hernán Valdés' *Tejas Verdes* (1974) are two of the best examples. Lafourcade weaves together explicitly documentary material with a fictional evocation of Allende's stream-of-consciousness ramblings on his government and its fate. The structural strategy of *Salvador Allende* resembles the conjunction of documentary materials and fictional narrative in Cortázar's *El libro de Manuel*, and in the representation of Allende's preverbal consciousness it bears affinities with Roa Bastos' *Yo el Supremo*. Because it does not convincingly portray the complexities of the Allende phenomenon, however, Lafourcade's work has never achieved recognition as an important post-1973 Chilean narrative.

Hernán Valdés is one of the most important writers who established themselves during the Allende period; his *Tejas Verdes*, subtitled *Diario de un campo de concentración en Chile*, recreates the time he spent after the 1973 coup in the Tejas Verdes camp, near the port of San Antonio. (A segment of *Tejas Verdes* appears in Skármeta's anthology [85-100]; for discussion, see Epple and Massey.) During the month of his internment Valdés was subjected to the torture and generally degrading treatment typical of such camps, and thus his account belongs to an extensive bibliography of fictional and documentary materials that treat the violence of repressive Latin American society. These materials focus on the use of torture, secret police, extralegal death squads, and clandestine jails for social and political control. From Eduardo Pavlovky's drama on professional tortures, *El Señor Galíndez* (1973), and novels on official torture like Manuel Puig's *El beso de la mujer araña* or Carlos Martínez Moreno's *El color que el infierno nos escondiera* (1981; *The Color Hell Hid from Us*) to the personal testimony by Jacobo Timerman, *Prisoner without a Name, Cell without a Number* (1980), there is a constellation of works in which it is difficult, and probably fruitless, to distinguish between the fictional and the documentary.

What is unique about *Tejas Verdes*, therefore, cannot be the voice it adds to the tragic chorus demanding recognition of human rights in Latin America: it would be impossible to provide a hierarchy for these voices, each powerfully eloquent in its own fashion. What is singular about Valdés' narrative is the conjunction of his unquestionably true statements regarding his personal experiences and his use of a hypothetical diary to portray those experiences. The diary format, particularly when an author uses it to transmit alleged fact, presupposes that the author can transcribe events on a day-to-day basis, in moments of recollection and reflection. Such a document should possess the spontaneity of the moment and the accuracy provided by immediate recounting. In contrast to chronological memoirs, which use the past tense to describe events, the diary uses the present tense to convey the continuity between an event and its prompt commitment to paper.

Valdés divides his diary into thirty-one dated segments, one for each day of his detention, and writes in the present tense. He recognizes in his preface, however, that since he was actually unable to maintain a diary during his stay at Tejas Verdes, what he presents is a legitimate recreation of what he would have written. Because prisoners lose a sense of time, as well as a sense of identity, under the barrage of physical abuse at a place like Tejas Verdes, the relative brevity of Valdés' internment lends credibility to his day-by-day recreation of

events. The preface is dated May 1974; and the closeness of dates serves to validate further Valdés' claims to accuracy.

Such a combination of circumstances testifies, of course, to Valdés' determination to bear personal witness to the terrible violation of human rights in Chile. His testimony speaks for the thousands who have died in places like Tejas Verdes or who have remained silent to avoid the risk of further persecution. Although Valdés writes from the safety of Barcelona, the juxtaposition of the restrictions of the concentration camp with the hypothetical recreation of the diary acquires, in terms of narrative discourse, a special meaning. The diary entitled *Tejas Verdes*, with its accurate descriptions of life inside the concentration camp, emerges as an ex post facto defiance of the silence and the loss of personal identity imposed by the extralegal prison system.

Ample evidence supports the allegation that strict silence is used as a strategy to destroy political prisoners, and the eloquence of the fictive day-by-day entries in Valdés' diary serves as a defiant counterpoint to the real, Draconian circumscriptions of imprisonment. By contrast, the only legitimate forms of communication become the demands for information imposed by the interrogation and torture sessions. The proscriptions against expression versus the demands for information, the imaginary worlds of the novelist versus the all too real world of political process, the semiconsciousness of the brutalized prisoner versus the eloquence of a personal testimony, the unreality of the experience of the moment versus the painfully vivid recall of a subsequent reflection—these are some of the juxtapositions Valdés' document uses to highlight the uniqueness of its narrative:

Hablar desde aquí de todo eso como de una realidad esfumada, como de una situación histórica única dilapidada por el temor, suena a pesadilla; pero más todavía reconocernos a nosotros mismos, en la medida en que hablamos, como sobrevivientes de esa realidad. Porque, si logramos salir de aquí alguna vez ¿qué seremos si no? En el mejor caso, individuos aislados, ocupándonos oscuramente de mantener nuestras vidas. Melancólicos de lo que no supimos hacer con la historia.

To talk about all this from here as though talking about a fuzzy reality, a unique historical situation decayed by terror, sounds like a nightmare. But even more so to recognize ourselves, as we talk, as survivors of that reality. Because if we are successful in finally getting out of here, what else will we be but survivors? The best we can expect is to be isolated individuals, obscurely concerned with sustaining our lives, melancholic about what we were incapable of doing with history.

(72; my trans.)

The deictic "aquí" 'here' of this passage assumes an ironic function because the diary defies the camp's restrictions against personal expression. As a reference to the locus of Valdés the prisoner, it alludes to the problem of continuity between the "situación histórica" of the narrator and of his colleagues and their imprisonment in Tejas Verdes: their personal suffering is not an isolated circumstance but part of an ideological process to which they bear symbolic witness. It is only in this way that the political prisoners can struggle against the psychological destruction sought by their jailers. But as the point of reference of Valdés the memorialist—the writer who allows himself the license of creating the diary he would like to have been able to maintain during his incarceration— "aquí" signals the problem of continuity between the timeless and nebulous domain of miserable suffering and the commitment to bear witness of the individual ten thousand miles removed from Tejas Verdes.

The artful strategy of interplaying silence and expressiveness—a strategy that is literary enough for a novelist of Valdés' qualifications—lends *Tejas Verdes* a power as documentary narrative quite beyond the work's validity as sociohistorical information and thereby frustrates the goal of the oppressors. In this sense, *Tejas Verdes* stands as a superb example of Latin American documentary narrative because it expressively defies the primacy of collective silence.

V

While the most renowned Latin American writers may write "testimonial literature"—literature that fictionalizes and allegorizes recognizable individuals and events in Latin American society and politics—relatively few have written specifically documentary narratives. Gabriel García Márquez provides a significant exception in *Relato de un náufrago que estuvo diez días a la deriva en una balsa sin comer ni beber, que fue proclamado héroe de la patria, besado por las reinas de la belleza y hecho rico por la publicidad, y luego aborrecido por el gobierno y olvidado para siempre* (1970; 'Story of a Castaway Who Was Lost at Sea for Ten Days in a Raft with Nothing to Eat or Drink, Who Was Proclaimed a National Hero, Kissed by Beauty Queens and Made Rich by Publicity, and Later Spurned by the Government and Forgotten Forever').[7] Published in 1955 as a series of newspaper articles in Bogotá's *El Espectador*, *Relato* would never have been reprinted in book form had not the young reporter gone on to become one of Latin America's most famous novelists. Indeed, García Márquez observes in his introductory note that he was persuaded to publish *Relato* solely because its publication would permit him to turn its royalties over to its true author, the forgotten seaman of a Colombian naval destroyer.

But *Relato* only functions as documentary narrative in the context of its republication. The seaman's narrative is not much more than a detailed description of the hardships faced by an individual afloat in an unprotected raft without provisions for ten days. Reminiscent of Hemingway's *Old Man and the Sea*, the narrative describes how the seaman survives because of his good physical condition, his calmness, and a determination probably born of military discipline. If the seaman's own ingenuous disclaimers give his statements merely the passing importance of a human-interest story, the basis on which *El Espectador* agreed to buy his story in the first place, how does *Relato* achieve importance as documentary narrative? García Márquez observes in his introduction that *El Espectador* and its eager reporter were unaware when it reluctantly agreed to buy Velasco's story (the newspaper felt that the topic had already been exhausted by the press) that the story would reveal an official cover-up of the events surrounding the incident. Whereas Velasco and seven crewmen who drowned were swept overboard in rough seas from the deck of a badly listing vessel, the official explanation said they had been lost during an unexpected storm that made any rescue attempt impossible.

What had made the destroyer *Caldas* list dangerously in the rough Caribbean seas between Cuba and Colombia was the heavy contraband cargo poorly distributed and inadequately lashed down on the deck. The cargo had been purchased in Mobile, Alabama, where the destroyer had been docked for eight months of repairs and refittings. The crewmen had used their pay during those long months to buy household appliances and other goods, and because of the double violation of transporting such cargo and transporting it on deck, the ship's officers were unquestionably compromised. Swept overboard when high waves broke the cargo loose, the seamen were left behind by the destroyer, which could not maneuver in the rough seas because of its poorly distributed weight. When rescue planes found no trace of survivors, a storm was declared responsible, and the case was closed. Velasco's appearance ten days later did not alter this story, and the hero's welcome he received was perhaps unspoken compensation for his abandonment by the *Caldas*.

In the subsequent recounting of his story to García Márquez, it soon became apparent that he spoke of two details that did not jibe with the official versions: the *Caldas* carried heavy cargo on deck, and there was no storm. The ensuing uproar—Colombia was ruled at the time by the dictator Gustavo Rojas Pinilla—cost Velasco his status as a hero and his job with the navy, sent García Márquez into the exile from which, ten years later, *Cien años de soledad* emerged, and resulted in *El Espectador* being closed down by the government. Thus the documentary meaning of *Relato* derives not from Velasco's narrative as such but from the accidental contradiction his story provided and from García Márquez' subsequent recontextualization in his presentation of the narrative in book form.

In the same way that the individual declarations gathered by Poniatowska provide little more than fragmentary versions of the events surrounding Tlatelolco and acquire their power as social and narrative document by virtue of the author's unifying conception, *Relato* attains its meaning from García Márquez' introduction. Although García Márquez as narrator does not intervene in Velasco's story, we may assume that the subject's "natural narrative" is not altogether untainted by authorial intervention. The presence of the reporter-interviewer, the questions he may ask overtly, and the conditioning he may provide covertly and even unconsciously contribute to the configuration of the narrative.

The text of *Relato* consists of Velasco's detailed reconstruction of events; read in conjunction with García Márquez' introduction, his tale acquires resonance as an unintentional exposé. A dramatic irony colors Velasco's representations because the reader knows what will happen and why: this information is superior to that of Velasco not only at the time of the adventure he describes but also, significantly, at the time of his declarations to *El Espectador*'s reporter. For example, Velasco refers repeatedly to the crew's acquisition of articles, to their special relationship with a salesman in Mobile who, because he spoke excellent Spanish without ever having been in Latin America, was particularly favored with their money, and to the way the contraband initially protected the seamen working on the deck of the *Caldas* from the waves before it swept them overboard. Read in conjunction with García Márquez' introduction, these references insistently foreshadow the impending disaster.

What makes such unconscious foregrounding especially interesting is that Velasco maintains that he developed a fear of the sea (after seeing the movie *Caine Mutiny*, he and his shipmates had discussed what they would do in such a storm). And he experiences a clear presentiment of trouble on the voyage back to Colombia, a voyage both routine and short. Yet, the references that foretell subsequent disaster are based on the storm that serves as the narrative catalyst of the *Caine Mutiny* and not on the improper stowage of the contraband the crewmen purchased while they enjoyed movies and other relaxations ashore. At the same time, the preoccupation with a storm at sea adds a further resonance: the government will cover the true circumstances of the seamen's fate by falsely attributing their loss to an unexpected storm.

On another level, the references to contraband become the central point in the interplay between untrustworthy official versions and the truth of Velasco's narrative as unintentional exposé. Again, this relation may only be perceived through the conjunction of the seaman's text and García Márquez' introduction. Two forms of contraband are symbolically interrelated in the text. There is the cargo stowed on deck in clear violation of military regulations. This cargo is the nucleus of Velasco's ordeal: its acquisition and its quantity bespeak the long stay away from home, and it prevents the *Caldas* from rescuing the men swept overboard. This contraband, which the seaman mentions simply as the material cause of his ordeal with no thought to its illegality, triggers the "contraband" newspaper interviews: because *El Espectador*'s articles inadvertently reveal both the truth of the forbidden cargo and the lie concerning the storm at sea, they become the object of persecution by the dictatorship. Truth is a contraband commodity in a repressive society, and reprisals for the "contraband" of *Relato* substitute for any judicial review of the officers of the *Caldas* and their accommodating superiors in the government. By the same token, *Relato*'s publication in 1970 acknowledges that its importance as a narrative document, beyond any intrinsic storytelling skills of the accidental literatus Luis Alejandro Velasco, derives from its unforeseen stature as contraband truth; and it is this quality that makes *Relato* an appropriate example of Latin American documentary narrative.

VI

Miguel Barnet's *Biografía de un cimarrón* (1966; published in English as *The Autobiography of a Runaway Slave*) exemplifies a subgenre of Caribbean literature that has acquired special prominence since the Castro revolution in Cuba in 1959: literature dealing with the black experience (see Schulman). Slaves were introduced early in the Caribbean, when the indigenous population was unable to survive the harsh conditions imposed by the Spanish conquerors. Barnet, whose *Canción de Rachel* (*Song of Rachel*) is one of the major narratives of the revolution, interviewed Esteban Montejo, a 105-year-old former slave who, after the abolition of slavery, became a peon on the sugarcane plantations that constitute the basis of Cuban economic wealth.[8] According to his own story, in an act of spontaneous rebellion he hurled a stone at one of the slave drivers and fled into the mountains, where he lived in solitude for several years as a runaway—hence the epithet *cimarrón*, which is used in the Caribbean to denominate a runaway slave (i.e., a maroon). When he discovers that the Spanish crown has abolished slavery, Montejo returns to civilization and becomes a wage-earning peon. Barnet's presentation is misleadingly titled, because only a small portion of Montejo's narrative is devoted to his personal suffering as a slave and his subsequent experiences as a runaway. There are ample assertions concerning the dreadful subhuman lot of the slaves and the scarcely improved conditions after the formal abolition of slavery. But Montejo's story concentrates more on his interest in women and on his descriptions of black folkways and customs in Cuba, traditional religious practices, and his own comings and goings, particularly his involvement in the struggle for Cuban independence from Spain that culminated in the American invasion of the island in 1898.[9]

Montejo's narrative, framed by Barnet's brief presentation, is perhaps the least novelistic of the documentary narratives I examine here (see Moreno Fraginals for comment on its ethnographic nature). Although critics recognize it as an important postrevolutionary text that is continuous with Barnet's creative fiction, it clearly belongs to the Cuban tradition of personal memoirs of social life. Barnet specifically introduces it as part of an ethnographic undertaking (and it was originally published, in 1966, by the Instituto de Etnología y Folklore in Havana). By the same token, there can be little question that *Biografía* has an ulterior social motive: the documentation of both the authentic folk culture of Cuba that the revolution sought to recover and the deplorable human conditions that justify the revolution and its subsequent programs. Montejo's symbolic status as a rebel against the institution of slavery, his participation in the struggle for Cuban independence, his membership in the Cuban Socialist Party, and, above all else, his representations of the solidarity first of the black slave society and subsequently of the black ethnic minority all attest to values promoted by the official mythopoesis of the Castro government. Thus, the correspondences between Montejo's declarations and the overall coherence of his narrative acquire meaning within postrevolutionary Cuban society by evoking intertextually an entire range of social and artistic documents.

If the postrevolutionary culture in Cuba constitutes a body of intertexts for the appropriate reading of Montejo's story, the ethnographic framework acts as a subtext that reveals the interplay between autobiographical documentary and social narrative. In a tone that would strike an American post–civil rights movement reader as somewhat patronizing, Barnet describes his early meetings with Montejo. The old man rambled on repetitively, without regard for chronology. Barnet claims that after he established the essential interest of the former slave's story, he prepared an inventory of chronologically based questions concerning the principal topics covered by Montejo. Barnet recorded and polished the man's replies and published them as *Biografía*. The editorial process involved a minimum of correction in order to retain the man's style and his sociolect, which includes archaisms, regionalisms, and socioeducationally determined solecisms; Barnet provides an appendix of vocabulary the nonspecialist reader might not recognize and footnotes clarifying some of the historical references.

There are several major problems with this framework. In the first place, the narrative cannot be read as a spontaneous declaration, free of intervening filters. There are the inevitable conditions imposed by the presence of the ethnographic interviewer and the instruments of his stenographic or electronic transcription, and Barnet makes it clear that Montejo's autobiography is based on questions elicited by the earlier, more rambling statements. However, Barnet does not present his questions in *Biografía* either as an integral part of the text or as an appendix. Montejo's narrative is divided into three segments of unequal length—"La esclavitud" 'Slavery,' "La abolición de la esclavitud" 'Abolition of Slavery,' and "La guerra de la independencia" 'War of Independence'—along with untitled internal divisions of similarly diverse length. The reader cannot reconstruct Barnet's questions, except by the rather unproductive process of generating questions based on discrete statements. For example, when Montejo says he can never forget the first time he attempted an escape, one could postulate Barnet's hypothetical question: "Tell me about the first time you attempted to escape." Like novels in which one speaker's words are transcribed while another's are represented by ellipses, *Biografía* presents as explicit text a narrative generated by a subtext conditioned by an interviewer's questions based on avowed ethnographic motives and sociopolitical interests.

Barnet accompanies these avowals of legitimate anthropological concern with the disclaimer that he intends to write literature. Such a disclaimer, though strategically important because of Barnet's identification with the contemporary Cuban novel, follows Barnet's frank admission that, in presenting Montejo's autobiography, he has added a level between Montejo's spontaneous declarations and the text we receive. In addition to restructuring the "natural narrative" through ethnographic questions, he felt constrained to copyedit the transcript for greater conciseness. These decisions, made by a highly skilled novelist, undoubtedly enhance Montejo's narrative. And in the process, although they do not justify our

reading *Biografía* as pseudoautobiographical fiction, they lend it a novelistic texture that disrupts significantly its "raw" documentary value.

The dominant narrative marker in *Biografía* is the controlling predicate statement "Yo vide" 'I saw.' It is immaterial whether this recurring phrase is consciously or unconsciously uttered, whether it is Montejo's own or Barnet's attribution. It has added emphasis because it is one of the principal archaisms (for "yo vi") in the text, and it clearly punctuates the narrative as an attribution of authenticity. By the same token, it is counterbalanced very carefully by statements to the effect that the narrator did not actually witness such and such an event or circumstance. That is, there is a clear interplay between what the narrator can claim as true by virtue of personal experience and what he can only report as claimed by others. In turn, such reportorial humility further authenticates the story because it lends credence to what Montejo maintains as personal experiences. This effect is especially noticeable when he refers to what the modern reader would likely take as traditional superstition rather than as verifiable fact: "Yo digo esto porque da por resultado que yo lo vide mucho en la esclavitud" 'I mention this because it turns out that I saw a lot of it during slavery' (32; my trans.).

Throughout his autobiography, Montejo recognizes the importance of his memory, for—to the extent that he can relate personal experiences to the sociohistorical panorama of Cuba—it gives continuity to his story and coherence to the information he is relaying. Thus he repeatedly stipulates the disjunction between the historical reality he clearly recalls and the imperfect memory of people today or between that historical reality and the changes that have occurred in Cuban society. Montejo's overriding concern is to explain how things were. His goal is to interpret for his audience (Barnet, in immediate terms; the anonymous reader of the text, in general) his life as a black slave and second-class citizen in Cuba. Although the resulting texture is narrative primarily because it has as an organizing point of reference the life of the first-person narrator, with little dramatic or active narrative, *Biografía* is a documentary with the undeniable novelistic traces I have outlined.

VII

It should be apparent that a clear unity underlies

the five works I examine in this study: all depend, for their defining structural principle, on the productive interfacing of a narrative explicitly framed by an author but attributable to historically "real" individuals. A sociopolitical continuity links Latin American novels from their origins in the late Renaissance chronicles of the Conquest, and an overwhelming testimonial quality characterizes the dominant strands of contemporary Latin American literature. Hence, any definition of documentary literature must go beyond the referential ties between texts and historical events.

Instead of pursuing a nebulous classification based on degrees of fictionality and referentiality, I have tried to identify those texts in which a credibly real story is given an explicit narrative framework by an intervening narrator. Not insignificantly, these narrators are acknowledged and often well-known novelists. Thus, although I avoid the question of fictionality by concentrating on essentially nonfictional documents, I give special prominence to the issue of narrativity, the ways acknowledged novelists frame their narratives and use standard narrative strategies such as complementary and contrapuntal juxtaposition (Poniatowska and Walsh), irony (García Márquez and Valdés), authorial editing and commentary (Walsh and Barnet), foreshadowing and echoing of events (García Márquez and Walsh), and disjunctive interplay between levels of text like natural discourse and transcribed narrative (Barnet and Valdés). These strategies do not make the five texts novels any more than the parables and other varieties of narrative make the Bible a novel. Rather, by invoking and echoing the structuring principles of mainstream contemporary Latin American novels, they underscore the continuity between imaginative literature and documentary in Latin American culture.

Arizona State University
Tempe

Notes

[1] Virtually all the major studies on Latin American literature make this point. See Fernández Moreno and the polemic of Collazos and Cortázar. Miguel Barnet, one of the authors I examine in this study, establishes fundamental criteria in "La novela testimonio: Socio-literatura" (*La canción de Rachel* 125–50).

[2] Social realism has yet to be adequately studied in Latin America. See, however, the monographs by Juan Carlos Portantiero and by Harry L. Rosser.

[3] There is little criticism on Poniatowska beyond brief notes. See Miller and González. Poniatowska speaks of *Noche* in *Vida Literaria*; the same issue contains commentaries by other writers.

[4] One can make such a summary statement only at great critical risk. Clearly, it accords with Carpentier's "lo real-maravilloso" and Carlos Fuentes' view of the contemporary Spanish American novel in *La nueva novela hispanoamericana*, in direct contrast to the "anamythopoesis" of hard-line Marxists like Hernán Vidal.

[5] See Fuentes' play *Todos los gatos son pardos* (1970), which views the massacre at Tlatelolco in the context of the Mexican Aztec-Christian-postrevolutionary sacrificial culture.

[6] Poniatowska dedicates her novel to her brother Jan, who died at Tlatelolco. Except in a few quotations, however, this personal relationship is virtually absent.

[7] Despite the universally recognized importance of García Márquez' writings, *Relato* has received only brief comment; see Müller-Bergh and Ruffinelli, "Diez días en el mar." See also Ruffinelli's "Un periodista llamado." The standard monographic study, by fellow novelist Mario Vargas Llosa, does not consider *Relato*.

[8] The difference between *Biografía* as a documentary novel and *Canción* as a testimonial novel is instructive. *Canción*, through the recollections of a fictional courtesan who is in retirement at the time of the Castro revolution, serves as a point of reference for the outlines of modern Cuban sociocultural history. See Chang-Rodríguez; Barnet, "Miguel Barnet charla"; and Bejel. Angel Luis Fernández Guerra treats the relation between Barnet's two major works.

For a thorough analysis of *Biografía* as an example of the innovative contributions of Cuban narrative, see González Echevarría. Although González Echevarría focuses on *Biografía* as a documentary novel, he emphasizes the sociocultural issue of literature versus history rather than the narrative strategies I stress here. Pedro M. Barreda does not consider the unquestionable "narrativity" of *Biografía*.

[9] The recent publication of Juan Francisco Manzano's *The Life and Poems of a Cuban Slave* demonstrates the continuing interest in Cuban slave literature.

Works Cited

Avellaneda, Andrés Oscar. "El tema del peronismo en la narrativa argentina." Diss. Univ. of Illinois 1973.

Barnet, Miguel. *The Autobiography of a Runaway Slave.* Trans. Jacosta Innes. London: Bodley Head, 1966.

———. *Biografía de un cimarrón.* México: Siglo XXI, 1971.

———. *La canción de Rachel.* Barcelona: Estela, 1970.

———. "Miguel Barnet charla con los editores de *Vórtice.*" *Vórtice* 2.2-3 (1979): 1-10.

Barreda, Pedro M. *The Black Protagonist in the Cuban Novel.* Amherst: Univ. of Massachusetts Press, 1979.

Barros Sierra, Javier. *1968: Conversaciones con Gastón García Cantú.* México: Siglo XXI, 1972.

Bejel, Emilio. "Entrevista: Miguel Barnet." *Hispamérica* no. 29 (Aug. 1981): 41-52.

Bissett, Judith Ismael. "Consciousness-Raising Dramatic Structures in Latin America's Theater of Commitment." Diss. Arizona State Univ. 1976.

Borello, Rodolfo A. "Novela e historia: La visión fictiva del período peronista en las letras argentinas." *Anales de Literatura Hispanoamericana* no. 8 (1979): 29-72.

Campos Lemus, Sócrates A. *El Otoño de revolución (octubre).* México: Costa-Amic, 1973.

Carpentier, Alejo. "De lo real maravillosamente americano." In his *Tientos y diferencias (ensayos).* México: Univ. Nacional Autónoma de México, 1964, 115-35.

Castellanos, Jorge, and Miguel A. Martínez. "El dictador hispanoamericano como personaje literario." *Latin American Research Review* 16.2 (1981): 79-105.

Chang-Rodríguez, Raquel. "Sobre *La canción de Rachel,* novela-testimonio." *Revista Iberoamericana* 44 (1978): 133-38.

Christ, Ronald. "The Author as Editor." *Review of the Center for Inter-American Relations* no. 15 (1975): 78-79.

Collazos, Oscar, and Julio Cortázar. *Literatura en la revolución y revolución en la literatura.* México: Siglo XXI, 1970.

"Coloquio sobre literatura chilena de la resistencia y del exilio." *Casa de las Américas* no. 112 (1979): 73-109.

Dorfman, Ariel. *Imaginación y violencia en América.* Santiago: Universitaria, 1970.

Epple, Juan Armando. "Esa literatura que surge de un cerco de púas." *Literatura Chilena en el Exilio* 2.1 (1978): 7-8.

Fernández Guerra, Angel Luis. "Cimarrón y Rachel: Un 'continuum.'" *Unión* 9.4 (1970): 161-67.

Fernández Moreno, César, comp. *América latina en su literatura.* México: Siglo XXI, 1972.

Ford, Aníbal. "Walsh: La reconstrucción de los hechos." In *Nueva novela latinoamericana.* Ed. Jorge Lafforgue. Buenos Aires: Paidós, 1969-72, 2: 272-322.

Foster, David William. "Augusto Roa Bastos's *I the Supreme:* The Image of a Dictator." *Latin American Literary Review* 4.7 (1975): 31-35.

Franco, Jean. "The Critique of the Pyramid and Mexican Narrative after 1968." In *Latin American Fiction Today: A Symposium.* Ed. Rose S. Minc. Takoma Park, Md.: Hispamérica; Upper Montclair, N.J.: Montclair State Coll., [1979], 49-60.

Fuentes, Carlos. *La nueva novela hispanoamericana.* México: Joaquín Mortiz, 1969.

———. *Todos los gatos son pardos.* México: Siglo XXI, 1970.

García Márquez, Gabriel. *Relato de un náufrago.* . . . Barcelona: Tusquets, 1970.

Goldar, Ernesto. *El peronismo en la literatura argentina.* Buenos Aires: Freeland, 1971.

González Echevarría, Roberto. "*Biografía de un cimarrón* and the Novel of the Cuban Revolution." *Novel* 13 (1980): 249-63.

Hellmann, John. *Fables of Fact: The New Journalism as New Fiction.* Urbana: Univ. of Illinois Press, 1981.

Hollowell, John. *Fact and Fiction: The New Journalism and the Nonfiction Novel.* Chapel Hill: Univ. of North Carolina Press, 1977.

Jitrik, Noé. *El no existente caballero: La idea de personaje y su evolución en la narrativa latinoamericana.* Buenos Aires: Megápolis, 1975.

Leal, Luis. "Tlatelolco, Tlatelolco." *Denver Quarterly* 14.1 (1979): 3-13.

Lyday, Leon F., and George W. Woodyard, eds. *Dramatists in Revolt: The New Latin American Theater.* Austin: Univ. of Texas Press, 1976.

Manzano, Juan Francisco. *The Life and Poems of a Cuban Slave.* Ed. Edward J. Mullen. Hamden, Ct.: Archon, 1981.

Massey, Kenneth W. "From behind the Bars of Signifiers and Signifieds." *Dispositio* 2 (1977): 87-92.

Miliani, Domingo. "El dictador: Objeto narrativo en *Yo el Supremo.*" *Revista de Crítica Literaria Latinoamericana* no. 4 (1976): 103-19.

Miller, Beth, and Alfonso González. "Elena Poniatowska." In their *26 autores del México actual.* México: Costa-Amic, 1978, 299-321.

Mora, Juan Miguel de. *Tlatelolco, por fin toda la verdad.* México: Editores Asociados, 1975.

Morello-Frosch, Marta. "La ficción se historifica: Cortázar y Rozenmacher." In *Actas del Simposio Internacional de Estudios Hispánicos.* Budapest: Akad. Kiadó, 1978, 401-11.

Moreno Fraginals, Manuel. "*Biografía de un cimarrón.*" *Casa de las Américas* no. 40 (1967): 131-32.

Müller-Bergh, Klaus. "*Relato de un náufrago:* Gabriel García Márquez' Tale of Shipwreck and Survival at Sea." *Books Abroad* 47 (1973): 430-66.

Paz, Octavio. *The Other Mexico: Critique of the Pyramid.* Trans. Lysander Kemp. New York: Grove, 1972.

———. *Postdata.* México: Siglo XXI, 1970.

Poniatowska, Elena. "Un libro que me fue dado." *Vida Literaria* no. 3 (1970): 3-4.

———. *Massacre in Mexico.* Trans. Helen R. Lane. Viking, 1975.

———. *La noche de Tlatelolco: Testimonios de historia oral.* México: Era, 1971.

Portantiero, Juan Carlos. *Realismo y realidad en la narrativa argentina.* Buenos Aires: Procyón, 1961.

Rodríguez Monegal, Emir. "David Viñas en su contorno." *Mundo Nuevo* no. 18 (1967): 75-86. Rpt. in his *Narradores de esta América.* Montevideo: Alfa, 1969-74, 2: 310-30.

Rosser, Harry L. *Conflict and Transition in Rural Mexico: The Fiction of Social Realism.* Boston: Crossroads, 1980.

Ruffinelli, Jorge. "Diez días en el mar." In *Sobre García*

Márquez. Ed. Pedro Simón Martínez. Montevideo: Biblioteca de Marcha, 1971, 207–09.

———. "Un periodista llamado Gabriel García Márquez." In his *Crítica en marcha: Ensayos sobre literatura latinoamericana.* México: Premia, 1979, 59–69.

Schulman, Ivan A. "Reflections on Cuba and Its Antislavery Literature." *Southeastern Conference on Latin American Studies* 7 (1976): 59–67.

Skármeta, Antonio, ed. *Joven narrativa chilena después del golpe.* Clear Creek, Ind.: American Hispanist, 1976.

Szichman, Mario. *La verdadera crónica falsa.* Buenos Aires: Centro Editor de América Latina, 1972.

Valdés, Hernán. *Tejas Verdes: Diario de un campo de concentración en Chile.* Barcelona: Ariel, 1974.

Vargas Llosa, Mario. *García Márquez: Historia de un deicidio.* Caracas: Monte Avila; Barcelona: Barral, 1971.

Vidal, Hernán. *Literatura hispanoamericana e ideología liberal: Surgimiento y crisis (una problemática sobre la dependencia en torno a la narrativa del boom).* Takoma, Md.: Hispamérica, 1976.

Walsh, Rodolfo. *Operación masacre.* Buenos Aires: Jorge Alvarez, 1969.

Weber, Ronald. *The Literature of Fact: Literary Nonfiction in American Writing.* Athens: Ohio Univ. Press, 1980.

Zavarzadeh, Mas'ud. *The Mythopoeic Reality: The Postwar American Nonfiction Novel.* Urbana: Univ. of Illinois Press, 1976.

"Through All Things Modern": Second
Thoughts on Testimonio

John Beverley

This is why Indians are thought to be stupid. They can't think, they
don't know anything, they say. But we have hidden our identity because we needed to resist, we wanted to protect what governments
have wanted to take away from us. They have tried to take our
things away and impose others on us, be it through religion, through
dividing up the land, through schools, through books, through radio,
through all things modern.
—Rigoberta Menchú, *I, Rigoberta Menchú. An Indian Woman in
Guatemala* [1]

To situate the title and the quote: These are second thoughts both
on the testimonio itself and on my own work on testimonio.[2] By *testimonio*

This paper had its genesis in a talk presented at a conference at the Kellogg Institute
of the University of Notre Dame entitled "Narrative Practices and Cultural Discourse In
Latin America," March 23, 1990. It will appear in a collection of papers from that conference edited by Steven Bell et al., *Critical Theory, Cultural Politics and Latin American
Narrative* (South Bend: University of Notre Dame Press, forthcoming).
1. Rigoberta Menchú, with Elizabeth Burgos, *I, Rigoberta Menchú. An Indian Woman in
Guatemala*, trans. Ann Wright (London: Verso, 1984), 170–71. All subsequent references
to this text will be cited parenthetically by page number only.
2. John Beverley, "The Margin at the Center: On Testimonio (Testimonial Narrative),"

boundary 2 18:2, 1991. Copyright © 1991 by Duke University Press. CCC 0190-3659/91/$1.50.

I understand a novel or novella-length narrative told in the first person by a narrator who is also the real-life protagonist or witness of the events he or she recounts. In recent years it has become an important, perhaps the dominant, form of literary narrative in Latin America. The best-known example available in English translation is the text that the passage above comes from, *I, Rigoberta Menchú*, the life story of a young Guatemalan Indian woman, which, as she puts it in her presentation, is intended to represent "the reality of a whole people."[3]

I want to start with the February 1990 elections in Nicaragua, which remind us of Jameson's redefinition of Lacan's category of the real as that which hurts. A decade after the revolutionary high tide of 1979–1981, it is clear that the moment of optimism about the possibilities for rapid social transformation in Central America has passed. Whether this represents a new, postrevolutionary stage in that region's history or simply a recession before the appearance of a new cycle of radicalization—perhaps also involving Mexico this time—is open to question. Testimonios like *I, Rigoberta Menchú*, or Omar Cabezas's *Fire from the Mountain* and Margaret Randall's *Sandino's Daughters* from Nicaragua, were very much part of the literary imaginary of our solidarity with or critical support for the Central American revolutions. So the electoral defeat of the Sandinistas, while it is certainly not absolute—there is still quite a bit of room for maneuver and struggle—must force us in any case to reconsider the relation between testimonio, liberation struggles, and academic pedagogy. I want to center this reconsideration in particular around the question of the relation of testimonio to the field of literature. This will in turn connect with some questions about what it is we do in the humanities generally, and particularly in connection with Latin American and Third World literatures.

I ended my reflection on the testimonio in "The Margin at the Center" with the thought that

> literature, even where it is infused with a popular-democratic form
> and content, as in the case of *testimonio*, is not in itself a popular-

---

Modern Fiction Studies 35/1 (1989): 11–28, a special issue entitled "Narratives of Colonial Resistance," edited by Timothy Brennan. This essay hereafter cited in my text as MC.
3. "My name is Rigoberta Menchú. I am twenty-three years old. This is my testimony. I didn't learn it from a book, and I didn't learn it alone. I'd like to stress that it's not only *my* life, it's also the testimony of my people. It's hard for me to remember everything that's happened to me in my life since there have been many very bad times but, yes, moments of joy as well. The important thing is that what has happened to me has happened to many other people too: My story is the story of all poor Guatemalans. My personal experience is the reality of a whole people" (1).

democratic cultural form, and (*pace* Gramsci) it is an open question as to whether it can ever be. How much of a favor do we do *testimonio* by positing, as here, that it has become a new form of literature or by making it an alternative reading to the canon (one track of the new Stanford civilization requirement now includes *I, Rigoberta Menchú*)? Perhaps such moves preempt or occlude a vision of an emergent popular-democratic culture that is no longer based on the institutions of humanism and literature. (MC, 26)

I might have added "no longer based, that is, on the university," because I believe that literature and the university (in the historically specific form each takes during and after the Renaissance) have been, appearances to the contrary, mutually dependent on each other and as such deeply implicated in the processes of state formation and colonial expansion that define early modern Europe. This legacy still marks each, making their interaction in contemporary processes of decolonization and postcoloniality at the same time both necessary and problematic.

Testimonios are in a sense made for people like us, in that they allow us to participate as academics and yuppies, without leaving our studies and classrooms, in the concreteness and relativity of actual social struggles ("we," "our," and "us" designate here the readers—or potential readers—of this journal). To borrow a passage from Bakhtin's definition of prose art in his essay "Discourse in the Novel" (with thanks to Barbara Harlow for bringing it to my attention), testimonios are texts whose discourses are "still warm from the struggle and hostility, as yet unresolved and still fraught with hostile intentions and accents." But they are (putting Derrida in parentheses here) still also *just* texts and not actual warm or, in the case of the victims of the death squads, not-so-warm bodies. I am not trying to guilt-trip people about being academics and yuppies. I am both. Russell Jacoby's critique of the academic encapsulation of the Left is wrong; the university is an absolutely crucial and central institution of late capitalist society. I believe in Gramsci's slogan of a long march through the institutions, and it follows that I think that our battlefield is the classroom and conference hall, that the struggle over the teaching and interpretation of literature has something to do with the production of new forms of ideological hegemony. As a pedagogic issue, the use of testimonio has to do concretely with the possibility of interpellating our students (and all readers are or were at one time students) in a relation of solidarity with liberation movements and human rights struggles, both here in the United States and abroad.

In the theoretical discussion on testimonio, much deconstructive

117

zeal has been spent on the fact that it is a mediated narrative: as in the case of *I, Rigoberta Menchú*, an oral narrative told by a speaker from a subaltern or "popular" social class or group to an interlocutor who is an intellectual or professional writer from the middle or upper class (and in many cases from a different ethno-linguistic position: the equivalent of what Peruvians call a *pituco*—white, upper class, culturally European, etc.), who then according to this subject position edits and textualizes the account, making it available to a similarly positioned national and international reading public as a printed book or pamphlet. The possibilities for distortion and/or cooptation in such a situation are many, as Gayatri Spivak has suggested in "Can the Subaltern Speak?" But one of the things that can be said in its favor is that it can serve as both an allegorical figure for, and a concrete means of, the union of a radicalized (Marxist) intelligentsia with the subaltern. Moreover, it is a relationship in which neither of the participants has to cancel its identity as such. Testimonios have become, in certain sorts of conjunctures, a discursive space where the possibilities of such an alliance can be negotiated on both sides without too much angst about otherness or "othering." Spivak is correct that "contemporary invocations of 'libidinal economy' and desire as the determining interest, combined with the practical politics of the oppressed (under socialized capital) 'speaking for themselves,' restore the category of the sovereign subject within the theory that seems most to question it."[4] But this is more a question—and not a simple one at that— of the ideology of the consumers of testimonio rather than its producers. Moreover, political struggle involves not only the critique of the forms of the dominant ideology but also the necessarily ideological production of new forms of identity. As Doris Sommer has noted, "To read women's testimonials, curiously, is to mitigate the tension between First World self and Third World other. I do not mean this as a license to deny the differences, but as a reminder that the testimonial subject is as complex and as available for coalitions as any other."[5]

I understand, of course, that "literature" is itself a matter of semiosis, of who defines what counts under what institutional circumstances. The political question is what is gained or lost by including or excluding under this name any particular kind of discursive practice. As in the Stanford civilization requirements, the pedagogic incorporation of testimonio in

4. Gayatri Spivak, "Can the Subaltern Speak?" in *Marxism and the Interpretation of Culture*, ed. C. Nelson and L. Grossberg (Urbana: University of Illinois Press, 1988), 278.
5. Doris Sommer, "No Secrets: Testimonio and Guarded Truth" (unpublished manuscript, 1988), version forthcoming in the special issue of *Latin American Perspectives* on testimonio.

the academy has strategically involved a theoretical-critical struggle to define it not just as an ethnographic document or "life history" but as part
of the canon of Great Works through which the humanist subject as such
is formed in a modern, multicultural curriculum.[6] The authorizing operation
of literary criticism, including "The Margin at the Center," in this regard
has been to articulate testimonio as a form of "minor" literature particularly sensitive to the representation or expression of subalternity. Fredric
Jameson gives it his imprimatur as an alternative to what he terms the
"overripe subjectivity" of the bildungsroman; Barbara Harlow makes it a
key form of Resistance Literature; Cornell publishes Barbara Foley's book
on "documentary fiction"—a category that subsumes the testimonio; Margaret Randall offers a "how to" manual for would-be practitioners of the
form; George Yúdice sees it as a Third World form of a postmodernism of
resistance; Juan Duchesne writes a doctoral dissertation at SUNY-Albany
on Latin American guerrilla narratives; Gayatri Spivak and Elzbieta Sklodowska caution against a naïve reception of the form; and so on.[7] Even to
arrive at the situation we are now in, where it has become fashionable to

6. Thus, for example, Allen Carey-Webb, who teaches an undergraduate course on world
literature based entirely on testimonios at the University of Oregon, notes of I, Rigoberta
Menchú: "[It] is one of the most moving books I have ever read. It is the kind of book
that I feel I must pass on, that I must urge fellow teachers to use in their classes. . . .
My students were immediately sympathetic to Menchú's story and were anxious to know
more, to involve themselves. They asked questions about culture and history, about their
own position in the world, and about the purposes and methods of education. Many saw
in the society of the Guatemalan Indian attractive features they found lacking in their
own lives, strong family relationships, community solidarity, an intimate relationship with
nature, commitment to others and to one's beliefs." See Allen Carey-Webb, "Teaching
Third World Auto/Biography: Testimonial Narrative in the Canon and Classroom," Oregon
English XII, no. 2 (Fall 1990): 8.
7. See, respectively, Fredric Jameson, "Third World Literature in the Era of Multinational
Capitalism," Social Text 15 (1986): 65–88, and his interview with Anders Stephanson,
Social Text 17 (1987): 26–27; Barbara Harlow, Resistance Literature (New York: Methuen,
1987); Barbara Foley, Telling the Truth: The Theory and Practice of Documentary Fiction
(Ithaca: Cornell University Press, 1986); Margaret Randall, Testimonios: A Guide to Oral
History (Toronto: Participatory Research Group, 1985); George Yúdice, "Marginality and
the Ethics of Survival," in Universal Abandon. The Politics of Postmodernism, ed. Andrew
Ross (Minneapolis: University of Minnesota Press, 1988), 214–36, and "Central American
Testimonio," essay forthcoming in a special issue of Latin American Perspectives on tes-
timonio; Juan Duchesne, "Las narraciones guerrilleras: Configuración de un sujeto épico
de nuevo tipo," in Testimonio y Literatura, ed. H. Vidal and R. Jara (Minneapolis: Ideologies and Literature, 1986), 137–85; Spivak, "Can the Subaltern Speak?" 271–313; and
Elzbieta Sklodowska, "La forma testimonial y la novelística de Miguel Barnet," Revista/
Review Interamericana 12/3 (1982): 368–80.

deconstruct in de Manian fashion this or that testímonio (Roberto González Echevarría was the pioneer of this in his article on Miguel Barnet's *Auto-biography of a Runaway Slave*[8]), still is to give it, in effect, a status as a literary text comparable to, say, Rousseau's *Confessions*.

This is fine and basically correct as far as I am concerned. There is no reason to suppose that Rousseau has anything more or less to tell us than Rigoberta Menchú or Esteban Montejo, the narrator of *Autobiography of a Runaway Slave*. But we must also understand why testimonio comes into being outside or at the margin of the historically constituted institution of literature in modern Western culture. At least part of its aesthetic effect—I mean this precisely in the Russian Formalist sense of *ostranenie* or defamiliarization—is that it is *not* literary, not linguistically elaborated or authorial. One symptom of this has been an ambivalence about the "artistic" as opposed to the "documentary" character of testimonio and about the distinction between testimonio per se and the more elaborated "testimonial novel" (*novela-testimonio*), such as those of Miguel Barnet (Capote's *In Cold Blood* would be an English-language equivalent).[9] Testimonio appears where the adequacy of existing literary forms and styles—even of the dominant language itself—for the representation of the subaltern has entered into crisis.[10] Even where its instrumentality is to reach in printed

8. Roberto González Echevarría, "*Biografía de un cimarrón* and the Novel of the Cuban Revolution," in his *The Voice of the Masters: Writing and Authority in Modern Latin American Literature* (Austin: University of Texas Press, 1985), 110–24.

9. An instance of this ambivalence may be found in the definition of testimonio in the contest rules of the prestigious literary prizes of Cuba's Casa de las Américas (it was the decision of Casa de las Américas in 1971 to offer a prize in this category that put testimonio on the canonical map of Latin American literature in the first place): "Testimonios must document some aspect of Latin American or Caribbean reality from a direct source. A direct source is understood as knowledge of the facts by their author and his or her compilation of narratives or evidence obtained from the individuals involved or qualified witnesses. In both cases reliable documentation, written or graphic, is indispensable. The form is at the author's discretion, *but literary quality is also indispensable*" (my translation and italics). But is there a determination of "literary quality" that does not involve in turn an ideology of the literary? Against a modernist bias in favor of textual collage and/or editorial elaboration in the preparation of a testimonial text, one could argue that a direct, "unliterary" narrative might have both a higher ethical *and* aesthetic status.

10. See for example the remarks of the great Peruvian novelist José María Arguedas on the difficulty of reconciling in his own work an inherited Spanish-language model of literariness with the representation of the world of Quechua- or Aymara-speaking Andean peasants: "I wrote my first story in the most correct and 'literary' Spanish I could devise. I read the story to some of my writer friends in the capital, and they praised it. But I came

form a metropolitan reading public culturally and physically distant from the position and situation of its narrator, testimonio is not engendered out of the same humanist ideology of the literary that motivates its reception by this public or its incorporation into the humanities curriculum; and in some cases it actively resists being literature. Let me give two examples, one from a contemporary Salvadoran testimonio, the other from *I, Rigoberta Menchú*.

Ana Guadalupe Martínez's testimonio *Las cárceles clandestinas de El Salvador* (The secret prisons of El Salvador) deals with her involvement in the Salvadoran guerrilla underground with the Ejército Revolucionario del Pueblo (ERP—Revolutionary Army of the People) and her capture, torture, and imprisonment by the army. She insists that her account is "the result of a collective and militant effort, and *has no intellectual or literary pretensions*; it is a contribution to the ideological development and formation of cadres on the basis of concrete experience that should be discussed and analyzed by those who are consistently immersed in the making of the revolution." Her co-prologuist, René Cruz, similarly notes: "There is considerable concrete experience which has been lost by not being processed and transmitted by militants, and another large part has been deformed in its essence by being elaborated by leftist intellectual intermediaries who adjust what they are relating not in relation to revolutionary needs but *in relation to the needs of fiction and bourgeois revolutionary theorizing*." [11]

The point about "no intellectual pretensions" is disingenuous, and there is more than a trace here of the intense sectarianism that has marked the Salvadoran revolutionary movement. "Leftist intellectual intermediaries" allude to the most famous modern Salvadoran writer, Roque Dalton, who

---

to detest more and more those pages. No, what I wanted to describe—one could almost say denounce—wasn't like that at all, not the person, not the town, not the landscape. Under a false language a world appeared as invented, without marrow and without blood: a typically 'literary' world in which the word had consumed the work." This quotation from "La novela y el problema de la expresión literaria en el Perú," in *Obras completas*, II (Lima: Editorial Horizonte, 1983), 196; my translation. Arguedas's solution was to develop a novel in Spanish, based stylistically and thematically on the tension between Spanish and Quechua. By contrast, there is the well-known example of the Kenyan writer Ngũgĩ wa Thiong'o, who, in 1977, after publishing a series of successful anticolonial novels in English, decided to write his novels, plays, and stories exclusively in his tribal language Kikuyu. See his *Decolonising the Mind. The Politics of Language in African Literature* (Portsmouth, NH: Heinemann, 1987).

11. Ana Guadalupe Martínez, *Las cárceles clandestinas de El Salvador* (México: Casa El Salvador, 1979), 12–14; my translation and emphasis.

also worked in testimonial forms,[12] and who, as it happens, was Martínez's adversary in an internal debate in the ERP in the mid-seventies over the direction of the armed struggle (a debate that led to his assassination by the leadership faction of the ERP that Martínez supported). Still, her point is worth taking. She wants to do something *other than* literature with her narrative and feels it would in some sense be compromised or betrayed by becoming literature, whereas Dalton, like Miguel Barnet, was concerned with the ideological and aesthetic problems of making testimonio a form of left modernist literature.

I, Rigoberta Menchú begins with a strategic disavowal of both literature and the liberal concept of the authority of private experience: "My name is Rigoberta Menchú. I am twenty-three years old. This is my testimony. I didn't learn it from a book, and I didn't learn it alone" (1). The quote at the start of this essay belongs with a series of passages in her text where Menchú explicitly counterposes book learning to direct experience or attacks the presence of no doubt well-intentioned schoolteachers in her village, arguing that they represent an agency of penetration and destruction of the highland Indian communities by the landowners and the Guatemalan state. Here are some others:

> When children reach ten years old [in our village], that's the moment when their parents and the village leaders talk to them again. . . . It's also when they remind them that our ancestors were dishonored by the White Man, by colonization. But they don't tell them the way it's written down in books, because the majority of Indians can't read or write, and don't even know that they have their own texts. No, they learn it through oral recommendations, the way it has been handed down through the generations. (13)

> I had a lot of ideas but I knew I couldn't express them all. I wanted to read or write Spanish. I told my father this, that I wanted to learn to read. Perhaps things were different if you could learn to read. My father said, "Who will teach you? You have to find out by yourself, because I can't help you. I know of no schools and I have no money for them anyway." I told him that if he talked to the priests, perhaps

12. See Roque Dalton's *Miguel Mármol* (San José: EDUCA, 1982), a reconstruction of the life of one of the founders of the Salvadoran Communist party, and his own autobiographical novel of the guerrilla underground, *Pobrecito poeta que era yo* (San José: EDUCA, 1976).

they'd give me a scholarship. But my father said he didn't agree with that idea because I was trying to leave the community, to go far away, and find out what was best for me. He said: "You'll forget about our common heritage." . . . My father was very suspicious of schools and all that sort of thing. He gave as an example the fact that many of my cousins had learned to read and write but they hadn't been of use to the community. They try to move away and feel different when they can read and write. (89)

Sometimes I'd hear how those teachers taught and what education was like in the villages. They said that the arrival of the Spaniards was a conquest, a victory, while we knew in practice that it was just the opposite. . . . This taught me that even though a person may learn to read and write, he should not accept the false education they give our people. Our people must not think as the authorities think. (169–70)

When teachers come into the villages, they bring with them the ideas of capitalism and getting on in life. They try and impose these ideas on us. I remember that in my village there were two teachers for a while and they began teaching the people, but the children told their parents everything they were being taught at school and the parents said: "We don't want our children to become like *ladinos* [in Guatemala, a Spanish-speaking white or mestizo]." And they made the teachers leave. . . . For the Indian, it is better not to study than to become like *ladinos*. (205)

One aspect of the archeology of Menchú's position here involves the Spanish practice during the Conquest of segregating the children of the Indian aristocracy from their families in order to teach them literacy and Christian doctrine. Walter Mignolo has observed that this practice

shows that literacy is not instilled without violence. The violence, however, is not located in the fact that the youngsters have been assembled and enclosed day and night. It comes, rather, from the interdiction of having conversations with their parents, particularly with their mothers. In a primary oral society, in which virtually all knowledge is transmitted by means of conversation, the preservation of oral contact was contradictory with the effort to teach how to read and write. Forbidding conversations with the mother meant,

123

basically, depriving the children of the living culture imbedded in the language and preserved and transmitted in speech.[13]

But it is not that, coming from a predominantly oral culture, Rigoberta Menchú does not value literacy or formal education at all. Part of the oedipal struggle with her father recounted in her story involves precisely her desire and eventually success as a teenager at learning first to memorize, then read, passages from the Bible in order to become a Catholic lay catechist (just as later she would learn Spanish and several other Indian languages because of the exigencies of her work as a peasant organizer and would lead a fight to have a school built in her community).[14] It is rather, as these passages suggest, that she does not accept literacy and book learning, and the narrative of cultural and linguistic modernization they entail, as either adequate or *normative* cultural modes. She is conscious, among other things, of the holistic relation between the individualization produced by the government schools and the attempts to impose on her community an agrarian reform based on private ownership of parcels (as opposed to its tradition of communal ownership and sharing of resources). That is why she remains a testimonial narrator rather than an "author"—a subject position that in fact would imply, as in the case of Richard Rodriquez's memoir *Hunger of Memory*, a self-imposed separation from her community and culture of birth (and a loss or change of name). As Doris Sommer has shown, even in the act of addressing us through the literary artifice of the testimonio—which is built on the convention of truth-telling and openness—Menchú is also consciously withholding information from us on the grounds that it could be used against her and her people by academically trained or advised counterinsurgency specialists: "Her testimonial is an invitation to a tête-à-tête, not to a heart to heart."[15] Menchú is aware, in other words, of something we may have forgotten since the Vietnam War: the complicity of the university in cultural (and sometimes actual) genocide. The concluding words of her testimonio are "I'm still keeping secret what I think no one

13. Walter Mignolo, "Literacy and Colonization: The New World Experience," in *1492–1992: Re/Discovering Colonial Writing* (*Hispanic Issues*, vol. 4), ed. R. Jara and N. Spadaccini (Minneapolis: Prisma Institute, 1989), 67.

14. Mignolo similarly is careful to distinguish in the same essay the literacy policies of the colonial and neocolonial state from the contemporary literacy campaigns instituted for example by the Cuban and Nicaraguan revolutions based on the methods of Paolo Freyre's "pedagogy of the oppressed," which he sees as a means of empowerment of the subaltern.

15. Sommer, "No Secrets: Testimonio and Guarded Truth," see n. 5 above.

should know. Not even anthropologists or intellectuals, no matter how many books they have, can find out all our secrets." (247)

We could say that Menchú *uses* the testimonio as literature without subscribing to a humanist ideology of the literary or, what amounts to the same thing, without abandoning her identity and role as an Indian activist to become a professional writer. This may be one way of answering Spivak's question in "Can the Subaltern Speak?" No, not as such (because "the subaltern is the name of the place which is so displaced . . . that to have it speak is like Godot arriving on a bus").[16] But the testimonial narrator like Rigoberta Menchú is not the subaltern, as such, either, rather something more like an "organic intellectual" of the subaltern, who speaks to the hegemony by means of a metonymy of self in the name and in the place of it. Testimonio is located at the intersection of the cultural forms of bourgeois humanism, like literature and the printed book, engendered by the academy and colonialism and imperialism, and subaltern cultural forms. It is not an authentic expression of the subaltern (whatever that might be),[17] but it is not (or should not be) easily assimilable to, or collectible *as*, literature, either.

My recent work with Marc Zimmerman on Central American revolutionary poetry[18] showed that it was not just a reflection or expression of an already constituted ideology of national liberation but rather a precondition for its elaboration; that something like the Sandinista revolution in Nicaragua depended in some significant ways on developments in modern Nicaraguan poetry initiated by the Granada Vanguardists in the 1930s under the influence of U.S. modernists like Stevens, Pound, and Eliot; that, in a strikingly postmodern way, literature was not only a means of revolutionary politics but also a model for it in Central America. Why this was the

16. Gayatri Spivak, "On the Politics of the Subaltern," interview with Howard Winant in *Socialist Review* 90, no. 3 (July–September 1990), 91. To anticipate the inevitable objections (see e.g., Benita Parry, "Problems in Current Theories of Colonial Discourse," *Oxford Literary Review* 9, no. 1–2 [1988]: 27–58): the subaltern of course speaks quite a lot, but not *to* Gayatri Spivak, so to speak. It is not to trivialize Che Guevara's example to observe that his eerily prophetic sense—noted in *Bolivian Diary*—of the blankness in the eyes of the peasants he encountered in the course of trying to establish a guerrilla *foco* in the Bolivian Andes might have been otherwise had he been able to speak their language, Aymara.

17. See on this point James Clifford, "On Collecting Art and Culture," in *Out There: Marginalization and Contemporary Cultures*, ed. Russell Ferguson et al. (Cambridge: MIT Press, 1990), 141–90.

18. John Beverley and Marc Zimmerman, *Literature and Politics in the Central American Revolutions* (Austin: University of Texas Press, 1990).

case had to do not only with the content of individual texts (i.e., with something that might be revealed by a hermeneutic or deconstructive analysis) but also with the way literature itself was positioned as a social practice by processes of combined and uneven development in Central American history.

As the late Angel Rama argued, a "republic of letters" (*ciudad letrada*) and the consequent normative role of literature and of the writer are among the basic forms of institutional continuity between colonial and contemporary Latin America.[19] The availability of literary texts through the medium of the printed book to an "ideal reader" is a historically and ethnically specific one, linked in Europe to the rise of the middle class, the commodification of literary production and distribution, and the corresponding growth of democratic forms of public education and a reading public, particularly in the nineteenth century. The mode of existence of literature in a caste-ridden, quasi-feudal society like colonial Latin America was in several respects quite different than this. To begin with, as Mignolo's comment illustrates, literature was itself a colonial import, with little or no continuity whatever with pre-Columbian discursive practices (where they existed, pre-Columbian texts were systematically destroyed). Most people in the colonies—perhaps 80 to 90 percent of the population—did not read at all, and many had no or only a rudimentary grasp of even spoken Spanish or Portuguese. In contrast to our contemporary concern with illiteracy (with its implicit equation of literacy, modernization, and democratization), however, this was regarded as a normal, even desirable, state of affairs. Access to written texts in Spanish or Latin was in itself a mark of distinction that separated colonizer from colonized, rulers from ruled, European from native.[20]

This was not just a question of functional literacy, however. The colonial fashion for the highly wrought and complex poetry represented by fashionable metropolitan models like Góngora involved the fetishization of writing as an aristocratic or sublime activity because it eluded, by its difficulty, the comprehension not only of the illiterate but also of those who might be functionally literate but not university-educated—sectors of the indigenous population to begin with, but also lower-class Creoles and the

19. Angel Rama, *La ciudad letrada* (Hanover, N.H.: Ediciones del Norte, 1984).
20. China, the Indian subcontinent, and Islamic Africa had written literatures before colonialism and in this sense differ from Latin America, which experienced a much deeper degree of European colonization both culturally and demographically. But I would argue that, whatever their links to the past, modern literatures in the Third World generally are also basically engendered by colonialism and imperialism.

castas or mixed-bloods. What such a literature transmitted to its readers—the *letrados* or men of letters (for they were almost always men)—in the urban centers of the colonial viceroyalties was not only a sign of aristocratic worth—*honor*—and connection to a distant metropolitan center but also a technique of power, an exercise or formal simulacrum of the ability to discern, organize, sublimate, and ultimately control productively.

This situation affected in part the nature of the literary text itself as a cultural artifact. In general, secular writing in the colonies was not intended for commercial publication and even less for a general reading public. There were printing establishments in the colonies, but—even at the end of the seventeenth century—a major project like the first anthology of the poetry of Sor Juana Inés de la Cruz required publication in Spain. It was common for literary texts to be available only in hand-lettered manuscript copies circulated privately to individual readers or special audiences (*tertulias*).

In its very form of circulation, then, but also in the cultivation of extreme forms of pedantry and linguistic complexity, Latin American colonial literature was not something intended for or available to everyone, certainly not for a socially amorphous public that could lay hold of it through the market in books. Literature (less anachronistically, *letras*, including, for example, history, biography, sermons, letters, and, especially, the essay), in other words, not only had a central role in the self-representation of the upper and upper-middle strata of Latin American colonial society; it was one of the social practices by which such strata constituted themselves as dominant. That is why for a neo-Machiavellian political theorist and moralist like the Jesuit Baltasar Gracián an "art of wit" (*arte de aqudeza*) based on the study of literary conceits (*conceptos*) was a prerequisite for the formation of the baroque man of affairs. (In general, it was via the curricula established by Jesuit pedagogy at the end of the sixteenth and the beginning of the seventeenth century that the new innovations in literature found their way into the hearts and minds of the colonial intelligentsia.)

This very acute sense of the power of literature—which involved both a recognition and an overestimation of its cultural importance—accounts for the prohibition by the colonial authorities of both the publication and importation of novels: the novel was quite literally seen as a medium incompatible with the assumptions of colonial rule (although it could, with heavy censorship, be tolerated in Spain and Portugal). This anomaly, however, also made of literature a place where the ambitions and resentments of Creoles, mestizos, and in some cases Indians or slaves could begin to take shape. The colonial intellectual was in the position of having to mediate in his or her writing between an empirically vivid American reality and an increasingly absent and abstract European model of civilization represented by literature. As in the case of the prohibition of the novel, problems of genre, style, decorum, neologism, and so on could easily become entangled and confused with political and social problems, and literature itself became both a sign of the colony's connection to metropolitan centers in Spain and Portugal (themselves, it should be remembered, only dubiously and recently European) and a practical medium for the elaboration of an ultimately anticolonial sensibility among the Creole upper and middle classes.

The later eighteenth century brought into this scene the sometimes clandestine influence of neoclassicism and Enlightenment literary models, Free Masonry, the Black Legend, Manchester School political economy, the French Revolution, and so on. But in a gesture of formal continuity with the colony, literature was also to be marked as a form of republican institutionality during the independence struggles of the nineteenth century. Latin American liberals—themselves formed pedagogically as *letrados*— saw the development of literature as a way to create a mentality appropriate for the consolidation under their authority of the newly independent republics. The new "national" literatures of Latin America therefore emerged in close connection both to state formation and to the *letrados'* own formation and incorporation into the state as, simultaneously, an intelligentsia and an actual or would-be ruling class. The literatures evolved with the process of social differentiation and status struggle of the members of this intelligentsia. The literatures served to define the letrados' group and personal identity, relationship to power and to other social classes or groups, sense of the defects and possibilities of development of the new societies, and, in a sort of feedback effect, a belief in the central role of literature and literary culture in assuring that development. But by reimposing, now under quasi-democratic and modernizing auspices, writing and literacy as standards of cultural performance, this liberal-romantic cult of literature put the predominantly oral practices of song and narrative of the indigenous population (a majority in some countries) and the mestizo peasantry and rural proletariat in a relation of subordination and domination, deepening the separation between a hegemonic Spanish-language print-based culture and subaltern cultures and languages that had been introduced with the colonial institution of literature.[21]

21. See Rama, *La ciudad letrada*; and in particular Alejandro Losada, "La literatura urbana como praxis social en América Latina," *Ideologies and Literature* 1, no. 4 (1977): 33–62.

The continued centrality of literature as a cultural form in Latin American society, revealed in the popularity of and critical hoopla about Boom narrative, involves something like a modernist (in the English-language sense of the term) revision of this ideology of the literary in its colonial and republican variants. In this revision, the development of new forms of literature is seen as intimately bound up with the question of economic and social modernization, by providing an agency for a progressive process of transculturation—the term was coined by the Cuban ethnographer Fernando Ortiz to describe the interaction of European and African elements in the formation of Cuban culture—involving a sometimes agonistic, sometimes beneficent combination of European and non-European, high and low, urban and rural, intellectual and popular cultural forms. Angel Rama was the most explicit proponent of this concept on the Left, relating it to the tasks of national liberation struggle in the sixties, but in one way or another it has tended to characterize Latin American literary criticism generally during the Boom and after (there is a neoconservative version of it in Octavio Paz, Emir Rodríquez Monegal, or Mario Vargas Llosa, for example). Directly or indirectly connected to this concept is the almost unchallenged assumption in Latin American literary history—its origins are in the work of Pedro Henríquez Ureña, the founder of modern Latin American literary criticism—that the writing of the colonial and independence periods represents a proto-nationalistic process of cultural *mestizaje* and differentiation. As Julio Ramos has noted, this assumption, which made literature and literary values the key signifiers of Latin American nationality for a national-bourgeois intelligentsia, became institutionalized as part of the ideology of the humanities in the Spanish-American university system in the early twentieth century, precisely as a response to the perceived threat represented by proletarianization and U.S.-style mass culture.[22]

I don't want to place myself in the position of denying the sometimes progressive role of literature and the humanities in Latin American society: among other things, such a position would undermine the argument I tried to develop in the book on Central American revolutionary literature. At the same time, the aversion or ambivalence of the testimonio toward literature that we have noted here (and, in a related way, the failure of the poetry workshop experiment in the Nicaraguan revolution championed by Ernesto Cardenal) suggests not only that cultural democratization must involve a

22. Julio Ramos, *Desencuentros de la modernidad en América latina. Literatura y política en el siglo XIX* (México: Fondo de Cultura Económica, 1990).

transformation of literature's dominant forms and character—most particularly a breakdown and renegotiation of the distinctions on which its status as a master discourse have rested—but also that literature itself (along with the concomitant standards and practice of "good writing") may in the process lose its centrality and authority as a cultural practice.

There is a critical moment in the introduction to *I, Rigoberta Menchú* where the interlocutor, the Venezuelan social scientist Elizabeth Burgos, debates with herself about what to correct in the transcription of the recordings of Menchú's conversations with her. She decides to leave in, for example, repetitions and digressions that she considers characteristic of oral narrative but, on the other hand, "to correct the gender mistakes which inevitably occur when someone has just learned to speak a foreign language. It would have been artificial to leave them uncorrected and it would have made Rigoberta look 'picturesque', which is the last thing I wanted" (xx–xxi).

One might object here that the interlocutor is manipulating the material the informant provides to suit her own metropolitan political, intellectual, and aesthetic predilections were it not for the fact that this is not something Menchú herself would have resisted or resented, since her point in telling her story to Burgos was precisely to make it available to metropolitan reading publics both in Guatemala and abroad. For what has happened between Menchú's speech and Burgos's preface is that her narrative has become both a "text" and "literary." There is perhaps no more mediated and editorially mutilated testimonial text in Latin American literature than the *Autobiography* of the Cuban ex-slave Juan Francisco Manzano, which was prepared in 1835 at the urging of the Cuban liberal Domingo Del Monte, corrected and edited by the overtly abolitionist novelist Anselmo Suaréz y Romero, and subsequently abridged and translated into English by the major agent of British imperialism in Cuba, Richard Madden. Sylvia Molloy has compared the unedited version of Manzano's original, handwritten manuscript with the published versions in Spanish and English. She concludes that

> The *Autobiografía* as Manzano wrote it, with its run-in sentences, breathless paragraphs, dislocated syntax and idiosyncratic misspellings, vividly portrays that quandary—an anxiety of origins, ever renewed, that provides the text with the stubborn, uncontrolled energy that is possibly its major achievement. The writing, *in itself*, is the best self-portrait we have of Manzano, his greatest contribution to

literature; at the same time, it is what translators, editors and critics cannot tolerate. . . . [The] notion (shared by many) that there is a clear narrative imprisoned, as it were, in Manzano's *Autobiografía*, waiting for the hand of the cultivated editor to free it from the slag—this notion that the impure text must be replaced by a clean (white?) version of it to be readable—amounts to another, aggressive mutilation, that of denying the text readability in its own terms.[23]

Can we take this, mutatis mutandis, as an allegory of both the production of testimonio and its incorporation into the humanities? What was at stake in the Stanford debate about the core curriculum was the opposition of two different reading lists—one traditional and Euro- and phallocentric, the other Third Worldist and feminist. But literature and the humanities as such—not to speak of Stanford's function in the formation and reproduction of class power in the United States and in the global economy—were never put into question. They were, rather, the condition of possibility of struggle over the curriculum and the reading lists in the first place. I understand this position, and it is one I pursue in my own work of presenting and interpreting texts in the classroom (which has included teaching courses on Central American revolutionary literature at, among other places, Stanford).

But in dealing with the testimonio, I have also begun to discover in myself a kind of posthumanist agnosticism about literature. I am not proposing that there is any more authentic or culturally effective ground than the one we are on as producers and students of literature in the academy, and in any case ideologies (even literary ones), like neuroses, defend themselves with very powerful and effective systems of resistance: nothing you experience in an essay of this sort is going to make you reconsider what you fundamentally believe. But in spite of Ernesto Laclau's point, which I consider extremely important in other contexts, that ideological signifiers do not have a necessary "class-belonging," the problem of testimonio indicates that literature cannot be simply appropriated by this or that social project. It is deeply marked by its own historical and institutional entanglements, its "tradition of service" so to speak. There may come a time when we have a new community of things we can call literature; but not now. Among the many lessons testimonio has to offer us is one that suggests

23. Sylvia Molloy, "From Serf to Self: The Autobiography of Juan Francisco Manzano," *Modern Language Notes* 104 (1989): 417.

that it is no longer a question of "reading against the grain," as in the various academic practices of textual deconstruction we are familiar with, but of beginning to read against literature itself.

Addendum on Postmodernism and Testimonio

I suggested in "The Margin at the Center" a complementarity between Latin American testimonio and First World postmodernism, noting that

> The reception of *testimonio* thus has something to do with a revulsion for fiction and the fictive as such, with its "postmodern" estrangement. *Testimonio*, if you want to look at it that way (and you are certainly not obliged to), could be seen as a form of postmodernist narrative closely related to established U.S. forms like drug or gay narratives, of which William Burroughs' *Junky* is perhaps the classic case, or Black, Chicano, and Puerto Rican autobiography (*The Autobiography of Malcolm X, Down These Mean Streets*), John Rechy's work, and so on. (MC, 15, n. 9)

Some second thoughts are perhaps also in order on this score. Clearly there is a problem in applying a term that is generally conceived in relation to the narcissism and anomie of "post-Fordist" capitalist societies to those represented in much of Latin American and Third World testimonio, which have not gone through the stage of "modernity" (in the Weberian sense) yet, or display an "uneven" modernity (what society does not, however?). Clearly, there is also a correspondence (sometimes quite direct, as in the case of architecture) between cultural phenomena identified as postmodernist and the present sensibility and strategies of transnational capitalism, which gives some credence to the idea that postmodernism may be a form of cultural imperialism. There is the related danger that the production of a "postmodernist sublime" in relation to Latin America may involve the aesthetic fetishization, as in Didion's *Salvador*, of its social, cultural, and economic status quo (as "abject," chaotic, carnivalesque, etc.), thereby attenuating the urgency for radical social change and displacing it onto cultural dilettantism and quietism. As George Yúdice has noted, the flux of late capitalist commodity culture that is seen as liberating by postmodernist theorists like Baudrillard may represent in fact new forms of oppression and subalternity for Third World peoples as it restructures and re-semiotizes their cultures. In the same vein, there is Neil Larsen's warning that, even where there is a "promise of subversion" in postmodernism, this "seems no more and no less genuine than that long-ago discredited pledge of the modernist vanguard to, as it were, seize hold of capital's cultural and psychic mechanisms without firing a shot."[24]

However, I think there is also an important sense in which the forms of popular-democratic cultural resistance to imperialism represented by and in testimonio themselves rise up on a postmodern terrain.[25] The two interrelated problematics that are generally taken as defining postmodernism are the collapse of the distinction between elite and popular (or mass) cultures, sometimes expressed as the loss of aesthetic autonomy (Jameson); and the collapse of the "great narratives" of Western progress and enlightenment—including both bourgeois and Marxist historicisms—with which the specifically aesthetic project of modernism was associated (Lyotard). Similarly, the aesthetic and ideological significance of testimonio depends on its ability to function in the historically constituted space that separates elite and popular cultures in Latin America and to generate postcolonial, non-Eurocentric narratives of individual and collective historical destiny. Where literature in Latin America has been (mainly) a vehicle for engendering an adult, white, male, patriarchal, "lettered" subject, testimonio allows the emergence—albeit mediated—of subaltern female, gay, indigenous, black, and proletarian "oral" identities. In this sense it is coincident with postmodernism rather than its other. It is true that part of what is designated as postmodernism is related to the rampant commodification and monopolization of even elite cultural production in late-capitalist societies, which also affects peripheral social formations (the small, national publishing houses that might have published Borges as a young writer, for example, are being taken over or displaced by multinationals concerned with retailing translations of international best-sellers); at the same time, as Benjamin understood, the loss of aura or desublimation of the art work

24. Yúdice, "Marginality and the Ethics of Survival"; Neil Larsen, *Modernism and Hegemony* (Minneapolis: University of Minnesota Press, 1990), xxxi.

25. I share Jameson's sense in the concluding remarks to his book on postmodernism that the concept, which has certainly been devoured by habitualization (and perhaps also by the current recession), is still worth using: "I occasionally get just as tired of the slogan 'postmodern' as anyone else, but when I am tempted to regret my complicity with it, to deplore its misuses and its notoriety, and to conclude with some reluctance that it raises more questions than it solves, I find myself pausing to wonder whether any other concept can dramatize the issues in quite so effective and economical a fashion." This quotation from *Postmodernism, or, The Cultural Logic of Late Capitalism* (Durham: Duke University Press, 1990), 410.

portended by mechanical reproduction can also be a very radical form of cultural democratization. Like testimonio, metropolitan postmodernism has involved in cultural production and consumption broad lower middle-class, working-class, and minority sectors of the population previously excluded in general from and by high culture forms like literature.

The critique of postmodernism by Latin American leftists[26] tends to set up a dichotomy between complex, anti-representational, value-leveling, high-culture forms of literature of the sort represented by Borges or Boom narrative in general and simple, lineal, representational, value-affirming, "popular" narrative forms like the testimonio. That some of the force of that dichotomy has necessarily crept into my own thinking about testimonio I think is evident from the above, but it needs also to be qualified. Although testimonio implies a challenge and an alternative to modernist literary models based on a subversion or rejection of narratives of identity, it is not, as we have seen, a completely autonomous form deriving directly from subaltern culture. It is (usually) a written transcription and textualization of a spoken narrative. The nature of any piece of writing—for example, the perceived qualities of testimonial as opposed to Boom narrative—is determined intertextually by its place in an already constituted discourse system. (Among the models Rigoberta Menchú mobilizes in constructing her testimonio is certainly biblical narrative, which, as a Catholic lay catechist, she knew intimately; there are clear traces of Cabezas's readings of Boom novels as a university student in his *Fire from the Mountain*, a text "spoken" into a tape recorder; and so on.) Rather than a clear dichotomy between a purely oral popular culture of resistance and a purely colonial and/or neocolonial written high culture, Latin American culture has involved since the colonial period a series of shifts and transformations between elite and subaltern forms. In its very situation of enunciation, which separates radically the subject-positions of the emitter and receiver, testimonio is a form of the dialectic of oppressor and oppressed, involved in and constructed out of its opposing terms: master/slave, literature/oral narrative and song, metropolitan/national, European/indigenous or African, elite/popular, urban/rural, intellectual/manual work.

Testimonio is no more capable of transcending these oppositions than more purely "literary" forms of writing or narrative: that would require social and cultural transformations capable of initiating literacy campaigns and developing the educational and economic infrastructures necessary to

26. See, for example, Yúdice's "Marginality and the Ethics of Survival."

create and sustain a mass reading public that have as a prior condition the victory of revolutionary movements in the first place. But testimonio does represent a new way of articulating these oppositions and thus of defining new paradigms for the relationship between the intelligentsia and popular classes. In this sense, it represents also a new sort of aesthetic agency in political struggles.[27]

If, however, testimonio has been in Latin America and elsewhere the "literary" (under erasure) form of both revolutionary activism and more limited defensive struggles for human rights and re-democratization, paradoxically and against the expectations of its original protagonists, it does not seem particularly well suited to become the primary narrative form of an elaborated socialist society like Cuba or even of periods of postrevolutionary consolidation and struggle, as in Nicaragua after 1979, perhaps because its very dynamics depend on the conditions of dramatic social and cultural inequality that fuel the revolutionary impulse in the first place. One of the problems revealed by the electoral defeat of the Sandinistas is that the identification portended in testimonio between a radicalized intelligentsia—represented by the FSLN leadership and upper and middle cadre—and the popular sectors had to some extent broken down. Coincidentally, one had begun to note a problematization of the formula of testimonio itself in Nicaragua: testimonios continued to be produced, but, except for those dealing with the contra war, they lacked the urgency of the testimonios of the revolutionary period (and testimonio must above all be a story that *needs* to be told, that involves some pressing and immediate problem of communication). We can conclude from this that, like postmodernism itself (and more particularly like its ancestor the picaresque novel), testimonio is a transitional cultural form appropriate to processes of rapid social and historical change but also destined to give way to different forms of representation as these processes move forward (or, as in the case of Nicaragua today, backward) to other stages, and the human collectivities that are their agents come into the possession of new forms of power and knowledge.

27. On this point, I find myself in sharp disagreement with Neil Larsen's Leninist "critique of aesthetic agencies" in *Materialism and Hegemony*, which I think has in common with a social democratic counterpart like Habermas's both the discomfort of what Gramsci called the "traditional intellectual" in the face of the emergence of mass culture and a corresponding nostalgia for a "rational" politics of clearly defined class-based parties.

31

Spanish American Testimonial Novel-
Some Afterthoughts

Elzbieta Sklodowska

Washington University

32

It has been long recognized that we cannot understand the specificity of various discourses without an appreciation of the role that interpretive communities play in producing meanings. In his well-known article, "How to Recognize a Poem When You See One," Stanley Fish develops an argument that "acts of recognition, rather than being triggered by formal characteristics, are their source. It is not that the presence of poetic qualities compels a certain kind of attention but that the paying of a certain kind of attention results in the emergence of poetic qualities" (105).

In this paper I will argue that in the context of Spanish American literature of the last two decades "paying of a certain kind of attention" to some of the previously neglected forms of nonfiction has resulted in the emergence of testimonio as a literary genre in its own right. Some rarely explored islands of Spanish American letters, such as women's writing, subaltern autobiography and minority experience, have come to be evaluated with "testimonio-seeing" eyes and the presence of the term itself in the language of literary criticism has become ubiquitous. The fact that we, the interpretive community of academic critics, have agreed to "recognize" testimonio and give it institutional legitimation is, arguably, one of the most important events of the past two decades in Spanish American literary history. I insist on the word "recognize," because the presence of testimonial qualities has been a time-honored trait of Spanish American writing since its inception and one could easily make a case for viewing it, along with realism, as a perennial mode of Western letters.

Despite all the critical attention it has received, testimonio remains undefined. In this case, the notion of genre is clearly "historically derived" rather than "logically prescribed" (Lohafer 11) and testimonio serves as a shorthand for a whole spectrum of narrative conventions. According to some critics, testimonio may show "family resemblance" to more established literary forms such as the picaresque narrative and the Bildungsroman. The new "genre," we are told, also relies on specifically forensic patterns of argumentation as well as on the narrative conventions of autobiography and the traditional realist novel. With the former it shares the split identity of the narrating/experiencing self, while with the latter it assumes an empiricist position. Unlike most classic autobiographies, however, it does not focus on the inner self, but on communal experience.

On the other hand, testimonio's creative use of the "life story" formula—as we know it from the studies of Oscar Lewis—places it within the tradition of the Chicago school of sociology with its concern for retrieving voices of people who had seldom been heard. In fact, the demarcation between testimonio and the life story is the most nebulous and L. Langness's definition of life story as "an extensive record of a person's life told to and recorded by another, who then edits and writes the life as though it were autobiography" (4-5) applies to testimonio as well.

Testimonio inevitably positions itself around the shifting borders of a well-known but elusive genre: the novel. As a matter of fact, for some testimonial writers, like Miguel Barnet, terms such as testimonio and novela testimonial become interchangeable. On the other hand, we have to recognize the fact that since the mid 1970s Spanish American testimonio ("raw" testimonies devoid of aesthetic elaboration) has had an important impact on shaping up the explicitly "literary" novels.[1]

By establishing an explicit interplay between factual and fictional, between aesthetic aspirations to literariness and scientific claims to objectivity, testimonio has consistently defied the critics departing from a traditional system of assumptions about truth and falsity, history and fiction, science and literature. While it is clear that an unambiguous definition of testimonio keeps eluding us, amidst the debates still resonating in the field of Latin American testimonio criticism there must be, one should assume, a fairly general agreement as to what testimonio represents. After all, if testimonio was given an identity in our recent (re)readings of Spanish American letters, this rereading must have been informed by a common understanding of what counts as testimonio.

I propose to look at two definitions of testimonio in order to approach this question. I start with these conceptualizations for two reasons. First and foremost, what they propose are true definitions and not simply a list of more or less distinct traits and relations. Secondly, these definitions stand out as the most ingenious attempts to break both the deadlock of "family resemblance" and the Aristotelian dichotomy between fiction and history. For George Yúdice,

> Testimonial writing may be defined as an authentic narrative, told by a witness who is moved to narrate by the urgency of a situation (e.g., war, oppression, revolution, etc.). Emphasizing popular, oral discourse, the witness portrays his or her own experience as an agent (rather than a representative) of a collective memory and identity. Truth is summoned in the cause of denouncing a present situation of exploitation and oppression or in exorcising and setting aright official history. (17)

When answering the question, "What exactly is a testimonio?" John Beverley and Marc Zimmerman write:

> a novel or novella-length narrative, told in the first person by a narrator who is also the actual protagonist or witness of the events she or he recounts. The unit of narration is usually a life or a significant life episode (e.g., the experience of being a prisoner). Since in many cases the narrator is someone who is either functionally illiterate or, if literate, not a professional writer or intellectual, the production of a testimonio generally involves the recording and/or transcription and editing of an oral account by an interlocutor who is a journalist, writer, or

34

social activist. The word suggests the act of testifying or bearing witness in a legal or religious sense. (173)

To any poststructuralist, Post-Boom or postmodern reader the giveaway in
Yúdice's definition is the notion of "authentic narrative." The critic succumbs
to what Foucault calls "the will of truth" and finds testimonio's authenticity in
an unquestioned origin of the word. We find ourselves in the heartland of
phonocentrism, as Christopher Norris has explained it, following Derrida:
"Voice becomes a metaphor of truth and authenticity, a source of self-present
'living' speech as opposed to the secondary lifeless emanations of writing" (28).
In both definitions testimonial writing is politically principled and strongly
action-oriented, which detracts from exploring its discursive armature. In strictly
formal terms, it is simply perceived as a curious brand of life document, autobiography and forensic patterns of confession, which takes the form of a novel.
All this does quite a bit, but not enough, to clarify how testimonio's technique
actually works. To help us delve further into the protocols governing testimonial writing and its recognition, I will focus on the intricate tension between
the indeterminacy of experience and the closure of discourse, between the act
of living/surviving/witnessing and the act of testifying/transcribing. I propose to test this terrain by using the notion of the differend, Jean-François
Lyotard's felicitous term coined in his meditation on the vicissitudes of testifying in the post-Holocaust era. Lyotard gives the name of a differend to

> the case where the plaintiff is divested of the means to argue
> and becomes for that reason a victim. If the addressor, the ad-
> dressee, and the sense of the testimony are neutralized, every-
> thing takes place as if there were no damages. A case of
> differend between two parties takes place when the "regula-
> tion" of the conflict that opposes them is done in the idiom of
> one of the parties while the wrong suffered by the other is not
> signified in that idiom. (9)

Four instances are needed, according to Lyotard, to constitute a phrase universe of testimonial contract as a truth-believing paradigm. First, an addressee—
someone not only willing to listen and accept the reality of the referent, but
also worthy of being spoken to. Then there is an addressor, a witness who refuses to remain silent. Third, a language capable of signifying the referent. Then
there is a "case" or the referent itself that "asks to be put into phrases, and
suffers from the wrong of not being able to be put into phrases right away"
(13). The referent, continues Lyotard, may be obliterated if silence results from
the denial of one or several of the preceding three instances (14). In other words,
testimony takes place only if the reality of a referent is established and in order
for this to happen all silent negations must be withdrawn and the authority of
the witness, addressee's competence and language's ability to signify must be

assured.

I am of course all the more aware that in the case of mediated testimonials Lyotard's model must be nuanced because it is further complicated by the fact that there are two levels of communication: first, the truth-believing effect has to be established between the two interlocutors and, secondly, between their collaborative text and the reader willing to approach it with "testimonio-see-ing eyes." Hence, I will further use the notion of veridiction—a crucial concept in the semiotic theory of Algirdas Julien Greimas—in my attempt to establish what mechanisms embedded in the highly mediated genre of testimonio might have inclined us to read it as truth-saying and how this celebration of authentic representation has occurred in the heyday of postmodernism when all notions of truth and meaning have become eroded.

According to Greimas, "truth-believing must be installed at the two extremities of the communication channel," thus creating a tacit agreement, a veridiction contract between the speaker and the addressee. Since discourse is "no longer considered as the representation of a truth exterior to it," and since "the enunciator is no longer presumed to produce true discourse, but discourses producing a 'truth' meaning effect" (368), the modern reader, Greimas contends, has to be persuaded to interpret the discourse as truth-saying.

After this theoretical detour, for the sake of brevity I will limit my discussion of the testimonial code of representation and communication to The Autobiography of a Runaway Slave, Miguel Barnet's/Esteban Montejo's foundational testimonio first published in Cuba in 1966 and a few years later (re)baptized as novela testimonial by the editor himself.[2] To simplify matters even further I will assume that it displays in miniature the narrative powers at work in mediated testimonials. I will analyze how a signifying referent—the fundamental tenet of any nonfictional discourse—is created when the testimony of a 105-year old illiterate former slave is transcribed by a young ethnologist of European background who has no direct knowledge of the facts he assembles into discourse.

In the introduction, Barnet, the addressee of the primary testimony, reviews his reasons, methods and intentions in recording and editing Montejo's life story, but the primary function of these editorial remarks is to present the text that follows as truth-saying and thereby forge a tacit agreement with the reader as to its irrefutable authenticity. In order to create an illusion of seamless, mutually (re)created reality, Barnet directs our attention away from his own persona and claims that he is an unobtrusive interviewer and a self-effacing editor. His visible presence is, indeed, limited to the margins of discourse comprised by the prologue, a number of somewhat random footnotes and—in the Spanish version—a glossary of Afro-Cuban terms. These traces of presence and authority provide us with a clue to Barnet's efforts to balance the freedom of "literary" creativity with the constraint of the testimonial "discipline." The prologue also exemplifies one of the most powerful strategies to control discourse. As Michel Foucault has persuasively argued in "Order of Discourse," commentary strives to exorcise "the chance element of discourse" and to reduce chance and multiplicity from "what might risk being said" (58).

Within the main text Barnet also follows what Greimas calls the strategy of "objectivizing camouflage" (685) whereby all "marks of enunciation" are erased. Barnet's veridictory technique of "objectivizing camouflage" relies on the obliteration of the context of the primary discourse: the interviewer's questions are eliminated and a simulacrum of a monologue supplants the original dialogue. All this is intended to support the editor's claim that it is indeed Montejo who is "the real author of this book" (8).

In terms of Lyotard's model, Barnet is the cornerstone of the bona fide testimonial contract. He can justly lay claim to being a competent addressee (a professional ethnographer), an engaged participant, whose sympathetic gaze should foster communication and eliminate silence. The actual extent to which Barnet as editor might have imposed his own choice of stylistic devices and reordered Montejo's original account is silenced and impossible to assess. Barnet admits, however, that in order to spare the reader Montejo's rambling stories he has necessarily had to paraphrase: "If I had transcribed his story word for word it would have been confusing and repetitive. I have kept the story within fixed time-limits, not being concerned to recreate the period in minute detail of time and place" (8). Whereas interweaving the various strands of the original dialogue may be perceived as a necessary evil, Barnet's method of distilling his interlocutor's speech is rather disquieting: "I wanted his story to sound spontaneous and as if it came from the heart, and so I inserted words and expressions characteristic of Esteban wherever they seemed appropriate" (7). By sifting out data, Barnet is performing a contradictory role: on the one hand he is a researcher, an engaged participant, whose own theoretical biases and sympathetic attitude should not interfere with the making of a scientific record. On the other, he is a writer who—despite his explicit disavowal of all literary intentions—pursues a narrative that would retrieve the past in the guise of a readable account. And from both of these points of view Montejo's account, derived from autobiographical remembrance, requires reconfiguring.

Barnet's preface is intended to create an illusion of a common front and give unity and uniformity to a project which ex definitione should address the issue of difference and not erase it. Unlike historians and ethnographers who over the past thirty years have begun to break their silence on the mechanisms of discursive authority, transcription and inscription (Hayden White, James Clifford, Clifford Geertz), Barnet makes claims to exhaustive understanding of his witness and does not view his own intervention as coercive or manipulative. Attempting to find his way between the Scylla of narrative chaos and the Charybdis of constraint, Barnet thus usurps the power as to what to reveal, how and when.

Exploring the tacit clauses of the testimonial contract, as it appears in The Autobiography of a Runaway Slave, makes us realize to what extent testimonio actually resembles discourses that Michel de Certeau calls "heterologies." An overriding concern that binds together discursive practices that fall into this category is that of capturing the voice reaching us from a distance: geographic, historic, cultural. In Certeau's words:

> The heterological operations seem to depend on the fulfillment of two conditions: an object, defined as a "fable," and an instrument, translation. To define the position of the other (primitive, religious, mad, childlike, or popular) as a "fable" is not merely to identify it with "what speaks" but with a speech that "does not know" what it says. . . .The fable is thus a word full of meaning, but what it says "implicitly" becomes "explicit" only through scholarly exegesis. (160)

Similar to the heterological mechanisms present in anthropological and psychoanalytic accounts—where the structuring force of scientific presuppositions determines inclusions and exclusions—in The Autobiography of a Runaway Slave it is the editor who warrants a story's "tellability" (Bruner's term). In all these cases the act of bearing witness calls for a guided dialogue. In each case the fragmentation of the original account is gradually transformed into a coherent and "complete" discourse.

Obviously, psychoanalytic, anthropological and testimonial contracts may differ in the degree of freedom they grant their informants in controlling the final text. In the case of The Autobiography the informant is not really allowed to control the production of the text. He is illiterate and consequently cannot read and contest Barnet's (in)version of himself. Barnet recalls, nevertheless, Esteban's concern as he was constantly looking at the interviewer's notebook and he almost forced his editor "to write down everything he said" (8).

It may be worthwhile to compare Barnet's prefatory remarks with another heterological discourse—Freud's introduction to what is probably his best-known case history, "Fragment of an Analysis of a Case of Hysteria." As Steven Marcus has demonstrated in his article "Freud and Dora: Story, History, Case History," when Freud specifies what it is that is wrong with his patients' stories, "the difficulties are in the first instance formal shortcomings of narrative: the connections, 'even the ostensible ones—are for the most part incoherent,' obscured and unclear; 'and the sequence of different events is uncertain'" (162). Among various types of narrative insufficiency, Marcus continues, Freud lists "amnesias and paramnesias of several kinds and various other means of severing connections and altering chronologies" (163). In a similar vein, Barnet underscores the problem of failing memory as related to Montejo's inability to tell a coherent, chronological story. "In many cases my informant was unable to remember precisely," he states on one occasion, to elaborate further: "Esteban's life in the forest is a remote and confused period in his memory" (8). The superseding voice of the editor is supposed to bring a restoration of order to this chaos, substitute for an absent voice, secure the "tellability" of the story, as it

38

indeed does, since one third of The Autobiography deals precisely with Montejo's survival in the forest.

While Barnet is unwittingly exposing the complex relations between the researcher and the witness, he does not seem concerned about the deeply unsettling implications of this situation. Curiously enough, when filling in the interstices of Montejo's voice, Barnet not only follows the rules of narrative "tellability" and the methodological guidelines of the discipline. I would argue that he also embarks on a search for his own identity through his encounters with Montejo. This yearning to know the "other," as the authors of "The Postmodernist Turn In Anthropology" point out, is yet another heterological trait and it "can be traced to the romanticism so frequently associated with anthropologists' scholarly pursuits. Traditionally, the romantic component has been linked to the heroic quest, by the single anthropologist, for 'his soul' through confrontation with the exotic 'other'" (25).

For Barnet the result of the testimonial transcription is cathartic also in a different way: "This book helps to fill certain gaps in Cuba's history," Barnet assures his readers. "None of the orthodox, schematically minded historians would ever have bothered with the experiences of a man like Esteban. But Esteban appeared on the scene as if to show that one voice from the heart of action is worth a vociferous chorus from the sidelines" (9).

I have argued elsewhere that Barnet's idea to commit Montejo's voice to paper might have been inspired by Fidel Castro's "Words to the Intellectuals."[3] In one of his three well-publicized speeches addressed to intellectuals in June of 1961, the Cuban leader recalled talking to an old woman, a onetime slave; he then confronted his audience at the National Library with the following rhetorical question: "Who could describe life under slavery better than this woman, and who can describe the present better than you?" (quoted in González de Cascorro 85). Like many other intellectuals of his generation and background, Barnet preferred to eschew the present and still keep his place "within the Revolution." Unlike Heberto Padilla or Edmundo Desnoes, who soon found themselves "out of the game," Barnet devised an acceptable formula: he became, in his own words, "a mediator for the voice of others," a scribe unveiling and reinterpreting the past on behalf of the Cuban people who, like Montejo or the old woman from Castro's anecdote, had no recorded history.

Contrasting Barnet's complaints about the incoherence of his interlocutor's story with the actual text signals the palimpsest-like structure of testimonial writing. Even when analyzed by a well-meaning reader who—like Yúdice—wants to see testimonio as an instrument of truth, The Autobiography of a Runaway Slave raises numerous questions as to why certain items were excluded or included. The title itself poses a challenge to Barnet's project: Montejo's autobiography—called biografía in the original—does not cover but a fraction of Montejo's life. From the introduction we learn that Montejo was an ardent supporter of the Cuban Revolution, but we have to take Barnet's word for it, since Montejo never really states it and the story comes to an abrupt closure fifty years before the Revolution, with a brief reference to the death of Máximo Gómez in 1905. Montejo's life after Independence is for the most part a ghost chapter, which can only be partly reconstructed from allusions dispersed throughout The Autobiography and from Barnet's next testimonial novel, Song of Rachel (1969). In a structural sense The Autobiography reveals Barnet's failure to fill the gaps and—as in Rigoberta Menchú's case—the failure of his "seduction" of the witness.

The Autobiography shows substantial editorial manipulations in the chronological division of the text (slavery-abolition-the War of Independence) and in the way its ethnographic material is organized by different topics and punctuated with dramatic reconstructions of historical events. This "belletrization" of ethnography, blurring considerable differences between two projects, two stories, two veridictory contracts becomes legitimate in Barnet's view since he writes out of a strong identification with his witness.[4] What is puzzling in this line of reasoning, however, is that Barnet's image of Montejo is blatantly heterological. At one point Barnet refers to Montejo's beliefs in the following manner: "His vision of the creation of the universe particularly appealed to me because of its poetic, surrealist slant" (8). This perception of the testimonial witness resembles the construction of the so-called magic realist narrative in that it frames the "other" as fantastically exotic. What we get instead of difference is awkwardness. The use of the term "surrealist" is so tainted with Eurocentric assumptions that its presence within testimonio is particularly disquieting. Moreover, it exemplifies the heterological practice of translation as domestication of alterity, perpetuating myths about the West and its "others."

Let us go now to the second and third instances of Lyotard's model—the witness and language. Montejo-the witness is portrayed in the prologue as rather willing to share his experiences, but, as we have already seen, Barnet underscores the problem of his failing memory and his inability to tell a chronological story. Even though the delimitation of territories between the editor and the witness is impossible, alongside the editor's efforts at embellishment and orchestration we hear—or want to hear—a different voice resonating beyond the strictures of the form. This voice that slips beyond the control of the author/ scribe will be called here Montejo's voice even though I realize it is just an echo of his voice.

First and foremost this voice challenges the editor's claim that we can reconstruct the world through accumulation of facts and their causal reordering. Montejo makes us acutely aware that the sense of totality suggested by such approach is treacherous and he testifies to the limits of witnessing, particularly in relation to religious tabu, traumatic experiences such as natural disasters or collective catastrophes and intimate personal dramas. "There are some things about life I don't understand," he admits in the opening line which sets the tone for the rest of the account. "Everything about Nature is obscure to me, and about gods more so still" (15). Moreover, there is even a discrepancy between his "real" name and the one he uses: "One of my surnames is Montejo," he explains, "after my mother who was a slave of French origin. The other is Mera. But hardly anyone knows this. Well, why should I tell people, since it is false anyway? It should really be Mesa, but what happened is that they changed it in the archives. . ." (17).

Even though some literary devices—such as irony, allegory, parables and symbols—are predicated upon the disjunction between appearance and substance, I would hesitate to interpret Montejo's silences in terms of a rhetorical ploy. Contrary to Doris Sommer—who has convincingly studied such "literary secrets" in another testimonial text, I, Rigoberta Menchú—I would like to emphasize that we are dealing here with very real secrets essential to the survival of the entire culture, and not with a belletrization of narrative gaps.

Montejo's restraint in disclosing certain aspects of his life is not only consistent with his personality but with the legacy of Afro-Cuban culture as well. In his study, Domination and the Arts of Resistance, James C. Scott demonstrates convincingly how different systems of oppression generate practices and rituals he calls "hidden transcripts of discourse." Ciphered language, Scott argues, constitutes one of the most powerful forms of everyday low-profile resistance in cases when direct vituperation or rebellion are considered too risky. Montejo's account gives ample evidence of the functioning of such "hidden transcripts" in the Aesopic folktales typical of the Afro-Cuban oral heritage. Occasionally he is more explicit about the atmosphere of discursive resistance that pervaded the entire slave culture: "These blacks made a secret of everything"—he recalls. "They have changed a lot now, but in those days the hardest thing you could do was to try to win the confidence of one of them" (36). Sometimes Montejo unmasks the meaning of Afro-Cuban "public transcript" which—out of fear—was constructed to appeal to the expectations of the powerful: "Santería used to be a religion for Africans, and even the Civil Guards . . . would have nothing to do with it," he recalls. "They would make some remark in passing like, 'What's going on here?' and the Negroes would say, 'We're celebrating San Juan.' But of course it was not San Juan but Oggún, the god of war. . ." (80).

This is by no means to say that Montejo's account is anti-testimonial. It is rather meta-testimonial. If indeed, as Susan S. Lanser has pointed out, the authority of the narrator hinges on his/her social identity (class, gender, race), honesty, competence and reliability and his/her privileged access to information and narrative self-consciousness, it may be Montejo's self-conscious stance that makes us truth-believing.

Montejo's self-reflexive account, obviously, does not escape its own prisonhouse of language. While he repeatedly displays his awareness of the equivocal nature of perception, understanding, communication and the very act of bearing witness he, nevertheless, considers himself a reliable narrator. Montejo claims he always "makes sure of the facts first" (122) and is quite suspicious of other people's stories. "You cannot put much trust in people," he contends, and then goes so far as to proclaim: "The truth is I don't even trust the Holy Ghost" (59). Despite the fact that Montejo has to preserve as instrument the very same language whose truth value he dismantles, by focusing on the holes between the warp and the woof of his story rather than on the perfect design itself, unlike his editor and unlike most testimonio critics, Montejo creates an internal system of self-questioning whereby he "inoculates" his story against external critique.

The narrator's ability to construct a truth-believing pact is put to the test when the fabric of experience becomes interwoven with such supernatural phenomena as headless riders, mermaids, spirits and demons. "I once told a young man about the little devil," recalls Montejo, "and he said I was lying. Well, it may sound like a lie, but it's the plain truth" (132). His skillful persuasion in such instances bears some affinity to so-called magic realism: very much like García Márquez in his celebrated levitation episodes, Montejo surrounds non-empirical phenomena with a vast array of everyday, material details that serve as assurances of plausibility and let him remain completely calm, almost aloof. This strategy is exemplified in the following portrayal of güijes whom he treats as personal acquaintances, although it is never clear whether he had actually met them or not. Montejo speaks about "little black men with men's hands and feet like . . . well, I never found out what sort of feet they had, but their heads were flattened like frogs', exactly like frogs'. Ave Maria, the fuss and commotion there was when the güijes appeared" (126). A similar technique is employed over and over again: "When witches appeared," asserts Esteban, "they took off their skins and hung them up behind the door and stepped out just like that, all raw" (127).

This rhetoric can succeed as long as he denies his audience—comprised in this case by Barnet and us, the readers—a full participatory experience. In other words, as long as we are less knowledgeable than the speaker and/or cannot verify his statements. That is why Montejo reminds us that at best we can only get one foot into his world. He first of all warns us that the ability to experience the supernatural is a privilege not everyone can enjoy. "Negroes had a natural tendency to see them," he concludes when talking about güijes. On a different occasion he stipulates:

> People who have the gift of visions see them almost every day; people who don't can still see them from time to time, though less often I wouldn't call myself a seer, though I have seen strange things, like a light which walked alongside me and kept stopping when it came to a place where there was buried money to be dug up, and then disappeared. . . .They don't appear now because I don't get about as much as I did, and the lights are a country thing. (127)

On the other hand, certain phenomena are just too rare to be verifiable. As far as the witches are concerned, for instance, Montejo explains matter-of-factly that "There aren't many of them left here, because the Civil Guard exterminated them all. They were all Canary Islanders, I never saw a single Cuban witch" (127).

Unlike his editor, who focused on the romanticized notion of bonding between the interviewer and the well-informed witness and underscored the researcher's capacity to elicit truth—Montejo is scarcely *en rapport* with anyone. His voice truly dramatizes the crisis of truth and the inevitability of (self)-deception. Moreover, Montejo's story, like that of Ginés de Pasamonte, resists closure: "I say I don't want to die, so I can fight in all the battles to come. And I'm not going into the trenches or using any of those modern weapons. A machete will do for me" (223). As Shoshana Felman and Dori Laub remind us in a recent book, in the testimony, language is in process and in trial, and it does not offer a final word on anything (5). Montejo—with his awareness of the impossibility of constructing a univocal narrative—stands as a witness to Barnet's anxiety about closure, and his voice generates its own, alternative rereading.

So while Barnet's introduction with its methodological contentions is cast in the mimetic frame, Montejo's voice brings us back to the notion of differend:

> In the differend, something "asks" to be put into phrases, and suffers from the wrong of not being able to be put into phrases right away. This is when the human beings who thought they could use language as an instrument of communication learn through the feeling of pain which accompanies silence (and of pleasure which accompanies the invention of a new idiom), that they are summoned by language, not to augment to their profit the quantity of information communicable through existing idioms, but to recognize that what remains to be phrased exceeds what they can presently phrase, and that they must be allowed to institute idioms which do not yet exist. (13)

Whereas Barnet wants to predispose the reader to view the text as seamless, Montejo tells us that language—including his own—reveals only inasmuch as it conceals as it thrives on dissimulation, camouflage, deceit, duplicity and not so benign lies. Montejo's narrative logic rests on the opposition between memory and experience, presence and absence, appearing and being, witnessing and testifying.

If definitions of testimonio are indeed symptomatic of what we look for when we read with testimonio-seeing eyes, this brief rereading of The Autobiography of a Runaway Slave tells us also what we tend to overlook. Yúdice, Beverley and Zimmerman find testimonio's authenticity in the voice of the victim, who has unquestioned power and right to "summon truth," "denounce," "exorcise," and "set aright." But they also tend to overcompensate for the internal discord we may find in specific texts and they direct our attention away from the problematic inscription of the differend. For these critics, the testimonial word that emerges from oppression is perceived as natural, pure, uniquely insightful and immune to ideological blindness.

Let us return to the initial concern of this paper—the critical perception and reception of Spanish-American testimonio within the context of the Boom and the Post-Boom. As I hope to have shown, testimonio is constructed in such a way as to, unwittingly, direct our attention to its own fissures. How was it possible then, that Barnet's text—built as it is around so many contradictions— instead of engendering some deconstructive readings ended up serving as a propitious model for the canonization of testimonio as a neorealist super-genre, a model of an "authentic narrative" for witnessing the unspeakable and narrating the unspoken experience of the Latin American subaltern? In other words, how was it possible to canonize testimonio as a discourse inverting the paradigm of subaltern (under)representation in Latin American letters?

I do not wish to launch a diatribe against the critics who fostered this process, partly because I would also have to say mea culpa. I can attempt to solve this paradox only by arguing that most critics did not read testimonial texts— they read the official voice of these texts, confusing the tongues of the editor and his/her surrogates. It is apparent that Barnet's attempt at genre making appealed to the practitioners of testimonio and critics alike because of his attractive claim to have devised the blueprint for a genuinely democratic and uniquely Latin American literary practice of harmonious weaving and blending of divergent voices. The reception of Barnet's project follows the critical trend that views all Latin American literature as an ongoing quest, a quest for a style which not only expresses the New World on its own terms, but also demonstrates an unrelenting commitment to the subaltern other.

Secondly, I think that this blind spot—which has had a galvanizing effect not only on testimonio criticism but on the perception of recent Spanish American narrative in general[5]—may have to do with a very legitimate concern of invalidating testimony, of transposing the reality of human suffering into nothing more than text. "If there is nobody to adduce the proof, nobody to admit it, and/or if the argument which upholds it is judged to be absurd," Lyotard warns us, "then the plaintiff is dismissed, the wrong he or she complains of cannot be attested. He or she becomes a victim" (9). It is likely that any reading of testimonio against the grain of its editorial voice would have been perceived as politically dangerous. I realize that there is a fine line between invalidating testimony and acknowledging, self-critically, "that what remains to be phrased exceeds what we can presently phrase" (Lyotard 13). Nevertheless, seeing testimonio as a seamless monument of authenticity and truth deprives it, in my opinion, of the ongoing tension between stories told and remaining to be told. More to the point, perhaps it also diminishes its potential as a forward-looking discourse participating in an open-ended and endless task of rewriting human experience. This task, in Lyotard's words, implies instituting

new addressees, new addressors, new significations, and new referents in order for the wrong to find an expression and for

44

the plaintiff to cease being a victim. This requires new rules
for the formation and linking of phrases. No one doubts that
language is capable of admitting these new phrase families or
new genres of discourse. Every wrong ought to be able to be
put into phrases. (13)

From the vantage point of today I would like to suggest that we take our cue
from the voice of the witness in testimonial texts. Testimonio's literary and
political power ultimately stems from the witness's ethos which, as we have
seen, remains unscathed by his or her sense of disorientation and discontinu-
ity. I would argue that if we allow for a similar dissonance in our critical enterprise, we will help in creating a discursive space in which the voice of the
differend will not be subjected to suffocation or cannibalization. Consequently,
we will be a step closer to recognizing the fact that testimonio does not provide
a solution to the problems of Latin American expression, but it continues the
same old quest in a new guise. In practical terms what it means is that we as
critics may also contribute to giving the differend its due.

One final quote from James Clifford's "Notes on (Field)notes" may help my
conclusion here concerning the critical operations performed on testimonio:

I am reminded of Roland Barthes' image of the sauce or glaze,
the nappe, which the French cuisine smoothes over and hides
the productive, transformative processes of the cooking.
Barthes makes this into an image for ideological, naturalizing
discourse. I have the impression that I can sometimes see
through the nappe of the finished ethnography—beneath the
unifying glaze, chopped meat. (64)

Ultimately, however, as any discourse, testimonio triggers its own rereading.
And then, beneath the unifying glaze of the editorial remarks and critical commentaries, we can sometimes see, if not chopped meat, at least rice and beans.

Earlier versions of parts of this paper were read at the MLA Convention in San
Francisco (December 1991) and Twentieth Century Spanish and Spanish-American Literature International Symposium at the University of Colorado, Boulder (November 1993).

Works Cited

Barnet, Miguel. "The Documentary Novel." Cuban Studies/Estudios Cubanos
11.1 (1981): 19-32.
Beverley, John. "'Through All Things Modern': Second Thoughts on

45

Testimonio." boundary 2 18.2 (1991): 1-21.

—.and Marc Zimmerman. Literature and Politics in the Central American Revolutions. Austin: Texas UP, 1990.

Bruner, Jerome. "The Narrative Construction of Reality." Critical Inquiry 18 (1991): 1-21.

Certeau, Michel de. The Practice of Everyday Life. Trans. Steven F. Randall. Berkeley: U of California P, 1984.

Clifford, James. "Notes on (Field)notes." Fieldnotes: The Making of Anthropology. Ed. Roger Sanjek. Ithaca-London: Cornell UP, 1990. 47-70.

Felman, Shoshana, Dori Laub. Testimony: Crisis of Witnessing in Literature, Psychoanalysis and History. New York and London: Routledge, 1992.

Fish, Stanley. "How to Recognize a Poem When You See One." American Criticism in the Poststructuralist Age. Konigsberg, Ira ed. Ann Arbor: U of Michigan P, 1981. 102-15.

Foucault, Michel. "The Order of Discourse." In Untying the Text. Ed. Robert Young. Boston: Routledge, Kegan Paul, 1981. 48-78

Franco, Jean. "¿La historia de quién? La piratería postmoderna." Revista de Crítica Literaria Latinoamericana 17.33 (1991): 11-20.

Glowinski, Michal. "Document as Novel." New Literary History 18.2.(1987): 385-401.

González de Cascorro, Raúl. "El género testimonial en Cuba." Unión 4 (1978): 78-89.

Greimas, Algirdas Julien. "The Veridiction Contract." New Literary History 20.3 (1989): 651-60.

Hesse, Douglas. "A Boundary Zone." Short Story at a Crossroads. Lohafer, Susan, and Jo Ellyn Clarey, eds. Baton Rouge: Louisiana State UP, 1989.

Khare R.S. "The Other's Double-The Anthropologist's Bracketed Self: Notes on Cultural Representation and Privileged Discourse." New Literary History 23.1 (1992): 1-23.

Langness, L.L. The Life History in Anthropological Science. New York: Holt, Rinehard and Winston, 1965.

Lanser, Susan Sniader. The Narrative Act: Point of View in Fiction. Princeton UP, 1981.

Lyotard, Jean-François. The Differend: Phrases in Dispute. Trans. Georges Van Den Abbeele. Minneapolis: U of Minnesota P, 1988.

Marcus, Steven. "Freud and Dora: Story, History, Case History." Literature and Psychoanalysis. Eds. Edith Kurzweil and William Phillips. New York: Columbia UP. 153-74.

Mascia-Lees, Frances, et al. "The Postmodernist Turn in Anthropology: Cautions from a Feminist Perspective." Signs: Journal of Women in Culture and Society 15.11 (1989): 7-33.

Montejo, Esteban. The Autobiography of a Runaway Slave. Edited by Miguel Barnet. Translated by Jocasta Innes. New York: Pantheon Books, 1968.

Norris, Christopher. Deconstruction, Theory and Practice. London: Methuen

46

Scott, James C. Domination and the Arts of Resistance: Hidden Transcripts. London-New Haven: Yale UP, 1990.

Shaw, Donald. "On the New Novel in Spanish America." New Novel Review 1.1 (1993): 59-73.

Sklodowska, Elzbieta. Testimonio hispanoamericano: historia,teoría,poética. New York-Frankfurt: Peter Lang, 1992.

Sommer, Doris. "Sin secretos." Revista de crítica literaria latinoamericana 36 (1992): 135-54.

Vidal, Hernán. "The Concept of Colonial and Postcolonial Discourse: A Perspective from Literary Criticism." Latin American Research Review 28.3 (1993): 113-119.

Yúdice, George. "Testimonio and Postmodernism." Voices of the Voiceless in Testimonial Literature. Gugelberger, Georg, and Michael Kearney, eds. Special issue of Latin American Perspectives 18.3 (1991): 15-31.

Zambrano, María. "La confesión: género literario y método." Anthropos-suplemento (marzo-abril 1987): 57-79.

Notes

1

When referring to Gustavo Pellón's chapter on "The Spanish American Novel: Recent Developments 1975 to 1990," Donald Shaw indicates that "the three most obvious new directions in the Post-Boom novel are the historical novel, the documental novel and the hard-nosed detective novel" (70). In my Testimonio hispanoamericano: historia, teoría, poética I argue that "en la década del ochenta el contrato testimonial se convierte en el recurso retórico más socorrido por los escritores más reconocidos del boom—basta citar Crónica de una muerte anunciada de Gabriel García Márquez e Historia de Mayta de Mario Vargas Llosa. En ambos casos la apropiación del formato testimonial es, en realidad, una desmitificación del mismo" (180).

2

See the English version of Barnet's "manifesto," "The Documentary Novel."

3

See my entry on Miguel Barnet in the Dictionary of Literary Biography: Latin American Fiction Writers, vol. II, ed. William Luis (forthcoming 1994).

4

For the discussion of "belletrization" and "formal mimesis" see Michal Glowinski, "Document as a Novel."

5

Hernán Vidal—who has done substantial work on testimonio—offers the following picture of Latin American literary criticism: "During the last few decades, these two modalities of development of Latin American literary criticism—the one technocratic and the other culture-oriented—have tended toward a frank enmity. One indication is the fact that the literary critical technocracy tends to congregate at the meetings of the Modern Language Association, while the culturalists gravitate toward the Latin American Studies Association" (116).

Gender Studies

Apuntes sobre la crítica feminista y la literatura hispanoamericana

JEAN FRANCO

«Sospecho que todo este palabrerío es tan sólo una forma de ocultar la pobreza de mi relato,» dice el narrador (masculino) de la novela *La hora de la estrella* de Clarice Lispector. Para las críticas feministas no es tanto la pobreza del material sino su escasez, lo que obliga a construir genealogías peregrinas saltando de Gertrudis Gómez de Avellaneda a Elena Garro, de Sor Juana Inés de la Cruz a Rosario Castellanos. Igual hacen las escritoras — de allí las genealogías de mujeres eruditas que presenta Sor Juana o la de una poeta contemporánea, Carmen Ollé cuando escribe:

> Clarice Lispector escribe rodeada de sus niños
> en el hogar.
> Sylvia Plath pensaba dejarlo todo en aquel caso.
> El occidente ha dado talentos como la Woolf cuya amistad
> con la Ocampo hizo decir á esta: yo como toda subdesarrollada
> tengo el hábito de escribir.

Todos sabemos que tales genealogías son estratégicas. Al señalar sus afiliaciones, las escritoras obedecen a una tendencia generalizada en toda la historia literaria latinoamericana que siempre ha sido no—canónica en relación con la literatura metropolitana y siempre ha proclamado sus afinidades y diferencias con otras literaturas a manera de banderas o consignas en la disputa de posiciones. Los que escribían las historias literarias latinoamericanas no encontraban correspondencias exactas con las historias metropolitanas. No podían identificar un período clásico ni tampoco precisar la «evolución» de la novela (the rise of the novel) como hacían los críticos ingleses. Tenían forzosamente que incluir en la

Dunkinfield, Cheshire, Inglaterra, 1924. Ha publicado, entre otros, los libros: *Introducción a la literatura hispanoamericana, La cultura moderna en América Latina, César Vallejo: The Dialectics of Poetry and Silence,* y numerosos artículos sobre literatura latinoamericana. Es profesora de literatura de Columbia University, New York.

historia literaria géneros no canónicos, textos tales como los cuadernos de bitácora de Colón, las crónicas de la conquista, las descripciones e historias del Nuevo Mundo, los libros de viaje y los programas políticos (por ejemplo, *El dogma socialista* de Esteban Echeverría). Al no poder trazar una historia del sistema literario, los autores se vieron obligados a cuestionar los límites de los géneros literarios, a crear unidades imaginarias a fin de enlazar el período de la conquista con la independencia. La «unidad» de la historia literaria se adscribía a su «originalidad» o a su «americanismo».

La teoría contemporánea parte de un examen consciente de la institucionalización de los géneros literarios, tarea de deconstrucción en la cual tiene particular interés el feminismo. Aquí quiero hacer hincapié en una distinción entre la teoría feminista y la crítica que rescata textos olvidados o reivindica el valor de textos del pasado. Esta crítica muchas veces define la literatura feminista en una forma muy general como «textos por mujeres.» Por ejemplo, en la antología de Angel y Kate Flores, *The Defiant Muse,* se trata de «una crítica de las vidas de las mujeres y de las injusticias que las mismas han debido soportar, en distintos tiempos y lugares en virtud de su sexo.» Esta versión de «la visión de los vencidos», como se ve, se limita al nivel «temático.» *Other Fires*, (otra antología reciente de escritura de mujeres latinoamericanas en traducción editada por Alberto Manguel) incluye un grupo heterogéneo de escritoras sin otro criterio que el hecho de que «su excelencia ha sido, hasta ahora, ignorada en Europa y EE.UU.»

La teoría feminista, en cambio, tiene una meta más ambiciosa. Falla como teoría si no logra cambiar el estudio de la literatura de modo sustancial. Debe, por lo tanto, abarcar una lectura de la cultura que altere sustancialmente los marcos del sistema literario y nos dé, al mismo tiempo, nuevos instrumentos de análisis. De allí, la cuestión central que quiero plantear ahora es si la teoría feminista en nuestro campo ha contribuido realmente al estudio de la literatura latinoamericana, lo que justificaría el dedicar una sesión entera de LASA al análisis del estado de la teoría y la crítica feminista. Mi respuesta a la pregunta es obviamente sí; de no serlo, no estaría aquí.

En primer lugar, la teoría feminista latinoamericana tiene que partir de una crítica de las instituciones y antes que nada, del sistema literario en sí mismo. Para realizar esta tarea, no es necesario que parta de cero, ya que sus intereses confluyen con los de otras corrientes y tendencias intelectuales; particularmente la deconstrucción, la semiótica y las teorías marxistas de la ideología.

La crítica deconstructivista, por los menos en la manera en que ha sido formulada por Jacques Derrida, contribuye de manera especial al análisis feminista porque demuestra lo arraigado que se encuentra lo binario en el pensamiento occidental y las oposiciones que produce: normal/anormal, serio/no serio, literal/no literal, lo central/lo marginado. Lo «femenino» siempre se alinea con el término «débil» de esta oposición. En segundo lugar, Derrida examina la imposición de límites y márgenes, de allí su cuestionamiento de «la ley del género,» mostrando que en realidad no hay tal ley y que el principio del género es inclasificable. El género, por lo tanto, no es un límite esencial sino imaginario. La deconstrucción propuesta por Derrida implica un examen de las instituciones que apoyan tanto las jerarquías arriba mencionadas, como los géneros — examen que no han continuado los discípulos americanos del crítico francés. De allí, la necesidad de una teoría feminista que estudie los géneros de discursos, la relación entre géneros de discurso e instituciones hegemónicas y se sumerja tanto en el estudio de los recursos que pueden establecer la autoridad textual, como en términos evaluativos tales como «dominio del lenguaje,» «profesionalización de la escritura», etc.

El marxismo, por su parte, contribuye de modo esencial a la comprensión de la hegemonía, la contrahegemonía y las ideologías que se forman en relaciones de lucha. Soy conciente de que existen grandes diferencias entre la deconstrucción y el marxismo, entre semiótica y análisis de la ideología. Sin embargo no soy la única en enfatizar la conjunción «y» más que la disyuntiva «o»— como se puede constatar leyendo algunos libros recientes tales como *Marxism and Literary History*, de John Frow, *Marxism and Deconstruction* de Michael Ryan, *Formalism and Marxism* de Tony Bennett—. Al igual que el marxismo, el feminismo no puede prescindir de estos aliados estratégicos. Sin embargo, tampoco es posible pensar el marxismo o la deconstrucción sin el feminismo, puesto que este último tiene por tarea investigar el sistema literario en relación con la jerarquización basada en la diferenciación entre lo masculino y lo femenino. La teoría feminista es, por lo tanto, una teoría que trata del poder expresado en términos analógicos a la diferenciación sexual que, a su vez, es determinada socialmente. La teoría feminista analiza la relación entre lo femenino y las instancias del poder y propone la misma pregunta que Derrida al decir: «¿Qué sucederá si tratamos un área de la relación con el Otro en el cual el código de señales sexuales no fuera ya determinante?»

Por otra parte, las feministas trabajan dentro de las instituciones académicas y tienen que enfrentar la manera mediante la cual la oposición masculino-femenino ha estructurado el conocimiento y ha enmascarado los propósitos de la evaluación académica. La teoría feminista, por lo tanto, no es simplemente el estudio de textos escritos por mujeres o el estudio de estereotipos de mujeres. No es lo mismo que la investigación de textos desconocidos escritos por mujeres, aunque tales investigaciones siguen siendo sumamente importantes. Cabe mencionar aquí las investigaciones llevadas a cabo recientemente en América Latina, en los talleres del Colegio de México, por ejemplo, en los centros de estudio de la Mujer, como el centro Flora Tristán en el Perú, en las revistas dedicadas a escritoras latinoamericanas y los congresos sobre la escritura femenina, todos los cuales nos han dado cimientos, datos específicos y los principios de una polémica fructífera sobre la validez de los conceptos del feminismo norteamericano en relación con América Latina.

Quizás la más lúcida exposición de esta última ocurre en el artículo de Sara Castro Klarén, «La crítica literaria feminista y la escritora en America Latina» que se publicó en *La sartén por el mango*. En este artículo, Castro Klarén advierte sobre los problemas de aceptar una identidad fija y universal para la escritura femenina, puesto que, en este caso, «Tendríamos pues que aceptar que basándonos en el estudio de unas cuantas escritoras —las que viven y escriben como miembros de una clase y sociedad específica en un momemto histórico determinado—, podríamos establecer una categoría universal de análisis, la que no sólo describe sino que exige una serie de temas, imágenes y posiciones ideológicas en relación a) a la tradición escritural dominada por el hombre, y b) a la imagen de la mujer, en esa sociedad y esa literatura. El estudio de este tipo de crítica literaria temática, y orientada hacia valores de personificación, revela un abordaje ingenuamente representacional y a veces resulta ser contradictoriamente a-histórica.» Partiendo del feminismo francés, especialmente de las teorías de Irigaray y Kristeva, Castro Klarén ataca la noción de «una identidad femenina como algo visible, fijo, constante y siempre igual a sí mismo.» Más cuestionable, sin embargo, es la equiparación que hace entre la discriminación que sufre la mujer y otros tipos de opresión —la racial, por ejemplo. Señala que la supresión y la exclusión de las mujeres del discurso patriarcal no es diferente de la exclusión que deriva del racismo: «Lo eterno femenino» se parece a «lo eterno buen salvaje.» Y añade, si como Gilbert y Gubar constatan, la misoginia patrista hace de «las mujeres monstruos sin habla, rellenos de un conocimiento indigesto, ¿no es ésta la misma imagen que Fernández Retamar reclama para América Latina en su rebelde Calibán?» Según Castro Klarén, por lo tanto, una teoría feminista latinoamericana tiene que partir de la premisa de que la lucha de la mujer está «cifrada en una doble negatividad; porque es mujer y porque es mestiza.» Sin embargo no explica cómo se puede emprender esta lucha sin una teoría que aclare las diferencias entre la opresión de la mujer y la opresión (por ejemplo) de los indígenas. Tal teoría tendría que ir más allá del Calibán de Fernández Retamar que conserva acríticamente la noción «heroica» de la tradición intelectual.

Castro Klarén tiene razón cuando ataca las tendencias universalizantes del feminismo metropolitano que, al igual que la teoría literaria en general, todavía no ha hecho ninguna tentativa de dar cuenta de las diferencias que marcan la literatura periférica en general. Es verdad que recientemente se notan algunos gestos de críticos como Jameson, Raymond Williams y Edward Said. Sin embargo, fundir la teoría feminista en una teoría general del colonialismo tampoco sirve. No es suficiente decir con Julia Kristeva que la «mujer» como categoría discursiva está incluída entre los marginados de la sociedad y «es la misma lucha... nunca puede darse la una sin la otra.» Definitivamente NO es la misma lucha. La jerarquía que subordina lo femenino a lo masculino no solamente se encuentra profundamente implicada en el lenguaje, sino que afecta la constitución de la subjetividad. Aunque no hay nada que impida a un hombre biológico «leer como una mujer», ni a una mujer biológica «leer como un hombre»— desde la posición de autoridad, por ejemplo— esto no significa que la diferencia no está marcada tanto en los textos como en las evaluaciones propuestas por la institución literaria. Ahora bien, una vez que se empieza a entender que esta jerarquía está en la base de la misma institución literaria, cabe investigar la manera en que se ha constituido la autoridad textual no sólo en el presente sino en distintas coyunturas históricas.

Se suele dividir la historia cultural latinoamericana en tres períodos: el colonial, el nacional y el período post-nacional. Aunque demasiado amplia, esta periodización nos permite efectuar una primera hipótesis. Durante el período colonial, la exclusión de la mujer de la esfera pública y de la adquisición del poder encontraba su apoyo en el dogma. Con la emergencia de la intelligentsia laica durante el movimiento de la Independencia, el dogma deja de ser la justificación de esta separación entre la esfera pública (masculina) y la esfera privada (femenina) que entonces pasa a depender de la constitución más débil de la mujer y de su rol prioritario en la reproducción de la familia. Con el cuestionamiento de la ideología del nacionalismo que ocurre en la época «transnacional» contemporánea, es posible, por primera vez, cuestionar la jerarquía masculina/femenina. Al mismo tiempo, el poder difuso de las sociedades contemporáneas tiende a diluir el poder contestatario del feminismo que viene a sumarse a una pluralidad de grupos y movimientos. La cuestión consiste en saber si es posible salvar la posición contestataria.

En cuanto a la historia de la literatura, resulta evidente que tiene su origen en el período nacional. Es precisamente porque estamos situados en un momento histórico que ha visto el derrumbe de la alegoría nacional (o de la nación como articulación de sentidos) y sus correlativas problemáticas de identidad nacional y cultura nacional, que nos es posible examinar desde otro punto de vista todo lo que ha significado la diferencia masculina y femenina en la articulación de esta alegoría. Cabe hacer notar que antes que la crítica, novelistas como Augusto Roa Bastos, Rodríguez Juliá, Luisa Valenzuela, Rosario Ferré y Jorge Ibargüengoitia ya habían sometido esta alegoría a la parodia. De hecho, una vez que se deja de considerar a la nación como una entidad natural o como el edificio que corona una construcción ineludible, el camino está abierto para un análisis de cómo la ideología de la nación ha determinado el canon literaria y cómo este canon siempre se ha basado en analogías sexuales.

La ideología laica y nacional de fines del siglo XIX, fundamenta el modo en que la intelligentsia no sólo articuló la historia de la literatura como una continuidad imaginaria sino que al mismo tiempo rechazó selectivamente inmensas áreas de la escritura colonial, particularmente la literatura religiosa. Al buscar un período clásico, una épica, esta intelligentsia encontro en la conquista y el descubrimiento elementos heroicos, descartando la literatura religiosa a la cual la mujer había contribuido en forma substantiva. Por ejemplo, en sus *Reseñas literarias* —que es un primer esbozo de una historia de la literatura mexicana —Ignacio Manuel Altamirano incluyó una carta en la que trata de guiar por el buen camino a una mujer que aspiraba a convertirse en escritora. Entre sus consejos de destaca una prohibición: no hay que leer a Sor Juana Inés de la Cruz «nuestra décima musa a quien es necesario dejar quietecita en el fondo de su sepulcro y entre el pergamino de sus libros, sin estudiarla más que para admirar de paso la rareza de sus talentos y para lamentar que hubiera nacido en los tiempos del culteranismo, y de la Inquisición y de la teología escolástica. Los retruécanos, el alambicamiento, los juguetes pueriles de un ingenio monástico y las ideas falsas sobre todo, hasta sobre las necesidades físicas, pudieron hacer del estilo de Sor Juana el fruto doloroso de un gran talento mártir, pero no alcanzaron a hacer de él un modelo.» A partir de esta prohibición (que los críticos católicos fueron los primeros en ignorar) se podía no sólo descartar la literatura colonial como obsoleta, sino también separar a las escritoras en potencia de una tradición propia.

Los elementos ideológicos estructurantes de las primeras historias de la literatura están dados por la idea de la nación, la originalidad de América y lo heroico. La originalidad americana y la formación de la nación justificaban la inclusión en el canon de textos no literarios, al mismo tiempo que aseguraban la exclusión de lo barroco y buena parte de la literatura colonial por su supuesta falta de originalidad. La historia de la literatura se convertía así en una genealogía de héroes de la emancipación cultural. En este sentido, la intelligentsia de América concordaba con Carlyle al decir que «la historia de lo que el hombre ha realizado en este mundo es básicamente la historia de lo que los Grandes Hombres han logrado aquí. Todas las cosas producidas en el mundo son propiamente el resultado material, la realización práctica y la encarnación de los Pensamientos de los Grandes Hombres.» De acuerdo con este criterio Rodó incluyó a Bolívar, Montalvo y Juan María Gutiérrez en el Mirador de Próspero. Bolívar es el «insuperable héroe epónimo» de «América nuestra.» «Porque la superioridad del héroe no se determina sólo por lo que él sea capaz de hacer abstractamente, valoradas la vehemencia de su vocación y la energía de su aptitud, sino también por lo que da de sí la ocasión en que llega, la gesta a que le ha enviado la consigna de Dios.» De la misma manera, Pedro Henríquez Ureña pensaba que la historia de la literatura de la América Hispana tendría que tomar en cuenta principalmente algunos nombres esenciales: Bello, Sarmiento, Montalvo, Martí, Darío, Rodó.

Es interesante que entre quienes han empezado a cuestionar los criterios que sirvieron de fundamento a estas primeras historias literarias se cuentan principalmente los críticos que estudian la literatura colonial (por ejemplo, Walter Mignolo y Rolena Adorno). Efectivamente, cualquier discusión sobre la investigación literaria actual tiene que empezar necesariamente por el reconocimiento del auge de los estudios de la literatura precolonial y colonial que es consecuencia directa de la emancipación del nacionalismo cultural. La reevaluación del barroco, el cuestionamiento del canon y de los límites de los géneros, el problema de Europa y su «Otro», los estudios de la semantización del discurso racista y colonial y el interés feminista tanto en la cultura de convento como en la principal figura de la literatura colonial, Sor Juana Inés de la Cruz, indican una reconfiguración extensiva de la historia de la cultura colonial. Las investigaciones de Josefina Muriel y Margarita Peña de la escritura feminista novohispana, los libros de historiadores como Asunción Lavrín, Silvia Arrom y Padre Martín; los estudios de Electa Arenal y Stacey Schlau sobre la cultura de convento, la nueva historia social que ha investigado las culturas de resistencia y que ha revelado una literatura satírica escrita durante la crisis de la colonia en el siglo XVIII, la catalogación de los archivos de la Inquisición que ha desenterrado poesía y teatro censurado — todo eso ha contribuido a la revisión de la historia cultural de la colonia.

Desde el punto de vista feminista se destacan tres campos de investigación: la literatura mística, los procesos de brujas y los estudios sobre la escritura de Sor Juana Inés de la Cruz y otras poetas menos conocidas. La mística sobre todo constituía una «sabiduría» accesible a la mujer. Como lo ha demostrado Michel de Certeau en *La fable mystique*, el misticismo presentaba problemas de orden epistemológico puesto que la palabra del sujeto y sus manifestaciones exteriores — arrobo, levitación — representaban la única prueba de la experiencia. De allí el afan del clero por tener testimonios escritos de la experiencia mística. Por otro lado, la mujer mística se comunicaba directamente con Dios o con los santos sin necesidad de mediación humana y sin necesidad de conocimientos especializados o habilidad en manejar el lenguaje legítimo. La mujer con su escasa educación podía, por lo tanto, llegar a la sabiduría mística e, inclusive, era más fácil para ella recibir este tipo de «favores» de Dios gracias a su temperamento blando que, por otro lado, también la volvía más dúctil y susceptible a las seducciones del demonio. Por esta razón, y por la dificultad de verificar la experiencia mística, los confesores hacían escribir a las monjas y así descubrían este continente ignoto de los sentimientos y los arrobamientos. De tal modo se constituyó un vasto archivo del inconciente colonial recogido en documentos cuya importancia para el estudio de la mujer empieza a ser valorada. Lo que interesa aquí no es la evidencia de una «escritura femenina» sino el estudio de la diferenciación ideológica entre la erudición racional a la cual sólo los hombres tenían pleno acceso y la sabiduría mística alcanzable aún por una mujer que no supiera latín.

Esta escritura recoge los sentimientos marginados del discurso oficial que no obstante buscaba la manera de controlarlos, oponiendo las verdaderas visiones a las visiones ficticias inspiradas por el demonio. El problema era distinguir la visión verdadera de la falsa y, como no existían pruebas objetivas, los confesores tenían que acudir al contexto. La vida de la monja o beata, su obediencia al confesor y al *status quo* constituían la prueba de la verdad de sus visiones. Las que trataban de burlar la vigilancia del confesor, de conseguir adeptas, eran las más susceptibles de ser denunciadas al Santo Oficio.

El ejemplo de la literatura mística es particularmente interesante porque la ausencia de una regla que permitiera la verificación interna demuestra que el criterio para juzgar la verdad era, en realidad, su conformidad con la ideología dominante. Cuando la iglesia pierde su hegemonía en el siglo XIX, la religión entera queda desterrada de la verdad y tiene que apoyarse en la creencia, o sea, en la esfera desvalorizada de la mujer. Por el contrario, en el siglo XX, con la rebelión contra la razón positivista, son los hombres los que se apoderan de la esfera de la creación y la imaginación, dejando a las mujeres el rol de ser las Gekreptens de la literatura.

Las investigaciones sobre la escritura de Sor Juana nos enfrentan con el otro lado del misticismo. Si el misticismo es permitido a la mujer a condición de que confirme el dogma, el conocimiento racional constituye un terreno mucho más conflictivo. La ejemplaridad de Sor Juana y su reivindicación del derecho de la mujer a la sabiduría, subyace en una serie de estudios importantes —de Georgina Sabat de Rivers, de Octavio Paz (*Sor Juana o Las trampas de la Fe*), Fernando Benítez (*Los demonios en el convento*) y Marie Cecile Benassy Berling (*Humanisme et religion chez Sor Juana Inés de la Cruz*)—. Este no es el lugar apropiado para una consideración detallada de estas investigaciones; se trata sencillamente de señalar la importancia de la escritura de Sor Juana como un camino totalmente opuesto al camino místico.

Por su contribución a la teoría feminista, quiero destacar el ensayo de Josefina Ludmer, «Las tretas del débil» publicado en *La sartén por el mango*. Usando el método estructuralista, Ludmer explica la generación del argumento de la «Respuesta a Sor Filotea» desde los términos «decir», «saber» y sus negativas. No puedo presentar en forma sucinta la densa argumentación de este ensayo, pero cabe subrayar sus conclusiones. Arguyendo que al emplear la carta y la autobiografía para desarrollar una tesis filosófica, Sor Juana derriba los límites de los géneros, Ludmer concluye «ahora se entiende que estos géneros menores (cartas, autobiografías, diarios), escrituras-límites entre lo literario y lo no literario, llamados también géneros de la realidad, sean un campo preferido de la literatura femenina. Allí se exhibe un dato fundamental: que los espacios regionales que la cultura dominante ha extraído de lo cotidiano y personal y ha constituido como reinos separados (política, ciencia, filosofía) se constituyen en la mujer a partir precisamente de lo considerado personal y son indisociables de él. Y si lo personal, privado y cotidiano se incluyen como punto de partida y pespectiva de los otros discursos y prácticas, desaparecen como personal, privado y cotidiano: ése es uno de los resultados posibles de las tretas del débil.» Apoyándose en un análisis de la lógica interna de la «Respuesta», Ludmer llega a señalar que la transgresión de los límites del género va mucho mas allá de la literatura y constituye una subversión de la diferenciación entre la esfera púlica (masculina) y la esfera privada (femenina).

Al pasar al período nacional se vuelve evidente que esta diferencia entre la esfera pública y la privada no cambia en su estructura fundamental, aunque ahora es la nación lo que justifica esta diferenciación. De ahí que el intenso esfuerzo realizado por la intelligentsia de principios del siglo XIX a fin de redefinir el lugar de la mujer nunca trasgrediera esta separación. Las mujeres no sólo se encontraron excluídas del saber/poder sino que ahora ni siquiera tenían el espacio cultural del convento. La casa constituía su esfera, llámese ésta casa grande, casa chica o casa verde. Al mismo tiempo, se definía la novela en términos de su misión cívica. Altamirano la considera «la biblia» del «nuevo apóstol»; escribir es una «misión patriótica». La novela es la épica moderna. Según Rodó es «la épica inexhausta y proteiforme de nuestro tiempo, orbe maravilloso donde cabe todo el infinito de la realidad, con su abreviada imagen.» No obstante la equiparación que se hacía entre estas aspiraciones épicas (que compartían tanto los naturalistas como los poetas modernistas) y la virilidad, escritoras como Clorinda Matto de Turner, Gómez de Avellaneda, Nelly Campobello y Juana M. Gorriti rechazaban el encasillamiento en una literatura doméstica. Aun así, hasta muy recientemente, la crítica seguía considerando a las escritoras como más aptas para explorar la vida interior. De esta manera, un crítico normalmente perspicaz —Angel Rama— en la introducción a su antología, *Novísimos narradores hispanoamericanos* (que incluye dos escritoras, Cristina Peri Rossi y Rosario Ferré) destaca los sentimientos (y no la sexualidad) como terreno propio de la escritora, citando como ejemplos, a Clarice Lispector, Armonía Sommers, Luisa Josefina Hernández y Beatriz Guido. Es aleccionador contrastar la manera en que Rama acepta implícitamente la división entre público y privado con un ensayo de Mary Louise Pratt sobre «Escritoras y nacionalismo literario.» En este ensayo, Pratt advierte que los críticos han intentado minimizar la escritura de las mujeres en el período nacional mediante el artificio de relegarlas de nuevo a la esfera de lo personal y doméstico a la cual ellas supuestamente pertenecen. Como demuestra Pratt, la poesía patriótica escrita por mujeres plantea un problema interesante porque «no se puede leer semejante poesía como si fuera generada en la esfera doméstica puesto que toma como tema el mundo público de la nación. La voz poética es la de la ciudadana.» A partir de allí, demuestra la posibilidad de analizar la poesía cívica de Gabriela Mistral destacando la forma en que glosa la alegoría nacional y el poema patriótico.

Este argumento lleva la discusión a otro terreno que trasciende la separación entre esfera pública y esfera privada. Sin embargo, no hay ninguna necesidad de restringirse a una discusión de poetas como Mistral que deliberadamente escogen temas cívicos. Se pueden emprender lecturas transgresivas de las mismas autoras mencionadas por Rama —Armonía Sommers, María Luisa Bombal, Clarice Lispector— demostrando que la supuesta esfera privada es para ellas una esfera pública. Todo esto sin mencionar autoras como Teresa de la Parra, Elena Garro, Rosario Castellanos, Rosario Ferré (*Maldito amor*), Isabel Allende, Elena Poniatowska, Marta Traba, Griselda Gambaro, Luisa Valenzuela, quienes han escrito parodias de la alegoría nacional o han transpuesto lo político en lo familiar.

Las escritoras latinoamericanas suelen negar que haya una escritura femenina. Muchas veces dicen que la escritura es neutral. Tenemos que entender esta negación como un rechazo al encasillamiento, recordando las Historias de Literatura que metían a las mujeres en un párrafo aparte al final del capítulo. La cuestión, sin embargo, está mal planteada. No se trata de averiguar si las escritoras tienen temas específicos o un estilo diferente a los hombres, sino de explorar las relaciones del poder. Todo escritor, tanto hombre como mujer, enfrenta el problema de la autoridad textual o de la voz poética ya que, desde el momento en que empieza a escribir, establece relaciones de afiliación o de diferencia para con los «maestros» del pasado. Esta confrontación tiene un interés especial cuando se trata de una mujer escribiendo «contra» el poder asfixiante de una voz patriarcal. En un artículo sobre Delmira Agustini, Silvia Molloy señala cuán diferente es esta confrontación en la vida real y en la literatura. En su correspondencia con Rubén Darío, Delmira Agustini «se aniñaba,» disminuyéndose así en relación con su maestro. Sin embargo, según Molloy, al escribir, Agustini, «forzosamente tiene en cuenta —y corrige— el texto precursor de Darío». Cita como ejemplo los poemas sobre los cisnes en los cuales Agustini interrumpe en forma violenta la armonía rubendariana. Por ejemplo, «Yo soy el cisne errante de los sangrientos rasgos / voy manchando los lagos y remontando el vuelo». Utilizando la terminología de Riffaterre se puede considerar el 'Nocturno' de Darío como el hipograma que glosa Agustini; su lenguaje poético «ensucia» el espejo transparente de contemplación narcisista con la mancha de la diferencia sexual, del mismo modo en que el pañuelo rojo de la Andaluza irrumpe en los sueños de inmortalidad de *Yo el Supremo* en la novela de Roa Bastos.

Podríamos inferir de estos ejemplos muy variados de la crítica contemporánea que no hay UNA escritura femenina pero sí que la intertexualidad es forzosamente un terreno de lucha donde la mujer se enfrenta con las exclusiones y las marginaciones del pasado. Tal como John Frow apunta en su discusión de la intertextualidad, «ésta comprende relaciones de dominación y de subordinación entre registros, y este choque, este antagonismo de lenguajes es una oposición de realidades — esto es, de universos éticos. El texto puede ser definido como un proceso de relaciones de contradicción discursiva, y es aquí donde se conforma y se desafía el valor ideológico y donde se genera la historicidad textual» (*Marxism and Literary History*).

El otro aspecto del texto en que la relación de poder se patentiza es en la situación de la enunciación. En este sentido, es interesante el uso del narrador masculino o de una voz poética masculina por escritoras como Rosario Ferré, Clarice Lispector y Cristina Peri Rossi. Estas escritoras desenmascaran la hegemonía genérica que ubica al narrador masculino en la posición de autoridad y de productor. Las mujeres «ventrílocuas» se instalan en la posición hegemónica desde la cual se ha pronunciado que la literatura es deicidio, la literatura es fuego, la literatura es revolución, la literatura es para cómplices, a fin de hacer evidente la jerarquía masculina/femenina.

No me parece accidental que en los últimos años se han publicado más obras literarias de mujeres que en todos los siglos anteriores. Estamos entrando en un período de crisis que ha visto el derrumbe de las «narrativas maestras» —las teorías globales y totalizantes basadas siempre en la exclusión de lo heterógeneo. Desde este punto de vista contemporáneo es relativamente fácil deconstruir los sistemas binarios del pensamiento colonial o nacionalista. Sin embargo el pluralismo también tiene sus riesgos: si todo es válido, nada importa. Las mujeres, tanto escritoras como críticas, tienen mucho interés en cuestionar la validez de un pluralismo que no trasciende el nivel del consumo.

OBRAS CITADAS

Rolena Adorno, *Guaman Poma. Writing and Resistance in Colonial Perú*, Austin, University of Texas Press, 1986.

Electa Arenal y Stacey Schlau, «Stratagems of the Strong, Stratagems of the Weak: Autobiographical Prose of the Seventeenth Century Hispanic Convent», de proxima aparición en Bella Brodzki and Celeste Schenck, *Life Lines*, Ithaca, Cornell University Press.

Silvia Marina Arrom, *The Women of Mexico City, 1790-1857*, Stanford, Stanford University Press, 1985.

Ignacio Manuel Altamirano, *La literatura nacional*, tomo 1, México, Porrúa, 1945.

Fernando Benítez, *Los demonios en el convento. Sexo y religión en la Nueva España*, 1985.

Sara Castro Klarén, «La crítica literaria feminista y la escritora en América Latina» en Patricia Elena González y Eliana Ortega, comps., *La sartén por el mango,* San Juan, Ediciones Huracán, 1984.

Michel de Certeau, *La fable mistique*, Paris, Gallimard, 1982.

Angel & Kate Flores, *Poesía feminista del mundo hispánico (desde la Edad Media hasta la actualidad)*, México, Siglo XXI, 1984.

Asunción Lavrin, *Latin American Women, Historical Perspectives*, Westport, Conn, Greenwood Press, 1978.

Alberto Manguel, *Other Fires. Short Fiction by Latin American Women,* New York, Clarkson N. Potter Publishers, 1986.

Luis Martín, *Daughters of the Conquistadores. Women of the Viceroyalty of Peru*, Albuquerque, University of New Mexico Press, 1983.

Walter Mignolo, «Cartas, crónicas y relaciones del descubrimiento y la conquista,» Luis Iñigo Madrigal, comp., *Historia de la literatura hispanoamericana, época colonial*, I, Madrid, Cátedra. pp. 57-116.

Josefina Muriel, *Cultura femenina novohispana,* México, UNAM, 1982.

Octavio Paz, *Sor Juana Inés de la Cruz o Las trampas de la Fé,* México, Fondo de Cultura Económica, 1982.

Mary L. Pratt, «Literary Women and Literary Nationalism,» MS. inédito.

Angel Rama, *Novísimos narradores hispanoamericanos*, México, Marcha, 1981.

Georgina Sabat de Rivers, «El *Neptuno* de Sor Juana: Fiesta barroca y programa político, *University of Dayton Review*, vol. XVI, n° 2 (Spring 1983), pp. 63-73.

LA IDENTIDAD CULTURAL Y LA
PROBLEMÁTICA DEL SER
EN LA NARRATIVA FEMENINA
LATINOAMERICANA

LUCÍA GUERRA CUNNINGHAN

**FINALISTA
PREMIO PLURAL 1987**

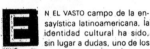

Vacíos y silencios
de la identidad cultural

Chilena. Catedrática, ensayista. Actualmente radica en Estados Unidos de Norteamérica, donde ejerce la actividad docente en la Universidad de California en Irvine y es investigadora en el departamento de español y portugués.

E N EL VASTO campo de la ensayística latinoamericana, la identidad cultural ha sido, sin lugar a dudas, uno de los temas más explorados y polémicos pues supone la reafirmación del ser americano no sólo a partir de una heterogeneidad de elementos endógenos sino también de diversos modelos culturales originados principalmente en Europa. Puesto que el concepto mismo de la identidad cultural pertenece a la tradición del pensamiento europeo de corte racionalista y logocéntrico, nuestros críticos y ensayistas se han visto en la necesidad de definir este concepto en términos abstractos y totalizantes, para lo cual han acudido a fuentes de tipo antropológico que enuncian sus principales elementos constitutivos. Así, se ha adoptado, por ejemplo, la definición de Miguel León Portilla para quien la identidad cultural estaría configurada por el idioma, los conjuntos de tradiciones, creencias, símbolos y significaciones, los sistemas, experiencias y destino en común, la posesión de un determinado territorio ancestral, la visión del mundo y el *ethos* o significado y orientación moral de una cultura.[1] Elementos más o menos concretos y comprobables que, en última instancia, se relacionarían con la *imago mundi*, con el imaginario colectivo o la figura que preside a la representación, puesto que ésta responde a modos peculiares de percibir y simbolizar el mundo. Por otra parte, la identidad cultural no sólo supone un conjunto de elementos semejantes y compartidos; se origina también en una dinámica de interrelaciones entre lo mismo y lo otro.

Dentro de este contexto, la identidad cultural de Iberoamérica en su literatura

sería un conjunto imaginario y distintivo de preocupaciones y respuestas, de temas, espacios, símbolos y motivos que se estructurarían en modelizaciones textuales. Es más, el fenómeno de la identidad cultural en dichos textos respondería a factores de tipo histórico o ideológico que, según investigadores como Fernando Aínsa, tendría sus raíces en un desfase o descolocación inicial del hombre latinoamericano con respecto a su entorno.[2] El viaje hacia el interior de la selva o los itinerarios hacia los espacios europeos representarían, por lo tanto, un proceso de búsqueda que yendo más allá de sus límites concretos trascendería al ámbito de lo ontológico y metafísico.

A primera vista, en este meticuloso y simétrico tejido conceptual, cada diseño parece tener su asidero en una visible totalidad empírica construida a partir de un contenido pluralista. Sin embargo, es importante hacer notar que la inclusión de los elementos culturales producidos por los grupos raciales subordinados se realiza, especialmente en la literatura, como producto de las mediaciones de una perspectiva blanca dominante que se ha apropiado del papel de sujeto creador de cultura. Es más, a través de sus procedimientos de abstracción y generalización, la perspectiva pluralizante difumina silencios significativos, voces marginales y signos de negatividad. Estas omisiones y mutilaciones han sido aún más graves en el caso de la mujer pues, según un

procedimiento ya típico de toda producción cultural hegemónica, bajo los falsos signos de ''hombre'', ''humanidad'' o ''valores universales'' se la ha incluido eufemísticamente, no obstante su posición de sujeto ausente.

De manera significativa, entonces, tanto en Europa como en América, una de las estrategias básicas de esta cultura oficial, creada por los hombres para reforzar un sistema patriarcal, ha sido anular las diferencias entre hombre y mujer cuando se trata de definir y generalizar con respecto a los seres humanos, aunque en los niveles más pragmáticos de la caracterología o la moral se ubique al sexo femenino en las zonas antitéticas de la actividad, la inteligencia y el vigor, atributos masculinos por excelencia. Y es precisamente como resultado de estas manipulaciones de la inclusión totalizante que la mujer, a diferencia de otros grupos culturales subordinados, ha carecido de una conciencia con respecto no sólo a su verdadera identidad sino también a los elementos específicos de su hacer en el mundo, a los rasgos característicos de su propia cultura hasta hace poco marginada al ámbito silenciado de la no-cultura.

En *El segundo sexo*, estudio señero sobre la problemática femenina en Occidente, Simone de Beauvoir demuestra que todas las interpretaciones de la realidad, los sistemas de conocimiento y los artefactos culturales han sido hechos según una perspectiva masculina dominante que los postula como la verdad absoluta. Sin embargo, en proliferas investigaciones recientes se ha puesto de manifiesto el hecho de que la mujer, tanto por su condición biológica como por el papel que le ha sido asignado en la sociedad, posee, no obstante su claudicación al orden masculino, una visión del mundo diferente.

otras versiones de la supuesta Verdad que la transgreden, la contradicen y la subvierten. Así, por ejemplo, en su ensayo "Le Temps des femmes", Julia Kristeva hace evidente el hecho de que en nuestra civilización predomina un concepto masculino del tiempo en el cual éste se postula como proyecto, teleología y linealidad, un tiempo eminentemente histórico cuya organización en la estructura, "punto de partida, progresión y llegada", es inherente también a los valores lógicos y ontológicos dominantes.[3] Sin embargo, la subjetividad femenina inserta en la recurrencia biológica de la menstruación posee otra modalidad de la vivencia del tiempo que mantiene un carácter de repetición y eternidad. Kristeva acertadamente afirma: "(en esta modalidad del tiempo) hay ciclos, gestación, la eterna recurrencia de un ritmo biológico que refleja el ritmo de la naturaleza e impone una temporalidad cuya estereotipación puede molestar pero cuya regularidad y unisonía con aquello que se experimenta como tiempo extrasubjetivo —tiempo cósmico— ocasiona visiones vertiginosas y una innombrable *jouissance*".[4] Por otra parte, se ha comenzado a construir toda una teoría que rescata las vivencias de la maternidad, hasta ahora generalmente representada por una perspectiva masculina a través de un vasto repertorio simbólico en el cual proliferan los signos de la madona, la madre abnegada o la madre terrible.

Tanto Julia Kristeva, en su ensayo titulado "La herética del amor",[5] como Lucía Piossek Prebisch, en "La mujer y la filosofía",[6] han puesto de manifiesto las implicaciones ontológicas de una condición del cuerpo femenino que, al convertirse en sede de otro, está sujeto a un orden y ritmo compartido con el reino animal y vegetal. Esta vivencia y transformación del cuerpo indudablemente afecta la posición de la mujer como sujeto y a la vez modifica las experiencias de la libertad y la capacidad de acción individual, razón por la cual Lucía Piossek Prebisch afirma "(en la maternidad), los proyectos individuales se entrecruzan en un momento

1. Miguel León Portilla. "Antropología y culturas en peligro". *América Indígena*, vol XXXV, N° 1 (enero-marzo 1975), pp. 15-27.
2. Fernando Ainsa. *Identidad cultural de Iberoamérica en su narrativa*. Madrid: Editorial Gredos, 1986.
3. Julia Kristeva. "Les Temps des femmes" 33/34 *Cahiers de recherche de sciences des texts et documents*, N° 5 (Invierno 1979), p. 5-9.
4. *Ibid*. La traducción es mía.
5. Julia Kristeva. "Herética del amor". *Escandalar*, vol. 6, Nos. 1-2 (enero-junio 1983), pp. 68-79.
6. Lucía Piossek Prebisch. "La mujer y la filosofía", *Sur*, Nos. 326-328 (septiembre 1970-junio 1971), pp. 95-101.
7. *Ibid.*, p. 99
8. Este importante fenómeno ha sido ampliamente analizado por Cheris Kramarae a nivel del génerolecto femenino en su libro titulado *Women and Men Speaking: Frameworks for Analysis*. Rowley, Massachusetts: Newbury House Publishers, Inc., 1981.

dado con los proyectos de la especie, que hacen del cuerpo humano no una forma ágil y centrífuga, apta para la aprehensión, transformación y dominio de la circunstancia, sino una grave y sensitiva materia que tiende a dejarse estar en el reposo y la espera".[7]

A pesar de que el cuerpo femenino es progenitor de una especificidad que origina una particular visión del sujeto y sus relaciones con el mundo circundante, por la primacía de la cultura masculina estas vivencias generalmente han carecido de un lenguaje, no han sido significadas en el nivel de interpretaciones filosóficas o modelizaciones artísticas, en otras palabras, no han adquirido la categoría de cultura, según los parámetros oficiales del falólogocentrismo. Y, en este sentido, la cultura femenina debe considerarse como un fenómeno típico de los grupos silenciados, pues no obstante poseer imágenes peculiares del mundo y de sí misma, la mujer generalmente las ha mantenido como imágenes subordinadas que no han logrado constituirse e imponerse como modos alternativos.[8]

Este importante fenómeno del silenciamiento y represión se da también en toda esa zona de la feminidad institucionalizada, de aquella condición que relega a la mujer al espacio doméstico, en su papel primario de madre y esposa. Ampliando y subvirtiendo un discurso filosófico ya tradicional, cabe preguntarse cuál es la visión del mundo para

dijo Lupercio Leonardo, que bien se puede filosofar y aderezar la cena. Y yo suelo decir viendo estas cosillas, si Aristóteles hubiera guisado, mucho más hubiera escrito. [10]

Anulando la disyunción masculina establecida a partir de los términos oponentes cocina y filosofía, sor Juana en su discurso los combina "irreverentemente" en un nuevo guiso en el cual el saber trascendental se nutre y se complementa con aquello catalogado como trivial, según los parámetros arbitrarios del sistema dominante. Es más, no obstante este gesto subversivo, la estrategia misma del candor "femenino" pone implícitamente de manifiesto otra disyunción esencial: el hombre en posición y posesión de lo trascendental y la mujer en los márgenes del saber.

Indudablemente, el aspecto más distintivo de la cultura femenina está en su triple marginalidad. Por una parte, la mujer, en su posición de segundo sexo relegado al espacio privado de la casa, tradicionalmente ha pertenecido sólo a medias a una nación sin poseer la posibilidad de participar activamente en el devenir histórico. Desde esta posición subordinada, ella ha adoptado pasiva-

un ser humano cuya existencia transcurre en el espacio cotidiano de la cocina donde la materia constantemente se corta, se cuece, se transforma y se consume. La voz de sor Juana Inés de la Cruz, primera mujer latinoamericana que significativamente puso en jaque las abstracciones y parcelaciones del pensamiento masculino dominante, al incorporar a través de "las tretas del débil" lo privado y cotidiano femenino, [9] resulta, en estos momentos, de un valor pertinente. En su Carta atenagórica. Respuesta a sor Filotea, escrita el primero de marzo de 1691, sor Juana de una manera estratégicamente candorosa, inicia un discurso femenino que legitimiza la cultura de la cocina al decir:

Pues, ¿qué os pudiera contar. Señora, de los secretos naturales que he descubierto estando guisando? Veo que un huevo se une y fríe en la manteca o aceite y por contrario, se despedaza en el almíbar; ver que para que el azúcar se conserve fluida basta echarle una muy mínima parte de agua en que haya estado membrillo u otra fruta agria; ver que la yema y clara de un mismo huevo son tan contrarias, que en los unos, que sirven para el azúcar, sirve cada una de por sí y juntos no. Por no cansaros con tales frialdades que sólo refiero por daros entera noticia de mi natural y creo que os causará risa pero. Señora, ¿qué podemos saber las mujeres sino filosofías de cocina? Bien

9. En su interesante estudio de la Respuesta de sor Juana Inés de la Cruz a sor Filotea, Josefina Ludmer analiza las discordancias entre el espacio que sor Juana se da y ocupa y aquél que le otorga la institución y la palabra del otro poniendo en evidencia las estrategias discursivas que sor Juana realiza desde su posición marginal y subordinada ("Las tretas del débil" en La sartén por el mango, editado por Patricia Elena González y Eliana Ortega. Río Piedra, Puerto Rico. Ediciones Huracán, 1984. pp. 47-54)

10. Sor Juana Inés de la Cruz. Obras completas. México: Editorial Porrúa, 1972. pp. 838-839.

11. Para un interesante análisis de este aspecto, se puede consultar el ensayo de Sigrid Weigel titulado "Double Focus: On the History of Women's Writing" (Feminist Aesthetics, editado por Gisela Ecker. Londres: The Women's Press Limited, 1985. pp. 59-80).

12. En nuestra aproximación crítica, adoptamos la definición de ideologema según la teoría de Julia Kristeva, para quien es tanto la racionalidad conocedora que integra la transformación de los enunciados en un todo (texto), como las inserciones de esta totalidad en el texto histórico y social; por otra parte, y desde el nivel de la intertextualidad, el ideologema es el encuentro de una organización textual dada con los enunciados que asimila en su espacio o a los que remite en el espacio de los textos exteriores (Ver El texto de la novela. Barcelona. Lumen. 1975)

mente las creencias, valores y sistemas impuestos por el sistema patriarcal sin reelaborarlos a través de un proceso de apropiación que pondría de manifiesto construcciones culturales alternativas. Es más, por los rígidos códigos impuestos al sexo femenino, el *ethos* o actitud moral del grupo dominante se desdobla y se restringe en un deber-ser que refuerza su papel de madre y esposa en los márgenes de la historia y reprime su sexualidad. Por otra parte, en su calidad de grupo colonizado, la mujer ha mantenido en forma precaria una cultura que se ha desarrollado de manera simultánea y silenciada puesto que, bajo una epistemología falologocéntrica, sus interpretaciones del mundo corresponden a lo catalogado como no cultura. Pero, a diferencia de otros grupos colonizados que están conscientes de la manipulación del otro, la relación sexual y familiar que ella

mantiene con el hombre la hace cómplice de una cultura dominante que al mismo tiempo la excluye.[11] Finalmente, el hecho de que esta cultura se origine en el cuerpo, en el ámbito doméstico y en lo cotidiano, triplica el fenómeno de la marginalidad dentro de una cultura dominante marcada por el racionalismo masculino.

En este contexto de marginaciones, la producción literaria de la mujer se caracteriza por la adopción de formatos literarios masculinos en los cuales la inclusión de las vivencias femeninas no produce modificaciones significativas en el nivel de modelos textuales, aunque pone de manifiesto una visión del mundo disidente. Y es precisamente en esta zona de la disidencia con respecto a los valores y preocupaciones de la cultura masculina dominante donde el concepto de identidad cultural surge como una ausencia, como un vacío que

construye a la negatividad, simultáneamente oponiendo a este silencio la preocupación por la identidad ontológica del ser femenino. En la marginal y marginalizada producción literaria de la mujer latinoamericana, el intento de autodefinirse posee un valor estructurante en un conjunto de textos que configuran, en nuestra opinión, una tendencia no suficientemente estudiada en su especificidad o evolución.

La estructura dialógica del ser femenino

En los textos narrativos que a continuación nos proponemos analizar, el ideologema básico[12] no apunta hacia las diferencias y semejanzas en un imaginario colectivo implícita o explícitamente comparado con aquel que presentan otros grupos culturales de la

hegemonía occidental; tampoco se establecen relaciones significativas de la identidad cultural con un espacio postulado como típicamente americano o "la otra orilla" que correspondería al *locus* europeo. Por el contrario, esta narrativa se estructura a partir de límites que revierten simbólicamente al espacio restringido de la casa anulando la categoría de lo cultural/territorial para insertar a la protagonista en un grupo estrictamente genérico —el sexo femenino concebido como un grupo que en todos los lugares del mundo vive la problemática de la subordinación. Ubicada, por lo tanto, en el género y no en la cultura nacional o continental, la escritora latinoamericana incursiona en la identidad femenina como problema ontológico inserto en una condición de alteridad con respecto al orden masculino. Es más, la representación misma de la feminidad supone la búsqueda de un ser mutilado y transformado por la imaginación masculina dominante, fenómeno que ha hecho afirmar a la escritora estadunidense Adrienne Rich lo siguiente: "Somos traducciones a diferentes dialectos/ de un texto que sigue siendo escrito en su lengua original."[13] Las diversas traducciones de lo femenino mediatizado por un sujeto masculino producen indudablemente deformaciones de un texto original —la feminidad— que no ha logrado construirse un lenguaje propio y debe irónicamente acudir a los diferentes dialectos como si éstos fueran la matriz auténtica.

Es a consecuencia de esta subordinación estética, reflejo de una situación social homónima, que el ideologema básico se construye a partir de un dialogismo entre lo masculino representado como lo absoluto imponiendo voces convencionalizadas de lo femenino y las resonancias que lo contradicen. Utilizamos el término "resonancia" porque la identidad femenina, como en su contexto histórico homológico, se construye en estos textos a partir del ser adjudicado por el orden masculino, y al compararse éste con el ser, según una perspectiva femenina, se produce una nueva versión que claudica, subvierte o denuncia al deber-ser. Y es precisamente esta configuración binaria y je-

rárquica de la identidad la que, en nuestra opinión, funciona como dinámica estructurante de la narrativa femenina que nos ocupa. En consecuencia, la problemática de la identidad se representa literariamente a partir de un sello visible y omnipotente sobre o por debajo del cual se tejen márgenes disidentes.

Si bien este ideologema funciona como una constante esencial, es importante notar que su elaboración particular pone de manifiesto no sólo los factores históricos en un momento determinado de la condición femenina sino también las estrategias ideológicas y literarias que funcionan como parámetros de una evolución de esta narrativa que, hasta ahora, se ha incluido erróneamente en las periodizaciones diseñadas para la producción masculina. En este sentido, las primeras novelas de Gertrudis Gómez de Avellaneda marcan en Hispanoamérica los inicios de la representación literaria de la identidad femenina. En *Sab* (1841), texto generalmente catalogado dentro de la tradición que aboga por la abolición de la esclavitud, el ser femenino convencionalizado se elabora a partir de modelos románticos que representan a la mujer como signo de la naturaleza, como reflejo armonioso de un orden divino suplantado por el injusto orden de la economía liberal. Carlota, entonces, por sus valores espirituales y su capacidad para amar, representa al sujeto romántico como figura que se margina y trasciende los valores pragmáticos de su sociedad del mismo modo como Sab, en su función homóloga, plasma el *leit-motiv* del buen

13. Adrienne Rich. *The Dream of a Common Language*. Nueva York: Norton, 1978, p. 51.
14. Para este importante aspecto de la novela, consultar el ensayo de Pedro Barreda Tomás titulado "Abolicionismo y feminismo en la Avellaneda. Lo negro como artificio narrativo en *Sab*" *(Cuadernos Hispanoamericanos*, vol. 342, 1978, pp. 613-626).
15. Gertrudis Gómez de Avellaneda. *Dos mujeres. Obras de la Avellaneda*, tomo V. La Habana: Imprenta de Aurelio Miranda, 1914, p 51.
16. Juana Manuela Gorriti. *El pozo del Yocci*, novela corta posiblemente escrita en 1863 y publicada por primera vez en Buenos Aires en 1876. Para este estudio utilizamos la edición de a Imprenta de la Universidad (Buenos Aires) 1929, p. 185)

salvaje. Si a primera vista el relato principal parece construirse a partir de los sucesos infortunados en la vida sentimental del esclavo, en el capítulo final se produce un cambio abrupto en el cual se postula el destino de Carlota como peor que el de un esclavo pues, bajo las cadenas perpetuas del matrimonio, ella está condenada a una muerte en vida. Es precisamente este desenlace el que pone en evidencia una estrategia fundamental de Gertrudis Gómez de Avellaneda quien, a través de una estructura palimpséstica, no sólo denuncia el poder aniquilante del orden masculino utilizando la figura literaria de Sab como recurso paradigmático de la esclavitud femenina[14] sino que también agrega un margen significativo al sujeto femenino romántico el cual en esta nueva versión está condenado al silencio, a fingir felicidad para mantener las apariencias, a una claudicación que ni siquiera merecerá una muerte sublime. En consecuencia, la trayectoria de la heroína se difumina en un vacío que contradice al matrimonio y la maternidad, como metas para la realización de la existencia femenina, postulando simultáneamente su identidad como una conciencia del no-ser que se enajena en el deber-ser.

Por otra parte, en *Dos mujeres* (1842), en un significativo proceso de inversión de las normas textuales, la autora subvierte el ser femenino convencional representado por Luisa oponiendo a él la figura de Catalina que se caracteriza como héroe romántico. El personaje catalogado por los otros como "mujer hombre"[15] resulta de la apropiación de lo masculino en sus atributos de genialidad, talento y poder creativo que al existir en una mujer producen el rechazo y la crítica de la sociedad. Es más, en esta transgresión de lo genérico y canónico concebido como innato según el orden masculino, Carlos es el personaje pasivo y sentimental. Tanto la defensa del adulterio, significativamente estructurada en la anulación de la disyunción folletinesca del bien y del mal, como la inversión de las oposiciones binarias de lo masculino y lo femenino, constituyen, sin embargo, gestos ideológicos y textuales condenados a reinsertarse en el sistema

convencional. Catalina, consciente del
hecho de que en la sociedad patriarcal
la mujer posee como único destino el
matrimonio, sinónimo de "cadena in-
sufrible e inquebrantable", renuncia a
su amante Carlos y simbólicamente se
encierra en un cuarto para suicidarse
asfixiándose. Difiriendo del simbolismo
masculino atribuido a la casa como *axis
mundi* o útero materno de los orígenes,
en *Dos mujeres* este espacio cerrado no
sólo funciona como signo de una situación sin salida sino que también, en un
repertorio simbólico típicamente femenino, aludirá a dicho espacio como *locus* por excelencia de una subordinación y dependencia sentimental con
respecto al sexo masculino que, en la
teoría de Simone de Beauvoir, posee la
posición de absoluto.

En estas novelas se plantea la condición femenina en los términos generali-
zantes de un orden patriarcal que se
impone como poder y que trasciende
todas las limitaciones del tiempo y del
espacio puesto que corresponde a lo
eterno, a aquello que no está sujeto a
las modificaciones del devenir histórico.
Los textos de Juana Manuela Gorriti
marcan en este sentido, un cambio
significativo al insertar la problemática
de la identidad femenina en un momento específico de la historia argentina, la dictadura de Rosas. Y es precisamente este acontecimiento el que
devela al absoluto masculino como signo de la violencia, de la ambición y de
la crueldad sin sentido; el hombre deviene, entonces, en "barro de
Adán" [16] en ser imperfecto y demo-
níaco que rompe la armonía creada por
Dios. Como poseedor del poder y de la
historia, lo masculino se simboliza en *El
pozo del Yocci* a través de la imagen del
águila, signo tradicional del sol y de la
guerra, mientras lo femenino, asociado
con el elemento indígena vencido, se
liga a la tierra, las aguas y la luna.
Aunque estos relatos se sitúan en un
acontecer concreto del devenir histórico, éste es observado desde una
perspectiva femenina que carece, por
su marginalización, de un ideario político y, a diferencia de sus coetáneos de
a Generación de 1837 Juana Manuela
Gorriti hace una remodelación moral y
cristiana de la circunstancia nacional.

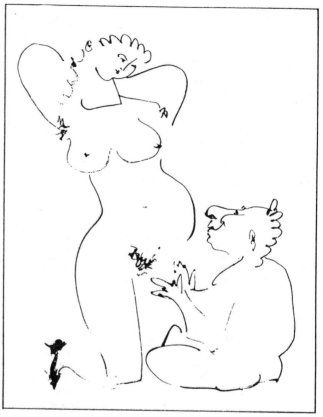

Así, la violencia de la dictadura se
plantea como sinónimo del mal, como
una bestialidad satánica que priva al
hombre de una humanidad concebida
según los principios católicos de amor
al prójimo, piedad y bondad.

En este contexto, que abstrae la historia con un objetivo moral, la identidad
femenina no sólo se sitúa fuera de toda
praxis modificadora sino que también se
la revierte a la zona consagrada de la
feminidad tradicional simbolizada por la
Virgen María. El ser femenino, cuyas
acciones sólo surgen del espíritu, el
amor o el instinto maternal, está limitado a ser testigo o víctima de la violencia sin poseer otra esfera de acción
que la de las predicciones, la enajenación o las apariciones fantasmales.
Marginalidad que refleja una condición
femenina originada por la infraestruc-
tura económica expresada por la autora
argentina en su visión misma de la circunstancia histórica que se resuelve, en
un nivel moral, con la utopía cristiana de
la armonía inminente bajo un poder
divino que establece cuotas medidas del
bien y del mal. Esta remodelización en la
esfera de lo divino está, de manera
significativa, determinada asimismo por
el orden masculino pues el héroe y el
tirano son sus únicos agentes activos.
En consecuencia, el aspecto más relevante de la identidad femenina está en
su tangencialidad con respecto al devenir histórico, visión que se reitera en
otras novelas contemporáneas en las
cuales se representa una circunstancia
histórica específica. Así, en *Hasta no
verte Jesús mío* (1969) de Elena Po-

niatowska. o *Estaba la pájara pinta
sentada en el verde limón* (1975) de
Albalucía Ángel. la mujer. lejos de ser
sujeto de la historia. se presenta como
signo de la subordinación social o exis-
tencial.

Un elemento importante en el dialogismo básico que se establece entre la
voz convencionalizada del orden masculino y sus resonancias en la imaginación femenina es. sin lugar a dudas. la
categoría del deber-ser que ha escin-
dido a la mujer en virgen o pecadora.
madre o prostituta. santa o bruja. Si en
algunos textos. como en *Aves sin nido*
(1889) de Clorinda Matto de Turner. *La
muñeca* (1895) de Carmela Eulate
Sanjurjo. o *Luz y sombra* (1903) de Ana
Roqué de Duprey. se reafirma el modelo
social de la maternidad sublime propi-
ciado por la moral patriarcal y teorizado
desde una perspectiva positivista por
Augusto Comte. el pecado o la amenaza
del no deber-ser constituye. sin lugar a
dudas. el núcleo más problemático de la
identidad femenina. *Blanca Sol* (1889).
de Mercedes Cabello de Carbonera.
marca. en este sentido. el inicio de una
tradición narrativa femenina que se genera en el ámbito conflictivo del pecado
que asume significados contradictorios
y claudica o transgrede la ética masculina. Así. la trayectoria de Blanca Sol
construye un tejido de doble faz en el
cual se dan simultánea y explícitamente
dos relatos. Por una parte. el relato de
''la torcida senda'' se configura a partir
de la moral disyuntiva del bien y del mal
y su instancia cardinal está en la caída
en la prostitución. Dentro de este sistema ético. Blanca Sol. como prostituta. es el anti-modelo de la feminidad
consagrada. Sin embargo. en un nivel
más problemático de la evolución de la
protagonista. ocurre simultáneamente
un relato situado en la esfera no-disy-
untiva del bien y del mal en el cual se
produce un proceso de iniciación que
culmina en el conocimiento de la de-
gradación de los valores de su sociedad
y la consecuente decisión de marginal-
izarse de dicho orden con la clara conciencia de que. si ella es ''una mujer
perdida'' todos los demás están también irremisiblemente perdidos
Consciente de que su matrimonio sin
amor ''no era más que la prostitución

sancionada por la sociedad''.[17] Blanca
Sol se rebela contra los falsos valores de
la aristocracia peruana que han hecho
del parecer y el poseer sustitutos del
verdadero ser y. yendo más allá del
adulterio que injustamente se le adju-
dicó. elige la prostitución. Pero si ''la
rabiosa indignación'' y ''el descaro''
parecen ser la senda de una afirmación
auténtica de la identidad femenina en la
transgresión del deber-ser. esta posibilidad se anula en los dos silencios que
se instauran en cada uno de los relatos
entretejidos: el silencio de Blanca Sol y
el silencio de la narradora. ''Ya llegará el
momento que lo diga todo'' (p. 189).
se dice la protagonista antes de recibir a
sus huéspedes en su papel de dueña del
prostíbulo. de empresaria de un trueque
comercial como cualquier otro en la
sociedad capitalista. Y este querer decir
queda en el nivel de un designio. de un
deseo y de una amenaza. La narradora.
por otra parte. concluye diciendo. ''Y
después de la cena hubo grande alga-
zara. loca alegría. cristales rotos. pala-

17. Mercedes Cabello de Carbonera. *Blanca Sol.*
Lima. Carlos Prince. Impresor y Librero Editor.
1894. p. 118.
18. En su conferencia presentada en Colombia en
1929. la autora postula un interesante concepto
acerca de la identidad femenina al decir: ''La
crisis por la que atraviesan hoy las mujeres no se
cura predicando la sumisión. la sumisión y la
sumisión. como se hacía en los tiempos en que la
vida mansa podía encerrarse toda dentro de las
puertas de la casa. La vida actual. la del automóvil
conducido por su dueña. la del micrófono junto a
la cama. la de la prensa y la de los viajes. no
respeta puertas cerradas. Como el radio. que tan
exactamente lo simboliza. atraviesa las paredes.
y quieras que no. se hace oír y se mezcla a la vida
del hogar. Para que la mujer sea fuerte. sana y
verdaderamente limpia de hipocresía. no se la
debe sojuzgar frente a la nueva vida. al contrario.
debe ser libre ante sí misma. consciente de los
peligros y de las responsabilidades. útil a la
sociedad. aunque no sea madre de familia. e
independiente pecuniariamente por su trabajo y
su colaboración junto al hombre. ni dueño ni
enemigo. ni candidato explotable sino compañero
y amigo''. *Ibid*. p. 685.
19. Según Luce Irigaray. la sexualidad femenina.
en su fluidez y multiplicidad. no sólo ha sido un
espacio vacío en la cultura occidental bajo los
parámetros de lo visible y lo fálico. sino que
también se opone a la tendencia falologocéntrica
de computar por unidades exactas. La sexualidad
femenina en el espacio múltiple de la vagina y el
estado de lo insaciable resulta así el sexo que no
es uno. *(Ce sexe qui n en est pas un.* París. Minuit.
1977)

bras equívocas y Blanca llegó hasta
¡Silencio!... No se debe describir el *mal*
sino en tanto que sirva de ejemplo para
el *bien*'' (p. 189). Aunque la posición
ética dominante en la novela parece ser
aquella que corresponde al relato de la
moral disyuntiva que revertiría al deber-
ser. en el discurso de la narradora se ha
producido una fisura que añade un
margen de ambigüedad haciendo de la
identidad femenina un signo oximorónico en el cual la confluencia simultánea de dos significados primarios pone
en evidencia una tensión que. lejos de
resolverse. se difumina en el silencio.

Es precisamente este espacio de
ambigüedades y silencios el que caracteriza a la narrativa femenina de la primera mitad del siglo XX. A primera
vista. este espacio resulta paradójico
puesto que la nueva ideología feminista
hacia los años veinte ha originado un
cambio cualitativo con respecto a una
toma de conciencia de la subordinación
social de la mujer y su derecho no sólo a
incorporarse a la educación. según el
proyecto decimonónico. sino también a
ser partícipe activo en la política. Sin
embargo. es importante hacer notar que
el movimiento por el sufragio universal
constituyó una instancia más en la serie
de claudicaciones que subsumieron la
individualidad femenina en el orden
masculino hegemónico sin modificar de
manera radical su condición. En consecuencia. durante este período se inten-
sifica la preocupación por la identidad
del segundo sexo que ahora imagina-
riamente se remodeliza a partir de ''lo
íntimo femenino'' aunque. de manera
homóloga a la circunstancia histórica. el
ser de la mujer permanece en una situación estática. Por lo tanto. en el
dialogismo que constituye el ideologema básico. las resonancias disidentes
con respecto a las voces convencionalizadas de lo femenino se multiplican y
diversifican. aunque al final claudican o
se diluyen en el vacío.

En un modo narrativo que utiliza los
recursos de la confesión o el diario
íntimo. la escritura se presenta como
una praxis del encierro. la frustración y
el fastidio; por otra parte. lo cotidiano
femenino logra instaurarse como suce-
so literario en una tradición masculina
que. al decir de Virginia Woolf. sólo ha

dado categoría estética a aquellos eventos que relacionan al hombre con el mundo de afuera. *Ifigenia* (1924) de Teresa de la Parra es, en este sentido, un texto clave, pues a través del espacio íntimo propone nuevos elementos configuradores de la feminidad: el cuerpo de la mujer y su relación con los artefactos del maquillaje, con la voluptuosidad de la ropa definida como segunda piel y con su imagen en el espejo. Apropiándose de la estructura del *Bildungsroman* tradicional, Teresa de la Parra irónicamente traza una trayectoria para su protagonista, quien de heroína rebelde y subversiva (modelo de la mujer nueva) se transforma en "señorita decente" sucumbiendo al orden patriarcal rígidamente resguardado por su abuela. Sin embargo, dada la perspectiva feminista de la autora,[18] los *leitmotivs* del silencio y el sacrificio adquieren significados que anacronizan tanto el contenido mitológico de la tradición griega como el concepto convencional de la identidad femenina. Ifigenia posee una clara conciencia social de su condición bajo la "divinidad omnipotente que tiene por cuerpo el egoísmo feroz de los hombres" (p. 493); también sabe que en su claudicación el verdadero holocausto es el que ha hecho de ella "un cuerpo sin

alma" (p. 492), razón por la cual el acto de asumir el mistificante espíritu de sacrificio posee una carga de ironía iluminada retroactivamente por la etapa rebelde de la protagonista. Si, en un nivel ya tradicional de la narrativa femenina, la claudicación se realiza como un acto de impotencia, dado el contexto ideológico de la novela y los elementos subversivos del desenfado presentes en los inicios de su trayectoria, ésta también adquiere el significado de anti-modelo.

En consecuencia, los labios sellados de la protagonista al final de *Ifigenia* son también una denuncia a viva voz, significado oximorónico del silencio que recurrirá en novelas tales como *El abrazo de la tierra* (1933), *Espejo sin imagen* (1936) y *Las cenizas* (1942), de María Flora Yáñez; *Extraño estío* (1944) y *El mundo dormido de Yenia* (1946), de María Carolina Geel, o *En soledad vivía* (1972), de Alicia Jurado. Es más, este silencio está precedido, como en el caso de *Ifigenia*, por un discurso femenino subversivo que, en estos textos, se nutre de la experiencia erótica vivida o imaginada en los márgenes convencionales de la casa burguesa. El deseo es, entonces, el elemento que instaura una nueva fisura en la voz institucionalizada del dialogismo sobre el ser femenino y,

en su calidad disidente, se contrapone al sistema ético dominante. Si bien el adulterio se plantea en la zona difusa de una ambigüedad que oscila entre el pecado y el derecho inalienable del cuerpo y el existir, la autentificación de la identidad femenina se da en la representación de una economía libidinal que hace de la mujer un ser intrínsecamente unido al agua y la tierra, una prolongación de la materia que ha sido subyugada y dominada por el impulso racionalizador de la civilización masculina. Transgrediendo el énfasis patriarcal en la penetración fálica, ésta se desplaza a una multiplicidad sensual que, según la teoría de Luce Irigaray, hace de lo femenino el sexo que no es uno.[19] Es más, la sexualidad femenina se plantea como la única vía que hace posible el hallazgo de la verdadera identidad inserta en un orden cósmico de infinitas gestaciones. Sin embargo, la identidad del ser femenino como sinónimo de la materia está condenada a un tronchamiento definitivo bajo el poder del orden masculino que en estos textos se metaforiza como la encarceladora convención social.

En la oposición Convención social versus Cuerpo femenino, subyace una interesante dicotomía entre civilización masculina y materia ancestral que plantea una significativa disidencia con respecto al concepto liberal de civilización y barbarie en la cultura masculina dominante en el continente hispanoamericano. Del mismo modo, los textos indigenistas escritos por mujeres modifican la tradición predominante al surgir, en nuestra opinión, de una identificación con los grupos marginales tanto por su posición de otro vencido y dominado (imagen especular de la condición femenina) como por su visión del mundo en la cual perduran una concepción del tiempo y una relación con la naturaleza que coincide con lo femenino. Así, en *Recuerdos del porvenir* (1963), de Elena Garro, las categorías falologocéntricas del tiempo y la realidad objetiva se diluyen y difuminan en el pueblo de Ixtepec, que mantiene las vivencias indígenas pese a la dominación de la Conquista española y la Revolución mexicana, subversión del vencido que se reitera significativamente en la oposición entre lo masculino y lo femenino representado por el general Francisco Rosas y Julia Andrade. El poder, la violencia y la energía racionalizadora ubicada en el presente y lo tangible se enfrentan con los escollos de la memoria, la intuición y lo impenetrable configurando espacios cognoscitivos irremisiblemente condenados a la incomunicación.

Rosario Castellanos ahonda en este conflicto postulando la posesión del lenguaje como elemento clave en todo sistema de dominación, tanto en aquel impuesto por el conquistador español como por lo masculino en la sociedad latinoamericana actual. *Balún Canán* (1957) y *Oficio de tinieblas* (1962) resultan, desde una perspectiva contemporánea, textos señeros con respecto a la relación entre discurso y estructuras de poder. Si el discurso ladino dominante impone la opresión y el silencio en el indígena, en las relaciones hombre-mujer se reitera esta estructura. Los personajes femeninos de *Oficio de tinieblas* son, en esencia, seres que no manejan las estrategias de un código lingüístico masculino, poniendo en evidencia una subordinación que se manifiesta en el silencio, en el monólogo interior, en la comunicación con un interlocutor imaginado.[20] Por

otra parte, Teresa, en su papel de narradora, transforma el lenguaje de instrumento de dominación en sistema sagrado que transmite lo mítico y perdurable —lo femenino e indígena que ha sido anulado por la civilización masculina occidental. Del mismo modo, la esterilidad de Catalina, que para los valores patriarcales es un signo negativo, se invierte pues ella en su función de *ilol*, no sólo se transforma en voz del pasado, presente y futuro de su pueblo; sino también en madre regestadora de los dioses ocultos. Es más, transgrediendo el signo de la Virgen María, Catalina asume un papel de sujeto modificador de la historia al ofrecer en sacrificio a su hijo adoptivo Domingo como la contrafigura indígena de Jesucristo, e insta a su pueblo a la rebelión. No obstante que el levantamiento de los indios es sofocado, la figura de Catalina perdura en la memoria de su pueblo transformándose así en símbolo de una libertad y esperanza que sobrevive en el devenir cíclico y mítico de una historia al margen de la linealidad occidental, del mismo modo como en el diálogo dispar entre lo masculino y lo femenino se mantiene latente un conjunto de valores que se oponen a las estructuras de poder impuestas por el patriarcado. En consecuencia, la representación literaria de lo indígena, más que responder, como en los textos masculinos, a una búsqueda de la identidad cultural, es la incursión feminista en el ámbito de los dominados y la reafirmación de un ser en constantes gestos subversivos.

En el contexto de una tradición literaria de corte metafísico, se observan también digresiones que resultan de un proceso de adecuación a la problemática y visión del mundo femeninas. Así, en *Las ceremonias del verano* (1966) de Marta Traba, el proceso de búsqueda de la identidad se traza en una trayectoria que corresponde a las etapas femeninas de la adolescencia, la adultez y la madurez y se presenta el problema de la

20. Para un excelente análisis de este aspecto, consultar el ensayo de Stacey Schlau titulado "Conformity and Resistance to Enclosure: Female Voices in Rosario Castellanos' *Oficio de tinieblas* (*The Dark Service*)". (*Latin American Literary Review*, vol. 12, N° 24 (primavera-verano 1984), pp. 45-57).

autonomía del ser dentro del sistema de valores de una sociedad latinoamericana dominada por la supremacía patriarcal. Significativamente, el conflicto de vivir para sí y desde sí se ilumina a través de la campesina Clemé, quien, como la figura del maestro sabio en la mitología masculina, enseña a la protagonista el camino de la verdadera existencia. De manera similar, Olga Orozco en *La oscuridad es otro sol* (1967) presenta el problema del ser y el estar en el mundo tomando en cuenta los papeles primarios asignados al hombre y la mujer. Superando todo condicionamiento social y genérico impuesto a su existencia, Lía se decide por la elección libre de comprender y abarcar su propio destino como único e individual, a través de la búsqueda de la realidad de su ser que se define como el desdoblamiento de Dios en máscara de todos.

El nuevo movimiento feminista iniciado hacia los años 70 ha resultado ser de una importancia vital para la reevaluación de la identidad femenina. El rechazo consciente de las imágenes y modelos impuestos por el orden masculino, la reivindicación del hacer femenino como praxis cultural y el proyecto ideológico de obtener un verdadero poder político han modificado, de manera significativa el ideologema básico sobre el cual se construye literariamente la problemática del ser. En este sentido, la narrativa de Rosario Ferré ha abierto una brecha importante. Si bien en *Papeles de Pandora* (1976) la identidad femenina se debate en el dialogismo ya observado en textos anteriores, en las relaciones entre la voz dominante del deber-ser se incorpora la rebelión y la ira, elementos que van dirigidos a la destrucción del orden patriarcal y burgués. Así, el *leitmotiv* de la venganza, que en "La bella durmiente" se realiza como un planeado acto de prostitución de parte de la protagonista burguesa, adquiere en "La muñeca menor" y "Marina y el león" los significados simbólicos de la invasión amenazante de los instintos, de la materia ancestral reprimida representada por las antenas furibundas de las chágaras y el elemento primordial del fuego. Por otra parte, la transgresión del orden masculino y burgués se realiza tanto en el nivel

del lenguaje como en el desdoblamiento de una identidad femenina que opta por lo catalogado como pecaminoso. Junto al lenguaje convencionalmente asignado a la mujer, se contrapone la blasfemia iracunda, la obscenidad y el vocablo despojado de todo eufemismo para designar los órganos sexuales. Del mismo modo, al motivo de la muñeca —signo que funciona como sinónimo de la feminidad bajo la estructura burguesa en su significado de pasividad, ornamentación artificial y enajenación de la realidad histórica— se contrapone la figura de la prostituta no sólo como símbolo del no-deber-ser sino también como personaje femenino que en su posición marginal ha mantenido una autenticidad erótica que la ética masculina ha aniquilado en la mujer por la rígida imposición de un código moral. Es más, fusionando las zonas convencionales de lo aceptado y lo prohibido, se postula la identidad femenina como un oximoron extendido en el cual ser mujer equivale simultáneamente a ser dama decente y prostituta. Fusión que en "Cuando las mujeres quieren a los hombres" se elabora a partir del motivo del doble (Isabel Luberza, Isabel la Ne-

gra) para resolverse en la absorción y subyugación de la dama por la prostituta. De este modo, los personajes femeninos iracundos, rebeldes y blasfemantes revelan, como Pandora, lo oculto, desenmascarando las imposiciones patriarcales a una identidad femenina que ahora asume una actitud beligerante.

Es precisamente en este contexto histórico, en el que se ha tomado conciencia de una cultura femenina reprimida y silenciada, donde comienza a surgir un nuevo concepto de la identidad, no ya subordinado o dependiente de las configuraciones sociales y simbólicas creadas por la cultura masculina dominante, sino como entidad en vías de asumir una verdadera autonomía e individualidad. *Las andariegas* (1984) de Albalucía Ángel marca, en nuestra opinión, el inicio de una nueva tendencia que intenta inscribir lo femenino en la historia y el futuro de Latinoamérica. Transgrediendo los formatos literarios tradicionales, la autora incursiona en un discurso que contradice la lógica, la objetividad y la linealidad de los discursos dominantes, explorando simultáneamente el espacio silenciado de la

memoria colectiva femenina. La escritura se construye así en acto fundador de una realidad inédita, develando asimismo la identidad femenina desde su propio centro —los círculos y semicírculos del sustrato mítico, literario e histórico que corresponde a las imágenes opacas del espejo patriarcal. La travesía de las andariegas deviene entonces en una búsqueda de los orígenes que es también una reafirmación y rescate de la historia y la cultura femenina deslizándose en los márgenes del hacer masculino y en una condición constante de exilio. Y es desde el ámbito legendario y mítico que se trasciende en viaje milenario a la utopía de la destrucción de la civilización masculina, representada por la ciudad de Nueva York, y al vuelo ascendente de las nuevas amazonas bajo la mirada sabia de la Tierra para iniciar un nuevo comienzo. Se produce así una nueva apertura que instaura la identidad femenina en el complejo significativo de lo ontológico, lo cultural y lo histórico, señalando el futuro de un verdadero ser que ha superado las mutilaciones, imposiciones y silenciamientos conjurados por el sistema patriarcal. **plural**

plural 21

Melodrama, Sex, and Nation in Latin America's *Fin de Siglo*

Francine Masiello

Gossip and public opinion come to play a distinguished role in Latin American narrative of the last *fin de siglo*. The gossip columnist, the reporter, and the intrusive neighbor take a central place in fiction to challenge established truths; they also question the uses of language in relation to the authority of the state. Recall, for example, the canonical novels of the late nineteenth century—*La bolsa*, by Julián Martel; *La charca*, by Manuel Zeno Gandía; *Pot pourri*, by Eugenio Cambaceres; *Oasis en la vida*, by Juana Manuela Gorriti—in which gossip alters the course of events and structures the major aspects of plot. It offers yet another way to classify private life, to name events and feelings, to set society in order. Moreover, it projects the anxieties of the times and allows individuals to speculate on the identities and to publicize the secrets of their neighbors. At the same time, gossip confuses reality and fiction; it disables the registers with which we earlier viewed modern culture and expands categories of analysis to accommodate new information. The voice of the intermediary also announces a tension between chaos and order insofar as it insinuates doubt regarding the identity of citizen subjects. Equally important, it depends for its growth on such topics as sex, crime, and perversion to confront passions and the complexity of social life.

Josefina Ludmer has observed, with respect to *gauchesca* literature, that the delinquent serves to organize the state from beyond.[1] From a

[1] Ludmer, *El género gauchesco: Un tratado sobre la patria* (Buenos Aires: Sudamericana, 1988).

Modern Language Quarterly 57:2, June 1996. © 1996 University of Washington.

post on society's edge, the criminal defines the boundaries of the state and strengthens the metropolitan center. In the same way, urban delinquents of the last decades of the nineteenth century taught by negative example. As wayward subjects, the prostitute, the thief, the pervert, and the dandy formed part of the social imagination of the times. But they also suggested that delinquency was everywhere to be found; even beneath the mask of the good bourgeois lay a delinquent *in potentia*. It was then the task of the gossipmonger and journalist to seek out these social misfits and even to rip off, once and for all, the mask of protection offered to the *gente decente*.

Late-nineteenth-century journalism is densely seeded with such reports, which contribute to the carnavalesque atmosphere of the period. Writers and journalists lamented the absence of public morality, the rise of social crimes, and the suspicious character of any figure who resisted the new state order; stories of double lives fascinated readers and reminded them of nearby transgressions. By the 1870s, coincidentally with general efforts to modernize Latin America, journalists pressed with increasing vigor for data about the behavior of the masses and about their private lives. By doing so, they called attention to the fragility of the social edifice and the failure of the state to control aberrance.

The zones of excess were always articulated as hybrid or marginal areas that confused delinquency and repressed desire. Latin American writers thus began to open their texts to representations of neurosis and hysteria; they studied sex crimes, deviation, and the corruption of home and society. Through rudimentary psychological inquiries, intellectuals tried to make sense of divergent human experience, while criminology was legitimated as a field on which to support the modern state.

In Argentina, for example, Kraft Ebbing's studies of crimes of passion were eagerly received in Spanish translation. Even José Ramos Mejía, in *Las neurosis de los hombres célebres* (1878), attempted to describe

Francine Masiello is professor of Spanish and comparative literature at the University of California, Berkeley. Her most recent books are *Between Civilization and Barbarism: Women, Nation, and Literary Culture in Modern Argentina* **(1992) and** *La mujer y el espacio público: El periodismo femenino en la Argentina del siglo XIX* **(1994).**

Latin American history in terms of the interior lives of important figures.[2] Rosas, Aldao, Monteagudo, Dr. Francia, Admiral Brown entered
Ramos Mejía's book as hysterics driven to seek power by their deliria.
In other words, the politics of the South were explained by psychobi-
ography. Equally important, social events were correlated to the
unchartable nature of desire. José Asunción Silva's hero of *De sobremesa*
(1896) constantly posed the question "¿Qué es la vida real?" [What is
real life?], while Clorinda Matto de Turner, in her novel *Herencia*
(1895), insisted that public life and desire were hopelessly intertwined.
Angel Rama rightly observes that "desire contaminated the totality of
operations that shaped the social milieu" of the late nineteenth century.[3] Explosions, excess, irrepressibility, crossovers of social identities:
fin de siglo literature was a sailor's never-learned lesson about the
unfathomable sea.

   In these pages I want to underscore the narrative excess that such
inquiries produced in literature, in newspapers, and in the gossip
columns of the period and then to explore their common bond of
melodrama. I focus on melodrama as a way to link the representation
of chaos and order in modern life. It plays with appearances and
deceptions; it juxtaposes the superficiality of the visible world with the
realm of feelings; and it insists on the perversity of gender relations as
the sine qua non of fiction and the language of the state. In addition,
melodrama links the crisis of modernity with the irrecuperable nature
of desire and provokes an inquiry into the very limits of representation. Thus it embraces the conflicts of excess and order in late-nineteenth-century culture.

   As such, it is impossible to narrate the *fin de siglo* without the structures of melodrama, whose voice is found in public opinion and gossip.
To develop my hypothesis, I want first to review a newspaper account,
typical of the interests of the times, and then several *fin de siglo* novels
to signal melodrama as the trope that joins periodical and literary discourses and the emerging crisis of individual subjectivities in relation
to the modern state.

   [2] Ramos Mejía, *Las neurosis de los hombres célebres en la historia argentina*, 2d ed.
(Buenos Aires: L. J. Rosso, 1932).
   [3] Rama, *Las máscaras democráticas del modernismo* (Montevideo: Fundación Angel
Rama, 1985), 86.

"Su Monstruosidad Espanta"
[His Monstrosity Inspires Fear]

I begin with a story published in 1883 in *Las calamidades de Buenos Aires*, a small Argentine newspaper whose subtitle *Diario viril* [Virile daily], brings all its yellow-press efforts together under the sign of gender. On the one hand, the newspaper occupies the space of the masculine, denouncing the effeminate state; on the other hand, it assumes the task of exposing sexual delinquency throughout Buenos Aires. *Las calamidades de Buenos Aires* thus offers some notable stories about urban sex crimes: an assistant police chief rapes a nine-year-old boy with the help of a female go-between; a prostitute steals from hotel guests; a homosexual judge stages a travesty of justice. Omnipresent homophobia and misogyny underlie the melodramatic narrative strategies of the yellow press. Together, they build a paradigm for Latin American fiction of the time.

Melodrama has been described by its linguistic extravagance in the field of realist representation.[4] In nineteenth-century fiction, it inserts a hyperbolic register into discourse. Because of its extreme bipolarity, it discovers the limits of language and marks the very essence of theatricality. As melodrama addresses a mass public, moreover, it shakes the world of feelings, awakens the audience's taste for horror and exploits its passion for violence, and opposes criminal and victim. Melodramatic inflections of the yellow press also link state corruption to horror.

One serialized tale covered for many months is about Zenon Lista, the assistant chief of police accused of raping the nine-year-old son of Italian immigrants. From the start the reporter assumes a hyperbolic tone. Exoticism, delinquency, and the revelatory power of the journalist frame the story, and an important theme runs its length: what name fits the crime? How might we classify it within the ordinary limits of language? From the start, then, a gap detected between reason and classification, on the one hand, and our immediate perceptions, on

---

[4] See especially Peter Brooks, *The Melodramatic Imagination: Balzac, Henry James, Melodrama, and the Mode of Excess* (New Haven, Conn.: Yale University Press, 1976); and Christopher Prendergast, *Balzac: Fiction and Melodrama* (London: Edward Arnold, 1978).

the other, leads us to speculate on ways to *feel* or experience the crime while giving it a name. Analytic and sensory reactions are drawn together; the nature of the crime demands both an intellectual and a physical response from the reader. Indeed, the story's novelty may well lie in its insistence on the physiological; through a visceral response to horror, readers might come to comprehend evil.[5] Of course, within the positivist package of late-nineteenth-century Argentina, all moral affirmations were defended through concrete, experiential responses. Hence a game of surface operations prevails; first, the immediacy of response is privileged in narration, and only later are readers expected to supply a proper interpretation of what has been seen.

Time and again, the journalist asks how the crime can be understood. Which categories of analysis can be used to inscribe its events? The writer even invokes Edgar Allan Poe to organize our conceptual framework:

> Edgardo Poe, el sublime borracho Edgardo Poe pudo haber apurado su fantasía para describir escenas tenebrosas y amalgamadas de horror, cuando hechos inverosímiles cuya misma inverosimilitud manifestaba la potencia extraordinaria de su embotada inteligencia.
>
> Pero Edgardo Poe no pudo encontrarse jamás con un Zenon Lista y con un Luis de Mare, porque entonces hubiera escrito la novela inmortal del más grande de los crímenes. Y no ha encontrado la personificación de estas dos individualidades, horrorosa la una y angelical la otra, porque los crímenes de la magnitud de que nuestros lectores conocen son un verdadero aborto entre los que han conmovido a las sociedades por medio de las mas fuerte sacudidas.[6]

[Edgar Poe, that sublime drunk Edgar Poe, was able to accelerate his fantasy of darkness and horror with improbable events whose very unlikelihood reveals the extraordinary powers of his average intelligence.

But Edgar Poe never met up with a Zenon Lista or a Luis de Mare, because if he had he would have written the immortal novel of the greatest of crimes. He never met these personalities—one awful,

---

[5] For an excellent discussion of sensationalist literature and the centrality of physiological reader response see D. A. Miller, *The Novel and the Police* (Berkeley: University of California Press, 1988), esp. "*Cage aux Folles*: Sensation and Gender in Wilkie Collins's *The Woman in White*" (146–91).

[6] "Luis de Mare: La víctima del asesino Zenon Lista: Horror y lágrimas," in *Las calamidades de Buenos Aires: Diario viril,* 15 March 1883, 3. My translations.

the other angelic—because crimes of the magnitude that our readers know are freakish even among those societies that have known great cataclysms.]

The comparison of terror between cultures suggests that this crime could not be repeated beyond the Latin American circuit. In effect, as Sylvia Molloy and Oscar Montero have noted, crimes of sexuality are valued as a way to confirm the originality of Latin America.[7]

Once private experience is beheld by a third party, it generates a political tension of its own. After all, who is the witness here? Not simply the reporter but also the prostitute, Cristina Almeyda; the two compete for the narrative space to produce their own stories and for the power of representation before the reading public. Journalist and prostitute take over the sentimental realm; in place of the republican mother, so frequently evoked in nineteenth-century fiction, we are left with the evil woman, an accomplice.[8] Later, however, even Almeyda is exiled from the discourse and denounced for her lies by the reporter. In effect, he, the carrier of public opinion, intervenes as the protective, good mother, while the child's father tells the story with "tears and a voice filled with horror" (3). Both home and state are sites where traditional representations of gender are inverted: the father fulfills domestic obligations, the reporter provides a supportive voice, yet the assistant police chief, as a representative of the state, violates the child. As a unit, they expel all women from the discursive network. The politics of domesticity are usurped by the state and by public opinion.

Through its titillating effect, the story brings us remarkably close to pornography; at the same time, it demands the response of the reader to bring about social justice. The dramatic force of the tale,

[7] Molloy, "Too Wilde for Comfort: Desire and Ideology in Fin-de-Siècle Spanish America," *Social Text*, nos. 31–2 (1992): 187–201; Montero, "Before the Parade Passes By: Latino Queers and National Identity," *Radical America* 24 (1990): 15–26.

[8] In *Between Civilization and Barbarism: Women, Nation, and Literary Culture in Modern Argentina* (Lincoln: University of Nebraska Press, 1992), I elaborate on the importance of republican motherhood in early-nineteenth-century Argentina and argue that 1880 (the moment of state consolidation, the rise of consumer culture, and increased attention to units of public exchange) marks a crucial transition in the discourse on gender and the representation of women. After 1880 the prostitute and the female criminal emerge as protagonistic figures in Argentine literature.

owing to its revelatory tone and emphasis on sensationalism, ushers us into the realm of melodrama. Thus we learn the tragedy of the victim, the poor child, the son of immigrants, who will never reach adulthood. A pen-and-ink portrait helps us visualize his innocence and pain. Finally, although the text tracks Lista's aggressions, his crime still refuses definition; neither reporter nor father and son can tell what happened.

Toward the end, the narration contrasts private and public lives to condemn the corruption of the state:

> En la vida privada del hombre hay cosas que no pueden descubrirse sin que la hediodez que despiden asfixie al imprudente que pretendiera hacerlo; pero cuando esas cosas o esos hechos ultrajasen los caracteres de la vida privada para ir a afectar al hombre público y a las instituciones, no hay más remedio que levantar el velo, volver la cabeza, y sacudir el latigazo que ha de convertirse en freno más tarde para la reproducción de esos y otros hechos escándalos y deprimentes.

> [In the private life of man, there are things that cannot be revealed without exposing the observer to an asphyxiating stench; but when these events surpass the limits of private life to affect public figures and institutions, there is no solution but to lift the veil, turn one's head toward the crime, and crack the whip that will later stop the reproduction of these and other depressing scandals.][9]

"Lift the veil"; expose the most scandalous details of domesticity; invade private lives to denounce what is seen in them; exercise social justice on the sexualized body: such projects inform the melodramatic text produced during Latin America's *fin de siglo*.

"Levantar el Velo" [Lifting the Veil]

I have cited this newspaper account to suggest the importance to turn-of-the-century society of melodrama, which organizes all inquiries about the conflict of public and private lives while bringing order to the emergent social body. But melodrama also dominates the so-called high culture of the late nineteenth century. Literary texts often refer

---

[9] "Asuntos asquerosos: Otros grandes escándalos," in *Las calamidades de Buenos Aires: Diario viril,* 11 February 1883, 3.

to sex crimes to underscore the corruption of national values. Passions disturb progress; decadence undermines public order. Moreover, melodrama projects an obsession, among elites, for the emergence of mass culture; by always minding the presence of new populations, the writer finally resorts to the literary form destined for them. *Amistad funesta*, by José Martí; the corpus of fiction by Eugenio Cambaceres; the detective series by Luis Varela; the naturalist fiction of Clorinda Matto de Turner; the novels of Mercedes Cabello de Carbonera: all take on the topic of private transgressions set against the rise of the modern state. They tell of social climbers, of the attempted founding of a new social order, and explicitly link sexual desire to the failings of Latin America. Their authors call on the uses of gossip, the power of social reporters, or the friendly *causerie et débat* that sets the stage for public morality and condemnation.

I would venture to say that the corpus of late-nineteenth-century fiction is based on "horror and tears." In *Amistad funesta* (1885), his only novel, Martí describes how jealousy and passion among the traditional social classes challenge progress in Latin America.[10] Before the retrograde vision of a provincial Central American oligarchy, the noble plan of Juan Jérez to found righteous nations ultimately stalls. The excess of passion—the very basis of melodrama—is generated by the women of the novel: Lucía Jérez, promised in marriage to Juan, her cousin, and her friend Ana, are both seen as inimical to Juan's liberal project. Hypersensitive, devoted to art and gossip, Lucía and Ana are joined in what Martí suggests is an unholy, erotic alliance. In the end Juan's plan fails because of Lucía's jealousy. Fearful that he will devote his attentions to another woman, she enlists an Indian to provide a weapon to murder her rival. Then Juan disappears, possibly murdered, and Lucía falls into Ana's arms.

Thus Martí announces the inability of family romance to structure a narrative of progress and also exposes a range of sentiments and gestures inadmissible in a future republic: "Aquí todo es pecado; contra la naturaleza" [Here sin abounds, against nature] (49). Like the chronicles of *Las calamidades de Buenos Aires*, Martí observes that America indulges a preference for perversion. The women in his novel insert a register of expression beyond liberal control; not only do they reveal

[10] Martí, *Amistad funesta* (Mexico City: Novaro-México, 1958).

their passion for each other, but they also rely on the complicity of sub-altern groups to get their way. In this double schema, domesticity confronts progress, and to shape the conflict, Martí turns to melodrama.

It has been said that the fundamental condition of the novel is its defense of privacy. One could argue also that the reader's private space and the private lives of characters are constantly interchanged in the reading systems proposed by fiction. Nevertheless, in late-nineteenth-century Latin American literature the private life is feared; characters set out to spy on its workings and to revile uncommon behavior. Accordingly, different registers meet violently; they force an encounter between liberty and spectacle, private life and public denunciation.

Not all literary texts, however, defend the voyeur's mission. Against Martí's project, in which passion must be controlled, other writers use melodrama to expose the malfeasance of meddlers. In Cabello de Carbonera's *Blanca sol* (1889), for example, the subversive nature of gossip is condemned.[11] The vox populi generates its own kind of horror, fragmenting the social whole that dominates the *fin de siglo*. Rumor and gossip, insofar as they give name to the manifestations of desire, inaugurate fantasies of adultery and crime.

In *Blanca sol* the eponymous heroine, untutored in ethical matters, yields to evil suggestions and falls into sin. The author sympathetically describes her as the helpless victim of slander. Yet at the close of the novel, in line with the principles of melodrama that always mark the overlapping of formerly separate lives, Blanca Sol indulges public speculation about her morality by turning to prostitution as a means of survival.

Cabello de Carbonera shows that the language of the gossipmonger or the newspaper reporters in her novel is simply incommensurate with daily experience. By equating public perception and language with deformations of reality, she opens an investigation into the cataloging of knowledge. She criticizes dictionary labels assigned to events, decries the bourgeois desire to define privilege with titles of nobility, and exposes lineages and identities founded on confected documentation or accumulated possessions and wealth. Most important, she explains that categories of knowledge cannot circumscribe desire.

---

[11] Cabello de Carbonera, *Blanca sol* (Lima: Carlos Prince, 1889).

What conclusions can be drawn from these observations? How might the cultural forms of *fin de siglo* Latin America be rethought? First, sexuality as a metaphor is necessary for shaping the ideological systems of both the novel and the state. Nevertheless, the Freudian family romance does not provide a paradigm for action, nor are gendered exchanges to be read as allegories of nation; instead, the state metaphorical system depends on images of perversion and takes definition (by analogy or opposition) before scandal. Second, the *fin de siglo* demands classification of all human knowledge; the catalog prevails as a hallmark of the times. Indeed, in Latin America's late-nineteenth-century literature, in which naturalism and *modernista* movements are represented as antithetical, intellectuals in both camps express the anxiety to name and shape new experiences and to discuss the details of private life in terms of excessive, unrepressed passions. In literature and the press, the struggle to open the registers of language is assumed by the reporter and the intrusive neighbor as shapers of public opinion and observers of progress. Third, to construct a narrative of late-nineteenth-century experience, intellectuals rely on an aesthetic juxtaposition of forcefully opposed visions; hyberbolic views of good and evil, of surface details and sentiments, clash on public and private agendas. Melodramatic form is invoked to describe bipolar worlds and, finally, to delineate the contradictory forces that result when individuals and public opinion face off. The texts examined above suggest different ways to consider the formation of a Latin American social community in the late nineteenth century. Using the tropes of confused identities, deception, and multiple lies, the authors of the *fin de siglo* investigate excess and try to lift the veil from citizens and their unnamed desires.

"WHO ARE YOU, ANYWAYS?": GENDER, RACIAL AND LINGUISTIC POLITICS IN U.S. CUBAN THEATER

LILLIAN MANZOR-COATS
University of California, Irvine

As the question in my title suggests I am interested in analyzing the ways in which configurations of Latino identity are constructed and represented in U.S. Cuban theater. By focusing on three musicals which were staged in New York, E. Miguel Muñoz' *The L.A. Scene*, Manuel Martín's *Rita and Bessie*, and Pedro Monge's *Solidarios*, I will analyze how these three plays, as a group, stage a trajectory within U.S. Cuban dramaturgy in which the simplistic "ethnic" tag is transformed. The trajectory I am suggesting is the following: a deconstruction of "traditional" gender constructs in Cuban culture in *The L.A. Scene*, a deconstruction of racial constructs in *Rita and Bessie*, and a reconfiguration of a Latino collective identity based on gender and race in *Solidarios*.

I must clarify the use of one term before proceeding: U.S. Cuban, as opposed to Cuban-American. As can be expected part of the problem lies in the term to the right of the hyphen; the term which, as Gomez Peña points out, refers to "this troubled continent accidentally called America" and "this troubled country mistakenly called America" (20). I reject the usage of Cuban-American because, in its inherent redundancy, it reproduces the cultural and political imperialist ideologies which have characterized the last two centuries of history in North and South America. In the nineteenth century, the independence of the Spanish colonies created a need for Europe to name and contrast that part of the two Americas which was not Anglosaxon. Thus, all of us became Latin Americans and were forced to produce a literature and a culture to prove that we indeed *were* Latin Americans.[1] In the twentieth century, not only is Cuba along with the rest of Latin America transformed politically and economically into the "backyard" of the United States but North America linguistically subsumes South America; the two Americas are reduced into one; America becomes synonymous with the United States. By using U.S. Cuban, I am also underlining the cultural transformations that have been taking place within the United States during the last fifteen years. Transformations which are now beginning to be recognized and which "aspire to reconceptualize 'America' in multicultural and multicentric terms that refuse the relativist fiction of cultural pluralism" (Flores and Yúdice 62).

These plays suggest that within this post-industrial and multicultural

society subject positions are constituted through a set of exchanges between race, gender and class. Identity seems to be understood as the different roles individuals undertake. As Flores and Yúdice have elaborated,
trends in ethnicity theory are not sufficient to account for the ways in which
Latinos are reconfiguring themselves. Racism, sexism, linguistic stratifica-
tion, discursive positions must all be considered. To talk about identity,
then, Latinos must take into account not only issues of racial and sexual differences but also how a subject is constituted through language and cultural
representations.[2]

   The L.A. Scene by Elías Miguel Muñoz is a one act musical about the artistic struggles of a "Cuban-American" musician in the United States in the
80's. The cast is comprised of five characters: Julian, a 33 year old Cuban
American musician; his younger brother Johnny; Geneia, their little sister
who is fifteen; Erica Johnson, an American rock star and Julian's "girlfriend"
and "partner"; and a female interviewer.

   The L. A. Scene is based on Muñoz's novel titled Crazy Love. This novel
Crazy Love is structurally mapped, organized around absence.[3] The text
proposes its organization— in the table of contents—around three "steps."
Steps which suggest not only musical rhythm but also progress and movement. Yet this proposal is overturned in that nowhere in this "table of contents" are the song lyrics nor Geneia's letters acknowledged, letters which
are the literal progression and development of time personal and
cultural—in the text.

   The novel is organized, instead, around the absence of Erica, whom
Julian calls his "ingeniously outre" (Muñoz 1989, 16).[4] The novel suggests
itself to be Julian's biography (Muñoz 1989, 150). Julian as author is writing
his biography pretending that he is telling it to Erica; his life story is thus addressed to Erica. Yet the reader never meets Erica except through
others—conversations between the band members, Geneia's letters,
Julian's stories. We never hear Erica's own voice, we only hear about her.
Thus the text is addressed to an unlocatable Other center that slips through
conversation as subject. That this Other is "woman" is not gratuitous, of
course. But this is not the place to discuss a reading experience based on
looking for woman.

   The play, interestingly enough, is structured around the novel's ab-
sences. That is, The L.A. Scene's organization is based on the presentation
and representation of Erica as a character, of Geneia's letter/ monologues
and of the songs' lyrics and music. The play, however, eliminates the direct
voice of Julian's grandmother and Julian's father. In the novel Julian's father,
Papi, occupies the 'male' position within a patriarchal structure. His voice is
the voice of Family. The grandmother in the novel is a cunningly domineer-
ing, manipulative, castrating woman; her voice is the voice of Tradition.

Together, Family and Tradition—Papi and grandmother—represent and enforce the dominant culture's constructions of sexuality and gender.

As Teresa de Lauretis has pointed out, gender is a representation and this representation of gender is its construction. In the case of the Caribbean culture in general, and of Cuban culture in particular, representations and constructions of masculinity and femininity seem to be guided by a simulatory move: to be male equals being macho, macho meaning the excessive and extreme presence of masculinity or male dominance. Thus, maleness is culturally coded as hypermaleness; the difference between macho—the hypersimulation of maleness—and male disappears. Constructs of femaleness seem to be more complicated. Femininity is either culturally coded as the silenced, absent other (in the form of Virgin/ mother, for example) or as excess (in the form of whore or panicky, hysteric female). It is these very notions of gender roles as sexual stereotypes that Papi's voice reproduces.[5]

The presence of Papi and the grandmother as characters is not needed in the play. Due to the economy of theater, it suffices to have one agent of patriarchy, and one castrating female. In the play, the character of Johnny is constructed to represent the agent of Patriarchy, and the character of Erica that of the manipulative castrating female.

The brother Johnny, from the very beginning, is presented as antagonistic towards Julian. Moreover he is the one who continuously alludes to stereotypical constructs of masculinity. In the very first scene he tells Julian: ". . . you were born singing, right? El Señor Canario. . . . A cute little bird" (6). In Cuban slang to call a man a "cute little bird," "un pájaro" is equal to calling him a "faggot". This metaphorical allusion to Julian's possible homosexuality is directly addressed as the play goes on. That is, he calls Julian "faggot" and "queer": "Faggot! . . . Papi was right. A boy shouldn't spend all his time in his room writing songs. . . Writing songs is for queers" (35).

Julian is aware of the fixity and artificiality of gender roles and their representation in Cuban, and Latin American society. Julian's bisexuality is, I suggest, a response and an alternative to the experience of forced masculinity. His sexual ambivalence calls into question the social construction of gender as a product of society as much as it calls into question how society produces, markets and consumes gender using a rhetoric of power and, ultimately, of violence. This hyper-social construction of sexuality and of gender according to biological difference is so overdone that it erases Julian's sexuality long before he even has the opportunity to choose.

Julian's bisexuality is thus informed by the social constructs which determine sexuality and gender as exposed in the violent representations of its own language. This language, however, Julian cannot escape. That is, Julian reproduces these very same rigid gender roles which he is trying to resist using the very same violent representations which have given him the choice to be either macho or a queer.[6] Early on in the play, for example, he talks about the young girls who dance to their music as "fat Latin mamas [who] bounce around" (14).

The language chosen by Julian is English, most of the time. Although it might seem that going against his "mother tongue" is Julian's most violent act,[7] his choice could also be read as Julian's refusal to be complicit with the violence inherent for him in the use of Spanish. Julian, as I have discussed, finds himself in a culture and with a language which prescribes and in-scribes his choice with the same violence as it pre-scribes and in-scribes "woman" and "man."[8]

I read Julian's linguistic preference, then, as analogous to his sexual preference: both moves point towards his rejection of violence, regardless of the contradictions with his choice. Julian's choice of English might also be interpreted mistakenly as a sign of assimilation into mainstream Anglo socie-ty. Complete rejection of the hegemonic language is, in the case of Latinos in the U.S., only an illusion of cultural independence. I say an illusion be-cause monolingualism—be it Spanish or English—would be the linguistic condition preferred by the monocultural Anglo society. If you speak only Spanish you remain in the margins, you have no access to the sociopolitical structure of the United States. If you speak only English then, as Ngugi would say and Richard Rodriguez has corroborated, you are the perfect post-colonial subject. Julian, and Muñoz for that matter, want to participate in the debate on transculturation and identity, and the use of English with-out the rejection of Spanish, is the most direct and effective avenue to them.[9]

Rita and Bessie, by Manuel Martín, is a musical about the blues singer Bessie Smith and the mulatto singer Rita Montaner. Using typical Cuban songs and Afro-American blues, the play contrasts racial and gender pre-judices in Cuba and the United States. The action takes place in an office of a theatrical agent on the top floor of the Chrysler Building in New York. The decor, costumes and music suggest a decadent 1930's movie set. Bessie is wearing a black satin dress, 1930's style, with a bow that adds a touch of theatricality to her costume. Rita has a red turban, clear plastic platform shoes and a matching purse. The turban and platform shoes suggest right away that she is playing the role of the Latin star of the 30's and 40's. The decor, besides suggesting a specific time and social space, also has a sym-bolic function: there is a window, covered from the outside by iron gates and framed in the inside by heavy burgundy drapes; moreover, the whole place seems to be suspended in mid-air. It is not until the end of the play that the spectator/ reader can assign meaning to this symbolic function. That the suspension in mid-air signals other-worldliness and that burgundy suggests death is corroborated at the end when the characters also realize that they are dead.

The language used by the two characters is an sign of racial and social class positionality. Bessie, from the very beginning, speaks in black vernacular while Rita's proper English, although spoken with an accent, makes her seem like a proper, educated lady:

> Rita: I don' t understand. I have an appointment.
> Bessie: So do I, honey.
> Rita: But he's expecting me.
> Bessie: He expects a lot of people, sugah'. You bet your sweet ass he ain't especially waiting for you.
> Rita: I beg your pardon?. . . (2)

That language serves as an accurate index of class status is soon corroborated. While both singers are waiting for the agent, Rita tells Bessie that she is the daughter of a pharmacist and a school teacher, that she went to the best schools in Havana, that she had a classical musical training with the best teachers and that in Cuba "color pigmentation didn't make a difference" (13). Bessie, on the other hand, never went beyond the sixth grade. In America, as she says, "no siree, no high class school for a nigguh'" (5). Moreover, she does not need to be taught to sing the blues; she sings from pain.[10]

Rita is the perfect example of those Caribbean subjects under colonialism that Frantz Fanon studied in *Black Skin, White Masks*. She has culturally assumed a racial identity, a white mask, which is not related to her racial body. Race for Fanon, like gender for de Lauretis, is not constituted by biological determination from within but from cultural overdeterminations from without.

Rita's "hallucinatory whitening" as well as her middle-class lady-like etiquette is unmasked for the audience through conversations that she has with imaginary characters off-stage which speak in a recorded voice. The function of these recorded voices can best be analyzed as analogous to what in film theory is called "space-off," that is, "the space not visible in the frame but inferable from what the frame makes visible" (de Lauretis 26). We hear the composer wondering "How do you think we can make her skin look lighter?" (10). In that space-off we also hear a younger Rita talking to another imaginary character who is using her rehearsal space: "What?... that she's having an affair with the station's producer? Listen, sweetheart, you better clear out of this place before the whole radio network knows you are getting laid by that miserable imbecile hick who's running the station. What?... That it has been a hard way to the top? And how would you know, when your only talent lies on a mattress and at the very bottom! Cunt! you are nothing but a cheap cunt!'' (12).

Rita's denial of her black skin is also paralleled by her refusal to see the cultural and ideological influence that the United States exerted on Cuba at the turn of the century, an influence which Bessie calls colonialism. Rita still holds on to some abstract notion of idiosyncratic national character saying that in Cuba everything was different. Rita also upholds the notion that art and politics do not go together. But this is also contradicted in the space-off where the censors try to shut her voice, a voice which she considers to be the voice of her people. The recorded voice of a policeman saying ''Just a little laxative to clean your tongue. You'll never use a microphone to insult our President'' (28) alludes to the infamous ''palmacristazos'' typical of the Batista regime as well as to the censorship which closed her television program in 1954.

When the agent finally arrives, (the agent's presence is signaled through his pre-recorded voice) the exoticism which made Rita famous and which she has also internalized as part of her self does not get her anywhere. In a scene which takes place like a musical duel, much like the d.j. clash of black culture, Bessie and Rita try to outdo each other. This duel does not impress at all the agent who tells Bessie that the blues are out and tells Rita that she is too ethnic; neither one of them is marketable anymore.

The body of the agent never occupies a physical space on stage. This is not surprising; the agent's voice, disarticulated from the agent as character, stands in the place of the distribution industry of music, an industry which is not attached to any one person specifically but which creates and conditions consumer's tastes and needs which it will then satisfy. That disarticulation is also representative of how the marketing and distribution of music is disarticulated from the production and consumption of music. The artist is finally alienated from its music once its listening becomes commodity fetishism.

The artist's alienation is further suggested in the play through the use of images suggesting enclosure, heat and suffocation. Rita and Bessie are literally and metaphorically caged in the agent's office; there is a power failure so they cannot use the elevator; the window is barred so they cannot be heard nor can they get any ventilation. They are both confined to the role and the space the industry has created for them. A role which has dictated the kind of music they are going to perform and a role which is analogous to the racial and gender role patriarchal society has dictated for them. It is finally this very industry which is going to silence their voice. No longer marketable, they are doomed to disappear from the music industry.

The two distinct spaces we were discussing—the stage and the space-off—are presented as coexistant in a contradiction that is never resolved. Rita as subject moves from white mask to black skin, from educated and proper to the "chusma criolla," from the perfect star to the sexually exploited artist, from the apolitical singer to a socially and politically committed artist from a famous ethnic singer to a non-marketable one. It is in the back and forth movement from these two spaces that the ideological representation of race, class and gender is constructed, or that the ideological construction of race, class and gender is represented.

Eventually, Rita becomes aware that she is the product of that music industry, the product of capitalist ideological simulation: "Hell! I made them accept me. Me, touring the world with a basket of fruit on my head and yards of muslin ruffles hanging from my waist. . . Impersonator! I became an impersonator. A Latin woman impersonating the Latin image that was demanded and expected" (41). She realizes that the imposed exoticism revindicated as a form of one's own personality is nothing more than an illusion.

Thus, even at the moment of truth, Rita is unable to discern between self and mask. She has become a living cliché of what the North American market has defined as Latinness. Always moving between stage and space-off, between Self and Other, between reality and hyperreality or simulation, neither she nor we can decide whether the mask has left a print on the face or whether the face has left a print on the mask (Piedra 6).

The play ends when both characters, and the audience, realize that they are dead. However, there is a move towards a coalition between the two characters. Not only do they do a final song together and walk out holding hands but Rita has incorporated aspects of Bessie's language. By calling Bessie "sister," Rita has become aware that they both share common subject positions: manipulated black women artists in a patriarchal capitalist society. Their "ethnic" and artistic differences—Cubanness and North Americanness, blues and Latin— give way to their commonalities. It is through their coming together, represented by their "harmonization," that they can finally "burst out" from the restrictive roles society has constructed for them.

It is precisely this harmonization, this coalition which is at the center of Pedro Monge's *Solidarios*. This one act play presents the lives of several Latinos in New York. Rather than focusing on their differences, the play demonstrates how they unite in order to confront the system and survive in Anglo American society. The action aptly takes place in the lobby of a building in New York. The lobby is that very locale in between the private space of home and the public space of the street. And it is in this in between space that the characters' private and public concerns come together.

The play begins with Carmen entering the stage singing Lalo Rodriguez' salsa hit "Devórame otra vez": "Carmen: Ven, devórame otra vez/ Ven, devórame otra vez/ Ven castígame con tus deseos. [Come, devour me once again/ Come devour me once again/ Come punish me with your

197

desires]"[11] This song immediately interpolates the audience and sets the time reference of the play; the audience knows that these characters are "living" in the present, the audience's present. Moreover, this is an important opening technique for the play since it is a Traveling Theater which serves the Latino community of Queens.

Carmen is socially and politically aware of their collective positions as "hispanics": "Las cosas van a cambial cuando comprendamos que la única solución es la unidad. . . Debemos dejarnos de líos y de criticarnos tanto: que si tú eres colombiana, que si los puertorriqueños somos esto o que si los cubanos son lo otro. Aquí somos hispanos nos guste o no porque así nos quieren ver los blanquitos" [Things are gonna change when we understand that the only way out is unity. . . We have to stop criticizing one another: you are Colombian, and the Puerto Ricans are like this, and the Cubans are like that. Here we are all Hispanics whether we like it or not because that's how the whities wanna see us] (9).

Their inferior subject position as "Hispanics" is first felt in the arena of language. In the building, if the others spoke English not only could they communicate with outside Anglo society, represented by the mailman, but they would have more power to exert some kind of control over their lives. To that outside hegemonic society, to speak English means to exist; if you are not heard it is as if you did not exist. That is why Carmen decides that she is going to teach her neighbors English: "Pa' que sepan que hablan" [So that they know that you speak] (10).

This struggle over language is excellently represented in the scene where the two immigration officers come to the building looking for Altagracia who is an ilegal alien. Since Carmen speaks English, she does not have to be bullied around by the two officers, representative of Anglo authorities. She is able to complain about the fact that they should also speak Spanish if they intend to go into Spanish neighborhoods. Moreover, she refuses to show them any paper or answer any questions until they show her their official papers and answer the kinds of questions she thinks are necessary to work with Spanish-speaking people. Carmen's attitude and actions signal to the officers that yes, she must be Puerto Rican; they do not have to worry about her.

This scene represents more than an attack on the monolingualism of both Hispanics and Anglos. It demonstrates that language, which in hegemonic society is usually a matter rooted in the private sphere, for Latinos becomes "the semiotic material around which identity is deployed in the "public sphere"" (Yudice and Flores 61). Language is thus part of a larger field of social and political representation and practices; it is directly related to issues of immigration legality, of education and of hiring practices in the service sector of the welfare state. Language is an integral aspect of culture and identity formation and it is indissoluble from economics and politics.

Since Carmen is able to speak both Spanish and English, she is able to hide, to mask Altagracia's identity as ilegal alien. She gives Altagracia the name of Caridad and talks to her as if she were Cuban. The name, of course, is the perfect cover up of her identity. Moreover, since Cubans are generally portrayed as haughty and fearless, the officers can spot them a mile away. Carmen, and the others, take advantage of that stereotype. She thus tells Altagracia: "Cuando regresen tienes que comportarte como si nada. Insúltalos para que vean que no tienes miedo" (23). [When they come back act as if nothing was going on. Insult them so that they see that you are not afraid.] And that is exactly what happens when the officers return.

These women respond to the power structure of anglo society through a cover up which is enforced linguistically and stereotypically. This cover up can be interpreted as an act of collective self-empowerment. As such, it points towards a cultural and political self-legitimation which is acted out, first, as subversive affirmation of hegemonic stereotypes, and then as "a negation of hegemonic denial articulated as the rejection of anonymity" (Yúdice and Flores 60).

The personal struggles and quarrels among the characters give way, at the end, to their collective struggle. Carmen is able to transcend her jealousy when she realizes that it is more important to help Altagracia against the immigration officers.

The question of "identity" is central to the three plays I have been discussing. However, this notion of identity can no longer be addressed in monolithic terms, the terms used traditionally to develop ethnicity paradigms.[12] Identity is presented as constantly shifting subject positions in relation to racial, linguistic and gender issues. The three are social constructs which are produced by experience and representation, through violent experiences and violent representations. Our Latino characters are caught between two different but equally repressive social traditions. Julian is fighting against and resisting, first, the social representations of gender inherent in Cuban culture, and second, the Latin ethnic tag that the mainstream Anglo society gives him. Rita's ambivalences and masks are also a product of two patriarchal societies with rampant racial prejudices. And in Solidarios we have the characters trascending their individual "ethnic" identities suggesting that the only way to survive and overcome being a "minority" seems to be through collective self-empowerment.

The problem of what language to use to name ourselves is of utmost importance. We can opt for Spanish, the original language which can almost ensure us silence or English, the imposed language which is going to give us a presence and a voice.[13] And we opt for both. With this choice, we situate ourselves on the border, on the margin, thus refusing to participate in an already given and monolingual "America."[14] By saying "English only, Jamás! Sólo inglés, no way" (Laviera, book cover) we are asserting our desire "to participate in the construction of a new hegemony dependent upon [our] cultural practices and discourses" (Flores and Yúdice 73).

This new border identity might suggest that Latino bilinguals in the U.S. are the perfect schizophrenics of postmodern culture. As Gustavo Pérez Firmat writes in his now often quoted poem "Bilingual Blues":

> Soy un ajiaco de contradicciones.
> Vexed, hexed, complexed,
> hyphenated, oxygenated, illegally alienated,
> psycho soy, cantando voy (164)

However, we, Latinos, suffer in our own flesh and blood the "indeterminacies" of postmodern culture, the inequalities of a "pluralistic" society. Moreover, it is through a strategic deployment of these indeterminacies that we are defining ourselves. For us, representation comes from within and is indissoluble from practice.

These three plays incorporate literally and metaphorically the question in my title, "Who are you anyways?" The plays might not offer a direct answer to that question. But what is certain is that these playwrights have, for the first time, an audience that acknowledges this question, an audience who recognizes itself as a collective addressee of a message. An audience whose answer, like the answer the plays seem to offer, is: "We are whom you have made us to be but we aren't going to be that forever.*

NOTES

*Funds for the research of this paper were provided by the Focused Research Initiative on Woman and the Image at the University of California, Irvine, and Ollantay Center for the Arts, New York. A version of this paper will be appearing in Ollantay Press. I would like to thank Erin Farrell for her research assistance, and the three playwrights, E. Miguel Muñoz, Manuel Martín and Pedro Monge for providing me with the scripts, their comments and for our endless discussions.

[1] The literature on Latin American identity is extensive; suffice it to mention Campra, Ardao.

[2] My analysis of identity is informed by de Lauretis' work on gender.

[3] I want to thank Joanne Barker for her discussions of Crazy Love in the undergraduate seminar at U.C. Irvine on "Hispanics in the United States".

[4] I read *outre* as a "other," that is, as a mispelling of *autre*. It could also be read as a double pun playing on excentricity and alterity.

[5] The machismo-virginity dichotomy seems to be prevalent not only among the U.S. Cubans but also among Chicanos and Puerto Ricans in the United States. See, for example, Carrier; Hidalgo and Hidalgo-Christensen; Kranau et al.

[6] This move seems to be typical among homosexuals. See carrier.

[7] See Vélez, for example.

[8] It should be noted that violence, in another context, is considered to be one of the unifying conditions of Latin American writing. The literature on violence and language in Latin America is extensive; see, for example Dorfman, Conte and Campra.

[9] The use of Spanish versus English is a very debated item within the U.S. Cuban communities, as may be expected. It is of interest to note that the adult's frequency of usage of Spanish with their children is something which differentiates U.S. Cuban from other Latino groups (García and Lega, 259).

[10] The fact that Bessie's blues, as well as her vernacular language, have "a defiantly racial sound" (Baker 95) is an indication that, as Baker has pointed out, "the quotidian sounds of black every day life become a people's entrancing song" (107).

[11] I do not have the space here to analyze the role of popular music in these plays. See Manzor-Coats for a study of the commodification of Latino music in the United States and its ideological implications.

[12] It is important to note that researchers in the social sciences have also used unidimensional models. These can only assess the degree of assimilation of values and behaviors of the "host" culture or the degree of retention of values of the original culture. They cannot account for bicultural individuals. See Garcia and Lega.

[13] Interestingly enough, the present struggle against this linguistic double subjection seems to be a repeat of the struggle Latin American writers were engaged in until very recently. See, for example, Campra and Fernández Moreno.

[14] I use the trope of "border culture' the way in which Flores and Yúdice, and Anzaldúa have developed it.

REFERENCES

Anzaldúa, Gloria. *Borderlands/ La Frontera: The New Mestiza.* San Francisco: Spinsters/ Aunte Lute, 1987.

Ardao, A. *Génesis de la idea y el nombre de América Latina.* Caracas: Centro de Estudios Latinoamericanos Rómulo Gallegos, 1981.

Baker, Houston. *Afro-American Poetics: Revisions of Harlem and the Black Aesthetic.* Madison: U of Wisconsin P, 1988.

Campra, Rosalba. *América Latina: La identidad y la máscara.* Mexico: Siglo XXI, 1987.

Carpentier, Alejo. *Tientos y diferencias.* La Habana: Unión de Escritores y Artistas Cubanos, 1974.

Carrier, J. M. "Mexican Male Bisexuality." *Journal of Homosexuality* (1985): 75-85.

Conte, Rafael. *Lenguaje y violencia en América Latina.* Madrid: Al-borak, 1972.

Cromwell, R. E. and R. A. Ruiz. "The Myth of Macho Dominance in Decision Making within the Mexican and Chicano Families." *Hispanic Journal of Behavioral Sciences* 1.4 (1979): 355-73.

de Lauretis, Teresa. *Technologies of Gender.* Bloomington: Indiana UP, 1987.

Díaz Ayala, Cristóbal. *Música cubana: Del Areyto a la Nueva Trova.* San Juan: Editorial Cubanacán, 1981.

Dorfman, Ariel. *Imaginación y violencia en América.* Santiago de Chile: Editorial Universitaria, 1970.

Fanon, Frantz. *Black Skins, White Masks.* Trans. Charles Lam Markmann. New York: Grove Press, 1967.

Fernández, Enrique. "La balada de Gloria Estefan." *Más* 2.1 (1990): 53-59.

Flores Angel and George Yúdice. "Living Borders/ Buscando America." *Social Text* 24, 8.2 (1990): 57-84.

Gomez Peña, Guillermo. "The Multicultural Paradigm: An Open Letter to the National Arts Community. *High Performance* (Fall, 1989): 20.

Hanchard, Michael. "Identity, Meaning and the African-American." *Social Text* 24, 8.2: 31-42.

Hidalgo, Hilda and Elia Hidalgo-Christensen. "The Puerto Rican Lesbian and The Puerto Rican Community. *Journal of Homosexuality*, 1976.

Ilich, Ivan. *Gender.* New York: Pantheon, 1982.

Kranau, J. E., V. Green and G. Valencia-Weber. "Acculturation and the Hispanic Women: Attitudes toward Women, Sex Role Attribution, Sex Role Behavior, and Demographies." *Hispanic Journal of Behavioral Sciences* 4.1 (1982): 21-40.

Laviera, Tato. *AmeRícan.* Houston: Arte Público, 1984.

Manzor-Coats, Lillian. "Devórame otra vez: Music, Ideology and Latino Gender Politics." In progress.

Martín, Manuel. *Rita and Bessie.* Playscript, 1986.

Monge, Pedro R. *Solidarios.* Playscript, 1989.

Muñoz, Elías Miguel. *Crazy Love.* Houston: Arte Publico Press, 1989.

Muñoz, Elías Miguel. *The L.A. Scene.* Playscript, 1990.

Padilla, Felix M. "Salsa Music as a Cultural Expression of Latino Consciousness and Unity." *Hispanic Journal of Behavioral Sciences* 2.1 (1989): 28-45.

Pérez Firmat, Gustavo. *Carolina Cuban.* In *Triple Crown.* Arizona: Bilingual Review Press, 1987.

Piedra, José. "His and Her Panics." Forthcoming. 1990.

Rodriguez Richard. *Hunger of Memory: The Education of Richard Rodríguez.* Boston: D.R. Godine, 1982.

Vélez, Lydia. "Separación y búsqueda como opción social en las novelas de Elías Miguel Muñoz." *The Americas Review* 18.1 (1990): 86-91.

Postmodernism
in Latin America

EL CONFLICTO DE POSMODERNIDADES

GEORGE YÚDICE
Hunter College

...en toda mi narración yo creo que doy una imagen de [mi pueblo]. Pero, sin embargo, todavía sigo ocultando mi identidad como indígena. Sigo ocultando lo que yo considero que nadie sabe, ni siquiera un antropólogo, ni un intelectual, por más que tenga muchos libros, no saben distinguir todos nuestros secretos. (Menchú, 1983: 271)

1. Más allá de la representación

En el pasaje, citado arriba, Rigoberta Menchú rechaza la posibilidad de una representación total y fiel de su pueblo, sea porque ella se niegue a ello, sea porque un enunciante de otra cultura no podría tener jamás toda la información necesaria ("nuestros secretos") para hacerlo. Al rechazar la representación, sin embargo, no se adopta una escritura —la *écriture*— que dramatice las aporías epistemológicas en las que se fundan, según Foucault (1977b), la literatura y filosofía modernas. Es decir, que si lo que se entiende por la *episteme* moderna es la contradicción entre representación objetiva (la labor del antropólogo o cualquier otro conocedor) y expresión subjetiva (fuente de la conciencia del individuo), el testimonio de Menchú no opta por ninguno de los dos partidos de la contradicción ni se entrega a la *jouissance* escritural, instalada en la contradicción misma a manera de vacío en el que se esfuma el sujeto cognoscente o a manera de espejo barroco, en el que se ve más bien la imagen del recurso reflexivo (pantalla, cuadro reduplicado) que la del sujeto/objeto (Sarduy, 1974: 78-83).

En otras palabras, el discurso de Menchú no depende ni positva ni negativamente del paradigma de la representación. El conocimiento de sí y del mundo se adquieren en la *práctica* de la sobrevivencia de la comunidad. Y el testimonio es parte de esta práctica. La voz enunciante no se identifica con el sujeto que conoce y se reconoce en la representación; el sujeto testimonial se forma como individuo a través de las prácticas de la colectividad, su conciencia grupal es también objeto de conocimiento, y su discurso obedece a factores éticos y estéticos arraigados en el *ethos* de la comunidad. La racionalización de la cultura en tres dimensiones autónomas (conocimiento objetivo, discernimiento moral-práctico y juicio estético) —establecida por Kant y atribuida a la moder-

© 1991 NUEVO TEXTO CRÍTICO Vol. IV No. 7 Primer semestre

nidad occidental por Weber — no rige la producción discursiva de Menchú. Las actividades estéticas (v.gr., fiestas), las prácticas religiosas y los rituales comunitarios por medio de los cuales se transmite el conocimiento y la identidad, todos son simultáneamente políticos. No se pueden separar las tres dimensiones atribuidas a la modernidad occidental. Asimismo, cuando se produce una representación, ésta responde siempre a imperativos ético-estéticos que tienen que ver con la reproducción de la comunidad.

Esta concepción práctico-estética del discurso no señala el advenimiento de un nuevo "orden de cosas" más allá de la modernidad. Si el discurso testimonial, tal como se lo ha caracterizado aquí, puede concebirse como un fenómeno *postmoderno* esto es porque implica una reformulación de los parámetros de lo que *una* herencia intelectual occidental (la hegemónica) ha entendido por "modernidad." El testimonio expresa, por una parte, la frustración para con las opciones ofrecidas por la cultura política representacional, siempre subordinada a los intereses de los sectores dominantes vinculados con los proyectos modernizadores en América Latina. Por otra parte, proyecta un mundo cultural distinto, lo cual no implica que éste se base en identidades esencialistas fundadas en mitos de orígenes como en ciertos discursos raciales (v.gr., el de Vasconcelos) o de identidad continental (el latinismo que proclama Rodó) o nacional (la soledad que para Paz define la esencia del ser mexicano).

El testimonio es sólo una de varias manifestaciones culturales que no se atiene a los parámetros de la modernidad. Los llamados nuevos movimientos sociales (étnicos, ecologistas, de mujeres, de *squatters*, de informales, etc.) que resisten incorporarse a la política representacional, así como la redefinición de la esfera pública por las comunicaciones de masas, en especial la televisión, y la creciente privatización de la cultura; todas estas manifestaciones rompen con el modelo kantiano-weberiano-habermasiano de la modernidad. No me parece, por ejemplo, que, como hace Habermas (1987: 321), deba aceptarse que sea una aberración cultural (distorsión del *Lebenswelt*) el que cuestiones cognoscitivas o éticas hoy día se elaboren estéticamente. Podría decirse, más bien, que el reconocimiento de lo estético en lo cognoscitivo, o de lo ético en lo estético, responden a estrategias necesarias para sobrevivr y obtener valor y poder en las sociedades contemporáneas. Pero para evaluar mejor cómo estas manifestaciones hacen necesario *repensar* los parámetros de la modernidad, será necesario hacer un recorrido, si bien breve, de su historia.

2. El orden de cosas moderno

Podría decirse, parafraseando a Anthony Wilden (1980: 467), que la ilusión fundamental de la modernidad es la creencia de que el hombre es el "territorio de su propio mapa." Pero esta condición moderna está minada, a la vez, por la brecha que la sucesividad temporal —la historia— abre entre el sujeto cognoscente y su representación —el mapa—. Para pensadores como John Locke, por ejemplo, la disyunción entre *mundo* (multiplicidad de sensaciones dadas simultáneamente a la inteligencia) y *conocimiento* (reorganización de las ideas aportadas por esas sensaciones) puede ser reducida y hasta eliminada por el *control* de las facultades asociativas. Sin este control, que "no hace sino seguir a la Naturaleza," la inteligencia produciría "quimeras" como la "unión de la Voz de una Oveja a la Forma de un Caballo" (Locke, 1985: 455). Es precisamente este control sobre la sucesividad en los "procesos mentales" (para asegurar que "lo espacial perdure en el tiempo") que Borges parodia en "Tlön, Uqbar, Orbis Tertius." En Tlön los procesos cognoscitivos no se ajustan a las leyes de la naturaleza — la ciencia — sino a los recursos de la ficción inherentes al lenguaje, instrumento de conocimiento y constitución del sujeto:

> Explicar (o juzgar) un hecho es unirlo a otro; esa vinculación, en Tlön, es un estado posterior del sujeto, que no puede afectar o iluminar el estado anterior. Todo estado mental es irreducible: el mero hecho de nombrarlo —*id est*, de clasificarlo— importa un falseo (Borges, 1956: 22).

Para Foucault, este énfasis en lo espacial — o, mejor, lo visual — emerge con el nuevo "espacio de conocimiento" que se abre cuando la naturalidad de la semejanza, *episteme* vigente hasta fines del siglo 16, da lugar a la exploración de la distancia que va de lo semejante a lo semejado. Si para el siglo 16, la "naturaleza" a conocer está atrapada en la "membrana fina" — si bien opacada por el paralaje — que superpone semiología [gramática de trazos] y hermenéutica [interpretación de signos], a partir del siglo 17 la naturaleza deja de estar "encarnada" en el lenguaje, pues se disuelve esta membrana-sutura entre lenguaje y mundo: "La peculiar existencia y la antigua solidez del lenguaje como cosa inscripta en el tejido del mundo fueron disueltas en el funcionamiento de la representación" (Foucault, 1973: 43). El discurso analítico-referencial de la nueva ciencia y del correlativo orden estético cultural (Reiss, 1982: 31) sustituye a la membrana intermediaria con una "instrumentalidad transparente," figurada en el telescopio galileano, metáfora en la que se puede visualizar la separación entre el sujeto cognoscente y el mundo de las cosas. Esa nueva instrumentalidad discursiva ya no mantiene vínculo necesario alguno con las cosas; sus signos son arbitrarios.

A esto se refiere Heidegger (1977: 135) cuando dice que en la "época del retrato del mundo" la opacidad de la encarnación cognoscitiva de antaño se ha hecho invisible en la modernidad, en la que "el hombre ha sido transformado en *subiectum* y el mundo en retrato." En la modernidad, pues, la antigua opacidad sólo se manifiesta como una "sombra invisible... proyectada alrededor de todas las cosas."

Es precisamente esta "sombra invisible" de la analogía que Locke quería expulsar por medio del control de la imaginación y de las otras operaciones asociativas necesarias para adquirir el auténtico conocimiento — i.e., no "quimérico" — del mundo. Para Foucault (1973: 43-44), la misma "sombra invisible" proporciona un *contradiscurso* que se da a "conocer" en la literatura autónoma:

> Y no obstante, a lo largo del siglo 19 y hasta nuestros días —desde Hölderlin a Mallarmé y hasta Antonin Artaud— la literatura logró una existencia autónoma, y

se separó de todos los otros lenguajes con una honda escisión sólo al formar una suerte de "contradiscurso" y al recorrer el camino desde la representación, o función significante del lenguaje, de vuelta a este ser primario que había sido olvidado desde el siglo 16.

3. Modernidad y heterogeneidad

Habría que preguntarse qué, exactamente, es lo que la literatura autónoma reconvoca ante el dominio de la representación. Para Heidegger (1977: 154), se revela la sombra, ese "espacio que ha sido retirado de la representación" en el que, si bien ocultado, mora el Ser incalculable. Esta morada se identifica en otros textos (Heidegger, 1975b: 222-223; 1975a: 203 y 206) como *lo poético*, que mide al hombre contra la divinidad, o como el lenguaje que "mide y establece las proporciones del mundo y de las cosas," "llamándolas así a instalarse en el intermedio de la dif-ferencia." El empleo de las palabras "incalculable," "medir," y "presenciar" para caracterizar lo que está más allá de la representación sugiere que Heidegger está dando aquí una versión del discurso de lo sublime, una de las metáforas privilegiadas de la heterogeneidad.

Frente a la enajenación —separación entre el yo y la otredad heterogénea que lo circunscribe y por ende define— endémica en la instrumentalización de los dispositivos de la representación, que luego lamentarán los románticos, la estética dieciochista revincula al yo con la heterogeneidad a través de la experiencia de lo sublime (Kant, 1952: 119-128). Esta heterogeneidad ("totalidad" de la naturaleza), no obstante, estará siempre subordinada a la razón:

> En un sentido literal y de acuerdo con su carácter lógico, las ideas no pueden ser presentadas. Pero si ampliamos nuestra facultad empírica de la representación (matemática o dinámica), con el propósito de alcanzar una intuición de la naturaleza, la razón inevitablemente toma la delantera, pues es la facultad encargada de la independencia de la totalidad absoluta, y suscita un esfuerzo mental, si bien ineficaz, para adecuar la representación sensorial a esta totalidad. Este esfuerzo, y el sentimiento de que la idea es inalcanzable por medio de la imaginación, es a su vez una presentación de la finalidad subjetiva de nuestra mente en el ejercicio de la imaginación conforme a los intereses de la provincia supersensible de la mente, y nos obliga subjetivamente a *pensar* la naturaleza misma en su totalidad como una presentación de algo supersensible, sin que podamos efectuar esta presentación objetivamente (Kant, 1952: 119).

Lo sublime, pues, es una heterología controlada, que oculta —"ensombrece"— y silencia el poder de lo supersensible, la hetereogeneidad.

Según Lyotard, lo sublime moderno corresponde a un ímpetu nostálgico que busca consuelo en la *forma* —mapa— de lo que está ausente (el conocimiento de la "totalidad"). Por nostalgia, Lyotard se refiere a la tentativa de *ver*, y así aprehender con la mirada (concebir, *concipere*), lo que está más allá de lo ostensible. La posmodernidad, por otra parte, no se define como algo más allá de la modernidad, de la representación, sino como el desplazamiento, dentro de la modernidad, de la *episteme* espacio-visual misma 'hacia la liberación de la heterogeneidad (impresentable):

> Lo postmoderno sería aquello que alega lo impresentable en lo moderno y en la presentación misma; aquello que se niega a la consolación de las formas bellas, al consenso de un gusto que permitiría experimentar en común la nostalgia de lo imposible; aquello que indaga por presentaciones nuevas, no para gozar de ellas sino para hacer sentir mejor que hay algo que es impresentable (Lyotard, 1987: 25).

Este desplazamiento hacia la incomensurabilidad impresentable ha sido, como reconoce Lyotard (1987: 93), la meta del "verdadero proceso del vanguardismo," no el combativo que procura crear un "nuevo hombre" sino el que se ha "dedicado a investigar los supuestos implicados en la modernidad." Esta investigación ha abierto no tanto alternativas específicas sino la potencialidad de la diferencia o la diferencia en toda su potencialidad, que, conforme a la teoría contemporánea que se considere, se identifica con el Otro (Lacan), lo abyecto (Kristeva), el poder afirmativo de lo heteróclito (Foucault), la *différance* (Derrida), etc. Podría decirse que a través de esta liberación de lo sublime cierta tendencia postestrucuralista que consitutye una de las versiones de la posmodernidad, identificada con el vanguardismo (desde Mallarmé y Lautréamont hasta Sollers y Sarduy), lleva a su última conclusión (y en su forma más encarnada, material, si bien *virtual*) no el reverso (el otro lado) sino el *elemento limítrofe que funciona como condición de posibilidad de la representación*.

El ejemplo más destacado de esta materialidad/virtualidad limítrofe es el *parergon* — marco — que desde una orientación representacional parecería ser ornamento (como en Kant) pero cuyo espesor sitúa al espectador en un espacio otro en o desde el cual desvanece el enfoque que discriminaría un dentro y un afuera o una conciencia cognoscente y un objeto a conocer, "invaginando" o transformando al sujeto en una suerte de cinta de Moebio (Derrida, 1978: 85-86). Es este el lugar de "La mujer" que "no existe" (Lacan, 1975: 68) sino como garante virtual de la fantasía fálica en la que se proyecta la impostura que es el hombre (Rose, 1982: 45-48). Y más generalmente, es este el lugar donde lo abyecto — secreciones, excremento — abruma al sujeto, corporeizándolo, injertándose en él como soporte virtual de la fantasía social (Kristeva, 1980: 10).

Se ve, pues, que esta vertiente posmoderna no destaca específicos sujetos marginados y oprimidos, pues no tienen el mismo valor que la privilegiada otredad generalizada. Más bien se identifica este posmoderno "hacerse minoritario" o "marginal" — mujer, animal, flor, piedra, etc. — con las "desterritorializaciones rizomáticas" de la *écriture* (Deleuze y Guattari, 1987: 291-292). Por desterritorialización se entiende un "hacerse minoritario" que aleja a todo sujeto de su identidad mayoritaria, desde donde se detenta el poder. Según Deleuze y Guattari, aun los negros, los judíos y las mujeres tienen que "hacerse negros, judíos y mujeres." Así, pues, el ser minoritario está más allá de toda identidad específica, que es *de facto* reterritorializadora. Los oprimidos, *qua* oprimidos, no son, pues, ese otro marginal o minoritario virtual que desterriorializa al sujeto enunciante. Resulta entonces que la "política" que todos estos pensadores atribuyen a la *écriture* y al "hacerce minoritario" es una *retirada*, mediante la actividad estética, de cualquier ejercicio de poder. Esta retirada corresponde a una *ética* de la "liberación" de todo lo que es heterogéneo al sujeto mayoritario (Kristeva, 1980: 208). Es la *etho-poética* — la estética del hacerse — que Rajchman (1986a: 169 y 1986b: 54) discierne en Foucault y Lacan.

4. ¿Écriture y posmodernidad en América Latina?

Parece lógico que la ética de la *écriture* que se viene considerando, con su apelación a la marginalidad, haya tenido un atractivo particular para los latinoamericanos, los cuales, según Borges (1964: 161), constituyen la otredad que pone en tela de juicio al sujeto mayoritario que es la cultura occidental:

> creo que los argentinos, los sudamericanos en general, estamos en una situación análoga [a los judíos y los irlandeses]; podemos manejar todos los temas europeos, manejarlos sin supersticiones, con una irreverencia que puede tener, y ya tiene, consecuencias afortunadas.

Estas "consecuencias afortunadas" se deben, conforme al argumento de Octavio Paz (1959: 152), a que la larga historia periférica de los latinoamericanos ha dado fruto en el momento en que la cultura occidental se ve encaminada a cultivar la marginalidad, debido a la disgregación producida por la segunda guerra mundial, la descolonización del tercer mundo y la concomitante pérdida de centralidad de los movimientos artísticos europeos:

> En efecto, hemos vivdo en la periferia de la historia. Hoy el centro, el núcleo de la sociedad mundial, se ha disgregado y todos nos hemos convertido en seres periféricos, hasta los europeos y los norteamericanos. Todos estamos al margen porque ya no hay centro.

Es decir, el latinoamericano, según esta orientación, puede ufanarse de encarnar el *parergon*: maginalidad, abyección, virtualidad, en fin, ese "no-ser-siempre-todavía" de que escribe Mayz Valenilla (1969: 92). Habiendo rechazado un ser latino-americano arraigado en orígenes esencialistas, escritores como Fuentes (1969) y Sarduy (1967, 1969 y 1982) ponen énfasis en el la construcción discursiva de lo latinoamericano. Para Fuentes (1969: 97-98), por ejemplo, la mengua del universalismo occidental abre la posibilidad de que se inventen nuevas formas de progreso y desarrollo. Esta tarea corresponde, desde luego, a los escritores, pues son los que manejan el material — la lengua — con que se constituyen la conciencia y la identidad:

> Pero si los hispanoamericanos somos capaces de crear nuestro propio modelo de progreso, entonces nuestra lengua es el único vehículo capaz de dar forma, de proponer metas, de establecer prioridades, de elaborar críticas para un estilo de vida determinado: de decir todo lo que no pueda decirse de otra manera.

A partir de "nuestra diferencia," de "nuestra marginalidad," pues, se puede realizar la potencialidad que elude al discurso hegemónico de occidente. La otredad latinoamericana, vehiculizada por los artistas de "nuestra lengua," se apropia del lugar de lo sublime.

En manos de Severo Sarduy lo cubano —entendido como superposición de tres culturas/ficciones (1967: 151)— se presenta como modelo del constante "hacerse" de que tratan Deleuze y Guattari: "Amb[os personajes, Auxilio y Socorro] quieren desaparecer, ser otras: de ahí la incesante transformación, la abundancia de afeites, de artificios" (1967: 152). La identidad cubana no se basa en un mito de origen sino, como dice Sarduy (1969: 68-69) respecto de Lezama Lima (y de Julián del Casal y de las observaciones que hace Cintio Vitier de la tradición poética cubana), en la superposición:

> No es un azar que Lezama, que ha llegado a la inscripción, al fundamento mismo de la isla, a su constitución como *diferencia* de culturas, nos reconstituya de ese modo su espacio. Cuba no es una síntesis, una cultura sincrética, sino una superposición. Una novela cubana debe hacer explícitos todos los estratos, mostrar todos los planos "arqueológicos" de la superposición —podría hasta separarlos por relatos, por ejemplo, uno español, otro africano y otro chino— y lograr lo cubano con el encuentro de éstos, con su coexistencia en el *volumen* del libro, o, como hace Lezama con sus acumulaciones, en la unidad estructural de cada metáfora, de cada línea.

Este "ser cubano" porta una carga —*jouissance*— que hace que hasta los "ideólog[os] postestructuralist[as] telquelian[os]" se den cuenta que su teoría es "una suerte de teología negativa en la que se fetichizaba el texto" (González Echevarría, 1987: 132). La "violencia de ese encuentro de superficies, como adición y sorpresa de lo heterogéneo yuxtapuesto" (Sarduy, 1969: 70), se establece como un "hacerse otro" mucho más radical, según esta lectura, que cualquier discurso enunciado por los escritores oriundos del centro de occidente. La idea de que la marginalidad —vis-à-vis occidente— le aporta un privilegio posmoderno a textos como los de Sarduy se encuentra en críticos como González Echevarría (1987: 133), para quien el "trascendentalismo contingente, local" hace posible "resist[ir] la interpretación global, y reten[er] algo de una simbología pre o post-moderna." Semejantemente, Linda Hutcheon (1989: 53) arguye que la parodia —según ella un modo de representación posmoderna— es un recurso útil de la perspectiva marginal para "mostrar cómo los modelos narrativos tradicionales —tanto historiográficos como ficticios—, que se basan en modelos europeos de cronología continua y relaciones de causa y efecto, son absolutamente inadecuados para la tarea de narrar la historia del Nuevo Mundo."

Si bien en las novelas del *Boom* se mantiene la autoridad de la enunciación, que, como afirma González Echevarría (1987: 250), se legitima mediante el metadiscurso del lenguaje como *non plus ultra* de la liberación (¿liberación de qué? habría que preguntar), en las novelas del post-*Boom* (que González Echevarría equipara con el posmodernismo) se "privilegi[an]...relatos locales que son la suma posible del conocimiento...." Y ¿qué es este conocimiento? Nada menos que una versión de lo que ya se ha considerado más arriba respecto de Lacan y otros pensadores postestructuralistas: que la impostura — máscara, copia, pantalla, etc. — es la condición de posibilidad de la identidad mayoritaria, paradigma de la existencia, del ser, etc.

> Sarduy invierte este hábito mental [de que la copia es lo débil]: la copia es lo más fuerte porque es lo que pone en movimiento, lo que genera la capacidad subversiva, cambiante en el modelo, que sólo sobrevive en la copia. (González Echevarría, 1987: 21).

Tenemos, pues, una manifestación más del escritor "periférico" que se instala en el privilegiado lugar virtual del *no ser* — simulacro hiperreal —, condición a partir de la cual se proyecta el "ser."

> El arte americano es travestismo, espectáculo Barroco. Lo americano sería aquí no ya secundario, sino aquello que *es* siendo secundario, y que al copiar lo europeo, al incorporar y asimilar visiblemente su forma, le da una vida que es tal vez la única que puede tener en la actualidad (González Echevarría, 1987: 217).

5. Otra versión de la posmodernidad: la transformación de la relación entre gusto estético y esfera pública

Lo que González Echevarría entiende por posmodernidad no es sino la apoteosis de *cierto* gusto estético que tiene una importante función de modelización de la formación de sujetos. Este gusto estético — gusto de la *jouissance*, gusto de la virtualidad, de la hiperrealidad— no es natural a todas las prácticas estéticas sino a aquellas que, como se vio más arriba, reclaman una ética de la libertad. Por libertad entiéndase la autonomía vis-à-vis cualquier ideología. Mediante la elección de una heterogeneidad absoluta, este tipo de esteta puede declarar su independencia, pues su posición marginal es lo que, estando allende toda ideología, define los contornos de lo socialmente "normal."

Ahora bien, en el caso de los Estados Unidos y de la Europa occidental se da una nueva versión de la heterología que se debe no sólo a la descolonización sino también al auge del consumismo y de la permeación de toda la vida por la simulación electrónica. Podría decirse que de los discursos subversivos — parodia, carnavalización, simulación a lo Bataille y Caillois —, que traen la carga de la transgresión y de lo sagrado (todavía anclados en el *cuerpo*), se pasa a lo abyecto y lo hiperreal, al simulacro estéril y obsceno a lo Baudrillard (1990: 27):

> Me gustaría hablar de una anomalía —aquella obesidad fascinante que se puede encontrar en cualquier parte de los Estados Unidos, aquella suerte de conformidad monstruosa al espacio vacío, de deformidad por exceso de conformidad que traduce la hiperdimensión de una socialidad a la vez saturada y vacía, en la que el escenario de lo social y del cuerpo desvanesce.

Lo que escritores como Sarduy y críticos como González Echevarría reclaman es que en América Latina, debido a su marginalidad, todavía cuenta el cuerpo, todavía cuenta lo sagrado, todavía cuenta la transgresión. Puede que tengan razón, pero ello se debería no a una escritura endémica en la esfera pública restringida de la literatura sino a las luchas culturales y sociales que procuran expandir el campo de lo público— espacio en el que se negocia la constitutción y satisfacción de necesidades, la sobrevivencia y reproducción de comunidades. Desde esta perspectiva, la *écriture* que se viene comentando sirve como entrenamiento estético para que se restrinja la comprensión de la heterogeneidad y de lo minoritario a una cuestión de arte entre actores de las élites. Por más que se inscriba la marginalidad, en el sentido sarduyano, se sigue esquivando no sólo el conocimiento sino la solidaridad con aquel agente que Gayatri Spivak llama sujeto subalterno. Este es el sujeto que se elude al inscribirse el artista/intelectual de las élites (metropolitanas y periféricas) a la esfera pública del "posmodernismo transnacional":

> ...sorprende a menudo observar cuán nítidamente cambian los ardides en ese campo en el que se codifica la producción de sujetos: la cultura política. Y las universidades, las revistas, los institutos, las exhibiciones, las series editoriales están abiertamente involucradas en este quehacer. Teniendo presente la constancia banal del aparato cultural de la sociedad transnacional, puede decirse que el cambio al transnacionalismo ha resultado en un tercermundismo más suave y benévolo en la universidad euroamericana...En este contexto nuevo la diáspora poscolonial adquiere un papel ideológico. Esta "persona" (sólo nos refereimos a una posición-de-sujeto aquí), que básicamente pertenece a una élite colaborativa, puede sentirse incómodo por diversas razones al devenir objeto de una benevolencia no cuestionada sólo porque es un habitante de este nuevo tercer mundo. El/ella está más a gusto produciendo y simulando el efecto de un mundo más antiguo constituido por los relatos legitimizadores de la especificidad y continuidad cultural y étnica, que nutren una identidad nacional casi perfecta —una suerte de "alucinación retrospectiva."
> Ello produce un "otro" conveniente para la posmodernidad transnacional...El crítico radical puede prestar su atención a este tercer mundo hiperreal para encontrar, en el nombre de una historia alternativa, un espacio arrestado que reprocha a la posmodernidad...Lo que disimula esta descripción a grandes rasgos es la tremenda complejidad del espacio poscolonial, en especial el espacio de la mujer [*womanspace*] (Spivak, 1989: 275-276).

La *écriture* que se ha considerado aquí no reproduce una "identidad nacional casi perfecta," en el sentido representacional, pero sí aboga por una mayor *autenticidad* subversiva y transgresora. Es decir, el *ethos* de esta *écriture* marginal es la declaración de que "la desconstrucción (o simulación, o hiperrealidad, o parodia, etc.) comienza con nosotros," declaración que ya hemos constatado en Borges, Paz, y Sarduy, y que Enrique Lihn (1980), a su vez, ha parodiado:

> no somos nada: remedos, simulacros o fantasmas: repetidores de lo que entendemos mal, esto es, a medias: organilleros sordos: los fósiles animados de una prehistoria que no hemos vivido aquí ni, por consiguiente, en parte alguna, puesto que

somos extranjeros autóctonos, transplantados de nacimiento en nuestros respectivos países de origen.

Pero, claro está, no basta esta "arqueología de las Bellas Letras" (Lihn) para poner en tela de juicio la función pública que desempeña este "mimetismo" legitimizador. Habría que modificar las instituciones a través de las cuales se reproduce la esfera pública en la que esta "marginocentralidad" estetizante se ciega ante las experiencias cotidianas de la gran diversidad de sujetos y actores sociales que consituyen América Latina.

Modificar instituciones implica reconfigurar los géneros discursivos y conductales a través de los cuales se forman sujetos y se reproduce —a nivel microfísico— la distribución de valor y poder. Ello requiere repensar el papel de la literatura y el arte, tal como se manifiestan en las escuelas, las editoriales, los museos, los institutos, los salones, las revistas y periódicos, y hasta los aparatos políticos. En América Latina se ha pasado de un modelo estético dominante según el cual el escritor/artista/intelectual lideraba y hablaba por las masas a un modelo autorreflexivo —en el que la única responsabilidad es la del lenguaje— como el que se comenta arriba respecto de Sarduy. Este desplazamiento de un modelo a otro deja de lado otra posible transformación: el abandono de la autonomía de la dialéctica representación/autorreflexividad.

Este abandono del modelo estético-literario vigente se encuentra en otro espacio social: los movimientos sociales —de indígenas, de mujeres, de ecologistas, de conscientización de las capas populares como favelados y *squatters*, etc.— cuya actividad se da al nivel de lo cotidiano. Es ahí dónde se inventan prácticas y se elaboran nuevos sentidos ante el fracaso de la política tradicional y de los grandes proyectos modernizadores/desarrollistas a partir de los años 50 y 60. Al situar esta actividad de transformación de instituciones a nivel de lo cotidiano no se está apelando a una ética-estética de representación —mostrar las condiciones míseras de los sectores populares— ni se está romantizando lo popular. El hecho es que casi sólo en la esfera de lo cotidiano, tanto en el "primer" como en el "tercer" mundo, es posible hoy día luchar por contrarrestar los efectos de los modelos de desarrollo económico y social que ponen en peligro la vida planetaria: políticas represivas para asegurar el éxito de las empresas transnacionales, el auge de la violencia debido a estas políticas y al narcotráfico, la deuda externa y los programas de austeridad impuestos por las instituciones financieras globales, la economía informal, la destrucción del ambiente, la dañina experimentación farmacéutica y médica impuesta a los sectores menos pudientes, etc.

No es la literatura, que corresponde a una esfera pública tradicional y elitista, la que se enfrenta a estas condiciones posmodernas. Junto a la tradicional esfera pública viene abriéndose otra, en la que se constituyen sujetos/actores sociales distintos. Su distinción estriba en el manejo diferente que hacen de los géneros discursivos y conductales. Como diría Bajtín (1985: 269), este es el espacio de la "reacentuacón de géneros," que hace posible la creatividad social. Y la razón por la cual se da esta actividad en lo cotidiano es su flexibilidad en comparación con la esfera pública oficial o formal. Bajtín puntualiza que la creatividad-reacentuación de géneros depende del·dominio de ellos, dominio que se logra institucionalmente. De ahí que se trabaje en un espacio al cual se tenga mayor acceso. Dominar géneros quiere decir haber tenido acceso a las instituciones que controlan el movimiento discursivo. En lo cotidiano, pues, se puede trabajar al margen de las instituciones formales y crear nuevas instituciones.

La pedagogía conscienitzadora de Paulo Freire y el movimiento de las comunidades eclesiales de base son dos ejemplos de actividades que han reacentuado géneros institucionalizados, creando a la vez instituciones alternativas que han tenido un gran impacto en la transformación de los sectores populares en América Latina y hasta en otros continentes. Es este el contexto en que emerge el testimonio, que no es exclusivamente una práctica política ni una forma literaria ni un ritual comunitario. El testimonio es una modalidad discursiva, reacentuación de géneros —autobiografía, examen de conciencia, evangelio, deposición, periodismo, propaganda, etc.— que se vincula a las instituciones alternativas de esta otra esfera pública.

Se ve, pues, que la constitución de esta otra esfera pública no implica una discontinuidad con respecto a la esfera pública formal sino una reacentuación. Hay continuidad de una a otra; la esfera pública alternativa incide en la otra y vice versa. De ahí que algunos escritores y etnógrafos profesionales, formados en la esfera pública formal, se conviertan en colaboradores —y no portavoces— en estas luchas de lo cotidiano. Se da, pues, un verdadero dialogismo que infunde la posicionalidad múltiple del sujeto de este tipo de actividad, dialogismo que contrasta sobremanera con la superposición que propne Sarduy y que sus comentadores conciben como una trasngresión a la autoría convencional. La transformación de la "presencia centralizadora de una voz autorial" (González Echevarría, 1987: 250) no se da realmente en la superposición sarduyana, pues la institución formal de la literatura, a la que pertenece su obra, no deja de imponerle el privilegio autorial. Este deseo imposible de trascender el poder que la esfera pública formal otorga a lo que se produce y distribuye a través de las instituciones que conforman lo literario es afín al deseo imposible del artista que procura trascender el privilegio del arte pero siempre en espacios —museos, galerías, plazas, etc.— demarcados para significar "arte."

En otras palabras, desde el lado del arte no se puede eludir el condicionamiento de la esfera pública formal. Esta es la lección que, según Burkhardt Lindner (1976: 83), aprendió la vanguardia histórica:

> En su pretensión de superar el arte en la praxis de la vida, puede considerarse la vanguardia como la tentativa más radical y consistente de mantener la autonomía del arte vis-à-vis todas las otras esferas sociales y darle así un sentido práctico. Así pues, la tentativa de liquidar el arte como institución no rompe con la época de la autonomía sino que *se manifiesta en el mismo nivel ideológico como fenómeno invertido.*

En contraste con las tentativas vanguardistas, las actividades (conscienti-zadoras, solidarias, etc.) de la esfera pública alternativa *no procuran hacer arte o literatura ni política tradicional* (Yúdice, 1990).

La conscientización típica de la actividad en esta otra esfera pública consiste en la interacción de discursos, ya no como objetos ajenos que hay que descifrar para extraer los valores deseados que encierran sino como el cuestio-namiento —"diálogo crítico y liberador" (Freire, 1979: 61)—, a la luz de la experiencia cotidiana, de los códigos ideológicos que vehiculizan los discursos. La conscientización implica otras bases de comunicación e interpretación, un marco epistemológico distinto que da prioridad al imperativo de sobrevivencia de la comunidad. Todo acto se evalúa conforme al *ethos* de la comunidad. Conscientización quiere decir obrar consciente y concienzudamente a partir de este *ethos*, que no está dado de antemano sino que está siendo en la praxis cotidiana.

La solidaridad con los otros es el fundamento de un conocimiento que deriva de la *fe*, entendida como *praxis*, en el sentido expuesto en las *Tesis sobre Feuerbach* de Marx (Silva Gotay, 1983: 256). Por praxis se entiende "transfor-mación del mundo" —cambio de circunstancias— a través de la cual se desa-rrolla la conciencia, haciendo posible la construcción de una *res publica* —esfera pública— distinta. Así pues, la praxis toma prioridad sobre cualquier noción de reflejo (Gutiérrez, 1979: 26) o "representación ideológica del mundo" (Silva Gotay, 1983: 239), lo cual no quiere decir que esta conscientización no apoye ciertas representaciones ideológicas en el contexto particular de su lucha por la sobrevivencia.

La formación del sujeto en estas luchas de lo cotidiano se da en esa esfera extraformal, al margen de o reacentuando los discursos vinculados con las instituciones oficiales. Este contexto explica la declaración que hace Domitila Barrios (1977: 163) en su testimonio *Si me permiten hablar*:

> Quiero esclarecer que, porque parece que hay gente que dice que me formaron, que su partido me formó, que no le debo mi conciencia y mi preparación a nada que no sean el llanto, el sufrimiento y las experiencias de mi pueblo. Quiero decir que tenemos mucho que aprender de los partidos pero que no deberíamos esperar que nos venga todo de ellos. Nuestro desarrollo tiene que venir de nuestra propia claridad y conciencia.

Para concluir habría que, por lo menos, mencionar otra versión más de la posmodernidad, la simulacional que Jameson (1986) define conforme a los siguientes criterios: 1) el auge del populismo estético, que acepta la cultura de masas y el kitsch, 2) la destrucción de la expresión del Ser (a lo Van Gogh) y el auge de lo simulado (a lo Warhol), 3) la mengua de la emoción con su concomitante remitencia a una profundidad humana (como en las pulsiones freudianas) y el surgimiento de la eufórica *jouissance* como experiencia de la muerte del sujeto (Lacan), 4) la sustitución de la parodia (transgresión) por el pastiche (conformidad), 5) la eliminación de la Historia por el "historicismo," es decir, por la espectacularización o simulación de todos los estilos del pasado,

6) la moda *retro* sin nostalgia emocional (*The Big Chill*), 7) la pérdida del pasado radical, 8) el narcisismo y la esquizofrenia sociales debidos a la desedipalización (Lasch), 9) la transformación de la obra y del sujeto en *texto* constituido por diferencias, 10) el sublime *Camp* o histérico que provienen ya no de la incapacidad de figurar o re-presentar la incomensurabilidad sino del terror de la existencia simulada, 11) la apoteosis del maquinismo capitalista de la tercera revolución industrial o cibernética, 12) la abolición de la distancia crítica, 13) la pérdida de coordenadas en el espacio urbano.

No creo que todos estos aspectos de la posmodernidad consumista/simulacional se circunscriban al llamado "primer mundo." Hemos visto ya que hay escritores e intelectuales latinoamericanos que se mueven en este mismo clima cultural. Lo que me parece que no vio claramente Jameson en ese ensayo clásico es que su versión de la posmodernidad se limita a lo que se produce y consume en la esfera pública oficial, hoy día en vías de simulación. En ese contexto, claro está, la política y la identidad, por ejemplo, se estetizan, resultando en presidencias del *marketing* como la del actor Reagan o en la identidad social que se porta en la camiseta o la calcomanía del automóvil. Pero en los mismos países de ese "primer mundo" se dan nuevos movimientos sociales que, como en América Latina, luchan por abrir nuevos espacios públicos alternativos. Puede decirse que se produce una culturalización de la política, pero ésta no es idéntica a la política estetizada y simulada por las comunicaciones de masas y el consumismo. De hecho, los nuevos movimientos sociales luchan por reacentuar la idea misma del consumo, es decir, transformar las instituciones a través de las cuales se satisfacen las necesidades de consumo de alimentos, servicios sociales y culturales y otras necesidades (Fraser, 1989).

Esta distribución de satisfacciones ya no se circunscribe a una política representacional, ni en América Latina ni en los Estados Unidos. Como se afirma arriba, el hecho de que los mayores peligros sociales se dan en lo cotidiano, las luchas por la distribución de satisfacciones tiene que ser necesariamente la de la cultura de lo cotidiano. Hoy día hasta los grandes conflictos internacionales (guerras, invasiones, crisis económicas, etc.) se perciben en términos locales. De ahí que surjan movimientos de solidaridad que trascienden fronteras nacionales (movimientos de mujeres, de grupos raciales y homosexuales, de protección del ambiente, etc.). Para volver momentáneamente al testimonio, el premio otorgado por Casa de las Américas a partir de 1970 fomentó la creación de una red de conexiones entre los movimientos testimoniados por activistas de diversos países. Y en Estados Unidos, los movimientos de solidaridad con y santuario para los sectores populares en los conflictos centroamericanos y de otras regiones, se valió del testimonio como vehículo concientizador tanto en las manifestaciones políticas como en las clases de literatura. La esfera pública alternativa que vengo comentando aquí, pues, no está limitada por fronteras geopolíticas sino que las cruza y concientiza acerca de lo que significan. Es en este movimiento a través de fronteras (geopolíticas, institucionales, genéricas, etc.) que se define lo que podríamos llamar la posmodernidad alternativa.

OBRAS CONSULTADAS

Bajtín, Mijail

1985 "El problema de los géneros discursivos." En *Estética de la creación verbal*. 2a ed. México: Siglo XXI.

Borges, Jorge Luis

1956 *Ficciones*. Buenos Aires: Emecé.
1964 *Discusión*. 3a ed. Buenos Aires: Emecé.

Bürger, Peter

1984 *Theory of the Avant-Garde*. Trad. Michael Shaw. Minneapolis: University of Minnesota Press.

Deleuze, Giles y Felix Guattari

1987 *A Thousand Plateaux. Capitalism and Schizophrenia*. Trans. Brian Massumi. Minneapolis: University of Minnesota.

Derrida, Jacques

1978 *La vérité en peinture*. París: Flammarion.

Foucault, Michel

1973 *The Order of Things. An Archaeology of the Human Sciences*. New York: Vintage.
1977a *Language, Counter-Memory, Practice. Selected Essays and Interview*. Ed. Donald F. Bouchard. Ithaca: Cornell University Press.
1977b "Language to Infinity." En Foucault (1977a): 53-67.
1977c "A Preface to Transgression." En Foucault (1977a): 29-52.

Fraser, Nancy

1989 "Women, Welfare, and the Politics of Need Interpretation." En *Unruly Practices. Power, Discourse and Gender in Contemporary Social Theory*. Minneapolis: University of Minnesota Press.

Freire, Paulo

1979 *Pedagogía del oprimido*. 22a ed. trad. Jorge Mellado. México: Siglo XXI.

Fuentes, Carlos

1969 *La nueva novela hispanoamericana*. México: Joaquín Mortiz.

González Echevarría

1987 *La ruta de Severo Sarduy*. Hanover, N.H.: Ediciones del Norte.

Gutiérrez, Gustavo

1979 "Liberation Praxis and Christian Faith." En Rosino Gibellini, ed. *Frontiers of Theology in Latin America*. Maryknoll, NY: Orbis Books: 1-33.

Habermas, Jürgen

1987 *The Philosophical Discourse of Modernity*. Trad. Frederick Lawrence. Cambridge: MIT Press.

Heidegger, Martin

1975a *Poetry, Language, Thought*. Trad. Albert Hofstadter. New York: Harper Colophon Books.
1975b "Language." En Heidegger (1975a): 187-210.
1975c "'...Poetically Man Dwells...'." En Heidegger (1975): 211-229.
1977 "The Age of the World Picture." En *The Question Concerning Technology and Other Essays*. Trans. William Lovitt. New York: Garland Publishing: 115-154.

Hutcheon, Linda

1989 *The Politics of Postmodernism*. London/New York: Routledge.

Kant, Immanuel

1952 *The Critique of Judgement*. Trans. James Cree Meredith. Oxford: Clarendon Press.

Kristeva, Julia

1980 *Pouvoirs de l'horreur. Essai sur l'abjection.* París: Seuil.

Lacan, Jacques

1975 *Le séminaire, livre XX: Encore.* París: Seuil.

Lihn Enrique

1980 *El arte de la palabra.* Barcelona: Pomaire.

Lindner, Burkhardt

1976 "Aufhebung der Kunst in der Lebenspraxis? Über die Aktualität der Auseinandersetzung mit den historischen Avantgardebewegungen." En W. M. Lüdke, ed. *"Theorie der Avant-garde."Antworten auf Peter Bürgers Bestimmung von Kunst und bürgerlich Gesellschaft.* Frankfurt: Suhrkamp. Citado en Bürger (1984).

Locke, John

1985 *An Essay concerning Human Understanding.* Ed. Peter H. Nidditch. Oxford: Clarendon Press.

Mayz Valenilla, Ernesto

1969 *El problema de América.* 3a ed. Caracas: Universidad Central de Venezuela.

Menchú, Rigoberta

1983 *Me llamo Rigoberta y así me nació la conciencia.* Barcelona: Argos Vergara.

Rajchman, John

1986a "Ethics after Foucault." *Social Text,* 13/14 (Winter/Spring): 165-183.
1986b "Lacan and the Ethics of Modernity." *Representations* 15 (Spring): 42-56.

Rose, Jacqueline

1982 "Introduction II." En Jacques Lacan and the *école freudienne. Feminine Sexuality.* Eds. Juliet Mitchell y Jacqueline Rose. Trad. Jacqueline Rose. New York: Pantheon.

Sarduy, Severo

1967 *De donde son los cantantes.* México: Joaquín Mortiz.
1969 *Escrito sobre un cuerpo.* Buenos Aires: Sudamericana.
1974 *Barroco.* Buenos Aires: Sudamericana.
1982 *La simulación.* Caracas: Monte Avila.

Silva Gotay, Samuel

1983 *El pensamiento cristiano revolucionario en América Latina y el Caribe.* 2a ed. Río Piedras: Cordillera/Ediciones Sígueme.

Spivak, Gayatri

1989 "Who Claims Alterity." En Barbara Kruger y Phil Mariani, eds. *Remaking History.* Seattle: Bay Press/Dia Art Foundation Discussions in Contemporary Culture, no. 4.

Yúdice, George

1990 "For a Practical Aesthetics." *Social Text,* 25 (1990).

Wilden, Anthony

1980 *System and Structure. Essays in Communication and Exchange.* 2a ed. Londres: Tavistock.

ACTA LITERARIA N° 15, 1990
Concepción (Chile)

POSTMODERNIDAD Y LATINOAMERICA (CON UN MODELO PARA LA NARRATIVA POSTMODERNA)

Alfonso de Toro
Universidad de Kiel (Alemania)

"En todas las ficciones, cada vez que un hombre se enfrenta con diversas alternativas, opta por una y elimina las otras; en la del casi inextricable Ts'ui Pên opta —simultáneamente— por todas. »Crea«, así, diversos porvenires, diversos tiempos, que también proliferan y se bifurcan [...] todos los desenlaces ocurren; cada uno es el punto de partida de otras bifurcaciones".
[...]
"Creía en infinitas series de tiempos que se aproximan, se bifurcan, se cortan o que secularmente se ignoran, abarca »todas« las posibilidades".
(Borges, "El jardín de senderos que se bifurcan", 170, 172)[1].

0. *INTRODUCCION*

Las siguientes páginas pretenden solamente proponer algunas ideas con respecto al fenómeno de la postmodernidad en relación con la narrativa latinoamericana. Esta restricción es necesaria frente a la amplitud y complejidad del debate de la postmodernidad. Intentamos, eso sí, poner de manifiesto que la postmodernidad es descriptible partiendo de una serie de elementos bases, y de esta forma también la novela latinoamericana postmoderna.

---

[1] *Ficciones* (Bruguera). Madrid 1985; cf. también la similitudes con Gille Deleuze/Félix Guattari: *Rhizome*. Berlin, 1977; fr. Paris, 1976).

1. GENERALIDADES

Lo que denota el término 'postmodernidad' y cuáles son sus características como sistema sigue siendo hoy en día, a pesar de un diluvio de publicaciones, altamente discutido, tanto dentro de una disciplina determinada como en la semiótica de la cultura: existen tan variadas tesis como autores que se han manifestado al respecto. El término se ha convertido con el tiempo en una metáfora poco convincente, en una idea fija, que se encuentra en todos los campos.

Frente a semejante situación es imprescindible aclarar las nociones del término en cuestión, y especialmente dentro de la ciencia literaria, donde observamos un fenómeno similar a aquél que se produjo cuando surgieron el estructuralismo, la semiótica y la teoría de la recepción, en que la terminología de estas disciplinas fue (y lo es aún) degradada a conceptos eclécticos que nada definían ni precisaban. Una semejante Babilonia impide una discusión seria, y ha conducido a que autores pertenecientes a siglos tan lejanos como Aristóteles y Rabelais, Cervantes y Gracián, Sterne y Baudelaire, Artaud y Joyce, Beckett y Borges, Heißenbüttel y Norman Mailer, Vonnegut y A. Robbe-Grillet, y no olvidemos a Nietzsche y Heidegger, Lyotard y Vattimo, U. Eco y muchos otros, se les califique de postmodernos, como ha sucedido últimamente también con la novela hispanoamericana en su totalidad[2].

Frente a esta definición inflacionaria, que a la vez es ahistórica, observa U. Eco en su "Postille a *Il nome della rosa*" en forma de sarcástica, que pronto llegaremos a Homero[3].

---

[2] Una semejante tendencia se encuentra en los trabajos de J. Barth: *The Literary of Exhaustion, en: Atlantic Monthly* 220 (1967) 29-43; The Literature of Repleneshment: Postmodernist Fiction, en: *Atlantic Monthly* 245 (1980) 65-71.

[3] U. Eco: Postille (1983), en: *Il nome della rosa* (1980). Milano (6 1985), pág. 528:

> "Malauguratamente 'post-moderno' è un termino buono »à tout faire«. Ho l'impressione che oggi lo si applichi a tutto ciò che piace a chi lo usa. D'altra parte sembra chi sia un tentativo di farlo slittare, all'indietro: prima sembrava adattarsi ad alcuni scrittori o artisti operanti negli ultimi vent'anni, poi via via è arrivato sino a inizio secolo, poi più indietro, e la marcia continua, tra poco la categoria del post-moderno arriverà a Omero".

La concepción de Eco es ahistórica:

> "Credo tuttavia che il post-moderno non sia una tendenza circoscrivibile cronologicamente, ma una categoria spirituale, o meglio un »Kunstvollen«, un modo di ope-

2. GENEALOGIA, HISTORIA Y PERIODIZACION DE LA POSTMODERNIDAD

2.1. Breve genealogía e historia del término 'Postmodernidad' y sus campos

Si el término 'Post-Modernidad' tanto semántica, histórica como sistemáticamente pretende tener algún sentido, no se debería partir de la premisa que el momento en el que manifestamos algo, es el moderno o vanguardista, ya que de esta forma la postmodernidad no podría tener lugar, lo cual sería insensato.

Desde un punto de vista histórico-cultural tenemos que diferenciar el término 'post-modernidad' actual, de aquel que estando relacionado con la historiografía y las ciencias naturales, se encontraba en oposición al de 'modernidad', es decir, con aquel que marca el comienzo del Renacimiento (1500) y de la Epoca Moderna inaugurada con Descartes (1596-1650) y la fundación de la *mathesis universalis*. Ese período se denominaba 'postmodernismo' y marca una época que comienza alrededor de 1875 (Toynbee), o también a partir de 1914 (Pannwitz)[4]. Frente a lo expuesto tampoco se debe confundir el término 'postmodernidad' con aquel de 'postmodernismo' de Federico Onís, que es de naturaleza cultural. Según éste, comienza el postmodernismo, como reacción al 'modernismo' (1850), alrededor de 1905-1914, pero poco o nada tiene en común con el término 'postmodernidad' que discutiremos aquí[5].

Bajo 'postmodernidad' entendemos un fenómeno histórico-cultural que aparece *después* de la 'modernidad' (ésta va desde 1850 hasta 1960..., de Baudelaire al comienzo de los años sesenta), es decir, en la segunda mitad de nuestro siglo.

---

rare. Potremmo dire che ogni epoca ha il propio post-moderno, cosi come ogni epoca avrebbe il propio manierismo (tanto che mi chiedo se post-moderno non sia il nome moderno del Manierismo como categoria metastorica)"; (*Ibid.*:p. 528).

[4] v. nota 6.

[5] Cf. Federico de Onís: *Antologia de la poesía española e hispano americana*. Madrid. 1934. Con respecto al postmodernismo en el ámbito hispánico: Octavio Corvalán: *El post-modernismo. la literatura hispanoamericana entre dos guerras mundiales*. New York (Las Américas Pub. Co.). 1961; Pedro Salinas: El cisne y el Búho: apuntes para la historia de la poesía modernista, en: *Literatura española del siglo XX* (México) (1949) 45-65; Beatriz Sarlo: La poesía post-modernista, en: *Historia de Literatura Argentina* (Buenos Aires. CEAL) 3 (1980) 98-113. También Charles Olson. poeta y ensayista. emplea este término para la época después de 1875.

Entendemos la postmodernidad no sólo como una consecuencia de la modernidad, como una 'habitualización", una continuación y cúlmine de ésta, sino como *una actividad de 'recodificación iluminada, integrativa y pluralista',* *que retoma, reconsidera un amplio paradigma, en especial de la cultura occidental, pero no solamente de ésta, con la finalidad de repensar la tradición cultural y de esta forma finalmente abrir un nuevo paradigma, donde se termina con los metadiscursos totalizantes y excluyentes y se boga por la 'paralogía', por el disenso y la cultura del debate. Yo osaría de calificar la postmodernidad como un 'Renacimiento recodificado'*[6]. La postmodernidad trata de poner en práctica en forma radical la actividad de la '*Verwindung*' (reintegrar) heideggeriana interpretada por Vattimo y Lyotard, como así la interpretación que da Lyotard a los términos freudianos de '*Verarbeitung*' (elaborar) y '*Erinnerung*' (memoria)[7].

En la historia de la cultura aparece el término como tal por primera vez en 1917 con Pannwitz, luego lo encontramos en 1934 en una antología literaria de Onís, y en 1947 en un libro de historiografía de Arnold Toynbee editado por C.D. Sommervellin[8].

---

[6] La discusión de la postmodernidad se puede dividir en tres grupos: uno que defiende la modernidad y rechaza la postmodernidad, un segundo que defiende la postmodernidad y rechaza la modernidad y un tercero que considera la postmodernidad como una evolución de la modernidad calificándola de "modernidad postmoderna".
Si se parte de la discusión histórica sobre el postmodernismo como lo ha planteado Rudolf Pannwitz (Die Krisis der europäischen Kultur, en: *ibid.: Werke.* Nürnberg 1917, Band II) o Arnold Toynbee (*A Study of History.* 1947) tenemos una alabanza al postmodernismo y una condenación de la modernidad. En oposición a esta tendencia se encuentra Arnold Gehlen (Über die kulturelle Kristallisation, en: el mismo: *Studien zur Anthropologie und Soziologie.* Neuwied/Berlin 1963, pp. 311-328 y Ende der Geschichte, en: el mismo: *Einblicke.* Frankfurt a.M. 1975, 115-133. Con respecto a la arquitectura, literatura, teatro, etc. v. nota 12,15,19 y: Roberto Venturi: *Complexity and Contradiction in Architecture.* New York 1966; Charles Jencks: *The Language of Postmodern Architecture.* New York 1977; Susan Sontag: Notes on »Camp« und One Culture and the New Sensibility, en: *Against Interpretation.* New York 1966; *Styles on radical Will.* New York 1969; John Barth v. Nota 2; Leslie Fiedler: The New Mutants, en: *Partisan Review* 1965; Cross the Border-Close the Gap., en: *Playboy* (december 1969), nuevamente impreso en: Marcus Cunliffe (Ed.): *American Literature Since 1900.* London 1975, pp. 344-366; Jerome Klinkowitz: *Literary Disruptions: The Making of a Post-Contemporary American Fiction.* Urbana III, 1975. Un panorama general ofrece Wolfgang Welsch: *Unsere postmoderne Moderne.* Weinheim 1988; Wolfgang Welsch (Ed.): *Wege aus der Moderne. Schlüsseltexte der Postmoderne-Diskussion.* Weinheim 1988.
[7] v. nota 11.
[8] El término ya se encontraba en 1870 en la pintura inglesa en oposición a la pintura impresionista.

Historia

La concepción postmodernista de Pannwitz resulta de una diagnosis negativa de la época anterior (entre 1850-1917). El Postmodernismo es definido positivamente: éste es un fenómeno conservador, el hombre postmodernista es deportivo, nacionalista, militarista y religioso, se dirige contra la modernidad a la cual le es inherente el nihilismo y la decadencia.

En la discusión actual, que comienza con Gehlen en los años 50[9], se analiza a la 'Posthistoria', respectivamente la Postmodernidad (después de la Segunda Guerra Mundial) en forma negativa: como una época carente de innovaciones, en la cual las posibilidades de desarrollo histórico se han agotado, en donde no existen actos creativos, sino formas meramente reproductoras de lo existente, que impiden la posibilidad de desarrollar nuevos valores, conceptos e ideales. Lo único que funciona es el aparato socio-económico de una siempre creciente sociedad de masas cuyos deseos y cuyas exigencias de consumo deben ser saciados. Demostraciones, protestas y otro tipo de actos subversivos se los considera ilusorios, como algo efímero, teatral, obsoleto y finalmente epigonal.

Somos por el contrario de opinión que la postmodernidad histórica comienza a desarrollarse durante los años 70 con los movimientos pacifistas, con el movimiento político-ecológico, con la perestroika, llegando a la cúlmine actual de su evolución con la desintegración de los sistemas estalinistas de Europa del Este, evolución a la que seguirá tarde o temprano un radical cambio del sistema político-militar de occidente.

Sociología

El término de postmodernidad se desarrolla en la sociología en EE.UU. a partir de 1958 con los trabajos de David Riesman (1958), se difunde luego con las investigaciones de Amitai Etzioni (1968), y la discusión llega a su cúlmine

[9] v. Nota 7 y del mismo autor: *Zeit-Bilder. Zur Soziologie und Ästhetik der modernen Malerei*. Bonn [2]1965; v.también Norbert Bolz: Die Zeit des Weltspiegels, en: *Ästhetik und Kommunikation* 63 (1986) 113-120.

con los análisis de Daniel Bell (1973, 1976 ff.). En Europa se realiza el debate con Alain Touraine (1969) y Jean Baudrillard (1971, 1981)[10].

En la socio-economía de Etzioni o Bell se argumenta en forma similar que en la historia. Se sostiene que el aparato socio-económico, que ha alcanzado una alta y diferenciada forma de producción, tiene la función de mantener el *status quo*, lo cual reprime las actividades en otros sectores de la vida. Bell acepta eso sí, en su diagnosis negativa del capitalismo norteamericano, que la cultura tiene una función subversiva, ya que ésta puede movilizar a las masas contra las exigencias de disciplina que implanta la producción capitalista.

Filosofía

En este campo se inaugura el paradigma de la postmodernidad con la filosofía de Jean-François Lyotard (1979) y Gianni Vattimo (1980), y partiendo de estos dos autores se descubren retrospectivamente a Michel Foucault (1966), Jacques Derrida (1967, 1972) y Gilles Deleuze (1968) como fundadores de la filosofía postmoderna[11].

La filosofía se despide del racionalismo y rigorismo cartesiano como así también de la metafísica. Ahora se da preferencia a la pluralidad de paradigmas concurrentes, a la diferencia, a la diseminación, a la heterogeneidad, a las distribuciones nómadas, a la deconstrucción, a la interculturalidad e intertextualidad, al disenso, al antagonismo. La filosofía postmoderna es absolutamente abierta, y se entiende en parte como una relectura creativa y transformadora de discursos establecidos en la tradición. No solamente recurre a la tradición filosófica de la época moderna, sino de la tradición occidental en su totalidad, para fundar un nuevo discurso filosófico con las características mencionadas.

[10] David Riesman: Leisure and Work in Post-Industrial Society, en: Eric Larrabee/Rolf Meyersohn (Ed.): *Mass Leisure*. Glencoe, Ill. 1958, 365-385; Amitai Etzioni: *The Active Society. A. Theory of Societal and Political Process*. New York 1968; Alain Touraine: *La société post-industrielle*. Paris 1969; Daniell Bell: *The Coming of Post-Industrial Society. A Venture in Social Forecasting*. New York 1973; *The Cultural Contradiction of Capitalism*. New York 1976; Jean Baudrillard: *L'Echange symbolique et la mort*. Paris 1976.

[11] Jean François Lyotard: *La condition postmoderne. Rapport sur le savoir*. Paris 1979; Gianni Vattimo, *Le avventure della differenza. Che cosa significa pensare dopo Nietzsche e Heidegger*. Milano 1980; *Al di là del soggetto. Nietzsche, Heidegger e l'ermeneutica*. Milano 1984, *La fine della modernità*. Milano 1985; Michel Foucault: *Le mots et les choses*. Paris 1966; Jacques Derrida: *L'écriture de la différence*. Paris 1967 y "Le fins de l'homme", en: *Marges de la philosophie*. Paris 1972, 129-164; Gille Deleuze: *Différence et répétition*. Paris 1968 y en colaboración con Félix Guattari: *Rhizome*. Paris 1976.

Arquitectura

En el campo de la arquitectura y del diseño se inaugura la discusión pro o contra la postmodernidad con Nikolaus Pevsner (1966) y Robert Venturi (1966), pero se llegará solamente a una teoretización amplia en los años '70 (1977) con los trabajos de Charles Jencks (cuya teoría de la 'doble codificación' la toma evidentemente de Leslie Fiedler), y del alemán Heinrich Klotz (1985)[12].

La arquitectura postmoderna (como así también el diseño) quiere crear una forma o estructura que sea capaz a la vez de considerar deseos particulares como generales e incorporar simultáneamente problemas arquitectónicos inmanentes, es decir de incluir elementos locales/regionales y particulares combinados con formas históricas. La reintegración o el redescubrimiento del ornamento, de lo figural, del color local, en un sistema integrador caracterizan este movimiento arquitectónico, como lenguaje radicalmente plural, como comunicación, metáfora que quiere o pretende provocar la fantasía del observador. La forma se acopla a un código 'socio-arquitectónico' con un metalenguaje lúdico, narcisístico, con una finalidad explicatoria y descriptiva. La combinación de diversos materiales (mármol, granito, concreto armado, ladrillo, vidrio, acero y plástico), colores y formas (geométricas, griegas-romanas, clasicistas, barrocas, estilo decor, y Bauhaus, etc.), como así también la recurrencia y retorno de elementos determinados: el aguilón o frontispicio triangular griego, renacentista y clásico, puertas o entradas ovaladas con claraboyas, formas de naves de iglesias, etc., son algunas de las características de la arquitectura postmoderna que se encuentran en diversos países y regiones.

---

[12] v.: Roberto Venturi: *Complexity and Contradiction in Architecture*. New York 1966; Nikolaus Pevsner: Architecture in Our Time. The Anti-Pioneers, en: *The Listener* (29 december, 5 january 1976); Charles Jencks: *The Language of Postmodern Architecture*. New York 1977; *Late Modern Architecture*. New York 1980; *Post-Modernism*. London 1987; Jürgen Habermas: Moderne und Postmoderne Architektur, en: *Der Architeckt* 2 (1982) 55-58 nuevamente impreso en: el mismo: *Die Neue übersichtlichkeit*. Frankfurt am Main 1985, pp. 11-29; Daniel Bell: *Immagini del Post-Moderno. Il dibattito sulla società post-industriale e l'architetura*. Venezia 1983; Jacques Derrida Point de folie-maintenant l'architecture, en: B. Tschumi (Ed.): *La case vide*. London 1986 y en el mismo: *Psyché. Invention del 'autre*. Paris 1987; Heinrich Klotz: Revision der Moderne. Postmoderne Architektur 1960-1980. München 1984; *Moderne und Postmoderne Architektur der Gegenewart 1960-1980*. Braunschweig/Wiesbaden 1987; Moderne und Postmoderne, en: Wolfgang Welsch (Ed.): *Wege aus der Moderne. Schlüsseltexte der Postmoderne-Diskussion*. Weinheim 1988, pp. 99-109. Sin lugar a duda es Venturi uno de los más fascinantes arquitectos tanto en la teoría como en la práctica.

La arquitectura es considerada como un signo narrativo, argumentativo, icónico y estético de gran variedad, como una ficción, como puente entre ideas poéticas (entre la belleza decorativa) y su utilidad (funcionalidad), como puente entre lo antiguo y lo nuevo, como humor, ironía y parodia.

Arte

Mientras que la práctica del arte postmoderno lo inicia Andy Warhol en los años 60 con el Pop Art y luego se desarrollan otras formas artísticas en EE.UU. y Europa, tales como el fotorrealismo, el neoclasicismo durante los años 70, la discusión teórica se inicia a partir de 1967. En 1980 se establece el término 'arte postmoderno' definitivamente en la crítica de arte[13].

Los artistas postmodernos reintroducen lo figurativo, emplean una fuerte masa de colores, la subjetividad, la metáfora y la alegoría. Así como en otros campos de la cultura recurren a toda la tradición artística occidental (y no sólo a ésta). Encontramos temas, estilos, técnicas y formas conocidas, realizadas en forma de cita distanciadora o paródica o reintegrados en un nuevo concepto, provenientes del renacimiento, del clasicismo, del impresionismo, del cubismo, del surrealismo, expresionismo, futurismo, dadaísmo, etc.). Se caracteriza no a través de la exclusión, sino de la inclusión de lo uno y lo otro[14].

Teatro

Mientras que en todos los otros campos de la cultura con la relativa excepción de la música, se inició una investigación científica de la postmoderni-

---

[13] v. los trabajos de Lewitt: Paragraphs on Conceptual Arts. en: *Artforum* 5 (1967) 72-83, 0-9 (New York 1969) und Sentences on Conceptual Arts., en: *Art-Languages* (England) 1,1 (1969); Brian O'Doherty: What is Post-Modernism?, en: *Art in America* 59 (1971) 19; Marshall Cohen (1971) y John T. Paoletti: Art. en: Stanley Trachtenberg (Ed.): *The Postmodern Moment. A Handbook of Contemporary Innovation in the Arts.* London 1985, pp. 53-80.

[14] Algunos de los pintores modernos serían: los americanos James Valerio, Bruno Civitico, John de Andrea; los italianos Carlo María Mariani, Lorenzo Bonechi, Franco Clementi, Sandro Chia; los alemanes Joseph Beuys y Christian Müller, el grupo de Berlín Occidental los "Nuevos Salvajes" (*Neuen Wilden*). Markus Lüpertz, Karl Horst, Dieter Hacker y Reiner Fettig; el ecuatoriano-berlinés Miguel Yaulema y Luis Suares Jofrá (San Juan/Argentina); cf. Heinrich Klotz: *Die neuen Wilden.* Stuttgart 1987; Charles Jencks: *Post-Modernims* (Academy Editions) London 1987; Klaus Honnef: *Kunst der Gegenwart.* Köln 1988.

dad, en el campo del teatro se encontró ésta al comienzo en la crítica, llamémosla periodística. Con cierto retardo comenzó la crítica académica a ocuparse del campo en discusión.

La práctica del teatro postmoderno comienza en los años 60 con el *Living Theatre*, el *Happening* y el *Open Theatre* en New York. Tendremos que esperar, eso sí, los años 70 y 80, es decir, al teatro de B. Shepard, Robert Wilson, Peter Brook, Heiner Müller, Tankred Dorst, Jean-Marie Koltès, Alberto Kurapel, Ramón Griffero y Fernando de Tavira, para que éste llegase a su real desarrollo.

En 1985 aparecen los trabajos de June Schlueter y Erika Fischer-Lichte, que describen determinadas formas del teatro postmoderno. En 1989 propuse un modelo general para un amplio trato de las diversas manifestaciones postmodernas[15].

El teatro postmoderno comienza en los años 70 y tiene las siguientes características: ambigüedad, discontinuidad, heterogeneidad, pluralismo, subversión, perversión, deformación, deconstrucción, decreación, es antimimético y se resiste a la interpretación.

Se trata de un teatro en el cual se celebra el arte como ficción y el teatro como proceso, *performance*, non-textualidad, donde el actor se transforma en el tema y personaje principal, donde el texto en el mejor de los casos es una mera base, en general carece éste de importancia. El texto es considerado como una forma autoritaria y arcaica. El texto es más bien un *performance script*. La idea de *performance* toma una tercera posición, mediadora y subversiva entre drama y teatro.

El teatro postmoderno se abre a todos los medios de comunicación (pluralidad de códigos: música, danza, luz, elementos olfatóricos), sin separarlos por rúbricas o géneros, y cualquier lugar pasa a ser lugar de teatro (cafés, garaje,

[15] June Schlueter: Theatre, en: Stanley Trachtenberg (Ed.): *The Postmodern Moment. A Handbook of Contemporary Innovation in the Arts.* London 1985, pp. 209-228; Erika Fischer-Lichte: Wilson/Heiner Müller »CIVIL warS« en *Historische und aktuelle Konzepte der Literaturge-schichtsschreibung.* Akten des VII. International en Germanisten-Kongresses Göttingen 1985. Tübingen 1986 vol. 11, pp. 191-201; Postmoderne Performance: Rückkehr zum rituellen Theater?, en: *Arcadia* 22 (1987) 55-65; Un resumen de mi trabajo, Hacia un modelo para el teatro-postmoderno aparece en *Gestos* 6 (1990), la versión original, en F. de Toro/K.A. Blüher/A. de Toro (Eds.): *Semiótica teatral y teatro latinoamericano* (Galerna). Buenos Aires 1990 y.en Italia Verso un modelo del teatro postmoderno, en: *Revista Teatrale* (Venezia) 1990.

casas de parqueo, *off-Brodway*, parques, iglesias, terrazas de edificios, *Happening* y *Open Theatre*)[16].

El actor se transforma en elemento-tema central, debe solamente representar a través de su gestualidad kinésica, a través de su actuar, de su percepción del mundo. En un teatro así concebido pierde la palabra su sentido, se actúa sin discurso, en base a meditación, gestualidad, ritmo, sonido, silencio, las acciones son instintivas, no se desprenden necesariamente de un entrenamiento. El teatro adquiere formas nihilistas, grotescas, llegando hasta el silencio (Robert Wilson), hasta el espacio vacío (Peter Brook).

El teatro postmoderno se resiste a la interpretación, el espectáculo no es más interpretable según parámetros semáticos tradicionales, los significados no son reducibles a una interpretación que den un sentido profundo, un mensaje, el teatro postmoderno tiene elementos de la ciencia ficción, maneja, juega, cita el lenguaje cotidiano, *ready mades* combinados según una técnica de montaje donde los fonemas son destruidos y altamente recurrentes; fragmentación, montaje y repetición son principios comunes de la organización performativa del teatro postmoderno; intertextualidad: empleo de citas de otros autores y textos de diversas épocas o de textos propios, mas sin función ninguna; transformación del texto en un collage tonal, donde los signos se han despedido de su función denotativa, es decir se han transformado en grafemas desemantizados; interculturalidad, es decir, la recepción de elementos de culturas extrañas en la propia, para producir un nuevo teatro.

El teatro postmoderno se manifiesta por lo menos en cuatro tipos de semiosis. La primera es aquélla de la representación total y de la integración de todos los géneros artísticos, o por lo menos de una gran cantidad de éstos, que definimos como: *teatro plurimedial o interespectacular* (aquí es posible la interpretación, mas no en la forma tradicional de buscar un sentido alegórico, profundo; es decir, los signos están acoplados a significados tanto retóricos como kinésicos); ej.: *Cosmopolitan Greetings* de Ginsberg/Gruntz/Liebermann/Wilson y Alberto Kurapel: *Prometeo encadenado* y *Tres performances*.

La segunda es aquélla en que se evoca la representación de una acción o mejor dicho pseudoacción narrativa, mas reducida radicalmente al gesto, que

---

[16] Con respecto al teatro latinoamericano podemos mencionar las obras de Alberto Kurapel: *3 performances teatrales* (Humanitas). Québec 1987; *Prometeo encadenado* (Humanitas). Québec 1989; Ramón Griffero: *Historia de un galpón abandonado. Espectáculo teatral* (manuscrito); Luis de Tavira: *La pasión de Pentesilea* (Universidad Autónoma Metropolitana). México 1988 y Marco Antonio de la Parra: *La secreta obscenidad de cada día* (Planeta. Biblioteca del Sur). Santiago / Chile 1988.

denominaremos *teatro gestual* o *kinésico* (la intepretación tradicional semántica se hace prácticamente imposible, no ofrece casi significados, sino significantes): ej.: R. Wilson/T. Dorst: *Parzival* y Luis de Tavira: *La pasión de Pentesilea*.

La tercera es aquella en que se emplea el discurso, la fábula, el espacio y tiempo teatral, mas como pseudodiscurso, pseudo-fábula, pseudoespacio y pseudotiempo. Lo hemos denominado teatro de *deconstrucción*. Se trata de una cita del teatro hablado, del teatro decadente, del teatro realista, del teatro o mejor dicho de la estética de *fin de siècle*, del teatro comprometido, del teatro pobre, del teatro social, del teatro del absurdo, del teatro historizante, sin ser nada de esto, sino citas, a través de las cuales constituye por deconstrucción, por montaje, su propio tipo de espectáculo. El espectador puede tratar de descodificar en forma semántica, coherente el texto espectacular. Que se trata de un intertexto y de una nueva forma de discurso teatral lo vemos p.e. en la fijación del texto, como texto dramático, por el contrario de *Parzival* y especialmente de *Cosmopolitan Greetings*; ej.: T. Dorst: *Der Verbotene Garten*, Jean-Marie Koltès: *Dans la solitude des champs de coton*, Ramón Griffero: *Historia de un galpón abandonado*.

La cuarta es aquella que retoma la tradición del teatro hablado tradicional con todos aquellos elementos del teatro hablado, como personajes bien definidos (nombre completo, profesión, relaciones personales privadas y profesionales). La diferencia con el teatro tradicional mimético radica en la negación de un mensaje, en la absoluta anonimidad del discurso. Este teatro lo clasificamos como teatro restaurativo tradicionalista.

Otros campos de la postmodernidad serían la teología, la danza, la moda, la cocina y el diseño[17].

2.2 *Periodización de la Postmodernidad*

Resumiendo, se puede fijar el comienzo de la Postmodernidad en 1960 con trabajos y obras de Sontag, Fiedler, Barth, Warhol, Sukenick, Mailer,

---

[17] Teología: Nathan Scott (1969) y también Marc C. Taylor (1984); Danza: Michael Kirby; Introduction, en: *The Drama Review* 19 (65-March 1975) 3; Cf. Sally Banes: Dance, en: Stanley Trachtenberg (Ed.): *The Postmodern Moment. A Handbook of Contemporary Innovation in the Arts.* London 1985, pp. 81-100; Cocina "La nueva cocina alemana" (Die neue Deutsche Küche), en: *Essen wie Gott in Deutschland.* Hamburg 1987.

Klinkowitz, Riesman, Gehlen, Etzioni, Touraine, Foucault, Derrida, Pevsner, Venturi, etc. Esta primera etapa va hasta alrededor de 1970.

La segunda etapa se desarrolla entre 1970 y 1979, aquí podemos contar autores tales como Baudrillard, Bell, Jencks, entre otros.

La tercera etapa comienza más o menos en 1979 y es hoy vigente. Contamos aquí a Robbe-Grillet, Duras, Eco, J. Marías, Montalbán, Azúa, Lyotard, Vattimo, Baudrillard, Bell, Klotz, etc.

3. *POSTULADOS PRINCIPALES DE LA POSTMODERNIDAD LITERARIA*

Las características fundamentales de la postmodernidad literaria se pueden resumir bajo el término acuñado por Fiedler del 'anti-arte' y de la 'doble codificación'. Según éstos se caracteriza la literatura (norteamericana) de la siguiente forma: es apocalíptica, antirracional, abierta y romántica, profética, desconfiada. La crítica literaria no se concentra en el análisis de la estructura de la obra, sino que quiere describir el proceso de experimentación lectoral, se transforma ella misma en arte, emplea la obra de arte para producir otra.

La literatura postmoderna tiene la tarea de llenar vacíos entre los límites de la cultura establecida y canonizada y la subcultura, entre seriedad y risa, entre las *belles lettres* y el *Popart*, entre élite y cultura de masas, entre crítica y arte, entre artista y crítica, entre arte y público, entre profesionalismo y diletantismo y amateur, entre lo real y lo maravilloso/mito. La primacía de la fantasía debe imperar sobre la sobriedad. Los géneros bases de la postmodernidad son según Fiedler el *Popart*, la pornografía y el Western[18].

---

[18] La tesis postmoderna de Fiedler representa una absolutización de una ideología, es decir, nos transmite un ideal subjetivo del autor sobre la postmodernidad, o cómo ésta debería ser. Por esto no se trata en el caso de Fiedler de una teoría de la cultura, la cual debería esforzarse por describir las diversas formas de la postmodernidad. Con esto crea Fiedler nuevos límites y cánones, lo cual está en abierta contradicción a la pluralidad propagada por él mismo, ya que debemos preguntarnos qué sucede con toda aquella literatura que no se ajusta a sus esquemas. La concepción de Fiedler describe solamente tres manifestaciones de la postmodernidad, en especial la norteamericana de los años 60 y allí aquella que se denomina subcultura, cultura alternativa, *Popart*. Fiedler nos da más bien un programa y no un término epocal o de estilo. De definitivo valor es el intento de Fiedler de cuestionar clasificaciones y definiciones de arte ya caducas, altamente elitarias, burguesas y discriminantes, creando así un espacio de reflexión legitima sobre las nuevas formas de arte y su crítica. Un semejante cambio se observa también en Roland Barthes en *Le plaisir du text*. Paris 1973 o en la obra de H.-R. Jauß: *Ästhetische Erfahrung und Literarische Hermeneutik*. München 1977, vol. 1.

Otros criterios no mencionados por Fiedler que incluirían otros países fuera de EE.UU. y que ampliarían el concepto de 'doble codificación' serían la 'deconstrucción', la 'intertextualidad', 'interculturalidad', la 'historización', la 'recepción/experiencia sensual-cognitiva del arte', la 'heterogeneidad', 'subjetividad', 'recreatividad', 'radical particularidad' o la 'diversidad' y por consecuencia la 'universalidad', como así también el 'minimalismo', la 'ironía', el 'humor', la 'fragmentación integrada', el 'collage' y un 'metadiscurso lúdico'[19].

La postmodernidad no se deja definir como la modernidad a través de la exclusión y a través de oposiciones, sino de la inclusión. Las oposiciones no representan incompatibilidades, sino posibilidades de nuevas manifestaciones.

---

[19] El término 'metadiscurso' podría ser causa de confusión en la doble forma que lo usamos. Lo usamos por una parte como estructura universal dentro de aquella filosofía que desarrolla modelos explicativos generales y deriva leyes generales, que con éstos pretende lograr la verdad científica. Por otra parte lo usamos como 'juego metadiscursivo', es decir, se refiere a indicaciones sobre los elementos y procedimientos usados en la ficción, sea en una forma reflexiva como en el *nouveau roman* o en una forma lúdica ficcional, como en las novelas a describir, es decir, incorporado a la acción, constituyendo un todo y no una división entre objeto-lengua y metalengua.
Otros autores que se han ocupado de la postmodernidad literaria serían: Ihab Hassan: *The Dismemberment of Orpheus. Toward to a Postmodern Literature.* Oxford University Press. 1971 (UB); POSTmoderISM, en: *New Literary History* 3,1 (1971) 5-30; Pluralism in Postmodern Perspective, en: *Critical Inquiry* 12 (1985/86) 503-520; Postmoderne heute, en: W. Welsch (Ed.): *Wege ausder Postmoderne. Schlüsseltexte der Postmoderne-Diskussion.* Weinheim 1988, pp. 47-56; Hoffmann, G. (Ed.): *Der zeitgenössische amerikanische Roman.* München 1988, vol. I-III; G. Hoffmann/A. Hornung/R. Kunow: 'Modern', 'Postmodern' and 'Contemporary' as Criteria for the Analysis of 20th Century Literature, en: *Amerika Studien* 22,1 (1977) 19-46; Michael Köhler: Postmodernismus: Ein begrifflicher Überblick, en: *Amerika Studien* 22, 1 (1977) 8-18; J. Peper: Postmodernismus: »Unitary Sensibility« (Von der geschichtlichen Ordnung zum synchron-environmentalen System), en: *Amerika Studien* 22, 1 (1977) 65-89; Andreas Huyssen: The Search for Tradition. Avantgarde and Postmodernism in the 1970 ths, en: *New German Critique* 22 (1981) 23-40; ibid.: Mapping the Postmodern, en: *New German Critique* 33 (1984) 5-52; Julia Kristeva: 'Postmodernism?', en: Harry R. Garvin: (Ed.): *Romanticism, Modernism. Postmodernism.* Lewisburg (Penn.) 1980, pp. 136-141; Douwe W. Fokkema: *Literary History, Modernism and Postmodernism.* Amsterdam/Philadelphia 1984; Stanley Trachtenberg (Ed.): *The Postmodern Moment. A Handbook of Contemporary Innovation in the Arts.* London 1985; A. Kibédi Varga: *Littérature et postmodernité.* Groningen 1986 Theo D'haen/Hans Bertens: *Postmodern Fiction in Europe and the Americas.* Amsterdam 1988; Nelly Richard: *La estratificación de los márgenes.* Santiago/Chile 1989.

4. *LA POSTMODERNIDAD LITERARIA EN LATINOAMERICA: LA NOVELA*

En un comienzo parece altamente difícil hablar de la postmodernidad en Latinoamérica, ya que, como hemos visto, se trata de un fenómeno global que tiene su origen fuera del continente latinoamericano, y como fenómeno global comparte una gran cantidad de características, especialmente en lo que se refiere al aspecto socio-económico, político y científico. Es precisamente esta globalidad lo que produce en Latinoamérica en un principio una fuerte actitud de rechazo.

Pero existen otras razones: una determinada corriente en Latinoamérica sigue no queriendo aceptar aquello que Borges formulaba hace ya decenios, que una gran parte de la cultura latinoamericana es parte indivisible de la cultura occidental.

La opinión de Borges se puede reformular constatando que Latinoamérica goza del privilegio de pertenecer a dos o más tipos de culturas.

Considerando una serie de aspectos ideológicos, sociales, étnicos y otros, sostenemos que Latinoamérica, constituida por un desgarrado sincretismo, se caracteriza por una gran disociación a todo nivel: el nivel cultural no tiene correspondencia con el económico, ni el económico con el social, y éstos con el político. Me refiero a que mientras Latinoamérica ya a comienzos de siglo goza de una gran poesía, y a más tardar en los años 50 se desarrolla una hiperactividad ensayística y novelística, permanecen los campos de la ciencia, economía, tecnología, industria y política en el subdesarrollo o en un modesto desarrollo; naturalmente que no olvidamos excepciones bien conocidas.

Se puede concluir, sin caer en la exageración, que la gran parte del continente no entró a la modernidad, y a los pocos países que entraron en cierta medida, el esfuerzo de modernización los condujo a la bancarrota, por lo menos momentáneamente.

A pesar de lo dicho podemos sin ningún problema hablar de la modernidad literaria latinoamericana que comienza por allí en 1888 y se desarrolla en varias etapas hasta principio de los años 60[20], y si aceptamos lo expuesto pues estaremos obligados a denominar y describir aquello que sucede en los años posteriores con otro término (a no ser que se quiera petrificar la modernidad), y esto es con el de postmodernidad.

---

[20] La primera etapa iría de 1888 (*Azul*) hasta 1925, la segunda de 1925 (*Residencia en la tierra*) hasta alrededor de 1955 y la tercera de 1955 (*El Acoso, Pedro Páramo*) hasta el comienzo de los años 60.

Esta propuesta que quiere incluir la disociación descrita no tan sólo para la modernidad, sino a la vez para la postmodernidad, persigue dos finalidades: una es el evitar que Latinoamérica quede fuera de la discusión general de un fenómeno de semejante envergadura, como ha sucedido ya tantas veces en la historia de la cultura, la otra es el describir el aporte propio de Latinoamérica a la postmodernidad[21].

No he sido jamás de opinión que Latinoamérica sea "diferente" y por esto no pueda estar englobada en fenómenos universales generales. Latinoamérica es tan diferente de USA o de Europa como lo es EE.UU. de Europa, Italia de Alemania y España de Francia, mas no por esto estos continentes y países se excluyen de servirse de toda la riqueza cultural de los vecinos. La famosa identidad y la acusada y demonizada hegemonía cultural bajo la que sufre presuntamente Latinoamérica son dos caras de un mismo mito, que ha postrado a Latinoamérica por períodos en el provincialismo cultural. La historia cultural de Latinoamérica ha demostrado ya hace decenios la falacia de esta posición: Neruda, poeta Universal, sale de la provincia, de un país subdesarrollado; Roa Bastos proviene de un feudo, Carpentier del azúcar, García Márquez de la superstición, Vargas Llosa, de un país culturalmente descastado. Mas todos fueron y son autores latinoamericanos en la medida que supieron emplear la cultura universal como suya, y con esto no perdieron su identidad, sino que la crearon. La identidad de un Borges, que vivió casi toda su vida en Buenos Aires (sostengo que Borges vivió más tiempo en B.A. que lo que cualquiera de los autores actuales han podido vivir en sus países de origen), es inconfundible

---

[21] El problema fundamental de Latinoamérica radica en los escasos medios de publicación. Son prácticamente inexistentes los fondos nacionales que permitan subvencionar libros en editoriales con distribución internacional como es lo usual en Europa y Norteamérica. El fenómeno se ha discutido desde mediados de los 80, primeramente en la sociología, con una carga ideológica muy grande y en la arquitectura; v. entre otros Maurizio Ferraris: Postmoderno, en: *Punto de Vista* (Buenos Aires) Nr. 21 (1984); 4-5 (1986); 31 (1987); 33 (1988); *Revista First* 19 (1988); 29 (1989); *Revista de Estética* (Centro de Arte y Comunicación de Buenos Aires) 5-6 (1987) 32-37; *Revista Universitaria* (Universidad Católica de Chile) 22 (1987) 38-43; Pedro Morandé: La cultura como experiencia o como ideología, en: *Revista Universitaria* (Universidad Católica de Chile) 22 (1987) 44-48; Fernando Pérez: La compleja superación de la sensibilidad y el ideal moderno en el terreno de la arquitectura, en: *Revista Universitaria* (Universidad Católica de Chile) 22 (1987) 49-55; Nicolás Casullo (Ed.): *El debate modernidad/postmodernidad*. Buenos Aires 1988; *Imágenes desconocidas. La modernidad en la encrucijada postmoderna*. Buenos Aires 1988; *Postmodernidad*. Buenos Aires 1988; Rosa María Ravera: *Estética y semiótica*. Rosario 1988; Pablo Oyarzún: La polémica sobre lo moderno y lo postmoderno en: v. Nelly Richard: *La estratificación de los márgenes. Sobre arte, cultura y políticas*. Santiago/Chile 1989.

a través de su escritura. El discurso artístico es lo que da identidad a una cultura y no solamente el lugar de origen.

Frente a este cuadro partimos de la base que en Latinoamérica naturalmente existe una postmodernidad, la cual entramos a describir en el campo de la novela.

4.1 *J.L. Borges o el comienzo de la postmodernidad*

J.L. Borges inaugura con *Ficciones* (1939-1944) la postmodernidad, no solamente en Latinoamérica, sino en general. Lo dicho podría ser interpretado como una contradicción, ya que hemos dicho que la postmodernidad es un fenómeno que se origina en EE.UU. y en los años '60. Si hubiese una semejante contradicción, ésta sería de carácter cronológico, no de carácter sistemático. A la obra de J.L. Borges le ha sucedido aquello que han experimentado muchas obras de la literatura universal: su discurso no se ha podido fijar históricamente visto, ni en lo que podríamos llamar la 'alta modernidad' o vanguardia, ni en la 'modernidad tardía', es decir, en aquella literatura que aparece en los años 50[22], y por la sencilla razón de que la escritura de Borges se encontraba ya en la segunda mitad del siglo XX. Este es también el lugar donde radica la incomprensión que produjo su obra por largo tiempo tanto en Latinoamérica como en Europa. Borges abrió dentro del paradigma de la modernidad, aquel de la postmodernidad, que atrajo la atención de algunos círculos literarios como aquél del *nouveau roman* y del postestructuralismo[23].

¿Cuáles son precisamente las características del discurso postmoderno borgesiano?

a)   El discurso literario: juego intertextual deconstruccionista, cita de otros autores de literatura ficcional y de textos ficcionales anónimos (Homero, Shakespeare, Cervantes, Flaubert, Joyce, Valéry, Chesterton, Kafka, *Las 1001 noches*, D'Annunzio, Agatha Christie), tanto de la cultura occidental como de otros sistemas;

---

[22] La modernidad europea puede ser periodizada de la siguiente forma: I. la modernidad joven que va de Baudelaire, pasando por Flaubert y Zola hasta comienzos del siglo XX (1850-ca. 1910/20; II. de Proust, pasando por Kafka, Woolf, Joyce, Dos Passos hasta Faulkner (1910/20-1939); III. de 1955 hasta comienzo de los años 60.

[23] La deuda del *nouveau roman* con Borges es considerable: ya se le conocía en Francia a más tardar de 1955.

b)   El discurso literario ficcional fantástico ("El Aleph", "Tlön, Ubqar, Orbis Tertius", "El Zahir", "La lotería en Babilonia", "El inmortal");
c)   El discurso filosófico, metafísico, teoría de la ciencia lógica (cita y empleo de filósofos, como Lull, Leibniz, Descartés, Berkeley, Hegel, Spengler, Kant);
d)   El discurso teológico (San Agustín y debates sobre la existencia de Dios y de la estructura del mundo);
e)   El discurso religioso/místico ("Los teólogos", "La escritura del dios");
f)   El discurso filológico ("La busca de Averroes", cita de la *Revista de Filología Española* o de la *NRF*, enciclopedias, mapas, etc.);
g)   El discurso genérico: ensayo, análisis literario ("Examen de la obra de Herbert Quain");
h)   El discurso detectivesco ("Abenjacán, el Bojarí muerto en su laberinto", "La espera", "El hombre en el umbral", "El jardín de senderos que se bifurcan", "La muerte y la brújula");
i)   El discurso de aventuras ("El sur", "El fin", "Abenjacán, el Bojarí");
j)   El discurso (pseudo-) realista ("El sur", "El fin");
k)   El discurso (pseudo-) cotidiano (cita de periódicos, revistas);
l)   El metadiscurso ("Pierre Menard, autor del Quijote", "El Aleph", "El inmortal", "La casa de Asterión", "La otra muerte");
m)   El discurso narrativo paródico, humoricidad;
n)   El discurso histórico;

La narración misma se caracteriza como sigue:

a)   Tono científico (mímesis científica, mas aquí como juego: superación del realismo decimonónico que era una mímesis científica más tomada en serio): citas de revistas filológicas, textos y autores existentes y no existentes;
b)   Autor omnisciente;
c)   Fábula consistente con una acción, lugares, tiempos y personajes bien delineados, mas luego deconstrucción, máscara, disolución, difusidad;
d)   Ambigüedad, resistencia a la interpretación;
e)   Alusión, sin solución;
f)   Deconstrucción de lo dicho, constitución de significados y su deconstrucción;
g)   Alusión autobiográfica;
h)   Mezcla absoluta de realidad y ficción, sin implicaciones ontológicas;
i)   Reflexión sobre la escritura y lo narrado;
j)   Pseudolocalismo (pseudoneocostumbrismo/pseudorrealismo);

k) Mito entre historia y lenguaje: semiotización, disgregación, diseminación del mito;

l) Disolución del narrador en tercera persona que se pierde a través de las contradicciones en su discurso, en primera persona: tiene muchas identidades y ninguna, es narrador y personaje a la vez, en relación consigo mismo o disociado;

m) Colectividad y repetición: la disolución del creador y del mito del genio; el texto como origen de la productividad;

n) Lector como activo co-autor: descodificación, deconstrucción de segundo grado.

1.1.1. *La Biblioteca de Babel*

En *La Biblioteca de Babel* se puede demostrar en forma ejemplar algunas de las características mencionadas.

El narrador incita a sus personajes y al lector a una búsqueda de significantes, dentro de la cual la búsqueda misma, el camino a recorrer es lo más importante, ya que si se encuentran significantes éstos permanecen herméticos. El bibliotecario babilónico se encuentra a la búsqueda del catálogo de los catálogos, es decir, no de un significado, sino de un principio de orden de la biblioteca, que es equivalente con el universo, esto es, con el lenguaje. En su búsqueda fracasa el bibliotecario, lo cual equivale en otros cuentos a la imposibilidad de descodificar el secreto que encierra un significado[24].

Borges niega la solución, y si se vislumbra alguna, es ésta tan arbitraria y contra la lógica del lenguaje que se puede prescindir de ella, como p.e. en "Tlön, Uqbar, Orbis Tertius", donde las cadenas sintagmáticas del lenguaje son deconstruidas. Por ejemplo: "no hay una palabra que corresponda a la palabra »luna«, pero hay un verbo que sería en español »lunecer« o »lunar. Surgió la luna sobre el río« se dice »hlör u fang axaxaxas mlö« o sea en su orden: hacia arriba »(upward)« detrás duradero-fluir luneció. (Xul Solar traduce con brevedad: upa tras perfluyue lunó. »Upward, behind the onstreaming it mooned«) [...] No se dice »luna«: se dice »aéreo-claro sobre oscuro-redondo o naranjado-tenue-del cielo«".

Los objetos son creados a través del lenguaje, a través de la fuerza de la fantasía como los hrönir, en "Tlön, Uqbar, Orbis Tertius".

---

[24] P.e. en La escritura del dios. Si se descubre/denomina el enigma, éste no es descifrable como en "El Aleph" o "Undr".

4.1.2 Undr

En *Undr* es la búsqueda mucho más radical aún que en el cuento anterior. Se tematiza el fracaso, la repetición de los mismos, la apocalipsis. Cuando Ulf Sigurdarson después de muchas aventuras regresa al pueblo de los ataúdes para descifrar el secreto por él buscado, le dicen que éste ha sido revelado y se llama *Undr*:

> "Ahora no definimos cada hecho que enciende nuestro canto; lo ciframos en una sola palabra que es La Palabra
> [...]
> Dijo la palabra »Undr«, que quiere decir maravilla.
> [...]
> — Está bien —dijo el otro y tuve que acercarme para oírlo—.
> Me has entendido"[25].

Con lo cual no se descifra nada, sino se mantiene el hermetismo.

4.1.3 Pierre Menard, autor del Quijote

En *Ficciones* (1944), precisamente en "Pierre Menard, autor del Quijote" (1939), J.L. Borges nos descubre la anticipación por analogía entre su discurso y la teoría de la recepción, la lingüística del texto, la semiótica, la deconstrucción, la intertextualidad y el palimpsesto.

La finalidad perseguida por Pierre Menard era la de escribir un segundo *Don Quijote* que estuviese de acuerdo con la época de su momento de producción. Menard no actualiza al héroe en forma recreativa, es decir, transformándolo en un personaje similar en relación con la época contemporánea, o en forma simplista, es decir, poniéndolo en un medio extraño a éste, p.e. en la Wall Street, sino que lo copia letra por letra, línea por línea[26].

Este cuento problematiza el fenómeno de la identidad/similitud y la dife-

---

[25] J.L. Borges, "Undr", en: *El libro de arena* (Alianza) (1975). Madrid [7]1986, pp. 66, 68.

[26] Cf. Alfred J. MacAdam/Flora H. Schiminovich: Appendix II. Latin American Literature and the Postmodern Era, en: Stanley Trachtenberg (Ed.): *The Postmodern Moment. A Handbook of Contemporary Innovation in the Arts*. London 1985, pp. 251-262 y Hans Robert Jauß. *Die Theorie der Rezeption - Rückschau auf ihre unerkannte Vorgeschichte* (Konstanzer Universitätsreden 166). Konstanz 1987, pp. 30ff.

rencia, es una mezcla de ficción y ensayo científico, de ciencia literaria y fantasía.

Al nivel del significante es el texto de Menard idéntico con el de Cervantes, pero a un nivel semántico-pragmático se diferencia plenamente de éste, ya que los sintagmas transpuestos en el tiempo han cambiado sus significados. Nos encontramos no con un palimpsesto semántico (= cambio de lexemas), sino con un palimpsesto pragmático (= permanencia de lexemas, transposición en el tiempo). Como ejemplo da Borges el capítulo I, 9 del *Don Quijote*: "cosa mal.hecha y peor pensada, habiendo y debiendo ser los historiadores puntuales, verdaderos y no nada apasionados, y que ni el interés ni el miedo, el rencor ni la afición, no le hagan torcer el camino de la verdad, cuya madre es la historia, émula del tiempo, depósito de las acciones, testigo de lo pasado, ejemplo y aviso de lo presente, advertencia de lo por venir"[27]. Esta frase que en tiempos de Cervantes —como dice el narrador— era una expresión retórica para el elogio de la historia, adquiere otra cualidad en la época de Menard, que es un contemporáneo de William James, el cual —como sabemos— relativiza en su *Pragmatism* (1907) el concepto metafísico de la verdad, proponiendo la fórmula: *verdadero es aquello que se confirma.*

Desde el siglo XIX adquiere la historia un estatus privilegiado, lo cual vale aún más para el siglo XX: ésta no es solamente una disciplina, que investiga una parte de la realidad, sino que es la fuente para la explicación del comportamiento, y con esto del origen de la vida y de la realidad. Frente a esta concepción se puede explicar —como también asegura el narrador— el fracaso de Flaubert en *Salammbô*, el cual trató de reconstruir el pasado, un propósito que el autor abandonará luego en *Bouvard et Pécuchet.*

Pierre Menard es uno de los textos más representativos del discurso borgesiano en cuanto éste sostiene que la realidad, y con esto nosotros mismos somos resultado del lenguaje, y así declara que la metafísica (¡la ciencia de las últimas razones!) es una rama de la literatura fantástica[28]. El postulado no es ya más *cogito ergo sum*, sino *escribo luego existo.*

Esta actitud es postmoderna, en cuanto Borges no le atribuye a la tradicional oposición entre realidad y ficción una cualidad ontológica. Ambas dimensiones poseen el mismo estatus, lo cual se articulará en la nueva novela a partir de los años 50 en lo '*real maravilloso*' o el '*realismo mágico*' o '*mítico*', como así también en la novela norteamericana de los años '60 en la llamada '*surfiction*'[29].

---

[27] Cervantes: *Don Quijote de la Mancha* (Espasa Calpe). Madrid [10]1975, p. 222.
[28] Tlön, Uqbar, Orbis Tertius, en: *Ficciones* (Emecé/Alianza). Madrid [2]1972, p. 24.
[29] Raymond Federman (Ed.): *Surfiction. Fiction... Now and Tomorrow.* Chicago 1974.

La apocalipsis en el sentido de repetición, de la negación del movimiento lineal, en el sentido de desenmascarar la existencia de la apocalipsis cristiana (Derrida[30]) se manifiesta en que la realidad se descubre como ficción a través de la recurrencia de lo dicho o escrito (= 'Negación de la originalidad, del novismo vs. acentuación de la intertextualidad y deconstrucción'). Para evitar la repetición y nuevas especulaciones de lo escrito, para evitar eso que él mismo ha emprendido, destruye Menard su manuscrito. Esta actitud estético-existencial es retomada y radicalizada por Italo Calvino en *Se una notte d'inverno un viaggiatore*[31]. Borges pone en claro que un texto no se puede entender aislado, sino solamente en relación con otros textos, lo cual pone de manifiesto en sus comentarios sobre Kafka: un autor no necesita conocer a sus antecesores para escribir como lo hace, sino que por el contrario, partiendo de un autor contemporáneo se descubren los pasados[32]. De esta forma se produce una disolución del Yo que pasa a ser una voz colectiva, que se manifiesta solamente en la palabra. Al fin queda solamente el lenguaje, el juego agonal lúdico que se impone y no el Yo (Lyotard[33]). Se pasa del autor como productor, al texto como productor, lo cual implica que todo autor es primeramente un lector, se pasa de la presunta originalidad al palimpsesto.

A pesar de ser J.L. Borges el primer autor postmoderno, su discurso no desenlazó un paradigma, sino, como hemos indicado, éste se constituye en los años '60. Debemos indicar que la obra de Borges se descubre como postmoderna partiendo de una perspectiva retrospectiva, así como Kafka se puede comprender a través de Borges (según este mismo), así se entiende la postmodernidad por medio de Borges, de la misma forma como partiendo de Lyotard y Vattimo, se descubre a Foucault y Derrida.

4.2 *La novela postmoderna latinoamericana*

A continuación quisiéramos, partiendo de las categorías expuestas más arriba, proponer algunas ideas para el trato de la novela latinoamericana desde

---

[30] Jacques Derrida: Point de folie-maintenant l'architecture, en: B. Tschumi (Ed.): *La case vide*. London 1986 y el mismo en: *Psyché. Invention del 'autre*. Paris 1987.

[31] (Einaudi, Torino 1979).

[32] v. J.L. Borges: Kafka y sus precursores (1960), en: *Otras Inquisiciones* (Alianza/Emecé). Buenos Aires/Madrid [5]1985, S. 107ff.; Cf. Eberhard Geisler: *Paradox und Metapher. Zu Borges Kafka-Rezeption*, en: *Romanische Zeitschrift für Literaturgeschichte* ½ (1986) 219-243.

[33] F. Lyotard: *La condition postmoderne*. Paris 1979; *Le Différend*. Paris 1983.

un punto de vista postmoderno. Esta propuesta quiere ser más una motivación que un modelo para reflexionar sobre el fenómeno en cuestión[34].

4.2.1. *La novela del 'metadiscurso, de la intertextualidad, deconstrucción e introspección': J. Cortázar, Rayuela* (1963)

Rayuela es una novela con una estructura particular en cuanto el autor le ofrece al lector tres posibles lecturas[35]. La primera consiste en leer el texto como está impreso, es decir, en forma lineal, sin saltos; en la segunda se propone leer los capítulos 1-56 y dejar los restantes fuera; la tercera, que es recomendada *expressis verbis* por el autor, ofrece un orden determinado de lectura que parte del capítulo 73 y luego se salta al capítulo siguiente, indicado al fin de ca-

---

[34] Algunos críticos partiendo del 'realismo mágico', de la pluralidad y de la estructura abierta de la *nueva novela* tienden a calificar la novela latinoamericana, si no de 1955, por lo menos de 1965 en adelante de postmoderna. Esta tendencia se descubre como un error ya que no todas las novelas del período mencionado tienen las características mencionadas tales como intertextualidad, deconstrucción, pluralidad, juego metatextual, parodia, ironía, humor, coloquialidad, discurso de subcultura, etc. Cuando se sostiene que *Cien años de soledad* es una novela postmoderna porque allí domina el principio del 'realismo mágico', porque existe un narrador omnisciente, una historia coherente, luego tendríamos que denominar también no solamente al *Don Quijote*, sino la Iliada y la *Odisea* como tales. Lo mismo vale para los términos de 'deconstrucción' e 'intertextualidad' que son patrimonio de la literatura desde hace siglos. Gran parte de la *nueva novela* pertenece a lo que hemos llamado 'modernidad tardía', esto es, a aquella novela que va de 1955 a comienzo de los 60, también en Europa, y que en Latinoamérica se extiende hasta los años 70, y que se caracteriza por la renovación, el experimento, la focalización de la historia y su traspaso a la consciencia de los personajes (*stream of consciousnes*), donde se problematiza la mímesis y se trata de encontrar una fórmula lingüística y narrativa propia. En los años 60 se comienza paralelamente a desarrollar la novela postmoderna, que por otra parte no es precisamente equivalente con lo que se está llamando 'novela del postboom'; al respecto v. Alfred J. MacAdam/Flora H. Schiminovich: Appendix II. Latin American Literature un the Postmodern Era, en: Stanley Trachtenberg (Ed.): *The Postmodern Moment. A Handbook of Contemporary Innovation in the Arts.* London 1985, pp. 251-262. En una forma similarmente ecléctica argumenta Brian McHalle: *Postmodernist Fiction.* New York/London 1987, pp. 12-27, el cual califica cualquier cantidad de autores de postmodernos sin darnos los más mínimos criterios clasificatorios; cf. también John Barth (The Literature of Replenishment, en: *The Friday Book: Essays and Other Nonfiction.* New York 1984, pp. 193-206) trata de calificar algunos autores latinoamericanos de postmodernos, lo cual ha sido refutado por O. Paz y Julio Ortega; v. Postmodernisme in Latin America, in: Th. D'haen and H. Bertens (Ed.): *Postmodern Fiction in Europe and the Americas.* Amsterdam/Antwerpen 1988, pp. 193-208.

[35] Capítulos para leer: 1-56 y capítulos prescindibles: 57-121.

da capítulo respectivo, etc. Esta lectura es compleja, pero encierra la clave de la comprensión del texto.

Rayuela se caracteriza también por su ironía, su humor, por su carácter lúdico, como así también por su variedad de discursos, tales como el parodístico, el deconstruccionista, el intertextual (frente a la novela realista histórica, cap. 34), el filosófico, el existencialista, el metalingüístico (con respecto a la teoría de la novela, en especial en la parte III, pero se encuentra prácticamente en toda la novela), y finalmente la representación de la heterogeneidad ('París vs. Buenos Aires').

Fragmentación y diversidad tanto al nivel del discurso como de la segmentación tipográfica de la novela producen una estructura abierta y nómada.

La variedad se concretiza también en los campos tratados, el mítico (Maga), en el del pensamiento y del conocimiento, en el de la teoría de la cultura y filosofía (Oliveira/París), en el del amor y la pasión.

Que *Rayuela* constituye un punto fundamental de cambio en la *nueva novela*, lo había ya hace algún tiempo constatado leo Pollmann[36]:

> Cortázars *Rayuela* [...] führt uns [...] ins Jahr 1963, in dem der Neue Roman Lateinamerikas an einer Wende steht [...], die auch als Ankündigung einer neuen These [...] gewertet werden kann.
> [...]
> Die Struktur von *Rayuela* steht also in der Auseinand-ersetzung mit dem europäischen Denken, mit der Versuchung zur Monokausalität oder auch nur zur gemä igten Vertikalität der Schraube.
> [Cortázar schuf] dieses Werk des strukturellen *Sic et Non*, des so spezifisch lateinamerikanischen *Sowohl als auch*.

4.2.2 La novela de la 'intrahistoria': 1975...

Bajo esta rúbrica contamos con novelas tales como las de Alejo Carpentier *El recurso del método* (1974), García Márquez *El otoño del patriarca*

---

[36] L. Pollmann: *Der Neu Roman in Frankreich und Lateinamerika.* Stuttgart 1968, S. 211-212 u. ff. und 215. Traducción: "*Rayuela* de Cortázar [...] nos conduce al año 1963, en el cual la Nueva Novela latinoamericana se encuentra en un momento de cambio [...], que se puede considerar como una nueva »tesis« [...]. La estructura de *Rayuela* se encuentra en el debate con el pensamiento europeo, con la tentación de la monocausalidad o con la moderada verticalidad del tornillo. [Cortázar creó] la obra del *Sic et non*, de la especificidad latinoamericana de lo *uno y lo otro*". Claro está que Pollmann considera esta novela, y las de este período, como cúlmine de la *nueva novela in sensu strictus* (a diferencia nuestra que la ubicamos desde *El acoso* y *Pédro Páramo*).

(1975), Carlos Fuentes *Terra Nostra* (1976), Roa Bastos *Yo El Supremo* (1977), Vargas Llosa *La guerra del fin del mundo* (1983) y García Márquez *El general en su laberinto* (1989).

Como ejemplo queremos solamente comentar la novela de Roa Bastos *Yo El Supremo* (1977).

La novela se concentra —como sabemos— en el período del dictador Dr. José Gaspar Rodríguez de Francia (1814-1840) como así también en el carácter de este personaje, que se caracteriza por una mezcla bizarra proveniente por una parte de la tradición del enciclopedismo francés del dieciocho (Rousseau, Montesquieu), de la época napoleónica y del romanticismo. Por otra parte, encontramos la mentalidad del autoritarismo patriarcal-feudal de la tradición de los terratenientes latinoamericanos. Esta novela de Roa Bastos no toma partido en pro o contra de la muy discutida y ambigua personalidad del dictador, sino que trata de aclarar la dimensión histórica de este personaje y de este período, que es representativo para la historia general de Latinoamérica hasta nuestros días, a través de una complejísima y diferenciadísima estructura siempre en evolución y cuestionando su propio discurso[37].

El marco general de la comunicación se caracteriza por la relación entre el Supremo y su secretario Policarpo Patiño, que a su vez es su escribano, como así también por la división del Yo del Supremo que se concretiza en una estructura Yo-El, y finalmente por dos editores, un corrector y un compilador.

La novela se puede estructurar partiendo de sus diversos temas en la forma siguiente: 1. 'El Pasquín; 2. Los apuntes, un texto que contiene los diálogos entre el Supremo y Patiño; 3. El cuaderno privado, en el cual el dictador lleva cuenta desde el comienzo de su gobierno —por propio puño y letra— de los gastos públicos, luego agrega —como indica el editor— diversos pensamientos, sucesos y reflexiones, tanto importantes como banales, sobre una gran gama de temas y campos sin un orden determinado. Este escrito es una especie de diario, un lugar de refugio, donde el dictador describe su política y su vida; 4. La circular perpetua que son decretos y dictámenes para los funcionarios es-

---

[37] El punto inmediato de partida de la novela es un pasquín anónimo, en el cual se encuentra escrito un texto con la misma caligrafía y estilo del dictador. En éste se ordena que el cadáver del dictador sea ultrajado públicamente y luego quemado, y que sus aliados políticos deben ser ejecutados. Con respecto a la autoría del pasquín existen varias posibilidades: una es que el autor sea el mismo dictador que emplea el pasquín como pretexto para aniquilar a sus enemigos; la segunda consiste en que el dictador mismo haya escrito el pasquín, mas, que debido a la división de su Yo, no lo sepa; y tercero, el pasquín puede haber sido escrito por sus enemigos como advertencia al dictador.

tatales que se los dicta a Patiño; 5. Las notas, que se encuentran en forma de notas a pie de página, por lo general se encuentran impresas con una letra más pequeña, estando separadas del texto principal, o se encuentran entrelazadas en el texto en forma de observaciones y breves digresiones (en total son 73); 6. Cuaderno bitácora, en el cual se describe en forma fragmentaria el pasado del dictador, y finalmente 7. Otros textos no clasificables que aparecen esporádicamente, muchas veces al borde del texto.

Yo el Supremo se puede considerar partiendo de su renovación lingüística y la forma intertextual del trato ficcional de la historia como una obra magistral y decisiva de la post-nueva novela, respectivamente de la postmodernidad literaria, y de aquéllas escritas en lengua española. El empleo de la intrahistoria, es decir, de la interacción de diversas series codificadas del conocimiento, aquí precisamente de la historia y la ficción, del empleo funcional de estos discursos con la finalidad de aclarar fenómenos radicados en la profundidad del sistema de la cultura que en su superficie aparecen al nivel del conocimiento como hechos irrefutables y en muchos casos contradictorios e inexplicables, el trato de la historia como un todo cultural, como un fenómeno semiótico, la intrahistoria como nueva forma de ver, es un objeto dominante en esta novela. A través de este procedimiento se interpretan por una parte las contradicciones, la pluralidad, las rupturas y la discontinuidad de la historia y de la cultura latinoamericana, en este caso concretizada en la personalidad del dictador y unida al empleo de diversos tipos de discursos y mediadores. Por otra parte se hace accesible la cultura de este continente a un lector ajeno a él.

4.2.3 *La novela del discurso de masas: 1968...*

A este grupo pertenecen novelas tales como de Manuel Puig *La traición de Rita Hayworth* (1968), *Boquitas pintadas* (1969), *The Buenos Aires affair* (1973), *El beso de la mujer araña* (1976), Mario Vargas Llosa *La tía Julia y el escribidor* (1977), Gabriel García Márquez *El amor en los tiempos del cólera* (1987) y Antonio Skármeta *Matchball* (1988).

Como ejemplo quisiéramos comentar la novela de Mario Vargas Llosa *La tía Julia y el escribidor*, que está constituida por diversas "historias" organizadas según el método de series de *radionovelas*.

Al comienzo tienen todas las historias el mismo estatus narrativo, es decir, el lector implícito cree que lo narrado realmente tiene lugar directamente en la ficción. La única diferencia entre las diversas historias radica en el hecho que mientras todas ellas tienen diverso contenido, son narradas por un narrador en tercera persona y su fin permanece abierto con la pregunta del narrador de cómo sería su final, hay otra que siempre retorna con un yo-narrador y que trata de la relación y vida de Mario y la tía Julia.

En el transcurso de la narración el lector se da cuenta que la narración en primera persona constituye el marco narrativo general, y las historias en tercera persona son parte del marco interno, como en *Las 1001 noches*[38], con lo cual tenemos más bien la estructura de una novela corta/cuento que de una novela. Esta estructura corresponde al estatus de las diversas historias que son la consecuencia de las *radionovelas* escritas por el boliviano Pedro Camacho para la Radio Central, es decir, escritas por un personaje que pertenece al marco narrativo general y que es calificado como "escritor decimonónico", con lo cual se establece una referencia con las novelas en episodios que se ponen de moda en los periódicos del siglo XIX.

Mientras a continuación las diversas historias permanecen independientes las unas de las otras, comienzan a desdibujarse los límites entre las historias singulares como resultado de una creciente pérdida de la memoria de Camacho, que se produce por su excesiva y obsesionada cantidad de trabajo. En un comienzo confunde éste los nombres y roles de los personajes pertenecientes a diversas historias, luego confunde las acciones hasta el punto en que Camacho se comienza a preguntar quién es quién. Especialmente evidente es esta situación en el cap. XVI[39]. Esta confusión es percibida por los locutores y auditores del programa (y por el lector), los cuales comienzan a preocuparse por la salud mental de Camacho, mas luego se interpreta la confusión como "un elemento de tensión" premeditado de Camacho y como una muestra más de su inconmensurable talento artístico.

La novela se caracteriza por su carácter fragmentario, por su heterogeneidad y diversidad. Esta introduce como referente, a través de un juego deconstruccionista, intertextual, como así también a través de la ironía y parodia, el género de la *radionovela* y de las mencionadas novelas episódicas, pero los temas de Camacho se diferencian por completo a los de este género, es decir, no tienen ni la cursilería ni el clisé de la novela rosa de radio (a lo Corín Tellado). Los episodios presentan una vasta gama de destinos, de personajes de diversísima proveniencia, que representan el paisaje completo de la sociedad peruana (y latinoamericana): tematiza a la oligarquía, a los intelectuales, a la gente de negocios, a la iglesia, a la pobreza, a la policía, a la gente media, a los

---

[38] El marco general está constituido por cifras impares 1,3,5 etc., y entre éstas se encuentran las *radionovelas*.

[39] Usamos la edición de Seix Barral/Biblioteca de Bolsillo, Barcelona 1984.

futbolistas, a las familias venidas a menos, etc.

La crítica no es aquí tan evidente como en las novelas anteriores de Vargas Llosa, sino que ésta se deja sutilmente en manos del lector implícito: solamente de la historia narrada sin comentario alguno, y sin el recurso a oposiciones binarias, se desprende una crítica social agudísima, sea a través de la descripción descarnada de concepciones morales rígidas hasta lo patológico, sea a través de la descripción de un autoritarismo enfermizo o de la pobreza más cruel y su adjunto, la violencia. Ejemplos serían el incesto entre Richard y su hermana Elianita (cap. II), la violación de una menor de edad y la negación del hecho por el violador que para probar su inocencia se corta el penis (cap. VI), o aquel episodio donde la hermana de Federico Tellez es devorada por ratas gigantescas y la transformación de Tellez en un déspota enfermizo que al final es asesinado por su propia familia (cap. VIII).

Los episodios de Camacho van teniendo crecientemente algo de horroroso y mórbido, la violencia y la eliminación de los personajes va siendo cada vez más monstruosa. De esta forma se deconstruye el modelo tradicional de la *radionovela* y se reemplaza por otro.

Este cambio se manifiesta claramente p.e. en el mencionado episodio del incesto, donde se emplea un discurso típico de la *radionovela*. Richard es la esencia misma de la perfección, proviene de la oligarquía, es por esto rico, un Adonis, un estudiante extraordinario, estupendo deportista y danzarín, un hijo mimado y admirado por toda la familia, un hijo ejemplar, es admirado y amado por todos sus amigos, en una palabra tiene todas aquellas características que se le dan en este tipo de literatura o de *radionovela* a chicos de la clase alta que salen algo de la mediocridad intelectual, que allí por lo general reina, y se les transforman en mito. A su hermana se le adjudican los mismos adjetivos. Mas luego caen en la infelicidad, en un tipo de desgracia que es sancionada por la sociedad.

La base de esta novela está constituida por una reunión de citas, tanto de contenido como formales, de los sistemas novelísticos de los siglos XVIII, XIX y XX, de Laclos, Balzac, Flaubert, Zola y Borges[40], donde los personajes siempre retornan, donde hay personajes que están afectados por "herencias genéticas". La diferencia con los sistemas decimonónicos radica en que Vargas Llosa no analiza la psique de los personajes, sus vitae y pasados como así tampoco sus problemas genéticos.

---

[40] A Balzac se le cita en cap. III, p. 65 y cap. XV, p. 329; a Zola en cap. II, p. 37; a Borges en cap. III, p. 59.

El modelo de Balzac se encuentra solamente como cita, no como sistema de base, p.e. en el cap. X, donde un suave joven, que tiene todas las características del héroe romántico, se radica en una pensión de mala categoría (como la Pensión Vauquer en *Le père Goriot*) en la cual éste desata su pasión hasta allí oculta y en una forma esquizofrénica y con una altísima carga criminal, tal que se transforma en un demonio, al cual se le encierra finalmente en un manicomio: el suave joven acuchilla al dueño de la pensión (que le tiene gran simpatía) mientras duerme, y luego viola o trata de violar a su mujer (esto no queda claro).

También Camacho, el escritor radial, concebido según parámetros del genio romántico, termina parando en el manicomio.

La *Education sentimentale* de Flaubert se encuentra inscrita en la relación entre Mario y Javier (como en la novela de Flaubert entre Frédéric y Deslauriers). Los amigos constatan después de algún tiempo que "han madurado psicológicamente"[41], lo cual es una reminiscencia de esta novela, como también de las observaciones que hace el narrador omnisciente en *Père Goriot* con respecto a Rastignac después de la muerte de Goriot.

La historia de amor entre Mario y su tía Julia es una ironización y casi parodia de *Liaisons dangereuses* (aquí también denominada "*juegos peligrosos*"[42]), en la cual las cartas se reemplazan por el teléfono, y los encuentros siempre acarrean peligro.

El juego metatextual se encuentra en todos aquellos momentos donde el narrador reflexiona sobre los procedimientos narrativos, o allí donde la ficcionalidad es descubierta como tal, y conocidos datos autobiográficos del autor son empleados como juego referencial.

En el cap. II, págs. 64-65 se citan los procedimientos realistas de la organización de los personajes y de la acción, los cuales son descubiertos como una alta mitización de la realidad y por esto como absolutamente carente de legitimación histórica y mucho menos científica. Camacho se basa para la creación de sus episodios radiales en un mapa de la ciudad de Lima, con la finalidad "de describir la vida real". Este objetivo resulta ser una ilusión y sus *radionovelas*, el producto de una imaginación desaforada. Camacho describe en forma arbitraria y sin conocimiento de Lima ni de sus habitantes, a los cuales les atribuye características tanto sociológicas como morales falsas, como constata Ma-

---

[41] Cap. XI, p. 249.
[42] Cap. IX, p. 196.

rio[43]. Con esto no solamente se descubre la ficción como ficción en el juego narrativo, sino que a la vez se tematizan los criterios de selección y de tipización de los personajes en la literatura decimonónica declarándola como un producto de la fantasía, a pesar de su ideología empirista.

Otros procedimientos citados se encuentran en aquellos episodios donde se pasa a lo fantástico, donde las acciones son absolutamente acausal, fragmentarias y sin explicación ninguna. En estos episodios se cita a Borges reflexionando sobre el '*salto cualitativo*', y citando así algunos postulados poetológicos de Vargas Llosa sobre la *nueva novela*[44].

Esta novela es finalmente una descripción de cómo nace una ficción, del proceso creador, mas por un camino opuesto al del *nouveau roman*[45].

---

[43] Cuando Mario protesta contra las clasificaciones contesta Camacho:
> "—No se trata de una clasificación científica sino artística —me informó [...]. No me interesa «toda» la gente que compone cada barrio, sino la más llamativa, la que da a cada sitio su perfume y su color. Si un personaje es ginecólogo debe vivir donde le corresponde y lo mismo si es sargento de la policía.
> Me sometió a un interrogatorio prolijo y divertido (para mí, pues él mantenía su seriedad funeral) sobre la topografía humana de la ciudad y advertí que las cosas que le interesaban más se referían a los extremos: millonarios y mendigos, blancos y negros, santos y criminales"; ibid.: III, pág. 65.

[44] Ibid. cap. III, pág. 58-59.

[45] Lo dicho se manifiesta p.e. cuando se describen las preferencias o los odios que tiene Camacho frente a temas y procedimientos que son una especie de hilo de Ariana en la novela: los argentinos tan odiados por Camacho son siempre presentados como criminales, sucios, ladrones y perversos (esto es producto de su experiencia profesional con argentinos), sus héroes son de una edad ideal de cincuenta años (que es su propia edad) y se parecen físicamente al radionovelista.

REALISMO MAGICO ENTRE LA MODERNIDAD Y LA POSTMODERNIDAD: HACIA UNA REMODELIZACION CULTURAL Y DISCURSIVA DE LA NUEVA NARRATIVA HISPANOAMERICANA

Emil Volek
Arizona State University

Wenn man etwas Bestimmtes tun und er-
reichen will, so muss man sich auch proviso-
rische beStimmte Grenzen setzen. Wer aber
dies nicht will, der ist volkommen wie der, der
nicht eher schwimmen will, bis er's kann. Er ist
ein magischer Idealist, wie es magische Real-
isten gibt. Jener sucht einer Wunderbewegung,
ein Wundersubjekt — dieser ein Wunderob-
jekt, eine Wundergestalt. Beids sin logisches
Krankheiten, Wahnarten, in denen sich aller-
dings das Ideal auf eine doppelte Weise offen-
bart oder spiegelt.[1]

Novalis, *Fragmente*, No. 576, Dresden, 1929, p. 222.

En los siguientes apuntes queremos volver sobre el tema del 'realismo mágico'. Bajo su bandera se suele reunir las obras más importantes de la narrativa hispanoamericana entre los años cuarenta y setenta. Para muchos, este concepto se ha convertido en sinónimo de la "nueva narrativa".[2] Otros lo han aplicado a cualquier obra literaria que mexclara lo que los críticos entendían como "la realidad" y "la fantasía", desde Cervantes en adelante, o hacia atrás [nota del lector: importante, Cervantes en el centro]. En ambas acepciones, se le ha manejado libremente, como una etiqueta aproximada según los intereses más variados y no siempre estéticos. Hacia el comienzo de los años setenta, el realismo mágico era una pasión popular. Algunos intentaron declararlo en

251

bancarrota ideológica o conceptual,[3] otros, ya sin sutilezas académicas, pidieron su muerte a gritos.[4] En fin, no se sabe por qué milagro del **vudú** se salvó del paredón intelectual. El tiempo y el razonable olvido han borrado esas especulaciones ardientes, y de a poco han vuelto a asomar algunas vindicaciones del sincrético concepto puesto en entredicho.[5]

Hoy nos parece particularmente extraño que se tuviera que negar un concepto histórico literario **americano** sólo porque sus presuntos tíos **europeos** pudieran haber guardado en las buhardillas también los íconos de Mussolini o de Stalin o sólo porque la crítica, como de costumbre, lo hubiera manejado mal.[6] Con esta lógica, hablaríamos como los académicos de Lagado, sin lenguaje y, a lo mejor, sin lengua. Además, el abominable **pedigree** del término que se le había armado para justificar su ejecución sumaria sufría de cierta amnesia histórica.

Aunque, debido a sus muchos abusos, este término pueda parecer completamente inútil [nota del lector: subrayado, **inútil**], no podemos olvidarnos de la problemática *real* que está detrás de él, a saber, la literatura hispanoamericana caracterizada por ciertos rasgos y cualidades, que nos incumbe investigar. Replantear la validez del 'realismo mágico' significa examinar la literatura que está representada, bien o mal, por este término. Por supuesto, esta compleja realidad simbólica podría designarse de otra manera y por otro[s] concepto[s]. Si, pese a los anatemas y a los deseos piadosos, el realismo mágico se niega a desaparecer del panorama, es tal vez precisamente por la presión de la literatura que lo sigue reclamando en ausencia de un conocimiento, conceptualización y denominación mejor.

Para que el término de realismo mágico pueda tener algún destino más allá del uso metafórico, hecho del que algunos ya dudan, debe adquirir contornos más precisos. Por supuesto, no puede tratarse de establecer ninguna casilla fija, sea transhistórica o transnacional, sino de construir un modelo flexible, que permita tomar en consideración y conceptualizar también cierta "dispersión" de los hechos; pero siempre un modelo inscrito en un contexto histórico y cultural hispanoamericano y occidental.

La historia del término es harto conocida;[7] pero es inexacta. Su origen no en Roh[8] sino en Novalis y en la literatura romántica le da una perspectiva histórica e ideológica distinta, aunque esto no cambia en nada la vaguedad de su definición.[9] Es sintomático que, en los fragmentos, Novalis se ocupe de la "magia" y del "idealismo mágico", y deje el significado del "realismo mágico" casi en cero, como una mera proyección negativa del otro término [nota del lector: en el realismo mágico, la proyección del "otro" se inscribe hasta en el significado original del concepto].

En cuanto a los protagonistas hispanoamericanos, dudamos que cuando Carpentier escribía el prólogo a *El reino de este mundo* [1949] [10] conociera el ensayo seminal de Borges sobre "El arte narrativo y la magia".[11] Ninguno de ellos se apoya en Roh. Si bien el punto de partida de ambos es la "realidad mágica", en Borges es la descrita por Frazer, mientras que en Carpentier es la de lo maravilloso surrealista y romántico aplicado a la realidad hispanoamericana. No sorprende que los dos proyectos apunten a cosas totalmente distintas.[12]

En cambio, en la crítica, Uslar-Pietri y Portuondo sí parten de Roh. En 1955, Flores canoniza esta línea, donde el "realismo mágico" tiende a confundirse con la literatura fantástica. En 1960, Alegría abre la discusión crítica a partir de Carpentier.[13] En un afán de rectificar el supuesto desplante de Flores, Leal traza un movimiento contradictorio: si bien identifica el realismo mágico con el proyecto carpentieriano, lo redefine a éste en los términos propuestos por Flores.[14] De cualquier forma, ninguno de los proyectos programáticos de los escritores ni las paráfrasis críticas llegan muy lejos.

En vista de este panorama, no tiene gran sentido dejarnos aprisionar por un supuesto significado original, porque el concepto no lo tiene. Si hubiera alguna duda, la nota con que Roh aclara el porqué del subtítulo de su libro es más que elocuente:

> Sobre el título "realismo mágico" no ponemos ningún énfasis particular. Como el niño tenía que obtener un nombre verdadero, y "postexpresionismo" expresa sólo el origen y la relación temporal, añadimos el segundo título cuando el libro ya estaba hacía largo tiempo escrito. Nos pareció, por lo menos, más adecuado que el de "realismo ideal" o "verismo" o "neoclasicismo", que sólo representan una parte de ese movimiento. Bajo "surrealismo" se entiende por el momento otra cosa. Con "mágico" en contraste con "místico" debería expresarse que el misterio **no penetra** en el mundo representado, sino que palpita tras él [lo cual se explicará quizás a lo largo del libro].[15]

Lo que nos proponemos bosquejar aquí es, pues, una revalidación sin cortapisas de un concepto "falso" y "construido" del realismo mágico;[16] un concepto, por decirlo así, fabricado a su imagen no desde las afirmaciones historiográficas o programáticas, sino desde varios contextos culturales, y cuya única justificación estriba en que tenga cierta utilidad instrumental. Se trata de armar un modelo del realismo mágico que nos permita entender mejor la temeraria o culpable realidad sígnica, literaria y extraliteraria, de su mundo referencial.

Comencemos por mirar el concepto mismo [notal del lector: **look and see** de Wittgenstein]: el 'realismo mágico', tal como nos lo encomendó Novalis y la crítica de la pintura postexpresionista alemana, es una denominación bipolar, ya por sí misma metafórica y ambigua, si no sincrética, paradójica y contradictoria. Porque, normalmente — o sea, desde ciertas normas —, "la realidad" y "la magia" se excluyen. En esta dificultad se incurre, en efecto, si se quiere entender el realismo mágico como un hecho de un solo plano, a saber, como un "método", una "actitud", etcétera.[17] En este caso, 'realismo mágico' no puede significar otra cosa que, digamos, "una mezcla de la fantasía y la realidad", donde y cuando quiera que se encuentre en la literatura o fuera de ella.[18] En el mejor de los casos, se sobreentiende una vaga postura epistemológica.[19]

Como esta concepción no aclara nada de específico ni en la literatura ni en la nueva narrativa, los críticos han intentado destacar algunos rasgos específicos, sea temáticos, estilísticos o técnicos en general [nota del lector: los procedimientos], que, según ellos, caracterizan las obras del realismo mágico; [20] pero estas tentativas han resultado poco satisfactorias.

Hay todavía otra importante consecuencia del transvasamiento de un término del dominio de las artes plásticas al de la literatura. La pintura postexpresionista presenta objetos y espacios, seres y enseres domésticos sencillos, cotidianos, pero envueltos en un aura de misterio. Es cierto que de una imagen más sencilla puede inferirse todo un mundo, tal como lo hace, por ejemplo, Heidegger a partir de los zapatos campesinos pintados por Van Gogh.[21] Pero la narrativa y, en particular, la novela hacen significativamente más explícito este modelo del mundo. No pueden no hacerlo[22]. Los "zapatos" serían, cuando más, sólo un "detalle" en un modelo de interacción social. La influencia de Roh sobre las definiciones del realismo mágico tiende a achatar su "realismo" y a borrar su dimensión de modelo del mundo.

Otra serie de equívocos se inaugura cuando se quiere entender el realismo mágico en el sentido de que la magia es "realidad" en algún lugar de este loco planeta. En esta dirección apunta otro término seminal, el de 'lo real maravilloso', invendtado por Carpentier para el Caribe a partir de la mirilla surrealista.[23] Muchos de los intérpretes del autor cubano, menos discretos, nos querían convencer de que ya la mera captación de esa "realidad" en una obra de arte produce de por sí "realismo mágico".[24] En estas interpretaciones, el concepto mismo de 'realidad' se maneja algo [nota del lector: ¿algo?] metafóricamente. Y se olvida también que lo real maravilloso americano, como quiera que se entienda, es sólo una materia prima de la creación artística, que puede ser plasmada de las maneras más diversas, en todos los registros y claves, desde los códigos iluministas y románticos hasta los vanguardistas y los que corresponden al propio "realismo mágico".[25]

Todas estas concepciones que hemos mencionado subsumen el realismo mágico y la literatura que representa en algo más general, o los identifican con alguna otra cosa. En el proceso, hacen abstracción de la estructura individual de las obras artísticas o, aún peor, la desfiguran [nota del lector: esto además del **misreading** cumún y corriente].[26]

Para poder dar una respuesta más matizada, tenemos que analizar el problema desde sus principios [nota del lector: no **principium** sino **principia**]. En las discusiones hasta el momento, la crítica ha dirigido la atención casi exclusivamente hacia el aspecto "mágico" y en su definición ha buscado la clave de la solución. Pero 'realismo mágico' es un término sincrético, bipolar.

Tenemos que prestar igual atención a los dos miembros. Además, ¿qué implicamos cuando hablamos del realismo mágico en el contexto cultural hispanoamericano y occidental?

Vayamos por partes. ¿Qué significa la palabra 'realismo' en el concepto del realismo mágico? Pero esta pregunta está inmediatamente diferida [nota del lector: otra vez Derrida y su musiquita] por otra preliminar: ¿qué es el 'realismo' en el arte? Lo único que está claro es que el realismo no es ninguna "realidad", sea "real" o "mágica", sino que es un concepto estético. Que lo demás ya no es tan sencillo, lo demuestran las incesantes y estériles discusiones sobre las "riberas" y las "modalidades" del realismo y hasta sobre la pertinencia de plantearse este problema. ¿No está acaso todo arte relacionado de tal o cual manera con la realidad? ¿No es acaso todo arte realista? En uno de los primeros trabajos desconstructivistas de la poética contemporánea, Roman Jakobson estableció toda una paradigmática de las posibles posturas frente al realismo y se divirtió con revelar su relatividad histórica e ideológica.[27]

El realismo en el arte se propone modelar "fielmente" su mundo referencial. Ese mundo puede ser, por ejemplo, los zapatos campesinos o todo un complejo mundo social balzaciano o faulkneriano. El primero es sólo un "detalle" en el segundo.

Frederico Engels lo ha expresado de manera clásica en una carta frecuentemente citada, dirigida a una curiosa señorita victoriana, M. Harkness: "Realismo, en mi opinión — escribe —, comprende además de la veracidad de los detalles también una representación verídica de los personajes típicos bajo circunstancias típicas."

En su gran obra, que sigue los avatares de la mimesis a lo largo de más de dos milenios de la cultura occidental, Erich Auerbach amplía en varios puntos el planteo de Engels:

> The serious treatment of everyday reality, the rise of more extensive and socially inferior human groups to the position of subject matter for problematic-existential representation, on the one hand; on the other, the embedding of random persons and events in the general course of contemporary history, the fluid historical background — these, we believe, are the foundations of modern realism.[28]

Es interesante observar hasta qué punto esta visión del realismo moderno está impuesta por el público que es su destinatario. Las clases medias y bajas se convierten en la medida del realismo: estas clases que han luchado por su dignidad social, exigen una representación seria de su vida diaria; infligen al arte su moral pública, victoriana; piden que su progreso hacia la hegemonía política se traduzca en una canonización alegórica en el mero centro de la nueva divinidad moderna, el "curso general de la Historia". El intento de enfocar, con la misma seriedad, las clases aún más bajas, las sociedades y las culturas "marginales", las minorías, es rechazado indignadamente como antirrealista [notal del lector: "naturalista" en el mejor de los casos].

Pero no es nada fácil hacer un modelo de la realidad. Como la "realidad" incluso de un objecto sencillo es infinita, aun el modelo más realista es siempre un tajo y atajo: interpreta, escoge, jerarquiza aspectos y, en efecto, **crea** un simulacro de la realidad, tal y como **se cree** que ésta existe; **es un modelo de un simulacro.** Si el modelo de la realidad es un modelo de un simulacro, el realismo es un acto de fe [not del lector: y también ha tenido sus inquisidores y sus autos de fe]. Y, por ejemplo, "lo real maravilloso americano" no es la realidad americana, tanto menos **la** realidad, sino **uno de sus posibles simulacros.**

En el sentido más abstracto, un modelo propone una "imagen del mundo". Según el simulacro del mundo referencial y la imagen de éste que se quiera dar, el modelo convoca los presupuestos científicos o metafísicos del conocimiento, las leyes naturales o sobrenaturales, los modos de vida social históricos o imaginarios.[29]

Por un lado, el contenido concreto del modelo realista debería variar según la realidad social y cultural que enfoca, porque, en distintas sociedades o períodos históricos, existen distintas normas y expectativas que determinan — prefabrican — lo que puede pasar por "real". Para evitar semejante escándalo de un realismo "ingenuo", el realismo moderno busca un árbitro en la razón científica, que en el mundo moderno ha ocupado el lugar tradicional de la divinidad. Apoyado en tan poderoso aliado, el realismo crítico del siglo XIX se proclama como la ineludible culminación de la Historia y desde este inezpugnable nicho dictamina quién es su legítimo precursor y quién simplemente corrió mal.

En todos sus avatares, la mimesis crea un simulacro de lo "típico", al que hay que entender no con el sentido de 'lo costumbrista' que esta palabra tiene en el contexto hispánico, sino como **lo representativo desde el punto de vista de la "máquina" social.** El realismo decimonónico pide un método científico para determinarlo. Como la sociología y la estadística no arrojan sino sólo precisamente el promedio gris, la triste mediocridad, la crítica pone en movimiento la ideología de la modernidad iluminista para salvar esta dificultad, haciendo surgir toda una teología en torno al héroe, conflicto y ambiente "típicos".

Entre las vicisitudes del modelo, el simulacro de la realidad referencial y la teología de lo "típico", la literatura que quiere ser una imagen fiel de la sociedad, inventa toda una "sociedad" según la mejor tradición literaria. En lugar de la realidad, se quedan sólo ciertos indicios convencionales que, bien o mal, hacen el "efecto de realidad".[30]

Lo "típico", la seriedad y el ejemplarismo pedagógico despiden del realismo decimonónico todo humor, juego y erotismo. Detrás de la cátedra narrativa se sienta el omnisciente maestro iluminado, quien da vueltas a las grandes alegorías onto-teológicas del proyecto moderno. Y al alumno, con el palo.

En la cresta de su poder, el realismo, por creer ser infaliblemente el más próximo a la realidad, quería ser también la medida de las otras modalidades de la representación. Esta ilusión no duró mucho. En el dominio social y de las realidades simbólicas, la ciencia seguía siendo, cuando más, conjetural. Y su propio desarrollo desigual en distintos dominios específicos contribuyó a romper la ilusión de poseer una imagen global, equilibrada, totalizadora, de la sociedad. El realismo, siempre a la corrida detrás de los últimos suspiros científicos, se fragmentó en "realismos". Ultimamente, el modelo realista del mundo ha sido degradado a sólo uno entre los "mundos posibles".[31]

La imagen del mundo constituye el nivel más abstracto del modelo literario. Las investigaciones lógicas de los "mundos posibles" son lindas y orondas, pero de por sí aclaran poco: mientras se limitan a trasvasar la lógica modal al terreno del arte, saltan los niveles mediatizadores (el lenguaje y los sistemas modelizantes secundarios como, por ejemplo, la narración), los elementos constructivos (los "detalles" y los indicios de la realidad) y la dinámica histórica de los contextos culturales. Con todos estos otros elementos, el modelo se complica aún más, se hace **sincrético, dinámico** y **relativo**. En fin, ¿qué otra cosa puede ser frente a la infinita realidad en devenir?

El estructuralismo intentó homologar los distintos niveles, sometiéndolos a los rigores de la limitada lucidez de los modelos linguísticos. Los resultados eran tan penetrantes como simplificadores, porque no sólo el mecanismo del lenguaje se proyecta sobre los otros niveles; también éstos impregnan el discurso y dejan en él inscritas sus señales. El discurso, sea literario o no literario, no es simplemente el lenguaje objeto de la lingüística sino ya un complejo **metalenguaje sincrético**.[32]

Dejamos de lado la problematicidad introducida por el lenguaje (todo el escándalo de la "crisis del lenguaje"), porque rebasa los límites de este resumen; sólo notamos su presencia, porque es una parte importante del contexto cultural moderno. La narratividad, como sistema modelizante secundario del discurso, fue demarcada tradicionalmente por la "historia narrativa" (**story, récit**).[33] Para Viktor Shklovski, la historia narrativa está definida por el planteamiento de un conflicto y por su resolución.[34] Este proceso narrativo se asemeja llamativamente a la estructura de la mediación mítica entre los contrarios, tal como la bosqueja Claude Lévi-Strauss en su ensayo seminal sobre la estructura de los mitos.[35]

Sin embargo, la mediación mítica también provee la historia narrativa tradicional con una apariencia de totalización y de un cierre ineludible. La experimentación en la narrativa moderna ha puesto en tela de juicio estos aspectos y la crítica postmoderna ha señalado tanto su carácter ilusorio y convencional, como también su índole peligrosa: la totalización y el totalitarismo son sólo distintos productos de la misma legitimación mítica.[36]

Un modelo del realismo en el arte tiene que operar con varios niveles ontológicos y epistemológicos heterogéneos. Por un lado está el simulacro del

mundo representado y sus indicios: primero, tenemos los elementos consti-
tuyentes, ambientales, individuales, y su veracidad de detalle, o sea, los
elementos omnipresentes, pero que no son suficientes para la definición
completa del realismo; segundo, tenemos el modelado de la interacción social
constituido por los personajes, conflictos y ambientes "típicos", o sea, que crean
el simulacro de la "representatividad"; tercero, tenemos los supuestos epistemológicos más generales, las normas y las instituciones sociales que determinan el "horizonte de la expectación" frente a lo real. Por otro lado, están los
recursos utilizados para la mediación: el lenguaje y los sistemas modelizantes
secundarios. Ninguno de estos elementos puede caracterizar el realismo por
sí solo. Pero hay más: todos estos componentes se convierten en abstracciones ininteligibles fuera de su contexto cultural.[37]

Este planteo del realismo no resuelve tampoco [nota del lector: no
resuelve] los mencionados problemas del relativismo histórico e ideológico de
la percepción de ciertas realidades representadas o de ciertos medios de su
representación como realistas o no realistas; pero permite tratarlos con más
sentido, inscribiéndolos entre el modelo sincrético general y el contexto cultural
histórico.

El contexto cultural del "realismo mágico" hispanoamericano es la literatura postrealista occidental, moderna y postmoderna.[38] El enfoque de las
culturas que, desde el punto vista de los centros hegemónicos, parecen ser
"marginales", sean culturas "primigenias" o simplemente "retrasadas", produce
un conflicto en la imagen del mundo: los supuestos epistemológicos válidos en
esas culturas son incongruentes con los principios científicos racionalistas de
la civilización occidental. El realismo latente, por ejemplo, la plasmación "seria"
de la vida cotidiana indígena, lleva al absurdo. Pero lo que es "absurdo" desde
un punto de vista, es "realidad" (simulacro de la realidad, dijimos) desde el otro.
Lo interesante es que en la "fe", postulada por Carpentier para la captación de
la "realidad maravillosa",[39] confluyen no sólo una postura realista "ingenua",
como opuesta al descreimiento surrealista y a la razón científica en general, sino
también la seriedad, con todo lo que implica de ciencia y erudición y de las
mencionadas exclusiones. Por ejemplo, su realismo mágico permite los actos
carnales, pero descarta el erotismo [nota del lector: lo descarna].

¿Cuáles son las "circunstancias típicas" en las novelas del realismo
mágico? Es toda una gama de **conflictos sociales**. La problemática social no
abarca sólo las viejas cuestiones de explotación, de desigualdad social y racial,
de "violencia", o sea, los temas característicos del realismo tradicional, sino
también los problemas más contemporáneos, o sea, existenciales, éticos y
epistemológicos, en la medida en que éstos tienen alcance intersubjetivo. Y lo
típico abarca también otras cuestiones importantes para la idiosincrasia de las
culturas americanas, tales como la relación del hombre americano y la Historia
(occidental, moderna), el choque de dos mundos, el mágico y el racionalista,

"moderno", etcétera.

En otras palabras, el polo "realista" de las novelas del realismo mágico no lo constituye simplemente el hecho de que la magia sea realidad, o simulacro de la realidad, en algún rincón del planeta, sino también **conflicto social representativo**.[40] De ahí que el tema de estas obras no es, digamos, "el mundo espiritual indígena", sino "el mundo espiritual indígena en la lucha contra las fuerzas de la explotación, el racionalismo y la modernidad" (ésta podría ser la "fórmula" temática de *Hombres de maíz*). Miguel Angel Asturias lo ha expresado con admirable claridad en una entrevista con Claude Couffon:

> Mon réalisme est magique parce qu'il relève un peu du rêve tel que le concevaient les surréalistes. Tel que le concevaient aussi les Mayas dans leurs textes sacrés. En lisant ces derniers, je me suis rendu compte qu'il existe un réalité palpable sur laquelle se greffe une autre réalité, créée par l'imagination, et qui s'enveloppe de tant de détails qu'elle devient aussi 'réelle' que l'autre. **Toute mon oeuvre se développe entre ces deux réalités: l'une sociale, politique, populaire,** avec des personnages qui parlent comme parle le peuple guatémaltèque; **l'autre, imaginative, qui les enferme dans une sorte d'ambiance et de paysage de songe.**[41]

Ahora bien: ¿qué significa lo 'mágico' en el realismo mágico? Funciona como un enfoque particular, como una perspectiva de la desfamiliarización (**ostranenie**), en la terminología de Shklovski,[42] de la mencionada problemática "realista". Esta perspectiva mágica tiene distintos componentes importantes.

En primer lugar, como material que informa la perspectiva de la desfamiliarización se escoge el mundo de las culturas primigenias de los indígenas y de los negros, concretamente, el simulacro surrealista o vanguardista de su mágica "realidad". Una variante menos etnocéntrica es el enfoque del mundo y de la cultura criolla popular, del campo y de la ciudad, surgida del barroco católico y del sincretismo colonial. Curiosamente, la modalidad etnocéntrica está más cargada de la herencia realista tradicional: la mencionada seriedad y las exclusiones que implica. Para la explosión de humor, juego y erotismo hay que esperar hasta el gran carnaval de la cultura criolla popular en *Cien años de soledad*.

La explotación del mundo de las culturas primigenias ha sido el rasgo más saliente [nota del lector: vendible] del realismo mágico hispanoamericano, porque parece ser el más original y típico — en el sentido costumbrista — del continente. Pero, es "original" y "típico", ¿para quién? Irónicamente, la visión de la realidad hispanoamericana como "mágica" surge no sólo bajo la tutela de las vanguardias europeas [nota del lector: y a la sombra de los cafés parisinos], sino que está dirigida a un público extraño: la clase media de las ciudades y el lector occidental en general. En este sentido, el realismo mágico latinoamericano es un artículo de exportación cultural [nota del lector: ya lo dije]. Además, se dirige a un consumidor seguro: a la Europa siempre ávida de las maravillas americanas.

En Europa occidental, que siguió [nota del lector: y sigue] como el árbitro supremo de la "bolsa de valores" en las letras hispanoamericanas, refleja el voto popular que fueran Asturias y García Márquez quienes ganaran el premio Nobel en la narrativa, mientras que un Borges o Cortázar se quedaron como eternos aspirantes. Siguiendo su largo ensueño con el "Nuevo Mundo", Europa prefirió — y prefiere [nota del lector: me imita] — los "indios" a sus contemporáneos urbanos, que le resultan demasiado semejantes.

Sólo esta "deslectura" secular, asumida a veces por los propios americanos, que convierte América latina en un **kitsch** para consumo doméstico, puede tal vez explicar por qué las formidables sátiras filosóficas y visionarias de un Borges fueron achatadas e interpretadas como un inocuo juego de un "genio solitario" y de su fantasía, y por qué pudieron quedar eclipsadas por las más simples "historias de la abuelita", que, dentro del mencionado horizonte de expectación, parecían mucho "más realistas" y afines a la supuesta "esencia" o "idiosincrasia" hispanoamericana.

Dentro de una perspectiva más americanista, sin embargo, el enfoque sobre el mágico mundo de las culturas primigenias o sobre la cultura popular criolla del campo y de la ciudad implica también un importante **viraje valorativo**: para el escritor, la mirada del indio, del negro o del hombre de pueblo [nota del lector: ¿y la mujer?] es **equivalente** y no inferior al hombre de la civilización "avanzada", "moderna". En Arguedas, la reivindicación emancipadora del indio está aún más complicada por su propio bilingüismo y por el plurilinguismo peruano.

Por un lado, esta emancipación artística tiene connotaciones democráticas y aun revolucionarias; por otro lado, participa de un movimiento histórico más amplio. El realismo mágico, que entra tan perfectamente en el horizonte de la expectación europea, es, paradójicamente, también una manifestación del desmoronamiento del eurocentrismo y es otro signo del actual malestar de la modernidad occidental. En esta situación y en la transfiguración artística particular, lo premoderno se ha convertido en uno de los primeros atisbos de la postmodernidad en Hispanoamérica.

En segundo lugar, el mundo mágico en cuanto material de la plasmación artística entra en simbiosis con las tendencias de la narrativa moderna y con los principios estéticos antimiméticos de la "vanguardia histórica". También por este lado, el realismo mágico se inscribe en la Historia cultural. Por una parte, el mito autóctono lleva a cabo la tendencia de la narrativa moderna (desde Thomas Mann hasta Joyce) a interpretar la cotidianeidad contemporánea en términos de un mito subyacente, porque en las sociedades primigenias la cosmovisión mítica *es* la realidad cotidiana. Por otra parte, el mito, en cualquier forma, permite naturalizar el cuestionamiento de los códigos y contratos miméticos históricos, legados por la novela realista decimonónica.

El mito subyacente convierte las obras en complejas, densas y totalizadoras estructuras simbólicas. Por un lado, el texto del mito, como lo ha señalado Lévi-Strauss, sirve como un mediador en las situaciones humanas y sociales elementales: produce un simulacro de mediación, de resolución, de superación de los contrarios. Con su movimiento tripartito, el mito ensaya el vals de la futura dialéctica hegeliana y ofrece también, a su manera, un simulacro de la totalización. Por otro lado, las "palabras" (los mitemas) y la sintaxis narrativa (el **mythos**) del texto mitico son **los universales** de la narración. De manera que el **mythos**, la forma narrativa del mito, subyace, según Aristóteles, a cualquier narración con historia (**story, récit**). Por este carácter doblemente elemental, el mito es potencialmente **universal**.

El aspecto mítico tiene todavía otra importante implicación para el discurso narrativo. Frente a las alegorías modernistas y postmodernistas, que figuran como unas islas estáticas en medio de la corriente discursiva, el mito subyacente permea el discurso de cabo a rabo y nos obliga a leerlo simultáneamente sobre varios niveles del significado. La interpretación de la cotidianeidad moderna por un arcaico texto mítico subyacente produce una tensión peculiar entre los niveles del significado y, así, desfamiliariza los dos polos.

Debido a la universalidad y a la desfamiliarización, la cosmovisión mítica indígena, negra o criolla se "desfolkloriza". Carpentier plantea agudamente este problema cuando declara en una oportunidad: "De lo que he tratado en mi obra es de **des-exotizar** la literatura latinoamericana sin cortarle sus raíces. He intentado encontrar en ella los elementos universales."[43] De esta manera, se evita el exceso del localismo costumbrista y del exotismo superficial [nota del lector: el Oriente modernista], pero se retiene lo suficiente como para abrir el apetito del público ávido de las Indias.

Por este lado de la totalización mítica y de las grandes proyecciones simbólico-míticas, el realismo mágico participa del grandioso proyecto moderno de la "novela totalizadora", que fue abrazado y protagonizado, por ejemplo, por Mario Vargas Llosa en otras corrientes de la "nueva narrativa", ya sin el andamiaje de la gran proyección simbólico-mítica.

Finalmente, tanto lo real como lo mágico son mediatizados por las técnicas narrativas más o menos experimentales. En este aspecto, el realismo mágico hispanoamericano es un "compañero de viaje" de las distintas fases de la experimentación vanguardista y postvanguardista, que se han manifestado en la narrativa europea e hispanoamericano desde los años cuarenta hasta la actualidad. El realismo mágico lleva la técnica experimental, el "estilo internacional", como una marca de su modernidad.

En total, hemos separado cuatro elementos fundamentales del modelo del realismo mágico hispanoamericano por armar: 1. la gama tradicional y moderna de los conflictos sociales (el "realismo"); 2. los simulacros de las culturas indígenas, negras y populares criollas como el material preformado de la perspectiva mágica ("lo real maravilloso"); 3. la proyección simbólico-mítica

universal, totalizadora, de la cotidianeidad; y 4. las nuevas técnicas experimentales. En todos estos aspectos, el realismo mágico está anclado en las distintas
facetas de la Historia cultural contemporánea y coparticipa de las distintas
corrientes de la "nueva narrativa".

Armemos el modelo. Los cuatro elementos mencionados crean en
conjunto la primera modalidad, la más fuerte y completa, del realismo mágico.
Si se pudiera quitar el rasgo valorativo del término, y bajo el riesgo de
linchamiento por los expertos críticos, diríamos que, en este museo arquetípico
de la plenitud, el realismo mágico bordea el **kitsch**.[44] *Al filo del agua, Hombres
de maíz, El reino de este mundo, Pedro Páramo, Los ríos profundos, Cien años
de soledad y José Trigo* representan cabalmente esta primera modalidad.

La pandilla de los cuatro elementos principales del realismo mágico no se
encuentra siempre en conjunto, ni con la misma fisonomía ni intensidad. Si
analizamos la gama de **neutralización** de los aspectos individuales, empiezan
a configurarse otras modalidades del realismo mágico. Así, por ejemplo, una
segunda modalidad aparece cuando en vez de un mundo mágico o folklórico
completo se dan cabida sólo algunos elementos de la mitología indígena (como
en *La región más transparente* o en *La muerte de Artemio Cruz*, o en "La noche
boca arriba") o sólo un clima mítico del continente (como en *Los pasos
perdidos*).

La neutralización total de este aspecto nos lleva a los gemelos y los
hermanos más urbanos del realismo mágico: a lo que podríamos llamar
realismo simbólico más bien que 'realismo fantástico', porque esta corriente
está apoyada sobre la proyección simbólico-mítica universal y totalizadora de
la cotidianeidad y no simplemente en algunos detalles realistas o fantásticos de
los objetos; o nos conduce directamente a la literatura *fantástica* (en el caso de
que se neutralice también el conflicto social "realista"). El "realismo mágico"
según Angel Flores, apoyado precisamente sobre los *detalles* realistas tal como
se dan en la pintura postexpresionista, se extiende precisamente entre el
realismo simbólico y la literatura fantástica. Representan el realismo simbólico
*El señor presidente, El acoso, El astillero, Sobre héroes y tumbas, El siglo de
las luces, 62. Modelo para armar, Cambio de piel, El obsceno pájaro de la noche*
y los hermosos dinosaurios de la modernidad como *Rayuela, Paradiso* o *Terra
nostra*, donde, a su vez, el realismo simbólico roza su brillosa plenitud de *kitsch*;
la narrativa fantástica la representan, a título de ejemplo, *Bestiario, Las armas
secretas, Aura* o *Concierto barrocco*.

De manera semejante, si se llega a neutralizar por completo la gran
proyección simbólico-mítica de la cotidianeidad, también salimos fuera de los
límites del realismo mágico. Las obras como *Hijo de ladrón, Coronación, La
ciudad y los perros* o *La Casa Verde* son, por decirlo así, sólo realistas, aunque
no en el sentido del realismo tradicional. Crean lo que podríamos llamar la línea
de realismo traditional. Crean lo que podríamos llamar la línea de *realismo
policromático*. En cambio, las obras como *Tres tristes tigres, De donde son los*

cantantes o *La guaracha del Macho Camacho*, aunque exploran los mundos de la cultura popular o la herencia de las culturas caribeñas, crean todavía otra línea, la de la *novela del lenguaje*. Y la neutralización de todos los elementos principales menos el discurso experimental lleva a *Cobra* y a la contrapartida hispánica del *nouveau nouveau roman* francés. Otras corrientes todavía han surgido en el límite entre la ficción y el documento.[45]

Por supuesto, cabe subrayar, por si acaso, que la pertenencia de una obra a tal o cual corriente de la "nueva narrativa" o a tal o cual modalidad del realismo mágico no dice de antemano nada acerca de su valor artístico. Y también que las corrientes de la nueva narrativa, que hemos enumerado sin ninguna pretensión de agotar su fenomenología, son como líneas de fuerza y que las obras individuales se mueven incluso entre varias de ellas. Consideremos a título de ejemplo, los mencionados dinosaurios del realismo simbólico moderno: el uso libre, irónico, desfamiliarizador, del dialecto porteño y los alardes de discurso experimental hacen de *Rayuela* también la primera novela del lenguaje, la primera lengüeta de la postmodernidad. O *Paradiso*, donde encontramos sorprendentes elementos de la cultura criolla popular, franquea también la frontera de los géneros literarios, convirtiéndose en un largo poema en prosa, gongorino y erótico por lo demás. Sólo *Terra nostra* parece que todavía busca la historia literaria que la absuelva.

Nuestro modelo de realismo mágico, que proponemos con un retraso no completamente debido a nuestra voluntad,[46] representata más bien un conjunto de coordenadas elementales de un mapa virtual que nos permite cartografiar los viajes imaginarios que hacen los escritores en cada obra particular. Y no sólo los viajes de las obras que se inscriben en la órbita del realismo mágico, sino que este modelo nos permite ver más diferenciadamente la propia nueva narrativa, más allá de las generaciones, la temática o los procedimientos llamativos con los cuales se ha querido encauzar [nota del lector: y encausar] sus múltiples corrientes.

NOTAS

1   "Cuando uno quiere hacer y alcanzar algo determinado, uno tiene que ponerse también ciertos límites provisorios. Quien no quiere hacerlo, se porta exactamente como quien no quiere nadar hasta que no sepa. Es un idealista mágico, tal como hay realistas mágicos. Aquél busca un movimiento, un sujeto maravilloso; éste, un objeto maravilloso, una figura maravillosa. Ambas actitudes son enfermedades lógicas, tipos de ilusión, en las que, no obstante, se revela o se refleja el ideal de una manera doble."

2   A partir del artículo pionero de A. Flores, "Magical realism in Spanish American fiction", *Hispania* No. 2(1955):187-92.

3   Emir Rodríguez Monegal, "Realismo mágico versus literatura fantástica: Un diálogo de sordos" y Roberto González-Echevarría, "Carpentier y el realismo mágico", en *Otros mundos, otros fuegos: Fantasía y realismo mágico en Iberoamérica*, ed. Donald Yates (East Lansing: Michigan State University, 1975), respectivamente. La ponencia de González-Echeverría desarrolla también este enfoque o desenfoque en su ensayo "Isla a su vuelo fugitiva: Carpentier y el realismo mágico", *Revista Iberoamericana* No. 86(1974):9-63.

4   Véase el testimonio de Lorraine Ben-Ur, "El realismo mágico en la crítica hispanoamericana", *Journal of Spanish Studies: Twentieth Century* 4.3(1976):158. En van argumentaba Enrique Anderson Imbert que "solamente a un fanático se le antojaría fijar en el pasado la significación de una palabra que todavía está muy viva en el presente", porque era el tiempo de los fanáticos. Véase su "Literatura fantástica, realismo mágico y lo real maravilloso", en *Otros mundos*, p. 41.

5   El realismo mágico resucita por el lado de "lo real maravilloso" americano. Inicia esta vuelta Jaime Alazraki, "Para una revalidación del concepto realismo mágico en la literatura hispanoamericana", en J. Alazraki et al., *Homenaje a Andrés Iduarte* (Clear Creek, Ind.: The American Hispanist, 1976), pp. 9-19. Irlemar Chiampi lo pasa por el crisol de (casi) todos los conceptos de la poética moderna, en su *Realismo maravilhoso: Forma e ideologia no romance hispano-americano* (Sao Paulo: Editora Perspectiva, 1980). Véase también Walter Mignolo, "El misterio de la ficción fantástica y del realismo maravilloso", en su *Teoría del texto e interpretación de textos* (México: UNAM, 1986), esp. pp. 152.-60.

6   Rodríguez Monegal acusa al realismo mágico del pecado de ser "reaccionario" porque los futuristas italianos reaccionaron y fueron reaccionarios y porque también "lo real maravilloso" de Carpentier fue una reacción, al surrealismo. *Op. cit.*, p. 31. En esta lógica, la 'reacción' en el sentido político y la 'reacción' como 'una acción en contra de' se funden maravillosamente.

7   El resumen más reciente se encuentra en Antonio Planells, "La polémica sobre el realismo mágico en Hispanoamérica", *Revista Interamericana de Bibliografía* 37.4(1987):517-29.

8   Realismo mágico constituye el subtítulo del libro de Franz Roh, *Nach expression-ismus: Magischer Realismus. Probleme der neuesten europaischen Malerei* (Leipzig, 1925).

9   Si el fallecido maestro uruguayo hubiera sabido que el término viene de uno de los escritores predilectos de Borges, tal vez contaríamos con una herejía literaria menos.

10   El prólogo fue recogido, bajo el título "De lo real maravilloso americano" y con algunas páginas introductorias [nota del lector: omisibles] que los sitúan en el contexto mundial, en sus *Tientos y diferencias* (La Habana: UNEAC, 1966), pp. 85-99.

11   *Discusión* (1932; Buenos Aires: Emecé, 1964), pp. 81-91.

12 Véase nuestro libro *Cuatro claves para la modernidad: Análisis semiótico de textos hispánicos. Aleixandre, Borges, Carpentier, Cabrera Infante* (Madrid: Gredos, 1984), esp. pp. 90-92 y 127-28.

13 Fernando Alegría, "Alejo Carpentier: Realismo mágico", *Humanitas* (Univ. de Nuevo León) No. 1(1960):345-72.

14 "El realismo mágico en la literatura hispanoamericana", *Cuadernos Americanos* No. 4(1967):230-35. Por ejemplo, Leal ni siquiera menciona la realidad *americana*; y sus ejemplos de "realismo mágico" son, entre otros, *Las armas secretas* de Cortázar y *Viaje a la semilla* de Carpentier e incluyen la novela mundonovista *Cantaclaro* de Gallegos (p. 33 y s.).

15 "Auf den Titel 'Magischer Realismus' legen wir keinen besonderen Wert. Da das Kind einen wirklichen Namen haben musste und 'Nachexpressionismus' nur Abstammung und zeitliche Beziehung ausdrückt, fügten wir, nachdem das Buch langst geschrieben war, jenen zweiten hinzu. Er erschien uns wenigstens treffender als 'idealer Realismus' oder als 'Verismus' und 'Neuklassizismus', welche je nur einen Teil der Bewegung darstellen. Unter 'surrealismus' versteht man vorläufig etwas anderes. Mit 'magisch' im Gegensatz zu 'mystisch' sollte ausgedrückt sein, dass Geheimnis nicht in die dargestellte Welt *eingeht*, sondern sich hinter ihr zurückhalt (was sich im Verlauf erklären mag)."

16 Para una propuesta de una poética decididamente constructivista véase nuestro *Metaestructuralismo: Poética moderna, semiótica narrativa y filosofía de las ciencias sociales* (Madrid: Fundamentos, 1986).

17 V.N. Kuteishchikova lo definió como 'método', en analogía con la teoría soviética del "realismo", en "El continente donde se encuentran todas las épocas", *Voprosy literatury* (Moscú) No. 4(1972):79; como 'actitud ante la realidad', Luis Leal, *op. cit.*, p. 232; como 'postura filosófico-literaria', A. Valbuena Briones, en "Una cala en el realismo mágico", *Cuadernos Americanos* No. 5(1969):233.

18 En este sentido amplio del término, Seymour Menton lo ha investigado en la pintura, en su *Magic Realism Rediscovered, 1918-1981* (London and Toronto: Associated University Presses, 1983). Más recientemente, también Fredric Jameson descubrió el realismo mágico e intentó aplicarlo al cine latinoamericano y polaco de los años ochenta, "On magic realism in film", *Critical Inquiry* 12.2(1986):301-25.

19 En esta línea hay que situar el trabajo de Floyd Merrell, "The ideal world in search of its reference: An inquiry into the underlying nature of magical realism", *Chasqui* 4.2(1975):5-17.

20 Así, por ejemplo, Valbuena Briones define el 'realismo mágico' como una "corriente estilística" (op. cit., p. 236); o A. Flores intenta delimitar ciertos rasgos representativos de la técnica (op. cit., pp. 189-92). El libro de Irlemar Chiampi representa una tentativa más comprehensiva.

21   En su trabajo seminal "Der Ursprung des Kunstwerkes", en *Holzwege* (1950; Frankfurt am Main: Vittorio Klostermann, 1964).

22   En la novela de Milan Kundera *Zivot je jinde* (La vida está en otra parte; Toronto: 68 Publishers, 1979; tr. *Life is Elsewhere*, New York: Knopf, 1974) se discute esta diferencia entre la lírica y la novela y sus implicaciones para la literatura conformista escrita bajo los regímenes totalitarios: la lírica puede tener vitalidad, mientras que la novela nace muerta.

23   En el mencionado prólogo a *El reino de este mundo* (1949). Emir Rodríguez Monegal ha estudiado este tema sobre el trasfondo del movimiento surrealista en "Alejo Carpentier: Lo real y lo maravilloso en *El reino de este mundo*", *Revista Iberoamericana* Nos. 76-77(1971):619-49.

24   Enrique Anderson Imbert, él mismo un excelente practicante del arte y de la literatura fantástica, señala las falacias de esta actitud, *op. cit.*, pp. 41-42,43.

25   Por ejemplo, un iluminista hablaría de la "barbarie" y de "vanas supersticiones"; el romántico, en cambio, cantaría al "buen salvaje", etc.

26   Por ejemplo, el mencionado prólogo a *El reino* terminó por distorsionar la visión crítica de una buena parte de la obra narrativa de Carpentier, porque la simple identificación con lo real maravilloso dejaba fuera sus características vanguardistas y neovanguardistas. En nuestra lectura de *Los pasos perdidos*, *Cuatro claves*, pp. 127-53, tratamos de poner el dedo en la llaga.

27   En el conocido ensayo "Sobre el realismo en el arte". También René Wellek ha estudiado el problema desde el punto histórico literario, véase "The concept of realism in literary scholarship", en su libro *Concepts of Criticism* (New Haven: Yale UP, 1965), pp. 222-55.

28   *Mimesis: The Representation of Reality in Western Literature* (1946; Princeton: New Jersey, 1974), p. 491.

29   Para un bosquejo parcial y preliminar de estas modalidades, véase Tzvetan Todorov, *Introduction á la littérature fantastique* (París: Seuil, 1970).

30   Roland Barthes se ha ocupado de este aspecto en "L'effet de réel", *Communications* No. 11(1968):84-89 (Trad. en T. Todorov, *French Literary Theory Today: A Reader* (Cambridge: Cambridge UP, 1982), pp. 11-17.

31   Para un resumen de estas investigaciones véase Thomas Pavel, *Fictional Worlds* (Cambridge: Harvard UP, 1986).

32   El círculo de Bajtin ha dado la primera formulación de este problema. En el terreno literario, el propio Mijail Bajtin ha estudiado la pluralidad del discurso con motivo de la relación de los discursos; en la lingüística, V.N. Voloshinov lo ha planteado con motivo

del discurso indirecto, véase *Problemas de la creación de Dostoievski* (1929) y *Marxismo y la filosofía del lenguaje* (1929; trad. *Marxism and the Philosophy of Language*, New York: Seminar Press, 1973), respectivamente. En la segunda edición, ampliada, de su libro (1963), Bajtin agrega unas consideraciones metodológicas, donde plantea la necesidad de un estudio metalingüístico del discurso, véase *Problems of Dostoevsky's Poetics* (Minneapolis: University of Minnesota Press, 1984), pp. 181-85.

33   El resumen de este aspecto se basa en una investigación más matizada, desarrollada en los capítulos centrales de *Metaestructuralismo*, pp. 129-89. Una confrontación de los enfoques estructuralistas y postestructuralistas se plantea en "Narrative, myth, history, and other f(r)ictions: The story from a metastructuralist point of view" (en preparación).

34   "La construcción del relato y de la novela", en *O teorii prozy* (Moscú: Federatsia, 1929), p. 71.

35   "La structure des mythes", *Anthropologie structurale* (París: Plon, 1958), p. 252s.

36   Jean-François Lyotard, *La Condition post-moderne* (París: Minuit, 1979).

37   Por eso fallan los catálogos de los "procedimientos realistas", tal como lo encontramos, por ejemplo en Philippe Hamon, "Un discours contraint", *Poétique* 16(1973): pp. 411-45. Al final, el autor mismo se da cuenta de que traza el rostro del realismo decimonónico.

38   Examinamos el aspecto postrealista en el ejemplo de *Los pasos perdidos*, en *Cuatro claves*, y de *Pedro Páramo*, en "*PP* de Jan Rulfo: Una obra aleatoria en busca de su texto y del género literario", *Revista Iberamericana* No. 150 (1990): pp. 35-47.

39   "De lo real maravilloso americano", *Tientos*, p. 97.

40   Aunque "lo representativo" represente sólo el simulacrum ideológico y prejuicioso de nuestro momento histórico.

41   C. Couffon, *Miguel Angel Asutrias* (París: Seghers, 1970), pp. 45-46 (el subrayado es nuestro).

42   Procedente de su manifiesto formalista vanguardista "El arte como procedimiento" (1917).

43   En una entrevista con G. Sucre, "Alejo Carpentier, *El siglo de las luces*", *Revista Nacional de Cultura* (Caracas) No. 180 (1967): 85. Carpentier conceptualiza este tema en "Sobre el folklorismo musical", en *Tientos*, pp. 37-50.

44   Matei Calinescu escribe perspicazmente sobre la relación de *kitsch* con la vanguardia y la (post) modernidad, en *Faces of Modernity* (Bloomington: Indiana UP, 1977), p. 225 y ss.

45   La literatura documental o testimonial la abordamos desde una perspectiva teórica en "Hacho/ficción/documento y la literatura: Hacia la lectura postmoderna de la de la crónica colonial, de la literatura testimonial y de otros géneros marginales o no literarios" (en preparación).

46   Este modelo fue propuesto en una ponencia escrita para el V Congreso de la Asociación Internacional de Hispanistas celebrado en Bordeaux, en 1974.   En pleno reino del mundo alucinante francés, un grupo de comunistas chilenos, prófugos entonces de la incipiente pinoche, tuvo por bien hacer un "juicio revolucionario" a los prófugos de otras latitudes y de otras noches.   Recuperado recientemente el texto, lo hemos puesto al día.   En el proceso, encontramos otro extenso manuscrito anterior sobre el tema, del cual también aprovechamos algunas partes.   Ha resultado un palimpsesto, una sobre-posición de los textos de distintas épocas.

Literary Whiteness and the
Afro-Hispanic Difference

José Piedra

Hablar de raza española es no saber lo que se dice . . .	To speak of a Spanish race makes no sense . . .
El lenguaje es la raza.	The language is the race
	Miguel de Unamuno[1]

Son griegas tus formas, tu tez, africana;	Your shape is Greek, your face, African;
tus ojos hebreos, tu acento español;	your eyes are Hebrew, your accent Spanish;
la arena es tu alfombra, la palma, tu hermana;	the sand is your carpet, the palm tree your sister;
te hicieron morena los besos del sol.	the kisses of the sun made you brown.

from an anonymous song documented in Mexico in the
nineteenth century[2]

'io compré un negro, crespo los cabellos,	'I bought a black man, curly hair, white teeth, swollen kisser.'
blanco los dientes, hinchado los beços.'	

an example of synecdoche used by Antonio de Nebrija in his
fifteenth-century book on Spanish grammar[3]

I

FOURTEEN HUNDRED NINETY-TWO should remind Hispanics of the publication of the first grammar of a modern European language, a fact overshadowed in historical records by the unification of the Spanish nation, the purification of infidels, and the launching of the New World adventure. Antonio de Nebrija's work billed the Castilian dialect as the "companion of the Empire," an appropriate grammatical endorsement of Spain's ethnic assertion, religious and racial bigotry, as well as the ultimate "civilized" weapon for political expansionism among the "illiterate."[4] Spanish grammar became the colonial pretext for the assimilation of otherness and others. Imperial grammarians established a test of literacy for Hispanic citizenship, which, if successfully passed, allegedly provided official entry into the Hispanic "Text of Otherness," a grammatical contract of servitude. Nebrija, in fact, not only announced the imperial qualities of language, but also explained in his text the ability of grammar to assimilate foreign words as well as foreign learners.[5] He proposed a language which would inherit the power structures of other literate societies and in the process would also Hispanicize non-literate societies. In the final process, Spanish would combine seductiveness with domination. Henceforth the grammatical and imperial "companion" was disseminated by conquerors and bureaucrats who unified in a rhetorical manner the differences of fate, faith, and race within the Hispanic empire. The final result was an "impure," but unified empire, combining aspects of the Latin, Hebraic, and Islamic models. The fact that the "impurity" of the system was not officially accepted only served to strengthen the imperial hold. Furthermore, it would offer outsiders a false sense of accessibility and a similarly false hope of equality within Spain's implicit, unofficial heterogeneity.

While preparing for an imperial career, Spain, as the dark child of Europe and the light child of Africa, opted for a linguistic unity over strictly ethnic, religious, and territorial determinism. Otherwise, national integrity might have lost itself in the long history of Iberian siege, spanning the Greco-Roman to the Afro-Islamic invasions and passing through what threatened Hispanophiles qualified as Jewish preeminence in commerce. Such interventions, however, did not forestall the deep-seated Spanish desire to associate with foreigners who were considered ubiquitous and important. Alfonso the Wise, for instance, established elaborate rules for the exchange between the different groups on Iberian soil. Beneath the cautionary acceptance of outsiders, Spaniards experimented with tactical assimilation aimed at national unity. Due to the state of siege of their territory, national unity could be forged only in theory, through language and cultural exchange. The work of Nebrija crystallized the most realistic form of unity available under siege. Nebrija, for instance, briefly discusses the linguistic contribution of Moors and Jews, ignoring their position of preeminence in occupied Spain.[6] He is chiefly concerned with the unification of the empire under the aegis of a grammatical mistress. From this tactical assimilation of the invader's contributions, Spain pieced together a language of survival and domination in both Africa and the New World. The transatlantic language offered cultural strength for the occupiers while promising syncretic assimilation for the occupied.

A strong common language was essential in the rhetorical war for transatlantic integrity. A unified linguistic front diluted the occupation armies' and master culture's hegemony; their imperial otherness led to a reasonably democratic syncretism of universal pretense. Latin and Castilian Spanish dominated as the vehicles of syncretism, absorbing knowledge from classical European, Islamic, and Judaic sources. Record keeping in Hispanicized languages, whether in Vulgar Latin or proto-imperialist Castilian, enticed the rest of the heterogeneous participants to partake in experiments of translation, teaching, and peaceful coexistence.[7] Columbus, for instance, a recent Italian convert to the Spanish system, expressed himself in these two languages.

Islands of universal knowledge emerged in the budding nation, supported by underground waves of linguistic pride.[8] The imperialist application of Aristotelian views of world unity and Nebrija's grammatical crusade should be considered as the hidden guiding lights for the pioneers of this aristocracy of the intellect with worldwide pretense. Spaniards had, after all, "discovered" Aristotle and the power of linguistic standardization at about the same time, and this much earlier than other European nations.[9] Under Islamic occupation, Iberian citizens learned the benefits of exploiting the symbiotic relationships with other cultures. The linguistic exploitation of knowledge gave the Hispanic "universities" an edge within "international" pockets of Iberian soil. Knowledge was assimilated as part of the Spanish zeal to control translations of the classics, thus creating a thriving European commerce in humanist books and scholars which is a considerable source for the ideology of the Renaissance. Individuals like Alfonso the Wise studied and translated the knowledge imported by "barbarians"—such as Moors, Jews, and to a lesser extent, sub-Saharan Africans. Theoretically, Iberians laid claims to Aristotelian thinking on world unity. In restricted diplomatic practices, they also prepared to turn such a thought into apologies for global control thinly disguised as a nationalistic pride in cultural (chiefly linguistic and rhetorical) prowess. The congenial systems of a rediscovered philosopher and a well-placed grammarian laid the groundwork for the exercise of the imperial hold. Europe, Africa, and America became the grounds on which Spain planned to practice enslavement justified as a rhetorical brokerage of universal knowledge.

Spanish interpreters stressed those aspects of Aristotelian theories of world unity and Nebrija's linguistic imperialism which proposed the conversion of outsiders to an official *written* dictum. If one is to follow Nebrija's interpretation, it establishes writing as the natural means of expressing Aristotelian world unity. After criticizing previous empires which spread themselves too thin without having the appropriate grammatical tools to uphold their unity, the Spanish imperial grammarian gives his ultimate endorsement of the power of writing: ". . . las letras representan las bozes, y las bozes significan, como dize Aristoteles, los pensamientos que tenemos en el anima" (". . . letters represent voices, and voices give meaning, according to Aristotle, to the thoughts we have in our souls").[10]

Those who opposed the written dictum would be forced to comply as slaves. Enslavement thus comes to be viewed as a harsh form of cultural apprenticeship. Slaves came to deserve a legitimate place in society as their behavior conformed to certain "inherited" rights as potential citizens. The Spanish view of slavery was tactfully disguised as citizen apprenticeship. Furthermore, whether enslaved or freed, every citizen was in fact subject to a degree of enslavement to the very same bureaucratic system that legitimized him.[11] Nebrija endorsed a similar system in his concept of language. He argued that language becomes a source of power when it provides an official "home" for the memory of all who contribute to the empire, and grammarians act as the official guardians of such a home. He considered grammar the system behind all imperial systems. As a propagandist extraordinaire, he was personally involved in "grammatical" interpretations of imperialism: official grammarian and Hispanist, rhetorician and humanist, biblical and secular editor, apologist and critic of the inquisition, royal historiographer and strategist of colonial campaigns. He managed his diverse imperialist interests while being an advocate of the accessibility to knowledge through the printing press.[12] Ultimately, he proposed his own book of grammar as a vehicle not only to conquer enemies, but to standardize and uphold the rights and duties of citizens and also to make friends of those who followed in the right path. Grammar constituted the core of a citizen's apprenticeship; it guided the recording and the actual making of history as the official channel of spreading "the truth." Grammar crystallized as the conquering envoy to new slaves and citizens. The Spanish empire used textual participation both as justification and vehicle of its abuses and as enticement for the abused.

First in Europe and then in the New World, written Spanish was projected as a centralized, self-consistent, and self-righteous textuality which invited outsiders to participate. The invitation glossed over potential differences—such as origin, faith, social standing, reason, and race. On paper, but not in practice, differences were minimized as alliances were maximized. Nebrija provided the New World with the justification for a cohesive Hispanic Text, he unified "otherness" under the grammatical self-righteousness of the colonial letter. Henceforth, the discourse of "the Hispanic self" disseminated within the discourse of Others (Moors, blacks, Jews) in occupied Spain was transformed into a unified discourse of Others within the Imperial "self"—as Spain subjected the "blood," "faith," and "letters" of previous settlers on the Iberian Peninsula as well as native Americans and African slaves in the New World to a bureaucratic test of integrity. Thus, by virtue of this assimilation and incorporation, the Others found themselves in a position of tactical compromise that was never to be forgotten in subsequent literature of Latin America. It was only those who considered themselves mediators between the extremes of the master culture and the potential slave who dared to challenge the uneasy compromise spun by the Hispanic Text.

Afro-Hispanics were among the mediators most profoundly affected by the Hispanic textual compromise. The unification of all races into the Text was propelled by many social, religious, and historical circumstances, chief among which were Spain's own racially ill-defined origins, its occupation by lighter and darker-skinned conquerors who imported their own black slaves and citizens, and the rest of Europe's prejudices about Spain's imprecise racial heritage. This constellation of circumstances led to a theoretical welcoming, on paper, of black newcomers under the far-reaching umbrella of a "Hispanic" race. This welcoming, however, was predicated on the supposition that knowledge and practice of the Hispanic ways would dissipate the more blatant differences when transcribed into writing, primarily through official syncretism and legal miscegenation. After these prerequisites for assimilation were satisfied, marginals were permitted a place in the world structure designed and led by Spaniards. Syncretism and miscegenation remained pages of theories which were liberally distorted by interpretations and chiefly practiced unofficially. Even for those who gained access to the bureaucratic means of swearing off their differences, there were far too many implicit variants that could be shed merely by explicitly declaring oneself Hispanicized. Spaniards, who had for centuries known Islamized Negroid peoples as conquerors, had now successfully transformed them into collaborators. In justifying its expansionist policies, the Empire applied a parallel rule to its conquest of sub-Saharan blacks under the guise of transforming them into political allies. The newcomers would serve a period of slavery while aiding the Hispanic search for new frontiers. It was the blacks, who, amidst all the mediators "officially" welcomed, experienced the most difficulty in proving their allegiance to the Hispanic—presumably blind and equitable—form of literary whiteness.

The concept of Hispanic "race" grew as a myth in print, rarely believed but mostly accepted as the unifying principle for the dissemination of Hispanidad. The voice of marginals was traditionally included in, but seldom allowed direct manipulation of, the printed page. And yet, enlightened Afro-Hispanics soon learned to use as publishing vehicles the very bureaucracies which monitored the integrity of printed materials. I have uncovered a significant number of these writers in official religious and secular records throughout the Spanish colonies; their works now come to light after centuries of burial as manuscript depositions for "crimes of difference."[13]

The issue of race has never subsided, solved only in the most fictional of rhetorical solutions. To this day, Hispanic unity is celebrated among Spanish-Americans as *Día de la Raza* ("Day of [the?] Race") on the date of Columbus's first landing. The race in question is a grand metaphor for unrealized promises of universal harmony offered by the Linguistic Mother of the Spanish New World. A "Grammar Day" would be a more appropriate celebration, albeit with caution, since it refers to the enlightened despotism of rules which set the terms of inscription for all Hispanic subjects.

Traditionally, all the peoples lagging behind the mythical Spanish-speaking race had to prove allegiance to the model in some court—a test required in particular from those "burdened" with visual differences. The ensuing tests of Hispanidad became cruel performances acted out by newcomers needing to partake of the world empire. Most newcomers desired to be counted, recorded, and declared *gente de razón* ("persons of reason"), a difficult trial for those adventurers who arose from the most uncertain strata of Iberian society.[14] From the outset, however, these future citizens found linguistic loopholes for the swearing-in.

At the turn of the fifteenth century, alongside the birth of the nation, the Spanish instituted the proof of *pureza de sangre* ("purity of blood") for those who wished to be Hispanic. In this way, the state attempted to ensure for each citizen a place in the imperial "genealogy." The issue of "purity of blood" involved a trial of faith, race, and national origin, depending on the issue in doubt. The end result was usually an auto-da-fé. This was the theatrical Spanish way to declare oneself faithful; the auto-da-fé, in fact, derived from the Spanish medieval plays which were secular adaptations of religious matters. Thus, the proof of Hispanic worth had become a theatrical production, words on an inquisitorial stage. The trial was no less staged; the suspected individual was publicly tried with all the pomp and circumstance of a pageant.[15] In fact many prominent black citizens "dramatically" accused themselves of crimes which could be proven untrue during the trial.[16] Their reason for this legal maneuver was to gain access to an official audience, often for their writing, or for defending rights which could not otherwise be brought to court, much less to the approval and/or mercy of the public at large. Significantly, the first item expected from the state in such trials was a genealogical account, intimately connected with the suspected individual's service to the Crown. Through the centuries, the suspect who could not pass such a trial would be denied in turn "reason" or "citizenship" until the eighteenth century, in which the trial was often relegated to a *prueba de hidalguía* ("proof of nobility").[17] After the Age of Enlightenment, a difficult combination of credentials could permit a marginal to qualify for citizenship: a letter of manumission (or other proof of freedom) and willingness to abide by mythical whiteness as incorporated by the pronouncements of the Spanish Royal Academy of the Language. These metaphorical dictates undermined the issue of race and, more broadly, of differences. Hence, acceptance into the system of Hispanidad was a far cry from an invitation to join the scores of "persons of reason" who occupied the elite positions in the dictatorship.

A light-colored nobody or an exceptional Moor, Jew, or Afro-Hispanic could, to some degree, swear off impurities and gain a fictional genealogy and a grammatical standing in the New World. Latin, the Law, the Faith, and the degree of Hispanic honor and nobility were claimed by the elite as badges, either automatically due in recompense for services rendered to the Crown or laboriously litigated in trials. Castilian and literature, parody and magic constituted the arsenal of the exceptional marginal person. Thus, most reasons for inquisitorial trials against marginals were linguistic and/or magical in nature; that is, individuals were accused of substituting for the official logic and written letter of the law some other form of expression. Even ventriloquism was considered a crime: *hablar por el pecho* ("to speak through the chest"); the accused was often charged with the ability to produce objects through words.[18]

Ventriloquism—a form of expression which bypasses the linguistic strictures of the Hispanic system—serves as a metaphor for the birth of literature in Spanish America. Prior to the discovery of the New World, it was primarily the highborn who were supposed to produce literature in moments of idleness. After the discovery, adventurers seeking nobility, honorary citizenship, or just freedom impersonated the voice of the idle rich as *littérateurs*. Nebrija sets an extreme example of prediscovery literary attitudes by ignoring the "official" example of the poetry of Alfonso the Wise. The intellectual king, however, made a good case for biases against the official status of literature by compiling poetry written not in Castilian but in Galician-Portuguese. Nebrija not only denies by omission the existence of literature in languages which coexist with Castilian on the Iberian Peninsula, but he also puts in question the worth of literature. He declares in the "Prólogo" of his *Gramática:* "I por que mi pensamiento y gana siempre fue engrandecer las cosas de nuestra nación, dar alos ombres de mi lengua obras en que mejor puedan emplear su ocio, que agora lo gastan leiendo novelas o istorias embueltas en mil mentiras y errores, acordé ante todas las otras cosas reduzir en artificio este nuestro lenguaje castellano, para que lo que agora y de aqui adelante enel se escriviere pueda quedar en un tenor, y estenderse en toda la duracion delos tiempos que estan por venir."[19] [And due to the fact that I put my intellect and desire to work toward the exaltation of our country's products, and that to give those who spoke my language works in which they would best use idle time, which they now waste reading novels or stories wrapped in lies and errors, my priority was to reduce the artifices of our Castilian language, so that whatever is written in it now and henceforth would fit into a mold, and would last forever into the future.]

According to Nebrija, fiction in the Hispanic Empire was in peril. And yet, Hispanic American fiction was born precisely from the elasticity gained by the official language. The creation of a Hispanic mold allowed the assimilation of viewpoints into "grammatically correct" writing. Orthography, syntax, and rhetoric were allies not just of historiography, but also of fiction. Discovery and conquest by force and by word cooperated without success in the attempted assimilation of differences. While the New World was created at the edge of an empire, discovered and named, conquered and renamed by outsiders, Hispanic American fiction was born on the margins of what was officially accepted as grammatical writing. The same adventurers and marginals who manipulated Nebrija's codified Castilian employed techniques of fiction to convey facts never experienced before. Columbus, who was not even a Spaniard, coated his unexpected finds in the New World with official-sounding words of consolation.[20] Such a tactical cover-up allowed him to experiment with fictional techniques without jeopardizing the semblance of truth and the power of convincing. On the contrary, fiction aided the rhetoric of truth devised by grammarians of imperialism such as Nebrija. Columbus's "mid-Atlantic" viewpoint creates a rhetoric of compromise aimed at preserving American differences within the Spanish textual molds.

From the outset, Hispanic American fiction recorded the opinions of extraordinary adventurers and relatively ordinary citizens who expressed themselves in the imperial language of tactical obedience. The emerging literatures walked a thin line between compromise and resentment in order to recreate a fictional Hispanic self within the factual mold. The recreation summarizes the sacrifices suffered by outsiders who "took advantage" of the Empire's offer to "cover" them with a utopic blanket of purity. This compromising offer translated into action Spain's own universal quest, under whose aegis the nation upheld a blind literary and Catholic whiteness.

In the New World, Hispanic discourse is reborn as a fictional manipulation of a rapacious grammar. Nebrija's textual guide yielded a new grammar assimilating nontraditional reality in instantly accepted, faithful words. The same could be said of historical records, the laws of the Indies, and the dictates of the Inquisition, which included local variants and fictional interpretations. Imperial grammar, history, law, and religion forged a wordy colonial bureaucracy, but the largesse of the mother language disguised a linguistic dominatrix which condemned dissident values to hierarchical classifications and stages of unpleasant conformity.

New World practitioners of the language of bureaucracy claimed rights as Creoles and as Christians almost as soon as they were willing to forgo their national or religious differences and officially join the Hispanic system. Conformity was sealed as a superficial, written allegiance; bureaucratic records provided labels for the pretender which indicated the degree of declared and feasible imitation of the official norms. Racial differences demanded a much greater commitment to imitation: either slow miscegenation toward the Hispanic model or an instant "certificate of whiteness" ensuring a place under the blind domination of the imperial grammar.[21] The present effort aims to trace the origins of Afro-Hispanic writings to factual and fictional differences within the model of literary whiteness.

II

Traditional literary history has it that black writings of literary significance began in the Spanish American world in the nineteenth century. At that time, the causes of abolition and liberation were well under way, presumably spurring Hispanics of all races to embrace the defense of the "darker" Others in their midst. The drive paralleled the legalization of a general Creole otherness against the one empire, echoing, further back in history, the Hispanic drive for a single national unity. With vicious circularity, texts embedded in literary whiteness mounted a rhetorical defense of black characters, who were used as the fictional mediators for ideas too daring for whites, such as surrendering to suppressed factual differences. The "rhetorical defense" placed black characters between fact and fiction, a convenient limbo to which newcomers were often confined by the dictates of the Old World. In the New World, the black mediators eventually emerged from their textual limbo to aid other Hispanics in a common adventure: as interpreters of the nature, language, and work orders of the conquerors for the native American *terra incognita*.[22]

Recent discoveries place the incipience of Afro-Hispanic literature early in the Colonial period, although such finds confirm the preponderance of a system of black mediation aligning itself with the general cause of Creole liberation.[23] Historians of Spanish America traditionally trace the ferment of Creole unrest to as early as the eighteenth century; black characters and writers joined in the projected restructuring of the rhetorical unity. However, whereas the growing wave of underground syncretism between white, black, and native values surfaced as a new enlightened unity, only the black characters', but not the black writers', mediation was considered acceptable. Creole rhetoric continued the campaign of the imperial language against difference, particularly from the pen of the openly different.

When the New World divided into new independent worlds in the Americas, the rhetorical empire was the first to show signs of unrest and the last to admit these signs or to crumble under the ensuing rebellious texts. To this day, language remains the relative dictator of Hispanidad. Nonwhites could write as long as they did not address the issue of difference, a stricture which practically denied them self-conscious literature. The first black writers who published in Vulgar Latin or in Castilian Spanish argued eminently neutral or white issues before they addressed their own difference.

Blacks who wished to write at all were encouraged to climb the imperial ladder of Hispanidad toward a rhetorical whiteness. Such whiteness stood as a symbolic acceptance of the system, where differences were reduced to rhetorical participation, in other words, loyalty and allegiance to a piece of paper. The monstrous system paid in bureaucratic complexity what it gained in plasticity and availability. Writing standards tacitly permitted tactical differentiations and a reserved form of racial "passing" for the imitators of the written norms.

The increased specificity of miscegenation tables and the proliferation of certificates of whiteness bespeak the tragic "opportunities" available to black applicants desirous of rhetorical conformity.[24] The tacit attempt to differ or the explicit desire to fail could produce the same result for the resentful imitators of Hispanic norms. The systematic impositions of such norms, however, could not erase certain differences. Those who failed could opt to revenge themselves against the white goals by exploiting the elusive opportunities which distinguish enlightened despotism from prior racial dictatorships. At the end of the eighteenth century, a substantial number of Afro-Hispanics asserted themselves beyond the alleged opportunities offered by the official discourse. But even before the peak of such a substantial wave of assertion, society was already "listening" while it brought to trial the first black writers openly resenting whiteness. In fact, Afro-Hispanics found in the trials of the Inquisition an unusual forum for their ideas; black writers even found judges ready to become their first literary critics.[25]

Before giving examples of the forbidden literature of the Afro-Hispanic Enlightenment, it would be expedient to compare its authors to exceptional predecessors and successors. An example of the former category is a late sixteenth to early seventeenth-century Afro-Spaniard, and of the latter a late eighteenth to early nineteenth-century Afro-Peruvian. Both writers dramatized the enslavement of marginals to the word, exemplified by their own names and careers. They also demonstrate that literary whiteness was, second only to pride in black aesthetics, the most difficult subject to communicate for the Afro-Hispanic *littérateur*. The examples serve to put in perspective other alternatives in establishing a mutually agreeable compromise between unofficial differences and the official model: either by progressive syncretism and miscegenation or by instantaneous certificates of whiteness.

The first example emerges from Spain's habit of conferring rather loose labels on newcomers during their "imperial apprenticeship." Citizens considered to be "low class" were enrolled under the uniform social label of *ladinos* (that disregarded race, creed, national or civil status), as soon as they spoke the rudiments of the official languages. Castilian Spanish and Vulgar Latin were considered as a progressive linguistic unity for this purpose. The rhetorical license was conferred upon black slaves who learned Spanish "within six months," and one black *ladino* became Juan Latino, the Latin grammarian and poet.[26]

For Latino, marrying into a "noble and white" Spanish family was simply a personal and social achievement, rather than an act of tactical miscegenation. Before his marriage, Juan had already experienced the scale of personal labels which named the stages of his acculturation. He had changed his slave name of "de Sessa," indicating his belonging to a "noble and white" Spanish master, to Latino, or "Latin," which lent the former black slave an old imperial bloodline and genealogy based on his own linguistic merits. Juan's Hispanicization took him a step beyond the midde-class Spanish meritocracy; he climbed the ladder of whiteness, nobility, and grammatical proficiency leading to the highest Latinesque strata of the Imperial chain. A noble, solicitous Spaniard, he served the Hapsburg dynasty and honored them with his literature.[27]

Within his restrictions, Latino manifested his defense of blackness when he viewed, with cautious anonymity and resentment, the African differences within the rhetorical blindness. In his own words:

Obvious Aethiopem Christum docet ore Philippus . . .
Ne Aethiopi iusta haec forte Philippe neges . . .[28]

[Phillip (II, Hapsburg King of Spain) instructs the found Ethiopian about
     Christ . . .
Do not deny, Phillip, to Ethiopians these just rights . . .]

And more explicitly:

Quod si nostra tuis facies Rex nigra ministris
displicet, Aetheiopum non placet alba viris.[29]

[If our black face, King, displeases your ministers,
Ethiopians do not like white ones on their males.]

The warring blacks, usually known in Spain as Moors and not by the effete cultural label of Ethiopians, are bound to learn the word of the Crown and Christ regardless of Latino's ironic plea on their behalf. The author's plea discreetly challenges the discourse of assimilation by taking the initiative and the official word in hand. The second excerpt suggests the limits of assimilation by contrasting aesthetic prejudices from both sides. Furthermore, Latino underscores the pursuit of whiteness as a weakness, considered unmanly among Ethiopians. In the Latin inscription he ordered for his own tomb, he cites among his accomplishments the dedication of his considerable knowledge to the service of the Hispanic ways as much as his *niggerrima* (blackest) origins.[30] Posterity was to judge him as much for his black origins as for his Hispanic goals.

The second literary figure of our concern wrote much more directly of the war of veiled assimilation and prejudices waged by Afro-Hispanics. José Manuel Valdés, the Afro-Peruvian physician, scientist, historian, and writer, lived during the transitional period after the Afro-Hispanic Enlightenment, when white writers attempted to manipulate the defense of blackness in their antislavery textual campaigns. Valdés witnessed his country's independence from Spain and assumed a low and bitter profile for his racial difference; his life vehemently unveils the imprints of marginality disguised by his writings. He bore the surname usually given by Latin American states to bastard children, one that is often found among writers born out of wedlock by one black parent. He wrote himself out of blackness by assuming an invisible self even when he addressed issues of marginality, as he did in his scientific and historical treatises.

It has been suggested that he received a certificate of whiteness to become a priest and a theoretician of medicine, even though he would not have needed it for practicing medicine, since many low-order ecclesiastical brothers and many surgeons in pre-nineteenth-century Peru were black.[31] In order to write, however, the same individuals had to reject symbolically all variables disturbing the empire's whitewashed, pure singleness of text. Valdés took to heart such a rule by carrying out the ultimate textual commitments to racial blindness. Not only did he receive and then renounce a certificate of whiteness, but he also refused to have his portrait painted.[32] Curiously, the only likenesses which remained were painted by Pancho Fierro, a black contemporary. The two watercolors by Fierro present the doctor obscured by a cape very much like the veils used by the *tapadas*, or women who hid their identities in the street. He also wears the sandals worn by the poor, in contrast to the rest of his clothing and the setting, which indicate the life of a gentleman.[33]

In spite of his self-imposed invisibility, and perhaps because of it, Valdés was able to deal in an impersonal fashion with the issue of minority-status people—women, the poor, and blacks. He introduced blackness into his more personal endeavors by fictionalizing the life of Saint Martin of Porras, the Afro-Peruvian saint from the turn of the sixteenth century. Actually, he received an official ecclesiastical commission to write his work. Only in his testament does he focus on his black genealogy—his posthumous wish conveniently tears the veil from his tactical pretense of racial neutrality.

By virtue of their language skills and controlled exertion of their differences, Juan Latino and José Manuel Valdés, children of at least one black parent, lived as virtually neutral Hispanics and only recreated their "selves" as Afro-Hispanics for posterity. For their pains and accomplishments they wore the letter of the empire written in blood over their identities and psyches. Both set important precedents in the history of black pride, making subtle but sure gestures of proud differentiation. Latino writes about anonymous *Aethiope* ("Ethiopian") warriors, Valdés about an illegitimate *pardo* ("brown") saint; both do so with awe and with sadness, against a background of rhetorical inequality. As a meager compensation for their efforts, less marginal interpreters of the Spanish language extended to them the honorable classifications of *Aethiope* and *pardo*, respectively.

III

The Enlightenment produced a new vocabulary of race and a fresh look at the mediating role of the different in the Spanish empire. This new vocabulary ultimately changed the European approach to otherness. Most enlightened Europeans, chiefly the French, considered Spanish-speaking people as their "wards," including white Spaniards and Spanish Americans. The French justified political takeovers as ways to "enlighten" the minds of Hispanics on issues such as liberty, equality, and fraternity—which ironically permitted French hegemony in both Spain and Mexico. The paradoxical wave of ideas divided Spanish American elites who supported either Spanish conservatism or French liberal ideology as cultural alternatives. Both extremes attempted to rally marginals to their cause. The attempts were either direct—recruiting the outcast as a taxpaying citizen and/or cannon fodder—or indirect—linguistic recruitment through elaborate tables of miscegenation, promising a place for everyone in the realm of the official word. The only difference between conservatives and liberals might have been their attitudes toward servitude. The pro-Crown conservatives promised improved conditions for the "slaves of the king"; the Francophile liberals promised improved conditions for the "slaves of the nation." The rhetoric, however, began to take a new turn as the institution of freedom from national boundaries or from international occupation now required a social choice from free citizens. The war of words came to be fought on the bases of the sociopolitical and economic advantages of recruiting supporters.[34]

Marginals, for instance dark-skinned individuals, confronted the very classifications which allowed them to be counted as citizens in positions more advantageous than that of the lowly, pure black. It was clearly not enough for enlightened blacks to be labeled with archetypal terms such as *Aethiope* or *pardo,* labels which covered a multitude of differences under the guise of "taming" a black ancestry into Hispanic conformity. In the enlightened New World, a detailed subdivision of categories of miscegenation and the proliferation of opportunities to become officially white became official policy. Both options steered clear of extremism in racial rankings by generating a contrived linguistic system. Nonwhites were encouraged to remain at a racially safe midpoint, indicated in the rhetoric of the empire by the term *moreno.* The etymological origin of this term is the conquering-conquered *moro,* or "Moor," a term which thus substituted for the concept of blackness one of an alleged neutrality.[35]

Afro-Hispanic authors must have been aware of the enlightened vocabulary's new ploy to "tame" them. I have found no evidence for their own use of such a vocabulary, or, for that matter, no evidence of any practical use by the authorities—in either birth certificates, censuses, or Inquisitorial records. However, we cannot assume that the new vocabulary was solely a theoretical issue, particularly because of the proliferation, during the eighteenth century, of the so-called *pinturas de castas* ("paintings of castes," or "miscegenation paintings").[36] We cannot assume either that these paintings were only aimed at enticing nonwhites to climb the socioracial ladder of whiteness. Along with the euphemistic, hairsplitting racial classifications we find in these paintings overt representation of "regressive" racial traits— such as *torna atrás* and *salto atrás* ("turn backwards" and "jump backwards").[37] I suspect that these paintings were used by ecclesiastical authorities for the purpose of marriage counseling. Each racial classification was portrayed with its parental source and the type of job, food, clothing, and other corresponding social benefits. A couple would thus become aware of the advantages or risks of their union vis-à-vis the white model race. The relative whiteness of the Spaniards themselves might have diminished the rhetorical "excellence" and "purity" of the model. Only at the time of marriage could the ecclesiastical authorities exert their influence. That would explain why the elaborate caste system does not appear at other times, such as in birth certificates, censuses, or during trials. At these other times ecclesiastical authorities consistently assigned very straightforward terminology to blacks. The aim was still assimilation under broad categories.

In documents of the Mexican Inquisition, for instance, one rarely finds qualifiers other than *negro*. *Mulato* is in fact the rare second choice, and *lobo* (the offspring of a black and native American union) follows.[38] However, during the eighteenth century, words which at one point had been considered defamatory nomenclature when applied to the national origin of whites became points of pride for black writers of Hispanic literature. The fact of the matter is that many whites themselves no longer considered such terms as derogatory, but rather as labels which identified them either as loyalists (for the *gachupín*, or Spanish-born immigrant) or advocates of independence (for the *criollo*, or New World-born) viewpoint.[39] When black writers were brought before the inquisitorial tribunals, there were curious debates about their national, rather than their racial classification. Despite such elaborate, and even idealized, categories of miscegenation, nonwhites struggled to be classified according to social and political standing, rather than race. There are even cases of individuals brought to trial at the Mexican Inquisition who refused all forms of citizen classification.[40]

Two writers of color from the eighteenth century, one from Mexico and the other from Colombia, illustrate the marginals' adamant attempts to name themselves as they pleased. The known autobiographical writings of these two people still exhibit the high price paid for their efforts at self-assertion. The texts of the Mexican are known through Mexican archival depositories, such as the Inquisitorial records; those of the Colombian appear in papers from secular tribunals. Although they both legally won their cases, chiefly by presenting essay-length letters to the authorities, the former was eventually declared a misfit, and the latter declared himself one.

José Ventura, an author who was officially declared "white," is one of the unsung defenders of true racial blindness during the Enlightenment. Even though brought before the tribunals of the Mexican Inquisition as a "Spanish heretic," his heresy was chiefly a linguistic one: he refused to be classified in terms of differences—racial, religious, or social.[41] Due to this refusal, his exact heritage still remains a mystery, and his effectiveness as an antiracist campaigner was greatly enhanced by his self-declared racial anonymity. He argued selflessly in favor of an impure and unorthodox image of Mexican selfhood, in which differences were admitted in reality but obliterated on paper for the sake of a democratic meritocracy. The Mexican Inquisition tried unsuccessfully to assimilate this humble man, an embroiderer by profession, into an imperial system which deprived him of the most elementary of choices: the definition of his self-image. Then the courts sought to find a legal cause for punishing his refusal. In fact, his many infractions against Church law became insignificant in comparison to his refusal to be cast as a member of a specific Hispanic caste. Thereby he created a formidable obstacle for a bureaucracy whose custom it was to introduce each case brought to trial by recounting the genealogy of the individual to place him or her in the proper socioracial category.

Ventura further jeopardized his fate by creating designs for embroidery in which he depicted social injustice, using himself as an example. Many of these sketched the rebellious message by presenting nude figures acting out their "sins" and revenge against society under the embellishment of an overlay of clothing or the suggestive bluntness of a prurient setting. The message was further driven home by his filling in some of the sketches—possibly not for sale—with volatile poetic captions, very much in the style of twentieth-century comic strips. For this complex of cultural heresies, Ventura was finally convicted by the secular legal system as a Creole pornographer. Ultimately, however, he was left relatively free to continue the expression of his moral violations, having been declared an "ethical" outcast and sentenced to life in an asylum for the insane. In spite of this tragic end, Ventura succeeded in making his antiestablishment points more than clear. His greatest victory may have been to point out for posterity that he could not be condemned for his refusal to remain racially neutral by the very system which promoted the caste system as a mechanism of assimilation pretending neutrality.

By means of his 1789 trial, through the writings and drawings included in the official record both in his defense and for the prosecution, José Ventura became a public self. The unabashedly Mexican writer assailed racial prejudices that were crucial to the definition of Mexico as a melting pot. The Mexico he portrays in his work was then barely a formed nation with a forced united front—a single mythical race, a single faith, and a single nationhood. After ironically accepting the inevitability of such a unilateral front, he proposed to base it on a tactical unity that openly incorporated plurality.

Perhaps no other text of Ventura's is as concise an example of the suffering experienced by Mexicans for claiming differences in writing as this letter to his daughter:

Querida hija de mi estimación, te remito esta carta en la cual verás el desengaño de la sanguinidad que por herencia te corresponde. Es cierto que Dios separó las formas de la naturaleza del hombre y también apartó las de la mujer. A unos los hizo blancos, a otros Amarillos, a otros Negros, a otros Pardos y cada generación a sus principios les daba vergüenza estar juntos y se fueron apartando: el blanco tenía su Rey, el Amarillo tenía su Rey, el Negro tenía su Rey y cada cual se hallaba en su lugar gobernando su cuerpo, el blanco en su blanca, el Negro en su Negra y el Amarillo en su Amarilla.

[Dear daughter of my heart, I am sending you this letter by which you will experience disillusionment with the blood line which is yours by heritage. It is true that God separated the forms of man's nature and also distinguished the forms of the woman. Some he made white, others Yellow, and others Black, and yet others *Pardo* (brown). And each generation in the beginning was ashamed to be together and they distanced themselves from one another: the white man had his King, the Yellow had his King, the Black had his King and each remained in his place governing his body, the white man in his white woman, the Black in his Black woman, the Yellow in his Yellow woman.

Mas esto asentado, tenemos por cierto que si queremos saber o indagar quiénes fueron nuestros Padres y la sangre y calidad que le asiste, hallaremos por nuestro Rey y Reyes anteriores que bajo de su corona hay blanco, hay Negro, hay Amarillo, hay Pardo, consintiendo los Reyes anteriores que el blanco se case con una Negra, el Negro con una blanca, el Amarillo con blanca y la blanca con un Pardo. Y así la Información no me cuesta ninguna dificultad el despacharla, bajo de cuyo supuesto te digo que bajo de este Imperio todos los que estamos somos españoles, porque el Rey de España a todos nos ha avasallado y avasalla. . . .[42]

[But once that has been settled, we know for a fact that if we want to ascertain or to investigate who were our Parents and the blood and quality (caste) which identifies them, we will find out that under our present and every previous King there have been white people, Black, Yellow, Brown, consenting such previous Kings for the white man to marry a Black woman, the Black to marry a white woman, the Yellow a white woman and the white woman a Brown man. And it is not difficult to dispense such Information, under whose aegis I can tell you that all of us here are Spaniards, because the King of Spain subjected and continues to subject us to servitude. . . .]

Ventura proceeds to attack native Americans who refused to become Hispanic while they lived under the control of the Spanish empire and suggests that the Indians, the original "citizens," act as the latest "newcomers" to the empire. In Ventura's view, they should realize their inability to claim "purity of blood" just like the other peoples gathered under the New World umbrella. Finally, the Mexican writer questions the justice of a bureaucratic system that supports one arbitrary and unjust God, one color, one government, and one standard of aesthetics without properly accounting for the "marginal" contributions.

Ventura's argument against the concepts of purity of blood and genealogy unveiled miscegenation as a historical fact which was part and parcel of the imperial system, while others opted for a metaphorical acceptance of whiteness. Whereas Ventura was persecuted by Church and Law for his overt choice to defend miscegenation, other individuals were rewarded by the Crown for their strategic and more acceptable desire to become officially white.

The second example in question is perhaps the most famous petition for "extinction of color," that of the *pardo* captain Pedro Antonio de Ayarza from Colombia, who petitioned the King of Spain on behalf of his son's rights. Ayarza's son had attended school and learned the basics of the humanities, as prescribed by the educational system of the time. By virtue of his race, however, the son could not obtain a formal degree or continue his professional studies. The King responded directly to Ayarza, bypassing the courts which normally interpreted the laws of the Indies, and yet adhering explicitly to the letter of those laws. The King's written permit circumvents racial differences in favor of an act of rhetorical blindness, whereby "the character of mulatto [a less desireable term than *pardo*] being held extinguished in him, he be admitted, without its serving as a precedent, to the degrees he may seek in the university. . . ." Thus José Ponciano de Ayarza became an honorary white lawyer by act of the royal pen, March the sixteenth of 1797.[43]

Whiteness was granted to Ayarza through a *documento de gracias al sacar* ("document of grace upon receipt"), a curiously legal and religious-sounding title for a Spanish certificate of whiteness. This type of rhetorical circumvention reveals much about the history of the people who devised it. The issue of "grace" euphemistically addresses both the rights and honors conferred upon a citizen which should already be his, at least according to utopic Spanish and Catholic principles.[44]

Unlike these representative examples of the black middle class, poets of the Afro-Hispanic Enlightenment remained reluctant to accept compromises with literary whiteness. The conciseness of form and looseness of message that poetry could convey served to disguise the effrontery of its authors. Although many poets were brought to trial for failure to toe the official line, others enjoyed the relative freedom of the paid itinerant improviser. The resulting self-assertive writing by all Afro-Hispanics is characterized by a parody of the very fabric of the imperial grammar. Citizens of all types read or heard this poetry, were prompted to cry or to laugh with or at the artists. However, the reader's emotive response was built upon the writer's tacit indictment of the linguistic system.

An important documented trial of an enlightened black poet was that of Baltasar de Esquivel by the Mexican Inquisition.[45] This author, somewhat like his compatriot José Ventura, tactically avoided a clear definiton in terms of race, religion, and nationality. However, unlike Ventura, from whom he learned to sew, he is much more candid about his blackness, his lax Catholicism, and his even laxer Mexican nationalism. His trial in 1753 records fragments of a fictional autobiography. He invented several selves, names, and origins, all of which enhance and ridicule a noble but illegitimate birth in an invented Spanish town full of heretics. The versions of his life narrated to the judges further coincide in describing a New World escape with a wet nurse, first to Havana—where he learned how to read, write, and sew—then to Mexico, where he was determined to serve the system as best he could.

The puzzled inquisitors were at odds to formalize an accusation against Esquivel, whom they called at first a *gachupín*, then of *calidad desconocida* ("unknown quality or caste"), and eventually a *criollo*. His assimilation into the text of the Inquisition, and thus of the official word of the Hispanic world, depends on his novelistic depositions. And yet, amidst the pages of his only known official record, his poetry transcends the ambivalence of his autobiographical narration:

Negro se te vuelva el dia
negro por sus negras horas
y negros trabajos pases,
pues de negro te enamoras.

To black shall your day turn
black as the black hours it bore
and black labors you shall endure
for it is black men you adore.

Con repetidos clamores
falsa, leve y sin fe
le suplico al cielo que
todas las tres pascuas llores
y con crecidos dolores
por tu infame tiranía
nunca tengas alegría
y para mayor quebranto,
pues a lo negro amas tanto
negro se te vuelva el dia.

With obsessive bouts of thirst
falsely, lightly, without faith
a cry to heaven I am to raise
for you to cry three holy births
and with the pains that burst
under your tyrannical concern
may happiness you never earn
and to your even greater sadness,
for much love placed on blackness
to black shall your day turn.

Quiera Dios que con afán
no tengas ningunos gozos
y que des tiernos sollozos
cuando otros cantando están,
y pues negro es tu galán
y negro el amor que imploras
ese negro a quien tú adoras
con voluntad tan veloz
lo mire como a un reloz
negro por sus negras horas.

May God set as a stubborn ploy
for you to lack in every pleasure
and to sigh softly under pressure
while others are singing with joy,
and as black is the man you enjoy
and black is the love you implore,
the black man whom you adore
with such a fast staying will,
as a clock you'll see him still
as black as black hours it bore.

Nunca del floreado pan
gustes sus blancas dulzuras,
sino unas semitas duras,
y por los días de San Juan:
más pobre te veas que Amán
y cuando a casarte haces
sea un negro con quien te cases
que de él mismo vivas harta
y que te traiga a la cuarta
y negros trabajos pases.

May you never of the flowery bread
taste the white sweetness it breeds
but some hard flowering seeds,
and by the feast of Saint John led
more than Haman may you have shed
and when to marriage you dare
be it a black choice you declare
and as you shall live full of him
to full quarter your life will ream
while black labors you shall bear.

Cuando el verano en primores	When the gala of summer showers
vista el campo de alegrías,	the ground with a robe of splendors
entonces con melarquías	just then melancholy renders
lágrimas tengas por flores,	your mood in tears instead of flowers,
ansias, penas y temores	anxieties, sorrows and fear of powers
tengas por minutos y horas;	feeling hours and minutes galore
pues a lo blanco desdoras,	as whiteness you begin to abhor,
quiera Dios por tu apetito,	may God feed your searching ploy
el que paras un negrito,	with the birth of a black baby boy,
pues de negros te enamoras.[46]	for it is black men you adore.

A critical lesson to be derived from this poem is the manner in which Esquivel defends "sacrificial blackness" as a rivaling part and intimate partner of the "victimizing whiteness" from which a mixed product emerges. The metaphorical usage of black and white as rivals is parodied by the incidence of intimacy between two representatives of the respective racial groups. No one is to blame for either the rejections in theory and the attraction in practice. The poet wishes for the partners of his portrayed affair to take full responsibility for their acts. Tradition as portrayed by Esquivel already contains an indication of cooperation between the races, often with tragic as well as triumphant consequences. For instance, the three holy births Esquivel suggests as dates to recall the responsibility of miscegenation correspond to official feasts of "naming" among Hispanic Catholics not ordinarily associated with such responsibility: January 6, the Feast of the Epiphany; June 24, the Feast of Saint John the Baptist, and the floating feast of Resurrection, often in March, when Christ acted out his divine role in God's name. The Feast of the Epiphany is implicitly interpreted as the feast of the mysterious conception of the global family. The Feast of Saint John is suggested as an improvised baptism of a new faith. The Resurrection was most likely suggested to be the decisive rite of faith toward the promise of an afterlife. These dates are, as it were, at the point of convergence between Judaism and Christianity, and thus are cruel remembrances of ethnic strife and the apparent triumph of one group over another. Furthermore, Esquivel sees both conflict and compromise from a relatively neutral perspective, until at the end of the poem the birth of a black baby boy serves as a reminder of the sacrifices still to be made for the blind acceptance of love. Both actors in this birth, the "black" man and his "white" lover continue to share their responsibilities. Esquivel, however, gives an added twist to the poem's social message by writing it from the perspective of the "white" or lighter colored woman who falls in love with a black man.

Esquivel endows the symbols of officially white, Western tradition with black responsibility, and vice versa. The offspring of interracial lovemaking certify the union of races and remind everyone of a painful joint responsibility. The poet elevates a love poem to the category of a racial model for society by "sanctifying" miscegenation with allusions to the Scriptures. Through his poetic manipulation of language the feasts of birth, baptism, and resurrection relate the culmination of Judeo-Christian tradition with the evocation of a biracial Chirst. In fact, the Judeo-Christian feasts live in symbiosis with Africa in Latin America. The subtext of this poem evokes the three most popular dates for Afro-Hispanic carnivals during colonial times. Esquivel's poem mimics and mocks the religious liturgy and official calendar by announcing their relationship with blackness.

In one last stroke of linguistic manipulation, the poem forces the reader to deal with an outsider to both the black and white codes vying for attention. Haman, the biblical figure who acted against the Jews, appears as a metaphor for him who pays a high price for his xenophobia. Haman's financial and social greed is the true motivation behind his attack on Jews. The feast of Purim celebrates a singular triumph: the miscegenation between a Jew (Esther) and a non-Jew (Xerxes, the Persian King) serves to save the rest of the bearers of the tradition. Esther, who appears in the Bible as a reluctant wife of Xerxes, asked her husband to put a stop to the massacre of her people as a favor to her. The biblical subtext suggests that Xerxes stops the Jewish massacre in exchange for the love of his wife. Purim, the celebration of this triumph of compromise, is in fact a carnival-like affair in the spring, a token celebration of freedom negotiated in a cross-ethnic compromise by Jews. Thus viewed, Purim is, beneath the official discourse, a feast of negotiated ethnic recognition through "miscegenation" and also through syncretic convergence with pagan rites like Saturnalia.

Esther and Esquivel, Purim and the Christian "carnivals" of naming, have much in common. The biblical character and the Afro-Hispanic writer make a compromise with "the one" power structure to save their respective people's lives and works. Haman and the other threats become assimilated into a concentric metaphorical language in Esquivel's poetry. The superstructure of whiteness, whether in the accepted Catholic or "unacceptable" Jewish manifestations, becomes both the subject and object of a text of blackness.

Esquivel's parodic participation in literary whiteness is a subtle indictment of the rhetorical system. Such a system never envisioned itself as an "opportunity" for the assertion of "differences"; on the contrary, it built itself as a "companion of the empire" in the assimilation of outsiders. Esquivel's autobiographical poetry follows the legacy of a discourse grammatically legalized by Nebrija on the verge of the Spanish empire, unsuspecting that its very effort of assimilation had its limits. The empirical grammar's proposed thoroughness in accounting for the variables of the others was based on a precariously obtained enlightenment which "lightened" the differences. Instead of total assimilation, the linguistic system created an all-encompassing bureaucracy large enough to encourage multiple interpretations and thus loopholes. Esquivel's poetry exploited the bases of the Hispanic tradition on faulty racial, ethnic, and cultural compromises. While he "lightened" his grammar of direct allusions to difference, he kept a rhetorical eye on the rebellious interpretations easily overlooked by the official bureaucrats. In fact, it appears that the inquisitors saw the racial tragedy rather than the triumphs of Esquivel's poem about miscegenation. Esquivel's ultimate triumph remains that this and other poems were kept for posterity by the inquisitors in its original booklet format attached to the records of his trial.

In a suite of poems included in his booklet, Esquivel reveals another angle of the implicit "blackness" of his poetic language versus the utopic "whiteness" of the model, that is, between the unofficial subtext of the official text. This time, the subtext of his work appears to be sanctioned by the formulas of courtly love against a background of Christian textuality. Esquivel manipulates such dual formulas in a style reminiscent of European courtly poets who subverted the standard metaphors of Western poetry in order to deal with forbidden love. The author purportedly overcomes the racial obstacle before the object of his desire by disguising his love in deliberately opaque language. His object of love is a *morena*—or dark Hispanic woman—whose ambivalent racial definition derives from a double etymology: treacherous fish of the depths or Moorish, that is, a proud and feisty Afro-Hispanic woman.[47] The worth and beauty of this *morena* is in the eyes of society as well as in the interpretation of a gluttonous language. The suite, buried in the Inquisition records, reads:

Amante es más justiciero	Lover is far more judicious;
aunque me anima el amor	although I am moved by love,
si le miro como amante	if I see him as a lover
le respeto como a Dios.	I respect him like God.
Amante de las almas	Lover of all souls,
esposo verdadero	true husband above all
que sólo tus piedades	for whom only your pity
al suelo te trajeron.	brings down to earth.

Como tan compasivo	Because of your compassion
por mi divino dueño	toward my divine master shed,
te cargas de mis culpas	you assume my load of guilt
y pagas lo que debo.	and pay what I owe in debt.
Señor sacramentado	Lord by sacrament delivered
que encubierto debemos	under cover we support
y descubierto muestras	while uncovered you exhibit
que eres señor inmenso.	your wide acceptance as lord.
Trigueño estás por el sol	From the sun you have darkened,
más que mucho sol bello	darker in beauty than any sun:
si es morena la madre	he whose mother is a *morena*
que el hijo sea trigueño.[48]	should have an equally dark son.

Parody still remains a disguise for frustrated action. The Afro-Hispanics who wrote literature, particularly poetry, suffered like no other Hispanics for their difference both on and off the record. On record, Afro-Hispanics allied themselves with the false compromises promised by the Imperial Grammar of the conquerors; hence, the results are reminders of a literature of resentment. This literature is heroic as much in its effort to transcend as in its skill to be assimilated by the enemy without calling attention to its differences. Of the Afro-Hispanic heroic acts, the most lasting is the visionary expression of blackness as an important element *within* the Hispanic culture. Transatlantic black culture in the Americas distills a philosophy of self-protection adaptable to the needs of nonspecifically black Latin Americans in search of their own "space" in the Hispanic world grammar. Afro-Hispanic writers learned to write "black" poems in Spanish, exploiting the built-in openness of the cultural proselytism and uncovering the built-in prejudice of literary images of blackness. Euro-Hispanics adopted this philosophy of writing when they argued in favor of their nationalism as a kind of "blackness."

National freedom and black liberation have traditionally coexisted as parallel aims in Latin America. Perhaps the ultimate proof is the employment by whites of black troubadours of freedom. Thus, many Afro-Hispanic writers tried by the tribunals of the system were free citizens who exploited the dubious liberal tendencies of their compatriots and won their cases. If at times the Inquisition intercepted their texts while they were likely being distributed from hand to hand among a select group, more often it was the writers themselves who brought their written materials before the judges. Those accused of violating some legal code often used their literature as a proof of worth, even though in fact they had to disguise or deny the contents of such literature.

Among the few known writers not tried by the Inquisition, two were itinerant performers who earned part of their livelihood from their "trade"—a further proof of their having become black heralds of liberal causes. The price they paid for their trade was the need to lighten the social implications of their black verse and their human worth as threats by deliberate use of self-deprecating humor. As buffoons, they engineered public displays of their oral talents and limited "publication" as grafitti artists or comic counterparts of white straightmen. The best known are Meso Mónica from the Dominican Republic and José Vasconcelos from Mexico, respectively known as "the little black Dominican poet" and "the little black Mexican poet."[49] It is fitting to end this essay by quoting their views of racial and social justice against the myth of one Hispano-Catholic whiteness.

Mónica comments on a basic source of rhetorical unity for the Spanish empire:

Aristóteles decía	Aristotle used to trace
(filósofo muy profundo)	(being in philosophy profound)
que en la redondez del mundo	to the fact the world is round
no existe cosa vacía.	the absence of all empty space.
Falsa es su filosofía	His philosophy I shall deface
según lo que a mí me pasa,	according to my own pleasure,
le discutiría sin tasa,	arguing without measure
y al cabo él se convenciera,	I shall undoubtedly win,
en el momento que viera	the instant he will have seen
las cazuelas de mi casa.[50]	at home my cooking pot's treasure.

Finally, Vasconcelos comments on the main racial image for rhetorical unity in the Spanish empire:

Calla la boca, embustero,	Your boasts, oh liar, do quench,
y no te jactes de blanco	by whiteness you cannot abide,
saliste del mismo banco	since you bear the same hide
y tienes el mismo cuero.[51]	from the same working bench.

Before the time of these two black poets, the Royal Academy of the Spanish Language had been founded as a bastion of the Imperial Grammar. The illusion of one pure, constant, and splendorous whiteness for all Hispanics exudes from its founding motto: *limpia, fija y da esplendor*—"cleanse, steady, and shine."

YALE UNIVERSITY

NOTES

1 Miguel de Unamuno, "Espíritu de la raza vasca," in *La raza y la lengua*, Vol. IV of *Obras Completas*, ed. Manuel Garcia Blanco (Madrid, 1968), p. 156.
2 From *El ruiseñor yucateco. Primera Parte. Canciones populares*, ed. Galo Fernández (Merida, Mexico, n.d.), p. 36. The song was collected in Yucatan by Juan Ausucua as the lyrics of a *guaracha*, imported from Cuba.
3 Antonio de Nebrija, *Gramática de la lengua castellana* (Salamanca, 1492), ed. Ignacio González-Llubera (Oxford, 1926), p. 122.
4 "Cuando bien comigo pienso, mui esclarecida Reina, i pongo delante los ojos el antiguedad de todas las cosas que para nuestra recordacion y memoria quedaron escriptas, una cosa hállo y sáco por conclusion mui cierta: que siempre la lengua fue compañera del imperio." [When in all honesty I think, my enlightened Queen, and place before my eyes all the ancient facts which have been left in writing for us to remember and to keep as memories, one fact stands out and makes me draw a sure conclusion: language has always been the companion of the empire.] Nebrija, p. 3. He also leaves up to the Queen command over language (p. 9).
5 Nebrija stresses the relationship between imperialism and linguistic assimilation (p. 7). He compares the imperial position of Spanish to other languages ("Prólogo," pp. 3–9) from which it not only inherited power through linguistic assimilation but to which it also owes linguistic derivation. He also proclaims the Spanish debt to languages with which it has come in contact (pp. 23–27, 77–78). Furthermore, Nebrija closely correlates the ability of Spanish to conquer and to seduce ("Prólogo," p. 8 and passim). Finally he dedicates Book V of the *Gramática* to the teaching of Spanish to foreigners: "Delas introducciones dela lengua castellana para los que de estraña lengua querran deprender" (On the preliminaries of the Castilian language for those who want to learn it as a foreign language); see pp. 141–70.
6 Alfonso the Wise used these two languages, Latin and Spanish, as the official ones; see Nebrija's discussion, pp. 5–6. Alfonso, however, compiled and/or wrote poetry in Galician-Portuguese. Literature was to be considered a separate linguistic domain.
7 Even though in his "Prólogo" Nebrija discusses Hebrew as a "power-language," he also points out that the dispersion of Jews around the world has weakened their civilization because it has eroded their linguistic unity. Moreover, he accepts but criticizes the influence of both Jews and Moors in the pronunciation and spelling of Spanish, comparing such "irregularities" to the barbarisms Latin grammarians imputed to outsiders' use (and abuse) of their language; see Nebrija, pp. 122–24.
8 Such as the School of Translators in Toledo, the Center for General Studies in Palencia, and the University of Salamanca, established between the twelfth and the thirteenth centuries. In these centers Latin and Castilian Spanish were the chief working languages.
9 The European rediscovery of Aristotle in Islamized Spain has been thoroughly documented; not so, however, the Greco-Roman legacy of citizens' enslavement to the system, suggested by many classical European writers, especially Plato and Aristotle. See Robert Schlaifer, "Greek Theories of Slavery from Homer to Aristotle," in *Harvard Studies in Classical Philology*, 47 (1936) 165–204, esp. pp. 166–70, quoted by David Brion Davis, *The Problem of Slavery in Western Culture* (Ithaca and London, 1966), p. 67. According to Schlaifer, Philemon was most explicit among the Greeks in his opinion that "the entire universe is viewed as a hierarchy of slavery, in which one's place on the scale mattered but little" (p. 190). Curiously there is a coincidence of names and an affinity of subject matter in Paul's epistle to a Philemon, in which the saint, when pleading to the commoner for pardoning a slave uses as an example his own "impris-

onment" to the kind word of Christ. As far as Nebrija's grammar being the "first" in modern Europe, see Nebrija, "Introduction" by González-Llubera, p. xliii.

10 Nebrija, p. 19.

11 See *Las Siete Partidas del rey Alfonso el sabio, cotejadas con varios códices antiguos, por la Real Academia de la Historia* (1807; rpt. Madrid, 1972), III, pt. 4, title 21, law 1 (p. 117); pt. 4, title 5, introduction (p. 30); II, pt. 3, title 5, law 4 (pp. 419–20). In these sections Alfonso the Wise discusses the nature of slavery as an "agreement" against "natural reason," and as a temporary institution that "should lead towards freedom." In vol. II, titles 16, 21, and 22 he discusses the citizenship advantages and the progression of slaves toward free participation in society. Moreover, newcomers to the Spanish empire had to abide by the conquerors' proposal to have them "speaking Spanish within six months." See *Colección de documentos para la historia de la formación social de Hispanoamerica. 1493–1810*, ed. Richard Koneztke (Madrid, 1953), I, 237–40.

12 Among his prestigious posts was that of Royal Historiographer. He was probably responsible for the introduction of the printing press into Salamanca, of whose university he was an influential young professor, or at least was involved in the editing and printing of the earliest Spanish books including a few of his own. He was editor of the Polyglot Bible under the supervision of Cardinal Cisneros, Inquisitor General, to whom he wrote an *Apologia*. He was also involved in the creation and running of universities and the introduction and management of humanist education in general. See Nebrija, "Introduction" by González-Llubera, pp. xiii–lxii. He also took active part in Spain's African campaigns.

13 I am indebted to the Menil Foundation, and particularly to Mme. Dominique de Menil and Ms. Karen Dalton, for giving me the opportunity and the encouragement to pursue the research which has yielded a movement of eighteenth-century black writers and artists in Latin America, as well as sporadic but important examples as early as the late sixteenth century.

14 The category "gentes de razón" becomes a bureaucratically difficult issue toward the end of the seventeenth century, as the children of miscegenation openly demanded to be included. Some suggest it was easier for the offspring of Latin American Indians alone or with Spanish partners to obtain such a classification; this seems to correlate with the fear of a black, as opposed to a native American, middle class. See Jonathan I. Israel, *Race, Class and Politics in Colonial Mexico, 1610–1670* (London, 1975), ch. 2.

15 For elaborate descriptions of the Inquisition as theater in which the word *teatro* ("theater") is used in the description, see *Documentos inéditos o muy raros para la historia de México*, ed. Genaro García (Mexico City, 1974), pp. 31–41, 92–93, 145.

16 Most of the self-accusations are of being Jewish, and it remains difficult to separate fact from fiction, particularly because many blacks enjoyed a symbiotic cultural relationship with Jews. See, e.g., García, ed. *Documentos inéditos*, pp. 150–51 and Solange Alberro's discussion of several examples in "Negros y mulatos en los documentos inquisitoriales," in *El trabajo y los trabajadores en la historia de México*, ed. Elsa Cecilia Frost, Michael C. Meyer, and Josefina Zoraida Vázquez (Mexico City, 1979), pp. 144–49.

17 Even a descendant of Nebrija went through a *prueba de hidalguía* during the eighteenth century, which served as a source of much of the biographical information on the famous ancestor. See Nebrija, "Introduction" by González-Llubera, p. xvi and n. 14.

18 There are many examples of such a crime in the manuscript collection "Ramo Inquisición" of the Mexican Archivos General de la Nación; few transcriptions, however, have been published. For a published example, see García, ed., *Documentos inéditos*, pp. 60–61.

19   Nebrija, p. 6.

20   See Christopher Columbus's *Journal*, tr. Cecil Jane (New York, 1960).

21   Elaborate miscegenation tables have existed at least since the early seventeenth century, as documented by Inca Garcilaso de la Vega, *Comentarios Reales de los Incas*, ed. Ángel Rosenblat (Buenos Aires, 1943). The "certificate of whiteness" refers to the *documentos de gracias al sacar*, mentioned by Alexander von Humboldt, *Political Essays of the Kingdom of New Spain* (London, 1814), I, 246–47, but in existence since at least 1789. See discussion of Pedro de Ayarza in the text.

22   Many free black Spaniards are represented in the early New World adventure; the chief occupation among those was that of "interpreters": of virgin nature (such as possibly Prieto, the pilot of one of Columbus's ships), of barbaric languages (such as Estebanico who "translated" for Cabeza de Vaca in Florida, and who also discovered what is today the southwest of the United States), of fate (such as the "soothsayers" who appear in colonial chronicles and other documents, for instance Juana García from Freyle's *El Carnero*), and of leisure (as Juan Cortés, the poet who improvised for the conquistador Cortés).

23   During the eighteenth century, the emergence of the Latin American Creole class as a political force changed the panorama of black slavery. Both members of loyalist and independentist camps attempted to attract Creoles to their ranks, and individuals of black ancestry were often included. A number of Hispanicized slaves were offered freedom in exchange for military and political support. Therefore, many of the freedom papers obtained were not necessarily associated with humanitarian views of abolitionism, but rather sought as a selective form of payment for services rendered.

24   The Enlightenment brought new euphemistic labels for categories of miscegenation, or *calidades* ("qualities," implying "castes"), whose chief purpose was to encourage free children of miscegenation to join the ranks of taxpaying and law-abiding citizens. Loyalists and independentists fought with rhetoric and other forms of coercion to enlist these new citizens in their causes.

25   Records of Inquisitorial trials which contain writing, such as the one concerning Baltasar de Esquivel (discussed later on in text), contain comments on the meaning and value of such writing; see the Archivo General de la Nación (Mexico), Ramo Inquisición, Vol. 988, folios 392–417.

26   The quote is a "campaign motto" issued by the Crown of Spain as an ordinance, collected in Konetzke, ed. *Colección de documentos*, I, 237–40.

27   Latino dedicated an epic poem in Latin to the Hapsburg dynasty; see Ioannes Latinus, *Fernandi Principis Navitate . . . Austrias* (Granada, 1573).

28   Latinus, p. 10.

29   Latinus, p. 10.

30   Valuarez B. Spratlin, *Juan Latino, Slave and Humanist* (New York, 1938), p. 21.

31   The black majority among pre-nineteenth-century Peruvian physicians is suggested by many statistics. See Manuel A. Fuentes, *Lima. Apuntes históricos, estadísticos, administrativos, comerciales y costumbres* (Paris, 1867), pp. 167–71. The work of black surgeons in Peru and Valdés's practice as a *cirujano latino*, i.e., "Latin-conversant surgeon," is also discussed by J. A. de Lavalle, *El Dr. José Manuel Valdés (apuntes sobre su vida y sus obras)* (Lima, 1886), pp. 3–4.

32   Information about a possible "certificate of whiteness" is discussed by Lavalle, p. 10. Paraphrasing Mendiburu, whose *Diccionario histórico y biográfico del Perú*, 11 vols. (1874–90; rpt. Lima, 1935) I have not been able to consult, Lavalle notes that Pius VII signed a Bull to exempt Valdés from "irregularidades de su nacimiento y el inconveniente de su color" [irregularities of his birth and the inconvenience of his color] in order to admit him into the sacred orders. Lavalle concludes that Valdés decided not to

make use of this Bull (pp. 10–11). Lavalle quotes from what he claims to have heard as a child about Valdés, who was then in his seventies (p. 26). Valdés, according to Lavalle, refused to be portrayed because "los negros salían muy feos en pintura" [blacks came out very ugly (badly?) in paintings].

33 Of the several portraits by Fierro mentioned by Lavalle, I have reviewed two similar watercolors in the Museo de Arte del Perú, Lima, in which Dr. Valdés's face is covered and he is wearing the sandals typical of the poor. One of the images includes a horse-drawn carriage and coachman waiting in the background.

34 See nn. 23 and 24.

35 The word has been in use since at least the early thirteenth century in Castilian (ninth century in Catalan) to indicate a Moor-like person. However, the implication of a proud, dark person becomes popular in Spanish America in the eighteenth century. For the usage in Spain, see "Moro," in Joan Corominas, *Breve diccionario etimológico de la lengua castellana* (Madrid, 1980), p. 404.

36 See Johanna Faulhaber, "El mestizaje durante la época colonial en México," in *Antropología física. Epoca moderna y contemporánea*, ed. Javier Romero Molina, Alfonso L. de Garay, Johanna Faulhaber, and Juan Comas (Mexico, 1976), pp. 69–119.

37 This classification was assigned to several racial combinations; see Faulhaber, p. 117.

38 Faulhaber, p. 112.

39 For a discussion of the etymological implications of these words see "Cacho 1." and "Criollo" in Joan Corominas, *Diccionario Crítico Etimológico Castellano e Hispánico* (Madrid, 1980), pp. 725–27 and 243–45, respectively.

40 For instance, José Ventura, discussed later in the text.

41 The biographical information about Ventura, his writings and drawings, are part of the records of his trial. See the Archivo General de la Nación (Mexico), Ramo Inquisición, Vol. 1505.

42 I have used the partial transcription of Ventura's letter, respecting his original choice of capitalization and emphasis, in the *Guía de forasteros. Estanquillo literario*, 1, No. 1 (Jan. 1984), 8–9.

43 The text of the "certificate" was published by John Tate Lanning, "The Case of José Ponciano de Ayarza: A Document on the Negro in Higher Education," in *The Hispanic American Historical Review*, 24 (1944), 432–51; see esp. p. 439. For more information about this case, see James F. King, "The Case of José Ponciano de Ayarza: A Document on *Gracias al Sacar*," *The Hispanic American Historical Review*, 32, No. 1 (Feb. 1952), Pt. 2, 640–47.

44 This was an implicit honor or *honra*, and a state of grace or *estado de gracia*, to which individuals were entitled as soon as they were declared Catholic believers and citizens by the respective forms of "naming," and as long as they behaved according to the principles they had "signed into."

45 I uncovered the trial of Baltasar de Esquivel, including his autobiographical and biographical sketches, letters, and poetry intercepted or voluntarily given as depositions, in the Archivo General de la Nación (Mexico), Ramo Inquisición, Vol. 988, folios 392–417.

46 Esquivel, folio 400 and verso.

47 A singular metaphorical association occurs early on in Spanish between the words *negro* and *fish*, particularly in literature. For instance, since the thirteenth-century *Cantigas* of Alfonso the Wise there are many occurrences of the expression "negro[a] como un pez" ("black as a fish"). Is this a veiled allusion to the *morena*? Possibly, if one accepts the double connotation of the word *morena* as the "dark and treacherous" fish (Latin *muraena*, English *moray*) and as a "low-lying" Moor or a Moor lying low not to be recog-

nized. This play on words can be found in Afro-Hispanic writings as late as the eighteenth century. An example of the Afro-Mexican Vasconcelos will be discussed later in the text.

48 Esquivel, folio 402^v.

49 For an introduction to the controversial careers of these two poets and examples of their works, see Eduardo Matos Moctezuma, *El Negrito Poeta Mexicano y El Dominicano ¿realidad o fantasia?* (Mexico, 1980).

50 Matos Moctezuma, p. 131.

51 Nicolás León, *El Negrito Poeta Mexicano y sus populares versos* (Mexico, 1912), p. 229.

Ethnic Issues

Minority Discourse and the African Collective: Some Examples from Latin American and Caribbean Literature

Josaphat Bekunuru Kubayanda

1. Origins and Definitions

Historically the seeds of Caribbean and Latin-American minority discourse and the African collective can be said to have been sown when Fray Bartolomé de Las Casas, by a spectacular (mis)use of what Césaire calls "Christian pedantry,"[1] recommended to the Spanish crown the importation of "more robust" native Africans to replace the "weaker" American Indians on the harsh plantations and mines in the New World. That single and singular (mis)judgement for which Las Casas later repented was, nevertheless, generally in keeping with the insensitivities of an expansionist Europe for which Africa and the rest of the then so-called "unknown" world represented something outside the possibilities of human civilization. Soon enough and in the long run, Las Casas's solution to the Indian labor problem was to have all kinds of complex consequences of a racial, moral, economic, sociopolitical and, least expected, literary nature. This article deals with some of the literary developments arising from that early European encounter with Africa in the New World. What is the nature of the imaginative writing in the present century of the descendants of those Africans who were, by the nature and effect of the colonial legal and political discourses, marginalized

---

1. Aimé Césaire, *Discourse on Colonialism*, trans. Joan Pinkam (New York: Monthly Review Press, 1972), 11.

and thus denied access to the Spanish language, Spanish official history, and Spanish power? In what ways can this literature be characterized as "minor" in the context of post-independence Latin America, a sub-continent which is in and of itself on the periphery? Why and how is this Black literary production different from dominant discourse?

One way to respond to these questions is to return in a general sense to Las Casas's formulation and to its impact on Black consciousness in Latin America. It seems to me that in theory, at least, there is almost no way a Black minority discourse of the Americas can be separated from the historical collective memory of the propositions of some of the learned secular and religious humanists of Spain, or from the specific legacies of slavery, dispersal, and other forms of marginalization. There is little chance that it can be divorced altogether from protest thought.[2] The union of writing, memory, and protest is what Césaire, for instance, suggests in his seminal study, *Discourse on Colonialism*: this, too, is the major concern of the novel *Chombo* (1981) by the Panamanian Carlos Guillermo Wilson, the son of immigrant parents from the West Indies for whom Spanish remains, to a large extent, the language of the majority culture.[3] The novel is about the experiences of those West Indians and their offsprings who were brought to build the Panama Canal. There is in it a particular passage which Wilson himself considers to be central to his preoccupations as a novelist.[4] It has to do with a female character, Abena Mansa Adesimbo, whose origins can be traced back to Jamaica and further back to the Gold Coast (modern Ghana). Like all the 100,000 Panamanian West Indians who helped to construct the canal, Abena's identity, her "africanidad,"[5] is portrayed as threatened with fragmentation and extinction by the dominant social and political discourse of the majority that is represented textually by the Catholic Church and by a secular Eurocentric order. Contrary to the wishes of the old woman Nenén, and in compliance with the pressures of the dominant society, Abena symbolically rejects the African

---

2. See, for instance, August Meier et al., eds., *Black Protest Thought in the Twentieth Century*, 2nd ed. (Indianapolis: The Bobbs-Merrill Company, 1971).

3. Carlos Guillermo Wilson, *Chombo* (Miami: Ediciones Universal, 1981).

4. At the thirty-nineth Kentucky Foreign Language Conference, 24 April 1986, Wilson read this piece from his novel and commented upon it extensively.

5. Wilson, *Chombo*, 59.

name given to her child on the grounds that it would make integration problematic for her baby. Thus, the latter is baptized against the wishes of Nenén whose voice throughout the novel is strengthened by the African collective, by the consciousness of the African element within a text and context where it is, as it were, under siege:

> On the eve of the Catholic baptism of the child, Nenén again showed her rejection of a religion which had allowed the bloody invasion of Ethiopia, and worse still, she rejected the priest of that religion — Bartolomé de las Casas — who had ruled in favor of the enslavement of Africans in the sugar plantations of the Americas.[6]

Thus it seems that a primary concern of this minority writing is with the apprehension of African humanity within particular spatio-temporal coordinates in which "no one colonizes innocently,"[7] in which the "threat to person and personality remains a complex arrangement of absurd hostilities and fateful consequences,"[8] in which the African is scathed and bruised in multiple ways.

> Between colonizer and colonized there is room only for forced labor, intimidation, pressure, the police, taxation, theft, rape, compulsory crops, contempt, mistrust, arrogance, self-complacency, swinishness, brainless elites, degraded masses. No human contact, but relations of domination and submission . . .[9]

Evidently the concept of the African collective as source of a Black Latin American minority utterance will not be properly grasped without a reference to this Césairean idea of "relations of domina-

---

6. Ibid., 59.
7. Césaire, *Discourse*, 17.
8. Lemuel A. Johnson, "The Dilemma of Presence in Black Diaspora Literature: A Comparativist Reading of Arnoldo Palacios' *Las estrellas son negras*," *Afro-Hispanic Review* 1, no. 1 (Jan. 1982): 3.
9. Césaire, *Discourse*, 27. Minority theory of discourse in general has, of necessity, to do with a critique of domination. One of the European theorists with something of direct relevance to minority discourse is Michel Foucault. Foucault sees and grasps the complexities of our present and our past, points out the power relations of our past and of our present, and suggests, like Césaire, the need to construct discourses of resistance.

tion and submission." The African collective is coextensive with historical referentiality and with both the real and preceived processes of discriminatory differentiation that Césaire's words suggest, that is, the New World type of social relationships in which cultural and racial differences sometimes appear harmful rather than helpful.

Minority discourse necessarily reflects cultural contacts and the problems that they generate and nurse.[10] When some of the problems of the real world of cultural contacts are translated into imaginative writing, as they are in the multiple texts in the Black Latin American literary tradition, we as real readers are invited, as it were, to consider the protagonists or the poetic voices, themselves nearly always completely "drained of their essence,"[11] as they pose and examine crucial group questions on genealogy, identity, and existential anguish. Who are *we*? What have *we* done? What has been done to *us*? What can *we* do? Where are *we* going? These are some of the major questions an Afro-Latin minority discourse addresses. As Deleuze and Guattari have convincingly argued, dominant discourse need not and usually does not pose these types of collective questions, the reason being that its cultural terrain has been relatively stabilized and "universalized" through colonial conquest and propagation.[12] In fact, Richard Terdiman also argues, with good reason, in his book *Discourse/Counter-Discourse* that "the dominant *remains dominant*," and even seemingly absorbs its antagonists into its fold.[13]

Minority literary discourse inhabits a traumatized and traumatizing world. We sense this in theory from many sources, particularly Edward W. Said's *The World, the Text, and the Critic*: we learn that there is no opposition between the text, with all the elements of textuality it may contain, and the world.[14] The discursive situation, continues

---

10.   Melville J. Herskovits's writings, especially *Acculturation: The Study of Culture Contact* (New York: J.J. Augustin, 1938) and *The Myth of the Negro Past* (1941; New York: Beacon Press, 1958), provide an early theoretical background from an anthropological perspective.

11.   Césaire, *Discourse*, 21.

12.   Gilles Deleuze and Félix Guattari, "What Is a Minor Literature?" *Mississippi Review* 22, no. 3 (Spring 1983): 15-33.

13.   Richard Terdiman, *Discourse/Counter-Discourse: The Theory and Practice of Symbolic Resistance in Nineteenth-Century France* (Ithaca: Cornell Univ. Press, 1985), 73.

14.   Edward W. Said, *The World, the Text, the Critic* (Cambridge, Mass.: Harvard Univ. Press, 1983), 49-50.

Said, reflects the gap between superior and inferior, colonizer and colonized, and, one might add, dictator and citizen. Language itself contains the world, and minority discourse borrows the language of the dominant world, which in its purely dominant form negates or diminishes the minority subject. What, then, does the minority literature do with such a dominant tongue? Shakespeare's Caliban is admittedly the supreme example in the Western literature of the minority subject crushed by the language of the majority. But Caliban saves himself through a counter-discourse which "deterritorializes" the borrowed English tongue with curses.

Nearly every Caribbean writer of note has commented upon the centrality of language in the expression of a Caribbean Self. Thus, for Roberto Fernández Retamar of Cuba, Caliban becomes, in cultural terms, the appropriate symbol of the islands.[15] For Césaire, as for Frantz Fanon, the minority writer eventually must attempt to cast away the cultural burden that the language of the majority, like French, imposes. This can be done, they propose, through a rebellious *don de sabotage*[16] or through a recontextualizing, reframing, or destruction of, in Guillén's words, "the purity of academe / the purity of grammarians / the purity of those who insist they have to be pure, pure, pure."[17] Should a new grammar be created? Can it be done, the perceptive reader wonders, when dominant discourse seems indestructible, when language, despite its apparent neutrality and innocence is, as Bernard Henri Levy writes in *Barbarism with a Human Face*, the pillar that supports dominant power and behavior? "Language *is* simply power, *the very form of power, entirely shaped by power.*" "We know that the regulation of language is the best preparation for the regulation of souls."[18]

I believe, then, that "the regulation of the souls" and the official prescriptions of history are among the most significant marks of the master discourse against which the minority literature of Afro-Latin

15.   Roberto Fernández Retamar, *Caliban: Apuntes sobre la cultura en nuestra América*, 2nd ed. (Mexico: Editorial Diogenes, 1974).

16.   Aimé Césaire, *Cahier d'un retour au pays natal/Return to My Nativeland*, pref. André Breton and trans. Emile Snyder (Paris: Editions Présence Africaine, 1971).

17.   Nicolás Guillén, "Digo que no soy un hombre puro," *La rueda dentada* (La Habana: UNEAC, 1972), 8 (my translation).

18.   Bernard-Henri Lévy, *Barbarism with a Human Face* (New York: Harper & Row, 1979), 32-33.

America pits itself. Minority discourse is circumstantially a counter-hegemonic discourse; it thrives on a counter-hegemonic vision also, which is not to suggest, as the reader might expect, that it is far from rational. My point is that minority discourse sounds dialectically rational. This is because it claims that the languages of power and the historical assumptions and distortions they have engendered endow their users, potentially at least, with a power-based vision of the world and with a consciousness that tends to devalue those who are different and less powerful. But I must point out that minority literature is not just jettisoned against the dominant canon and its hegemonic centers, but also is immersed in those substratum African/African-American linguistic forms customarily thought to be outside the possibilities of creativity.

I chose this topic because Black Latin America is a minority area par excellence, historically and culturally. It has produced minority writers (who write in the major European languages) of considerable importance, some of whom rank among the best in the Spanish language. Among them are Zapata Olivella, Nicolás Guillén, Arnoldo Palacios, Adalberto Ortiz, Jorge Artel, and others. Reading them one can observe their marginality within the larger Latin American society and within the Spanish tradition, a marginality sometimes promoted by critical neglect and by a cultural stress on the "Latin" to the exclusion of the non-Latin in Latin America. To counter-balance this, Black minority discursivity provides a linkage with Africa, although this again is often ignored by those who fail to appreciate what is being done cross-culturally in Third World letters. Indeed, one of the fascinations for me of this topic is what it has to say about writing and, by implication, about critical reading and about our knowledge of the cultural realities of Latin America. The rest of my essay, then, is divided into two major sections which investigate the nature, context, and function of minority texts from Afro-Latin America.

2. Discourse, Power, and the African Continuum

Because colonial language legitimized the colonial and neocolonial orders, because in Latin America and the Caribbean, in particular,

the colonial language (be it French, Spanish, or Portuguese) reinforced the hierarchical relationships between the colonials, the white
criollos (creoles), and the Indian and African populations, and because the colonial functions of language were carried over into the
post-independence period, the language question was/is taken very
seriously. There was almost bound to develop among the *conquistadores*,
and later the *caudillos* (political bosses) and dictators of Latin America, a hegemonic rhetoric. At the same time that this was happening
in the dominant culture, there emerged among the minorities a
counter-hegemonic discourse. Examples would include Indian
(both oral and written), Jewish, Chicano, and Afrocentric literatures,
the latter of which is my primary concern here.

How does a Black Latin American counter-discourse work? First,
as in Césaire's *Return to My Nativeland* and Juminer's *Bozambo's Revenge*,[19] it takes the metropolitan language and "deterritorializes" it
by creating with it a style almost unrecognizable within the standard
discursive practices of the metropolitan centers and the administrative
strongholds of Latin America. Its function is clearly one of reversal at
the level of speech; however, it also raises and nurtures a combative
consciousness through linguistic subversiveness. Second, a Black minority counter-discourse introduces a new set of discursive features,
which include the cohesive and symbiotic relationships of oral and
written discourses, the presence in print of paralinguistic cues usually denied to the writer in the formal linear tradition of Europe, the
use of "regularitites" and other sociolinguistic patterns from the African continuum rather than from the standard reservoir of the
culturally and historically dominant discourse of the crown, cross,
conquistador, or *caudillo*.[20] Here its function is the affirmation of the
roots of a minority culture. It has a collective value because its goal
is to arouse and nourish a collective sensibility.

Negritude's role in all this is not small. It liberated the creative
minds of the Black writers so that they could create literary ironies to
counteract some of the monolithic formulations of the dominant

---

19. Césaire, *Return*, and Berténe Juminer, *Bozambo's Revenge*, trans. Alexandra B.
Warren (Washington, D.C.: Three Continents Poem, 1976.)
20. For further reading, see J.B. Kubayanda, "The Linguistic Core of Afro-Hispanic
Poetry: An African Reading," *Afro-Hispanic Review* 1, no. 3 (Sept. 1982): 21-26.

discourse. For the African minorities, or lettered minorities in the Latin world, the dominant discourse — from the *conquistadores* to Conrad and Kipling — presented itself as political discourse or, as González Echevarría better phrases it, "the voice of the masters."[21] This was particularly the case whenever the dominant discourse was confronted with the phenomenon of the Other, especially the so-called African *tabula rasa*, the cheap African slave labor market, and the mystery of the African jungle. *Bozambo's Revenge* confronts the dominant discourse and savagely strips it of its logic by turning its tide backwards so that primitive Europe is colonized by civilized Africa. Language use as we know it through formal education thus breaks down almost completely, as the dream of the minority group takes over the structure of the text. Like Juminer, Césaire takes that unilinear, monocausal master view of Africa and of things African, deflates its certainties, and projects the possibilities for a multi-dimensional reality beyond the imperial dreams of the master discourse of France and colonial Martinique.

The desire and the quest for a genuinely plural reality are at the heart of minority discourse. The African presence in the New World, according to Césaire, not only undermines mainstream monolithism but makes possible, theoretically at least, a unique multifacetedness which admits to collective or multiple existence in America. This in itself represents a sociocultural and humanistic attempt at innovation by those who, ironically, have invented nothing and humiliated no other race. Very often readers have failed to see this ironic twist of language in Césaire, and therefore have missed one of the salient characteristics of Caribbean minority discourse in general.

To underscore my thesis, one also has to look in a very special way at the Dominican Pluralist movement in poetry since 1975, especially Manuel Rueda's *Con el tambor de las islas*.[22] Going beyond the earlier tradition of drum poetry (cultivated by Guillón, Palés Matos of Puerto Rico, and Jorge Artel of Colombia), *Con el tambor* uses the multi-

---

21.   Roberto González Echevarría, *The Voice of the Masters: Writing and Authority in Modern Latin American Literature* (Austin: Univ. of Texas Press, 1985).

22.   Manuel Rueda, *Con el tambor de las islas* (Santo Domingo: Editora Taller, 1975). The Pluralist movement in the Dominican Republic of which Rueda is chief advocate is essentially experimentalist in nature. Its purpose is to force a new way of reading upon us and, thus, to suggest a new way of looking at the world.

vocal sounds of the Caribbean drum to great creative advantage: to represent the Caribbean people, to create a complex counter-linearity, a network of plural forms and of poetic "blocks" in one semantic or structural unit, calligraphs and *dragramas* (the drama of the word and the human person), all of which function as signs of several currents in the text and in the world. By implication, Rueda sees drum language, the language maligned and persecuted almost incessantly by the colonial discourse and order, as the medium not only for a new poetic discourse, but for a new voice against absolutism in writing and reading. Set in the mountains of Santo Domingo, *Con el Tambor* takes us to the beginning of things when there was the drum which produced a pure, primeval language of several sounds, realities, and possibilities. But that was before writing and its one-dimensional representation of time and space, as well as its support for dominance, came into being. Drum language came from the gods and therefore puts no limits on truth, whereas writing is a human creation and, therefore, an extension of human folly and limitations. However, when drum music is mixed, in a particular discursive space, with the written word, it provokes a response from us; it shocks us into participating and into seeing the simultaneity of things. The architecture of the poem *Con el tambor* is clearly a mixture of musical forms and writing: the words shout or sing to us with different letter sizes and colors and without the spatial crowding that we observe in linear writing.

I have said that the Black minority literature of Latin America introduces fresh Afrocentric discursive features for an affirmation of a "minor self" against the possibilities of cultural disappearance. Langston Hughes's famous poem "I Too Am America" is most demonstrably paradigmatic of that legacy of self-affirmation, which is partly what Henry Louis Gates describes as "integrity."[23] To complete that sense of self, Black minority literature, even when it uses a European language, seeks rhythmic reintegration into the signs and substance of

---

23.   Henry Louis Gates believes and has argued, contrary to scholars like Wayne Booth, that writing has never been "neutral," that in fact it has nearly always served some definite purpose. To this extent, Black writing, for Gates, is not value free; rather it serves to preserve the "whole" from being destroyed. See Gates, "Criticism, Integrity and the Black Idiom," conference on "The Nature and Context of Minority Discourse," Univ. of California, Berkeley, 26 May 1986.

the Afro-American and African traditions. It is fundamentally a written expression of reconnection and reappropriation. And this takes many forms. As argued in another paper, African rhetoric, whether oral-traditional or written-modern, relates to ancestry and to the natural agencies of revitalization or integrity (the baobab or palm trees, for example), and to textual categories like play jokes, riddles and proverbs, ritual narratives, mortuary or lament rites (dirges), musical formulae, and occasionally ideophonic sequences.[24]

It is neither possible nor desirable here to go into the details of each of these elements, but I would like briefly to mention what I believe to be a veritable *magnum opus* in Latin American letters of the present age. I am referring to *Changó, el gran putas* (1983) by Manuel Zapata Olivella of Columbia.[25] *Changó* is an ancestral novel, a novel in search of integrity. Written over a twenty-year period, *Changó* is the stunning result of novelistic maturation, the embodiment of a ritualistic and epic language in Spanish that belongs to and celebrates the Yoruba cosmogony, especially the god Shango (Changó), god of life, dance, and war, the three elements of blackness that Zapata Olivella himself says he sees in Colombia and in Latin America.[26] For this reason no New World novel is closer to the African utopian core than *Changó*. The falsely vulgar word *"putas"* in the title has confused Zapata Olivella's readers, but it really refers to something other than "Holy Fucker." This "something" is a textual entity almost more powerful than the Christian God or Devil and, because of its resilience, is seen by Zapata Olivella to be "applicable to the Blacks who have managed to survive the slave raids in Africa, the tremendous conditions of misery and hunger to which they were subjected during the Middle Passage, and who managed to survive all the slave regimes in this continent."[27] Thus, we have the coalition of two "divine" images, one from the Columbian Pacific Coast (*putas*), the other of African origin (Shango). This coalition at the imaginative level

---

24.   J.B. Kubayanda, "Notes on the Impact of African-Oral-Traditional Rhetoric on Latin American and Caribbean Writing," *Afro-Hispanic Review* 3, no. 3 (Sept. 1984): 5-10.
25.   Manuel Zapata Olivella, *Changó, el gran putas* (Bogotá: Editorial Oveja Negra, 1983).
26.   Interview, Yvonne Captain-Hidalgo, "Conversación con el Doctor Manuel Zapata Olivella," *Afro-Hispanic Review* 4, no. 1 (January 1985): 26-32 (my translation).
27.   Ibid., 30.

seems to produce the New World ideal, or the minor writer's desire for a genuine cultural synthesis, an enduring new wholeness, rather than an acculturative structure (that is, a movement from inferiority to superiority), which is the cornerstone of dominant discourse when it encounters minority voices. *Changó* shows in a unique way that minority literary discourse, being naturally pluralistic in conception and form, does feed on and is, in turn, fed by more than one tradition. This, I believe, is a major advantage for a minority discourse — an advantage, because it is connected to a kind of cultural heroism which eschews narrowness.

3. Minor Literary Reconstructions of History

Earlier I claimed that Afro-Latin literary discourse is embedded in a particular sociopolitical and historical context. Its primary function is not to make an accurate description of historical events, but rather to raise the national conscience by addressing questions that have to do with the minor self *vis-à-vis* the national identity or sovereignty, and with the perceived conflicts between freedom and autocracy, between Utopia and reality. Its purpose is not to record the "facts" but to reach a deeper *meaning* and to project a minority ethos. It indirectly argues against the anti-meaning movement in literary or critical scholarship. And one can understand why a literature congruent with a culture of questioning, of resistance, of the recuperation of one's roots, and of self- and national renewal, will be involved with definitions and significations. The Black Latin American idiom is therefore deconstructionist only to a point: it deconstructs the binary space in chronological history that allows "the master," as Fanon said of colonial Algeria, to laugh at "the slave." But its tendency, in symbolic terms, to destroy the negative constructions of history or of repressive power is underscored by a corresponding desire for "bio-power" (Foucault), that is, the "solidaristic" means to manage the repressed self throughout history, the harrowing effects of domination notwithstanding.[28]

A clear example of what I am talking about is the maroon novel in Spanish which, briefly stated, redefines and rejects the standard

---

28.   François Ewald, "Bio-Power," *History of the Present* 2 (Spring 1986): 8-9.

structures of the dominant historical discourse. I regard the maroon narrative as a good illustration of minority discourse in Latin America for the reasons that follow. Maroon narrative or poetry deals with marooning and with an underground discursive scheme unfamiliar to dominant discourse. The term "marooning" refers to the guerrilla resistance movements among Blacks that spanned the seventeenth, eighteenth, and nineteenth centuries in the Americas, especially the Haiti of Macandal, the Brazil of the *quilombos* (African encampments), the Jamaica of Cudjoe, the Surinam of Baron and Araby, the Cuba of José Antonio Aponte, the Mexico of the Mandingo rebels, the Ecuador (specifically Esmeraldas) of Illescas, and the Virginia of Nat Turner.[29] Marooning enabled the runaway slaves both to challenge and to escape the plantation or post-plantation order. But it was also intended to articulate, as independently as possible and within the colonial structure, the sociocultural and spiritual modes of being of the minority activists. It made it impossible for the dominant order to assume complete control of the discursive world. Today, marooning is considered an important minor historical paradigm for minorities in certain Latin American and Caribbean countries, particularly Cuba and the French Caribbean, who are reexamining their histories in order to redefine themselves without the perspectives of the metropolitan hegemonies. As a result, marooning is increasingly being given a new place in both the historical and intellectual domains of the Caribbean, and the maroon figure is becoming, in imaginative literature, protagonist rather than object of history. My thesis is that there is a correlation between this maroon discovery and the concerns, content, and context of the minority texts examined below.

Although certain works, like *Juyungo* by Adalberto Ortiz, *Cuando los*

---

29. On this subject see, among other studies, Eugene D. Genovese, *From Rebellion to Revolution* (Baton Rouge: Louisiana State Univ. Press, 1979); Sally and Richard Price, *Afro-American Arts of the Surinam Rain* (Berkeley: Univ. of California Press, 1981); Mary Jane Hewitt, "An Overview of Surinam," *Black Art* 5, no. 1 (1981): 4-28; José Luciano Franco, "Palenques de Frijol, Bumba y Muluala," in *Plácido y otros ensayos* (La Habana: Ediciones Unión, 1964); Thomas Flory, "Fugitive Slaves and Free Society: The Case of Brazil," *The Journal of Negro History* 64, no. 2 (Spring 1979): 116-130; and Patrick J. Carroll, "Mandinga: The Evolution of a Mexican Runaway Community, 1735-1827," *Comparative Studies in Society and History* 19, no. 4 (October 1977): 488-505.

guayacanes florecían by Estupiñán Bass, and *Chombo* by Carlos Guillermo Wilson, are set mainly in the twentieth century, Hispanic-American maroon novels often take place in the nineteenth century. Diaz Sanchez's *Cumboto* is situated in a Venezuelan community of fleeing Blacks; Miguel Barnet's *Biografía de un cimarrón* focuses on an ex-maroon's recollections of nearly one hundred years of personal marooning; and César Leante's *Los guerrilleros negros* deals with the period immediately following the 1812 widespread slave revolts throughout the island of Cuba.[30] This nineteenth-century setting is not without explanation. As evidenced by several studies of the plantation economy, the 1800s saw the emergence of fully-fledged slave societies in the Latin regions, especially Cuba and Brazil, which profitably turned from precapitalist toward capitalist development by becoming world producers and suppliers of sugar and coffee. That economic boom, however, contributed much to a dramatic worsening of the social conditions and race relations in Latin America. At the same time that the social rigors became pronounced internally, Latin American countries were either intensifying their emancipation drives against Spain or consolidating their newly-won freedom. Thus, the maroon consciousness, essentially a minority consciousness in the context of Latin America, was seemingly alert to what appeared to be a great historical paradox, that is, the white *criollo's* increasing drive for independence set alongside a continually potent chattel slavery and system of social injustice. In addition, as witnessed by the observations of the main maroon speakers in the works mentioned earlier, the maroon consciousness appeals to a new discourse vital to a new thinking and to the expression of a revolutionary stream of writing in Latin America. As the paragraphs which immediately follow will confirm, that vitality of the maroon creative act almost corresponds to the indomitable spirit or ethic of authentic liberation.

Nothing testifies more tellingly to that minority spirit of disso-

---

30. The principal maroon texts used here are: Adalberto Ortíz, *Juyungo* (Buenos Aires: Americallee, 1943); Miguel Barnet, *Biografía de un cimarrón* (Buenos Aires: Editorial Galerna, 1968); Ramón Diaz Sánchez, *Cumboto* (Santiago: Editorial Universitaria, 1967); César Leante, *Los guerrilleros negros* (Mexico: Siglo XXI, 1979); Estupiñan Bass, *Cuando los guayacanes florecían* (Quito: Editora Casa de la Cultura Ecuatoriana, 1954); and Carlos Guillermo Wilson, *Chombo*.

nance than the numerous discursive units concerning the clearly conflictive relationships between the national covenant and the African maroon presence. For example, in one such dissident discourse, the protagonist-narrator in *Los guerrilleros* states: "I did not know the word fatherland . . ." ("Desconocía la palabra patria . . .").[31] The speaker's psychic anguish and self-confession seem to be rooted, as I have argued earlier, in the maroon view that there is a fundamental historical contradiction in Latin America. This view undermines simple readings of reality and deconstructs, as it were, those monological forms of nationhood which the maroon narrator confronts. Barnet describes this as "the false myth of a unified nation."[32] Esteban Montejo, the maroon protagonist of *Biografía* who is similar to the narrative voice in *Los guerrilleros*, lives by an ethic of refusal:

> When slavery was ended, I ceased being a maroon. From the people's shouting I knew that slavery was over and I came out (of my hiding place.) They shouted: "Free at last." But I didn't really believe it. For me it was (all) a lie.[33]

This skeptical view that official history is no more than a deception was underscored early enough by some nineteenth-century Cuban cultural historians, such as Martin Morúa Delgado, who advocated a genuine unification and an open extention of sovereignty to all the Cuban nationals. This, he hoped, would turn Cuba away from the "tortuous paths" of the colonial era.[34] The maroon text's commitment to the principle of full emancipation constantly comes to the fore through a language that contradicts the textual and political claims of the old *raison d'état*, or those of the nascent *criollo* superstructure. The Blacks talked about full emancipation because there was a great uncertainty about the social implications of unfettered freedom. Indeed, uncertainty bred fear which in turn led to a nearly schizophrenic conditioning of the *criollo* mind regarding the Black

---

31.   Leante, *Los guerrilleros negros*, 11.
32.   Miguel Barnet, "The Culture That Sugar Created," *Latin American Literary Review* 18, no. 16 (Spring/Summer, 1980): 40.
33.   Barnet, *Biografía*, 62.
34.   Martin Morúa Delgado, *Integración cubana y otros ensayos*, ed. Alberto Baeza Flores (La Habana: Editorial Comisión Nacional Del Centenario de Martin Morúa Delgado, 1957), 64 and 196.

minorities. According to the Cuban essayist, del Valle, any African assertiveness in the nineteenth century was considered one of the two most serious misdemeanors that could be committed against the Hispanic-American public policy and administration, the other being any form of agitation of sociopolitical significance.[35]

Yet, against this backdrop, maroon writing throbs with ideals of self-government and is striking for its language of strident probing and resoluteness. In context, it is subversive of the dominant order in that it looks for its own truth beyond that of established reality; it addresses not only the question of the unilateral projections of the pre-independence period but also the *criollo* ideological articulations of post-independence including those of the so-called revolutionary eras. To the maroon frame of mind, a questioning deconstructionist mind, the old-time servitudes seem to reappear in the new society as part of a real or perceived stasis, that is, as the constancy of things, which is the base of "black rage."

This textual pinning of a note of cruel immutability on official history and historiography does not degenerate into resignation as may be expected; rather it leads in literature to modes of rupture with the modalities of the past, such as the sugar culture of Cuba, the Canal culture of Panama (*Chombo*), or the peonage of Ecuador (*Juyungo; Cuando los guayacanes florecían*). In consequence one often finds in maroon literature not just forms of protest but plain *licentia* which Cicero, long before the emergence of modern society, described as a "figure of diction and thought" or "a frankness of speech" occurring when a subordinate reprehends her superior for an ethical transgression.[36] Its literary focus is on verbal reversions and inversions; its functions include an undermining of the conventional formalities and orthodoxies and a broadening of our horizon of questioning. A good example of *licentia* is found in *Los guerrilleros* where the maroon captain, Gallo, lampoons the Catholic priest who acts as mediator between the government

---

35. Francisco G. del Valle, *La vida literaria en Cuba (1936-1940)* (La Habana: Cardenas, 1938), 8. Also see Charles Minguet's unpublished study, "Le Noir dans la Sensibilité et l'Idéologie des Creoles Americains à l'Epoque de l'Independance (1780-1816)," Colloquium on Negritude in Latin America, Dakar, Senegal, 7-12 Jan. 1974.

36. See Cicero, *Ad C. Herpennium Libri IV*, trans. Harry Caplan (Cambridge, Mass.: Harvard Univ. Press, 1954), 371.

forces and the rebel maroon troops.[37]

The expressive militancy I have been discussing is often highlighted by symbolic weaponry. Textually, the machete functions almost like the sword in the epic of Old Europe. Historically, it was the maroon hero's weapon of war, his companion, a powerful arm arrayed against the guns, hounds, and horses of the slave captors and conquistadors. The machete, to some extent, is turned into the symbolic agent that orders the literary worlds of Barnet and Leante, and those of Carpentier (*En reino de este mundo*), Ortiz (*Juyungo*), Olivella (*Chambacú* and *Cuentos de muerte y libertad*), Bass (*Cuando los guayacanes florecían*), and Wilson (*Chombo*).

The reason for the prevalence of this warring symbol in the texts of Black minorities in Latin America can be found in unofficial history: throughout colonial Africa and Latin America certain "natives," like the Asante warriors of the Golden Stool, the Afro-Cuban and Afro-Peruvian maroons, and the Saramaka of Surinam, frequently resorted to the machete as a major weapon of freedom. In the Cuban Wars of Independence, Montejo recalls in the *Biografía*, "the machete was the weapon for battle. Our commanding officers (Maceo and Maximo Gómez) would tell us: Upon arrival raise your machetes"[38] But there is in all this widespread use of the machete a fairly strong suggestion that the maroon experience of life, an experience going back to the beginnings of the New World, had itself opened up all of America to the possibility of liberation. To this extent, the machete has been transformed from a simple, ethnic weapon of self-protection to a broader sign of new trends of thought and action; it has become, in Barnet's words, "the epic of our nation (Cuba)."[39]

Maroon literature, it is suggested here, comes alive in epic narrative or heroic ballad; it is energized not just by machetes alone, but also by fictional and historical figures who are almost always fired by flights of moral ambition and activism. The maroon narrative or poem, however, scarcely indulges in the types of fantasied feats that mark most European epics from the *Iliad* to *Paradise Lost* (one exception being the Spanish *El Mío Cid*). All the same, the maroon text of-

---

37. Leante, *Los guerrilleros*, 200.
38. Barnet, *Biografía*, 164.
39. Barnet, "The Culture," 53.

ten takes a biographical or autobiographical form, portraying minority children and youths, male and female, as sources of national energy, as symbols of revolt against injustice, and as agents of some virtue. Natividad in *Cumboto* supplies corroborative testimony. Unlike the adult Roso and his West Indian ancestors who founded Cumboto, Natividad physically cannot oppose the enslaving structures at hand. Nevertheless, his mission in the story reflects an epic consciousness and a psycho-ethical awareness germane to the poetics of marooning: Natividad is resolved and succeeds in influencing the secluded aristocratic world of his master and friend Federico, thereby deconstructing the simple binary master-servant opposition which the politics of the story and the facts of history seem to uphold. It is true that the one event in the novel that kindles the imagination of Natividad is the heroic flight from the Caribbean and the resettlement on the Venezuelan coast long before the arrival of the European planter class. But unable to trace his blood parents and thus unable to fix meaning in exclusive terms, Natividad, as speaking person, becomes the voice of the entire community and ends up being Federico's only reliable companion and spiritual adviser. His success seems to signify for him an overall defeat of the monolinear expectations that his world has laid upon him. There is thus not an irreconcilable conflict between his sign and that of others; rather there is only an obvious *différance*, a trace of the substance of his sign in the other.

Conclusion

What conclusion can one draw about Black Latin American minority discourse? What will become of it? Will it get absorbed by the dominant discourse? Will it disappear on its own? I think that the problem is epistemological, that is, it has to do with the organization and dissemination of knowledge. Thus, to paraphrase Said again, the answer lies more with the readers and critics of minority literature than with the creators of that literature: " . . . critics create not only the values by which art is judged and understood, but they embody in writing those processes and actual conditions in the *present* by means of which art and writing bear significance."[40] In other words, all liter-

---

40. Said, *The World*, 53.

ary discourse, including minority discourse, is dependent upon a certain critical responsibility. I believe there is a real Black Latin American literary tradition, just as there is a distinct Black North American literary tradition. One of the dangers that arises is what happens if minority *critical* discourse ignores the minority *literary* discourse which continually interacts with both the dominant and marginal cultures. Another possible danger might be a failure to apply to minority literature the critical theories now being developed by Said, Spivak, Gates, and other scholars who are concerned with literary works and cultural objects outside the dominant canons set up by the West. In any case, Black Latin American minority discourse is an important one that will play an increasingly significant role in Latin American scholarship. As argued above, and as corroborated by other readers,[41] it has all kinds of possibilities. First, Black Latin American minority discourse forces us as readers to reconsider some of the so-called "universals" of history, to abandon monolithic reading, and to open our minds to multiple readings of reality. Second, it nourishes and is nourished by some of the most cogent cultural values of traditional Africa. Third, it is inseparable from the integrity of the race, but it does not attempt to raise the latter above all others; it simply affirms and reclaims its roots where the dominant culture overrides or tries to override the marginal groups. Finally, it rejects the politics of control, especially where this control is cultural. This is because minority discourse operates from the awareness that, as Kenyan writer Ngugi wa Thiong'o has put it, "once you control how a people look at themselves, you can in fact make a move in any other direction."[42]

---

41. I am thinking, for instance, of Richard Jackson's already extensive scholarship on the literature of Black Latin America, especially his book *Black Writers in Latin America* (Albuquerque: Univ. of New Mexico Press, 1979).

42. Hansel Ndumbe Eyoh, "Language as Carrier of People's Culture: An Interview with Ngugi wa Thiong'o," *UFAHAMU* 14, no. 3 (1985): 156.

REMEMBERING THE "DISREMEMBERED": MODERN BLACK WRITERS AND SLAVERY IN LATIN AMERICA

By Richard Jackson

> I am the contradiction of my history
> I am the one chosen to rewrite it.
>
> —Blas Jiménez

I. Introduction

The slave experience in Latin America and in the United States is being rediscovered with unprecedented frequency and artistry in black literature and in criticism today. If we stretch the concept of "black literature" to include literature on black themes by black and nonblack writers alike, then the theme of slavery truly has become a constant, especially but not exclusively in Cuba, Brazil and the United States, the three countries where the institution had its longest run. Slavery is an enduring theme, and it is appropriate that writings and discussions of the topic in these countries are peaking at this time, since they coincide for the most part with the centenaries of the abolition of slavery in the United States in 1963, in Cuba in 1986, and in Brazil in 1988.

It is appropriate that we talk about slavery also in the context of the upcoming commemoration in 1992 of the 500th anniversary of Columbus's first voyage to America, the fifth centenary of what has been called the meeting of two worlds. We should talk about it because slavery was a reality for most of those 500 years since Columbus, almost 400 years of it in some areas. Few topics during the life of this continent since the first arrival of Columbus have generated more interest among historians, creative writers and literary critics than blacks in bondage. Slavery informs, for example, some of the most popular and best-known novels in South America written in this century. *Matalaché* (1926) by the Peruvian Enrique López Albújar immediately comes to mind, as do the Venezuelan novels *Las lanzas coloradas* (1931), *Pobre negro* (1937), and *Cumboto* (1950) by Arturo Uslar Pietri, Rómulo Gallegos, and Ramón Díaz Sánchez, respectively, as do other titles I will mention later.

Frank Tannenbaum's famous little book *Slave and Citizen: The Negro in the Americas* fueled interest in the comparative approach to slavery when it was published in 1946, the same year as the appearance in English translation of Gilberto Freyre's classic *The Masters and the Slaves*, both published by A. A. Knopf in New York. There have been many studies since these landmark works appeared that have carried forward the debate regarding slavery in the New World. Much of the writing on slave history now is being done not only by historians but by creative writers and filmmakers as well, who are turning to the past in order to better understand and establish tradition for

131

the present. In much of the literature and film in Latin America today, black resistance to oppression, especially in Cuba, takes more center stage than the passive acceptance and romantic passion that characterized some of their nineteenth-century anti-slavery predecessors.

The film *The Other Francisco* sets out to correct flaws writer-director Giral found in *Francisco*, Anselmo Suárez y Romero's nineteenth-century anti-slavery novel, replacing frustrated romance with armed rebellion. César Leante's recent novel *Los guerilleros negros* (1976) also brings to life the black slave rebel so often missing from the pages of nineteenth-century anti-slavery novels. Miguel Barnet's *Biografía de un cimarrón* (1966) uses a live informant with experience in slavery as a door to history remembered. This ex-maroon told his story to Barnet, who reconstructed it from tape recordings. Reinaldo Arena's novel *La loma del Angel* (1981) was characterized recently by Ed Mullen as a work that recognizes the power of slave resistance and its ultimate historical consequences.

All of this writing or rewriting of slave history is not just a symptom of our time. Some of it started back in 1838, when several white intellectuals first took Juan Francisco Manzano's slave autobiography and created their own versions out of it. Manzano's slave autobiography is really the only slave autobiography we have in Latin America. The document he left us is a remarkable account of a suvivor of slavery who willed himself the knowledge to be able to write about it. Writing for Manzano was a heroic act as it was for Plácido, his free black contemporary, but especially for Manzano, because slaves were not supposed to do it. I wanted to just mention Manzano and Plácido here because there is kind of a recent critical resurrection of both of these early black writers who wrote during slavery times. Joe Kubayanda, for example, not too long ago, went so far as to say that Plácido's combativeness clearly anticipated the Black Renaissance of the 1920s, the Civil Rights movement of the 1960s and the *afrocubanismo* of the 1930s. He believes as well that the writings both of Manzano and Plácido reflect a pioneering, original attempt to create a literature of resistance, freedom and justice.

These are precisely the same thematic concerns that link these early black voices against slavery to modern black writers who have taken up the subject in their literature. In addition to the recent appearance of a great deal of critical work on slavery, including a panel held in New Orleans in March 1988 as part of the annual meeting of the Latin American Studies Association[1] there are such modern landmark creative works by black writers as Alex Haley's *Roots* (1976), Manuel Zapata Olivella's ambitious Afro-Colombian novel *Changó, el gran putas* (1983), and Toni Morrison's recently acclaimed novel *Beloved* (1987). I will concentrate here on modern black authors and on some of the strategies they use in remembering slavery in literature. Black writers today approach slavery through myth, by recreating intimate histories, and sometimes by reversing symbols, a technique of inversion perhaps used first by Martín Morúa Delgado in *Sofía* (1891), where he placed a person who was for all intents and purposes white in a black slave situation; this technique has since been used, with variations, by Nicolás Guillén, Carlos Guillermo Wilson, and Manuel Zapata Olivella, to name a few. The search for the intimate history of the black slave is especially evident in the Afro-Cuban poetry of Nancy Morejón, the Brazil-oriented literature of

132

Gayl Jones, the black American author who is a specialist on Brazilian slavery, and in Toni Morrison's new novel *Beloved*, which the 1987 Pulitzer prize-winner researched, in part, in Brazil. Morrison's novel, like Zapata Olivella's *Changó, el gran putas* (1983), takes mythical realism, a key narrative strategy, to new and ambitious heights.

II. Reversing Symbols: Slavery and the Vindicationist Perspective

> a man alone, imprisoned by
> whiteness . . . defying the white
> cries of a white death. . . .
>
> —Aimé Césaire

Black authors today are looking at slavery not only to correct the distortions of history, but also to radically change the legacy of color symbolism and the negative impact of blackness on the human mind. They do this in the first instance by bringing a black or vindicationist perspective, rather than an ideological position, to bear on the question of slavery, in effect, approaching the subject through an inversion of symbols not unlike the Black Muslim interpretation of whites as the original white devils, "the source of all humanity's evil."[2] In a clear reversal of "the usual racist symbolism," Carlos Guillermo Wilson, for example, speaks in his novel *Chombo* (1981) of *black* harmony upset by the depraved *white* sheep (rather than black sheep), "the root of all the race's calamity."[3]

Much of slave literature today focuses on the Middle Passage, including blacks who did not make it through. The slave crossing provides the mythic core for much of the new generation literature on the slave experience in Latin America, and figures prominently, for example, in the recent work of Cuba's Nancy Morejón and the Afro–Dominican Blas Jiménez. Afro–Central American writers of West Indian descent remember in their work a *double* Middle Passage, the original Atlantic slave trade and the "new" Middle Passage, the subsequent "scatteration process" from the Caribbean to Central America (Smart 93). In Cuba, much of Nicolás Guillén's poetry recalls the Atlantic crossing. When he writes "I came on a slave ship," or when he asks "Do you know my other surname . . . the one that crossed the sea in chains," or when he states: "So many ships, so many ships / so many blacks, so many blacks," we know his perspective on slavery will not be that of the "friendly master," nor will slavery be idealized. Such Afro-Hispanic authors as Manuel Zapata Olivella and Carlos Guillermo Wilson start their spiritual journey into the black American past below the slave-ship deck. They take us down inside the slave-ship hold, but they bring us up topside as well, through the eyes and thoughts of black slave rebels determined to mutiny, maim and salvage their dignity.

The model for Middle Passage literature could easily be Robert Hayden's well-known poem "Middle Passage" (1945), where we find all the elements of that "voyage through death / to life upon these shores."[4] Black writers today are returning to the

133

inhuman cruelty of that journey across the Atlantic and are finding new ways to recreate artistically the unspeakable inhumanity those "shuttles in the rocking loom of history" represented. Hayden's poem has been called "an epic in miniature,"[5] since he achieves in a few narrative voices the epic sweep of a much larger work. The same powerful irony we find in his poem can be seen as well in Zapata Olivella's own epic, the novel *Changó, el gran putas* (1983). Both authors let the evidence condemn itself. Both turn the horror of the slave trade back upon the perpetrators through a technique of inversion, where the slave traders are shown to condemn themselves through their own words and by their own actions.

Through ironic inversion both authors lead the reader to impressions directly opposite to what one would expect, given the words we read. Log books and ship diaries are the source of much of these words, written by uneasy crew, who fear rebellious blacks, crazy laughter and other manifestations beyond their comprehension. The "bright ironical names" of the slave ships that open Hayden's poem—*Jesús, Estrella, Esperanza, Mercy* (Hayden 68) also reappear in kind in Carlos Guillermo Wilson's unpublished novel *Afroexiliados*, where the name of the slave ship *Nazareno* belies the cargo on board. Perhaps the best-known of these historical slave ships with "pleasant" sounding names would be the *Amistad* (Friendship), because of the Cinquez rebellion on board. Cinquez is the hero of Hayden's poem, a historical figure who has become a symbol of freedom for blacks. Unlike the many black voices who become spiritual leaders in *Changó, el gran putas* and *Afroexiliados*, Cinquez does not speak in Hayden's poem, nor does he need to, because we know what he did. Hayden's "Middle Passage" represents a synthesis of historical voices recalling the inhuman cruelty of a people transported as chattel. To Zapata Olivella the transporters themselves are the animals, "white" animals, as he, like Carlos Guillermo Wilson, reverses racist historical symbolism by attaching negative connotations to the color white.[6]

The same slave crossing motifs inform the works of Hayden, Zapata Olivella and Wilson. The sexual element, for example, in Hayden's poem (66), where the "Crew and Captain lusted with the comeliest of the savage girls kept naked in the cabins"[7] becomes in Zapata Olivella's work "the *mandinga* woman tied to his bed," and in Wilson's "The young black women kept on deck were repeatedly raped." Other motifs include blacks in chains, the stench, blood, hatred, and the ever-present sharks, "the white hungry sharks" (Wilson 18) waiting to devour black bodies who leaped or were thrown overboard, and madness: "Lost three this morning leaped with crazy laughter / to the waiting sharks, sang as they went under" (Hayden 65). In a passage similar to this one from Hayden's poem, Zapata Olivella has written: "We had to throw that crazy slave overboard. It was bewitched and it laughed . . . even after it was swallowed up by the sea" (78). Present most of all in their works is "the timeless will" or the spirit of Shango that has enabled blacks to survive this "white horror," as Wilson names the Middle Passage (17). Both Wilson and Zapata Olivella reverse symbols as they try to give broad epic sweep to their accounts of remembered history. Hayden shocks the reader often through irony, as do Wilson and Zapata Olivella at times, but Hayden's Afro-Hispanic counterparts want the reader to see blacks taking control through aggressive action, deception, refusal to cooperate, and planned revolt designed to make blood flow that for the first time "is not ours" (Zapata Olivella 37).

134

Wilson and Zapata Olivella, in their detailed accounts of black rebellion, focus on black vengeance and the fear and confusion the slave captors had of the unknown. They leave nothing to the imagination in their return to the Middle Passage, because they evoke that voyage through death with the decided purpose of making the contemporary reader smell the stench and feel "the shackles, the iron rings, and the chains."[8] Wilson especially overloads with *tremendista* description in order to better shock and sensitize the complacent reader of today to the "white" horrors of the past. Guillén does the same thing by using "white" slaves in *El diario que a diario* (*The Daily Diary*) (1972), one of his last works.

White slaves did exist, but few of today's readers know it. Guillén uses white slaves in this work not to educate the public on this point but to raise white consciousness about the repulsive nature of black slavery, which everybody does know about. The expectation of finding black slaves where white slaves are mentioned makes this reversal work whether or not white slaves existed. Guillén puts white slaves in situations traditionally associated with blacks simply to catch the readers' attention, and to make them think. The strategy works because the reader is not prepared for the way the Afro-Cuban author turns history upside down. By making his slaves white Guillén not only attacks the repulsive nature of slavery, but, like Carlos Guillermo Wilson, attacks reader complacency as well. Role reversal, reversing symbols and ironic inversion are all techniques or variations of the same strategy black writers use to create art and to educate the public. Martín Morúa Delgado started it off in 1891 with his novel *Sofía*. Black writers in Latin America today are still doing it.

III. Intimate Histories: Slavery and the Black "Womanist" Perspective

> Slavery eliminated neither
> heroism nor love.
>
> —Sherley Anne Williams

Black writers, especially black women writers, are telling the intimate history of slavery through a black "womanist" perspective, a term in current usage that goes beyond the goal of sociopolitical freedom to restore "the place of love, growth and healing as satisfactory solutions to both life and literature."[9] The term, which originates with Alice Walker, embraces love and tenderness, and we find these qualities in abundance in the recent literature of several black women writers who have written about slavery, among them, Nancy Morejón, Gayl Jones and Toni Morrison. All of them look within and focus on the interior life of the slave, on the intimate history and the human experience of slavery as that institution affected love, feelings and what family life there was.

Black American female authors are in the forefront of the search for the inner world of the slave and for the true slave voice. They in particular have turned to Brazil, especially Gayl Jones, who is an expert on that country's slave history. Even Toni

135

Morrison, as I indicated earlier, researched Brazilian slave records for the intimate and personal history of her story of American slavery: "I went to slave museums but they weren't much help: little handcraft things slaves had made. No chains or restraining devices. In Brazil, though, they've kept everything. I got a lot of help down there."[10] More Brazilian help for creative writers in the United States is now available in the Mattoso volume *To be a Slave in Brazil 1550–1888*, which was just recently published in English.[11] Mattoso researched a variety of primary sources for this volume in an effort to reveal the inner world of the slave. Since slaves in Brazil left no written records, she had to turn to other sources in search of the slave perspective, which she was able to reconstruct from wills, inventories, judicial records and other papers that tell something about what it was like being a slave in Brazil. In her documentary work Mattoso adopted the standpoint of the slaves themselves, and tried to convey something of their thoughts, feelings and attitudes.

Nancy Morejón tried to do the same thing with the black slave woman in Cuba. Elizabeth Fox-Genovese chose the quotation "Slavery is terrible for men, but it is far more terrible for women" in a recent discussion of the burdens, wrongs and sufferings slave women endured.[12] These words call to mind Nancy Morejón's poetry, where the Afro-Cuban recreates similar accounts of the black slave woman's determination and progress from slavery to freedom. The black womanist perspective characterizes much of Morejón's poetry. She is perhaps best known for her poem "*Mujer negra*" ("Black Woman"), but she has done a good deal more. Slavery informs much of her work. The slave role of the black woman persona surfaces, for example, in "*Mirar adentro*" ("Looking Within"), when she writes: "*del siglo dieciseis data mi pena*" ("From the sixteenth century dates my suffering").[13] Slavery appears in "*Madrigal para cimarrones*" ("Madrigal for Runaway Slaves"), where she singles out the "*belleza tan dura*" ("hard beauty") of the hearts of the black runaway slaves who through their own actions resurrect their lives, taking their liberty "*como a niños / como a dulces niños*" ("like children, sweet children"). The black man "*como esas flores invernales / del trópico, siempre / tan asombrosas y arrogantes*" ("like those tropical winter / flowers, so stunning and / arrogant always") figures prominently in her slave poetry.

Most of all, Morejón has written of the black woman, the black slave woman, and of the awakening of the kept black slave woman who asks: "*¿Por qué le sirvo? / ¿Adónde va en su espléndido coche / tirado por caballos más felices que yo?*" ("Why do I wait on him hand and foot? / Where does he go in his lavish coach / drawn by horses that are luckier than me?"). It is the black slave woman in this poem "*Amo a mi amo*" ("I Love My Master") who, to the bewitching sounds of drum beats, comes to realization and takes knife in hand, and the black slave woman in "*Mujer negra*" that come to mind when we consider slavery in her poetry. In "*Mujer negra*," Morejón's intimate history of the black woman in America begins with the Middle Passage: "*Todavia huelo la espuma del mar que me hicieron atravesar*" ("I still smell the foam of the sea they made me cross"). Echoing Robert Hayden's well-known line "Voyage through death to life upon these shores," from his poem "Middle Passage," she writes: "*Me dejaron aquí y aquí he vivido / . . . aquí volví a nacer*" ("They left me here and here I've lived / . . . here I came to be born").

Morejón's "Black Woman" traces the history of the black slave woman exploited

136

and abused sexually, physically and mentally in America, in this new land *"donde padecí . . . azotes"* ("Where I suffered . . . the lash"), where *"sembré, recolecté y las cosechas no comí"* ("I planted seeds, brought in the crops, but never ate those harvests"). Morejón's black slave woman grew strong in hope and spirit, rising up eventually in rebellion, seeking the only independence possible: *"el palenque"* ("the free slave fort") in the hills where black slaves fled. Her poem culminates a century later, when descendants of the black slave runaway now down from the hills share in the creation of a new Cuba. Morejón's intimate history of the black slave woman from slavery to a freedom taken by her own hands finds its parallel and culmination in the larger framework of nation-building. Morejón tells in her poetry the intimate history of Cuba, which has at its essence a slave past. It is a fact that Morejón is a "woman formed in the Revolution"[14] but her poetry is very much based in history—both slave history and contemporary Cuban history. Morejón honors past heroes. Her poem "Black Man" does honor to "the dignity and suffering of millions" (Weaver xv). Her poem "Black Woman" honors the momumental black female figure who "moves through Cuban history, from the slave-crossing, through years of labor, experience and humiliation," to today (Weaver xv).

Morejón has said that she wrote this poem, which has been called as fine a treatment of slavery as any written in her generation,[15] in an attempt to reconstruct through an epic, first-person voice a part of Cuban history: namely, the story of the black women of her country; in this she has succeeded admirably. Much like other black writers today who recreate the slave past, Morejón takes the reader inside the mind of the slave whose master cannot even begin to understand. Morejón gives voice to the slave woman who curses *"esta lengua abigarradamente hostil que no mastico"* ("this language so stubbornly hostile I can't spit it out"). African slavery is a history of horror and hell, but it is also one of struggle and resistance. This history, as much as the new Cuba where *"ahora soy"* ("now I exist"), is a source of the strength, independence and freedom she feels. The black female persona in "Black Woman" feels the same.

Morejón's black slave woman rebelled and fled to an African stronghold in the hills in Cuba. In *Song for Anninho* (1981), a long narrative poem, Gayl Jones takes us inside Palmares, the best known of the free slave settlements founded by escaped Africans in Brazil, to tell a tender story of hope and black love, the love story of a black man and woman during colonial times.[16] Robert Hayden defines the "Middle Passage" as a "voyage whose chartings are unlove," using the term "unlove" to denote a total absence of love or compassion in this trade in human lives. Jones charts some of this unlove in her first novel *Corregidora* (1975), but the other side of love is her story in *Song for Anninho*. *Corregidora* is, in a sense, an intimate history of the black woman's experience of utter degradation. On one level the novel is contemporary, but Corregidora, the name of the protagonist, comes from the Portuguese slave master who raped his slaves, some of them his own daughters and granddaughters. *Corregidora* bears witness to the sexual exploitation of black women and focuses on the brutality and the sexual abuse black women have suffered from the days of slavery to today. Jones tells this story through the eyes and feelings of female victims of that perverse behavior. Jones is a student of Brazilian slave history, and she has researched the

137

personal stories of black slaves. Her novel is human-centered in that she goes inside the feelings of the participants in history.

In *Song for Anninho* Jones takes Palmares, a symbol of black freedom, struggle and resistance even today, and explores the flesh-and-blood relationships among individuals that sustained that rebel slave community and made it work. Most of all Jones contrasts sadism and sexual abuse with true black love in the midst of slave revolt. Both the tale of sexual exploitation in *Corregidora* and the story of black love between slaves in *Song for Anninho* are told from the minds of the female protagonists. Almeyda is the voice in the narrative poem. We see through her eyes. We hear her private conversations with self and with others. We feel the slaves' desire for freedom, but we also see the intimate relationship among slaves. Slave revolt frames the work, but just as she contrasts the personal story of her female protagonists in *Corregidora* with the broad impersonal telling of the Portuguese slave master and the social types he represents, so too does Jones, in *Song for Anninho*, probe the psychology of her characters and the human relationships that motivated them in their slave stronghold. Jones has researched her subjects well, and "what I learned," Almeyda tells Anninho, is that "we loved not to escape the pain but in spite of the pain."[17] Sustaining love at a time of severe cruelty and sadism is her theme: "How one could keep loving / at such a time. How we could look at each other with tenderness. / And keep it, even with everything." Gayl Jones tries to capture the feelings of the people inside Palmares before its final destruction, described below in a letter from Domingo Jorge Velho or one of his captains to the Portuguese Overseas Council, dated February, 1694:

> During the second watch that night, between the fifth and sixth of February, suddenly and tumultuously [Zumbi] with all his people and the equipment which could follow him through that space, made an exit. The sentinels of that post did not perceive them almost until the end. In the rear guard Zumbi himself was leaving, and at that point he was shot twice. As it was dark, and all this was taking place at the edge of the cliff, many—a matter of fact about two hundred—fell down the cliff. As many others were killed. Of both sexes and all ages, five hundred and nineteen were taken prisoner.[18]

Song for Anninho is also an account of their escape from Palmares, of Almeyda's mutilation at the hands of Portuguese soldiers, and of her memories of better times with Anninho. Times were tough, but through flashbacks Almeyda recalls the "good place" that was Palmares, good because "it was like the place / we lived before / like in our country." She remembers the kindness and the love of Anninho for her that extended beyond simply getting "between her knees." In a larger sense *Song for Anninho* is a spiritual journey through memory over time, a remembering beyond Palmares that establishes a place for blacks in the world. In this same larger sense, *Song for Anninho* is a story of hope and freedom, of perseverance and the will to survive. Through remembering one can not just survive destruction but "survive at loving."

In the end, *Song for Anninho*, perhaps more than anything else, is a song of the immortality of symbol, of Zumbi, of heroism, and of an enduring and sustaining love

138

that transcends actions, death and hardship. This love between two black slaves on the run is Jones's plea for tenderness, and for the "young ones" not to forget "the tender ways . . . the ways a man must be with a woman, the ways a woman must be with a man." The way it was even in the midst of the danger, the hardness, the horror, the adventure, and the war on Palmares. Gayl Jones, like black Brazilian writers, recognizes that Palmares represents "a type of African *continuum*"[19] a link or conduit through which African traditions of resistance and love of freedom were reinforced and passed on. Blacks today, she seems to realize, have much to learn from the Quilombo tradition of black solidarity and black love.[20]

Toni Morrison, who, like Gayl Jones, approaches slavery through the intimate histories of the people trying to live through it, recently spoke about omissions in slave narratives written for abolitionist readers during the nineteenth century. She believes that since blacks were addressing sympathetic whites they tactfully suppressed feelings of outrage that might offend their hearers. They "forgot" many things, and "'most importantly—at least for me,' Morrison said, 'there was no mention of their interior life.' " Morrison recreates this interior life in *Beloved* "with a moving intensity no novelist has ever approached before."[21] Morrison's new novel tells a very old story. Stripped down, *Beloved* has at its center the story of Sethe, a slave girl who "split to the woodshed to kill her children."[22] Sethe chose death for them since they could not grow up in freedom to a "livable life."

The external reality of slavery is a given, but Morejón, Morrison and Jones display their assessment of it by exploring its effects on the personal lives and feelings of individuals who are for the most part black women. Gayl Jones has recognized and has explained her preference for the intimate history. Toni Morrison has done the same: "Usually a book on slavery," she has said, "is about slave masters, the institution—a predictable plot. When I say *Beloved* is not about slavery, I mean that the story is not slavery. The story is these people—these people who don't know they're in an era of historical interest. They just know they have to get through the day. I deal with five years of terror in a pathological society, living in a bedlam where nothing makes sense. . . . But these people are living in that situation, and they survive it— and they are trying desperately to be parents, husbands and a mother with children."[23]

Morrison talks of these people in the present tense as though she has put herself into their past, seeing them in their struggle as it is unfolding. There is no story or history more intimate and personal than the family, and the author attacks the absurd logic that tore it asunder in slavery: "Slavery depends on the absence of a family. You can't have families if you're going to have slavery because then you're got another family, then another, then a clan. People start getting furious and say 'give me back my daughter,' 'give me back my wife.' So they had to destroy the family."[24] *Beloved* has been called a "vividly unconventional family saga,"[25] in which the author goes to the core of the family fabric which is the mother instinct, even in a slavery designed to distinguish it. "I started out wanting," Morrison has said, "to write a story about the feeling of Self. Women feel themselves best through nurturing. The clipping about Margaret Garner stuck in my head. I had to deal with this nurturing instinct that expressed itself in murder."[26]

Morrison does a good deal more than just recount a true tale of infanticide. That

139

event is the factual and intimate center of her novel both structurally and emotionally, but she builds layers onto it, recreating in the process the cruelty and terror of plantation life in the 1850s and after. Always she gives us the perspective of the black slaves who lived in those times and who suffered the moral abomination and outrage that was slavery. Desperation perhaps is a key word here, because people get desperate when all seems lost. Returning to slavery after having escaped it was to lose everything, which is why Sethe tried to kill all her children and herself too—to avoid going back. Morrison's novel covers a time when even freedom was no paradise. *Beloved* shows that even after slavery, "daily reality for the freed slave continued to be a matter of perpetual struggle,"[27] a fact of black life all over, even in the Spanish-speaking world and in Brazil.

Freed slaves in Spanish America had similar problems and obstacles to overcome and in some cases were treated worse than slaves; they were certainly considered far more dangerous. One of the discoveries discussed in the Matusso volume regarding Brazil was that even in freedom, freed black Brazilians had to often resort to humility, obedience and loyalty to survive and adapt to Brazilian society. Morrison does not write about Brazilian slavery, but the Brazilian documents she used helped give her the perspective necessary to get inside the slave's mind. Matusso's volume tries very hard to do the same thing. Morrison understands that bondage is bondage whatever the system. Black slaves in Brazil had no concept of that fact, namely, that they were in Brazil and therefore should somehow have a different mindset from black slaves in slavery elsewhere. Morrison understands this, and for this reason relied on the interior evidence wherever she could find it, and she did find help in Brazil. While her novel focuses on "the holocaust of slavery and the blood-soaked years afterwards; the vicious tools used to humiliate slaves, the grotesque prison chain gangs,"[28] in the United States we know that the slave mentality she recreates reflects the difficulty of living black slaves faced everywhere.

IV. Mythical Realism: Slavery and the Mythical Perspective

> Myth is the very core of the . . .
> literary artifact and criticism must
> attend to this central feature.
>
> —Carmen Virgilio and Naomi Lindstrom

The continuum of human experience is a very big part of Toni Morrison's *Beloved* (1987) and Manuel Zapata Olivella's *Changó, el gran putas* (1983). It is at the level of mythical realism where these two novels meet. Each author tells a harrowing tale of staggering proportions, but in both cases their starkly realistic narrations are overlaid with a mythical quality as much ghostly as lyric. Both novels border on the supernatural in that Zapata Olivella uses "dead" narrators in his Afro-Colombian novel, and Morrison uses a reincarnated baby grown up. Both work from an African world-view, where the dead interact with the living. Beloved, to be sure, is the ghost of Sethe's murdered baby, but she is also a symbol or representative of the many millions who died in passage, which is Morrison's way of paying homage to or remembering those who never made it into slavery. Beloved, more than anything, speaks for all the "disremembered," and Morrison's novel, like Zapata Olivella's, reminds present-day blacks of their responsibility to remember the past and to learn from it. Slavery for these writers becomes a collective experience, which is why their telling of it often takes the form of myth. They remember slavery in narrative forms that are sometimes stunning, especially when their remembering moves outside of chronological time.

Black writers today also are rejecting negative racist myths about blacks, including the "myth of the Negro past," which holds, in effect, that all worthwhile achievements and discoveries of human society originated in the white Western world and that black ancestors were "out of it."[29] These kinds of myths, in fact, are not really myths at all, but "persistent lies . . . too often taken to be ageless truths," to use Robert Bringhurst's excellent distinction between the older sense of the word myth ("ageless truth") and what it has become or how it is often used today ("persistent lie"). Real myths teach humility; lies teach pride, he has said, adding: "The claim that the Emperor is divine, or that the Jews or the Blacks are inferior . . . these are all myths in the second and more recent sense of the word. All of them are lies. . . . Real myths are stories that are rich and nourishing. . . . It is a persistent lie that the emperor is divine, but it is an ageless truth that the emperor has no clothes. . . . Our lust for control and our appetite for pride . . . lead us to trade good mythology for bad history."[30]

As Nicolás Guillén did throughout his life, black writers today are fighting myth with myth, replacing persistent lies, or bad history, with good mythology. They do this in part, as we have seen, by reversing symbols, which involves rejecting white myths about blacks, turning white symbolisms completely around, and reinstating in their place a black mythology, or black myths of their own. The concept of whites as the original white devils is a part of a black mythology that retells or recreates history from the black vindicationist perspective discussed earlier. A mythological approach to slavery has always been reflected in symbolic oral tales and in oral poetry, which speak of survival strategies and of the slaves' fight for liberty, and of their rebelliousness. Defiant blacks and runaway slaves figure in proverbs as well, and this oral literature at times becomes a social statement reflecting black slave heroism, much of it contradicting collective racist beliefs about blacks. Black myths are built on a black mythology grounded in part on an African cosmovision, on the sum total of African collective beliefs.

It is clear to anyone reading it that *Changó, el gran putas* is thoroughly grounded in mythology, "an African mythology,"[31] one that breaks down walls between the past and the present, between the living and the dead, between fact and fiction, and between myth and reality. Zapata Olivella's ambitious novel indeed has the combination of myth and history, of truth and lie, as Marvin Lewis has said, that is necessary to the most enduring works of fiction.[32] *Changó* will endure as have the characters, both historical and mythical, that populate his novel. The author himself, like Mackandal and other black heroes in the work, has become a myth custodian, one who traces black history from the mythological beginnings through the Middle Passage forward, moving his characters through a mythical realism that transcends time. *Changó* provides insights into the continuum of black resistance first on board ship, then during the first 100 years and after, right up to our time.

Manuel Zapata Olivella moves from white myths to black mythology by rejecting the myth of the docile slave with no rebellious spirit, replacing that persistent lie with black heroes of mythic proportions. What the Afro-Colombian author does is to retell the story of slavery through the voices and participation of the custodians of the ancestral past, some, as in the Haitian Revolution, mixing myth and politics, or in a word, voodoo.[33] *Changó* is indeed a literary work "spawned by the cultural intertext of slavery"[34] and by the mythic forces that inspired the quest for freedom in the Black Diaspora. Y. Captain-Hidalgo[35] was the first to refer to Zapata Olivella's *Changó* as a projection of mythical realism, a term she uses to define the collective belief or faith of a people who accept the mythical as real, certainly as possible, especially during the Haitian Revolution, which represents to many black humanity's coming of age for the first time in the New World in a political sense.

What sustains Zapata Olivella's novel is the sense of mission that motivates the major figures or myth custodians in the work to foment and encourage freedom, not only in Haiti, but elsewhere in the New World as well. It is not surprising, therefore, that Haiti, which has been described as "the greatest hell on earth"[36] for blacks at that time, represents the most clear account of the collective faith of a people in their destiny foretold. Nor is it coincidental that this "voodoo rebellion," which guided slaves in Haiti to rise up and feel invincible, would produce Mackandal, certainly one of the most famous *maroons* in black history. It was inevitable that Mackandal and other symbols of black resistance, Toussaint L'Ouverture among them, who in their heroic exploits rival the mythological gods themselves, would appear in *Changó*. Zapata Olivella gives legendary historical figures in his novel the mythical status they deserve and have earned.

V. Conclusion

With Manuel Zapata Olivella leading the way, black writers in Latin America today continue to see it as their duty to combat the stigma associated with the black slave past. It is not an easy task when that legacy is perpetuated both in literature and in life. In the Spanish Caribbean,[37] for example, as in other Latin American areas, there is an extensive folk literature based on black themes that reflects the inheritance of slavery. Its favorite subject is ridicule of blacks, an offshoot of the prejudice that originated with slavery. Black writers in Latin America today confront that legacy, or "the slavery model," Marvin Lewis has called it.[38] Lewis is discussing Peru, where he finds blacks still bearing the burden of slavery, but the effects of slavery have been felt all over.

The same burden applied, for example, in Cuba, where during the greater part of this century life for blacks was "not significantly different from slavery."[39] Nelson Es-

142

tupiñán Bass's novels often show similar situations for blacks in Ecuador where, certainly during the early part of this century, many lived in "virtual slavery."[40] In this century "the slave master has become the owner and the slave is now the worker."[41] Only the terminology has changed. It would seem, then, that while black writers are rewriting slave history, the legacy of the slave past, while inspiring black unity, continues to "cast a heavy shadow,"[42] one that hampers their efforts to overcome the stigma associated with that legacy.

Notes

1. Two of the participants on the panel in New Orleans—Lorna Williams, who organized it, and William Luis—have under way major book-length studies on the experience of slavery in Cuban fiction. The papers they gave were, respectively, "Negating *Cecilia Valdés*: Morúa Delgado's *Sofía*" and "Juan Francisco Manzano's *Autobiografía*: Suárez y Romero's Version." The program also included Antonio Vera Léon's "Barnet-Montejo: *La escritura y el cimarronaje*," and Edward J. Mullen's "Reinaldo Arena's *La loma del Angel*: The Rewriting of History in Cuban Fiction." See also Jill Ann Netchinsky, "Engendering a Cuban Literature: Nineteenth Century Antislavery Narrative (Manzano, Suárez y Romero, Gómez de Avellaneda, A. Zambrana)," diss., Yale U, 1986; Henry Louis Gates, Jr., "The Literature of the Slave," *Figures in Black: Words, Signs, and the Racial Self* (New York: Oxford UP, 1987), 59–163, and other recent works by Gates, including *The Slave's Narrative* (1984), which he edited. See also John Sekora and Darwin T. Turner, eds., *The Art of Slave Narrative* (Macomb, IL: Essays in Literature Books, 1982), and the highly useful updated bibliography on slavery and the slave narrative in the notes to Sekora's recent article, "Black Message/White Envelope: Genre, Authenticity, and Authority in the Antebellum Slave Narrative," *Callaloo* 10.3 (1987): 482–515. Just out is *Slavery and the Literary Imagination*, D. E. McDowell and Arnold Rampersad, eds. (Baltimore: Johns Hopkins UP, 1989).
2. Ian Smart, *Central American Writers of West Indian Origin, a New Hispanic Literature* (Washington, DC: Three Continents, 1984), 84.
3. Smart 83, 84. This kind of reversal even appears in black comic strip humor. Witness this conversation in "The Middletons": "Dad, did you go to college?"—"Yup, we all did, all except George. He didn't care about education or responsibility."—"Who's George?"—"He's the white sheep of the family."
4. Robert Hayden, *Selected Poems* (New York: October House, 1966), 65. All parenthetical references are to this text.
5. Fred Fetrow, *Robert Hayden* (Boston: Twayne, 1984), 306.
6. Manuel Zapata Olivella, *Changó, el gran putas* (Bogota: La Oveja Negra, 1983), 89; Carlos Guillermo Wilson, *Chombo* (Miami: Ediciones Universal, 1981), 18.
7. Hayden 66.
8. Wilson, *Afroexiliados*, unpublished ms., 25.
9. Clyde Taylor, "Black Writing as Immanent Humanism," *Southern Review* 21.3 (1985): 795.
10. Walter Clemons, "The Ghosts of Sixty Million and More," *Newsweek* 28 Sept. 1987: 75.
11. Katia M. de Quierós Mattoso, *To Be a Slave in Brazil 1550–1888*, trans. Arthur Goldhammer (New Brunswick: Rutgers UP, 1986).
12. Elizabeth Fox-Genovese, "A Manifold Challenge," rev. of Harriet Jacob's *Incidents in the Life of a Slave Girl, Written by Herself*, ed. Jean Fagan Yellin, *Times Literary Supplement* 4 Dec. 1987: 1340.
13. All quotations and translations are from Nancy Morejón, *Where the Island Sleeps Like a Wing: Selected Poetry*, ed. and trans. Kathleen Weaver (San Francisco: Black Scholar Press, 1985).
14. Miguel Barnet, *Where the Island Sleeps*, x.
15. Julio Finn, *Voices of Négritude* (London: Quartet Books, 1988), 169.
16. Gayl Jones, *Song for Anninho* (Detroit: Lotus, 1981). All quotations are from this edition.
17. Gayl Jones, "Work in Progress," *Obsidian* 2.2 (1976): 41.
18. Reprinted in Ronald M. Rassner, "Palmares and the Freed Slave in Afro-Brazilian Literature," *Voices From Under: Black Narrative in Latin America and the Caribbean*, ed. William Luis (Westport, CT: Greenwood, 1984), 221.
19. David Brookshaw, *Race and Color in Brazilian Literature* (Metuchen, NJ: Scarecrow, 1986), 290.

143

20. Gayl Jones's interest in the African presence in Latin America continues in her recent publication, *The Hermit Woman* (Detroit: Lotus, 1983), a collection of poems. "The Machete" tells the story of the rebellion of a "band of *cimarrones*/wild black men" and an African slave woman who kills her mistress. Her narrators for the most part continue to be women, and the question of love and commitment even in difficult times continues in this recent work.
21. Reported in Walter Clemons, "A Gravestone of Memories," *Newsweek* 28 Sept. 1987: 74.
22. Toni Morrison, *Beloved* (New York: Knopf, 1987). All quotations are from this edition.
23. Toni Morrison in an interview with Miriam Horn, "Five Years of Terror," *U.S. News and World Report* 19 Oct. 1987: 75.
24. Toni Morrison in "Five Years of Terror," 75.
25. Carol Rumens, "Shades of the Prison House," *Times Literary Supplement* 16–22 Oct. 1987: 1135.
26. Clemons 75.
27. Rumens 1135.
28. Deirdre Donahue, "The Lyrical World of Toni Morrison," *U.S.A. Today* (1987), 1D.
29. James B. Webster, in Michael Bradley's *The Black Discovery of America* (Toronto: Personal Library, 1981), xiii.
30. Robert Bringhurst, "Myths Create a World of Meaning," *The Globe and Mail* 7 May 1988: C1.
31. Ian Smart, rev. of Zapata Olivella's *Changó, Afro-Hispanic Review* 3.2 (1984): 31.
32. Marvin Lewis, *Treading the Ebony Path: Ideology and Violence in Contemporary Afro-Colombian Prose Fiction* (Columbia: U of Missouri P, 1987), 118.
33. See Janice Lee Lidell, "The Whip's Corolla: Myth and Politics in the Literature of the Black Diaspora: Aimé Césaire, Nicolás Guillén, Langston Hughes," diss., U of Michigan, 1978, 8–9.
34. Lewis, *Treading the Ebony Path*, 118.
35. Captain-Hidalgo, "The Realm of Possible Realities: A Comparative Analysis of Selected Works by Alejo Carpentier and Manuel Zapata Olivella," diss., Stanford U, 1984, 57.
36. Franck Bayard, "The Black Latin American Impact on Western Culture," *The Negro Impact on Western Civilization*, eds. Joseph S. Roucek and Thomas Kiernan (New York: Philosophical Library, 1970), 293.
37. Samuel Feijoo, "African Influences in Latin America: Oral and Written Literature," in *Africa in Latin America*, ed. Manuel Moreno Fraginals (New York: Holmes, 1984), 145–69.
38. Marvin Lewis, *Afro-Hispanic Poetry 1940–1980* (Columbia: U of Missouri P, 1983), 49, 115.
39. William Luis, "History and Fiction: Black Narrative in Latin America and the Caribbean," *Voices From Under: Black Narrative in Latin America and the Caribbean*, ed. William Luis (Westport, CT: Greenwood, 1984), 201–21.
40. Henry Richards, "Nelson Estupiñán Bass and the Historico-Political Novel: From Theory to Praxis," from Estupiñán Bass's *When the Guayacans Were in Bloom*, trans. Henry Richards (Washington, DC: Afro-Hispanic Institute, 1987), 213.
41. Luis 24.
42. Robert Brent Topin, "From Slavery to Fettered Freedom: Attitudes Toward the Negro in Brazil," *Luso-Brazilian Review* 7.1 (1970): 3–12.

144

Politics, History, and Nation

Politics, Literature and the Intellectual in Latin America

BY ENRICO MARIO SANTÍ

(For Nivia Montenegro)

Our subject is vast, and to attempt to cover it in an essay this size is perhaps mad. The reader may also wonder how a professor of literature can presume to address the complex and tumultuous world of politics and the intellectual in Latin America. I would wonder myself, were it not for the fact that literature and the writer — the poet, the novelist, the playwright,the essayist — continue to play a crucial role in the shaping of that world. In fact, so closely has the institution of literature been identified with the political debates among Latin American intellectuals, that often general discussions on the subject take the terms writer and intellectual to be synonymous, despite their obvious differences. Not too long ago, for example, *The New York Times Magazine* carried a long and interesting piece by Alan Riding on "Revolution and the Intellectual in Latin America" which featured a number of literary celebrities — notably, García Márquez and Octavio Paz, but also Borges, Cardenal, Cortázar, Fuentes, Rulfo and Vargas Llosa, among others.[1] Despite the comprehensive title, Riding's piece focused exclusively on these writers and their ideological differences without ever mentioning the existence of other Latin American intellectuals who are not literati — ar-

---

[1] *The New York Times Magazine* (March 13, 1983), pp. 29-40.

tists, economists, historians, journalists, academics — and who presumably participate as well in the same debate. More significant, I think, is that despite this glaring absorption of the intellectual by the writer, Riding's piece contains hardly any discussion of literature per se. The works of these writers indeed provide the background and identity that make their political differences significant, but these works are never discussed. It is only in the final paragraph of the piece, when Riding's need to justify his approach becomes evident, that he mentions how this political debate "has contributed to the region's literature," and concludes, hurriedly and cryptically, that "Latin America's social models may so far have failed, but its writers have made the failures memorable."

I realize of course, that I may be asking of Riding's journalism a scholarly precision which it never intended. Be that as it may, what interests me about his article, and which I would like to make the theme or at least the goal of my essay, is the significance of Riding's omission of literature from his discussion of the role of the writer in the current political debate in Latin America. I wish to explore, in part, the paradox that this omission dramatizes — the virtual exclusion of literature from the concept of the intellectual while at the same time calling upon the writer to represent that intellectual. The paradox is not, to be sure, a cultural phenomenon which is peculiar to Latin America. It constitutes, rather, one more version of the general problematic that binds literature and the intellectual; and even more generally, of the contradictory relationship between the intellectual and his own discipline. About this general relationship I shall have more to say later. My immediate purpose, in citing this telling example from *The New York Times*, was to demonstrate that literature does play an important role in that debate — indeed, to judge from its systematic exclusion from articles like Riding's — a much more crucial role than would appear at first sight. Consequently, any serious discussion of the relationship between the writer and the intellectual cannot simply chronicle from the outside, as it were, the broad political opinions that writers may or may not share. It must also broach those specific problems, complex and slippery as they are, that are peculiar to the writer and to literature as both human experience and as an institution.

Before attempting to take up the specific literary question that I have just raised, let me begin as broadly as possible and review with you some of the themes that constitute the current political debate among Latin American writers and intellectuals. My comments must be necessarily general, more in an attempt to outline a conceptual framework that would help us understand the various positions than to give a comprehensive or exhaustive survey. It is true that, as Riding points out, at the heart of this debate, "is the search for new political models for a continent....viewed as desperately in need of change". Within the growing strategic importance that the Third or underdeveloped world assumes in the East-West conflict, the question of a reliable political and economic model for Latin America has become, to say the least, urgent. The United States and Soviet Union continue to provide, of course, the alternative models of development. But in a continent where democratic political institutions are constantly on the verge of collapse and the local economies suffer from a chronic instability, despite the proximity to and influence of the United States, the prestige of a Western democratic model has waned. At the same time, however, the continuing economic failure, repressive policies and militarization of the Soviet Union have cast doubts on its own viability as a model for Latin America, particularly as that model has already been proven a failure in the areas of economic and ideological dependence, as the case of Cuba demonstrates.

It would of course be too simple to say that all of the positions assumed by Latin American writers and intellectuals derive from this debate regarding political models. At the same time, however, one must admit that the implicit choice of models determines not only the various ideological positions but, more importantly, different concepts of the intellectual. Should the writer and intellectual be a dissident and adopt, for example, a constantly negative position toward the State; become a permanent critic of government, as it were, in defense of a universal ethic or morality? Or should he be a public defender instead; attempt to identify, that is, the social and political problems that require immediate redress and thereby take the side of so-called revolutionary governments and national liberation movements which make these problems their object of reform? I put this question in an either/or formula, reductive though I find it, because this is the way that most Latin American intellectuals themselves often pose it. García Márquez will ask, for example, "how can the intellectual enjoy the luxury of debating the destiny of the soul when the problems are of physical survival, health, education, ignorance, and so on?" Octavio Paz, on the other hand, will assert that "as a writer, my duty is to preserve my own marginality before the State, before political parties, before all ideologies and before society itself."[2] Thus while intellectuals of the left, such as García Márquez or Mario Benedetti, will accuse their liberal counterparts of selling out to American imperialism because of the liberals' occasional criticism of the Cuban and Sandinista Revolutions, liberal intellectuals, such as Octavio Paz or Mario Vargas Llosa, will charge their counterparts on the left with support of so-called revolutionary causes and governments for the sake of opposing United States influence in the area, even while allowing that kind of support to curtail their freedom to criticize those same cases and governments.

I am deliberately overstating the rift between the two sides for the sake of clarity. In reality, the distinctions between the two groups are not as clear-cut, although the issues remain as real. Neither Octavio Paz nor Mario Vargas Llosa spend their days, as García Márquez apparently hints, debating the destiny of the soul. In the current intellectual scene I can think of no more outspoken critic of concrete political and social issues ranging from Mexico's one-party system to birth control — than Octavio Paz. Likewise, Vargas Llosa's actions on behalf of certain causes — like freedom of the press in his native Peru and the fate of Argentina's "disappeared" — is also well-known. At the same time, both García Márquez and Benedetti, like the late Julio Cortázar, have been able to speak out against Washington's complicity with repressive military dictatorships and in support of the Cuban and Sandinista revolutions

[2] *El ogro filantrópico* (Barcelona: Seix Barral, 1979), p. 306. All translations, here and elsewhere, are mine.

precisely because they assume a marginal position both as exiles and as critics. I suspect, therefore, that what divides these groups is more strategy than substance, although there are clear substantial differences, of course. All of these writers oppose dictatorial regimes; all of them criticize, albeit in various degrees, the pervasive influence of the United States; and all of them defend intellectual freedom. What does divide them, I think, is two things: one, localized issues which both determine and reflect their implicit choice of political models; and two, each group's skeptical views of the other's intellectual status. I want to pursue the second of these divisive reasons.

A moment ago, I described the reciprocal opinions of liberal and left intellectuals. We can now refine that description by adding these two statements. First, in suppressing any criticism of the socialist countries that actively support national liberation movements in Latin America, intellectuals of the left are accused by their liberal counterparts of ideological dogma, thus betraying in effect their role as critics and reformers. As Vargas Llosa stated recently, in a spirited debate with Benedetti, "I criticize equally all of those regimes that throw their adversaries into exile (or into jail, or kill them off) while he (Benedetti) seems to think all this is somehow less serious if it's done in the name of Socialism."[3] Second, in withholding blanket support of national liberation movements and criticizing all dictatorial regimes equally and without distinction of their ideological sign, the liberal intellectual is accused by his counterpart on the left of diluting any specific criticism of the United States, thus betraying their social conscience. "How can we be content," writes Benedetti in the same debate with Vargas Llosa, "if every minute a Latin American child dies of hunger and disease; if every five minutes there's a political murder in Guatemala; if 30,000 people have disappeared in Argentina?"[4] As we can see, then, what is at stake in each of these positions is nothing less than the very identity of the intellectual. One ceases being an intellectual as soon as the other side believes you to have betrayed the essence of intellectual identity: unceasing criticism and reform, in the case of the

[3] *Vuelta*, 92 (July, 1984), p. 51.
[4] Ibid., p.48

liberal; conscience and solidarity, in the case of the left.

It would perhaps seem obvious to us, standing safely outside of the debate, that the figure of the intellectual includes or should include *both* of these functions. The intellectual should be, at once, the unceasing critic of society and of the state, ever alert to point out deceit, irresponsibility or mismanagement in the public domain; but the intellectual should also be the conscience of society and the state, the keeper of cultural and social values, the mirror in which society reflects itself in order to legitimize the status quo. The first, critical or reformist function determines a negative, marginal position before society at large. The intellectual points out problems and wrongdoings and suggests ways of resolving them. The second, moral function determines a positive, central position in society. The intellectual defends policies and actions and justifies their implementation. I would venture, however, that it would be difficult to get Latin American intellectuals to agree on the distribution of functions which I am offering here. Whereas the liberal (certainly Paz and Vargas Llosa) would be the first to describe him/herself as the true conscience, the first to appropriate a moral function to his or her criticism, though not necessarily a central position in society, the intellectual of the left (García Márquez or Benedetti), on the other hand, would argue instead that in denouncing the hidden complicity between Washington and military regimes, for example, it is s/he who fulfills a truly critical, negative position. The problem, of course, is that both positions are correct because descriptions of the type that I have made rest ultimately on the point of view chosen to evaluate the debate.

One can gather, then, that much of the problem of discussing the subject of the intellectual in Latin America revolves around our lack of an adequate vocabulary to describe such a figure. It would certainly be tempting, in this regard, to apply concepts about the intellectual developed in Europe to a description of the Latin American version. I am thinking in particular of the categories formulated by Antonio Gramsci, the first (and in my opinion the most acute) modern Marxist to make the intellectual the central part of his sociopolitical analyses. As we know, Gramsci says that intellectuals are

usually of two kinds: *organic* intellectuals, who appear in connection with an emergent social class and who prepare the way
for that class's conquest of civil society by preparing it ideologi-
cally; and *traditional* intellectuals, those who seem to be un-
connected with social change and who occupy positions in
society designed to conserve the traditional processes by which
ideas are produced — teachers, writers, artists, priests and so
forth.[5] But if we were seriously to apply these Gramscian
categories we would immediately run into problems. The organic intellectual's ideological work on behalf of the emergent
class would certainly fit certain aspects of the intellectual of
the left. But the defensive, almost reactionary dogma with
which the left guards its political advances would seem to draw
them closer to Gramsci's definition of the traditional intellectual. Conversely, the traditional intellectual's established position in society would seem to describe the liberal intellectual's
privileged status; and yet, the pluralism which the liberal intellectual advocates would seem to counter the traditional conservative process by which ideas are produced in the
underdeveloped societies of Latin America.

Compounding the difficulty attendant to the lack of a
general theory of intellectual production in the Latin American
tradition are the intrinsic difficulties stemming from the concept of the intellectual itself, what I earlier referred to as the
general paradoxical relationship between the intellectual and
his discipline. "The intellectual," wrote Jean-Paul Sartre in one
of his many *meddling* essays, "is someone who *meddles* in what
is not his business."[6] Indeed, in order to qualify as an intellectual, what Sartre calls "a specialist in practical knowledge,"
one must stand apart from one's particular specialization, take
cognizance of its universal implications, and discuss these implications publicly. Charles Oppenheimer and Carl Sagan, for
example, were a physicist and is an astronomer, respectively;

[5] See "The Function of the Intellectuals" and "The Different Position of
Urban and Rural-type Intellectuals", in *Selections from the Prison
Notebooks*, ed. Quintin Horare and G.M. Smith (New York: International
Publishers, 1971), pp. 3-23.

[6] *Between Existentialism and Marxism* (New York: Random House, 1974), p.
230.

but it was only when both scientists began to discuss publicly the implications of their research for the threat of nuclear war that they actually joined the ranks of the intellectual. (Noam Chomsky and Andrei Sakharov are two other names that come to mind.) How does this paradox work in the case of the writer? Must the writer, along with the physicist, the astronomer and the linguist, stand apart from his particular work and take cognizance of its universal implications before s/he can become an intellectual? For Sartre, whose views on the subject are revealing, the answer is no. "The writer," he says, "is not an intellectual *accidentally*, like others, but *essentially*."[7] That is, unlike the physicist, the astronomer or the linguist, the writer, by the very nature of his work, is always engaged in the contradiction between the particular exigencies of his craft and the universal implications of his message. Moreover, the writer makes of that contradiction the theme and substance of his work.

"Not all intellectuals are writers," writes Octavio Paz, "but all (or almost all) writers are intellectuals."[8] To Paz's succinct formula, with which I agree, of course, I would simply add the following: Indeed, all writers are intellectuals *but* their intellectual status will be recognized insofar as they address something other than their writing, insofar as they meddle, that is, in what is not their business, namely literature. This is not, incidently, my own personal opinion; I am merely describing an institutional reality. Nobody would deny, for example, that Jorge Luis Borges was an intellectual; and yet, the fact that in his last few years Borges devoted himself almost exclusively to literary concerns and no longer wrote about politics — and when he did speak about politics it was to thank an honoring regime like Pinochet's Chile or to praise democratic elections, like the recent ones that ousted the Argentine junta and put Alfonsin in power — cast Borges, in the public eye at least, as a curious non-intellectual of sorts. Is it by chance, I wonder, that in his piece Riding refers to Borges as a poet ("the continent's greatest living poet") or that he should barely mention Borges, or Juan Rulfo, another famous non-meddler, in

[7] Ibid., p. 284.
[8] *El ogro filantrópico*, p. 20.

the course of his discussion of other literary celebrities whom he does not hesitate to call "intellectuals"? Thus, while the writer would seem to be the essential, rather than the accidental, intellectual, still he appears to fall prey to the same paradox that riddles the figure of the intellectual in general. Indeed, in the case of the writer that paradox seems to loom even larger. For when the physicist and the astronomer discuss publicly the universal implications of their work, they punctuate their discussion with precise details of their research for the simple reason that everyone expects them to share those details. And yet, when the writer discusses publicly the universal implications of his writing, or of literature in general, how can he possibly do this without risking a loss of his status as an intellectual? The question, in other words, is how can a writer be an intellectual and still remain a writer?

Facing this particular quandary of the writer as intellectual, liberals like Octavio Paz and Vargas Llosa have given an answer with which I happen to sympathize. The essence of the writer as intellectual, they say, is determined by his creative use of language, which thereby presupposes his undertaking a critique of language — precisely the medium that intellectuals must use in order to exchange ideas. Such a critique does not necessarily produce, as opponents from both left and right have charged, an irresponsibly aestheticist or solipsistic form of literature — texts that comment on their own aesthetics while excluding all historical and existential issues. Rather, in making language the object of his criticism, the writer opens himself and his work to the realm of systematic inquiry, to an analytical reason and doubt that necessarily binds his writing to his historical and political context. In this sense, writing, like politics, becomes as Octavio Paz points out, "the space where political freedom is displayed — circus, arena, theatre, tribunal, philosophical academy, scientific laboratory and open-air church, all rolled into one."[9] Vargas Llosa, less lyrically perhaps, has put it this way: "The literary vocation is born out of one man's disagreement with the world, out of his detection of the deficiency, the emptiness and the rubbish that sur-

9 Ibid., p. 302.

round him."[10] If statements such as Paz's and Vargas Llosa's sound primitive and perhaps even naive to an American or European ear, it may be because they advocate the kind of minimal level of intellectual freedom which already forms part of a modern Western consciousness but which in Latin America, languishing on the margins of the West, has been the exception. On the other hand, by posing such a primitive position, in restating the minimal conditions of intellectual activity, one achieves a distinct advantage over Western discussions of the intellectual which, in the case of the writer at least, as we have seen, lead to a quandary. Such a restatement restores, that is, the intellectual essence of the writer by pointing to the centrality of language — the medium that embodies the writer, identifies the intellectual and allows for the critical exchange of ideas.

In order to exchange ideas critically we must have, as a minimum, a willingness to establish a dialogue with others — those whose ideas are opposite, or at least different from, ours. Dialogue means sharpening our language in order to communicate our ideas, sharpening our reason in order to question those ideas with which we happen to disagree, and sharpening our conscience in order to have the courage to modify ideas whenever we are persuaded by the dialogue. These truisms are the staple of any liberal intellectual establishment, such as that of the American university, but unfortunately not those that prevail in Latin America. The predicament of the intellectual in Latin America, I fear, is that while differences of opinion do abound, very little face to face exchange of these differences actually takes place. Disagreements either with the State or among intellectuals themselves are taken as betrayals, breaches of conduct and personal affronts, rather than as the necessary and healthy differences stemming from one's intellectual and moral conscience. Simply to understand, as he does, the important issues of his history, society and culture is not enough for the intellectual. Such understanding often stagnates for the lack of a meaningful circuit of exchange. And yet, as C. Wright Mills wrote once about the predicament

---

[10] *Contra viento y marea* (1962-1982) (Barcelona: Seix Barral, 1983), p. 135.

faced by the post-War American intellectual:

> Knowledge that is not communicated has a way of
> turning the mind sour, and finally of being forgotten.
> For the sake of the integrity, discovery must be effec-
> tively communicated. Such communication is also a
> necessary element in the search for clear under-
> standing, including the understanding of one's self.
> For only through the social confirmation of others
> whom we believe adequately equipped do we earn the
> right of feeling secure in our knowledge.[11]

The historical roots of this tragic absence of intellectual
dialogue in Latin America are well known. A heritage of
violent conquest and colonization; a climate of authoritarianism stemming from the anti-modern spirit of the
Counter-Reformation; the fracture of a single culture into
twenty-one artificial republics; the endemic weakness, since
Independence, of democratic institutions; the wholesale absence of liberal values. With this desolate background, it is no
surprise that since Independence the Latin American intellectual has pursued the question of his or her cultural identity,
and that he should have pursued it, by and large, in exile.
What exactly is Latin America, who exactly is the Latin
American and what do these things mean, are the questions
that underlie much of the literature written in Latin America,
from Simón Bolívar to Carlos Fuentes, during the 19th and
20th centuries. The questioning itself, however, has often suffered under the very fragmentation that elicits it. For usually
the question is not who exactly is the Latin American, but
rather who exactly is the Argentine, the Brazilian, or the
Cuban? What is the national psychology of the Peruvian? Or,
how do we arrive at an ontology of the Mexican? Such questions may seem silly to us jaded Americans, but they have been
felt to be and are of course necessary to Latin Americans; and
they are interesting and useful insofar as they stem from and
refer back to the broader cultural context which they attempt

[11] *Power, Politics and People*, ed. Irving Louis Horowitz (New York: Oxford
University Press, 1963), p. 300.

to interrogate. Such questions about cultural identity reflect, in turn, other more fundamental, less rarefied questions. Why are we so bad off, how did we get this way, and how do we get out of this mess? The question about identity — the ontological question, if you will — thus becomes indistinguishable from the question about process — the historical question; and these two questions, in turn, merge into one broad social question: what is the history of relations not only among the Latin American nations themselves, but between Latin America and the rest of the world?

Such a monumental history, essential though it is, still awaits its Arnold Toynbee — and I am certainly not it. But whereas Latin America has lacked encyclopaedic historians of the breadth and talent of Toynbee it does have a tradition of equally encyclopaedic writers whose work makes up in visionary depth what it has lacked in scholarly breadth. In other words, it has been in the language of literature, rather than in that of strict scholarship, that the Latin American intellectual has always asked the fundamental questions about his or her cultural identity. Which thus means that the answers that literature has provided have themselves posed other (or perhaps the same) questions in a perhaps endless chain of historical interpretation. The late visionary style of a writer like José Martí — Cuba's foremost 19th century poet and one of the principal figures of Latin American intellectual history — stems, for example, from a desperate attempt, toward the end of his short life, to synthesize historical wisdom, moral judgment, political action and poetic insight. The argument of an essay like "Nuestra América" (Our America) (1891), in which Martí pleas for the self-knowledge and self- government of Latin America through original ideas and original institutions, cannot be divorced from its rhetorically-charged language and visionary sweep. It would not be excessive to say that in this particular essay Martí's critique of the dual faults of provincialism and servile imitation, so rampant in the politics and culture of 19th century Latin America, is couched in an intricate poetic logic where ideology becomes indistinguishable from metaphor. In my own literal and surely crude translation of two of the essay's memorable sentences: "We were but a mask: underwear made in Britain, vest made in Paris, coat from the United States, and a little beret made in Spain...Let our wine be made of bananas; it may turn out bitter but it is still our wine." Of course, banana wine exists only in language, in Martí's metaphor for cultural independence; but the metaphor itself embodies a will to invent, or invent anew, a synthesis which Martí found lacking in the fractured colonial mask of 19th century Latin American society. Intellectuals of the left today claim Martí, with all good reason, as a precursor of their own anti-imperialism; but they somehow always manage to overlook that Martí's revolution, carried out throughout a lifetime of exile, actually takes place in language, and therefore that his contributions to ideology presuppose a linguistic critique of certain received ideas of his time.

The poetic logic and visionary sweep of a writer like Martí therefore deceive us into dismissing his work as unscientific and perhaps even politically useless. Indeed, Martí was a critic of Positivism, so we can expect his style to reflect an abiding distrust of scientific method and a sympathy for intuitive understanding. And yet his work, like that of any writer and thinker, has limits and problems — particularly insofar as that work both unveils and conceals the broader question of cultural identity. In this sense Martí is no different from most 19th century Latin American intellectuals, whose anti-analytical prejudice left an equivocal legacy. They urge us, on the one hand, to assume our cultural identity, but they never inform us, on the other, about how exactly that identity came about, let alone what that identity means in relation to other cultures. They urge, in other words, the pursuit of ontology, without pursuing the more significant details of history, and ultimately ignore, for the sake of self-definition, the social context that necessarily determines that identity.

One can find a useful corrective to such a legacy, I believe, in the historical meditations of a writer like Octavio Paz. In a series of essays on the subject of history and society — starting with the classic *Labyrinth of Solitude,* which dates from 1950, and on with the *Critique of the Pyramid* (1969), *El ogro filantrópico* (1978), *Sor Juana Inés de la Cruz* (1982), and *Tiempo nublado* (1983) — Paz has sought to uncover the hidden traumas, so to speak, of Latin American history. I use the word trauma advisedly, for Paz's intention in these and other essays has been nothing less than to psychoanalyze Latin American history; to do psychohistorical interpretations of certain moments and institutions in the hope that such interpretations might effect an eventual therapy. Paz himself would prefer calling his essays "moral criticism," "the description of a harmful, hidden reality," as he has stated, rather than a straight psychohistory, and there is good cause to follow him on this.[12] *The Labyrinth of Solitude,* for example, describes certain traits of the Mexican character — hermeticism, hypocrisy, formality, the death wish, violence, etc. — which are explained as symptoms of psychic conflicts caused by historical traumas — the violence of the Spanish Conquest, the humiliation of the Indian during the Colonial period, the ensuing bad faith of Mexican intellectual and political movements like the Porfirato and even the Mexican revolution. In this sense, the history of Mexico, from the Aztecs to the present, becomes a kind of text which the poet, as a privileged reader, can decipher in terms of the traumas found in the day- to-day behavior of today's Mexican.

One may or may not agree with Paz's original and at times inventive links between symptoms and traumas in the course of his argument. But one cannot deny that unlike earlier attempts to describe the Mexican character, such as Samuel Ramos's *Profile of Man and Culture in Mexico* (1934), Paz's solid grounding in history represents a breakthrough. Such a breakthrough is possible, moreover, because unlike previous attempts to deal with the subject, undertaken mostly by academics (philosophers or social scientists), *The Labyrinth of Solitude* was the work of a writer, and specifically of a poet. In fact, Paz has stated on occasion that his original plan was to write a novel about Mexican history, but that once he wrote it he decided to change it into an essay because the only good thing about the novel turned out to be the characters' dialogue, which of course discussed ideas about Mexico. Even the title — *El laberinto de la soledad* — is poetic, let alone the goal of the

[12] *El ogro filantrópico.* p. 20.

book: one poet's reading of history for the sole purpose of feeling himself (and making others feel) less lonely. Although the influence of Marx, Freud and Nietzsche is evident throughout the book, what is ultimately interesting about it is the personal, almost intimate attitude that Paz assumes toward his subject. Neither Marx, nor Freud, nor Nietzsche, not even the Sartre of *Being and Nothingness* — had ever granted loneliness the status of a separate philosophical category. But Paz had, if not as a philosophical category at least as an existential reality, scrutinized it in his early introspective poetry as well as in a brilliant earlier essay entitled "Poetry of Solitude and Poetry of Communion", partly devoted to Saint John of the Cross. As the central formula of that early essay had been that "the poet starts out from loneliness, and guided by desire, goes toward communion," so Paz's reading of Mexican history follows such an itinerary to end, finally, in the discovery of loneliness as a universal human problem rather than a specifically Mexican trauma. To quote from the haunting lines of the last chapter: "There in open loneliness, transcendence awaits us too: the hands of other lonely people. For the first time in our history, we are the contemporaries of all men."[13]

In citing the examples from Martí and Paz I have attempted to show how the cultural and political meditations of the Latin American intellectual necessarily involve a literary consciousness. This consciousness flares up, as Martí's daring metaphors dramatize for us, even at those moments when the notion of literature seems to be furthest removed from the writer's mind, involved as he is in the unmediated moral reading of his society. There is something of this in Paz's statement that historical knowledge, being neither quantitative nor subject to constant laws, falls halfway between science and poetry. "The historian," says Paz, "makes descriptions like a scientist and has the visions of the poet. History allows us to understand the past, and also, at times, the present. More than a

---

[13] My translation from *El laberinto de la soledad* (1950; Mexico: Fondo de Cultura Económica, 1973), p. 174. Incidentally, I would prefer to translate Paz's *soledad* as "loneliness" intead of "solitude", as it is usually rendered. Loneliness refers more precisely to Paz's theme of the lack of intimate association with, rather than a wilful separation from, others.

form of knowledge, history is a form of wisdom."[14] Thus poetry or literature would seem to constitute not just the formal or rhetorical framework of the historical text — its "mode of encodement", to use Hayden White's handy term — but the very essence and justification of the historian's task, the very source of its meaning, as it were. The historian, just like the writer as intellectual, would therefore appear to be constituted by a literary or poetic consciousness which he does not and indeed cannot acknowledge, but without which — without "visions" and "wisdom" in Paz's view — his identity would not be possible.

We readily accept the opposite view, of course — literature can be historical, philosophical, or political without any loss of its specificity. In fact, the more historical, philosophical or political, the more modern and indeed the more literary we believe that literature to be. The appeal to modernity is in fact that — an appeal to immediacy, to action, to the anti-historical moment that can be experienced through the senses, through sentiment, through any medium that is *not* language. Literature feeds upon its own self-denying gestures, and the abandonment of literature (as in Cervantes and Flaubert) is itself one of the greatest literary themes. It is significant that some of the most representative texts of modern Latin American literature also dramatize this paradox. Pablo Neruda's *Heights of Macchu Picchu*, for example (a poem I always like to come back to), narrates a flight out of the alienation of the modern world and into the pre-Columbian past that the ruins of the famous Incan city represent. The speaker, whom I now take to be a figure of the Latin American intellectual, ascends to the ruins searching for an unmediated contact with a past untouched by the distortions wrought by five centuries of Western domination. And yet, the poem shows us not only that the speaker's flight cannot be a flight out of time, for he remains locked into the present, but that the very meaning of the ruins he so anxiously sought is constituted by the very history he attempted to avoid. That history includes, of course, the speaker's own literary consciousness, held to be an ac-

---

[14] *El ogro filantrópico*, p. 21.

complice of Western cultural domination; and the poem goes on to implement that consciousness as a subversion of the Western library.[15] The poem's flight out of literature and into the mode of historical action ends up affirming the role that literature plays in the realization of that action. A similar pattern emerges from Alejo Carpentier's *The Lost Steps*, the novel of an alienated Latin American musicologist's voyage from New York City to the South American jungle in search of primitive musical instruments. After locating the instruments in a remote jungle village where he feels at home at last with himself and his context — he decides to return to civilization one last time in order to bring back the paper that will allow him to write down his musical *magnum opus*. When the musicologist returns to the jungle, however, he discovers that the signs that marked the way to the village have been covered over by the torrential rains, and therefore that this flight into the jungle, and the implicit rejection of the historical world, is impossible. The only world given to the intellectual is the present, however corrupt and disenchanting he may find it. I want to quote you from the last lines of the novel: "The gloomy mansions of romanticism, with its doomed loves, are still open. But none of this was for me, because the only human race to which it is forbidden to sever the bonds of time is the race of those who create art. They not only must move ahead of the immediate yesterday, represented by tangible witness, but must anticipate the song and the form of others who will follow them, creating new tangible witness with full awareness of what has been done up to that moment."[16]

Both *Heights of Macchu Picchu* and *The Lost Steps* are allegories of the plight of the Latin American intellectual called upon to explore his cultural identity, tempted to abandon literature for the world of committed action, and forced always to return to literature as the ground of his personal identity and the field of that action. Both texts narrate a process of con-

---

[15] For such a reading of the poem, see my *Pablo Neruda: The Poetics of Prophecy* (Ithaca and London: Cornell University Press, 1982), especially pp. 104-175.

[16] *The Lost Steps*, 2nd ed. Trans. Harriet de Onís (New York: Alfred Knopf, 1971).

version to the cause of that historical action, only their common argument further describes that conversion as an open, infinite process, ever subject to eventual scrutiny and revision, as if anticipating, as the end of *The Lost Steps* tells us, "the song and form of others that will follow." Both *Heights of Macchu Picchu* and *The Lost Steps* are classics, to be sure, of modern Latin American literature. And yet the knowledge — and the *wisdom*, as Paz would have it — including political knowledge and wisdom, that these two classics, among other texts, have to offer, have been little heeded by most Latin American intellectuals, including, alas, Neruda and Carpentier themselves. Throughout the twenty odd years following the publication of his poem, Neruda remained an obedient Stalinist, a virtual accomplice of the Soviet mass murders, persecutions and the Gulag. Carpentier, in turn, went on to become a solemn, respectful bureaucrat in Paris, where he lived for the better part of his last twenty years, enjoying all the comforts and luxuries that he so piously denounced as an echo of the regime that he served.

Fortunately, however, the wisdom of literature is distinct from the human foibles of its authors, and literature tells us things that authors themselves are incapable of articulating, except of course in the very literary language which they seem condemned to ignore, or at least to misunderstand. If literature constitutes, as I have tried to argue, a separate valid mode of knowledge or wisdom, then it will be necessary to develop a reading method that would respect that mode and not simply reduce it to another master discourse. Philosophers, historians, politicians, social scientists, journalists like Alan Riding, and even some literary critics, are fond of invoking and using literary texts for the purpose of illustrating ideas and theories. Literature, in this restricted sense, becomes an object to be interpreted and decided upon by the master discourse of *other* disciplines — which thereby become the subject that decides where meaning lies and what to make of it. A reversal of such a scheme whereby philosophy, history, politics, *The New York Times* and even literary criticism itself would become the object of interpretation of literature would not only allow literature to be heard, but also would probably uncover the arbitrary and ultimately fictional strategies that are at work in preserving the power structures of those disciplines. Literature, in this other, unrestricted sense, would become that "minor horror" which Jorge Luis Borges, our intellectual nonintellectual *par excellence*, once invoked as his idea of Paradise: "a vast, contradictory library, whose vertical deserts of books run the incessant risk of metamorphosis, which affirm everything, deny everything, and confuse everything — like a raving God."[17]

---

[17] "The Total Library", in *Borges: A Reader*, ed. E. Rodríguez Monegal and Alastair Reid (New York: EP. Dutton, 1981), p. 96.

La literatura urbana como praxis social en América latina

Alejandro Losada

1. INTRODUCCION

El objetivo de estas notas es la formulación de un paradigma que permita comprender el fenómeno literario latinoamericano como praxis de diversos grupos sociales en la etapa de expansión preindustrial.

Entiendo por etapa de expansión preindustrial un fenómeno económico y político, cuyos efectos multiplicadores se localizan en un ámbito específicamente urbano en lo que atañe a sus perfiles modernizantes. Comprende un ciclo más amplio y, por otro lado, uno más limitado de lo que desde un punto de vista socioeconómico se ha caracterizado como la etapa de «expansión hacia afuera», cuando se consolida institucionalmente un nuevo tipo de Estado nacional basado en los recursos de exportación primaria [1]. Lo propio de este período es que, si bien las nuevas naciones latinoamericanas participan en el proceso de expansión económica de la etapa industrial burguesa, no cambian su estructura tradicional ni modernizan de la misma manera sus relaciones sociales. El impacto del proceso, en cambio, se percibe localizadamente en la vida urbana, sobre todo donde se asientan las instituciones del Estado nacional, y en los estratos medios tradicionales que se incorporan a su expansión. Habrá que esperar que ese Estado tenga la suficiente posibilidad de dominar las fuentes de recursos y de desarrollar las fuerzas productivas para que su acción transforme toda la formación social [2]; o bien que la ciudad capital se convierta en ciudad «primada», se diferencien los sectores formándose el secundario y el terciario incorporados a la vida de la metrópoli, para que se produzcan significativos cambios cuantitativos y cualitativos que transformen la relación entre las personas y las clases, la forma en que se estructura y comunica la sociedad, las actitudes de los sujetos hacia sí mismos y hacia un mundo exterior y, en general, las funciones que puede cumplir en uno y otro contexto la producción cultural [3].

Desde un punto de vista social, este período puede ser llamado como el de las culturas dependientes, en cuanto que es una producción realizada por estratos medios articulados más o menos directamente a la vida del Estado y a las élites dominantes tradicionales. Se diferencia, tanto de las culturas cortesanas producidas por la misma élite dominante, como de las culturas relativamente autónomas producidas en la vida metropolitana. Estas últimas, ya sea porque se producen en función de un público anónimo que estimula la demanda como un mercado; ya sea porque se elaboran en la marginación desde una situación de proletarización o de aislamiento aristocrático; o ya sea porque se integran a un grupo politizado que tiene un comportamiento revolucionario con respecto al sistema social vigente, se diferenciarán esencialmente de las culturas dependientes. En los tres casos —cuando el escritor produce para un público competitivo, cuando lo hace para sí mismo como un personaje aislado, o cuando se integra a un grupo revolucionario— el cambio cualitativo fundamental ha sido la ruptura de la articulación de la cultura y de sus productores con las élites que dominan el poder. Este hecho acontece precisamente cuando comienza a expandirse la metrópoli, a constituirse un Estado burocrático, empresario y represivo, a formarse, diferenciarse y ampliarse los sectores secundarios y terciarios y a padecer una crisis de legitimidad política el dominio de las antiguas oligarquías exportadoras, que no pueden afrontar el liderazgo de un inevitable proceso de industrialización que destruirá la estructura tradicional sobre la que garantizaban su dominio.

A un mayor nivel de generalidad, nuestra tesis afirma que la producción cultural urbana latinoamericana no puede ser comprendida como un hecho social si se la considera directamente referida a un punto de vista macrocultural, es decir, en aquello que tiene de semejante con la evolución literaria de los países industriales. Esto, y no otra cosa, han propuesto quienes han dividido sus procesos siguiendo el desarrollo estilístico de las literaturas de los países industriales (clasicismo, romanticismo, naturalismo, modernismo, vanguardismo, contemporánea). En este trabajo precisamente proponemos un paradigma donde al menos tres de los cuatro primeros estilos —y en algunos países los cuatro— pueden ser interpretados como distintas variaciones de un mismo fenómeno cultural (ilustración borbónica colonial, romanticismo peruano-mexicano, modernismo peruano-mexicano-chileno-argentino). Pero, por otro lado, estas notas afirman que tampoco es suficiente entenderlo como literaturas «republicanas» o «nacionales», ya que se trata de producciones de pequeñas élites ilustradas que, en coyunturas estructuralmente semejantes, intentan una praxis social en unas pocas direcciones que se repetirán sin trascenderse, hasta aproximadamente los años que siguen a la primera guerra mundial.

Desde un punto de vista específico de interpretación de la cultura, nuestra tesis afirma que ella desarrolla el comportamiento de ciertos grupos ilustrados dependientes de las élite soligárquicas, cuya característica básica es la tentativa histórica de representar la modernidad en medio de una resistente estructura social predominantemente tradicional. Estas literaturas representan las diversas actitudes de clientelazgo, de radicalización abstracta y de coopción reprimida, que han podido desarrollar aquellas élites cuando optaron por la modernidad. Significan, en realidad, la imposibilidad que encontraron de desarrollar una cultura moderna en una vida urbana tradicional. Se dará acá otra faceta de ese choque entre estructura e historia, donde se entiende por estructura un grado relativo de desarrollo de las fuerzas productivas, un determinado modo de producción y un específico patrón de relaciones sociales y de distribución, en el que participan estos grupos productores de cultura; y se entiende por historia los diversos comportamientos y proyectos de cada una de las clases y fracciones de clase, posibilitados por aquella estructura social. La cultura, en la mayoría de los casos, será producida por un pequeño grupo que es una fracción de los llamados estratos medios tradicionales, es decir de aquellos sectores dedicados a la administración, las profesiones liberales y los servicios —sobre todo educativos y artísticos— en una sociedad estructurada rígidamente, en una ciudad cuya vida está determinada en función de las élites y no de otros sectores medios o industriales. En estas notas la cultura será estudiada simultáneamente, como un resultado de la ampliación y dinamización muy relativa de aquella estructura tradicional —que gracias a la expansión de la exportación introduce perezosamente algunos rasgos de la modernidad; y cómo el comportamiento de los sectores medios, que tratan de ampliar esa modernidad y, finalmente, chocan contra los estrechos límites tradicionales donde les está permitido desarrollarla.

La base para la formulación de este paradigma será el estudio de la literatura romántica como praxis social en la primera etapa de afirmación de la República del Perú, tal como se encuentra desarrollada en la obra de Jorge Basadre. Posteriormente, discutiré sus planteos comparándolos con otros casos más amplios, para formular al final el paradigma básico que permita la comprensión de la cultura latinoamericana dependiente de las oligarquías exportadoras como praxis de diversos grupos sociales.

En la obra de Basadre, al nivel más aparente, el romanticismo es la expresión artística de unas pocas docenas de jóvenes en medio de una intensa vida urbana. Nace vinculado a los nuevos centros de enseñanza, al modernizado espectáculo artístico teatral, al cultivo de un nuevo patrón de prestigio social, a la expansión de las actitudes y las doctrinas más radicales de España y Francia en los nuevos países latinoamericanos y a la primera generación ilustrada que ha crecido, se ha formado y se ha incorporado a la élite social durante la afirmación de la República. Se desarrolla acompañando el proceso de autoconsolidación, de diferenciación social y de lucha por su lugar en la sociedad de esa juventud, constituyendo uno de los principales canales por donde pueden desarrollar su comportamiento social. Finalmente, se consolida, después de quince años, como uno de los rasgos principales de aquella generación, condensando un aspecto de la personalidad social que ha producido la específica experiencia republicana.

Sin embargo, a un nivel más general, el mismo hecho aparece articulado a otros dos fenómenos que, aparentemente, tendrían poca relación con la cultura. Por un lado, como un efecto del proceso general de expansión económica y de consolidación institucional de la nueva nación. Y, por otro, como un comportamiento de aquella generación con respecto a los principales actores sociales de su tiempo. Por lo tanto, el movimiento romántico puede ser estudiado como uno de los tantos fenómenos dependientes de un cambio importante a nivel estructural; puede ser interpretado como uno de los aspectos donde se plantean las contradicciones, las alianzas o la integración entre diversos actores sociales; y se lo puede considerar en referencia a la propia generación productora. En el primer caso, el intérprete se mueve a nivel estructural. En el segundo, a nivel histórico inmediato de la dinámica social permitida por aquella estructura. Y, en el tercero, al nivel inmanente de una conciencia social. Aludiremos brevemente a cada uno de los tres aspectos, tal como se pueden percibir en la obra de Basadre.

2. EL NIVEL ESTRUCTURAL

Desde un punto de vista estructural, Basadre describe el período como el momento en que se diseña un nuevo orden social que en parte reemplaza y en parte continúa el orden colonial[4]. Este hecho nos permite articular el proceso de producción literaria con una formación social concreta, de manera que podamos diferenciarlo de otros movimientos románticos que produjeron los países industriales, los países europeos periféricos y otras nuevas naciones latinoamericanas. Los dos hechos relevantes que diferencian este ciclo del anterior son un nuevo modo de articulación y expansión económica asociada a los países industriales y la constitución política de la nación. En este último aspecto, el caso peruano podría ser considerado como semejante al resto de los países de la región. Pero un rasgo fundamental que caracteriza esta etapa de desarrollo se dará en el Río de la Plata o en México sólo algunas décadas más tarde: la reconstrucción del aparato productivo y el acelerado aumento de los recursos del Estado en base a la exportación de productos colocados en los mercados internacionales. Este período, que ha sido llamado de «expansión hacia afuera»[5] vivirá un intenso proceso de modernización social, consolidación del Estado, estabilización de un régimen político basado en algún tipo de participación restringida, la afirmación de la ciudad primada, la asociación al capital internacional comercial y financiero, la mayor demanda de bienes y servicios y, finalmente, la formación de un excedente que se volcará en el orden del bienestar y de la cultura, teniendo en cuenta el efecto de demostración europeo. Todo ello implicará la aceleración del proceso de urbanización, una mayor ampliación del sector terciario, el aumento relativo de la movilidad social y la incorporación limitada de estratos medios a la burocracia, el comercio, la política y la cultura, acompañando un proceso amplio de institucionalización.

Lo que queremos hacer notar es que el romanticismo en el Perú se producirá en una circunstancia estructuralmente similar y con características internas semejantes al modernismo en el Río de la Plata, en Chile o en México. Uno se desarrollará entre 1840 y 1880 y, los otros, entre 1890 y 1910. De manera que el factor fundamental para determinar las características de un movimiento cultural —aun desde un punto de vista expresivo, estilístico y formal— no es la difusión que se desarrolla a partir de los países dominantes del proceso de expansión del capitalismo, sino de las posibilidades y cambios que se realizan en cada formación social. Aquel proceso económico e institucional, en el Perú y más tarde en los otros países, creará nuevas demandas ocupacionales e instituciones para formar los nuevos cuadros administrativos y profesionales, amplía un poco el proceso de participación democrática y de movilidad social, produce una relativa especialización de la cultura y da nueva importancia al talento individual y al papel que puede desarrollar la personalidad moderna en la vida social. El movimiento romántico en el Río de la Plata (1840-80), en cambio, está integrado a una matriz diferente. En el país del Pacífico se produce a partir de la expansión de la riqueza y de la consolidación del Estado y se articula a sus dinamismos. En el Río de la Plata, al contrario, es una reacción en contra de la anarquía institucional y el estancamiento económico. En un caso acompaña a un particular proceso de modernización del orden establecido y, en el otro, es una lucha contra la estaticidad del orden establecido para introducir la modernidad. En el Perú se dará como un modo de integración a la clase dirigente y, mediada por ella, a Europa; en el cono sur, en cambio, como un combate contra la clase dirigente que no quería ni podía incorporarlos, con el auxilio de las flotas y los comerciantes europeos. Una y otra situación estructural condicionarán que el romanticismo sea, en uno y en otro país, dos literaturas radicalmente diferentes. Esta es la distancia que va entre Echeverría, Mármol, Sarmiento y Hernández, por un lado, y Luis B. Cisneros, Salaverry, Felipe Pardo, Manuel A. Segura y Ricardo Palma por otro.

El hecho relevante que indica la permanencia del antiguo orden es una estructura social que, en sus componentes abrumadoramente mayoritarios, permanece subordinado a un ordenamiento rígido y jerárquico. A diferencia de como se realizó el proceso de expansión del capitalismo en los países industriales, la incorporación de esta nación a la nueva etapa del sistema no produce un fenómeno general de traslado de la población desde el sector agrícola al urbano industrial; tampoco ocasiona una ampliación significativa de las clases medias. El acceso a la propiedad y a la riqueza, al poder y al prestigio, a la administración, al comercio y a la burocracia, al clero y a la cultura, sigue restringido para un pequeño grupo que se encuentra muy cercano a la cúspide de la pirámide social. Y esta élite, a pesar del desarrollo económico relativo (el presupuesto nacional se duplica varias veces en dos décadas) sigue en su gran mayoría controlada por las pautas coloniales de producción, acumulación de capital y falta de inversiones, distribución de los ingresos y los gastos, relaciones de dependencia con respecto al mercado comercial, industrial y financiero externo, relaciones de clientela, de familia o de pertenencia hacia el propio estrato social. En su proyecto de modernización no se contemplaba la posibilidad de la formación de un mercado interno, la consolidación de un capitalismo nacional y de un proyecto de industrialización que podría romper aquel rígido orden social [6].

Actualmente es casi un lugar común en el análisis de las causas del subdesarrollo de los países latinoamericano el hecho de que se vincule la persistencia del orden tradicional con la dependencia económica, es decir, con un tipo de economía articulada al orden capitalista industrial como productora de productos primarios exportables. Esta situación dejaría a las élites modernizadoras encerradas en una doble limitación. Externamente, se mantendrán dependientes del mercado y del capital internacional, sin poder reestructurar suficientemente la formación social nacional. Internamente, tenderán a consolidar aquella estructura social rígida, según pautas señoriales de la colonia [7]. Este hecho se produce de manera más crítica en aquellos países donde el nuevo proceso productivo se organiza en base a la existencia anterior de una fuerza de trabajo amplia, organizada y sometida, ya se trate de las culturas amerindias, del Brasil o del sur de los Estados Unidos. Se encontrará, en cambio, mitigado en aquellas otras regiones donde la nueva producción obedece a una planificación empresarial *(pioneers),* en base a la inmigración o a la contratación de una fuerza libre de trabajo [8], como es el caso de los países del Atlántico. De allí que en el Perú el proceso tienda a consolidar las pautas dominantes de la colonia, donde existía con anterioridad un patrón de comportamiento señorial basado en la explotación de la propiedad de la tierra y de una mesa de trabajo organizada, articulada a un Estado que consolidaba los privilegios desde el exterior: era una estructura patriarcal, donde la élite dominante ponía todo su empeño para diferenciarse de la masa de la población, consolidar su privilegio con signos culturales de prestigio, emitiendo una especie de veto hacia la participación en los bienes del sistema por parte de las otras clases y razas [9]. Por otro lado, la situación del Perú recuerda aquella otra manera en que se diferencia el desarrollo económico despendiente, ya sea que se realice a partir del control nacional de la producción o bien se lleve a cabo a partir de una economía de enclave [10]. En el primer caso, la élite se convierte en empresarial, tiende a tomar en sus manos las decisiones que se refieren a la inversión y el control de la producción, procura formar un Estado nacional que subordine las fuentes de capital y los recursos a su propio interés y, por consecuencia, produce un dinamismo que hace imposible mantener una estructura social tradicional. En el caso de la economía de enclave, en cambio, la élite tiende a convertirse más en intermediaria y administradora que en empresaria, no asientan su dominio sobre el control de un nuevo sistema productivo que aproveche todas las fuentes de recursos físicos y humanos de su territorio, mantiene las funciones tradicionales del Estado, donde más se trata de distribuir y gratificar a la clase privilegiada que de transformar y dinamizar la sociedad, tiende a aislarse tanto de los dirigentes regionales, que basan su poder en la hacienda tradicional, como de la masa del pueblo, y cada vez más se diferencia de la mayoría. El resultado último de este proceso de enclave es que, al cabo de algunas décadas, se ha constituido una oligarquía urbana modernizada en base al usufructo de los recursos del enclave disfrutados como un privilegio o una renta señorial, a cuyo alrededor se han incorporado pequeños estratos sociales dedicados a la administración, los negocios, la burocracia, la milicia y la cultura.

El hecho decisivo que queremos hacer notar se refiere a la posibilidad que tendrán los estratos medios modernizadores, en medio de este panorama estructural, para proponerse objetivos revolucionarios que destruyan la estructura tradicional. Su espacio será la ciudad de Lima, es decir un centro cultural y administrativo que alrededor de 1840 tenía aproximadamente 50.000 habitantes, entre los cuales se contaban un tercio de blancos, un millar de clérigos y religiosos, 10.000 entre esclavos e indios y otro tercio de castas intermedias. A finales de la década del cuarenta todo el grupo activo dominante sostenía un periódico por suscripción —El Comercio— y ellas no llegaban al millar. Así, Luis Benjamín Cisneros (1864) podrá hablar de las 2.400 familias decentes que componen la sociedad limeña. En esta isla constituída por el influjo de un Estado en expansión, ¿qué tipo de metas, qué problemas y qué comportamientos estarán permitidos para una pequeña burguesía profesional que quiere representar la modernidad?

Comparando la situación del mismo grupo en el Río de la Plata, el contraste se manifiesta claramente. Unos y otros se ven arrastrados a dos proyectos sociales y culturales diferentes que, al final del proceso, llevará a unos a ser cooptados y asimilados a la clase dominante modernizadora y, a otros, a la revolución para destruirla y suplantarla. Por esta razón, cuando a continuación resumamos el intenso dinamismo social y político donde chocan diversos actores a lo largo del período, tal como aparece en la *Historia* de Basadre, debe ser interpretado como un juego social posible, muy limitado, dentro de las estrechas alternativas permitidas por esta rígida realidad estructural. Porque ese comportamiento, a muy mediano plazo, estará condicionado por esas características del proceso de institucionalización y modernización realizado a partir de una economía de enclave, en medio de una sociedad tradicional predominantemente agrícola, donde se encuentra sometida una enorme masa indígena. En esta matriz básica los nuevos productores de cultura pertenecientes a los estratos medios, a pesar de todos sus programas radicales, sólo podrán hacer planteos individualistas y abstractos y terminarán reprimiendo todas sus expectativas al hecho de que ellos se identifican con ese puñado de dirigentes que usufructúan los privilegios, y se diferencian de la masa tradicional de su sociedad. Para decirlo en una palabra, el hecho de que ésta sea una cultura dependiente de su integración a los grupos tradicionales de poder ocasionará que sus productores reduzcan su horizonte al de la élite dominante. El intelectual parecerá agredir, tratará de diferenciarse y se mostrará románticamente opuesto tanto a los sectores tradicionales como a las élites dominantes, pero ello no impedirá que se identifique con estas últimas y acomode sus expectativas a su proyecto histórico. Porque, en definitiva, ellos serán también los beneficiarios de los frutos de la expansión como sector que se ha incorporado a la élite y los disfruta como privilegio patrimonial. Por ello no imaginarán realmente ninguna medida eficaz que tenga un efecto estructural y transforme la rígida sociedad en que se movían, moderarán todo planteo radical a lo que le permite la permanencia del sistema e, inclusive, no les estará permitida una producción artística subjetiva que trasgreda la realidad de su incorporación a las pautas sociales de una élite dominante. Y esto influirá radicalmente, quizás como el factor más importante, en las características negativas del romanticismo y la cultura peruana republicana.

3. EL COMPORTAMIENTO SOCIAL

Probablemente sea posible simplificar la matriz estructural donde se desarrollará el romanticismo y, en general, toda la producción cultural republicana, entendiéndola como sujeta a una contradicción irresoluble. Los términos se oponen y se neutralizan mutuamente cuando se trata de incorporarse a un proceso de transformación económica y social que, a su vez, consolida la estructura social y las pautas de relación tradicionales; o que se esfuerza en construir un Estado nacional en base a la modernización de un enclave urbano que lo diferencia del resto de la sociedad; o que organiza instituciones democráticas fortaleciendo el privilegio y la diferenciación social. De alguna manera los términos de esa contradicción estaban presentes en la conciencia de las élites republicanas. Sin embargo, no lo estaba de la misma manera la contradicción misma. Ellos podían hablar acerca de la situación moral del indio, de la irresponsabilidad y del despilfarro de la plutocracia, de la violencia en el sistema electoral y, aun, del fracaso de la República; pero no tomaban como materia de elaboración la incoherencia que implicaba la lucha por un orden social moderno que, a su vez, tenía como condición de posibilidad la necesidad de injertarse, como un cuerpo extraño, dentro de un orden tradicional, consolidándolo y diferenciándose de él.

La experiencia social inmediata, en cambio, que se refiere al choque y a las alianzas de varios actores sociales, es la materia propia que será elaborada por la conciencia social. En este nivel es posible interpretar el romanticismo no sólo como el resultado de un condicionamiento estructural, sino como un comportamiento social; es decir, como conducta de un grupo frente a los demás grupos sociales, que tiene conciencia de sus fines, acumula y elabora el resultado social de sus acciones, reformula sus metas y explica ideológicamente su situación en el mundo.

Es posible distinguir tres tendencias en el romanticismo peruano, que se articulan a las tres etapas por las que se desarrolla el proceso de maduración de la primera generación juvenil formada durante la República. Para simplificar, en otro trabajo las hemos llamado populismo ilustrado, utopía revolucionaria y aristocraticismo intimista [11]. Señalaremos únicamente las líneas básicas por donde se desarrolla el comportamiento social de la generación. No reproduciremos, en cambio, por razones obvias [12], cómo ese comportamiento se traduce en la formulación de una estética y en obras literarias.

a) *El populismo ilustrado*

El populismo ilustrado es un rasgo del primer momento de producción cultural de este grupo juvenil, cuando se dirige a un público urbano poco cultivado utilizando los recursos melodramáticos que pueden lograr un efecto inmediato en un sector plebeyo dominante de la cultura. El relato de Basadre muestra a este grupo adoptando las nuevas formas románticas, tratando de triunfar delante de un auditorio tradicional que ahora se apasiona por las formas europeas y «modernas» del espectáculo. Fue una producción efectista, que no se dirigía a descubrir un nuevo horizonte sino a conseguir el éxito social. Significaba, más que una tarea profesional o creadora, una búsqueda de prestigio donde la juventud pretendía ser aprobada por la clase dirigente tradicional. Las pautas de su comportamiento les estaban dictadas por la demanda de ese público urbano —vinculado al Estado— que buscaba un espectáculo novedoso y formas delicadamente trabajadas en medio de lo tremendista, lo espectacular, lo fácilmente accesible a su burda sensibilidad [13]. Era un nuevo proyecto artístico moderno y europeo, cuyos límites se encontraban en que, a través del éxito en la escena, podían incorporarse al grupo dirigente tradicional y usufructuar los privilegios y los beneficios de la expansión.

Esta figura puede ser comprendida en las relaciones generales de clientela en que se desarrollan las vinculaciones sociales en los grupos tradicionales. Se da acá dependencia, protección, ascenso y seguridad social por la vinculación a la élite, expectativa de participar en los beneficios del sistema gracias a un comportamiento adecuado. Lo que tiene de interesante la *Historia* de Basadre es que ese comportamiento tiene muy poco de obsecuente y cortesano, en que los actores sociales dominantes no están absorbidos por la élite tradicional y en que el proceso de sanción de la opinión pública urbana es un hecho relativamente anónimo y democrático. Esto dará a la nueva generación la sensación de que su éxito está logrado en un terreno competitivo y democrático gracias al talento. El clientelazgo, como la futura coopción, no procederá con la claridad cortesana de la colonia, sino que se hará presente por la represión inconsciente y, más adelante, por la falta de un instrumento racional adecuado para poder elaborar el significado de la experiencia social. Para decirlo en pocas palabras, creían estar en un ámbito democrático y moderno, mientras vivían integrados a un mundo tradicional y privilegiado.

Por ello, tal será el choque entre sus expectativas y la realidad social, que esta generación abandonará a los pocos años toda tentativa de dar razón —al nivel de la conciencia— de su existencia social. Si hablamos acá de clientelazgo y de coopción, estos conceptos no se podrán desprender directamente de su comportamiento consciente —que significaba precisamente lo contrario— sino de la parábola que describirá ese comportamiento dentro de los marcos estructurales que hemos descrito.

Por esta razón, si decimos que la relación más relevante que tuvo esta generación estaba condicionada por la presencia de los caudillos militares, hay que atender alguna vez a la *Historia* de Basadre para comprender qué significan en la República las palabras «caudillo» y «ejército», superando aquel estereotipo romántico creado por Sarmiento en la persona de *Facundo* (1845), que ha influido tan fuertemente toda la concepción histórica liberal y todavía sigue determinando las interpretaciones contemporáneas [14]. Para Basadre, los caudillos y el ejército significaron la única instancia en que, a través de un proceso de «democracia directa», se logra una cierta permanencia en la vida del Estado en el orden nacional. Desde un punto de vista social, por otro lado, son el canal por donde se pueden cumplir las aspiraciones de sectores mestizos medios para tener acceso a los privilegios de la clase dirigente; es decir, permiten un proceso restringido de democratización de la vida social. En esa épcca había cambiado la composición de la cúspide de la élite social, quedando desprestigiada, emigrada o vencida la antigua burocracia virreinal y la primitiva aristocracia terrateniente colonial. Ellos no sólo no representarán sus intereses, sino que se opondrán a la influencia política de los plantadores costeños, entrando en alianza con los hacendados del interior para tener poder militar. Están permanentemente rodeados de la clase pequeño-burguesa profesional, los periodistas, los ideólogos liberales y los abogados, que encuentran en ellos un acceso al poder. Por otro lado, no tienen el carisma «machista» que los hace conquistar a las masas. Antes, al contrario, tienen una relación problemática con el pueblo bajo urbano, que les presta sólo un apoyo condicionado, encontrándose desbordados más de una vez por la reacción popular o parlamentaria. Por ello es casi infantil seguir pensando a esos caudillos como absorbidos por la ambición, ya que la mayoría no pretende crear una sólida red de familias o de clientelas. Entregan el poder a sus sucesores, limitan su poder con las Asambleas o los Consejos de Estado, no se enriquecen ni se identifican con definidos intereses económicos. En este período, el caudillo más bien parece un mediador entre los diferentes grupos de presión o de poder que un sujeto que subordina todos los grupos al propio autoritarismo dominador. Si son básicamente pragmáticos no se comprende su conducta si no se los ve comprometidos, dentro de lo posible, con el proyecto de constituir una nación soberana y una sociedad algo más democrática, más moderna y más justa [15].

La nueva generación no tendrá una relación directa con la clase dominante del poder del estado —militares y profesionales ilustrados—; su incorporación estará mediada por el éxito social delante de la opinión pública urbana. Es una consagración festiva y democrática, nacida de una ovación espontánea a quienes —como Corpancho, Ricardo Palma o Luis Benjamín Cisneros— demuestran ser jóvenes de talento para poder proponer al público burdos dramas construidos «a la manera» moderna europea. Acá también hay que superar aquella imagen de la sociedad republicana como de una élite enclaustrada en sus privilegios coloniales y reconocer que el «pueblo» urbano es realmente un nuevo actor social, presionando como opinión pública —a veces armada— para determinar el curso de los acontecimientos, oponerse a los hechos consumados o sancionarlos. Precisamente este tema es una de las constantes de la obra de Basadre. El ha mostrado cómo ese pueblo tenía ya una participación activa, como muchedumbre aulica y religiosa, como participante en el espectáculo artístico, en la fiesta ciudadana o simplemente como opinión tumultuaria, ya en la colonia. Después explica cómo se constituye con una nueva fisonomía social a partir de la Emancipación. Su comportamiento lo hace entronizar o deponer caudillos, tiende a combatir al absolutismo autoritario y provoca la caída de mandatarios (Monteagudo, Bolívar, Gamarra, Santa Cruz, Salaverry, Vivanco, echenique), aunque a veces se identifique con los mismos. No se encuentra tampoco pasivo frente a la élite plutocrática, como se puede comprobar en la constante oposición al círculo de Echenique, que después renacerá contra el recién fundado civilismo. Es un personaje que se mueve activamente, sosteniendo una intensa vida periodística, una inusitada vida artística (teatro, poesía, ballet, ópera, conciertos, toros), una participación peligrosa en los períodos electorales, un eco al comportamiento parlamentario y una actitud imprevisible frente a los caudillos. Es frente a ese público que se expondrá la nueva generación para, con su aplauso, ganar prestigio y conseguir ser incorporada por la nueva élite dirigente mestiza. Es, como se ve, un clientelazgo muy sofisticado, que se puede percibir por las evidencias de que ese público y esa élite imponen una especie de control social con su expectativa que, por otro lado, estaba estimulando la aparición de talentos que representaran la modernidad [16].

La obra de Basadre permite interpretar la formación y la entrada en escena de la joven generación romántica como un fenómeno directamente articulado a estos nuevos actores sociales —clase mestiza militar e intelectual modernizante y pueblo urbano constituido en opinión—. Todos ellos vivían, en 1848, una situación diferente del pasado. Ahora se trataba de consolidar la nación, afirmar las instituciones, administrar la expansión económica, incorporarse a la modernidad. Todo ello era posible de imaginar gracias a un recurso controlado por una nueva élite social, donde los factores dominantes ya no eran la raza, la sangre, el capital o la familia, sino los caudillos militares, el grupo intelectual ilustrado y la opinión pública urbana. La nueva generación nacerá a partir de su pertenencia a esta situación todavía tan firmemente arraigada al pasado, pero decidida a incorporarse al futuro tomando el camino restringido de la modernización de la vida social de la propia élite urbana. Aquellos dirigentes verán en ellos, con declarada complacencia, su propia incorporación a la modernidad. Palma recuerda que, en su tertulia, un ministro les decía: «En el certamen del siglo, el que no alza la voz es porque nada tiene que decir. El reinado de la inteligencia se afirma en el mundo, y el hombre de verdadero talento pasa el Rubicón, dejando atrás a la aristocracia de la sangre y a la aristocracia del dinero.» Recordará, también, que casi todos ellos llegaron a figurar ventajosamente en el foro, en los Ministerios o en la diplomacia, mientras que en su época de estudiantes eran sólo «pobres de solemnidad» (1886). Más tarde, cuando maduren, estos jóvenes llegarán a despreciar al pueblo y a esa élite ignorante. Sin embargo, en este primer período, como estudiantes del colegio San Carlos o del Guadalupe, dispuestos a incorporarse al sector dirigente de su sociedad, a ganar prestigio y a asumir todos los gestos que les aseguren el éxito social, su producción tendrá todos los caracteres de una integración social, donde se cumple lo que se espera de una juventud promisoria, bajo el control de una clase tradicional que, en ellos, ve el resultado de su propia opción por dirigirse hacia la modernidad.

b) *El radicalismo abstracto*

Habíamos dicho que los dos rasgos característicos de este período son la expansión económica y la consolidación institutional. En su primera etapa (1845-1851) este doble movimiento clausura un proceso de anarquía social y de indefinición nacional. Su efecto más inmediato es la creación de un nuevo espacio urbano, económico y cultural, donde los actores sociales se vinculan entre sí teniendo en cuenta una agenda de cuestiones significativamente diferente de la que dominaba el horizonte de los años anteriores. Ya no se luchará a favor o en contra de la Emancipación; tampoco se discutirá la forma en que se han de constituir las nuevas naciones ni el problema más inmediato será la guerra. Hay un voto más o menos unánime por la forma que tomó la soberanía nacional después del fracaso de la Federación, y por los principios democráticos que comienzan a dominar las instituciones del Estado a partir del primer gobierno de. Castilla (1845). Es decir, toma cuerpo una especie de consentimiento en un proyecto básico de modernización. Sin embargo, aceptadas la nación, sus instituciones liberales y las metas del progreso social, producida una relativa calma temporal, comienza una intensa lucha por ganar el poder político. Basadre tiene razón en indicar que, mirando en perspectiva, ésta es una época de normalidad donde los problemas son más administrativos que políticos. Pero esto no contradice que, a lo largo de toda la década del cincuenta, aquella generación todavía esté obsesionada por el problema de las revoluciones, por la anarquía y por la lucha de las facciones partidistas personalistas. Por ello quizás sería más ajustado describir este proceso como determinado por una doble tendencia donde se compaginan el consenso y la lucha. Existiría cierta unanimidad en aceptar el nuevo orden nacional, económico e institucional y en la necesidad de introducir una serie de cambios que transformaran la sociedad. Pero se dará una intensa pugna política por controlar el poder del Estado y por tener en sus manos el ritmo del proceso de transformación. En esta lucha, los dos nuevos actores sociales que se enfrentarán serán la recién reconstituida plutocracia conservadora que se organiza alrededor de la figura del Presidente Echenique, y la pequeña burguesía profesional que constituye, por primera vez de manera independiente, un partido liberal. En medio de esta lucha, la generación romántica supera el primer perfil de su personalidad social, que estaba articulado a los grupos dominantes y al pueblo frívolo urbano, intentando un comportamiento político diferenciado. Las características de esta segunda tendencia, que concreta de una manera muy particular el movimiento general del romanticismo occidental, son un rasgo de las características de la lucha del partido liberal en esta sociedad tradicional. Ambos seguirán el mismo movimiento como un todo indiferenciado y ambos terminarán en el fracaso.

Los hechos dominantes del período podrían resumirse en una doble tentativa frustrada. Por un lado, los plantadores terratenientes costeños y los descendientes de la antigua nobleza virreinal tratan de beneficiarse de la creciente prosperidad del Estado, haciéndose pagar sus propiedades destruidas o los daños sufridos por las guerras. Por otro lado, el Partido Liberal trata de tomar el poder y de realizar una revolución institucional utópica. Los hechos se van sucediendo de manera anecdótica, donde el grupo de Echenique comienza a ser acusado de inmoralidad, exclusivismo y corrupción por gente de su propia clase, hasta que se hace enormemente impopular. Este grupo, por otro lado, se enfrenta a los antiguos caudillos militares (Castilla, San Román, Vivanco), que comienzan a urgir una definición de Echenique frente a una posible guerra con Bolivia. Finalmente, Echenique colabora con los grupos conservadores que desean retomar el poder que había caído en manos de los liberales en Ecuador y en Nueva Granada. En Lima se encontraban algunos liberales chilenos y se vivía una intensa efervescencia ideológica, donde se propagaban los ideales abstractos de una organización social libre, democrática, feliz y productiva nacida de una decisión constitucional. Había que tomar el poder y, por decreto, transformar la sociedad. Los caudillos hacen la revolución, los liberales los apoyan, el pueblo y la masa trabajadora (indios y esclavos) se movilizan decididamente en favor de ese movimiento que les promete la abolición de la esclavitud y del tributo y, después de una intensa lucha militar, el movimiento triunfa. Las instituciones representativas quedan en manos de los liberales, que se dedican a dictar una nueva Constitución, mientras la guerra se prolonga otro año por una lucha de facciones caudillescas. Las medidas liberales eran tan impopulares que, al poco tiempo, se habían enemistado con el clero, con los grupos medios beneficiarios de los derechos adquiridos, con el ejército y los caudillos, con la antigua plutocracia y con el pueblo urbano. Un oscuro coronel disuelve la Convención y, cuando regresa Castilla triunfante, los puede desconocer y organizar su gobierno con grupos moderados conservadores, algunos de los cuales habían sido ministros de Echenique. De esta manera, fracasando los conservadores y los liberales, el caudillo militar aparece de nuevo tomando las riendas del Estado como un moderador pragmático que trata de mantener el poder personal pero, al mismo tiempo, busca legitimidad en su capacidad para conciliar los intereses, incorporarlos controladamente a la fusión y los beneficios del poder público y representar el papel de árbitro entre ambos.

Lo que deseo hacer notar es que, en medio de esta intensa lucha político-militar-ideológica, para un observador que se ubica en un período que abarque más o menos un siglo, más son los puntos de coincidencia que las divergencias entre los antagonistas. Acá se manifiesta esa contradicción entre conciencia histórica y limitaciones estructurales, que nos permite juzgar desde nuestra perspectiva el hecho de que esa conciencia no podía elaborar la verdadera situación en que se encontraba y se mantenía en un terreno abstracto y utópico, que define tanto al liberalismo como a esta tendencia del romanticismo peruano. El hecho básico era que había un excedente acumulado que debía ser empleado. Para decirlo con la frase de Basadre, se había llegado a la situación de un Estado rico en un país empobrecido. Unos y otros tenían, igualmente, un proyecto limitado de desarrollo económico y de organización social. Simplificando, podríamos decir que, en su visión, el lugar preferencial lo tenían los productos de exportación como fuente de recursos. Entre ellos, el Estado se desentendía del fomento de un nuevo aparato productivo y se dejaba absorber por el problema de la administración de la explotación del guano. La renta producida tenía, como primer destinatario, el aparato remozado y ampliado del propio Estado. Una parte significativa debía ser empleada en obras públicas, donde tenían preferencia los transportes y el ornato urbano. Otra parte debía estimular indirectamente la producción minera y agrícola de exportación, e invertirse en la preparación de cuadros profesionales que llenaran las funciones demandadas por la nueva etapa. Una cantidad no despreciable favorecerá la repartición más equilibrada de los beneficios y de las cargas en sectores no tradicionales, como los grupos mestizos que alguna vez habían servido en la burocracia y en el Ejército (los derechos adquiridos), los esclavos y la masa indígena (abolición de la esclavitud y del tributo). En todo el juego de organización, administración y reparto de estos recursos, el papel predominante lo debía tener el Estado. No entra en su visión una modificación de la estructura económica, un plan de desarrollo industrial, una posibilidad de dominar las fuentes de capital del interior, un plan de acumulación de riquezas para crear un capitalismo agresivo continental, una redistribución de la tierra o un mayor dominio de las fuerzas políticas o productivas.

Los problemas que discutirán los liberales tienen un doble aspecto. Por un lado, se oponen concretamente a que la plutocracia domine y se beneficie como un grupo de privilegiados de estos recursos. Pero, por otro, el plan de Echenique, que él mismo llama liberal, no era muy distinto de esa matriz general que defendía la misma generación que lo combatía [17]. Podían tener diferentes posiciones ideológicas y tratar de imponer diferente ritmo a los cambios, pero unos y otros se preocupaban por la nación, la democracia, los indios y los negros y ambos limitaban su proyecto a los mismos objetivos. Para decirlo en pocas palabras, la lucha se entablaba por el modo en que se administraban y repartían los recursos, no por los objetivos de la administración. Ni unos ni otros discutieron sobre el modo de posesión de los medios de producción o sobre la modificación de la estructura social tradicional. Los problemas serán la consolidación de la deuda pública, su conversión, los negocios del guano, los adelantos de los consignatarios, los empréstitos, las obras públicas o el modo de liquidar la deuda contraída con la liberación de los esclavos. En el fondo, los liberales pensaban que ellos podían administrar esos recursos de una manera más racional, democrática y moderna y se indignaban que no se atendiera su talento. Pero en la vida cotidiana tenían ya un enorme sentido de autosuficiencia que se basaba no en que ellos fueran más capaces y más rectos que los ricos y los caudillos, sino en que representaban el progreso humano y podían realizar una sociedad ideal.

En esta época es notable el hecho de que la juventud romántica liberal extrae su identidad no del modo en que se articula a su sociedad, de los intereses que representan o del lugar privilegiado que ocupan en la estructura general, sino de un ideal específicamente literario. Era como si se sintieran diferentes, y aun los más aptos para tomar el gobierno, porque representaban ideales librescos y abstractos. Una intensa literatura politizada representa esta actitud, expuesta suficientemente por Basadre: Manuel y Francisco Bilbao, Juan Espinosa, Manuel Alvarado, Luis Benjamín Cisneros, los hermanos Gálvez o Alberto Ureta eran sobre todo ideólogos. Se habían formado en el periodismo y en la cátedra. Sus ideas mantenían una crítica institucional, se deleitaban en la retórica programática que defendía un ideario utópico y grandilocuente, como lo refleja el ensayo de Francisco Bilbao (1855) o la idea de la revolución que manifiesta la vida de Salaverry de Manuel Bilbao (1852). Propugnaban la necesidad de un Estado sin Congreso, sin sistema representativo indirecto que viciaba las elecciones, en base a comicios permanentes donde se consultaba directamente la voluntad del pueblo en cada una de las cuestiones, con un tribunado dependiente y revocable por el mismo pueblo, con la guardia nacional alerta, con un ejército minúsculo cuyos jefes debían ser nombrados por la tropa y cuyas armas nunca debían ser autorizadas a disparar contra el pueblo, con múltiples colegios, asilos, hospitales, cajas de ahorro y otras instituciones de asistencia. Con esto quiero hacer notar que existe casi una inmediata relación entre una ideología abstracta y utópica y, por otro lado, la producción intelectual liberal producida en una sociedad tradicional que se manifiesta imposible de transformar. La expansión del romanticismo y del liberalismo es un fenómeno mundial o, al menos, relacionado con las sociedades nacionales que se encuentran articuladas a la expansión del capitalismo industrial. Los grupos que lo adoptan para definir su propia identidad son ordinariamente de pequeña burgusía profesional. Pero el modo en que se realizará esa tendencia en una coyuntura tradicional, o en otra revolucionaria, será totalmente diferente. Los segundos, como Italia o el Río de la Plata, tomarán como materia de elaboración la propia batalla contra el orden tradicional y deberán imaginar un proyecto revolucionario alternativo, donde se edifique otro orden social. De ahí que los emigrados rioplatenses tengan en su agenda problemas como la inmigración masiva, la inversión de capitales, la erradicación de los sistemas políticos y de las clientelas tradicionales regionales, la construcción de un Estado empresario, la educación forzada, la productividad de la fuerza de trabajo tradicional y la seguridad del capital. En medio de esta lucha, el romanticismo intentará configurar la imagen de los antagonistas, atenderá al hombre popular, tomará como tema los grandes ciclos históricos de formación y destrucción del orden tradicional y será, simultáneamente, simbólico y racional, buscando, al mismo tiempo, proponer objetivos políticos concretos y movilizar las pasiones para poder alcanzarlos.

A partir de esta experiencia histórica juvenil, vivida en medio de esta inmóvil estructura social, es posible, en cambio, interpretar la ideología y el destino frustrado que le cupo a la tendencia política del romanticismo liberal en el Perú. Se caracterizará por su contenido ético y principista, utilizando una apasionada retórica revolucionaria, pero no por ello dejará de mostrarse incapaz de utilizar su aparato conceptual para intentar un análisis de la realidad social de su país o de su propio comportamiento y, por lo tanto, de formular un programa político concreto. Este desfasase entre su ideología y vivencia de lo que era la realidad, con la sociedad que ellos pensaban que estaban llamados a dirigir, origina su pronto fracaso. Y su consecuencia será el abandono de todo proyecto político independiente y una resignada retracción de la conducta social. El año posterior a la disolución de la Convención, los liberales intentan otra revolución y aun el asesinato político, debiendo emigrar. Parten los Gálvez, Ricardo Palma y Luis Benjamín Cisneros. Pero pronto los veremos nombrados representantes de su país en el extranjero y, poco más tarde, estarán nuevamente incorporados a la Administración y a los negocios. Se limitarán a colaborar a regañadientes en lo económico-administrativo, divorciados de su pueblo y bajo el dominio del mismo grupo dominante que habían combatido. Desde el punto de vista de la producción cultural, esto ocasionará también la renuncia a la actitud triunfalista frente a la realidad social y, con ello, a utilizar la razón para interpretarla, servirla y transformarla. Reprimirán todo estímulo para elaborar la experiencia histórica, no intentarán comprender la vida social, no se volcarán sobre su medio, sino que se reducirán a la interioridad. Y acá estará la razón más honda por la que las mayores creaciones de la literatura peruana republicana se negarán a nombrar o a elaborar los problemas más importantes de su experiencia social y se dirigirán, en cambio, a compensar, en la interioridad, los desencantos y las frustraciones de la vida social.

c) *El aristocraticismo intimista*

A partir de los últimos años de la década del sesenta dominará en el ambiente social limeño un nuevo espíritu preocupado por lo práctico, lo bursátil, lo atildado y, salvo momentos excepcionales, lo sedentario. Fue un ritmo aburguesado, en una situación aparentemente próspera y confiada. En 1866 se instaura la dictadura de Mariano Ignacio Prado, triunfante en la revolución nacionalista contra Pezet, con un gabinete liberal de «talentos», como lo llama Casós. El 2 de mayo, que se combate contra España, es una jornada cívica multitudinaria que deja una sensación de triunfo no sólo contra la agresión, sino contra el mismo estado de disgregación social que vivía la élite dirigente. Se instaura un reformismo progresista democrático que buscaba reordenar el sistema hacendario, moralizar la vida del Estado, reorganizar el aparato administrativo y enfrentar el grave problema económico de una posible bancarrota del Estado. Al poco tiempo se enfrenta nuevamente el Poder Ejecutivo con el Congreso Constituyente, los liberales se ven hostigados por todos aquellos que defienden sus «derechos adquiridos», por el Ejército, por los hacendados, por los propietarios de predios rústicos y urbanos y, aun, por los indios, pues todos ellos se oponen a las reformas y al nuevo sistema impositivo que intentaba sanear las fuentes de recursos del Estado. Ante el ambiente revolucionario, un ministro liberal manda a deportar a Castilla, a quien llama «el obrero más infatigable del desorden» (1867) y se da una Constitución liberal. A los primeros enfrentamientos con el Presidente, Casós pide el enjuiciamiento del Poder Ejecutivo, presenta un proyecto por el que la Asamblea reasumiría aquella facultad en la persona de su Presidente y convocaría al Ejército para defenderla, hasta que se produce la revolución de 1868, dominada por la reacción caudillista y conservadora. En esta época termina la presión liberal que se mantuvo constante veinte años, siempre esperando dar la batalla definitiva tantas veces soñada para dominar el poder y lograr la transformación del país. El país, entonces, parece permanecer conminado por el ímpetu de la expansión económica pero, también, por el caudillismo militar y los sectores conservadores, manteniéndose la sensación de corrupción en el manejo de los negocios del Estado, usufructuados por los consignatarios del guano y los beneficiarios con una serie de prebendas conseguidas en las sucesivas revoluciones [18].

Ante este panorama se consolida el abandono de las posiciones políticas y de los planteos ideológicos de los liberales y se afirma su incorporación a la élite dirigente y al mismo ritmo simultáneamente aburguesado, caudillesco y venal de esa sociedad, justificándose con la colaboración racional, administrativa o ilustrada que aportaban. Se da, por lo tanto, una adhesión a aquel proyecto básico con el que la clase dirigente, que habían combatido, imaginaba la organización de la sociedad y del Estado y el modo en que han de encarrilarse las relaciones sociales, constituyendo un grupo de profesionales, de técnicos, de diplomáticos y de artistas que no sólo no es disidente ni contestatario, sino que es la faceta moderna donde la misma clase tradicional reconoce su propio progreso social. Esta ambigua reincorporación de los antiguos liberales produce la necesaria reacomodación ideológica y, con ella, la escisión entre la personalidad pública y privada y la referencia del nuevo arte, con nuevos lenguajes, temas y funciones, a esta última. En 1862, por ejemplo, Pedro Gálvez, el antiguo radical, regresa encandilado de la Corte de Napoleón III y se dedica a preparar un proyecto de Moneda y de Banco de emisión, depósito y descuento organizado en forma de sociedad anónima, con grandes privilegios para el Estado, colaborando con tareas de tipo administrativo y mostrando una moderación política tan manifiesta que se hace evidente que, por sobre el revolucionario del Colegio Guadalupe, ahora vive el pragmático, el realista y el administrador de los gobiernos guaneros [19]. Casós, a pesar de su demagogia revolucionaria en las Asambleas, abandona su escaño a cambio de un cargo en Europa en 1867. Ricardo Palma y Carlos Augusto Salaverry, apoyan la revolución de Balta y el primero es su bardo y su cronista; el segundo, su secretario, después nombrado diputado en las Cámaras. El mismo Salaverry cantó las glorias de Castilla, de Balta, del difunto Manuel Pardo, de Francisco García Calderón y publicó sus poemas gracias a una subvención del Estado, mientras cumplía una misión en Europa, en 1872. De esta época, y no de antes, es ese apoyo incondicional de los principales dirigentes de la élite dominante a la literatura —a estos poetas y esta literatura (y no del período romántico liberal)— cuando estos literatos ya pertenecían por derecho propio a la misma élite social [20].

El romanticismo nació en vinculación directa con el pueblo y con la élite dirigente como un populismo ilustrado; se desarrolló articulado a la lucha del Partido Liberal como un radicalismo aristocrático; a partir del fracaso del proyecto liberal en 1858 se produce una crisis sobre su significado social. Ya no puede vincularse con el público urbano, con la clase dominante o con el partido revolucionario y toda relación con la sociedad se vuelve problemática. Se produce, entonces, una liquidación definitiva de las dos tendencias anteriores y la producción cultural se referirá predominantemente a la vida privada. Aquellas dos etapas duraron escasamente ocho años y no logran constituir una tendencia literaria dominante, crear su propia tradición y madurar hasta dar obras de suficiente relevancia estética. Esta última opción, en cambio, señala la etapa de consolidación de la literatura republicana y formula un proyecto cultural y una doctrina estética que serán reconocidas por la conciencia oficial como «la cultura peruana». Aquéllas no fueron sino tentativas de la joven generación modernizada por asumir un perfil social que terminaron en el fracaso. La modernidad no puede ser realizada vinculada a la antigua élite dirigente ni al pueblo urbano tradicional; tampoco pudieron optar por una personalidad social autónoma que, ganando el ejercicio del poder estatal, impusiera su dominio sobre la realidad nacional. La primera realización del modo de ser republicano, resultado de su opción por la democracia, por la independencia y por la articulación con la modernidad europea, se resuelve en una especie de compromiso donde el individuo se incorpora resignado a una sociedad tradicional que no puede modificar, pero se identifica íntimamente con una modernidad que no puede tampoco representar. Y este será el perfil esencial que caracterizará a toda la producción cultural de las élites ilustradas mientras se mantengan dependientes de su incorporación a la élite dominante y no se encuentra en situación de intentar una revolución social.

Toda esta generación tuvo el problema de cuál había de ser su relación artística con la sociedad y con la experiencia de la propia individualidad. La primera solución de Cisneros (1861-1864) intentó idealizar la misma vida social limeña, que consideraba repugnante y degradada, seleccionando algunos aspectos bellos y «poéticos», frente a la evolución de un estilo aburguesado que acentuaba la misma corrupción que combatía. La solución no podía persistir alegremente como había ocurrido en los narradores franceses que escribían con la misma intención. Si se leen los poemas amorosos de Salaverry teniendo en cuenta su otra faceta laudatoria e ideologizante con los gobernantes de turno, se podrá percibir el sentido de esa interiorización sensitiva y melodiosa que ha representado el más delicado e intenso lirismo de su época [21]. Su poema «El héroe y el bardo» (refiriéndose a él y Balta) muestra una concepción de la función del poeta como aquel que está en un ámbito superior («Dios... / A vos os abrió el campo de la guerra... / a mí... / Vuelos para dejar la tierra / y lira para cantar ilustres hechos... / Vuestra gloria será en lo venidero / de las leyes salvar el arca santa... / Y mi gloria mayor cantar la vuestra»). Cuya función es idealizar la figura de los que detentan el poder. La misma idealización del yo, de sus sentimientos íntimos y de sus experiencias amorosas empañan la vivencia directa de la vida en una visión idílica, rítmica y armoniosa que lo encuadra en un marco alejado y le trata de insuflar un matiz de amable belleza [22]. Hacer poesía se convertirá —como diría Machado a propósito del Modernismo— en un idear afeites para una tarea cosmética, donde se trata de ocultar la realidad circundante y la experiencia cotidiana con un barniz de idealismo que permite soportarlos. Y de allí que no será muy difícil poder relacionar todo este modo de producción de un tipo peculiar de cultura con su más alta realización en el período modernista. Porque toda ella está soportada por esa escisión entre arte y vida social, entre cultura y vida cotidiana, entre poesía y experiencia inmediata. El modo de producción del Modernismo se consolidará cuando esta tendencia incipiente sea cultivada por profesionales de la belleza y del lenguaje que se dediquen con ahínco a la tarea de abolir la experiencia cotidiana amputando todas sus impurezas hasta convertirlas en una experiencia estética. Serán maestros en el escamoteo deliberado de todas las aristas de la realidad, aun de la propia vivencia, y expertos en el oficio artesanal que sabe encontrar palabras, ritmos, imágenes, contextos y melodías que permitan trasladarlas a una esfera distante, autónoma y casi autosuficiente del canto poético. Se tratará precisamente de suprimir aquello que entrega la vida sin negarlo, a través de un nuevo lenguaje que la reintegra a un universo orquestal y sonoro. No habrá modo más eficaz de justificar ideológicamente el proyecto de una clase social sin nombrarla ni cantarla —que también lo hicieron— ya que se realizará en base a la escisión entre la existencia y la conciencia, refiriendo la cultura solamente a un reino ideal de belleza y procurando que no interfiera en la vida de la sociedad o del propio yo, sino que las purifique, que las transforme y las idealice [23]. Si tenemos en cuenta que el mismo estadio de frustración y desencanto, seguido por un similar movimiento de interiorización realizado en la marginalidad, ha dado por resultado las memorias de Pruvoneda, las de Echenique, las de Orbegozo, las de Mendiburu, las de Valdivia, de Francisco Calderón, de Távara, de Lasalle o de Cáceres [24], percibimos la oposición que se plantea entre todos aquellos que han apelado a la producción de la cultura para configurar su relación consigo mismos y con el mundo, y aquellos otros que la han utilizado para olvidar, compensar y ocultar esa realidad. No será al acaso, entonces, que estos poetas y escritores se puedan incorporar aproblemáticamente a la antigua élite social que compatieron y que, a su vez, esa misma élite eleve sus producciones a la categoría de la cultura oficial, los reconozca, los prestige y los recompense, mientras aquella otra producción caiga en el olvido. Esta literatura ya no puede ser llamada legítimamente romántica sino en el sentido peyorativo que tiene este concepto para referirse al emocionalismo sensiblero referido predominantemente a la subjetividad privada. Mientras la etapa anterior, a pesar de su fijación esencialista en el pasado de la ilustración, tenía el carácter definido de un subjetivismo romántico porque significaba la configuración del individuo en su propio lenguaje como opuesto a su mundo, este subjetivismo reblandecido no es sino un vago sustituto para ciertos momentos privados que no define la personalidad burguesa que la produce. No es ya un ideal, sino una idealización forzada de lo real. No implica una relación con el mundo sino que trata de olvidar esa relación. Y si la producción de la crónica y de la costumbre ilustrada buscaba entender el medio; si la sátira pretendió agredir a la sociedad a la que inevitablemente se pertenece; si la memoria apela al recuerdo para dar coherencia a la experiencia pasada —donde se interpreta el destino individual a la luz de sus relaciones sociales y de los procesos históricos— la novela sentimental burguesa no es una explicación, no es una utopía, no es una agresión sino un compromiso, al nivel más superficial de la vida privada, con la sociedad degradada a la que resignadamente el nuevo individuo se reincorpora. Implica la renuncia a que la cultura intervenga en la historia, la renuncia a que las existencias de un espíritu insatisfecho se inmiscuyan en las relaciones sociales, la renuncia a buscar la propia identidad a partir de una problematización de la propia imagen y la renuncia a diseñar un horizonte humanizado de la existencia. Todo ello compensado con la ternura de la vida íntima y la belleza contenida en un lenguaje idealizado .Esta doctrina estética, que como se ve es una toma de posición frente a sí mismo frente a la sociedad y frente a la cultura, dominó el horizonte oficial peruano los próximos cincuenta años y persistió aún más tarde, por ejemplo en la idea que se tuvo del fin de la enseñanza de la literatura nacional hasta hace muy poco tiempo.

4. LA AUTOCONCIENCIA GENERACIONAL

En su primera etapa, el romanticismo peruano fue un espectáculo social. En la segunda, estimuló un comportamiento político. A partir del fracaso liberal se convertirá en un aristocratismo intimista, referido a la vida privada. Desde entonces, esta generación define una nueva posición social y se consolida la finalidad de su producción cultural. Sus gestos no significarán la búsqueda de prestigio como en el primer caso; tampoco se articularán a la lucha por el dominio del poder, como en el segundo; desaparecerán de su horizonte la opinión pública urbana, la relación de clientelazgo con respecto a los representantes del Estado y el apetito de poder. La cultura se convertirá así en una especie de código diferencial, propio de un sector social cultivado, que lo distingue de la misma manera que lo podría hacer un cargo burocrático, la posesión de una fortuna, la pericia profesional y una cátedra en la universidad. La cultura ya no será un puente para fundar una relación social, ni un instrumento para conseguir un objetivo político, sino una cualidad de la subjetividad. Lo más notable, sin embargo, de esta inversión, es que perderá también todo sentido afirmativo, indagatorio o crítico, y dejará de ser la proyección de una personalidad social, para reflejar solamente una crisis de identidad. No definirá al sujeto social que la produce, sino que es la tentativa por la que ese sujeto evita autodefinirse, escamotea de su conciencia su propia experiencia social y le asigna a la producción cultural la tarea de suprimirla, desfigurarla y configurarla nuevamente, trasladándola a un fingido reino de belleza, ironía, rencor o melancolía.

A partir de mediados de la década de 1860 se estabiliza la fisonomía del llamado romanticismo peruano como idealización interiorizada de la vida privada, tal como lo percibimos en el espacio cultural que presuponen las novelas de Cisneros, los poemas de Salaverry o las tradiciones de Palma. Estas obras tienen como supuesto básico la oposición entre la vida artística y la vida social, entre la cultura y la vida cotidiana. Este desenlace del movimiento no resulta imprevisible si tenemos en cuenta el marco estructural en donde debió desarrollarse este dinamismo histórico. Lo que resulta más difícil de explicar, en cambio, es la aparente contradicción entre la progresiva radicalización política y el fracaso de esta generación, por un lado, y la distinta resolución artística con que formalizó esa experiencia en el nivel del arte y de la cultura, por otro. Si esa generación luchó contra los caudillos, contra el poder clerical y contra la plutocracia; si intentó reemplazar al Ejército con las Guardias Nacionales y con la Convención; si urgió la liberación de los esclavos y luchó por la abolición del tributo y si se opuso a que las instituciones del Estado fueran administradas como una posesión patrimonial: ¿cómo es posible que esa misma generación no dirija la reflexión sobre esa frustrada experiencia social para narrarla, explicarla o elaborarla, y defienda en cambio que la función del arte consiste en la espiritualización de los sentimientos privados y en la creación de un ámbito que obtiene su validez de su independencia de su medio social? Los párrafos anteriores nos entregan la explicación que, como hemos visto, no se encuentra solamente a nivel estructural sino que es el resultado de un comportamiento histórico en esa situación estructural.

La obra de Basandre nos permite estudiar la producción cultural como un proyecto social. No se trata sólo de obras literarias sino también de conductas, es decir, de relaciones sociales diseñadas a partir de una determinada posición en medio de una concreta formación social. A la búsqueda de prestigio en un momento de consolidación institucional y de expansión económica correspondió una producción espectacular, melodramática y efectista. El apetito de poder y la autoafirmación generacional proyectó símbolos utópicos y eligió lenguajes que le permitieran diferenciarse como grupo de los demás sectores sociales, imaginándose a sí mismos como mártires y como héroes, capaces de forzar el curso de la historia. El fracaso político significará la muerte de los ideales sociales modernizadores y, también, el vaciamiento ideológico. El comportamiento ahora estará dominado por el pragmatismo político colaboracionista que se justifica hablando del aporte de la razón en una sana administración de los negocios del Estado y, no menos, teniendo en cuenta que allí está también su propio interés económico y social. El pragmatismo desilusionado, cuando puede ser cooptado por una élite que administra una sostenida expansión económica, formula la escisión entre la vida pública y privada como dos órdenes irreconciliables y obliga a la cultura a no trasgredir sus nuevos límites. Será, por eso, una cultura cooptada, más que represiva, reprimida. La tónica cultural de la primera etapa de consolidación de la República (1860-1910) no sólo estará determinada por el subdesarrollo económico y social —éste sería el elemento estructural— sino también por el fracaso del proyecto liberal y por la coopción de la antigua clase que la asocia, la identifica con sus propios horizontes y la compromete con un proyecto de modernización limitada que les prohíbe nombrar todos los elementos que quedan fuera de su acción.

Además de aquella dimensión estructural y de este perfil histórico social, las diversas etapas del romanticismo constituyen la cambiante autoconciencia de una generación. En un primer momento, ellos se pensaron a sí mismos teniendo en cuenta el efecto que producía su comportamiento frente a las expectativas de sus jueces benevolentes, que esperaban ver en ellos el ejemplo de su propia incorporación a la modernidad. En el segundo período, la imagen con que se interpretan a sí mismos está tomada de símbolos ideales abstractos, buscando legitimar su pretensión de tomar el poder, no en el hecho de que representan concretos intereses sociales, sino aquellos elevados ideales que eran el verdadero motor de la historia. En el tercer período no se definirán en función de la élite dirigente, ni tampoco alegarán que ellos concretizan históricamente hechos ideales. Más bien se podría decir que, a partir de 1860, ellos se niegan a formular su propia imagen, no quieren definirse a sí mismos y se muestran incapaces de establecer una relación ingenua entre su conciencia y su experiencia social, reflejando una crisis de identidad. Ser una generación moderna, en el Perú republicano, significaba simultáneamente pertenecer y sentirse ajena a la realidad social. Desde su punto de vista ilustrado, ellos podían definir exactamente los términos de la oposición en que se debatía la coyuntura histórica, representados por una sociedad tradicional volcada hacia el pasado y una sociedad moderna europea tensionada hacia el futuro. Pero no se podían definir a sí mismo ya que, al mismo tiempo, pertenecían y eran ajenos a uno y a otro, sin poder sentirse espontáneamente identificados con ninguno de los dos. La producción romántica representa la tentativa de un grupo social para darse una personalidad social y definir la propia identidad, produciendo en sus obras diversos comportamientos para alcanzar precisos objetivos sociales. Esto es ya una cultura burguesa que ha de ser articulada, no a una raza, un tipo o una síntesis cultural, sino: (a) a una evolución estructural, donde esta producción cultural secularizada se encuentra sostenida por nuevos estratos sociales, que cumplen con ella nuevas funciones sociales; (b) a un comportamiento social de esos sectores con respecto al poder, a las clases, a las posibilidades de desarrollo histórico de su sociedad y a las funciones que puede cumplir la *propia* cultura para sostener ese comportamiento; y (c) al esfuerzo de formular una autodefinición de la propia identidad. Es por lo tanto una producción específicamente restringida a una élite ilustrada fracasada y, finalmente, cooptada por los representantes del poder.

Las características del romanticismo peruano, por lo tanto, deben ser explicadas por la imposibilidad que tuvo una élite ilustrada de desarrollar una cultura moderna en una sociedad estabilizada con pautas tradicionales —causa estructural—, en una determinada coyuntura histórica modernizante que provocó el fracaso y la coopción de la tentativa liberal —causa histórica—. No es sólo un movimiento imitativo, que tiende a parecerse a un país central. Ni es la expresión de un tipo social regional, que muestra cómo ha elaborado la fusión de razas en un nuevo medio, produciendo un nuevo tipo cultural. Es una praxis de un pequeño grupo social, donde entraron en conflicto la tentativa de imitación de la modernidad y el choque contra la realidad tradicional. Y por ello tampoco puede llamársela una literatura «nacional».

Es convincente la reiterada tesis de Basadre, donde afirma que la gesta emancipadora y las sucesivas luchas nacionales tuvieron eco multitudinario[25]. Esto significaría que, a nivel de la producción de la cultura, las tendencias y los productos intelectuales, ya sean las Constituciones, los periódicos, los discursos o las obras literarias, significarían la cultura de toda la nación. Las cosas, sin embargo, podrían ser planteadas de otra manera. No se trata de que la gran mayoría indígena y la ya amplia clase urbana iletrada no pudiera tener conciencia actual de todos estos problemas sino que, en definitiva, si toda esta producción podría representar sus intereses históricos confusamente entrevistos cuando participaban en las luchas nacionales. Este argumento tendría que explicar la diversidad de intereses a los que se incorporaban y se siguieron sucesivamente incorporando hasta que la lucha toma un acento anticivilista y antioligárquico con el pierolismo costeño y, más tarde, clasista con las rebeliones indígenas y las luchas obreras de este siglo. Pero, más que eso, se trata de comprender que el movimiento por la emancipación y, después, por la organización de la República a lo largo de los últimos dos siglos, ha sido un fenómeno inducido por la revolución democrático-burguesa de los países industriales. Y si es posible decir que la nación como totalidad se articula progresivamente a ese movimiento con el inicio de la República, hay que tener en cuenta que el impacto de esa ola expansiva no es el mismo en la élite ilustrada, en la que se incorpora a parte de la antigua clase dominante y dirige los negocios del Estado, ni en la mayoría popular. El dinamismo con que se forman estas élites ilustradas, con que progresan y ascienden rápidamente a los altos niveles de la sociedad, con que se reclama su colaboración, con que se vinculan a la sociedad europea y se desvinculan de la nacional es tal, que pronto se produce un grave desfase entre ellos y su realidad social. Es en ese momento cuando se plantean con agudeza el tema de su propia identidad y de una imagen del mundo, de la historia y de sí mismos que de alguna manera elabore su experiencia social, que no es sino la manifestación, al nivel de la conciencia, del gravísimo problema de su modo de pertenencia a la sociedad nacional, a la élite dirigente y a la moderna sociedad europea. Por ello, la producción de su cultura se ve también problematizada y no puede ser directamente referida a la sociedad nacional y, tampoco, a la élite dominante, sino que ha de ser vista como la producción de un horizonte de un grupo diferenciado y sometido a graves contradicciones con su medio social [26].

La producción romántica no agota la cultura del Perú republicano, ni siquiera la del sector social ilustrado. En el mismo nivel social encontramos aquellos otros que no tuvieron una experiencia ni de truinfo, ni de coopción social, y que producen la sátira, la memoria o la novela crítica. Vinculado al público urbano medio se producen la costumbre, el relato de viajes y la comedia nacional. La gran masa indígena y campesina, mientras tanto, seguía viviendo y recreando la cultura tradicional. Basadre ha tenido el mérito enorme de llamar la atención sobre toda esta producción que, en su conjunto, muestra hasta qué punto un concepto de cultura nacional que tratara de incluir la idea de síntesis armónica, de expresión de un tipo de comunidad homogénea, puede resultar inadecuado. Y muestra también el proceso de selección de los textos que puede realizar la «cultura oficial», donde se consagran como «canónicos» una serie de producciones irrelevantes, quedando en el olvido todas aquellas otras que obedecen — o pueden provocar— otro tipo de comportamiento y sustentar un diferente proyecto social.

5. LOS ESTRATOS MEDIOS EN LA ETAPA DE EXPANSION PREINDUSTRIAL

¿En qué matriz básica se desarrolló el comportamiento de los estratos medios ilustrados en la segunda mitad del siglo XVIII?[27] A partir del ascenso al trono de Carlos III (1759), comienza en el Imperio español un proceso de modernización desde arriba, que tiene su origen en una decisión política de quienes se encuentran en la cúspide de la pirámide social y es instrumentado por un programa estatal. Los dos principales objetivos eran solucionar la dependencia y el estancamiento económicos y fortalecer el poder militar. Para lograrlos, el rey escoge un cuerpo de administradores desvinculado de los intereses dominantes, que no pertenecen a los sectores privilegiados tradicionales, reclutándolo entre la baja nobleza, la clase burguesa acomodada y entre sectores medios que habían hecho carrera en el ejército, el clero o en pequeñas universidades de provincia. La ideología ilustrada de este grupo lo prepara para revisar las instituciones, sanear la administración, racionalizar la producción, fortalecer la economía del Estado y fomentar un nacionalismo económico expansivo. Cuando se comienza con las reformas se produce una oposición decidida entre quienes estaban interesados en mantener el *status quo* tradicional. A partir de entonces el programa se restringe a una serie de ajustes administrativos dentro del sistema imperial tradicional, sin dañar los intereses ni los privilegios establecidos. En medio de este cuadro global, los estratos medios tienen las siguientes posibilidades: 1) En un período de expansión y de cambios, se produce una demanda de nuevos tipos humanos para llenar nuevas necesidades y funciones. Este grupo encuentra entonces la posibilidad de ser incorporado a la élite dominante gracias a que han cumplido una «carrera» que muestra su competencia y su talento. Sin embargo, a quien sólo tenía talento y no títulos de nobleza únicamente se le abría esa posibilidad a través de la protección de un hidalgo, un noble o un personaje influyente. El talento disponible para cumplir una nueva función social se encuentra condicionado, desde un principio, por la realidad del clientelazgo. 2) La posibilidad que tienen estos nuevos estratos de desarrollar una acción se deriva del hecho previo de que existe una decisión del poder político absoluto, que tiene necesidad de llenar nuevas funciones administrativas, económicas y militares. Es decir que el programa de modernización que ellos deberán cumplir nace de una decisión «desde arriba», frente a la cual los estratos medios dependientes no tienen poder de decisión. 3) Por ello, el límite de sus posibilidades estará dictado por el sistema social en cuyo conjunto se integran y, en particular, por los sectores privilegiados que componen la élite a la que se incorporan. Ellos eran llamados para realizar algunos ajustes, no para transformar el sistema o para derrocar a las clases dominantes. Ellos vivirán esa contradicción donde se los llama para representar la modernidad dentro del horizonte de una clase que los promueve, les pide su iniciativa, los estimula, pero, en definitiva, los constriñe como condición de sobrevivencia. Resumiendo, estos estratos, unidos al poder político, son los instrumentos de ese poder para realizar algunas reformas. Sin embargo, los condicionamientos básicos en que deberán desarrollarlas nacen de su posición dentro del sistema general de estratificación, donde sólo pueden desarrollar comportamientos de clientelazgo, de radicalismo dependiente y coopción. Serán los representantes de una modernidad limitada por un encuadre tradicional.

Germani [28] analiza la situación de los estratos y de las clases medias, comparando los efectos del proceso de expansión en los países industriales y en los de América Latina. Los elementos comunes a una y otra región se derivan de la similitud en cuanto a la ubicación en la estructura social global. Sin embargo, mientras el proceso se cumple en Europa a partir de una economía industrial que transforma rápidamente la organización social tradicional, en los países de economía primaria de exportación se retrasan los efectos modernizadores de la expansión. Los elementos básicos del sistema son los siguientes: 1) En la cúspide de la pirámide social se encuentran las oligarquías modernizadoras que se benefician del proceso de exportación, manteniendo el poder en base a una democracia restringida y limitando los cambios al horizonte que les permite sus propios intereses de clase. Se da acá una inversión de la situación europea, ya que los intereses de clase de una y otra región se dirigen hacia metas diferentes: la urbanización, la industrialización, la liberación de la fuerza de trabajo, la formación del sector secundario y terciario, en Europa, y a mantener la rígida estructura social tradicional y el dominio sobre la tierra, en América Latina. 2) Los estratos medios tienen una relación contradictoria con esas oligarquías. Por un lado, mantienen una actitud de oposición que tiende a ampliar el proceso de participación democrática, defender la justicia social y proponen doctrinas ideológicas más avanzadas (legales y constitucionales), llegando inclusive a liderar movimientos populares en contra de esas mismas oligarquías. Una vez incorporadas al aparato del Estado, tratarán de aplicar medidas reformistas que tocan al modo de administrar sus recursos, tendrán cierta inquietud nacionalista, tenderán a dictar leyes sociales que contemplan la situación de las clases bajas y a favorecer la movilidad social, sobre todo dando mayores oportunidades de educación. Pero, por otro lado, su lucha contra la oligarquía se limita a favorecer la democracia formal o la reforma constitucional, sin herir realmente su posición de predominio; sus pautas de prestigio los hace identificarse con esa misma oligarquía diferenciándose de la gran mayoría de abajo y teniendo con ellos actitudes paternalistas o vicarias; y el límite de sus reformas se encontrará precisamente en que nunca se plantean la posibilidad de modificar esencialmente el sistema de propiedad de los medios de producción, o la forma privilegiada en que se distribuyen los beneficios y las oportunidades en una rígida estructura social. En síntesis, representan una tendencia progresista en su sentido democrático y social, luchan contra las injusticias y desean favorecer la movilidad, pero se identifican con el sistema social y con la élite dominante. Esta identificación, y la consiguiente constricción de su propio horizonte a los intereses de la clase dominante, son los rasgos más nítidos para definir que su aparente radicalización ideológica, democrática y social, termina cooptada por una élite dominante que los admite en su seno y los hace participantes de sus privilegios. Como se puede comprender, la matriz básica no ha variado esencialmente: 1) Se da acá también un movimiento de transición y de expansión, donde se crean nuevas demandas de sectores medios vinculados a la acción del Estado; 2) se realiza un programa restringido de modernización, pronunciado «desde arriba», que tiene como límite la situación privilegiada de una élite en medio de una estructura social que resiste rígidamente a los cambios; 3) El movimiento de modernización está representado por los sectores medios ilustrados que han hecho carrera gracias a su talento. Pero ellos también constituyen una élite dentro de una inmensa mayoría que no ha tenido esa posibilidad. Y aunque sean más progresistas, democráticos y tengan una mayor inquietud social que sus pares del siglo xviii, en definitiva unos y otros se identifican con la élite dominante, y encuentran el límite de su propia actividad en el horizonte de esa élite y del mismo sistema social estratificado que no imaginan transformar, terminando incorporados a la cúspide privilegiada de la pirámide social.

Podemos volver ahora a nuestra distinción entre condicionamientos estructurales y acontecimientos históricos. No hay duda de que Basadre ha dado un importante llamado de atención, para que en adelante se evite la simplificación con que la gran mayoría de los científicos sociales aluden a la transición de la colonia a la República. Al menos para el Perú, no se puede afirmar que la independencia sólo significó una toma del poder político por parte de las élites privilegiadas criollas [29]. Pero, por otro lado, nos parece que esta matriz básica puede ser utilizada para trazar la parábola que, como conjunto, describe el empeoramiento de los estratos medios del período y, aún, de otros períodos siguientes que se desarrollan durante esta misma etapa hasta la aparición de los movimientos revolucionarios de clase media de los años 20 y 30 de este siglo. En este sentido, la descripción de Germani conviene más para el movimiento pierolista y para tendencias culturales como el primer indigenismo, la novela crítica urbana de principios de siglo y el modernismo, incluyendo algunos aspectos del radicalismo de González Prada. El romanticismo, en cambio, se parece más al siglo xviii (clientelazgo, radicalización abstracta, coopción) que a la primera década del siglo xx, aunque los tres mantienen los rasgos básicos de su cultura como un comportamiento social. Inclusive, las reflexiones sobre las élites liberales que realizara el mismo Basadre [30], y que después continuó realizando una y otra vez [31], se acercan explícitamente a esta interpretación.

6. PARADIGMA DE LAS CULTURAS DEPENDIENTES DEL PODER COMO PRAXIS SOCIAL

Aprendiendo en la obra de Jorge Basadre cómo es posible interpretar un movimiento cultural como proceso histórico dentro de una determinada matriz estructural, podemos ahora formular un paradigma que permanecerá válido mientras se den las mismas condiciones. Las variables serían las siguientes:

1) Un sistema social en proceso de estructuración a causa de la expansión económica y la consolidación del poder central, incorporando sectores intermedios tradicionales a un programa restringido de modernización.

2) Una estructura social rígida, sin demasiadas posibilidades de transformación global, manteniendo el predominio de la organización tradicional.

3) Un grupo intelectual productor de cultura, identificado con la élite dominante modernizadora dentro de esa estructura tradicional, perteneciente a estratos medios también tradicionales.

En esta situación, el intelectual se mantendrá incorporado a las élites dominantes, diferenciándose del pueblo mayoritario. El romanticismo peruano será el primer movimiento republicano que mostrará cuál es la posibilidad de realizar una cultura burguesa moderna en una situación de dependencia de las élites dominantes tradicionales. No será el primer movimiento de este tipo, ya que en condiciones semejantes se produjo la cultura colonial durante la Ilustración. Ni será el último, ya que esta matriz se reproduce casi exactamente en las diversas tentativas culturales que se realizan hasta el movimiento modernista, mientras la cultura se mantenga producida en un ámbito urbano restringido y se encuentre dependiente de la oligarquía tradicional.

La permanencia de esta matriz también explicará la persistencia de las posibles variantes de esta cultura específica, articuladas a las posibles actitudes que le está permitido tomar al estrato intelectual medio frente al poder, frente a las posibilidades de desarrollo histórico y frente a las diversas clases de su sociedad. Ellas son las siguientes:

a) Cuando predomina una situación de clientelazgo dependiente, la tendencia a producir una cultura «moderna» de tipo aproblemático, efectista y espectacular, que llame la atención a la sensibilidad del público sin cuestionarlo.

b) Cuando se intenta asumir una actitud de independencia, se trata de producir actitudes radicales, críticas, contestatarias, utilizando la prédica emotiva más cercana a la retórica que al análisis racional, buscando escandalizar o agredir más que fundar un nuevo horizonte, utilizando la analogía dramatizante para convencer. No intentarán, en cambio, una actitud revolucionaria donde se diseñe una alternativa real al sistema vigente, se analice la realidad social y se escoja un nuevo público desvinculado de la élite dominante.

c) Cuando este estrato se encuentre cooptado, o sea incorporado a la élite dirigente, se dará una cultura reprimida, interiorizada, referida a la vida privada, con tendencia al aristocratismo purista y espiritualista.

Estas tres tendencias básicas pueden percibirse ya en el período de la Ilustración, pero se repiten con mayor claridad en el período siguiente al romanticismo, tanto en el Perú como en los otros países que viven un proceso de expansión limitada.

La cultura dependiente dentro de esta etapa de modernización significa la cultura de la transición entre aquella cultura cortesana, estereotipada y producida por los miembros de la clase privilegiada que se dio durante la colonia; y la futura producción cultural del intelectual proletarizado, que dentro de una metrópoli que tiene una nueva estructura social diferenciada en clases y sectores, escribe de manera anónima para un público o, desdichadamente, sólo para sí mismo. Es la cultura de la modernización restringida y controlada por la élite tradicional dentro de la urbe preindustrial y que fue el rasgo más característico de los grupos intelectuales del primer período republicano. Tendrán que entrar en crisis el sistema social y el liderazgo de las élites oligárquicas privilegiadas y aristocráticas, formarse los sectores secundario y terciario, movilizarse políticamente las clases medias para que aparezcan nuevos grupos de intelectuales —esta vez tratando de articularse, no a las élites oligárquicas, sino a un cierto internacionalismo cultural y a los nuevos movimientos sociales que trataban de superar aquella situación social— para que se produzca un nuevo sistema cultural.

NOTAS

[1] Gino Germani, *Sociología de la modernización*, Buenos Aires, Paidós, 1969, pág. 53; Fernando Henrique Cardoso y Enzo Faletto, *Dedendencia y desarrollo en América Latina*, Buenos Aires, siglo XXI Editores, S. A., 1971, págs. 38-53.
[2] Richard Newbold Adams, *Energy and Structure: A Theory of Social Power*, Austin, University of Texas Press, 1975, págs. 266-274.
[3] Richard P. Schaedel, «El tema central del estudio antropológico de las ciudades hispanoamericanas», *Revista de Indias*, Madrid, núm. 127-130, enero-diciembre, 1972, págs. 56-86.
[4] Jorge Basadre, *Historia de la República del Perú*, 5.ª ed., Lima, Editorial Universitaria, 1968, VII-X, XXVI-XXIX.
[5] Germani, *op. cit.*, págs. 53-56.
[6] Stanley J. y Barbara H. Stein, *La herencia colonial de América Latina*, 2.ª ed., México, Siglo XXI Editores, S. A., 1971.
[7] Theotonio dos Santos, *Dependencia y cambio social*, Santiago de Chile, Centro de Estudios Socioeconómicos, Universidad de Chile, 1970.

[8] Richard Morse, «The Development of Urban Systems in the Americas in the Nineteenth Century», *Journal of Interamerican Studies and World Affairs*, Miami, vol. 17, núm. 1, febrero 1975, págs. 4-26.

[9] Sergio Bagú, *Estructura social de la colonia*, Buenos Aires, El Ateneo, 1952, págs. 49-51, 72-77.

[10] Cardoso y Faleto, *op. cit.*, págs. 48-54.

[1] Alejandro Losada, *La producción romántica y la formación de la sociedad republicana (El caso peruano, 1840-1880)*, en preparación.

[12] Alejandro Losada, «La consolidación del romanticismo como afirmación del modo de ser de la aristocracia intelectual republicana», *Apuntes*, Lima, en prensa.

[13] Basadre, *op. cit.*, págs. 630-634.

[14] Eric Wolff y E. C. Hansen, «Caudillo Politics: A Structural Analysis», *Comparative Studies in Society and History*, Nueva York, vol. IX, págs. 168-179.

[15] Basadre, *La iniciación de la República*, Lima, F. y E. Rosay, 1929, I, 109-130; II, 411-413. *La multitud, la ciudad y el campo en la historia del Perú*, 2.ª ed., Lima, Editorial Huescarán, 1947, pág. 238. *Introducción a las bases documentales para la historia de la República del Perú con algunas reflexiones*, Lima, Editorial P. L. V., 1971, págs. 305-309, 401-411.

[16] Basadre, *La multitud, la ciudad...*, págs. 139-264; *Introducción a las bases documentales...*, págs. 311-312, 365, 403-407.

[17] José Rufino Echenique, *Memorias para la historia del Perú*, Lima, Editorial Huascarán, 1952, I, 196-201.

[18] Basadre, *Historia*, págs. 1395-1458, 1687-1703.

[19] *Ibid.*, pág. 1395.

[20] Luis Alberto Sánchez, «La literatura peruana», *Derrotero para una historia cultural del Perú*, Lima, Editorial Ediventas, S. A., 1966, págs. 960-963.

[21] Alberto Escobar, *Carlos A. Salaverry*, Lima, Editorial Universitaria, Biblioteca Hombres del Perú, 1966, XXXV.

[22] *Ibid.*, pág. 64.

[23] Angel Rama, *Rubén Darío y el modernismo*, Caracas, Universidad Central de Venezuela, 1970, págs. 105-124.

[24] Basadre, *Introducción a las bases documentales...*, págs. 93-104.

[25] Basadre, *Historia*, págs. 256-274.

[26] Alejandro Losada, «Los sistemas literarios como instituciones sociales en América Latina», *Revista de Crítica Literaria Latinoamericana*, Lima, núm. 1, primer semestre 1975, págs. 39-61.

[27] Stein, *op. cit.*, págs. 96, 161, 177.

[28] Germani, *op. cit.*, págs. 218-221.

[29] *Ibid.*, pág. 219; Stein, pág. 156.

[30] Basandre, *Perú: problema y posibilidad*, Lima, F. y E. Rosay, 1931, páginas 49-104.

[31] Basadre, *Introducción a las bases documentales...*, pág. 185.

Latin American Literary Criticism and Immigration

Marc Zimmerman
University of Illinois, Chicago Circle

1. The Advances of Socio-Historical Criticism

As many of us are quick to point out, great advances have been made in the past several years with respect to the socio-historical study of Latin American literature. New methodologies developing in literary studies have enmeshed with perspectives developing in the social sciences to create a new range of possibilities for historical and critical analyses of texts, movements and currents. The traditional canon of works has been questioned, and the doors opened to the study of a whole series of genres and modes of written expression, so that the very definition of the object of study has been questioned and transformed. Intensified work on countries and regions that have been neglected or given scant attention has enhanced our understanding of the richness and diversity of Latin American literatures, their varying rhythms of development, their varying relations with and distances from varied social totalities. Studies directed toward the multi-lingual, multi-cultural Caribbean area led to a certain problematizing of our object, and of our overall theoretical apparatus, implying a need for grasping regional totalities and relations among works, writer-groups and larger social sectors before establishing a firmer basis for a comprehensive or reconstructed totalistic theory.

In terms of approach, we have participated in a shift from rather simplistic Marxist and historicist perspectives to an enriched focus on the relative autonomy of "literary practices" and the importance of "relative literary systemicity" as forces mitigating against any socio-economic, ideological or even class reduction of literary phenomena; and we have carried out an application and

384

then critique of dependency theory and Althusserian perspectives, ever in function of a more complex and adequate grasp of social formations and processes, as well as socio-economic relations. We have seen a gradual shift in emphasis, too, from a concern with the social explanation of the production of texts to a concern with their functioning in distinct social formations as part of a cultural or counter-cultural field.

Ultimately all roads have led to the bases for constituting a new history of Latin American literature in function of regional, historical and cultural differentiations, and in terms which see "literature" as the varied written expressions of social groups in varying degrees of conformity or opposition to the ideological and formal determinations of evolving local, national and international apparatuses which have acted to assure the extended reproduction of the relations necessary to the socio-economic and political system in which these determinations are operative. And in all this there has been a shift from a focus on literature as a received phenomenon to a focus on all written and expressive forms—on a shift, then, from *belles lettres* according to dominantly European models, to "cultural expression," from institutionalized ideological and even cultural manifestations to those connected with everyday life, seen as a kind of creative cauldron of compensations, resistances, condensations of oppositions to forces of domination.

Nevertheless, while the bases in method and knowledge for a new totalistic approach have grown, while a process of institutionalization has taken place which has made many of the advances noted possible, and while many of those who have participated in this movement have themselves become institutionalized and thus enabled to carry on their work, other forces have been developing which have raised questions about the value of the ongoing project and the functions it could serve, its overall impact on the social totality in which it operated and the social totality which it had as object.

Of course changes in the world economic and political order, as well as the place of the U.S. in the midst of these changes had much to do with both our advances in socio-criticism and our latest sense of uncertainty about its purpose, effect and future. Since the early 1970's, the capitalist countries have suffered stagflation, internal crisis and a series of realignments within their internal and external relations; meanwhile, underdeveloped nations have undergone nationalist, religious and cultural turmoil, so that the configuration of global power relations and possibilities has changed considerably. Many advanced countries have been crippled; underdeveloped countries, oil-rich or not, capitalist or not, have been unable to underwrite or attract the ever-escalating sums required for modernization. The conflict between capitalist and socialist policies and powers, between advancing and declining capitalist states, between these states and multinational corporations on the one hand and developing national liberation struggles and established governments of national liberation on the other hand—all these have had a far-reaching impact on economic and political policies and strategies, on ideological and cultural structures and on the expressive artistic systems in which literary systems and specific literary expressions are born and operate; they have also had impact on the institutions and entities in which the study of literature takes place.

As for Latin America, the fall of Allende and the seeming collapse of many revolutionary movements led to the exile of many progressive scholars, critics and writers from the Southern Cone and other points. The entry into a period of reflux, paralleled, some would claim, by a twilight of the Latin American narrative boom had actually helped to dynamize the new developments in Latin American literary studies. But the new order which emerged globally at the same time would not only facilitate but simultaneously put constraints on the whole process and eventually tended to neutralize much of its hoped for effects, even as a new revolutionary wave, this time from Central America, gave even deeper importance to literary-historical studies. At the very moment when socio-historical approaches to Latin American literature seem on the threshhold of significant totalizations and applications in grand synthetic and national literary histories, we find ourselves questioning the value of such a field as a pedagogical and practical force. The decline of U.S. resources of education, the consequent pressure on academics, the elimination of many promising teachers from the academy, the scarcity of committed, advanced students to carry on the work, the erosion of the force of literature and literary criticism (or rather the neutralization of the space for such endeavors)—all these and other dimensions come together to present us with a sense of uncertainty. Indeed, the need to delimit, neutralize and rechannel left-tending Latin American studies becomes even more crucial as Central American revolutionary movements are seen as a threat to U.S. hemispheric hegemony, at a time when a reduced globlal position makes "local" hegemony seem all the more important. Advanced Marxist literary studies as applied to Latin America has come to seem just an alternative academic approach in a vapid pluralistic democracy of discipline; the possible social effect of our work, indeed even our effect on most of the students we teach, is rendered quite minimal in the total constellation of forces affecting social consciousness and action.

At the same time, another not unrelated matter, too much ignored in our past efforts at theoretical totalization, the process of immigration and its implications for Latin American literary history studies and their effect, came to bear strongly on the very conditions of literary creation and analysis.

2. Immigration, Latin America and Literature

Of course immigration has long been an international phenomenon of great significance as both an effect and causal factor in the functionality and development of socio-economic and political forces and institutions. Obviously world economic tendencies as they impact specific regions and policies are essential in determining the flow and impact of immigration; and these broader tendencies then create new contexts for a whole series of problems which confront home base and host countries involved in particular immigration processes. A study of immigration causes and effects with respect to home-base countries is very important in plotting the future development of these countries and their international role; such study is also important in understanding the future of immigrant populations in host countries. Inevitably the consequences of immigration for the host countries and their particular constituencies are of vital concern, especially with respect to questions of economic, social and cultural adjustments, impact on pre-existing institutions and forms, technological and overall productive development, employment, housing and an array of issues affecting social dynamism, public policy, law and politics. Ultimately immigration related issues affect and potentially transform the very nature of host countries and the very world order of which they are a part. Thus, to the degree that immigration has become an essential dimension and expressive form of world socio-economic development, it is a key issue for understanding all things which are said to relate to that development. Indeed, the general normative observations set forth here are especially relevant to Latin America and the Caribbean in their relation to the U.S. While immigration is a global phenomenon, and while recent key migrations include the exodus from Southeast Asia and Eastern Europe, the movement of Mediterranean guest workers to Northern Europe, and such Latin America-related phenomena as the Japanese movement to Brazil, the Salvadoran movement to

Honduras, the Guatemalan movement to Mexico and the more longstanding Columbian movement to Venezuela, still, for Latin America, the chief issue must be the massive and still growing movement of peoples to the U.S. This latter movement signals important and deep structural processes which are important even for literary studies.

Just as the decline in U.S. world hegemony led politicians and strategists to give more attention to Latin American and Caribbean social formations, and just as Grenadan and Central American revolutionary currents broke lose, the rate of immigration from these and adjacent areas accelerated. Of course, these phenomena were not unrelated. To cite just one connection: As U.S. and homegrown Latin American capitalists invested heavily in capital-intensive enterprises, rising growth rates betokened new levels of immiseration and stirred new waves of revolutionary unrest and migration. As U.S. products became less competitive in the world market, more U.S. capital migrated to Latin America, and the immigrants who were increasingly forced to move north became subject to a process aimed at bringing down the price of labor to thus stave off the further export of industry and capital.

While the total process has been far more complex than can be grasped by any one pattern, still the overall implications of U.S. decline and its effect on large numbers of Latin American and Caribbean workers, as well as our overall hemispheric economic and social life, have not escaped notice. And yet Marxist literary critics were not in the forefront of considering this dimension of our times. Perhaps they were fetishized by their own objects of study, by their theoretical syntheses and above all by their concern for the literary movements in the Latin American countries they studied and, in many instances, with which they identified. It is not that they never mentioned the phenomenon, but we are speaking here of a real, operationally implemented concern. Even when we verbally acknowledged a need to include, say, Chicano literature as at least a problematic part of our Latin American object of study, even as more and more refugees and exiles, or their sons and daughters, began to write a literature of migration and exile, little attention was given to such work except to the degree that it could be assimilated to concerns with home base countries. Indeed, I believe that it was not until the Chilean literature of resistance in exile appeared, so qualitatively distinct in contours as to demand a mutation in critical frame, that say, Chicano, and U.S. Puerto Rican or Cuban literatures began to attract an attention that could begin to impinge on the theoretical systhesis toward which we were heading. The whole syncretic process of the internationalization of a specifically Latin American mode of literary production tied to the concrete circumstances of Latin America was slipping between our fingers. And only now, before a phenomenon that has been developing for any number of years, are we persuaded to consider that we can have no theory or theoretically-guided study of literature expressive of Latin America if we do not pose the question of how Latin America and its literary expressions have extended north and of how Latin American literature, however hybridized and mutant, was part of a world which most of us had opposed to Latin America.

Suddenly, after several years of affirmative action, when Spanish Departments and Latin American Studies programs have held on and in some cases thrived in relation to the growing importance of Latin America and the Latin American presence in the U.S., we find ourselves saying (and this at a moment when affirmative action is dying) that the issue of immigration and the literatures of immigration may be a very important dimension of our work.

If we are saying that Marxist literary study extends now beyond the realm of traditional literary criticism and to deal with the contours of everyday life, then what more apt phenomena than the ones posed by immigration? The issue is no longer peripheral, parenthetical or tangential, but the very stuff of our work, because it is increasingly the substance of many Latin American lives. And clearly in this country the question is not simply that of Chicano literature (indeed that literature poses a particular problematic instance with relation to the question of totality, since it is both a literature indigenous to the Southwest and a literature of immigration). And isn't it a coincidence that Latin Americans involved in our field bring up this subject just at a time when at the theoretical level they are talking about everyday life? Can it be that the subject of immigration encroaches on the everyday life of the researchers, and has been a business they have lived without ever wanting to confront it as a subject matter until, turning a corner, they find it staring them in the face?

For, our proposed object of study, immigration and its culture and literature, is certainly one of the hardest objects of study for U.S.-based Latin American Latin Americanists, if only because they are so very directly part of the object of study. And it is an object which the force of our socio-economic system has perhaps made them want to stand apart from—as so many middle class Latin American immigrants (or those who have risen in class once here) have wanted to stand apart from those lowly economic refugees, those *mejicanos* and *caribeños* with their beaded curtains, and loud stereos, their dashboard Christs and macho crosses hanging from their necks—those people whose treatment in a racist country threatens the status and sense of being of the Latin American middle class, and the life experience of their children. The very value which Chicanos celebrate in function of *La Raza* are values which even Marxist Latin American Latin Americanists, as respectable members of the middle class, may instinctively seek to avoid. And yet, if as I have insisted elsewhere, Latin American socio-criticism constitutes a veritable mode of production interior to the literary system which Latin American literature, the problem for the critic is especially compounded, for the exterior object of study becomes a mirror.

So there, turning the corner, the critics see that even the literature of exile (of political immigrants after all!) may also be a literature of exiles who will never return and whose distance from home grows each day as they sit in one place dreaming of home. And this literature—it may, stylistically, structurally, somehow, have more in common with certain works of Chicano literature than of the literature in the home base. And so we begin to take note, and we must, simply because hardly any subject can be more symptomatic to Latin America today and to the situation of Latin American critics whose own lives and writings are the causes and effects of immigration. And if we are concerned about distances (between the critics and the reality they treat, between the literary texts and the people they however mediatedly express), the phenomenon of immigration as fact and object of study will provide many of the answers. And if solidarity work with Latin American struggles provides some extra-professional means for bridging the gap back to Latin America, and if in this work, we suffer perplexities and frustrations (as well as certain naïve pleasures) when we try to work with other homebase immigrants or other Latinos, are we not once again facing the same issue in another guise?

Reconstructing Latin American literary history, we come to realize that the issue has always been there (we think of Martí and so many countless others). But immigration and its context have undergone innumerable transformations, and never has the issue been so extensive and profound as it is today. Never has it affected so many; never has it been so much the expression of social formations in crisis; whole socio-economic systems, whole peoples and cultures. Over one hundred thousand leave Cuba; Haitians drown off the Florida coast; thousands are fleeing from Central America; Puerto Rico, in the face of Reagonomics, prepares for another massive exodus; Dominican undocumenteds flood New York; and now with the peso devaluation, what may we expect from *nuestro querido* Mexico?

If we are concerned about the practice of Latin Americanist Marxists in this country at a time when the pedagogical function seems to be shrinking for even certain of our more advantageously placed colleagues to specialized studies for ever more tiny and elite elites and basic language skills for future technicians and low-level technocrats, the question of Latin American immigration poses a whole area for creative and responsible activity in the very areas of everyday life, cultural expression, mass media, sex role transformations, etc. with which we are becoming increasingly able to deal. And what issue confronts us more directly with domestic concerns and even the future of the U.S. workingclass in ways that connect so decisively with Latin America?

What are the implications of immigration for Latin America and the U.S. and for the particular areas of culture, ideology and literature in which our work as critics is situated? What are the parameters of our object? What are some of the problems and tasks before us? In what follows, we will look at just certain dimensions and possibilities of an enormous yet-to-be mapped out field.

3. Latin American and Caribbean Immigration: Population and Culture

The first effect of continuing Latin American and Caribbean immigration is the fact made so much of in the past few years, that the "Hispanic" population is fast becoming the largest U.S. minority. An important dimension of this fact is that the vast majority of this population is of working class origin and destination, although this is not to underestimate the growing immigration of business and professional people, including many intellectuals. Indeed the heterogeneity of the incoming peoples combined with the already existing heterogeneity of those Latinos already here (reactionary Cuban lumpen, radical and reactionary professionals, etc., etc.) mitigates against overestimating the significance of mere numbers: the U.S. Latino population hardly forms a *bloc*, and even among many sectors with similar objective interests, it is extremely difficult to build effective unity. Nevertheless, in focusing on the workingclass dimension which predominates in this growing population, we may note the general trend by which the U.S. is experiencing potentially unsettling repercussions resulting from its modes of expansion and domination, according to which the long-standing exploitation of Latin American and Caribbean peoples is becoming more and more a situation which has turned inward on the U.S. itself.

For reasons stated above and many others, it is very difficult to specify the implications of projected Latino population growth for the future. While immigration has often offered the possibility for dynamizing host country development, the problems for immigrant population and for the populations among which the immigrants come to live and work, seem the dominant phenomenal dimension of our current social reality. Such problems have their effects on cultural and literary transformations and on the total system of which teachers of culture and literature are a part.

One such problem stems from the fact that material conditions in U.S. society have led to a racist attitudinal set which tends to lump all Latin Americans together, and from the fact also that such an attitudinal set feeds back on and tends to reproduce the very material conditions which produce it. We may already observe that even among non-Chicano or Puerto Rican Latinos with more privileged class and educational backgrounds significant numbers (sometimes even the children of immigrating Latin American professionals) are gradually coming to share the problems of their more dominantly working class Chicano and Puerto Rican "cousins" and are becoming less and less distinct from them in their situations and interests. This process has its positive side if we think of potential alliances among Latin American workers, but the negative side consists of the class differentiation which has been developing within a framework of exploitation and manipulation. But in spite of this last factor (which is inevitably a crucial one for considerations of potential Latino unity in actual class struggle), it is nonetheless true that what happens to the vast majority of Latin Americans here who are working class will be important to all U.S. Latinos. Inversely, since we are discussing what will potentially constitute a very significant proportion of employed or unemployed U.S. workers, what happens to U.S. Latinos will be important for the future of the U.S. Finally, since people absorb and react to historical events through the mediations of culture as complex and process, the question of Latin American culture as a specifically evolving and variable synthesis of several Latino and U.S. majority and minority complexes becomes a matter of growing importance for all people in this hemisphere.

The initial prospect seems bleak enough. Without some dramatic transformations or policy changes, current trends would lead to a situation in which a vast and growing population of unskilled, poorly educated workers, many of them mono-lingual in Spanish or French, would be inserted into a society based on advanced technology and capital-intensive labor; we would have a population needing housing, social services, education and jobs in a nation whose own logic of capitalist development may well leave it ill-prepared to deal with the problems it has engendered. Indeed, since the median age of this population mass would be significantly lower than the U.S. majority population, the U.S. would face an extenuation of an already existing polarization between an older, mainly White population (though with some strategic Latino intermediaries) which increasingly monopolizes wealth, resources and power, and a younger, mainly non-white population numerically dominated by Latin American and Caribbean immigrants and their children, who will be waging an ever more difficult struggle to maintain and win access to institutions and resources in which the majority has lessening interest and commitment.

To the questions for immigration theory and overall policy posed by this prognosis, we may add an array of issues pertaining to the legal and political status of immigrants, as well as to the corporate and even military stake in immigrant concerns. But without elaborating on these points, we may take note of all the problems and dangers which a consideration of Latino immigration poses. Given our premise about the role of culture, we may then make the following assumptions (really just some of many possible ones) about the future:

1. In the coming years, U.S. Latinos will be a people going through a conflictive and painful process of transformation marked by constant, contradictory efforts to hold on to their existing cultural patterns and identifications while modifying and transforming them in an effort to maintain relative balance with changes in society at large.

2. In this period of transition, some Latinos will seek to acculturate fully into capitalist or "Anglo" society, but vast numbers will hardly make the effort. For each one who wishes to do so, there will be many others so alienated by a society based on class domination, institutionalized racism and oppression, that they will not want to integrate themselves. And even many Latino workers who may want to will be unable to integrate themselves adequately in the U.S. mainstream, because their marginalized role as cheap labor source will be all too convenient for certain powerful groups in this country.

3. Thus many Latinos will continue to seek their solace from the wear and tear of social domination in what they can salvage of their traditional cultural values and relations.

4. But Latin American cultural complexes will not be able to remain the same in a changing world, and if U.S. society evolves along its present road, Latino culture may prove less and less able to meet its old needs, of providing all which the governments of class domination have not provided. In this circumstance, we may expect to see a possible extenuation of the worst things that are already happening to large numbers: Increased unemployment, increased poverty, increased crime and drug abuse, increased enmity between newly arrived and more established sectors, increasing hostility toward Latinos from other parts of Latin America and toward other minority groups, the breakdown of families and whole communities, the survival and assertion of only the most negative, superficial and regressive dimensions of culture.

5. In fact, unless Latinos can develop their culture in ways which integrate a progressive political dimension able to overcome certain community splits based on certain aspects of the culture itself, unless Latinos can form viable alliances and struggle effectively for their future, large numbers will be sunk in the backwaters of North American life in a society that will move toward a greater division of rich and poor, haves and have-nots.

6. A politically progressive study of U.S. Latino culture involves examining prevalent and potential modes of Latino identification in function of their possible activation in forging group unity, alliances with other Latinos, oppressed minorities and class sectors. Identification with popular struggles in Latin America and elsewhere is a dimension of what is at issue here. The ultimate end is to find bases for generating a viable and organizable political response to conditions of exploitation and exclusion.

7. Crucial in the study of U.S. Latino culture is the ability to grasp both Latin American and U.S. dimensions. But class and academic division have left Latin Americanists mainly external to developments in U.S. Latino Studies, and only a few figures like Gilberto López and the late Joseph Sommers have worked comfortably in both Latin American and U.S. Latino Studies. Given the factors specified above, it is important to break down the barriers between fields, and to launch a more integrative approach to the question. The following additional hypotheses provide a partial, provisional basis for further work:

8. Efforts by Chicano and U.S. Puerto Rican specialists to define their cultural complexes in themselves are important. But these complexes can only achieve full definition when seen as differential, historically changing phenomena in relation to Latin American, Caribbean and U.S. Latino realities as they in turn relate to North American and the wider world beyond.

9. Especially important and symptomatic in any analysis of U.S. Latino culture is the fact that it is not a phenomenon with fully meaningful geographic parameters. While the U.S. Southwest has inevitably dominated pioneering efforts in Chicano Studies, for example, successive waves of immigration from different parts of Mexico and varying patterns of migration from and to different parts of the U.S. have led to a complex and often subtle grid of historical differentiation and convergences that must be recognized and defined in any effort to conceptualize and forge some ultimate unitary theory about present and future realities of Chicano culture. In the studies necessary for formulating such a theory, increased emphasis will have to go to those groups not from the Southwest itself.

10. Further, Latino culture requires differentiation from other U.S. minorities or ethnic cultures, and from strictly immigrant complexes, first because of the longstanding Mexican and Indian presence in the U.S. and second, because of the ongoing two-way immigration pattern between the U.S. and Mexico, the U.S. and Puerto Rico.

11. While aspects of U.S. development and U.S. Latino history and culture generate tendencies of increased Latino diversification and disunity (including class and political differentiation) and while certain cultural dimensions (e.g. extended family structure) vitiate efforts to forge broader social unity among Latinos (as well as other, non-Latino groups), there are nevertheless other factors, resulting mainly from the effects of domination, which suggest greater future Latino unity and greater impact on Latino and U.S. American sub-totalities.

12. One of the most complex and crucial dimensions of Latino unity is the retention of characteristics which have been variously defined as "pre-capitalist," "early capitalist," "pre-industrial," "Catholic," "dependent," etc. It has been argued that these characteristics render Latinos as relatively "dysfunctional," "under-privileged" or "underdeveloped" in the vast rationalized productive system governing U.S. society; but such characteristics may well prove to be a source of strength against the corrosive effects of capitalist advance.

13. While Latinos are slow to absorb the values and productive patterns of dominant Whites, their situation in U.S. cities has led to hostility toward and yet "lateral acculturation" with other minority cultures. However reluctantly, Latinos are both recipients and generators in the syncretic process of lateral working-class acculturation which stands as a prime potential source for a positive Latino future in united struggle with other workers.

14. The particular place that Latinos tend to occupy in the workforce is, of course, a fundamental factor both in their preservation of "dysfunction" cultural characteristics and their potential for alliances and action. But the unique place of Latinos between Latin American and U.S. workers makes the analysis of Latino culture important for a consideration of future transformations in the U.S. and the possible forging of international class alliances that will affect capitalism in the Americas.

15. In a progressively oriented study of Latino culture, or any culture for that matter, distinctions must be made between a group or sub-group's ideology of culture and culture itself—also between the specific cultural products (in art, music, literature, etc.) and the "little traditions" of the oral and popular traditions—of language, social interaction, etc.: between what people say they believe and do and how they actually behave in concrete situations. Thus actual cultural analysis from a socio-historical perspective must relate cultural products to more mass concerns and actualities. There must be some determination of the relation between the "ideologues" of a people's culture and the people's culture itself.

16. Ideally, a socio-historical study of Latino culture from the perspective established here must involve a synthesis of contributions from specialists in several disciplines as they address our focus: specialists in anthropology because our object is culture; specialists in sociology because culture is not "class-innocent"; specialists in history, because culture is historical and involves a grasp of patterns of industrialization, urbanization, modernization, acculturation and resistance; specialists in socio-linguistics because language is the most overt and objectifiable mode of cultural expression and communication, linking everyday life to broader historical currents; specialists in literature, since the literature of Latin American immigration in its dramatic arc of development and elaboration is the lived nexus between the oral tradition and the "print culture" world or advanced

capitalism both in its external imperialist and internal domestic manifestations.

4. Latin American Immigration and the Question of Literature

In the context of the above considerations about U.S. Latino culture, it would be valuable here to supplement the very impressive work which has been developing about the questions of Chicano and U.S. Puerto Rican literature with some observations and working hypotheses that would have reference to both Latin American and U.S. Latino literature in function of our focus on immigration. At a conference on the Caribbean sponsored by the Institute for the Study of Ideologies and Literature in the fall of 1978, Roberto Márquez addressed himself to the impact of immigration on Caribbean writers in a way that is very valuable for our concern. Since his comments were never published, I take the liberty of quoting him at length:

> The problem of immigration...requires thorough investigation before it can be fully integrated into a theoretical schema governed by the notion of totality. Indeed the immigration issue pressures a more acute historical precision with respect to a totalistic orientation that could otherwise be too abstract, lax, romantic or unrigorous...My sense is that [many twentieth century Caribbean writers]share several characteristics with [a figure like] José Martí...Martí spent almost all his life outside the Caribbean area. Is he any less a Caribbean writer? Hostos is another example, so that even in the 19th century, the problem is not one that can be dealt with in terms of geographical location. Yet, when we come to the 20th century, the problem seems to become more complex, for the fact of residence, say, in the U.S. even for five or ten years creates a veritable *problematique* out of the question of integral Caribbean identity. That is why the issue of immigration needs to be sorted out in a theoretical and historical manner which affects our overall conception of Caribbean society and literature.

> While it is...correct to see Claude MacKay's Harlem as a transposed Caribbean setting, the precise coordinates of this transposition are difficult to define. ...Nevertheless, by seeing MacKay as a transitional figure between the 19th century and our present moment, we can begin to locate a significant dimension of the conceptual apparatus we require. A constant dimension of the immigration process has consisted in the fact that the immigrants have brought with them their entire sense of class structure into contexts that have not provided the social buttressing for this structure. In the capitalist center, the fact of class is generally superceded by national origin, and indeed "Caribbeanness" tends to outweigh and homogenize both class and national differences. The distictions that existed in the home environment...between some anonymous sugar worker and a George Lamming are minimized by a foreign productive structure and by a social process which says that both men are Jamaican or Caribbean or black.

It is more than a coincidence that the Negritude movement is at once a movement of immigration and a movement whose contradictions in terms of class perspective stemming from the immigrant situation did not prevent its being accepted by many Caribbeans at home and in foreign centers as an indigenous phenomenon. Immigration from the Caribbean was already becoming a general occurrence in the 1920's; even then it was more a phenomenon of push than of pull...And the fact is that the salient features and contours of negritude were determined by the immigrant push. ...It is also more than coincidental that it is in London that Caribbean immigrants whose native language is English come to realize that they are from the Anglophone Antilles, and not just from Jamaica, Barbado or Guyana. Indeed, within certain linguistic and cultural parameters, both national and pan-Caribbean consciousness are intensified by the push-out process...The writers are pushed out because they can't make a living, because they have no place to publish. Structurally their situation is similar to that of the field hands; the relation of both groups to the mode of production is untenable. Once outside their class differences are outweighed by their more or less common cultural *desajuste* in a new geo-cultural setting, where, we might add, racism cooperates with the needs for cheap labor to lump the two groups together. Thus features of their native mode of production and the ones which dominate the world to which they migrate both serve to define them as composite. And obviously the same composite crosses over distinct national identities. This composite typing in the immigrant centers inevitably poses a *problematique* for those who are its object; they must come to terms with it.

For a countless number of reasons, then, the phenomenon of migration and what it means in its historical and geographical variations has to be looked at very carefully, because this phenomenon dovetails back and becomes central to the question of Caribbean identity...Recently Puerto Rican migration has vied with the migration of right wing Cuban middle sectors and exiles and migrant workers from all other parts of the Caribbean. Thus the class and political dimensions of immigration have multiplied; in addition, the dimension of lateral acculturation with dominant and minority groups...in the host country have become increasingly complex. These matters have greatly complicated Caribbean realities...Of course what is complication and fragmentation at one level may be the basis for greater richness and unity on another. But ultimately the question of immigration must be given the theorization it requires if we are to arrive at an adequate approach to Caribbean culture and literature.

On the basis of Márquez's comments, whose richness I can only partially reflect here, I offer the following hypotheses which I believe helpful (though by no means sufficient) in the examination of Caribbean literature and in the overall effort to develop a theoretical perspective on the immigration process in relation to literature:

1. Caribbean immigration to the imperialist centers involves a transposition of cultural values and norms tied to one local mode

of production, to the values and norms of a second mode which in fact conditions the very functionality and efficacy of the first.

2. The immigration process involves the immigrant's cultural and even psychological "de-centering" from imperialist contradiction to the more determinant contradictions of capitalism itself.

3. This shift derived from immigration tends to homogenize Caribbean class, national, cultural and today even linguistic differences in function of the core capitalist dichotomy of capital and labor, so that while some Caribbeans from the middle sectors may aspire to and succeed in maintaining or securing their non-working class status, the force of the dominant host society's ideological and productive necessities will tend to displace large numbers toward the laboring (which often means, unemployed or under-employed) sector.

4. In this circumstance, Caribbean immigrants, while perhaps attempting to 'assimilate white dominant class values, will often grasp those values through the filter of the oppressed group which dominates the productive sphere to which they have been relegated.

a. This historical and geographical variable conditions the process of lateral acculturation among immigrants and means that in New York, Caribbean peoples will tend toward "Newyorican" norms, which will in turn be conditioned by U.S. Black; in the Southwest, Hispanophone Caribbean norms will tend toward the Chicano, etc.

5. The immigration experience may lead to the most negative possibilities: unemployement, acculturation into lumpen patterns of drugs, prostitution, loss of viable cultural identity, etc.; it may involve the most radical *de-creolization*. However, it may, as in the case of the negritude movement, involve an actual intensification of positive creolization.

a. The stereotyping, domination and concrete exploitation of Caribbean immigrants may have the positive effect of giving them a sense of class consciousness which they could not perhaps have as easily acquired in the imperialist context of their home base; their lateral acculturation process is a dialectical one which involves a sharing of tendencies (though obviously in the center of domination)—which means that while they obviously remain Puerto Rican, Jamaican or whatever, they may become simultaneously "de-centered" from their national core identity and incorporate more Pan-Caribbean and then international working class dimensions.

6. Given the large return rate of Caribbean immigrants from the U.S. (the Haitian, Jamaican and Dominican farmworkers returning from Florida, the constant ebb and flow of Puerto Rican return rates), the negative and positive resultants of the hybridization process re-enter the Caribbean reality, and begin to modify it. Contradictions external to the islands not only penetrate through the importation of goods, through mass media and tourism, but through the returning Caribbean peoples, who bring along their new parcel of contradictions as integral elements of their identity to disseminate at home.

7. Obviously, a Marxist perspective seeks out the means for countering the negative developments and for intensifying and instrumentalizing the positive dimensions of this process. In this sense Marxist *literary* studies of the Caribbean require the full examination of several very important matters—for example:

a. The degree to which immigrant and non-immigrant Caribbean writers are able to grasp the social processes involved in the immigration movement, especially those processes which relate to sectors other than their own.

b. The degree to which immigrant writers, either by their pre-immigration or post-immigration formation, in fact (and in spite of their claims to shared experience with other immigrating social sectors) begin to distance themselves or relate themselves to a more totalistic Caribbean identity.

c. The degree to which they take on metropolitan majority or minority patterns in literature—to undergo the influence, say, of dominant culture writers like Conrad, Faulkner or Pynchon, or an "internal minority migrant" artist like Wright or Ellison, or a more cosmopolitan minority figure like Ernie Gaines or John Williams.

8. We need to see what theoretical parameters we can establish, to specify the overwhelming complexities we have been describing: the degree to which the writers in fact say what the people are saying; the degree to which the cultural distance immigration or the very practice of writing implies ultimately dilutes or intensifies the capacity for totalistic Caribbean expression; the degree to which externally generated creolization has its reverberations on the metroplitan center (for immigration certainly means that Caribbean norms do influence the metropolitan norms—e.g., MacKay influences Ellison—which influence the Caribbean); and finally, then, the degree to which the immigration experience, and immigrant literature act on the culture and literature of the Caribbean home base.

These hypotheses are only meant as general guides to future work in which the Caribbean focus here may be expanded to overall Latin American immigration. In such work we would have to reach the point of being able to deal with the question of immigration in relation to specific themes, modes and genres, and a whole series of formal considerations. In this direction, three further points whith respect to Caribbean immigrant writers may help to articulate and refine the literary dimensions of our hypotheses:

1. Immigrant writers are not only a product of the class of value sets developed around two modes of production (as in hypothesis 1); to the degree that they establish themselves as writers, they are subject to the social relations of production pertaining to their particular productive sphere—this in spite of the fact that their Caribbean immigrant status makes them marginal to those relations in their new work center and in their home base.

2. Further, Caribbean immigrant writers are simultaneously installed in a specifically and historically determinate literary mode or sphere of production, and in one or more subdivisions of this mode. They may work in function of a Caribbean subset of literary production, or, say, in a U.S. dominant or minority subset—or in some hybrid context; further, they may work in one or more literary modes or genres of the literary "mode of production." However, whatever these writers produce in their productive sphere can only be a modification or transformation of what that sphere already contains or allows.

3. The degree to which that mode, then, is initially distanced from expressing immigrant concerns or Caribean concerns will condition the distance which a given Caribbean immigrant writer must go to express the social groups basic to Caribbean identity and unity.

To be sure, the suggestions I make with respect to Caribbean literary modes and genres are ones which are very difficult to consider—especially if one wishes to sort out and pinpoint the impact of immigration (as opposed even to imperialist penetration) on these complexly determined literary matters. Why is it, Márquez asks, that Caribbean poetry is more homogeneous in levels of achievement and forms of expression than is the Caribbean novel? And he adds:

> Whatever the sociological and specifically cultural and literary reasons for differences between Anglo and Hispanophone novelistic

practices, they are clearly multiple, involving the greatest complexity among interacting processes. Among these processes, immigration undoubtedly makes its contribution. But ultimately we must ask how we are to measure that contribution and how we are to elaborate a proper theory enabling us to trace the materialization of an effect.

All of these and other objections that could be raised have their validity. But as Márquez finally admits, the fact that we must acknowledge our current inadequacy on this score should not prevent us from applying those concepts and notions about which we feel reasonable sure, to carry on what we trust are more or less adequately scientific and useful studies of Caribbean culture and literature.

Again, I believe these remarks can be extended to Latin American literature, and I also believe it would be very valuable to carry out future developments along the lines of theory, compilations and analyses of Caribbean and Latin American immigrant literature within an overall framework of immigration studies. It is to certain suggestions in this regard to which I will now turn.

5. *Suggestions for Work on Latin American Literature and Immigration*

In an effort to explore the hypotheses raised as well as the difficulties cited above, I would propose that the phenomenon of immigration (as well as exile and displacement, as related processes) be one of the primary areas of exploration among Latin Americanists (and of course Latin American literature specialists) in the years to come. But I say this within the frame of a concern for the future study of historical, cultural and literary phenomena of the homebase as well as the host countries. Indeed, I believe that by centering on the question of immigration and immigration culture (the expression of that experience), we can well justify more careful and practically oriented examinations of homebase developments, as well as their transformations in this society, their impact here and finally their impact back on the homebases. To take a rather sensationalistic example, it seems no coincidence that at a time of great conflict and mass migration from El Salvador, Reagan is discussing the establishment of "free enterprise zones" in the U.S.; in the midst of great and growing unemployment, too, armies of rightwing Latin American exiles are being trained: does this suggest a possible future for U.S. Latinos being displaced from the labor market? Immigration studies provide a particular locus for understanding cultural and literary developments in the context of overall transformations of international capital in which homebase and host nations are implicated.

In order to carry out our proposal, we would ideally make use of such centers of immigration and of immigration studies as New York, Washington, Chicago, Los Angeles, etc., with given specialists in given centers focusing on their particular priorities. In Chicago, the two main streams of Puerto Rican and Mexican immigration are caught up in waves of immigration from other Caribbean points, and the Central American immigration has been exponential. In addition, like New York, Chicago has massive immigration from many other points of the globe, as well as a massive internal migration population, including Chicanos from the Southwest. And yet while we have a Latino Institute and various entities that carry out various kinds of work related to immigration, we have no institution focused according to the parameters we have suggested. Ultimately it would be necessary not only to work in our two traditional literary and Latin Americanist frames (MLA and LASA), but also in the frames of established general and specifically Latin American immigration institutional developments. Such organizations as New York's Centro de Estudios Puertorriqueños possibly offers us an expandable model. In this context, we have much to learn, but it is also true that our emphasis on culture and literature will dimensionalize the work of such existing institutions. If no such institutes exist where we think they sould be, then we shoud work with others to establish them. And here we should note that it is important that the centers be multidisciplinarian, but that when possible, literary specialists should participate in their formation and development as early as possible, because if not, our concerns and what we have to offer will receive little space.

There is of course something tremendously creative in all this, because to the degree that we choose to focus on immigration literature in the context of immigrant cultural expression, then we must not only be investigators and analysts, but creative producers, promoters and participants in immigrant culture.

Our first task might be to establish seminars in which we work with students to survey community resources and issues. Out of the seminars could come more permanent interdisciplanary curricula and bibliography, as well as the beginnings of a library or archive of materials, which would include whatever holdings we could acquire and reference materials which would indicate other local, regional and national holdings, special and individual collections, etc. For example, in Chicago one researcher has gathered copies of old magazines, newspapers, clippings, dance and banquet programs, etc. reflecting the evolution of Chicago's Mexican communities. With reference to our own modest resource library, steps were taken last year to catalogue and cross-reference existing Chicago materials on Central America, and to gather initial materials on other primary homebase centers of Latin American immigration to Chicago. At a certain point in development of modest university-based programs and libraries, it would become valuable to utilize or set up a local consortium frame of universities and community-based organizations (cultural centers, etc.) to develop a more coordinated city plan.

As the macro-organizational work is going on, our work with students in class is very important. We need to have students working on projects which help to build our library and increase our knowledge at all levels; we need to form student cadres who will continue the work when their class-work ends. Projects could be as simple as clipping articles from local newspapers, developing a bulletin board of current happenings, etc. But more ambitious things have been attempted, even with undergraduates and have worked. Students have gathered materials from the community, done oral history projects, factual studies of community organizations, agencies, associations, groups, cultural producers, etc. Other projects suggest themselves:

1. A survey of daily life and recreation in immigration centers takes on special importance in a time of high unemployment. The organization of unemployed time as well as traditionally defined "leisure time" should yield special insights. What are the most popular songs in the cantinas? What records do people pay to hear, to own? What requests do people make of strolling musicians? What do they sing when the spirit moves them? What kinds of books and magazines are available in libraries, grocery stores, etc.? What do people buy and read?

2. Oral history tape and also photograph libraries are relatively easy to develop, and represent great riches for studies of immigration culture; developing video libraries is also a not too expensive possibility.

Obviously, along with the library and curriculum components of our work we need to establish journals or other publication frameworks which would disseminate our materials and our findings, offering opportunities for student and community research and cultural expression. These publications can be of the simplest nature (mimeographed, photo-copied, whatever—meant for classroom use, sharing among centers, etc., perhaps in the style of the Centro de Estudios Puertorriqueños monograph series. But from our point of view, perhaps the most important task would be to establish the means for placing, developing and publishing local and regional immigration cultural expression and providing a basis for analyzing it. In this context, our creative use of our critical skills is essential. The selection and editing of the cultural materials and fragments entail a series of ideological choices bound on the one side by our concern with historical accuracy (too narrow a selection aimed at highlighting a progressive trend may simultaneously distort its rather minor role in the constellation of immigrant tendencies) and our concern with cultural and ultimately political effect.

For our purpose is ultimately political. We would not simply be reflecting and expressing Latino immigration culture in its historical development and proliferation of expressive modes, but we would be playing on possibilities, affecting future production, if only by creating our own vehicles, and we would also be proliferating effects on those Latinos and non-Latinos who would read our publications, attend our exhibits, film showings, etc. The emphasis would indeed fall on our creative function in developing and promoting projects and collaborations, in writing grant proposals at a time of severe cutbacks, for one or another aspect of our total project. Also it would take a good deal of time before a mass of cultural expressions could accrue that would provide the basis for rich theoretical and critical elaborations, although from the inception of this work, we must be guided by a sense of theoretical frame, a sense of global process, a sense of unity about the nature of processes in home base and host populations, because we would be trying to feed into the more progressive possibilities of the immigration population in their participation in this society and the effects this society has on home bases.

To the degree that our conern with regional and local phenomena results in products of a certain expressive richness, we will in fact be helping to create a richer basis for the elaboration of the literature of immigration and U.S. minorities.

In the work on literature itself, of course, distinctions must be made among three Latin American literatures being created in the U.S.:

1. A literature of "middle-class" Latin Americans who happen to live here for reasons of exile or transplantation as part of the "brain drain." Whether progressive or reactionary, this literature tends to integrate itself with dimensions of the overall "high literature" literary systems, the works standing as Caribbean, Central American, Argentine, etc. or even, as an effect, North

American majority or "international." Relations between this literature and the phenomenon of worker immigration are very distanced and mediated, perhaps emerging in certain linguistic or stylistic transformations of varying significance in terms of internal dynamics of the work or its relation with the world. Here it is a matter of degree, for the Chilean exile poet from the Allende period, still thinking himself Chileno, not integrating into a Latino group that functions as an ethnic minority, middle class in social status, a professional or intermediary between Latinos and the large rationalized structures of modern U.S. life, nevertheless can write more broadly and openly, less symbolically and restrainedly about the Chilean experience that they could if they were to approach similar materials in present-day Chile.

2. Another, less *"culta"* literature with form and theme dictated very much by the immigration experience itself, a literature that draws perhaps on other immigrant literatures but that grows out of the mass of Latin American workers in this country, even if the writer is basically a son or daughter of immigrants so that already sufficient distance exists between the writer and the mass so that the act of writing itself (whether in "mother tongue" or adopted language) can occur at a level of elaboration sufficiently high to constitute a relatively coherent text. The usual treatment of writers of such often crude and unschooled literature is to encourage them to "develop," that is, to take on what is seen as meaning for them to enter into the categories of those writers we note as beloging to the first literary mode, rather than seeing how their expressive experience may be enriched by a greater relation with a third mode:

3. This is the literature not even produced as literature, but as the product of oral history, as grafitti, etc. The raw material of the other two literatures mentioned, this literature involves the pattern of daily speech, the songs and variations of songs, the jokes—the very spontaneous creative, syncretic and dynamic reproduction of the experience of everyday life which remains then as part of everyday life in the creation of further patterns. One of our goals should be the recording of such materials and in critical practice, of making it available to the writers of literatures 1 and 2, so that they may draw upon it in the creative development of an ever richer literature.

Implicit in all this is not the creation of a left literature, but of a literature and culture which sustains its relation to broad numbers of people, and maintains and develops its creative possibilities, so that the prospects for a progressive culture are kept ever alive, though never imposed. Indeed, the effort to impose a sense of history and consciousness which does not grow out of the concrete development of a people can often lead to negative results. Pushing too hard, say, on the crisis of El Salvador may create resistance in a Latino community not carefully prepared to hear the message.

The goal of our work is not the mere focus on local communities but on their role in a larger national and international totality, and their value as models for tracing the links between all phenomena subject to international and local determinations. We are not only interested in particular Latino subgroups, but their interactions with other immigrant groups, minority and dominant groups in the configuration of patterns existing today and the possible patterns (and alliances) for tomorrow.

Work along these lines is very much open to Marxist Latin American literature specialists (and especially the Latin Americans among them) who have already a grounding in the history, cultural development and literature of home-base areas and who can then begin to develop a knowledge of immigration and acculturation effects which ultimately feed back into an enriched knowledge of the homebase. Such work also gives Latin Americanists a local area of study and practice and provides those in remote places with very minimal immigration influx with a framework of ties to nearby regional centers where they can apply their and their students' expertise and intellectual interests. While much of the work involved feeds into the practical and implies an action on culture and ideology, it also implies a theoretical frame for action and the increased enrichment of that frame which ultimately remakes our conception of Latin American cultural and literary history, as well as our ability to understand it as it develops in the future. In this sense, the growing consciousness of U.S. Latino immigrant populations and of their cultural products feeds in and affects homebase literary production, not only because some of the exiles and immigrants return, but because their works and experiences, as well as writings about them do. The fullfledged development of this dimension of Latin American and Caribbean studies suggest an actual praxis on literature, the kind of multi-leveled intervention of which Marxist intellectuals often dream. We cannot be sure of all the results; we can only hope that some of them will be roughly as progressive as the intentions. But the project I am proposing does provide a logical place for the insertion of U.S. Latino and other minority students in gradated studies and activities that can even begin in their early formative years. My own experience has been thus, as undergraduate

Latinos and other minority students have worked on developing Central American political poetry projects, and in the development of a newspaper, *La Opinión Latina*, as well as a journal, *Ecos* (both of them centering on immigrant issues and culture). And they are now saying they want to work on other projects, ones delving into the communities of Chicago, others reaching out into the larger world. In this way, the object and subject of study come together in ways that propogate creation and hope.

THE NOTION OF OTHERNESS
WITHIN THE FRAMEWORK OF
NATIONAL CULTURES

HERNÁN VIDAL
University of Minnesota

Why are we now so assiduously talking about Otherness in academic Latin American literary criticism? Our profession undergoes periodical cycles of modernization when we introduce in our reading new analytical, descriptive and interpretive theories and methodologies, which publishing trade marketing makes fashionable according to strategies not always clear in their origin, inception and intention. The vogue of such technologies is apparent in professional conferences, symposia and publications, where we witness demonstrations of their degree of efficacy by scholars who achieve recognition precisely by means of such demonstrations. These modernization cycles are also marked by the clear predominance of certain topics of research generated by the heuristic capabilities of the technologies involved. A demonstrational effect is thus created whereby scholars are motivated to join the latest vogue out of prefessional responsibility and commitment to renovate their critical tools. In this way we maintain and upgrade our professional credibility.

During the last decades we have had sequences and convergences of structuralism (French or otherwise), psychoanalytical archetypal criticism, various Marxist and semiotic trends, and deconstructionism. Ungenerous comments label this as "trendism." In a more constructive approach perhaps we should ask whether —following Thomas Kuhn[1]— literary criticism is a paradigmatic scientific discipline, a question that has tormented some of the social sciences for years.[2] Kuhn designates a science as paradigmatic when long-standing consensus is achieved among practitioners regarding models that best define its subject matter, the revelant phenomena to be observed within it, and their interpretation according to the laws, theories, and hypotheses provided by the models. Scientists working within a paradigm are not innovators, but puzzle-solvers who conduct as many studies as possible in order to confirm the validity of the established models, until enough anormalities are detected and the existing paradigms are discarded and replaced. If this description is correct, and if we are skeptic about our profession, we might say that the diversity of technologies being applied indicate literary criticism is certainly not a paradigmatic discipline; if we are tepid about it, we might say it is a pre-paradigmatic field; if we are positive, we might say that, quite the contrary, it is multiple-

paradigmatic. Yet unless we come up with concrete sociological information about how the cycles of modernization take place, the change in
technologies within our field will tend to have a highly erratic, irrational,
non-cummulative aspect; we do not set common tasks the profession will
accomplish until a new technology will be necessary. Some of these
technologies simply bring back very old topics to the research agenda,
although with a new jargon.

The coming 500th anniversary of the Conquest and Colonization of territories in America by Spain, sponsored by the Spanish government under
the very problematic slogan "Encounter of Cultures," has perhaps introduced another element into the problem of professional retooling. Now we
have an institutional intervention with a clear origin and intention —the pro-
motion of scholarship dealing with the Spanish-American historical and intellectual interface. In particular, this intervention has led many literary
critics in the Latin American field to respond to the research promoted by
integrating the anthropological notion of the Other to their work and applying it to Colonial literature. On the positive side, this intervention has been
one more incentive for the growing interest in Colonial literature studies
and the expansion of interdisciplinary trends in our field. Yet given the way
in which new analytical and interpretive tools are usually adopted, I do not
think there has been a generalized discussion of the ideological implications
of this new adoption.

From a socio-historical perspective, this paper is intended to make a
contribution in this sense by situating the notion of the Other within the
broader concept of national culture in Latin America. I will work with a
Gramscian concept of national culture: it is the articulation and neutralization of various other alternatives of social and economic development projects by the hegemonic capacity of a power block. My main argument will
be that the knowledge we may now acquire about the way in which radically different cultures are represented epistemologically and discursively cannot be separated from two of the major cultural preoccupations in Latin
America at present —the critique of the application of foreign models of
social and economic development in the area as the basis for the protection
or violation of Human Rights: the right of nation States to self-
determination, and within autonomous nation-States, the right of native
people to the preservation of their culture and civilization. Once the notion
of Otherness is situated among these issues, the result is a chain reaction;
the problem of self-determination implicitly entails the creation of nation-
States with autonomy enough to allow the population to arrive at a consen-
sual definition of national needs, priorities and systems for social, cultural
and economic development without distorting influences from abroad. On
its turn, the consensus required for such definitions within high ethnic and
cultural heterogeneity brings back to the research agenda problems now

traditional in Latin American studies —those of cultural synthesis, articulation, syncretism, and the national identity, now in its contemporary modulations.

The thrust of my arguments is to move the implicit implications of the use of anthropological concepts in literary criticism to the frontiers recently shown by discourse analysis as it has become more pervasive among literary critics: i.e., literature is only one of the symbolic forms created in the self-reproduction of society and should not be privileged exclusively in culturally oriented research programs. Full understanding of literature's social nature requires that it be placed comparatively among other clusters of discourse that define the historicity[3] of a society —i.e., the cultural models trying to become hegemonic in a society as orientation of the process of capital accumulation: the nature of the "good life," the ideal image and gender of human beings, and the various forms of knowledge needed to achieve them. If this is the case, the approach I am proposing reinforces the contemporary tendency in the human sciences to blur their boundaries, particularly as it pertains to the crucial importance now being given to the narration strategies of research findings.[4] If so, then perhaps we should take the next step and come to the realization that literary criticism could be understood as a discipline within symbolic anthropology. Once in this new realm, perhaps two benefits would accrue. First, from the socio-historical perspective we could come to the conviction that at least this type of literary criticism finds objective, scientific paradigms in the cultural models that regulate capital accumulation; second, the way would be open for debates similar to those that continuously engage ethnographers and anthropologists vis-a-vis their contribution either to the subjugation or self-determination of peoples. I will discuss the first issue at the end of this paper.

The need for such a debate appears obvious if we take into consideration that the notion of "the Other" encapsulates the sense in which anthropology elaborates its object of study: understanding the logic that brings together the institutionality, the functions, the symbology, and the process of self-reproduction of radically different cultures. Johannes Fabian[5] explains that in order to constitute their object, anthropologists have always anchored their perspective in the present tense of European(ized) cultures as a fixed point in time from which to turn their interpretive gaze onto that radically different Other. Thus time was turned into a spatial dimension allowing for a taxonomic scheme; that fixed point was sequentially erected into a paradigm of religious redemption of civilization, and then of modernity. The characteristics of that Other came to be judged within an evolutionary scale in which the differences appear to be rudimentary manifestations of entities containing the potentials and the urge to move towards redemption, civilization and modernity. Fabian argues that no anthropolo-

gical trend —either evolutionist, diffusionist, functionalist, relativist, structuralist or semiotic— has ever been able to surmount this ethnocentrism.
Together with the use imperialist powers have made of anthropological
knowledge in their colonial or neo-colonial enterprises, this ethnocentrism
has caused in conscientious and progressive anthropologists a continuous
feeling of crisis in their profession, the need for public self-flagellation, and
expression of guilt, remorse and nostalgia for the disappearance of primitive
cultures under the homogenizing effects or control of transnational
capitalism.

For Fabian nowhere is this crisis more clearly exposed than in the dislocation between direct field experience and the way anthropologists narrate
their ethnographic reports. Responding to the professional demand of using
technical paradigms and jargon, at the moment of narrating anthropologists
must deny the experience of direct communication and cohabitation with
human beings who show similar capacities to make symbolic sense of their
space, time, actions, and the capacity to build a cultural identity in a present
tense shared both by the observer and the observed. Anthropologists must
rhetorically distance and separate themselves and proceed to place these
human beings in a theoretical framework that turns them into archeological
objects in an evolutionary continuum that consciously or unconsciously
contrasts progress, development, and modernity with their negative mirror
images: stagnation, underdevelopment, tradition. Fabian refers to this
dislocation as "denial of coevalness" and "allochronism" evolutionary sequences and their concomitant political practice of colonialism and imperialism may look incorporative. After all, they create a universal frame of
reference able to accommodate all societies. But being based on the
episteme of natural history, they are founded on distancing and separation.
There would be no *raison d'etre* for the comparative method if it was not the
classification of entities or traits which first have to be separate and distinct
before their similarities can be used to establish taxonomies and
developmental sequences. To put this more concretely: what makes the
savage significant to the evolutionist's Time is that he lives in another Time.
Little needs to be said, I assume, about separation and distancing in colonialist praxis which drew its ideological justification form Enlightenment
and later evolutionism" (26-27).

Fabian's arguments are an effort to distill the core meaning of the
historical development of anthropology, so he had to carry them on at an
extremely high degree of abstraction. Nevertheless, anthropological discussions must secure a firm base in the actual workings of particular cultures to
be of any theoretical value. For my purposes I will be anchoring my
arguments on the cultural experience of Chile during the last two decades
under a militarized Liberal regime. This will demand that I discuss the notion of Otherness by means of an abrupt juxtaposition of Liberalism and the

Socialist alternative of organizing society, since the struggle for these two cultural models brought about the institutional crisis in Chile. My narrative, though, will try to expand the Chilean case as a typical Latin American experience for the discussion of Otherness.

At first sight it would seem that the notion of the Other has no place in the critical language of a Latin American progressive intellectual. After more than a hundred years of apparent political independence we are direct heirs of the Liberal project of the early 19th century towards the formation of strong, independent nation-States, based on the material progress gained from participation in the rising international capitalist market. The emerging Liberals envisioned these new States with an integrating capacity stemming from the development of cohesive, homogenizing master narratives of national identity diffused by the educational system among ethnically diverse populations, once the Liberal project became hegemonic. During the 20th century this project showed its contradictions when these very same national master narratives, as used by the middle and working classes, became obstacles in the Liberal utopia of a free world circulation, accumulation, and transfer of capital. With the demise of the Liberal cultural-nationalist project, the ideal of autonomous nation-States was raised by the national bourgeoisies, the middle classes and the Socialist revolutionary movement. All contemporary critical thought originated in these sectors has been sustained by anti-imperialist and anti-dependency notions, vying either for a protected national capitalism or for an institutional rupture towards Socialism. Throughout the recent decades these trends have evolved into a deeper awareness about the disintegrating effects of an unrestrained transnationalized economy on the national policies. Within these nationalist parameters, what sense could it make to look at one's own national culture with an imperialist gaze, as if some of its components actually were that radically different Other?

I am afraid posing the question in this way is simply submitting to Liberal ideologies of national cohesiveness which the actual reality of dependency easily disavows. Ever since its inauguration as a satellite of Spain and Portugal, and later under the influence of England, the United States, and nowadays the ubiquitous transnational conglomerates —the "global economy"—, Latin American material and symbolic production has been carried on within the framework of combined and uneven development. These various Metropolis have selectively integrated some aspect of material production in the satellite economies into their control, in response to the changing cycles of commercial demand in the international market. Following directives generated abroad, the local seat of production of such commodities is turned into the locus of modernity vis-a-vis the science and technology used, the productive methods, systems, and equipment employed, and the deployment of an administrative, distributive infrastruc-

ture, and means of communication. The new pole of development eventually forces the reconstellation of the old, outdated productive systems so
that they may serve a supporting role for the modern one. Thus the most ancient forms of primitive communism still surviving in the hinterland may be
brought to function together with sierra located semi-feudal latifundia, urban industry still based on mechanical means of production, and the most
efficient electronically controlled, foreign market oriented enclaves. In
these conditions, the capitalist system maintains and self-reproduces by
means of various forms of strategic gate-keeping of the key positions in the
networks of distribution and circulation —oligopolies, clientelism,
gamonalismo, ladinismo, for example. These "hinge" devices function
simultaneously to maintain and articulate cultural fragmentation in a
pyramidal sharing of political power and appropriation of economic
surplus. At the representational level, this constellation of diverse modes of
production is complemented with a kaleidoscopic mosaic of symbolic
systems that may abruptly juxtapose and confront in simultaneous coexistence pre-Columbian magical world-views with the latest, most modern
forms of scientific cultural discourse. The foreign symbolic capital circulated
by the media and the educational systems, the accumulation of master narratives of national identity, the persistence of pre-Columbian and African
folklore and the massive migrations of the population throughout the national territories and beyond, according to economic fluctuations controlled
from abroad, generate forms of creolization which fuse together all kinds of
expressive elements in complex patterns of cultural synchretism. Julio
Cotler[6] has referred to this process as urban ruralization and rural urbanization. Alejo Carpentier theorized the artistic implications of combined and
uneven development with his notion of "real maravilloso." Cultural synchretism is a spontaneous response of populations who must carry on their
lives and reproduce themselves within the boundaries of a nation-State and
the cultural models accumulated therein, yet responding to dynamic factors
emanating from a productive logic outside their control.

Within the framework of combined and uneven development the Latin
American intellectual castes have traditionally played the role of internaliz-
ing and adapting to local conditions the foreign symbolic capital brought by
the historical cycles and waves of dependency. The prototype of this role
emerged during the Conquest of America, when the anthropologist priests
separated young children from their indian communities to serve as in-
formers on their logic, organization and resistance strategies. Later on the
prototype was readapted by means of scholarships and fellowships to obtain advanced academic degrees abroad. During the independence movements of the 19th century an urban based intelligentsia articulated a
historical script defined by the tenets of Enlightenment, a script which certain sectors of the commercial and land-owning oligarchies felt inclined to

pursue; the creation of secular societies, with organic ties with the international market, nation-States in which the irrationalities grafted into the minds of the Latin American popular masses by the religious world-view of the old Mercantile Spanish and Portuguese Empires would be eradicated and replaced with a modern, rational, scientific, and technical administration of society. From then on the various fissures in the combined and uneven development mosaic came to be discussed under the bracket of Civilization versus Barbarism. At the material level, Liberals projected the synthesis of these components by diffusing from the main cities the civilization they imported from the advanced capitalist countries. At the ideological level, the Liberals expected to arrive at the cultural synthesis by creating, institutionalizing and disseminating master narratives of national cohesiveness articulated by imported ideologies. In this sense Liberalism attempted a cultural synthesis from the top. Liberal intellectuals have always had to adopt the imperialist gaze and observe the rest of the national culture as that radically different Other. Yet the long term chronological rythm required by a peaceful cultural synthesis clashed with the speed needed by the national economy to readjust to the rapid cycles of commodity booms and busts in the international market. Given this predicament, governments based on free trade policies have always been tempted to use State military force to achieve fast solutions to the contradiction between actual national needs and international market demands. Military force is the panacea for securing real estate for export production in the hinterland through genocide of native peoples, and for neutralizing social upheaval against chronic foreign indebtedness, inflation, periodic devaluations of the local currency, substantial price increases, and the fall of living standards which are endemic in a Liberal economy. Such upheavals reinforce among Liberals the suspicion that barbaric elements do exist among the masses —whether they are called indians, anti-socials, communists or subversives.

The Liberal need to secure the national territory for unimpeded circulation of capital, for the establishment of foreign production enclaves, and a migrating labor force that will move around in response to the productive calendar disrupt the myths of nationality:[7] the notion of a "we" gathered together in a community sharing similar historical experiences and future projects sedimented in an ongoing creation of symbols and master narratives of national identity, the notion of "the people" (*lo popular*) as a fundamental sense of collective justice that will satisfy the dignity requirements even of the most dispossessed sectors of the population, the notion of citizenship that demarcates the channels and procedures by means of which individuals will have the right and obligation to participate in the national projects. In its starkest repressive forms militarized Liberalism cancels this symbolic universe and exhibits itself as sheer domination. At this point Liberal intellectuals have lost all legitimacy as articulators of the national, in-

tegral common good and become spokesmen for the non-nation. In compensation, and in line with the geopolitics of the Doctrine of National
Security, they shift their arguments towards the apology for the total continuity and parity between the elitarian civilization they represent locally
and the rest of the Western-Christian world.[8] The dislocations introduced
into the national community by transnational capitalism are covered with
an enthusiasm for hundreds of anecdotes that illustrate the adventure of fast
change in modernization and excite a superficial nationalism.[9] The national
symbology and the folklore of the native peoples submitted to genocide are
turned into exotic commodities attracting tourists, ornaments, ceremonies,
rituals, carnivals and festivals to be performed within tourism complexes
and enclaves, and images that may create an aura of prestige and a recognition factor for the exports of a country. In present day Liberalism the fissures
of dependent, combined and uneven development have become permanent and the "barbaric" component of the national culture freezes into a
marginal, estranged Other, permanently unemployed or underemployed,
that has no place in the economy and in civilization. The barbarians can only be exorcised by means of the repressive tactics of Low Intensity Warfare,
welfare handouts or pious statements about the need for society to accept
the "human cost" of modernization. Using Fabian's language, in its crisis
Latin American Liberalism has achieved the maximum denial of coevalness
and allochronism.

  For intellectuals responding to the Socialist utopia the feasibility of the
Latin American cultural synthesis posits two fundamental issues: first, the articulation of an anti-imperialist revolutionary movement representing all
organized social sectors affected by dependency —bourgeoisie and middle
classes whose economic survival is imperiled by transnational finance
capital and conglomerates, peasantry dispossesed of their land, marginalized and active working class and second, articulating the interests of
heterogeneous ethnic groups in the anti-imperialist struggle and future
society in such conditions that their cultural identity will be preserved, and
their autonomy will be promoted. Among them Marxist-Leninist vanguard
parties will be present or will later evolve. Traditionally these parties have
congregated disaffected bourgeois and middle class intellectuals, and the
most socially minded elements of the working class; therefore they contain
a seminal experience of cultural synthesis. The critical thought behind these
movements exposes the fragmentary, dislocating, distorting, marginalizing,
polarizing effects that transnational capital introduces into the national
social relations. A call is made for a liberation movement that will establish a
sense of balance, proportion, continuity, integration, and justice in the projects of social and economic development.[10] In order to implement this
strategy, a new national State must be created, with enough autonomy to
define in independent terms the real national needs, allocate the resources

required to satisfy them, and open autonomous spaces and decision making mechanisms for the participation of ethnic groups. Since the transnationalized local bourgeoisies and their external allies are not expected to relinquish their power peacefully, some kind of military capability must be assembled. In concerting and assembling the revolutionary front and articulating its political platform, in waging the military campaigns, the urban, enlightened, literate intellectuals must develop the capacity to interact with most heterogeneous sectors in terms of race, ethnia, language, and literacy. This interaction can bring on fundamental and mutual changes of life-style and world-view that inaugurate a new, more democratic cycle in the national culture —the rise of the New Man/ Woman. This cultural synthesis will be accelerated and deepened if the conditions are there to move forward from the bourgeois-democratic to the Socialist revolution. During this process the experience of cultural synthesis gained within the Marxist-Leninist parties becomes a way to institutionalize the new social relations. These revolutionary movements are an attempt to produce the cultural synthesis from the social base, maximizing coevalness, and erasing allochronism. Although the difficulties entailed are enormous, the accomplishments of the Cuban, Nicaraguan, and Salvadoran revolutions, and the Indian participation in the Guerrilla Army of the Poor and the Organization of the People in Arms in Guatemala, the Shining Path and the Revolutionary Movement Tupac Amaru in Peru illustrate the feasibility of the synthesis.

Keeping in mind the imperialist history of the notion of the cultural Other, fully maintaining it within Socialist revolutionary interpretive parameters is questionable. Although it can be argued that progressive intellectuals in dependent societies may be as ignorant of the ethnic heterogeneity of their national culture as any European, the social project entailed is essentially different. Knowledge will not be gathered and narrated to subjugate the Other or to satisfy open-ended academic requirements, but to visualize some form of popular political agency or to expedite practical alliances towards national liberation. If produced within political party structures, much of this knowledge will unfortunately remain reserved due to security exigencies. Yet some important aspects of it will reach the general public through various sources: post-facto testimonials, the production of intellectuals gathered in think-tanks who do sociological research or theorize in order to orient party lines or to participate in national debates, from party-affiliated or progressive, independent academic scholars who want to test or upgrade the validity of certain social theories or ascertain the historical and cultural meaning of specific conjunctures. The problem here is to produce knowledge of society from the perspective of the dispossesed and for the dispossesed so as to clarify the existing system of alienations that reproduces their subordinate status. This is the first step in charting the long-range strategies and practical organizational and mobilizational tactics, so that the dispossesed will have better access to the benefits of collective material and symbolic production. In the Marxist-Leninist parlance this is the notion of "partisanship" or "tendentiousness," which is ground zero for all cultural analyses and interpretation. The theologians of liberation would refer to it as the "option for the poor." The challenge here is for intellectuals to come out of their middle class social identity, their habits and reflexes, and make their own the cause of the dispossessed, whose milieu and culture are often alien to their experience. As previously indicated, in the Marxist-Leninist tradition the vehicle for this transformation has been the vanguard party and the party cell. Here the efforts, minds and living styles of people from all walks of life are fused together in the process of meeting the political tasks set by the organization. Thus these personnel are turned into organic intellectuals who collectively represent, elaborate and act on the preoccupations and interests of the working classes.

Due to the externally generated dynamics of social change in a situation of dependency, all Marxist and Marxist-Leninist oriented parties and intellectuals must strive to update their concept of the popular classes and popular culture. The constant renegotiation of the ways in which the local economies are periodically reinserted in the international market profoundly modifies class relations. In a limited sense, this entails the displacement of the problem of the radically different Other to another context. This context is the changes and generational shifts among militants, which forces the party bureaucracy to renovate and reinforce among them the experience of the heterogeneity in the national culture for mobilizational purposes. Despite these changes and shifts, the pool of acquired knowledge and experience still remains in the institutional memory through various interactions: the recollections of old and/ or retired militants, the permanent efforts made to recruit from among that heterogeneity, the assets in exile, if the vanguard party is undergoing severe repression at home.

The definition of the popular classes is perhaps the simplest issue and has been solved through a functional approach. They are the classes and fractions of classes most threatened in their interests by imperialist penetrations; therefore they are those who may potentially participate in a national liberation front as a consequence of their objective and subjective situation. Perhaps later on they will also participate in propelling the institutional rupture towards a Socialist State. Quite the contrary, the definition of the subtantive nature of the popular culture —an immanentist approach— is the most debated issue for historical materialism, because, on the one hand, the existence of a "national soul" being gradually expressed through historical time is an unacceptable idealist philosophical contrivance, and on the other, the notion of a nation's "peculiar social physiognomy" or "collective personality" has not been theorized. Nevertheless, an effort at a substantive definition of popular culture must be attempted because in both revolutionary scenarios —bourgeois-democratic and Socialist— the most subordinate social classes become the mass for political and military manoeuvering. Therefore, knowledge of their customs, mentality, and symbolic universe is imperative for the creation and maintenance of a revolutionary front composed of disparate social and ethnic elements, and for the efficacy of the leadership conducting the movement.

It would appear that these requirements force historical materialist theoreticians to the rush conclusion that a popular culture exists prima facie, on the basis of the materialist notion that all human beings, because they are human beings, cannot but acquire and create meanings and patterns of behaviour out of the array of symbolic and material instruments historically accumulated in a society. It stands to reason, then, to think that the subordinate classes do possess their own, distinctive culture, elaborated from whatever access they have had to the instrumental pool, according to the orientations dictated by the administration of the hegemonic cultural model. The theoretical crisis comes at the moment of defining that distinctiveness substantively, while at the same time avoiding the trap of an essentialist "expression of the soul of the people." At this point we discover that the question is being begged, because it is illogical to prove the existence of an entity by starting from the promise that the entity already exists. The question becomes even more complicated when the definitions of the concept of culture brought to bear clash among each other.

This issue lies at the core of the debate on the nature of popular culture recently generated by Néstor García Canclini.[11] Fusing the concept of hegemony from Antonio Gramsci and Pierre Bourdieu's concept of reproduction of domination through the administration, access to, and acquisition of symbolic capital, García Canclini defines "popular cultures" as "configurated in a process of unequal appropriation of the economic and cultural capital of a nation or ethnicity by its dominated sectors, and by the real and symbolic comprehension, reproduction and transformation of general and specific conditions of life and work" (47). Later on he explains: in a sense, the boss and the lineworker share the same work in the same factory, seeing the same television channels, etc. (although obviously form different perspectives that generate different decoding); but at the same time economic and cultural options exist that differentiate them, separate jargons, and communication channels distinctive for each class. Both spaces, that of the hegemonic and that of the popular culture, are interpenetrated, so that the typical language of the lineworkers or the peasants is in part a construction of their own and in part a resemantization of the language of the mass media and political power, or a specific way to allude to social conditions common to all (for example, jokes about inflation). In a reverse sense, there is also this interaction: "the hegemonic language of the media and the politicians, to the extent it wants to reach the population as a whole, will have to take into account the particular forms of popular expression" (pp. 48-49). Then García Canclini concludes: "Conceiving (the popular cultures) in this way, we distance ourselves from the two predominating positions in the scholarship addressed to the issue: the immanentist interpretations formulated in Europe by romantic populism and by nationalism and conservative indigenism in Latin America, and on the other hand, by a positivism that, concerned about scientific accuracy, forgot the political sense of the symbolic production of the people" (p. 49).

Upon commenting on this endeavour, José Joaquín Brunner [12] has called attention to the tautological and paradoxic nature of the Gramsci-Bourdieu combination in García Canclini. If we follow the Bourdieu component of the definition, we will arrive at the conclusion that popular culture is constituted by the ways in which the subordinate classes internalize their domination, a fact so basic in historical materialism that needs no redundant elaboration. Then, if we follow the Gramscian component, we have to realize that culture must be understood as the expression of an existing hegemony. Therefore it is composed of a number of indispensable elements: a specific, unified conception of the world that binds together the various sectors of a power block, an integrative capacity to articulate within its power other world-visions vying for hegemony, neutralizing their hostility while showing animosity towards them, a specialized intelligentsia charged with the articulation, elaboration and readaptation of that world-view, an organizational base for its production and dissemination among the population in order to orient its behaviour to the convenience of the dominant class through consensus or conformism and identifiable social sectors that function as the preeminent encarnation of that world-view. Because they have never been part of a power block, these ingredients are beyond the reach of the dominated classes; their symbolic production appears dispersed, disparate, inarticulated, uncohesive. It is, therefore, quite evident that here we are meeting a paradox in García Canclini's arguments; in order to define the concept of popular culture he uses theoretical concepts that deny its existence.

To solve the impasse Brunner recommends returning to Gramsci's notion of folklore to designate what García Canclini calls popular cultures. For Gramsci the subordinate classes possess folklore, not an elaborate, systematic, politically organized and centralized culture. Folklore is not a conception of the world, but multiple, juxtaposed conceptions of life surviving through history like mutilated, contaminated documents reflecting the impact of the various hegemonic cultures in fragmented, disfigured images, in capricious combinations, accumulated like strata that touch upon the gross in various degrees, all of which orients the practice and the beliefs of the dominated classes. Folklore decants a philosophical stance that Gramsci calls common sense. It is folklore of philosophy and, again, it is expressed in dispersed, incoherent, incongruent ways, correlative to the social and cultural position of the subordinate masses. For Gramsci, the liberational aspects of folklore will be part of the raw material for the Socialist revolution and the inauguration of a new State and hegemonic culture. An appropriate educational system must carefully separate the submissive aspects of folklore from the liberational ones, so that a folkloric world-view will gradually be left behind. This should eventually lead to the birth of a modern national-popular mass culture, expressing a revolutionary power block articulated on the basis of the philosophy of praxis.

Gramsci spoke as a Marxist-Leninist about a cultural synthesis similar to the one being attempted in Latin America. The Socialist utopia was the integrating element of that synthesis at the dawn of Socialism in Europe, while the system was being built in the Soviet Union. Gramsci relied on the notion of the vanguard party for the conduct of the revolutionary process and the institutionalization of the new national-popular culture. Nowadays progressive Latin American intellectuals speak in the midst of very insecure redemocratization processes in the countries affected by Fascism, the collapse of the European Socialist block, the crisis of Socialism in the Soviet Union, and the impact it has on the Cuban, Nicaraguan, and Salvadoran revolutions. The severe internal strains occuring in the Latin American Communist movement have strengthened the influence of Social Democracy. Social-democratic intellectuals are displacing the issue away from a definition of the popular classes and popular culture, and into the theme of strengthening the more spontaneous micro-institutions of civil society vis-a-vis the political parties and the State. They would like to see the emergence of multiple, independent movements voicing neighborhood, community, ethnic, gender, and environmental concerns. They have abandoned the dialectic notion of the relative organic totalization of the different levels of praxis in a social formation and have come close to American Liberal pluralism; the dictatorship of the minorities can only be neutralized by the activation of multiple social agencies confronting each other in free conflict and competition, without State intervention. Therefore, these intellectuals condemn the instrumentalization of community based movements by political parties. Following Jürgen Habermas in many respects, they see no difference between the present outcome of Socialism in Europe and the social pathologies created by the bureaucratic administration of capitalism.

At this point in Latin American history, intellectuals in the Socialist tradition stand between a rich theoretical legacy, a deep crisis in the Socialist utopia and the need to reorient scholarly endeavours. What should be done?

My suggestion is amplifying priorities for research. The discussion of popular culture should also consider that Socialism is a subculture. In this sense two considerations are in order. On the one hand, the crisis in the

Socialist camp —los Socialismos reales— will not necessarily mean a decrease in the disintegrating effect of transnational capitalism in the Third World. Quite the contrary, if the invasion of Panama serves as an index, the lack of a counterbalance from the remnants of the Socialist camp may expand its scope and violation of Human Rights. The struggle to defend Civil, Social, Economic and Cultural Human Rights will probably increase. On the other hand if the utopia of Socialism is the grounding for the most effective, integral implementation of all Human Rights, the collapse and crisis of the Socialismos reales simply means that it is the party bureaucracies implementing the Socialist project who have failed, not necessarily the utopia. We therefore need to differentiate between the Marxist and Marxist-Leninist parties as bureaucratic institutions and the Socialist subcultures surrounding, supporting, and criticizing them. Perhaps the continuance and future dissemination of the Socialist utopia in Latin America will depend on that subculture and not on the party bureaucracies as we now know them.

Historical experience shows again and again that the party cadre and membership are an elite that do not totally account for the mass mobilizations of the subordinate classes. These parties become political vanguards only to the extent that they can objectively represent libertarian aspirations that motivate such mobilizations. This means that the vanguard parties are credible administrators of the Socialist ideals and symbology only to the extent they can erect themselves as points of political reference both before the popular folklore and the much more structured philosophical worldview of independent, Socialist oriented intellectuals. In other words, there are carriers and producers of a surplus of Socialist symbolic meaning outside party structures who circulate around, through, and into the political programs projected by the party bureaucracies. These are independent, well educated agents of all social classes who produce music, art, literature, and discuss, teach, and open spaces for a Socialist ethos in everyday life, without becoming members of political institutions, or doing so temporarily. They are the product and outcome both of the efficacy of the party bureaucracies in disseminating Socialist ideals, theories, and symbols, and of the periodic credibility failures of these bureaucracies. Some of them are children of actual or ex-party members. They represent and move within social circuits that reproduce personalities structured and consciously acting according to an ethos deeply commited to social justice, that generate peculiar life-styles where budgeting time and resources for such commitments is possible, that motivate particular selections of professions and trades, perhaps oriented to social service and the social science. To the extent that these spaces and social circuits do exist in societies where Socialism is not hegemonic, I think we are talking about a Socialist subculture. Within the realm of a Socialist counter-hegemony, this subculture stands half-way between the inarticulateness of popular folklore and the highly structured discourse of the vanguard party bureaucracy that guides the party line towards the possibility of a revolutionary national State.

If the Socialist utopia cannot be reduced to party bureaucracies, we need to understand the origin and present expression of this subculture. Informally jotting down a possible research agenda for Latin American literary criticism and discourse analysis, it would be fruitful to go back and look into the Socialist trends and the literature produced within the radicalized Liberalism and Positivism, and into the Anarchist and Anarcho-Sindicalist thought and literature of the 19th century and beginnings of the 20th. What happened to this symbolic expression when Marxism-Leninism arose with the Soviet revolution and the Communist parties were founded? What tensions did Stalinism create among Socialist itellectuals? It would be important to direct a new gaze on exemplary, conflictive figures such as José Revueltas and members of the Grupo de Guayaquil. Research re-evaluating the connection between the Socialist utopia and the aesthetic vanguardism of the first half of this century and that of the Boom fiction —already underway in work such as Nelson Osorio's and Guido Podestá's— should be deepened. We need to understand better how Socialist symbolic capital circulates among Christians, producing such synchretisms as Liberation Theology. The poetics of Liberation Theology still remain to be decoded. The defense of Human Rights movement is rapidly moving to a position parallel to Socialism with the concept of Basic Needs in the United Nations discussion of new strategies of development the protection of Human Rights is better assured by styles of development carried out in an autonomous, global, integral way, based on the internal needs of each society, with the initiative residing in the social base and not in the State bureaucracy. This kind of convergence makes the Human Rights movement suspect of being a Communist front of those who believe in the Doctrine of National Security.

Finally, let me move towards a conclusion by trying to profile the consequences of my arguments for Latin American cultural hermeneutics. I do not think one can proceed to apply the anthropological notion of Otherness —as it has been done in some recent approaches to Colonial literature— without first filtering it through the present condition of most Latin American societies, that of being dependent national cultures, with a combined and uneven economic and cultural development. Otherwise, literary critics would be playing the fiction of observing the Conquest of America with total proximity, either with the wonder of the conqueror or the horror of the conquered, which is a strange, romantic, and perhaps perverse way of freezing history. Our situation in contemporary reality shows, quite the contrary, that the Other —ethnic heterogeneity within the national cultures— must be understood within the still mostly unresolved task of building autonomous, sovereign national States, with the free capacity to decide on the appropriate style and the desired system of social and economic development, based on the recognition and most ample implementation of Human Rights. The very fact that we can use the notion of Otherness within the framework of the Latin American national cultures —either directly, as in the Liberal proyect, or displacing it to the discussion of popular culture, as in the revolutionary Socialist project— attests to the unfinished task of a cultural synthesis necessary for the new autonomous national States. It appears to me that this is the vertebrating factor of the Latin American cultural evolution. In these conditions, then, discussing Otherness turns out to be not a romantic freezing of time, but some sort of contemporary archeology: we can witness in the here and now a trauma similar to that of the original Conquest with the periodic reconstructions of dependency, with new actors, new cycles in the expansion and modernization of capitalism, yet with the same application of military violence, and the same gross violations of Human Rights.

Nevertheless, on the positive side this contemporary archeology also shows that the resistance to the periodic traumas of dependency has grown in an ascending spiral of complexity. Hundreds of years ago it was the suicide of indians and black slaves as rebellion against forced labor and deportation; it was *cimarronaje*; it was indian malones and wars; it was also spontaneous or planned revolts led by figures like Tupac Amaru; it was *bandidaje*, smuggling, and *caudillismo*, it was peasant uprisings. Then, in a crucial qualitative advance, it was artisans' mutual aid societies, positivist Socialist parties, anarchist groups, the rise of democratic middle class parties, the organization of trade unions, the Mexican revolution, the accreditation of Communist parties, then the rise of Socialist parties, the organization of huge labor confederations, the Cuban revolution, the Popular Unity in Chile, the Nicaraguan, and Salvadoran revolutions. Socialism became a viable, concrete possibility. Enzo Faletto[13] argues that the entire modern Latin American social history makes sense only if we consider that the Socialist utopia ceases being the working classes exclusive social project and gradually becomes a national project. Only then Socialism becomes an axis generating struggles for or against such a possibility. Thus the various forms of populism emerging in the first half of the 20th century —*varguismo, cardenismo, peronismo, ibañismo*— must be dialectically considered both as an effort to preserve capitalism by derailing certain sectors of the working class away from Socialism and into supraclass, personalistic ideologies and movements, and at the same time as a kind of mobilization that could have taken place only because the masses were enticed by disfigured Socialist aspirations. Reformist movements such as the Christian Democracy could only come to the fore because they promised to partially fulfill the contents of a radical Socialist program —the agrarian reform, for example— with a massive influx of financial aid from the United States. Conservatives and militarized Liberals discredit the Christian Democracy alleging that its reforms simply generate a stronger impetus towards Socialism. In their minds the last resort is the use of military force, which paradoxically brings on both a defeat of Socialism and another confirmation of the potency of its utopia in Latin America.

To conclude, my arguments point to a hermeneutic procedure; from the perspective of a socio-historical literary criticism and discourse analysis, cultural analysis and interpretation must proceed by detecting the contradictory axes of articulation —the equality of contradictory terms— that generate the production of symbolic forms within social formations as an index of the class struggle. In Alain Touraine's terms, these axes constitute the historicity of societies by revealing the ideological discursive production of organized social sectors vying for control of the cultural models that orient the process of economic surplus accumulation— conceptions of "the good life," of the ideal human being produced by the good society, and of the knowledge necessary to produce both. In this procedure it is imperative that cultural analysts direct their gaze at the central contradictions generated by such conflictive axes because "the truth" as social production cannot be located within any of the discourses vying for control of the cultural model of a society but in the total ensemble of these discourses. In my arguments I have designated that axis as the succesive attempts to produce a cultural synthesis of dependent, capitalist combined and uneven development by Spanish and Portuguese imperial mercantilism, Liberalism in the 19th century, and neo-Liberalism and Socialism in the 20th century. In no way does it mean that understanding the logic of the ensemble of cultural discourses gyrating around such axis would force cultural analysts to pretend they are dispassionate observers hovering above and beyond human folly —although technocratic personalities might tend to take such a stance. It is indispensable, though, to find a long duration synchronic normative base permitting the interpretive imputations addressed onto the shorter duration, diachronic events being analyzed. I have found that synchronic base in the Human Rights movement The United Nations Declarations of Human Rights and its complementary Covenants contain all the rights accumulated by the human species through revolutionary struggle: the Civil and Political rights specified in the Magna Carta of 1215, and those created by the American and French revolutions; the Social, Economic, and Cultural rights created by the Mexican and the Soviet revolutions, and all the 20th century anticolonial movements. They serve as a critical base to address the violations of Human Rights committed both by Liberalism and Socialism. In the end the hermeneutic procedure described posits a firm paradigm for the study of symbolic forms in the historicity of social formations. It also erases the interpretive boundaries between most of the social sciences, literary criticism and discourse analysis. I suggest, then, we may as well take a higher, vaster ground of endeavour and proclaim literary criticism as a discipline within symbolic anthropology.

NOTES

[1] Thomas S. Kuhn, *The Structure of Scientific Revolutions.* 2nd ed. (Chicago: Chicago University Press, 1970).

[2] Stanley R. Barrett, *The Rebirth of Anthropological Theory* (Toronto: University of Toronto Press, 1984); Marc Augé, *The Anthropological Circle. Symbol, Function, History* (Cambridge: Cambridge University Press, 1982).

[3] Alain Touraine, "Historicity." *The Self-Production of Society* (Chicago: University of Chicago Press, 1977).

[4] George E. Marcus and Michael M. J. Fischer, *Anthropology as Cultural Critique. An Experimental Moment in the Human Sciences* (Chicago: The University of Chicago Press, 1986).

[5] Johannes Fabian, *Time and the Other. How Anthropology Makes Its Object* (New York: Columbia University Press, 1983).

[6] Julio Cotler, "The Mechanics of Internal Domination and Social Change in Peru." Irving Louis Horowitz, ed., *Masses in Latin America* (New York: Oxford University Press, 1970).

[7] Guillermo O'Donnell, "Tensions in the Bureaucratic-Authoritarian State and the Question of Democracy." David Collier, ed., *The New Authoritarianism in Latin America* (Princeton: Princeton University Press, 1979).

[8] As an index see multiple ideological perspectives in Hernán Godoy Urzúa, coordinador, *Chile en el ámbito de la cultura occidental* (Santiago de Chile: Editorial Andrés Bello, 1987).

[9] Joaquín Lavín, *Chile: la revolución silenciosa* (Santiago de Chile: Editorial Zig-Zag, 1988).

[10] See Anthony Brewer, *Marxist Theories of Imperialism A Critical Survey* (London: Routledge & Kegan Paul, 1980); Ronald H. Chilcote, *Theories of Development and Underdevelopment* (Boulder, Colorado: Westview Press, 1984).

[11] Nestor García Canclini, *Las culturas populares en el capitalismo* (La Habana: Casa de las Américas, 1981).

[12] José Joaquín Brunner, "Notas Sobre Cultura Popular, Industria Cultural y Modernidad." Materiales de Discusión. Programa FLACSO, Santiago de Chile, No, 70, junio 1985.

[13] Enzo Faletto, "Estilos Alternataivos de Desarrollo y Opciones Políticas. Papel del Movimiento Popular." Documento de Trabajo. Programa FLACSO, Santiago de Chile, No, 118, julio 1981.

Acknowledgments

Fernández Retamar, Roberto. "Caliban: Notes Towards a Discussion of Culture in Our America." *Massachusetts Review* 15 (1974): 7–72. Translated by Lynn Garofala, David Arthur McMurray, and Robert Márquez. Reprinted with the permission of Massachusetts Review, Inc.

Mignolo, Walter D. "Occidentalización, imperialismo, globalización: herencias coloniales y teorías postcoloniales." *Revista iberoamericana* 61 (1995): 27–40. Reprinted with the permission of the International Institute of Ibero-American Literature.

Luis, William. "Culture as Text: The Cuban/Caribbean Connection." *Translation Perspectives* 6 (1991): 7–20. These essays were first presented at a SUNY Conversation in the Disciplines in 1991 and subsequently printed in *Translation Perspectives* VI. Reprinted with the kind permission of the copyright holder the Research Foundation of the State of New York.

Foster, David William. "Latin American Documentary Narrative." *Publications of the Modern Language Association* 99 (1984): 41–55. Reprinted by permission of the Modern Language Association of America. © 1984 Modern Language Association of America.

Beverley, John. "'Through All Things Modern': Second Thoughts on *Testimonio*." *Boundary* 18, no.2 (1991): 1–21. Reprinted with the permission of Duke University Press.

Sklodowska, Elzbieta. "Spanish American Testimonial Novel—Some Afterthoughts." *New Novel Review* 1, no.2 (1994): 31–47. Reprinted with the permission of *New Novel Review*.

Franco, Jean. "Apuntes sobre la crítica feminista y la literatura hispanoamericana." *Hispamérica* 15: 45 (1986): 31–43. Reprinted with the permission of *Hispamérica*.

Guerra Cunninghan, Lucía. "La identidad cultural y la problemática del ser en la narrativa femenina latinoamericana." *Plural* 205 (1988): 12–21. Reprinted with the permission of Compania Editoiral Excelsior S.C.L.

Masiello, Francine. "Melodrama, Sex, and Nation in Latin America's *Fin de siglo*." *Modern Language Quarterly* 57 (1996): 269–78. Reprinted with the permission of *Modern Language Quarterly*.

Manzor-Coats, Lillian. "'Who Are You, Anyways?': Gender, Racial and Linguistic Politics in U.S. Cuban Theater." *Gestos* 11 (1991): 163–74. Reprinted with the permission of *Gestos*.

Yúdice, George. "El conflicto de postmodernidades." *Nuevo texto crítico* 4, no.7 (1991): 19–33. Reprinted with the permission of *Nuevo texto crítico*.

Toro, Alfonso de. "Postmodernidad y Latinoamérica (Con un modelo para la narrativa postmoderna)." *Acta literaria* 15 (1990): 71–99. Reprinted with the permission of *Acta literaria*.

Volek, Emil. "Realismo mágico entre la modernidad y la postmodernidad: hacia una remodelización cultural y discursiva de la nueva narrativa hispanoamericana." *Inti* 31 (1990): 3–20. Reprinted with the permission of Inti Publications.

Piedra, José. "Literary Whiteness and the Afro-Hispanic Difference." *New Literary History* 18 (1987): 303–32. Reprinted with the permission of John Hopkins University Press.

Kubayanda, Josaphat Bekunuru. "Minority Discourse and the African Collective: Some Examples from Latin American and Caribbean Literature." *Cultural Critique* 6 (1987): 113–30. Reprinted with the permission of Oxford University Press.

Jackson, Richard. "Remembering the 'Disremembered': Modern Black Writers and Slavery in Latin America." *Callaloo* 13 (1990): 131–44. Reprinted with the permission of Johns Hopkins University Press.

Santí, Enrico Mario. "Politics, Literature and the Intellectual in Latin America." *Salmagundi* 82 (1989): 92–110. Reprinted with the permission of Skidmore College.

Losada, Alejandro. "La literatura urbana como praxis social en América Latina." *Ideologies and Literature* 1, no.4 (1977): 33–62. Reprinted with the permission of the Prisma Institute.

Zimmerman, Marc. "Latin American Literary Criticism and Immigration." *Ideologies and Literature* 4, no.16 (1983): 172–96. Reprinted with the permission of the Prisma Institute.

Vidal, Hernán. "The Notion of Otherness Within the Framework of National Cultures." *Gestos* 11 (1991): 27–44. Reprinted with the permission of *Gestos*.